POSSIBLE WORLDS

POSSIBLE

AN INTRODUCTION TO LOGIC AND ITS PHILOSOPHY

WORLDS

RAYMOND BRADLEY
NORMAN SWARTZ
Department of Philosophy
Simon Fraser University

HACKETT PUBLISHING COMPANY
Indianapolis • Cambridge

Published in the United States of America
by HACKETT PUBLISHING COMPANY, INC.

Copyright © 1979 by Raymond Bradley and Norman Swartz

Published in Great Britain
by Basil Blackwell Publisher

Printed in the United States of America
Second Printing, 1981

Library of Congress Catalog Card Number 79-51037
ISBN 0-915144-60-3
      0-915144-59-x (pbk)

Cover design by Richard L. Listenberger
Art for cover by James Felter, Centre for the Arts,
    Simon Fraser University

Interior design by James N. Rogers

For further information, please address
Hackett Publishing Company, Inc.
P.O. Box 55573
Indianapolis, Indiana   46205

To the members of our families, of whose company we were too often deprived during the years spent writing this book

Contents

2 PROPOSITIONS   65

Preface

Talk of possible worlds is now a commonplace within philosophy. It began, nearly three hundred years ago, within philosophical theology. Leibniz thought it reassuring to say that although our world contains much that is evil, it is nonetheless the best of all possible worlds. Few philosophers today find this statement very plausible. Nevertheless, talk of the set of all possible worlds — when stripped of the suggestion that the actual world is better than any others — is nowadays frequently invoked as a means of illuminating other areas of philosophy. Ethics, epistemology, philosophy of psychology, philosophy of language, and — most notably of all — logic, are all benefiting from the insights of what is called "possible worlds semantics".

Unfortunately, most current talk of possible worlds is still regarded as the province of professionals; little of it has filtered down to those who are just beginning to learn their philosophy. Yet there is no good reason why this should be so. Although the higher reaches of possible-worlds semantics bristle with technical subtleties, its basic insights are really very simple. This book explains what those insights are and uses them to construct an integrated approach to both the philosophy of logic and the science of logic itself.

This approach, we believe, is especially suited to the needs of those who have difficulty with symbols. There are many persons who would like to learn something of philosophy and logic but who, because they are put off by the severely formal manner in which the logical part of philosophy is usually presented, are deterred from pursuing their intent. Their alienation is unfortunate and needless; we try to prevent it by taking more pains than usual to ensure that logical concepts are well understood before they are symbolized. Indeed, it is only in the last two chapters that the powers of symbolism are systematically exploited. Then, again, we would like to think that our approach will be helpful to those for whom symbolism holds no terrors but for whom the difficulty lies rather in seeing how there can be any real connection between the formal results of logic and the substantive inquiries undertaken in other parts of philosophy. Their intellectual schizophrenia reflects the fact that the rarefied results of formal logic resemble those of mathematics more closely than they do those of metaphysics, epistemology, and the rest. But it neglects the fact, which we here emphasize, that the basic concepts of formal logic are hammered out on the same anvil of analytical inquiry as are those of other parts of philosophy. Grounding logic in talk of possible worlds, we believe, is one way of making logic seem more at home with its philosophical kin.

Many of the arguments presented in this book are, and need to be, matters for philosophical debate. Yet seldom have we done more than hint at the parameters within which such debate arises. There are three main reasons for this. First, we believe that the kind of questioning which we hope this book will generate is likely to be deeper if it is provoked by sustained argument for a single coherent point of view rather than if it stems from exposure to an eclectic display of divergent doctrines. Secondly, we are confident that serious students will, sooner or later, be treated — by their reading or their teachers — to arguments which will put ours into a broader perspective. Thirdly, we could not hope to do justice to competing points of view without making this book even longer than it is.

Students in three countries — Australia, New Zealand, and Canada — have been the guinea pigs for the general approach and parts of the material in this book. We have benefited from the criticisms of many and also from the encouragement of the few who have gone on to become professional teachers of philosophy. We are indebted to scores of fine young minds.

Specific acknowledgements go to two institutions and to a number of individuals. The Canada Council and the President's Research Grant Committee of Simon Fraser University have provided generous financial assistance for some of the research and editorial work on this book. Three research assistants, Michael Beebe, Jeffrey Skosnik, and Moira Gutteridge, have assisted in the preparation of the manuscript: their help in compiling the references and index, in preparing some of the graphics, and in commenting on the manuscript, has been invaluable. Many professional colleagues have offered criticism and encouragement. We are especially indebted to Sidney Luckenbach, California State University at Northridge, Malcolm Rennie, Australian National University, and an anonymous reviewer for Basil Blackwell, our U.K. publisher. Each of these philosophers has offered extremely valuable comments on the manuscript. Even though we have not adopted all their suggestions, we hope that they will like the final version and will recognize their own contributions to it. Charles Hamblin, University of New South Wales, is the philosophical godfather of this book: his early unpublished classification of modal relations gave rise to the worlds-diagrams herein; his success in introducing students to logic through modal, rather than truth-functional concepts, has served as a model for our approach.

Responsibility for the final shape and substance of the book lies squarely with the authors. The book contains many imperfections. We are aware of some of them but have not wished to fall prey to the perils of perfectionism by further delaying publication. Besides, we trust that errors of which we are not yet aware will be communicated to us by those who think the possible worlds approach worth promoting and who would like to see it brought closer to that state of perfection which only a non-actual possible world is likely ever to contain.

NOTE ON THE SECOND PRINTING

All typographical errors known to us have been corrected. Substantive changes occur on pages 78, 143, 146, 286, 295 and 296.

To the Teacher

Approach

Three main features determine the complexion of this book: (1) the way we characterize the *subject matter* of logic; (2) the way we characterize the *methodology* of logic; and (3) the fact that we present the science of logic in its *philosophical* rather than in its formal guise.

(1) The *subject matter* of logic, as we present it, is explicated mainly in terms of metaphysical talk about the set of all possible worlds and the ways in which concepts apply and propositions are true or false within those worlds.

Philosophical reflection about the foundations of logic — and of mathematics, for that matter — tends to make *metaphysical realists* (Platonists, if you like) of us all. Both of us (the authors) would, if we could, happily live with the economies of nominalism. But, like so many others, from Plato to Gottlob Frege, Hilary Putnam, and David Lewis, we have felt compelled to posit a modestly rich ontology of abstract entities. Our own catalog extends not only to numbers and sets, but also to concepts and propositions and — above all — to possible worlds. Those of you who think it possible to be more parsimonious will probably relish the task of showing how it can be done. At the very least, you should find our arguments grist for your own philosophical mills.

One of the chief attractions of the Leibnizian metaphysic of *possible worlds* is that — as Kripke, Hintikka, and others demonstrated in the early 1960s — it enables us to give a semantical underpinning to much of the machinery of formal logic. And it enables us to do this in a way which flows naturally from the simple intuitions which most of us — laymen and philosophers alike — have about such concepts as consistency, inconsistency, implication, validity, and the like. We are all (if we have any logical insights at all) disposed to say such things as: that an argument is valid just when its premises imply its conclusion; that one proposition (or set of propositions) implies another just when it isn't possible for the former to be true in circumstances in which the latter is false; that one proposition is inconsistent with another just when it isn't possible for both to be true; and so on. It is only a short step from these modes of talking to those of Leibniz's possible worlds. And the step is worth taking. For once we take it, we have at our disposal an extremely powerful set-theoretic framework in terms of which to explain all these, and many other basic concepts of logic and philosophy.

The set-theoretic framework which does so much of this explanatory work is depicted in this book by means of what we call *worlds-diagrams*. Our worlds-diagrams are grounded, in chapter 1, in simple and pictureable intuitions about the ways in which the truth-values of propositions may be distributed across the members of the set of all possible worlds. They are elaborated, in chapters 5 and 6, in such a way as to yield a new and effective decision-procedure for evaluating sentences and sentence-forms within propositional logic, both truth-functional and modal.

The logic whose formalism most adequately reflects our Leibnizian intuitions about implication, necessity, and the like is, of course, *modal* logic. More particularly, we believe and argue that it is that system of modal logic which C. I. Lewis called S5. Like William and Martha Kneale, we are persuaded that S5 is the system whose theses and rules "suffice for the reconstruction of the whole of logic as that is commonly understood".[1] We give to modal logic in general, and to S5 in particular, both the philosophical and the pedagogical primacy which we believe is their due. This is why, for instance, we introduce the modal concept of logical implication (what Lewis called "strict implication") early in chapter 1 and postpone discussion of the truth-functional concept of material conditionality (often

---

1. *The Development of Logic*, Oxford, Clarendon Press, 1962, p. 583.

misleadingly called "material implication") until chapter 5. It is, you will undoubtedly agree, a purely empirical question as to whether this order of presentation is pedagogically viable and desirable. We believe that it is — on the basis of experience. But we await the reports of others.

(2)   The *methodology* of logic, as we present it, is explicated in terms of epistemological talk about the a priori methods of analysis and inference whereby knowledge of noncontingent propositions is possible.

The epistemology of logic is an essential, though often neglected, part of the philosophy of logic. We try to treat it with more than usual care and thoroughness.

Chapter 3 serves as an introduction to *epistemology in general*, with as much emphasis on noncontingent propositions as on contingent ones. To the question, What is the *nature* of human knowledge? we answer with a version of defeasibility theory. It would have been nice, perhaps, to have espoused one of the currently fashionable causal theories of knowledge. But causal theories, though plausible for cases of experiential knowledge, do not seem able — as at present formulated — to account for the kinds of a priori knowledge which we have in mathematics and logic. To the question, What are the *limits* of human knowledge? we answer by arguing for the unknowability in principle of at least some propositions: of some contingent ones by virtue of the falsity of verificationism; of some noncontingent ones by virtue of the truth of Gödel's Proof. To the question, What are the standard *modes of knowledge-acquisition* for humans? we offer two answers. One has to do with the natural history, as it were, of human knowledge: with its sources in experience and its sources in reason. The other has to do with the Kantian dichotomy between empirical and a priori knowledge: with whether or not it is possible to know a proposition by means other than experience. The two distinctions, we argue, are by no means equivalent. Thus it is, for example, that we are able to accommodate Kripke's claim that some necessary propositions of logic are knowable both experientially and a priori without in any way compromising Kant's belief in the exclusiveness and exhaustiveness of the empirical/ a priori distinction. The upshot of all this is that we offer ten different categories — rather than the usual four — under which to classify the epistemic status of various propositions; and further, that our knowledge of the truths of logic turns out to be possible under just two of them.

Although we acknowledge, with Kripke, that parts of the subject matter of logic may on occasion be known experientially, it by no means follows that appeal to experience forms part of the distinctive methodology whereby that subject matter may be systematically explored. On the contrary, we argue, the methodology of logic involves two wholly a priori operations: the ratiocinative operations of *analysis* and of *inference*. In chapter 4 we first show how analysis — "the greater part of the business of reason", as Kant put it — and inference can yield knowledge of noncontingent propositions; and then go on to illustrate, by surveying the three main branches of logic — Propositional Logic, Predicate Logic, and (what a growing number of philosophers call) Concept Logic — the sorts of knowledge which these methods can yield.

(3)   The *philosophy* of logic which we present in this book is resolutely antilinguistic in several important respects.

With respect to the *bearers of truth-values*, we argue against those who try to identify them with any form of linguistic entity, such as sentences, and quasilinguistic entities such as sentences taken together with their meanings. Propositions may be expressed by linguistic entities and apprehended by language-using creatures; but their existence, we hold, is not dependent upon the existence of either of these.

With respect to the notion of *necessary truth*, we argue against those who suppose that necessary truth can somehow be explained in terms of rules of language, conventions, definitions, and the like. The truth of necessary propositions, we hold, does not require a different kind of explanation from the truth of contingent propositions. Rather it consists, as does the truth of contingent propositions, in "fitting the facts" — albeit the facts in all possible worlds, not just in some.

With respect to the notion of *a priori knowledge*, we argue against those who suppose that a priori knowledge is best explained in terms of our understanding of words and sentences and of the linguistic rules, conventions, or definitions which they obey. The linguistic theory of the a priori was never so persuasive as when it went tandem with the linguistic theory of necessary truth. But having rejected the latter we felt free, indeed obliged, to reject the former. Our alternative account of a priori knowledge relies, as already noted, on the twin notions of analysis and inference. It is, of course, propositions and their conceptual constituents which — on our view — are the proper objects of analysis. We try to show how what we call "constituent-analysis", when combined with possible-worlds analysis (roughly, truth-condition analysis), can yield knowledge both of the truth-value and of the modal status of logical propositions. And we try to show, further, how rules of inference may be justified by these same analytical methods.

In short, we replace linguistic theories about truth-bearers and necessity with an ontological theory about propositions, possible worlds, and relations between them. And we replace the linguistic theory of a priori knowledge with an epistemological theory which gives due recognition to what philosophers have long called "the powers of reason". This is not to say that we ignore matters having to do with language altogether. On the contrary, we devote a lot of attention to such questions as how sentential ambiguity may be resolved, how ordinary language maps onto the conceptual notation of symbolic logic, how sentence-forms can be evaluated in order to yield logical knowledge, and so on. But we resist the view that the theory of logic is best viewed as a fragment of the theory of language. Just as the subject matter of logic needs to be distinguished from its epistemology, so both — on our view — need to be distinguished from theory of language.

Many philosophical theses, other than those just canvassed, are developed in this book. We touch on, and in some cases discuss at length, the views of dozens of philosophers and a few mathematicians. This is seemly in a book whose primary emphasis is on the philosophy, rather than the formalism, of logic. And it serves to explain why we have found room in this book for little more than a brief sketch (in chapter 4) of the broad territory of logic, and why chapters 5 and 6, although lengthy, do no more than introduce the elements of propositional logic (truth-fnctional and modal, respectively). Which brings us to:

Place in a Curriculum

The book is written so as to be intelligible, and hopefully even intriguing, to the general reader. Yet it is expressly designed for use as a textbook in first- or second-year courses at colleges and universities. It is not designed to replace handbooks in 'speed reasoning' or informal reasoning. Nor is it designed only for those students who plan to go on to more advanced work in philosophy and logic.

As we see it, *Possible Worlds* could, either in part or as a whole, serve as an *introduction to philosophy in general* — as an introduction, that is, to the logical and analytical methods adopted by contemporary analytical philosophers.

It could, either in part or as a whole, serve as an introduction to formal logic, in particular — as a philosophical introduction to the basic concepts with which formal logicians operate. So viewed, it should be used as a *prolegomenon to the standard curricular offerings in logic programs:* to all those courses, that is, which develop natural deduction and axiomatic techniques for propositional logic, quantification theory, and the like. For we touch on these and such-like matters only for purposes of illustration (if at all).

Again, the book could, either in part or as a whole, serve as the text for a belated *course in the philosophy of logic* — as a way of opening up philosophical questions about logic to those whose introduction to logic has been of the more traditional formal kind. It has been our experience — and that of countless other teachers of logic — that the traditional approach, of plunging students straight into the formalism of logic, leaves so many lacunae in their understanding that additional instruction in the philosophy of logic is sooner or later seen as a necessity. Our own preference, of course, is to preempt these sorts of problems by introducing logic, from the outset, as an integral part of philosophy — to be more specific, as that part of philosophy which serves as a foundation for mathematics, but whose most intimate philosophical ties are with metaphysics on the one hand and with epistemology on the other. But those of you who do not share our pedagogical predilections on this matter may nevertheless find that *Possible Worlds* will help your students, later if not sooner, to understand why logic is as important to philosophers as it is to mathematicians.

Ideally, the material in this book should be covered in a single course of something like 40 – 50 lecture hours. Alternatively, the material might be spread over two courses each of 20 – 25 lecture hours. Barring that, one will have to design shorter courses around particular selections from the book's six chapters. Here are two possiblilities:

A short course on 'baby' formal logic, which keeps philosophical discussion at a minimum and maximizes formal techniques in propositional logic, could be structured around chapters 1, 5, and 6 (with chapter 4, perhaps, being treated in tutorial discussions).

A short course on philosophical logic, which maximizes philosophical discussion and minimizes formal techniques, could be structured around chapters 1, 2, 3, and 4.

Still again, the book may be used as an ancillary text for courses whose primary focus is importantly different from ours. For example, for courses in philosophy of language, teachers may wish their students to read chapter 2; for courses in epistemology, teachers may wish their students to read chapter 3; and for courses which — like so many general introductions to philosophy — include a brief survey of logic, teachers may wish their students to read chapter 1 and selections from chapter 4.

Some Practical Hints

Many of the exercises — especially in chapters 1, 5, and 6 — since they require non-prose answers — may be more readily corrected (perhaps by exchanging papers in class) if the instructor prepares *worksheets* for students to complete.

Exercises which require the completion (e.g., by addition of brackets) of *worlds-diagrams* are best handled by distributing photocopies of figure *(1.i)*. We hereby give our permission for the unlimited reproduction of this figure.

You may find it useful to make the progressive construction of a *glossary of terms* a formal requirement in the course.

Finally, much of the material in the book lends itself to testing by *multiple-choice examinations*. We would be happy to send sample copies to teachers whose requests are made on departmental letterheads.

To the Student

Most of you already understand that logic is theoretically important as a foundation for mathematics and practically useful as a set of principles for rational thinking about any topic whatever.

But what may not be clear to you is that logic also forms an integral part of philosophy.

Since this book aspires to introduce you to logic in its philosophical setting, a few words of explanation are in order.

What, for a start, is philosophy? More concretely: What is it to be a philosopher? Our answer — which will suffice for present purposes — is this:

> To be a philosopher is to reflect upon the implications of our experience, of the beliefs we hold, and of the things we say, and to try to render these all consistent — or, as it were, to try to get them all into perspective.

Four of the terms we have just used are particularly significant: "reflect", "implications", "consistent", and "perspective".

Philosophers are, first and foremost, *reflective* persons. We believe — as did Socrates — that an unexamined life is shallow, and that unexamined beliefs are often mischievous and sometimes dangerous. This is why we tend to be perplexed about, and to inspect more carefully, matters which less reflective persons either take for granted or brush aside as of no practical value. Any belief, dogma, or creed — social, political, moral, religious, or whatever — is subject to the philosopher's critical scrutiny. Nothing is sacrosanct; not even the beliefs of other philosophers. Do not be dismayed, then, to find in this book arguments which criticize other philosophical viewpoints; and do not be disturbed, either, if your teachers when dealing with this book find reason to criticize our own viewpoint. Out of such dialectic, philosophical insight may be born and progress towards truth may be made.

Of the notions of *implication* and *consistency* we shall have much to say before long. For the moment, it will suffice to say that one way a philosopher, or anyone else for that matter, has of testing the credentials of any belief or theory is to ask such questions as these: "Is it *implied* by something we already know to be true?" (if so, it must itself be true); "Does it *imply* something we know to be false?" (if so, it must itself be false); and "is it *consistent* with other beliefs that we hold?" (if not, we are logically obliged, whether we like it or not, to give up at least one of them). Plainly, if you wish to be able to answer questions such as these you will need to know a good deal about the concepts of implication and consistency themselves. But these concepts are *logical* concepts. Little wonder, then, that logic is — as we said at the outset — an "integral part of philosophy". The trouble is, however, that when — with others in coffeehouses, pubs, or university classrooms, or, alone, in moments of reflective solitude — we ponder such deep philosophical questions as those about existence, freedom, responsibility, etc., most of us do not know how to handle, in the requisite disciplined way, the logical concepts on which such questions turn. Learning a little logic can help us to get our thinking straight in philosophy as well as elsewhere.

As for trying to get everything into *perspective*: that, it is probably fair to say, is usually thought to be the most distinctive goal of philosophers. You will need to learn a good deal of logic, and a lot more philosophy, before achieving the kind of lofty vantage point reached by such great thinkers as Plato, Aristotle, Leibniz, Hume, Kant, Russell, and Wittgenstein. But one must begin somewhere. And perhaps one of the best places to start is by reflecting on the fact that the world of human experience is but one of many that could have been — that the actual world is, as we shall say, only one of many possible worlds. Thinking about other possible worlds is — as Leibniz recognized — a way of getting our own world into perspective. It is also — as we try to show — a way of providing both an introduction to, and secure theoretical foundations for, logic itself. Hence, the title of this book.

Possible Worlds

1. THIS AND OTHER POSSIBLE WORLDS

The Realm of Possibilities

The year is A.D. 4272. Lazarus Long is 2360 years old. Although he has been near death many times, he hasn't — unlike his biblical namesake — required the intervention of a miracle to recover. He simply checks himself (or is taken by force) into a Rejuvenation Clinic from time to time. When we last hear of him he is undergoing rejuvenation again. The year is now 4291 and Lazarus is being treated in his own portable clinic aboard the star-yacht "Dora" after traveling back in time to his birthplace in Kansas and being "mortally wounded" in the trenches "somewhere in France".

All this, and much more, happens to the Lazarus Long of Robert A. Heinlein's novel *Time Enough for Love*.[1] In his novel, Heinlein starts with a framework of persons who actually lived (e.g., Woodrow Wilson and Kaiser Wilhelm II), of places that actually existed (e.g., Kansas City and France), and of events that actually occurred (e.g., U-boat attacks and the entry of the U.S. into World War I), and builds up a world of fictional persons, places, and events. He carries us with him, in make-believe, to another world different from our actual one: to a merely possible world.

How much of this other possible world is believable? How much of it is *really* possible? Much of it is credible. For instance, there *could* have been a man named "Ira Howard" who died in 1873 and whose will instructed his trustees to set up a foundation devoted to the prolongation of human life. For all we know, Ira Howard may be just as historical a personage as Woodrow Wilson. To be sure, Ira Howard *may* be just as much a creature of Heinlein's imagination as is Minerva — a computer become flesh and blood and one of Lazarus' many mistresses. But this matters not. For, whatever the historical facts happen to be, we can always suppose — *counterfactually*, as we say — that they might have been otherwise. We constantly make such suppositions in the world of real life. The world of fiction needs no special indulgence. We easily can, and daily do, entertain all sorts of unactualized possibilities about past, present, and future. We think about things that *might* have happened, *might* be happening and *might* be about to happen. Not only do we ruefully ask "What if things *had been* thus and thus?"; we also wonder "What if things *are* so and so?" and "What if things *were to be* such and such?" Counterfactual supposition is not mere idle speculation. Neither is it just a fancy of the dreamer or a refuge for the escapist. Given that we are so often ignorant of what *is*, we need a rich

---

1. New York, G.P. Putnam's Sons, 1973.

sense of what *might be.* In matters of practice, we need to consider alternatives where knowledge is denied us. In matters of theory, we need to consider hypotheses where facts are unknown.

Actuality is, as it were, surrounded by an infinite realm of possibilities. Or, as we might otherwise put it, our actual world is surrounded by an infinity of other possible worlds. No wonder then that fiction writers like Heinlein have little difficulty in beguiling us with their stories of possibilities, most of which will never be actualized. Might there not come a time when incest will be socially and legally acceptable, when human life will be prolonged by periodic visits to Rejuvenation Clinics, when computers will be embodied in human flesh, or when travel from one galactic colony to another will be a commonplace? Maybe our everyday counterfactual suppositions are much more mundane. But who among us would rule the exciting ones entirely out of order? The fact is that we can, and do, conceive of social and legal, biological and technological, and perhaps even of physical, possibilities which the world of fact may never encompass.

What are the limits to the possible?

But are there not limits of some sort to what we can conceive or suppose to be possible? Does just anything go? How about time-travel, for instance? In Heinlein's novel, Lazarus recounts how he assumed a biological age of thirty-five so as to travel back in time twenty-three hundred years to observe how things were in his childhood and (as it turns out) to fall in love with his own mother.

SOME EVENTS IN THE LIFE OF LAZARUS LONG, SENIOR MEMBER OF THE HOWARD FAMILIES

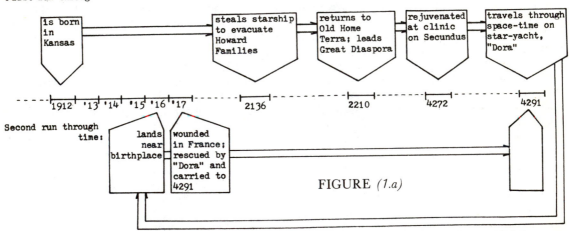

FIGURE *(1.a)*

Could time-travel occur? Can you be sure that there is not some other possible world in which it occurs even if it never occurs, or will occur, in our actual world? Is there any paradox in the idea of Lazarus observing himself as a four-year-old? See exercise 4 on p. 25.

Many of us may feel that the very concept of time-travel is paradoxical. If time-travel were possible then should we not be able to imagine a person traveling back in time and fathering himself? But is this really possible? Our minds boggle a bit. It is supposed by some that here we have reached the limits of conceivability, and that the world which Heinlein portrays through Lazarus is, in this respect at least, not in any sense a possible world. This, as it happens, is the view of another of the novel's characters: Carolyn Briggs, chief archivist of the Howard Foundation. As she put it in her Preface to the Revised Edition of Lazarus' memoirs: "An apocryphal and obviously impossible tale of the last events in his life has been included at the insistence of the editor of the original memoir, but it cannot be taken seriously." On the other hand, some of us may feel that time-travel, of the kind that Lazarus is supposed to have undertaken, is not wholly inconceivable; that paradox can be avoided; and that a world in which time-travel occurs may someday be seen to be possible if and when our concepts of space-time become more sophisticated. We may want to agree with Carolyn's predecessor — Justin Foote, chief archivist emeritus — when he appends the following note to her Preface: "My lovely and learned successor in office does not know what she is talking about. With the Senior [i.e., Lazarus], the most fantastic is always the most probable."[2]

But whatever we say about time-travel — whether we think it falls within or beyond the limits of possibility — it is certain that some things are *not* possible no matter how sophisticated our concepts become. The supposition that time-travel both *will* occur sometime in the future and will *not* occur anytime in the future, is a case of point. It takes us, in a sense, beyond the bounds of conceivability. It is not just paradoxical. It is, as we say, flatly self-contradictory. A supposed world in which something literally both is the case and is not the case is not, in any sense, a possible world. It is an impossible one.

Possibility is not the same as conceivability

So far we have spoken as if the boundary between the possible and the impossible were a function of human psychology: as if, that is, it coincided with the boundary between that which we find conceivable and that which we find inconceivable. Yet, while there is a great amount of overlap between what is conceivable and what is possible, the two are not the same.

In the first place, it should be clear on reflection that our inability to conceive of a certain state of affairs does not imply the impossibility of that state of affairs. Notoriously, there was a time when our ancestors thought it inconceivable that the earth should be round. Yet obviously the possibility of the earth's being round was in no way limited by their inability to conceive it.

Secondly, our seeming ability to conceive of a certain state of affairs does not imply the possibility of that state of affairs. For many centuries, mathematicians sought a means of squaring the circle (sought a procedure whereby to construct for any given circle a square of equal area). Plainly, they would not have done so unless they thought it conceivable that such a procedure existed. Yet we now know, and can prove, that the squaring of the circle is wholly beyond the bounds of possibility — that the concept itself is self-contradictory.

But if, as our first argument shows, conceivability is neither a necessary condition (conceivability is not *needed* for something to be possible), nor, as our second argument shows, a sufficient condition (conceivability doesn't *suffice* to establish possibility), what then *are* the conditions for something's being possible?

One might be tempted to answer that it is *conceivability without inconsistency* or *coherent conceivability* — not just conceivability itself — which is the measure of possibility. After all, although certain of our ancestors apparently did not have the psychological capacity to conceive of the earth being round, the concept of the earth being round is itself a perfectly coherent or self-consistent concept and hence is one of which they could — in the requisite sense — have conceived without inconsistency. And, again, although generations of mathematicians thought that the squaring of the circle was a goal which one could intelligibly pursue, we now know that they could not conceive of that goal without inconsistency.

Unfortunately, this answer will not do; or rather, it will not do from the standpoint of those who wish — as we do in this book — to explain the principal concepts of logic in terms of the notion of a possible world. For among those principal concepts are the concepts of consistency and inconsistency. And if we then invoke the concept of consistency in order to explain what a possible world is and how a possible world differs from an impossible one, we expose ourselves to a charge of circularity.

---

2. *Time Enough For Love*, p. xvii. [It will be our practice to give the complete bibliographical reference only on the first occasion in each chapter of our citing a work. Thereafter we shall omit the details of publication.]

Our predicament is apparently this. On the one hand, we wish to avoid *psychologism,* viz., any form of theory which makes logic a function of human psychology. In its older form, psychologism held that the laws of logic were "the laws of thought". It treated the science of logic as if it were a branch of psychology concerned with the description of how human beings actually reason. Psychologism, in its traditional form, is now dead, largely as a result of the efforts, early in this century, of Frege, Russell, and Wittgenstein. We wish to avoid introducing it in a new form. Yet that is what we would be doing if we were to explain the principal concepts of logic in terms of possible worlds and then go on to explain possible worlds themselves in terms of the purely psychological concept of conceivability. On the other hand, we wish to avoid the *circularity* in which we would be involved if we tried to define possible worlds in terms of the logical notion of consistency, and then later defined consistency in terms of possible worlds.

Fortunately, there is a way out of this predicament. We can avoid circularity and still not be trapped by psychologism. Consider, for a moment, how the charge of circularity in definitions may in other cases be avoided. We look in a dictionary, for example, to find out what it is for something to be complex and find that the concept of complexity is opposed to that of simplicity; we try to find out what it is for something to be simple and find that the concept of simplicity is opposed to that of complexity. Yet such a circle of definitions can be, and standardly is, broken. It is broken by *citing examples:* sometimes by ostension (pointing); sometimes by naming; and sometimes by description. Thus, in the present case we can avoid the trap of circularity — and at the same time, the seduction of psychologism — by citing clear-cut examples (they are often called "paradigm examples") of possible worlds, and equally clear-cut examples of impossible worlds. Intuitively, we would want to include, among the possible worlds, worlds in which there are more objects than in the actual world (e.g., in which the earth has two moons); worlds in which there are fewer objects than in the actual world (e.g., in which the earth has no moon at all); worlds in which the same objects exist as in the actual world but have different properties (e.g., in which the long-supposed "canals" on Mars turn out, after all, to be relics of some past civilization); and so on. And intuitively, too, we would want to include, among the impossible worlds, worlds in which circles can be squared, worlds in which there is an even square root of nine, worlds in which time-travel both does and does not occur, and so on.

To be sure, descriptions can be given of worlds about whose possibility or impossibility we have no clear intuitions. But for nearly any distinction that we care to think of there will be problematic cases lying near the borderline of that distinction. The case of worlds in which time-travel occurs is just such a case; and so, until recently, was the case of worlds in which more than four colors are needed to demarcate between countries on a plane map. But the difficulty of deciding, for certain cases, on which side of the distinction they are to be located should not be allowed to discredit the distinction itself. The distinction between possible and impossible worlds is grounded in an appeal to paradigm cases. We do not have to be able to settle all boundary disputes in order to have a secure enough footing on which to proceed in our attempts to explain the workings of logic.

Possible worlds: actual and non-actual

Let us pause at this point and reflect, in philosophical fashion, on some of the things we have been saying. We have been working with a threefold distinction, which is implicit in much of our thinking, between the actual world, worlds which are non-actual but possible, and worlds which are neither. But what precisely do we mean by "possible world"? More basically still: What precisely do we mean by "the actual world"?

When we speak of "the actual world" we do not mean just the planet on which we live. Nor do we mean our solar system, or even our galaxy. We have spoken of the actual world in an all-encompassing way so as to embrace all that really exists — the universe as a whole.

Again, when we speak of "the actual world" we do not mean just the universe as it is now, in the present. When we identify it — as above — with all that really exists, we are using "exists" in a timeless sense, so as to encompass not only what exists now but also what once existed in the past and what will come to exist in the future. The actual world embraces all that was, is, or will be.

Now it is clear that the actual world is a possible world. If something actually exists then it is obviously possible that it exists. On the other hand, not everything that possibly exists does so actually. Not all possible worlds are actual. It follows, therefore, that the actual world is only one among many possible worlds: that there are possible worlds other than ours. Moreover, given that by "the actual world" we mean — as we agreed a moment ago — everything that was, is, or will be the case, it follows that by "another possible world" we do not mean some planet, star or whatnot that actually exists and which is located somewhere "out there" in physical space. Whatever actually exists, it must be remembered, belongs to the actual world even if it is light-years away. Other, non-actual, possible worlds, are not located anywhere in physical space. They are located, as it were, in conceptual space; or rather, as we may prefer to say, in logical space.

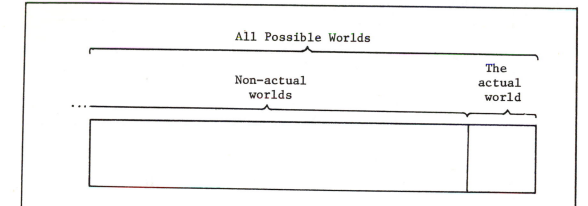

FIGURE *(1.b)*

Our world (everything that actually was, is, or will be) is only one of an infinite number of possible worlds. It is the actual world. The others are non-actual.

Note that in this and other similar diagrams we represent an infinite number of possible worlds by a rectangle of finite size. The rectangle may be thought of as containing an infinite number of points each of which represents a different possible world. It is only for the sake of diagrammatic convenience that we represent the actual world on this and a few subsequent figures by a segment of the rectangle rather than by a single point. From a logical point of view the actual world has little (if any) claim to privileged status. Indeed, in most of the worlds-diagrams featured later we shall have no need to make mention of the actual world, let alone to feature it prominently.

Note, further, that the bracket for non-actual worlds is left open at the left-hand side of this diagram and all diagrams on which the actual world is featured. This is to signify that there are more non-actual worlds than we have here depicted. The class of non-actual worlds contains all possible worlds other than the actual world and contains as well all impossible worlds. Every impossible world is a non-actual world.

Logical possibility distinguished from other kinds

By "a possible world", it should be emphasized, we do *not* mean only a *physically* possible world. Countless worlds which are physically *im*possible are numbered among the possible worlds we are talking about. Physically possible worlds form a proper subset of all possible worlds; or, to make the contrast somewhat sharper, we might say that the set of physically possible worlds forms a proper subset of all *logically* possible worlds.

A physically possible world is any possible world which has the same natural laws as does the actual world.[3] Thus the logically possible world depicted in Charles Dickens' novel *David Copperfield* is a physically possible one: no event in that novel violates any natural law. On the other hand, Washington Irving's short story *Rip Van Winkle* describes a physically impossible world: a world in which a person sleeps without nourishment for twenty years. The latter circumstance, a person's living for twenty years without nourishment (energy intake), violates certain laws of thermodynamics. Nonetheless, although such a situation is thus physically impossible, it is not logically impossible. In

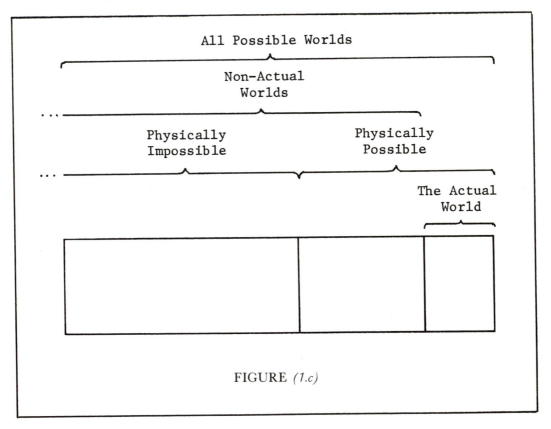

FIGURE *(1.c)*

3. Note that, on this account, the notion of a physically possible world is parasitic upon (needs to be defined in terms of) the broader notion of a logically possible world. Similarly, a state of affairs is physically possible, it is usually said, if its description is *consistent with* the natural laws (of the actual world). Yet the relation of consistency — as we show in section 4 — is itself to be defined in terms of possible worlds, i.e., of *logically* possible worlds.

some non-actual, physically impossible, but logically possible world in which the natural laws are different from those in the actual world, Rip Van Winkle does sleep (without nourishment) for twenty years. Of course, not every physically impossible world will be logically possible. The physically impossible world in which Rip Van Winkle sleeps for exactly twenty years without nourishment and does not sleep for twenty years without nourishment is a logically impossible one as well.

The class of *logically* possible worlds is the *most inclusive* class of possible worlds. It includes every other kind of possible world as well: all those that are physically possible and many, but not all, that are physically impossible; and it includes all worlds which are technologically possible, i.e., physically possible worlds having the same physical resources and industrial capacity as the actual world, and many, but not all, which are technologically impossible.

Very many different subsets of the set of all logically possible worlds may be distinguished. Many of these are of philosophical interest, e.g., physical, technological, moral, legal, etc. But we shall not much concern ourselves with them. For the most part, in this book our interest lies with the largest class of possible worlds, the class of logically possible worlds, and on a few occasions with the class of physically possible worlds. It is only in more advanced studies in logic that the special properties of various of these other subsets are examined.

Hereinafter, whenever we use the expression "all possible worlds" without any further qualification, we are to be understood to mean "all *logically* possible worlds".

The constituents of possible worlds

How are possible worlds constituted? It may help if we start with the possible world that we know best: the actual one. Following Wittgenstein, we shall say that the actual world is "the totality of [actually] existing states of affairs", where by "a state of affairs" we shall mean roughly what he meant, viz., an arrangement of objects, individuals, or things having various properties and standing in various relations to one another. It will help, however, if we adopt a slightly different terminology. Instead of the terms "objects", "things", and "individuals" we shall adopt the more neutral term "items".[4] And in addition to the terms "properties" and "relations" we shall adopt the more generic term "attributes".[5] An item (object or thing) is whatever exists in at least one possible world: physical objects like Model T Fords and starships; persons such as Woodrow Wilson and Lazarus Long; places such as Old Home Terra (the earth) and Secunda; events such as World War I and the Great Diaspora of the Human Race; abstract objects such as numbers and sets; and so on. An attribute (property or relation) is whatever is exemplified or instanced (has instances) by an item or by items in a world; properties such as being red, being old, being distant, or being frightening; and relations such as being faster than, being a lover of, being more distant than, or being earlier than. Typically, items are the sorts of things we would have to mention in giving a description of a possible world; they are things we can refer to. Attributes are the sorts of things that characterize items; they are the sorts of things which we ascribe to the objects of reference.

Now it is clear, from the examples just given of items and attributes, that items exist in possible worlds other than the actual one, and that attributes are instanced in possible worlds other than the

---

4. Other terms which play roughly the same role in philosophical literature are "particulars" and "logical subjects".

5. The term "attribute" with the meaning we have given it was introduced into recent philosophical literature by Carnap. As he put it: "In ordinary language there is no word which comprehends both properties and relations. Since such a word would serve a useful purpose, let us agree in what follows that the word 'attribute' shall have this sense. Thus a one-place attribute is a property, and a two-place (or a many-place) attribute is a relation." *Introduction to Symbolic Logic and Its Applications*, New York, Dover, 1958, p. 5.

actual one. How, then, do non-actual possible worlds differ from the actual one? They may differ in three basic ways. Other possible worlds may contain the very same items as the actual world but differ from the actual world in respect of the attributes which those items instance; e.g., differ in respect of the Eiffel Tower being purple, the Taj Mahal being green, and so on. Or they may contain at least some items which do not exist in the actual world (and ipso facto differ in respect of some attributes); e.g., they may contain Lazarus Long or Sherlock Holmes. Or still again, they may lack certain items which exist in the actual world (and ipso facto differ in respect of some attributes); e.g., they may lack Stalin or Shakespeare.

Some philosophers have thought that other possible worlds can differ from the actual one only in the first of these three ways. Other philosophers insist that they can differ from the actual one in the other two ways as well. Our own thinking in the matter is evident: in choosing the world of *Time Enough for Love* as our example, we are allowing the existence of non-actual possible worlds some of whose items do not exist in the actual world. In chapter 4, section 6, we will explore briefly some of the consequences of being less generous.

EXERCISES

In this and subsequent exercises, it is essential that one assume that all the terms being used have their standard meanings, e.g., that "square" refers to a plane, closed, four-sided figure having equal interior angles and equal sides. To be sure, for any word or sentence we care to think of, there will be possible worlds in which that word or sentence will mean something altogether different from what it means in the actual world. This fact, however, in no way tells against the fact that what *we* refer to by the word "square" has four sides in all possible worlds. The exercises posed ask whether the claims *we* are here considering are true in any possible world; and this is a wholly distinct matter from whether our words might be used by the inhabitants of other possible worlds to make different claims.[6]

Part A

For each of the following, say whether there is a logically possible world in which it is true.

1. *Frederick, of Gilbert and Sullivan's "Pirates of Penzance", has reached the age of 21 years after only 5 birthdays.*

2. *There is a square house all of whose walls face south.*

3. *Epimenides, the Cretan, spoke in truth when he said that everything that Cretans say is false.*

4. *Mt. Everest is lower than Mt. Cook.*

5. *Mt. Everest is lower than Mt. Cook, Mt. Cook is lower than Mt. Whistler, and Mt. Whistler is lower than Mt. Everest.*

6. $2 + 2 \neq 4$.

7. *The Pope believes that* $2 + 2 \neq 4$.

8. *The Pope knows that* $2 + 2 \neq 4$.

6. For more on this point, see our discussion in chapter 2, pp. 110ff, of the uni-linguo proviso.

9. *No objects are subject to the law of gravitation.*

10. *There is a mountain which is higher than every mountain.*

Part B

The following quotations are for reflection and discussion. For each of them try to decide whether the circumstance described could occur (a) in a logically possible world, and (b) in a physically possible world.

1. " 'All right,' said the Cat; and this time it vanished quite slowly, beginning with the end of the tail, and ending with the grin, which remained some time after the rest of it had gone." (Lewis Carroll, **Alice's Adventures in Wonderland & Through the Looking Glass**, New York, Signet Classics, 1960, p. 65.)

2. "As Gregor Samsa awoke one morning from uneasy dreams he found himself transformed in his bed into a gigantic insect. He was lying on his hard, as it were armor-plated, back and when he lifted his head a little he could see his dome-like brown belly divided into stiff arched segments on top of which the bed quilt could hardly keep in position and was about to slide off completely. His numerous legs, which were pitifully thin compared to the rest of his bulk, waved helplessly before his eyes." (Franz Kafka, **The Metamorphosis**, 1912, translated by Willa and Edwin Muir, New York, Schocken Books, 1948, p. 7.)

3. "NAT BARTLETT is very tall, gaunt, and loose-framed. His right arm has been amputated at the shoulder, and the sleeve on that side of the heavy mackinaw he wears hangs flabbily or flaps against his body as he moves. . . . He closes the door and tiptoes carefully to the companionway. He ascends it a few steps and remains for a moment listening for some sound from above. Then he goes over to the table, turning the lantern very low, and sits down, resting his elbows, his chin on his hands, staring somberly before him." (Eugene O'Neill, **Where the Cross is Made**, copyright 1919 by Boni and Liveright. Reprinted in **Twelve One-Act Plays for Study and Production**, ed. S. Marion Tucker, Boston, Ginn and Co., 1929, pp. 202, 208.)

2. PROPOSITIONS, TRUTH, AND FALSITY

Truth and falsity defined

Items (i.e., objects, things), we have said, may exist in possible worlds other than the actual one. Likewise, attributes (i.e., properties and relations) may be instanced in possible worlds other than the actual one. Consider, now, any arbitrarily selected item and any arbitrarily selected attribute; and let us name them, respectively, a and **F**. Then we can *define* "truth" and "falsity" as follows:

and

(a) it is *true* that a has **F** if, and only if, a has **F**;

(b) it is *false* that a has **F** if, and only if, it is not the case that a has **F**.

These definitions tell us, for instance, that where "*a*" stands for Krakatoa Island and "**F**" stands for the property of being annihilated in a volcanic eruption, then

It is true that Krakatoa Island was annihilated by a volcanic eruption if and only if Krakatoa Island was annihilated by a volcanic eruption and again, that

> It is false that Krakatoa Island was annihilated by a volcanic eruption if
> and only if it is not the case that Krakatoa Island was annihilated by a
> volcanic eruption.

These definitions accord with the insight which Aristotle, more than two thousand years ago,
expressed thus:

> To say of what is that it is not or of what is not that it is, is false, while
> to say of what is that it is, and of what is not that it is not, is true.[7]

Several points about these definitions are worth noting:

(i)   Although Aristotle's account suggests that it is persons' sayings which are true or false (i.e.,
which are, as we shall put it, the bearers of truth-values), our account in (a) and (b) leaves open the
question as to what it is which is true or false. There is no doubt that sayings, along with believings,
supposings, etc., are *among* the things which can be true or false. But many contemporary
philosophers prefer to say that it is primarily *propositions* which have the properties of truth or falsity
(i.e., that it is primarily propositions which are bearers of *truth-values*), and would hold that the
things persons say, believe, suppose, etc., are true or false just when the propositions which they utter,
believe, or entertain, etc., are true or false. For the reasons given at length in chapter 2, we adopt the
latter way of talking.[8] If we let the letter "P" stand for the proposition that *a* has **F**, we can restate (a)
and (b) as

> (a)*   The proposition P (that *a* has **F**) is true if and only if *a* has **F**;

and

> (b)*   The proposition P (that *a* has **F**) is false if and only if it is not the case
> that *a* has **F**.

(ii)   Our account, in (b) and (b)*, of the conditions in which the proposition that *a* has **F** is false,
allows for two such conditions: the possible state of affairs in which the item *a* exists but fails to have
the attribute **F**; and the possible state of affairs in which the item *a* does *not* exist. Since an attribute
can be instanced by an item in a possible world only if that item exists in that possible world, the
failure of an item to exist in a given possible world precludes it from having any attributes whatever
in that world.

(iii)   Strictly speaking, our account — and Aristotle's — of what it is for a proposition to be true
or false applies only to propositions which ascribe *properties* to items. But it is easily enough extended
to deal with those propositions which ascribe *relations* to two or more items. We can deal with
so-called "two-place" attributes (i.e., relations holding between just two items) as follows: where P is
a proposition, *a* and *b* are items, and **R** is the two-place attribute (relation) which P asserts to hold
between *a* and *b*, then P is true if and only if *a* and *b* stand to each other in the relation **R**, while P is

7. *Metaphysics*, Γ, 7(1011[b] 26 – 27), *The Basic Works of Aristotle*, ed. R. McKeon, New York, Random
House, 1941.

8. A proposition, we shall argue, is to be distinguished from the various sentences which language-speakers
may use to express it, in much the same way as a number is to be distinguished from the various numerals
which may be used to express it.

false if and only if it is not the case that *a* and *b* stand in the relation **R**. And accounts of truth-values for other relational propositions involving three or more items may be constructed along similar lines. Alternatively, we can deal with relational propositions by pointing out that whenever an item *a* stands in a relation **R** to one or more other items, *b, c,* etc., *a* can be said to have the *relational property* of standing in that relation to *b, c,* etc. And since relational properties are properties, the straightforward account given in (a) and (b) suffices.

(iv)   The account of truth which we are here espousing has been described variously as "the Correspondence Theory", "the Realist Theory", or even "the Simple Theory" of truth. In effect, it says that a proposition, P, is true if and only if the (possible) state of affairs, e.g., of *a*'s having **F**, is as P asserts it to be. It defines "truth" as a property which propositions have just when they "correspond" to the (possible) states of affairs whose existence they assert. It is a "realist" theory of truth insofar as it makes truth a real or objective property of propositions, i.e., not something subjective but a function of what states of affairs really exist in this or that possible world. And it is a "simple" theory of truth insofar as it accords with the simple intuitions which most of us — before we try to get too sophisticated about such matters — have about the conditions for saying that something is true or false.

(v)   If it seems to some that this theory is overly simple and not profound enough, this is probably because it is deceptively easy to confuse the question "What are the conditions of truth and falsity?" with the question "What are the conditions for our *knowledge* of truth and falsity?" It is not surprising, as a consequence, that the most commonly favored alleged rivals to the Correspondence Theory are the so-called Coherence and Pragmatist Theories of Truth. Proponents of these theories tend either to deny or to ignore the distinction between a proposition's *being* true and a proposition's *being known* to be true. We may accept the coherence theorist's claim that one way of getting to know what propositions are true is to determine which of them cohere with the rest of the beliefs that we hold to be true. And we may also accept the pragmatist's claim that one way of getting to know what propositions are true is to determine which of them it proves useful or practical to believe. But at the same time we would wish to point out that neither claim warrants *identifying* truth with coherence or truth with practical usefulness. And further we would point out that both theories are parasitic upon the "simple" theory of truth. The pragmatist states that certain hypotheses *are* useful; the coherence theorist states that certain sets of beliefs *are* coherent. Yet each, in so doing, is implicitly making a claim to the *simple* truth of *these* propositions. The concept of simple truth, it seems, is not easily dispensed with. Even those who would like most to avoid it cannot do so.

Truth in a possible world

It should be evident from our definitions (i) that a proposition, P, may assert that an item *a* has attribute **F** even if *a* exists only in a non-actual possible world, and (ii) that P will be true in that non-actual world provided that in that world *a* has **F**. Let us use the letter "W" (with or without numerical indices) to refer to any possible world of our choosing (e.g., the world of Heinlein's *Time Enough for Love*). Then our definitions allow us, for instance, to assert the truth in some specified possible world, W_1, of the proposition that Lazarus Long has the relational property of being a lover of Minerva even though in some other specified possible world, W_2 (e.g., the actual world), he does not exist and a fortiori does not have that property. Likewise, they allow us to assert the falsity in some specified possible world, W_2, of the proposition that Lazarus had Minerva as a lover even though in some other specified possible world, e.g., W_1, that proposition is true. Needless to say, they also allow us to assert that a proposition is true (or false) in some *unspecified* world, W; or, as we shall later put it, to assert that a proposition is possibly true (or false, as the case may be).

Truth in the actual world

It follows from what we have just said that — contrary to what is often supposed — the expressions "is true" and "is false" do *not* mean the same as "is actually true" and "is actually false". To say that a proposition is actually true (or false) is to say that among the possible worlds in which it is true (or false) there is the actual world. Thus, for instance, the proposition that Canada is north of Mexico is actually true because in the *actual* world Canada stands in the relation of being north-of to Mexico, i.e., has the relational property of being north of Mexico. And equally, the proposition that Lazarus has Minerva as a lover is actually false because in the *actual* world Lazarus fails to exist.

The fact that "true" does not mean "actually true" should be evident from two considerations. First, if it did, then the occurrence of the qualifier "actually" would be wholly redundant (pleonastic). Yet, as we have already seen, it is not. Secondly, if it did mean the same, then persons in other possible worlds would not be able to invoke the concept of truth without thereby making claims about *this* world, the actual one in which you and we find ourselves. Consider, for illustrative purposes, Lazarus' claim (on the first page of the narrative of *Time Enough for Love*): "It's true I'm not handy with the jabber they speak here." The year is A.D. 4272 and the place is the fictional Howard Rejuvenation Clinic on the fictional planet of Secundus. Lazarus asserts that a certain proposition, viz., that he doesn't have facility with the local language, is true. We understand him to be saying something which is true of the fictional world in which he exists. Yet if "true" *meant* "actually true" we should be obliged to understand him as saying something very different — as saying something about his lack of facility with a language that exists in the actual world which you and we inhabit.

Although "true" does not *mean* "actually true", it can be — and often is — used to *refer* to actual truth; what matters is *who* uses it. When persons in the actual world claim that a proposition is true they are claiming that it is true in their own world; and since their world is the actual world, it turns out that they are attributing actual truth to the proposition. However, when a person in a non-actual world attributes truth to a proposition, he is attributing to that proposition truth in his *own* world; and since his world is *not* the actual world, it turns out that he is attributing non-actual (but possible) truth to that proposition.

The myth of degrees of truth

It is worth pointing out that it is implicit in both Aristotle's account and the one in (a)* and (b)* that truth and falsity do not admit of degrees. Although there is a common manner of speech which fosters this belief — for example, "Jones' report was more true than Roberts'" — strictly speaking this manner of speech is logically untenable. A proposition is either wholly true or wholly false. There is no such thing as partial truth. Consider the simplest sort of case, that in which a proposition P ascribes an attribute **F** to an item *a*: P is true if *a* has attribute **F**, otherwise P is false. There is no provision, no room, in this explication of truth, for P to be anything other than wholly true or wholly false; for either *a* has the attribute **F**, or it is not the case that *a* has the attribute **F**.

There is, however, a way to reconcile the common manner of speech just reported with the stringencies of our definition of truth; and that is to regard such utterances as "Jones' report was more true than Roberts'" as elliptical for something of this sort: "A greater number of the details reported by Jones were true than those reported by Roberts." Similarly, an article in *Time* magazine[9] which bore the title "How True is the Bible?" could instead have been better presented under the title "How Much of the Bible is True?"

9. Dec. 30, 1974.

3.   PROPERTIES OF PROPOSITIONS

Among the items which exist in various possible worlds must be included propositions; and among the attributes which propositions instance in various possible worlds are the properties of truth and falsity. In every possible world each proposition has one or other of these properties of truth and falsity. But truth and falsity are not the only properties which propositions can have. By virtue of the fact that in any given possible world, a proposition has either the property of truth or the property of falsity, we can distinguish other properties which a proposition can have, viz., possible truth, possible falsity, contingency, noncontingency, necessary truth, and necessary falsity. These are properties — *modal properties* we shall call them — which propositions have according to the way in which their truth-values are distributed across the set of *all* possible worlds; according, that is, to whether they are true (or false) in just some, in all, or in none of the totality of possible worlds.[10] In distinguishing them we begin to approach the heart of logic itself.

Possibly true propositions

Consider, for a start, those propositions which are true in at least one possible world. The proposition that a particular item, Lazarus, had a particular attribute, that of having lots of time for love in his twenty-three hundred odd years, is a case in point. It is a proposition which is true in that possible though (so far as we know) non-actual world of Heinlein's novel. We shall say that it is *possibly true*, or again that it is a *possible truth*. Another example of a proposition which is true in at least one possible world is the proposition that Woodrow Wilson was president of the U.S. in 1917. In this case, of course, one of the possible worlds in which the proposition is true is also the actual one. Nevertheless it makes sense to say that this proposition is a possible truth even if, in saying so, we are not saying all that we are entitled to say, viz., that it is also an actual truth. For actual truths form a subclass of possible truths. A proposition is a possible truth, then, if it is true in at least one possible world — actual or non-actual. A proposition is *actually true* if among the possible worlds in which it is true there occurs the actual world.

In saying of a proposition that it is true in at least one possible world it should not be thought that it is also being claimed that that proposition is false in some other possible world. When we say that a proposition is true in some possible worlds we leave it an open question as to whether that proposition is true in all other possible worlds as well, or is false in some of those other possible worlds.

Possibly false propositions

How about propositions which are false in at least one possible world? Such propositions, we shall want to say, are *possibly false,* or are *possible falsities.* Now some (but, as we shall see later, not all) propositions which are possibly true are also possibly false. The proposition that Lazarus had lots of time for love is not only possibly true, because there is a possible world in which it is true; it is also possibly false, because there are other possible worlds — our own actual one among them — in which (so far as we know) it is false, i.e., actually false. Similarily, the proposition that Woodrow Wilson was president of the United States in 1917 is not only possibly (as well as actually) true, because there is a possible (as it happens the actual) world in which it is true; it is also possibly false, because there are other possible worlds — our own actual one *not* among them — in which it is false.

10. Note that although attributions of noncontingent truth and noncontingent falsity *will* count as attributions of modal status, the corresponding attributions of contingent truth and contingent falsity will *not*. The reason for allowing an ascription of contingency to count as an ascription of modal status but not allowing ascriptions of contingent truth or contingent falsehood is given in chapter 6, section 5.

Contingent propositions

Any proposition which not only is true in some possible worlds but also is false in some possible worlds is said to be a *contingent proposition*. A contingent proposition, that is, is both possibly true and possibly false. The proposition about Woodrow Wilson is contingent and happens to be true in the actual world, while the proposition about Lazarus is contingent and happens to be false in the actual world. The former is a possible truth which *could* have been false, even though as a matter of actual fact it is not; the latter is a possible falsity which *could* have been true, even though as a matter of actual fact it is not.

Contradictories of propositions

Suppose we have a proposition which is contingent and true in the actual world, such as the proposition that the U.S. entered World War I in 1917: then it is true in some possible worlds, including the actual one, but false in all those possible worlds in which it is not true. What might such a possible world be in which it is false that the U.S. entered World War I in 1917? It could be, for example, a possible world in which the U.S. entered World War I, not in 1917, but in 1918; or, it might be a possible world in which World War I never took place at all, perhaps because universal peace had been established in that world some years earlier, or because mankind had managed to destroy itself quite accidently in 1916; or again it might be a possible world in which the North American continent, and hence the U.S., simply did not exist. In each and every one of these latter possible worlds, and in countless others besides, it is false that the U.S. entered World War I in 1917, or in other words, it is true that it is not the case that the U.S. entered World War I in 1917.

Let us call any proposition which is true in all those possible worlds, if any, in which a given

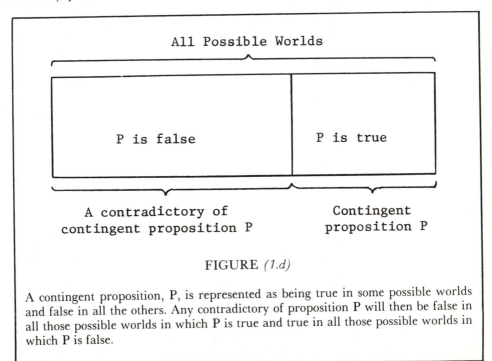

FIGURE *(1.d)*

A contingent proposition, P, is represented as being true in some possible worlds and false in all the others. Any contradictory of proposition P will then be false in all those possible worlds in which P is true and true in all those possible worlds in which P is false.

proposition is false, and which is false in all those possible worlds, if any, in which a given proposition is true, a *contradictory* of that proposition.[11] Then the proposition that it is not the case that the U.S. entered World War I in 1917 is a contradictory of the proposition that the U.S. did enter World War I at that time, and vice versa. The proposition that it is not the case that it did, since it is a contradictory of a true contingent proposition, will be contingent and false. It will be false, that is, in all those possible worlds, including the actual one, in which the U.S. entered World War I in 1917. Again, suppose we have a proposition which is contingent and false, such as the proposition that no fighting occurred in France during World War I. Then, although this contingent proposition will be false in some possible worlds including the actual one, there will be other possible worlds in which it is true. These other possible worlds will be precisely those in which a contradictory of that proposition, e.g., that fighting did occur in France at that time, will be false.

Noncontingent propositions

We have just been talking about those propositions which are both possibly true *and* possibly false. They are, we said, the contingent propositions. Are there any propositions which are *not* both possibly true and possibly false? Any propositions which are just the one and not the other? Any propositions, for instance, which could not possibly be false, i.e., which must be true? Or again, any propositions

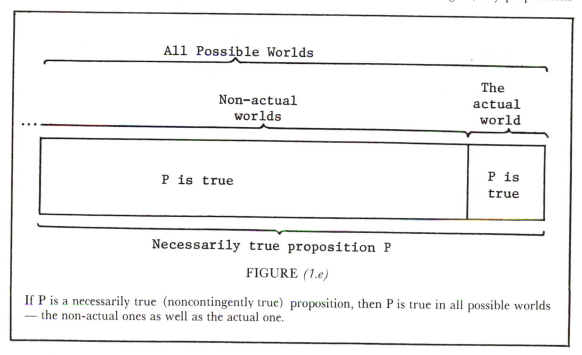

FIGURE *(1.e)*

If P is a necessarily true (noncontingently true) proposition, then P is true in all possible worlds — the non-actual ones as well as the actual one.

11. It is commonly said that a proposition has one and only one contradictory. If this claim were true, we ought, accordingly, to speak of *the* contradictory of a proposition rather than, as we have here, of *a* contradictory. However, subsequently in this chapter — after we have made a distinction between propositional-identity and propositional-equivalence — we will show that every proposition has an infinite number of non-identical equivalents and hence that every proposition has an infinite number of non-identical, but equivalent, contradictories.

which could not possibly be true, i.e., which must be false? Such propositions, if there are any, would not be contingent. They would be what we should want to call *noncontingent* propositions.

Consider, first, what it would be like for there to be propositions which *must be true*. Such propositions we should call *necessarily true* propositions. A necessarily true proposition would, of course, be a possibly true proposition. Indeed, since it would not only be true in at least one possible world but true in *all* possible worlds, it would also be true in the actual world. See figure *(1.e)*.

A necessarily true proposition, in short, would be both possibly true and actually true. But it would not be contingent and true. For a true contingent proposition, remember, is false in some possible world, whereas a necessarily true proposition — since it would be true in every possible world — could not be false in any. A necessarily true proposition, then, as well as being both actually and possibly true, would be *noncontingently true*.

Can we give an example of such a proposition? Examples abound, and we shall examine many in the course of this book. But for present purposes we shall satisfy ourselves with a particularly straightforward example.

It is a fairly obvious fact that not only can we ascribe truth and falsity (and other attributes) to individual propositions, but also we can ascribe various attributes to *pairs* of propositions. For example, we can assert of a pair of propositions (1) that neither is true, (2) that only one is true, (3) that at least one is true, or (4) that both are true, etc. In asserting something of a *pair* of propositions one is, of course, expressing a proposition which is itself either true or false. For example, if one were to assert of the two false contingent propositions

> *(1.1)*   Benjamin Franklin was a president of Spain,

> *(1.2)*   Canada is south of Mexico,

that one or the other of them is true, then the proposition which one has expressed is itself, obviously enough, contingent and false.

Our ability to ascribe truth to neither of, or to one of, or to both of, etc., a pair of propositions, provides a means to construct an example of a necessarily true proposition.

Necessarily true propositions

Consider the case in which we ascribe truth to one or the other of a pair of propositions. We can, of course, do this for any arbitrarily selected pair of propositions whatever. But let's see what happens when we do so in the case of ascribing truth to one or the other of a pair of contradictory propositions. Take, for instance, the contradictory pair

> *(1.3)*   The U.S. entered World War I in 1917;

> *(1.4)*   It is not the case that the U.S. entered World War I in 1917.

As we saw, *(1.3)* is true in all those possible worlds in which *(1.4)* is false, and *(1.4)* is true in all those possible worlds in which *(1.3)* is false. So in every possible world one or the other is true. If we then assert of such a pair that one or the other is true, the proposition we express will be true in all possible worlds. This proposition will be

> *(1.5)*   Either the U.S. entered World War I in 1917 or it is not the case that the U.S. entered World War I in 1917.

The same holds for any pair of contradictories whatsoever. Think of any proposition you like: for example, the contingent proposition that you (the reader) are now (at the moment of reading this sentence) wearing a pair of blue jeans. It doesn't matter whether this proposition is actually true or false. Being contingent, it is true in at least some possible worlds — even if not the actual one — and false in all those in which it is not true. Now think of a contradictory of that proposition, e.g., that it is not the case that you are wearing a pair of blue jeans. Whether this latter proposition is actually true or false, it will be true in all those possible worlds in which the proposition that you are wearing blue jeans is false, and false in all those possible worlds in which this proposition is true. Finally, then, think of the proposition that *either* you are wearing a pair of blue jeans *or* it is not the case that you are wearing a pair of blue jeans. This latter proposition, just like the proposition *(1.5)*, is true in all possible worlds, and hence, like *(1.5)*, is necessarily true.

Any proposition which asserts of two simpler ones that either one or the other is true, i.e., that at least one is true, is called a *disjunctive* proposition: it *disjoins* two simpler propositions each one of which is a *disjunct*. The disjuncts in a disjunctive proposition need not be contradictories of one another, as they are in the case of *(1.5)*. For instance, the proposition that either you are wearing a pair of blue jeans or you are dressed for a formal occasion is a disjunction whose disjuncts are *not* contradictories of one another. But in the case when disjuncts are contradictories, it follows, as we have seen, that the disjunction itself is necessarily true.

It is important not to think that the only necessarily true propositions are those which assert of a pair of contradictories that one or the other is true. Later we shall cite examples of necessarily true propositions which are not of this sort.

Necessarily false propositions

Consider, now, what it would be like to have a noncontingent proposition which *must be false*. Such a proposition we should call a *necessarily false* proposition. A necessarily false proposition would, of course, be a possibly false proposition. Indeed, since it would not only be false in at least some possible worlds but false in *all* possible worlds, it would also be false in the actual world. A necessarily false proposition, in short, would be both possibly false and actually false. But it would not be contingent and false. For a false contingent proposition, remember, is true in some possible world whereas a necessarily false proposition — since it is false in every possible world — is not true in any. A necessarily false proposition, then, as well as being both actually and possibly false would be *noncontingently false*.

What would be an example of such a proposition? Again, our ability to say something about the way truth and falsity are distributed between the members of a *pair* of propositions gives us the means of constructing an example of a necessarily false proposition.

Just as we can say of any pair of propositions that one or the other of them is true, we can also assert of any pair that *both* are true. But consider what happens when we say of a pair of propositions that they both are true in the case in which the two propositions happen to be contradictories. Consider, again, the contradictory pair of propositions *(1.3)* and *(1.4)*. Suppose we were to assert of them that they both are true. The proposition to this effect would be

> *(1.6)*   The U.S. entered World War I in 1917 and it is not the case that the U.S. entered World War I in 1917.

It is easy to see that there is no possible world in which this latter proposition is true. For, as we saw earlier when discussing the limits of possibility and conceivability, a supposed world in which something literally both is the case and is not the case is not, in any sense, a possible world; it is an

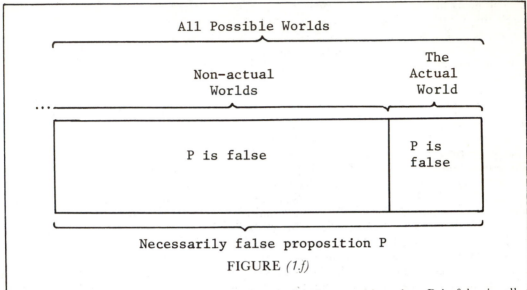

Necessarily false proposition P

FIGURE *(1.f)*

If P is a necessarily false (i.e. noncontingently false) proposition, then P is false in all possible worlds — the non-actual ones as well as the actual one. Such propositions are also said to be *self-contradictory, self-inconsistent,* or *logically impossible.*

impossible one. The case we considered earlier was that of the supposition that time travel both *will* occur sometime in the future and *will not* occur at any time in the future. We can see that it, like the case we are presently considering, involves ascribing truth to two propositions one of which is a contradictory of the other. And perhaps we can also now see why we earlier said that that proposition was *self-contradictory,* and why we would now want to say that the present case is also self-contradictory. For if any proposition ascribes truth to both members of a pair of contradictories, then that proposition is one which has a contradiction within itself.

Any proposition which asserts of two simpler ones that both of them are true, is called a *conjunctive* proposition: it *conjoins* two simpler propositions each of which is called a *conjunct.* The conjuncts in a conjunctive proposition need not be contradictories of one another, as they are in the case of *(1.6).* For instance, the proposition that you are wearing a pair of blue jeans and your friend is wearing a pair of tweeds is a conjunction whose conjuncts are *not* contradictories. But in the case where conjuncts are contradictories, it follows, as we have seen, that the conjunction is necessarily false.

More about contradictory propositions

A simple way of describing the relation which holds between two propositions which are contradictories of one another is to say that in each possible world one or other of those propositions is true and the other is false. This description has two immediate consequences which we would do well to note.

First, note that any contradictory of a contingent proposition is itself a contingent proposition. For if a proposition is contingent, i.e., true in some possible worlds and false in all the others, then since any proposition which is its contradictory must be false in all possible worlds in which the former is true, and true in all possible worlds in which the former is false, it follows immediately that this second proposition must be false in some possible worlds and true in some others. But this is just to say that the latter proposition is contingent.

Second, note that any contradictory of a noncontingent proposition is itself a noncontingent proposition. For if a proposition is noncontingently true, i.e., true in all possible worlds and false in none, then any proposition which is its contradictory must be false in all possible worlds and true in none, which is just to say that it itself must be noncontingent, and more especially, noncontingently false. Similarly, if a proposition is noncontingently false, i.e., false in all possible worlds and true in none, then any proposition which is its contradictory must be true in all possible worlds and false in none, which is just to say that it itself must be noncontingent, and more especially, noncontingently true. In short, if one member of a contradictory pair of propositions is necessarily true or necessarily false, then the other member of that pair must be necessarily false or necessarily true respectively. To cite an example of such a pair we need only return to propositions *(1.5)* and *(1.6)*: *(1.5)* is true in all possible worlds and *(1.6)* is false in all possible worlds; they are, in short, contradictories of one another.

Between them, then, a proposition and any contradictory of that proposition divide the set of all possible worlds into two subsets which are *mutually exclusive* and *jointly exhaustive*. One of these subsets will comprise all of the possible worlds, if any, in which the former proposition is true, and the other subset will comprise all of the possible worlds, if any, in which the latter proposition is true. Each possible world will belong to one or the other, but not to both, of these subsets.

Some main kinds of noncontingent propositions

So far, the only example cited of a necessarily true proposition was the disjunction of a pair of contradictories, viz., *(1.5)*; and the only example of a necessarily false proposition was the conjunction of a pair of contradictories, viz., *(1.6)*. Yet many noncontingent propositions are of kinds very different from these. In what follows, we cite some other kinds of examples (in no special order), all of necessarily true propositions. It should be evident, from what we said in the previous subsection, that the contradictories of each of the necessarily true propositions cited will be necessarily false.

1.   One main kind of necessarily true proposition is exemplified by

> *(1.7)*   If something is red then it is colored.

Note that this proposition is true even in those possible worlds in which there are no red things. To assert *(1.7)* is simply to assert that *if* anything is red then it is colored; and this proposition is true both in worlds in which there are red things and in worlds in which there are not.[12] Philosophers have spent time analyzing the *reasons* for the necessary truth of propositions like *(1.7)*. Properties, in general, tend to come in *ranges:* ranging from the more or less specific to the more general. Thus the property of being located in Ray Bradley's drawer in his desk at Simon Fraser University is a highly specific property. Or, as we shall prefer to say, it is a highly *determinate* property. The property of being located in British Columbia is less determinate; that of being located in Canada even less so; that of being located in the northern hemisphere even less so again; and so on. As we proceed along the scale of increasing generality, i.e., decreasing determinateness, we come finally to the least determinate property in the range. This is the property which, intuitively, falls just short of the most general of all properties — that of being a thing — viz., in the present instance the property of being

12. It has become standard practice, in the past hundred years or so, to construe sentences of the form "All . . . are. . . ." as if they said the same as sentences of the form "For anything whatever, if it is . . . then it is. . . ." On this account, the sentence "All red things are colored" expresses the necessary truth *(1.7)*.

located somewhere or other. Such properties we shall call *determinable* properties. Determinable properties are those under which all the more or less determinate properties of the range are subsumed. They are those which we would cite if we wished to give the least determinate possible answer to such general questions about a thing as: "Where is it?" (location); "How many are there?" (number); "How heavy is it?" (weight); "What color is it?" (color); and so on. Plainly, on this analysis, the property of being colored — of having some color or other — is a determin*able* property under which the relatively determin*ate* property of being red is subsumed. To be red is, therefore, ipso facto to be colored; and nothing could possibly be red without being colored.

2.   In the light of this understanding of determinable properties, we are able to give a characterization of a second main kind of necessary truth; that of which

(1.8)   Any event which occurs, occurs at some time or other

is an example. This kind of proposition is sometimes called a *category proposition* (or even a categorial[13] proposition): it is that kind of proposition in which a determinable property is truly ascribed to an item of a certain sort, or (as we shall say) of a certain *category*. Just as determinate properties are subsumable under highly general determinable properties, so are particular items and classes of items subsumable under highly general categories of items, e.g., the categories of material objects, of events, of persons, of mental processes, of sounds, and so on. Now what distinguishes items belonging to one category from those belonging to another is just the set of determin*able* (as distinct from determinate) properties which are essential to such items.[14] Material objects and shadows, for instance, share certain determin*able* properties, e.g., having some number, some shape, and some location. And these determinable properties are *essential* to them in the sense that nothing could possibly be a material object or a shadow if it lacked any of these determinable properties. By way of contrast, the determin*ate* properties, which particular items in a given category happen to have, are *not* all essential. The determinate property of being in Ray Bradley's drawer, for instance, is not essential to his copy of *Anna Karenina* although the determinable property of being located somewhere or other is. What makes material objects and shadows comprise different categories is the fact that, though sharing certain determinable properties, they do not share others. They do not share, for instance, the determinable property of having some mass or other. And neither of them has the determinable property which seems distinctive of propositions, viz., being true or false. The question as to what the essential determinable properties of items in a given category turn out to be, is one which we cannot pursue here. Suffice it to say that any true proposition which, like *(1.8)*, ascribes to items in a certain category a determinable property which is essential to those items, will be necessarily true. And so, for that matter, will be any true propositions which, like

(1.9)   Propositions have no color

deny of items in a certain category that they have a certain determinable property.

---

13. Note the spelling of this term. Do not confuse it with "categorical". The two are not synonyms.

14. A related kind of necessary truth, that which truly ascribes essential properties to so-called *natural kinds* — as, for example, the proposition that gold is a metal — has recently been the subject of much philosophical discussion. See, in particular, Saul Kripke, "Naming and Necessity" in *Semantics of Natural Language*, ed. Harman and Davidson, Dodrecht, D. Reidel, 1972. Kripke, somewhat controversially, maintains that having atomic number 79 is an essential property of gold.

3.   Still another main kind of necessary truth is exemplified by the *relational proposition*

> *(1.10)*   If Molly is taller than Judi then it is not the case that Judi is taller than Molly.

The necessary truth of this proposition, it should be noted, is not in any way a function of which particular items it asserts as standing in the relation of being taller than. Rather, it is a function of the essential nature of the relation of being taller than; of the fact, that is, that no matter what possible worlds or what possible items are involved, if the relation of being taller than holds between two items, x and y, in that order, then it does not also hold between x and y in the reverse order. This fact about the essential nature of the relation of being taller than is sometimes referred to by saying that the relation of being taller than is an "asymmetrical" relation. It is a fact about the relation of being taller than which serves to explain why not only *(1.10)* but countless other propositions, viz., *any* propositions of the form

> *(1.11)*   If x is taller than y then it is not the case that y is taller than x

are necessarily true. More generally, the property of being asymmetrical is essential to countless other relations as well, e.g., being the mother of, being older than, being the successor of, and so on. And for each of these relations there will be countless necessarily true propositions analogous to *(1.10)*. In chapter 6, section 6, we will investigate other of the essential properties which relations may have: (a) symmetry or nonsymmetry (as alternatives to asymmetry); (b) transitivity, intransitivity, or nontransitivity; and (c) reflexivity, irreflexivity, or nonreflexivity. We will see that every relation has at least one essential property drawn from each of (a), (b), and (c), i.e., has at least three essential properties *in toto*. That this is so provides a rich source of necessary truths. For all those propositions whose truth can be ascertained by an appeal to a fact about an essential property of a relation will themselves be necessary truths.

4.   In saying that propositions of the several main kinds discussed so far are logically necessary truths we are, it should be noted, using the term "logically necessary" in a fairly broad sense. We are not saying that such propositions are currently recognized as truths within any of the systems of formal logic which so far have been developed. Rather, we are saying that they are true in all logically possible worlds. Now, in this broad sense of the term, the *truths of mathematics* must also count as another main kind of logically necessary truth. Bertrand Russell and A. N. Whitehead, it is worth mentioning, tried soon after the turn of this century to show that the truths of mathematics were logically necessary in the rather stricter sense of being derivable in accordance with the rules of and from the axioms of then-known systems of formal logic. But whether or not they were successful — and this is still a topic for debate — there can be little doubt that mathematical truths are logically necessary in the broader sense. Indeed, it seems that early Greek philosophers recognized them as such well before Aristotle laid the foundation of formal logic in the third century B.C. The true propositions of mathematics seemed to them to be necessary in a sense in which those of history, geography, and the like are not. Admittedly, they doubtless would not then have offered a "true in all (logically) possible worlds" analysis of the sense in which mathematical truths seemed to them to be necessary. But such an analysis seems to fit well with their judgments in the matter.

It may seem to some that there are two important classes of exceptions to the general account we are giving of mathematical truths. The first has to do with propositions of what we often call *applied* mathematics. If by "propositions of applied mathematics" is meant certain true propositions of physics, engineering, and the like which are inferred by mathematical reasoning from other propositions of physics, engineering, etc., then of course such propositions will not count as necessary truths but only as contingent ones. But then it is misleading even to say that they are, in any sense, propositions of mathematics. If, on the other hand, we mean by "propositions of applied mathematics" certain propositions which, like

> *(1.12)*   If there are 20 apples in the basket then there are at least 19 apples in the basket

are *instances* (i.e., applications) of propositions of pure mathematics, then our account is sustained. For there are no possible worlds — even worlds in which apples, baskets, and whatnot fail to exist — in which a proposition like *(1.12)* is false. This sort of mathematical proposition should be distinguished from propositions about the physical results of putting things together, e.g.,

> *(1.13)*   One liter of alcohol added to one liter of water makes 2 liters of liquid

which not only is not necessarily true but is contingent and false. (See chapter 3, p. 170).

A second supposed exception has to do with the propositions of geometry. Thus, it may be said that although there was a time when propositions like Euclid's

> *(1.14)*   The sum of the interior angles of a triangle is equal to two right angles

were universally thought to be necessarily true, we now know much better: the development, in the nineteenth century, of non-Euclidean (e.g., Riemannian and Lobachevskian) geometries in which the sum of the interior angles of triangles are asserted to be more than or less than (respectively) two right angles, shows that *(1.14)* is not necessarily true. In effect, the objection is that with the advent of non-Euclidean geometries in the nineteenth century, we have come to see that the answer to the question as to what is the sum of the interior angles of a triangle, is a contingent one and will vary from possible world to possible world according to the natural laws in those worlds.

But this objection fails to make an important distinction. It is correct so long as by "triangles" it refers to physical objects, e.g., triangles which surveyors might lay out on a field, or paper triangles which one might cut out with scissors. But there are other triangles, those of pure geometry, whose properties are *not* subject to the physical peculiarities of any world. These idealized, *abstract* entities have invariant properties. What the advent of non-Euclidean geometries has shown us about *these* triangles is that we must distinguish various kinds: a Euclidean triangle will have interior angles whose sum is equal to two right angles; a Riemannian triangle, angles whose sum is greater than two right angles; and a Lobachevskian triangle, angles whose sum is less than two right angles. Specify which kind of abstract triangle you are refering to, and it is a necessary truth (or falsehood) that its angles sum to two right angles, less than two, or greater than two.

5.   Among the most important kinds of necessarily true propositions are those true propositions which ascribe *modal* properties — necessary truth, necessary falsity, contingency, etc. — to other propositions. Consider, for example, the proposition

> *(1.15)*   It is necessarily true that two plus two equals four.

(1.15) asserts of the simpler proposition — viz., that two plus two equals four — that it is necessarily true. Now the proposition that two plus two equals four, since it is a true proposition of mathematics, is necessarily true. Thus in ascribing to this proposition a property which it does have, the proposition *(1.15)* is *true*. But is *(1.15)* necessarily true, i.e., true in all possible worlds? The answer we shall

want to give — and for which we shall argue in chapter 4, pp. 185-88, and again in chapter 6, p. 335 — is that true propositions which ascribe necessary truth to other propositions are themselves necessarily true, i.e., logically necessary. As Hintikka has put it:

> It seems to me obvious that whatever is logically necessary here and now must also be logically necessary in all logically possible states of affairs that could have been realized instead of the actual one.[15]

Similar considerations lead us to say further that any true proposition which ascribes necessary falsity or contingency to another proposition is itself true in all possible worlds, i.e., is necessarily true. And the same holds for true propositions which, like

> *(1.16)*   The proposition that there are 20 apples in the basket is *consistent* with the proposition that the basket is green

assert of two simpler propositions that they are logically related by one of the *modal* relations, implication, equivalence, consistency, or inconsistency (discussed in the next section).

  6.   The preceding five kinds of necessary truth are not wholly exclusive of one another and are certainly not exhaustive of the whole class of necessary truths. There are other propositions which are true in all possible worlds but for which it is difficult to find any single apt description except to say that they are propositions whose truth can be ascertained by *conceptual analysis*. When Plato, for instance, in his dialogue, *Theatetus,* analyzed the concept of knowledge and came to the conclusion that knowing implies (among other things) believing, he provided grounds for us to ascertain, as being necessary truths, a host of propositions, such as

> *(1.17)*   If the Pope knows that there are nine planets then the Pope believes that there are nine planets.

That hosts of such necessary truths exist should be evident from the fact that the analytic truth which Plato discovered is quite general, admitting countless instances ranging from the Pope's knowledge (and consequent belief) about the number of the planets to the knowledge (and consequent belief) that most of us have about the earth's being round, and so on. Likewise, when a moral philosopher analyzes the concept of moral obligation and concludes that being morally obliged to do something implies being able to do it, that philosopher establishes that a host of propositions, of which

> *(1.18)*   If the foreign minister is morally obliged to resign then he is able to do so

is only one instance, are necessary truths. Characteristically, philosophers — in their analyses of these and other concepts which figure centrally in our thinking — are not trying to compete with scientists in discovering contingent truths about how the actual world happens to be constituted. Rather, they are trying to discover what is *implied* by many of the concepts which scientists and the rest of us take for granted. And the propositions in which they report their analytical discoveries, if true, are necessarily true.

---

15. Jaakko Hintikka, "The Modes of Modality" in *Acta Philosophica Fennica,* vol. 16 (1963), pp. 65–81.

Summary

Much of what we have said so far concerning worlds — actual and non-actual — and concerning propositions — true and false, contingent and noncontingent — about items in these worlds can be summarized in the following diagram:

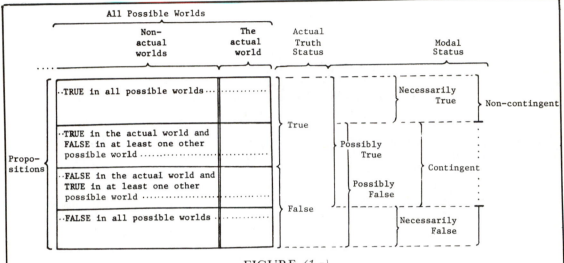

FIGURE *(1.g)*

Note that only those propositions are contingent which are *both* possibly true *and* possibly false, whereas those propositions are noncontingent which are *either* not possibly false (the necessarily true ones) *or* not possibly true (the necessarily false ones).

Other important relationships between classes of propositions may be read off the diagram in accordance with the following rule: if the bracket representing one class of propositions (e.g., the necessarily true ones) is contained within the bracket representing another class of propositions (e.g., the actually true ones), then any proposition belonging to the former class is a proposition belonging to the latter class. For instance, all necessarily true propositions are actually true, although not all actually true propositions are necessarily true.

EXERCISES

1. *For each of the following propositions, say (1) whether it is contingent or noncontingent, and (2) if noncontingent, then whether it is true or false.*

    a. *All aunts are females.*

    b. *On April 13, 1945, all females are aunts.*

    c. *If a bird is entirely black, then it is not also white.*

    d. *All black birds are black.*

     e. All blackbirds are black.

     f. Some squares have six sides.

     g. No mushrooms are poisonous.

     h. It is illegal to jaywalk in Moscow.

     i. Whenever it is summer in New Zealand, it is winter in Canada.

     j. What will be, will be.

2. *Briefly explain why each of the following propositions is* false.

     k. If a proposition is actually true, then that proposition is also contingent.

     l. If it is possible for a proposition to be true, then it is possible for that same proposition to be false.

     m. Even though a proposition is actually false, it need not be.

     n. If a proposition is noncontingent, then it is actually true.

     o. If a proposition is possibly true, then it is contingent.

3. *Write a short story such that a person reading that story could tell from subtle clues that there is no possible world in which all the events related occur.*

4. *Does the concept of time-travel really generate paradoxes? Here is what Lazarus says about the matter when discussing it with two of his descendants before making his own time-trip: "That old cliché about shooting your grandfather before he sires your father, then going* fuff! *like a soap bubble — and all descendants, too, meaning both of you among others — is nonsense. The fact that I'm here and you're here means that I didn't* do *it — or won't do it; the tenses of grammar aren't built for time-travel — but it does* not *mean that I never went back and poked around. I haven't any yen to look at* myself *when I was a snot-nose; it's the era that interests me. If I ran across myself as a young kid, he — I — wouldn't recognize me; I would be a stranger to that brat. He wouldn't give me a passing glance. I know, I* was *he." Discuss. (Robert A. Heinlein,* Time Enough For Love, *p. 358.)*

*   *   *   *   *

Symbolization

Much of the success and promise of modern logic, like that of mathematics, arises from the powerful and suggestive symbolization of its concepts. From time to time, as we introduce and discuss various of the most fundamental concepts of logic, we will also introduce symbols which are widely accepted as standing for those concepts.

    Already we have casually introduced some of these symbols as when, for example, we used the capital letter "P" of the English alphabet to represent any arbitrarily chosen proposition; when we used "*a*" to represent any arbitrarily chosen item; and when we used "**F**" to represent an arbitrarily chosen attribute.

    Let us extend our catalog of symbols even more. We have just introduced several of the most important concepts of modern logic. They are standardly represented in symbols as follows:

(1)   The concept of falsity: "∼" [called *tilde*[16]]

(2)   The concept of possibility: "◇" [called *diamond*]

(3)   The concept of necessary truth: "□" [called *box*]

(4)   The concept of contingency: "▽" [called *nabla*]

(5)   The concept of noncontingency: "△" [called *delta*]

Each of these symbols may be prefixed to a symbol (such as "P", "Q", "R") which stands for a proposition, to yield a further propositional symbol (e.g., "∼ P", "◇R"). Any sequence of one or more propositional symbols is called a "formula".[17]

Each of these symbols may be defined contextually as follows:

"∼ P" $=_{df}$ "The proposition P is false"[18] [or "It is false that P"]

"◇P" $=_{df}$ "The proposition P is possible" [or "It is possible that P"]

"□P" $=_{df}$ "The proposition P is necessarily true" [or "It is necessarily true that P"]

"▽P" $=_{df}$ "The proposition P is contingent" [or "It is contingent that P"]

"△P" $=_{df}$ "The proposition P is noncontingent" [or "It is noncontingent that P"]

These symbols may be concatenated, that is, linked together in a series, as for example, "∼ ∼ P". This gives us the means to express such propositions as that P is possibly false ("◇ ∼ P"), necessarily false ("□ ∼ P"), impossible ("∼ ◇P"), etc.

Certain of these combinations of symbols are sometimes unwittingly translated into prose in incorrect ways, and one should beware of the pitfalls. In particular, combinations beginning with "▽" and "△" prove troublesome. Consider, for example, "▽P". There is a temptation to translate this as "it is contingently true that P," or equivalently as "P is contingently true". Neither of these proposed translations will do. The correct translation is "It is contingent that P is true." Why? What exactly is the difference between saying on the one hand that P is contingently true, and on the other, that it is contingent that P is true? Just this: to say that P is contingently true is to say that P is both contingent and true; to say that it is contingent that P is true, is to say only that P's being true is contingent, i.e., that P is true in some possible worlds and false in some others. Clearly, then,

---

16. Rhymes with "Hilda".

17. In later chapters we will distinguish between formulae which are constructed so as to make sense (i.e., which are well-formed) and those which are not. The exact rules for constructing well-formed formulae within certain systems of symbols are given in chapters 5 and 6.

18. The "$=_{df}$"-symbol may be read as "has the same meaning as" or alternatively as "equals by definition". The expression on the left side of the "$=_{df}$"-symbol is the expression being introduced; it is known by the technical name *definiendum*. The expression on the right hand side of the "$=_{df}$"-symbol is the one whose meaning is presumed already understood and is being assigned to the definiendum. The right hand expression is called the *definiens*.

to say that a proposition is contingently true is to say *more* than merely that its truth is contingent. In other words, the expression "P is contingently true" is to be rendered in our symbolic notation as "P and $\triangledown$P." It is thus incorrect to translate "$\triangledown$P" alone as "P is contingently true." Similarly, "$\triangledown \sim$ P" is to be translated as "it is contingent that it is false that P"; and not as "P is contingently false."

An easy rule to bear in mind so as to avoid mistakes in translations is this: Never translate "$\triangledown$" or "$\triangle$" adverbially, i.e., with an "ly" ending; always translate them as "it is contingent that" and "it is noncontingent that" respectively. Adverbial translations in the other cases, i.e., for "$\square$" and "$\lozenge$" are freely permitted: "it is necessarily true that" and "it is possibly true that" respectively.

EXERCISES

1. Let "A" stand for the proposition that Canada is north of Mexico. Translate each of the following expressions into English prose.

    (a) $\sim A$ (f) $\sim \lozenge \sim A$ (k) $\triangledown A$ (p) $\triangle \sim A$

    (b) $\sim A$ (g) $\square A$ (l) $\triangledown \sim A$ (q) $\sim \triangle A$

    (c) $\lozenge A$ (h) $\square \sim A$ (m) $\sim \triangledown A$ (r) $\sim \triangle \sim A$

    (d) $\lozenge \sim A$ (i) $\sim \square A$ (n) $\sim \triangledown \sim A$

    (e) $\sim \lozenge A$ (j) $\sim \square \sim A$ (o) $\triangle A$

2. For each of the cases (c) through (r) above say whether the proposition expressed is true or false.

3. Letting "A" now stand for the proposition that all squares have four sides, say for each of the expressions (a) – (r) in question 1, whether the proposition is true or false.

4. Explain why "$\triangle$ P" is *not* to be translated as "P is noncontingently true" but as "it is noncontingent that P is true." Find a proposition of which it is true that it is noncontingent that it is true, but of which it is false that it is noncontingently true.

5. Say of each of the following which is true and which is false. (Note: it is actually true that some cows are infertile.)

    (s) It is contingent that some cows are infertile.

    (t) It is contingent that it is not the case that some cows are infertile.

    (u) It is contingently true that some cows are infertile.

    (v) It is contingently false that some cows are infertile.

6. Say for each of the following whether it is true or false.

    (w) It is noncontingent that $2 + 2 = 4$.

    (x) It is noncontingently true that $2 + 2 = 4$.

    (y) It is noncontingent that it is false that $2 + 2 = 4$.

(z)   *It is noncontingently false that 2 + 2 = 4.*

7.   *Explain the difference in meaning in the two phrases "noncontingently true" and "not contingently true".*

4.   RELATIONS BETWEEN PROPOSITIONS

Just as the modal properties of propositions are a function of the ways in which the truth-values of those propositions singly are distributed across the set of all possible worlds, so the *modal relations* between propositions are a function of the ways in which the truth-values of the members of *pairs* of propositions are distributed across the set of all possible worlds. We single out four modal relations for immediate attention, viz.,

inconsistency; consistency; implication; and *equivalence.*

In terms of these we will find it possible to explain most of the central logical concepts discussed in this book. Yet these modal relations, we shall now see, can themselves be explained — in much the same way as the above discussed modal properties — in terms of possible worlds.

Inconsistency

Two propositions are *inconsistent* with one another, we ordinarily say, just when it is necessary that if one is true the other is false, i.e., just when they cannot both be true. Translating this ordinary talk into talk of possible worlds we may say that two propositions are inconsistent just when in any possible world, if any, in which one is true the other is false, i.e., just when there is no possible world in which both are true.

Inconsistency is a generic modal relation. It has two, and only two species: contradiction and contrariety.

Contradiction is that species of inconsistency which holds between two propositions when they not only cannot both be true but also cannot both be false. As we saw in section 2, it is a relation which holds between, e.g., the contingent propositions

and

(1.3)   The U.S. entered World War I in 1917

(1.4)   It is not the case that the U.S. entered World War I in 1917;

and also holds between, e.g., the noncontingent propositions

(1.5)   Either the U.S. entered World War I in 1917 or it is not the case that the U.S. entered World War I in 1917

and

(1.6)   The U.S. entered World War I in 1917 and it is not the case that the U.S. entered World War I in 1917.

In any possible world, one or other of the propositions in a contradictory pair is true and the remaining proposition is false. Where two propositions are contradictories of one another there is no possible world in which both propositions are true and no possible world in which both propositions are false. To repeat: contradictories divide the set of all possible worlds into two mutually exclusive and jointly exhaustive subsets.

Contrariety is that species of inconsistency which holds between two propositions when although they cannot both be true, they nevertheless can both be false. Consider, for instance, the relation between the contingent propositions

and

> *(1.3)*   The U.S. entered World War I in 1917
>
> *(1.19)* The U.S. entered World War I in 1914.

Plainly, if one member from this contrary pair is true, the other is false. The truth of one excludes the truth of the other. So if two propositions are contraries it must be that at least one is false. Moreover both may be false. After all, we can conceive of its having been the case that the U.S. entered World War I neither in 1914 nor in 1917 but rather, let us suppose, in 1916. Thus while propositions *(1.3)* and *(1.19)* cannot both be true, they *can* both be false. There is some possible world in which *(1.3)* and *(1.19)* are false. Between them, then, the propositions of a contrary pair do not exhaust all the possibilities. In short, contraries divide the set of all possible worlds into two mutually exclusive subsets which are *not* jointly exhaustive.

Both members of the contrary pair just considered are contingent propositions. Can noncontingent propositions also be contraries? Can a noncontingent proposition be a contrary of a contingent proposition? As we have here defined "contrariety", the answer is "Yes" to both questions.[19] Consider, first, two propositions which are necessarily false. Since there are no possible worlds in which either is true, there is no possible world in which both are true. That is to say, since both are necessarily false, they cannot both be true. But equally, since both are necessarily false, they are both false in all possible worlds, and hence there is a possible world in which both are false. Hence, since two necessarily false propositions cannot both be true, but can both be false, they are contraries. Consider, secondly, a pair of propositions one of which is necessarily false and the other of which is contingent. Since there are no possible worlds in which the necessarily false proposition is true, there can be no possible worlds in which both it and the contingent proposition are true. To be sure, there will be some possible worlds in which the contingent proposition is true. But in all those possible worlds the necessarily false proposition will be false. Hence, even in those possible worlds it will not be the case that *both* are true. Moreover, both propositions may be false. They will both be false in all those possible worlds in which the contingent proposition is false. Hence, since two propositions one of which is necessarily false and the other of which is contingent cannot both be true, but can both be false, they are contraries.

Necessarily false propositions, it is clear, are profligate sources of inconsistency. Every necessarily false proposition is a contradictory of, and hence inconsistent with, every necessarily true proposition. Every necessarily false proposition is a contrary of any and every contingent proposition. And every necessarily false proposition is a contrary of every other necessarily false proposition. Indeed, we need only add that the term "self-inconsistent" is a synonym for the term "necessarily false", in order to conclude that a necessarily false proposition is inconsistent with every proposition whatever, including itself, i.e., that a necessarily false proposition is *self*-inconsistent.

From the fact that two propositions are inconsistent it follows that at least one is *actually* false. For since, by the definition of "inconsistency", there is no possible world in which both members of an inconsistent pair of propositions are true, every possible world — including the actual world — is a world in which at least one of them is false. Inconsistency, we may say, provides a guarantee of falsity. But the converse does not hold. From the fact that one or both of a pair of propositions is

---

19. Historically some logicians have used the terms "contradiction" and "contrariety" as if they applied only in cases in which both propositions are contingent. For more on this, see the subsection entitled *"A Note on History and Nomenclature"*, pp. 53–54.

actually false, it does not follow that they are inconsistent, i.e., that in every possible world one or both of them is false. Thus *(1.4)* and *(1.19)* are false in the actual world. Yet they are not inconsistent. This is fairly easy to show. Consider the fact that *(1.19)* is contingent and hence is true in some possible worlds, in particular, in all those possible worlds in which the U.S. entered World War I in 1914. But in each of these possible worlds, it turns out that *(1.4)* is also true: any possible world in which the U.S. entered World War I in 1914 is also a world in which it is not the case that the U.S. entered World War I in 1917. And this is just to say that in all those possible worlds in which *(1.19)* is true, *(1.4)* is also true. Hence there is a possible world in which these actually false propositions are true together. In short, from the fact that they are false in fact it does not follow that they are inconsistent. Being false in the actual world, it turns out, provides no guarantee of inconsistency.

EXERCISE

Can two propositions be contraries as well as contradictories of one another? Explain your answer.

*   *   *   *   *

Consistency

What does it mean to say that two propositions are *consistent* with one another? Given that we already know what it means to say that two propositions are *in*consistent with one another, the answer comes easily: two propositions are consistent with one another if and only if it is not the case that they are inconsistent. It follows that two propositions are consistent if and only if it is not the case that there is no possible world in which both are true. But this means that they are consistent if and only if there *is* a possible world in which both are true.

As an example of the modal relation of consistency, consider the relation between the contingent propositions

and

> *(1.3)*   The U.S. entered World War I in 1917

> *(1.20)*   Lazarus Long was born in Kansas in 1912.

Whatever other relation may hold between them, plainly the relation of consistency does: it need not be the case that if one is true the other is false; both can be true. No matter what the facts happen to be about the actual world (no matter, that is, whether either *(1.3)* or *(1.20)* is actually true), it is possible that both of them should be true — which is just to say that there is at least one possible world in which both are true.

If two contingent propositions happen both to be true in the actual world, then since the actual world is also a possible world, there is a possible world in which both are true, and hence they are consistent. Actual truth, that is to say, provides a guarantee of consistency. But the converse does not hold. From the fact that two propositions are consistent it does not follow that they are both true in the actual world. What does follow is that there is *some* possible world in which both are true; yet that possible world may be non-actual. Thus *(1.3)* and *(1.20)* are consistent. Yet they are not both true in the actual world. *(1.3)* is true in the actual world and false in some non-actual worlds, while *(1.20)* is false in the actual world and true in some non-actual worlds. Hence propositions can be consistent even if one or both is false. In short, consistency does not provide a guarantee of truth.

Since a necessarily true proposition is true in all possible worlds, a necessarily true proposition will be consistent with any proposition which is true in at least one possible world. It will be consistent, that is, with any contingent proposition and with any necessarily true proposition. It will be inconsistent only with those propositions which are not true in any possible worlds, i.e., with necessarily false ones.

Implication

Of the four modal relations we are currently considering, it is probably implication which is most closely identified, in most persons' minds, with the concerns of philosophy in general and of logic in particular. Philosophy, above all, is concerned with the pursuit of truth; and logic — its handmaiden — with discovering new truths once established ones are within our grasp. To be sure, philosophers and logicians alike are concerned to *avoid inconsistency* (since the inconsistency of two propositions is a sufficient condition of the *falsity* of at least one of them) and thus to *preserve consistency* (since the consistency of two propositions is a necessary — but not sufficient — condition of the *truth* of both). But it is in *tracing implications* that they most obviously advance their common concern with the discovery of new truths on the basis of ones already established. For implication is the relation which holds between an ordered pair of propositions when the first cannot be true without the second also being true, i.e., when the truth of the first is a sufficient condition of the truth of the second.

Like the relations of inconsistency and consistency, the relation of implication can be defined in terms of our talk of possible worlds. Here are three equivalent ways of so defining it:

(a)   a proposition P implies a proposition Q if and only if Q is true in all those possible worlds, if any, in which P is true;

(b)   a proposition P implies a proposition Q if and only if there is no possible world in which P is true and Q false;[20]

(c)   a proposition P implies a proposition Q if and only if in each of all possible worlds if P is true then Q is also true.

As an example of the relation of implication consider the relation which the proposition

(1.3)   The U.S. entered World War I in 1917

has to the proposition

(1.21)   The U.S. entered World War I before 1920.

Whatever other relations may hold between (1.3) and (1.21), plainly the relation of implication does. All three of the above definitions are satisfied in this case. Thus: [definition (a)] (1.21) is true in all those possible worlds in which (1.3) is true; [definition (b)] there is no possible world in which (1.3) is true and (1.21) is false; and [definition (c)] in each of all possible worlds, if (1.3) is true then (1.21) is true.

To say that a proposition Q *follows from* a proposition P is just to say that P *implies* Q. Hence the relation of following from, like its converse, can be explained in terms of possible worlds. Indeed, the explanation can be given by the simple expedient of substituting the words "a proposition Q

---

20. Definition (b), it should be noted, amounts to saying that P implies Q if and only if the truth of P is *inconsistent* with the falsity of Q. Implication, in short, is definable in terms of inconsistency.

follows from a proposition P" for the words "a proposition P implies a proposition Q" in each of the definitions (a), (b), and (c) above.

In terms of the relation of implication (and hence in terms of our talk of possible worlds) we can also throw light on another important logical concept: that of the *deductive validity* of an inference or argument. True, we have not hitherto had occasion to use the words "deductively valid". Yet it will be evident to anyone who has even a superficial understanding of the meanings of these words that much of our discussion has consisted in marshalling deductively valid arguments and drawing deductively valid inferences.[21] Time and again we have signaled the presence of arguments and inferences by means of such words as "hence", "consequently", "therefore", and "it follows that"; and implicitly we have been claiming that these arguments and inferences are deductively valid. But what does it mean to say that an argument or inference is deductively valid? As a preliminary it may help if we remind ourselves of some familiar facts: that it is propositions from which and to which inferences are drawn. Consider, then, the simplest sort of argument (or corresponding inference) which features just one proposition as its premise and just one proposition as its conclusion; and let us designate the premise "P" and the conclusion "Q". Then we can reformulate our question by asking: What does it mean to say that an argument or inference from P to Q is deductively valid? To say that an argument or inference from a proposition P to a proposition Q is deductively valid is just to say that P implies Q, or (conversely) that Q follows from P.[22] Deductive validity, then, which is a property of arguments or inferences, can be explained in terms of the modal relations of implication and following from. And, like them, it can be explained in terms of possible worlds. In this case, we need only adopt the expedient of substituting the words "an argument or inference from P to Q is deductively valid" for the words "a proposition P implies a proposition Q" in each of the definitions (a), (b), and (c) above.

A casual reading of our three definitions of "implication" may suggest to some that only true propositions can have implications. After all, we defined "implication", in (c) for instance, as the relation which holds between a proposition P and a proposition Q when in all possible worlds if P is *true* then Q is also true. And we illustrated the relation of implication by citing a case where a true proposition, viz., *(1.3)*, stood in that relation to another true proposition, viz., *(1.21)*. Does this mean that false propositions cannot have implications? Does it mean, to put the question in other words, that nothing follows from false propositions, or that deductively valid arguments cannot have false premises?

Not at all. On a more careful reading of these definitions it will be seen that they say nothing whatever about the actual truth-values of P or Q; i.e., that they say nothing at all about whether P or Q are true in the actual world. Hence they do not rule out the possibility of a proposition P implying a proposition Q when P is not true but false. In (c), for instance, we merely said that where P implies Q, in all possible worlds Q will be true *if* P is true. We have not *asserted* that P is true in the actual world but merely entertained the *supposition* that P is true in some world or other; and that is something we can do even in the case where P is false in the actual world or even where P is false in all possible worlds.

21. When persons draw a conclusion out of a proposition or a set of propositions they can be correctly said to be "inferring a proposition". Inferring is something persons *do;* it is *not* a logical relation between propositions. It is not only grammatically incorrect to speak of one proposition inferring another, it is logically confused as well. See H.W. Fowler, *A Dictionary of Modern English Usage, 2nd Edition*, revised by Sir Ernest Gowers, Oxford, Clarendon Press, 1965, p. 282.

22. Note that here we are defining "deductive validity", not "validity" *per se.* Later, in chapter 4, we shall define the wider concept of validity.

Moreover, we might just as easily have chosen to illustrate the relation of implication by citing a case where a false proposition implies another proposition. Consider such a case. The proposition

(1.19)   The U.S. entered World War I in 1914

is contingent and happens to be false; it is false in the actual world even though it is true in at least some non-actual worlds. Does this (actually) false proposition have any implications? (Equivalently: Do any other propositions follow from *(1.19)*? Can any other proposition be inferred with deductive validity from *(1.19)*?) Obviously enough, the answer is: Yes. A false proposition, like a true one, will have countless implications. For instance, the false proposition *(1.19)* implies all the countless propositions that we could express by uttering a sentence of the form "The U.S. entered World War I before . . . " and filling in the blank with the specification of any date whatever later than 1914, e.g., 1915, 1916, 1917, etc., etc. The crucial difference between the implications of a false proposition and the implications of a true proposition lies in the fact that on the one hand, a false proposition has implications some of which are false — as is the proposition that the U.S. entered World War I before 1915 — and some of which are true — as is the proposition *(1.21)* that the U.S. entered World War I before 1920 — while, on the other hand, a true proposition has implications all of which are true.

Here, then, are two important logical facts about the relation of implication. (i) All the implications of a true proposition have the same truth-value as that proposition, i.e., they 'preserve' its truth. For this reason implication is said to be a *truth-preserving* relation. In tracing out the implications of a true proposition we can be led only to further true propositions, never to false ones. Or, in other words, the only propositions that follow from or can be inferred with deductive validity from propositions which are true are propositions which are also true. (ii) The implications of a false proposition need not have the same truth-value as that proposition. Some of the implications of a false proposition are themselves false; but others are true. Implication, we may say, is *not* falsity-preserving. Among the propositions which follow from or can be inferred with deductive validity from propositions which are false, there are some true propositions as well as some false ones.

These simple logical facts have important practical and methodological applications when it comes to the pursuit of truth. By virtue of (i), it follows that one of the ways in which we can advance the frontiers of human knowledge is simply to reflect upon, or reason out, the implications of propositions we already know to be true. This is, paradigmatically, the way in which advances are made in mathematics and logic. But it is also the way in which unrecognized truths can be discovered in other areas as well. Many of the advances made in technology and the applied sciences, for instance, occur because someone has reasoned out for particular circumstances the implications of universal propositions already accepted as true in the pure sciences. By virtue of (ii), it follows that we can also advance the frontiers of human knowledge, negatively as it were, by testing the implications of hypotheses whose truth-values are as yet unknown, weeding out the false hypotheses, and thus narrowing down the range of alternatives within which truth may yet be found. An exploratory hypothesis is put forward and then tested by seeing whether its implications 'hold up' (as we say) in the light of experience. Of course, if a hypothesis has implications which experience shows to be true, this does not entitle us to conclude that the hypothesis itself is true. For as we have seen, there always are some implications of a proposition which are true even when the proposition itself is false. But if, on the other hand, a hypothesis has any implications which experience shows to be false, this does entitle us to conclude that the hypothesis itself is false. For as we have seen, there can be no false implications of a proposition in the case where that proposition itself is true. Hence if any of the implications of a hypothesis turn out to be false, we may validly infer that that hypothesis is false.

These two facts about the relation of implication are reflected in the standard methodology (or 'logic' as it is often called) of scientific enquiry. The cost of ignoring them, when one is conducting scientific research or when one is pursuing knowledge in any field whatever, is that the discovery of truth then becomes a completely haphazard matter.

Two further important logical facts about the relation of implication deserve notice and discussion. It follows from the definitions given of implication that: (iii) a necessarily false proposition implies any and every proposition; and (iv) a necessarily true proposition is implied *by* any and every proposition whatever. Conclusion (iii) follows from the fact that, if a proposition P is necessarily false then there is no possible world in which P is true and *a fortiori* no possible world such that in it both P is true and some other proposition Q is false; so that [by definition (b)] P must be said to **imply Q. Conclusion (iv) follows from the fact that if a proposition Q is necessarily true then there is no possible world in which Q is false and *a fortiori* no possible world such that in it both Q is false and some proposition P is true; so that [again by definition (b)] Q must be said to be implied by P.**

These conclusions, however, strike many persons as counterintuitive. Surely, it would be said, the necessarily false proposition

> *(1.6)* The U.S. entered World War I in 1917 and it is not the case that the U.S. entered World War I in 1917

does not imply the proposition

> *(1.2)* Canada is south of Mexico.

And surely, it again would be said, the necessarily true proposition

> *(1.7)* If some thing is red then it is colored

is not implied by the proposition

> *(1.20)* Lazarus Long was born in Kansas in 1912.

For the propositions in the first pair have 'nothing to do with' each other; they are not in any sense about the same things; one is 'irrelevant' to the other. And the same would be said for the propositions in the second pair.

These admittedly counterintuitive results are ones to which we devote a good deal of discussion in chapter 4, section 6, pp. 224–30. For the present, just three brief observations must suffice.

In the first place, (iii) and (iv) ought not to be viewed solely as consequences of some recently developed artificial definitions of implication. They are consequences, rather, of definitions which philosophers have long been disposed to give; indeed, comparable definitions were adopted by, and the consequences recognized by, many logicians in medieval times. Moreover, they are immediate (even if not immediately obvious) consequences of the definitions which most of us would *naturally* be inclined to give: as when we say that one proposition implies another if the latter can't *possibly* be false if the former is true; or again, as when we say that one proposition implies another just when if the former is true then *necessarily* the latter is true.[23] Once we recognize this we may be more ready

---

23. For discussion of an ambiguity, and a possible philosophical confusion, lurking in these natural ways of speaking, see chapter 6, section 3.

to educate our intuitions to the point of recognizing (iii) and (iv) as the important logical truths which they are.

Secondly, it is not hard to understand why our uneducated intuitions tend to rebel at accepting (iii) and (iv). For the plain fact of the matter is that most of the instances of implication which we are likely to think of in connection with the inferences we perform in daily life, or in scientific enquiry, are instances in which the relation of implication holds between *contingent* propositions; and one contingent proposition, as it happens, implies another only if there *is* a certain measure of 'relevance' to be found between them — only if they are, in some sense, 'about' the same things. Not surprisingly, then, we are inclined to indulge our all-too-common disposition to *generalize* — to suppose, that is, that all cases of implication must be like the ones with which we are most familiar. Had we, from the beginning, attended both to the consequences of our definitions and to the fact that they allow of application to noncontingent propositions as well as contingent ones, we might never have come to expect that all cases of implication would satisfy the alleged relevance requirement when, in the nature of the case, only some do.

Thirdly, in chapter 4, section 6, pp. 224–30, we press the case further for acceptance of (iii) and (iv) by showing, among other things, that those who are disposed to reject them are likely to have other *competing* and even more compelling intuitions on the basis of which they will be strongly disposed, as well as logically obliged, to accept (iii) and (iv). But the detailed argument on that can wait.

EXERCISES

1. *Explain the difference between asserting (1) that Q is a false implication of P, and asserting (2) that it is false that P implies Q.*

2. *Give an example of two propositions such that the latter is a false implication of the former.*

3. *Give an example of two propositions such that it is false that the former implies the latter.*

*   *   *   *   *

Equivalence

Once we have the concept of implication in hand it is easy to give an account of the modal relation of equivalence. To say that a proposition P is equivalent to a proposition Q is just to say that they imply one another, i.e., that not only does P imply Q but also Q implies P, i.e., that the relation of *mutual* implication holds between P and Q.

Now the relation of implication, as we have already seen, can itself be defined in terms of possible worlds. It follows that the relation of equivalence is likewise definable.

Consider once more how we defined "implication". Any of the definitions, (a), (b), or (c), will do. Let us choose (a). There we said that a proposition P implies a proposition Q if and only if Q is true in all those possible worlds, if any, in which P is true. Suppose, now, that P and Q are equivalent, i.e., that not only does P imply Q but also Q implies P. Then not only will Q be true in all those possible worlds, if any, in which P is true, but also the converse will hold, i.e., P will be true in all those possible worlds, if any, in which Q is true. It follows that where two propositions are equivalent, if there are any possible worlds in which one of them is true, then in exactly the same worlds the other is also true. More briefly, two propositions are equivalent if and only if they have the same truth-value in precisely the same sets of possible worlds, i.e., there are no possible worlds in which they differ in truth-value.

As an example of the relation of equivalence consider the relation which the contingent proposition

>   *(1.2)*   Canada is south of Mexico

has to the contingent proposition

>   *(1.22)*   Mexico is north of Canada.

Even if we were merely to rely on our untutored intuitions most of us would find it natural to say that these two propositions are equivalent. But now we can explain why. We can point out that not only does *(1.2)* imply *(1.22)*, but also *(1.22)* implies *(1.2)*. Or, getting a little more sophisticated, we can point out that in any possible world in which one is true the other is also true and that in any possible world in which one is false the other is false. It matters not at all that both propositions happen to be false in the actual world. As we have already seen, false propositions as well as true ones can (and do) have implications. And as we can now see, false propositions as well as true ones can be equivalent to one another.

Noncontingent propositions as well as contingent ones can stand in relations of equivalence to one another. Indeed, if we attend carefully to the definition we have given for equivalence it is easy to see: (i) that all noncontingently true propositions form what is called an equivalence-class, i.e., a class all of whose members are equivalent to one another;[24] and (ii) that all noncontingently false propositions likewise form an equivalence-class. Conclusion (i) follows from the fact that if a proposition is necessarily true it is true in all possible worlds and hence is true in precisely the same set of possible worlds as any other necessarily true proposition. Conclusion (ii) follows from the fact that if a proposition is necessarily false it is false in all possible worlds and hence is false in precisely the same set of possible worlds as any other necessarily false proposition.

These two conclusions strike many persons as counterintuitive. Surely, it would be said, there is a *difference* between the necessarily true proposition

>   *(1.5)*   Either the U.S. entered World War I in 1917 or it is not the case that the U.S.
>   entered World War I in 1917

and the necessarily true proposition

>   *(1.23)*   Either Canada is south of Mexico or it is not the case that Canada is south of
>   Mexico.

After all, the concepts involved are not the same. One of these propositions makes reference to an item called "the U.S." and to an event that occurred at a specific moment in time. The other makes reference to two very different items called "Canada" and "Mexico" and to the geographical location of one with respect to the other. How, then, can the two propositions be equivalent? Likewise, it would be said, there is a difference — a conceptual difference, one might say — between the necessarily false proposition

---

24. In this book we are using the term "equivalence-class" as a synonym for "a class of equivalent propositions". On this reading, it is possible for a proposition to belong to several equivalence-classes. More standardly, however, the term "equivalence-class" is used in such a way that a proposition can be a member of only one equivalence-class. There should be little cause for confusion. The more usual conception of equivalence-class can simply be regarded as the logical union of all the equivalence-classes (as here defined) of a proposition.

> *(1.6)*   The U.S. entered World War I in 1917 and it is not the case that the U.S. entered World War I in 1917

and the necessarily false proposition

> *(1.24)*   Canada is south of Mexico and it is not the case that Canada is south of Mexico

which prevents us, in any ordinary sense of the word, from saying that they are "equivalent".

The same problem arises in connection with contingent propositions. Let us see how.

Consider, for a start, the fact that any proposition which asserts of two other propositions that both are true will be true in all and only those possible worlds in which *both* are true. After all, in any possible world, if any, in which one were true and the other false, the claim that both of them are true would be false. Suppose, now, that we want to assert of a contingent proposition that both it and a noncontingently true proposition are true. Then the proposition in which we assert their *joint* truth will be true in all and only those possible worlds in which both are true together. But they will be true together only in those possible worlds in which the contingent proposition is true. Hence the proposition which asserts the joint truth of two propositions, one of which is contingent and the other of which is necessarily true, will be true only in those possible worlds in which the contingent proposition is true. But this means that any proposition which asserts the joint truth of two propositions one of which is contingent and the other of which is necessarily true will itself be contingent and equivalent to the contingent proposition. For example, suppose that we have a proposition which asserts both that a contingent proposition, let us say

> *(1.2)*   Canada is south of Mexico

and that a necessarily true proposition, let us say

> *(1.5)*   Either the U.S. entered World War I in 1917 or it is not the case that the U.S. entered World War I in 1917

are true. This will be the proposition

> *(1.25)*   Canada is south of Mexico and either the U.S. entered World War I in 1917 or it is not the case that the U.S. entered World War I in 1917.

Then it follows from what we have said that *(1.25)* is true in all and only those possible worlds in which it is true that Canada is south of Mexico, i.e., in which *(1.2)* is true. But this means not only that *(1.25)* is contingent but also that it is true in precisely the same set of possible worlds as *(1.2)*, and hence that *(1.2)* and *(1.25)* form an equivalence-class, i.e., are equivalent.

But are *(1.2)* and *(1.25)* *identical?* Our intuitions are likely to rebel at the very suggestion. And this is for the very same sorts of reasons which would lead them to rebel at the suggestion that the necessarily true propositions *(1.5)* and *(1.23)* are identical.

Perhaps the first point that needs to be made in reply to these objections is that the sense in which we are saying that two contingent propositions *may* be equivalent, and that any two necessarily true propositions *are* equivalent, and that any two necessarily false propositions *are* equivalent — is simply that which is conveyed in our definition, viz., that members of each of these sets of propositions have the same truth-value in the same set of possible worlds. We are *not* claiming that equivalent propositions are identical with one another. To be sure, there are uses of the term "equivalent" in ordinary discourse which foster the idea that "equivalent" is a precise synonym for "identical". For instance, someone who says that a temperature of zero degrees Celsius is equivalent to a temperature of thirty-two degrees Fahrenheit might just as well claim that the temperature as measured on one scale is the same as, or is identical with, the temperature as measured on the other scale. But the claim that two propositions are equivalent is not to be construed in this way. Two propositions can have identical truth-values in identical sets of possible worlds without themselves being identical. They can be identical in *these* respects without being identical in *all* respects. That is to say, they can be equivalent without being one and the same proposition. Draw a distinction between equivalence and identity, and conclusions (i) and (ii) no longer will seem counterintuitive. Similarly, we shall then be able, with consistency, to say that the two equivalent contingent propositions *(1.2)* and *(1.25)* are likewise non-identical. What *would* be counterintuitive would be the claims that all necessarily true propositions are identical with one another, that all necessarily false propositions are identical with one another, and that all equivalent contingent propositions are identical with one another. For then we should have to conclude that there are only two noncontingent propositions — a single necessarily true one and a single necessarily false one; and that all equivalent contingent propositions are identical.

But precisely how is the distinction between propositional equivalence and propositional identity to be drawn? More particularly, since we have already said what it is for two propositions to be equivalent, can we give an account of propositional identity which will enable us to say that propositions may be equivalent but non-identical?

It is worth noting, for a start, that discussions of identity — whether of the identity of propositions or of people, of ships or of sealing wax — are all too often bedeviled by difficulties even in posing the problem coherently. We can say, without any sense of strain, that two propositions are equivalent. But what would it mean to say that two propositions are identical? If they are identical how can they be *two*? Indeed, how can we sensibly even use the plural pronoun "they" to refer to that which we want to say is *one*? One's head spins, and we seem to be hedged in between inconsistency and futility. One of the greatest philosophers of the twentieth century, Ludwig Wittgenstein, put it aphoristically:

> Roughly speaking, to say of *two* things that they are identical is nonsense, while to say of *one* thing that it is identical with itself is to say nothing at all.[25]

One way out of this incipient dilemma lies in the recognition that on most, if not all, of the occasions when we are tempted to say that two things are identical, we could equally well — and a lot more perspicuously — say that two linguistic items symbolize (refer to, mean, or express) one and the same thing. Instead of saying — with all its attendant awkwardness — that two people, let us say Tully and Cicero, are identical, we can say that the names "Tully" and "Cicero" refer to one and the same person. Instead of saying that two propositions, let us say that Vancouver is north of Seattle and that Seattle is south of Vancouver, are identical, we can say that the sentences "Vancouver is north of Seattle" and "Seattle is south of Vancouver" express one and the same proposition.[26] This essentially, is the solution once offered, but subsequently rejected, by the great German philosopher and mathematician, Gottlob Frege. As he put it:

25. Ludwig Wittgenstein, *Tractatus Logico-Philosophicus*, trans. D.F. Pears and B.F. McGuinness, London, Routledge & Kegan Paul, 1961 (original edition published in German under the title *Logisch-Philosophiche Abhandlung*, 1921), proposition 5.5303.

26. Further reasons for adopting the distinction between sentences and propositions will be developed at length in chapter 2.

What is intended to be said by $a = b$ seems to be that the signs or names *'a'* and *'b'* designate the same thing.[27]

Although Frege's suggestion works well enough when we want to make specific identity-claims, it does not enable us to avoid the dilemma when we try to formulate the conditions of identity for things quite generally, things for which there are no linguistic symbols as well as for things for which there are. As it stands, Frege's claim suggests that we should be able to say something along these lines: "Two signs or names *'a'* and *'b'* designate the same thing if and only if. . . ." (where the blank is to be filled in by the specification of appropriate conditions of identity). But it is just plain false that to make an identity-claim is, in general, to assert that two expressions have the same reference. Frege's reformulation works well enough in the case of items which happen to have been named or referred to by someone or other in some language or other. But are there not at least some unnamed items, for which linguistic symbols have not yet and perhaps never will be, devised? Surely there must be identity-conditions for these items as well. Yet if this is so, how can we even begin? As we have already seen, we can hardly start off by saying "Two things are identical if and only if . . ."

In order to give quite general identity-conditions for any items whatever, we would do well to, as it were, 'turn the problem around' and ask for the conditions of *non*-identity. We would do well, that is, to ask, "Under what conditions should we feel compelled to say that there are *two* items rather than just one?" Not only is this way of putting the question paradox-free, but it also avoids the limitations implicit in Frege's formulation.

The answer which commends itself to most thinking people, philosophers and nonphilosophers alike, is essentially that which has come to be known as Leibniz's Principle. Leibniz put it this way:

> There are never in nature two beings which are exactly alike in which it is not possible to find an internal difference. . . . [28]

In effect, Leibniz claimed that it is impossible for *two* items to have *all* their attributes — including relational ones — in common. Putting the point in still another way: there are two items rather than one if and only if one item has at least one attribute which the other does not.

Armed with this account of identity, let us return to the task of distinguishing between propositional equivalence and propositional identity. Can we give an account of the conditions of propositional identity which will enable us to preserve our intuitions that propositions may be equivalent and yet non-identical?

It seems clear that what guides our intuitions when we insist that propositions, contingent and noncontingent alike, need not be identical even when they are members of the same equivalence-classes is something like Leibniz's Principle. We note that in each of the problematic cases preceding, one proposition has at least one attribute which the other lacks, and so conclude — in accordance with Leibniz's Principle — that the two, though equivalent, are not identical.

Let us call any attribute which serves to sort out and differentiate between two or more items a *differentiating attribute*. Then we may say that what guides our intuitions as to the non-identity of

27. Gottlob Frege, "On Sense and Reference", in *Translations from the Philosophical Writings of Gottlob Frege*, ed. P. Geach and M. Black, Oxford, Basil Blackwell, 1952, p. 56.

28. G.W.F. Leibniz, *Monadology*, trans. R. Latta, London, Oxford University Press, 1965, Section 9, p. 222. This principle is widely known as the Principle of Identity of Indiscernibles. More aptly, it might be called the Principle of Non-Identity of Discernibles.

the equivalent contingent propositions *(1.2)* and *(1.25)* is the fact that there is at least one differentiating attribute which makes them non-identical. Indeed there are several. The attribute of making reference to the U.S. is one of them: it is an attribute which *(1.25)* has but *(1.2)* does not. And there are still further differentiating attributes which, in the case of these two propositions, serve to differentiate one from the other: *(1.25)* makes reference to an event which *(1.2)* does not; *(1.25)* makes reference to a date which *(1.2)* does not; and so on. In short, the items and attributes to which one proposition makes reference are not entirely the same as the items and attributes to which the other makes reference. Hence the propositions themselves are not the same but different.

Similarly, by invoking Leibniz's Principle we may distinguish the two equivalent noncontingent propositions *(1.5)* and *(1.23)*: *(1.5)* refers to the U.S., *(1.23)* does not; *(1.23)* refers to Canada, *(1.5)* does not; etc. Once again, we may conclude that two equivalent propositions are not identical.

To sum up, equivalent propositions cannot differ from one another in respect of the attribute of having the same truth-value in the same sets of possible worlds. But they can differ from one another in respect of other attributes. Identical propositions, by way of comparison, cannot differ from one another in respect of this or any other attribute. They have all of their attributes in common.

In chapter 2, section 2, we return to the problem of drawing a line between propositional equivalence and propositional identity and come up with a more precise statement (in section 3) of the conditions for propositional identity.

EXERCISES

1. Which propositions *(a. – e.)* are inconsistent *with which* propositions *(i. – v.)? Which* propositions *(a. – e.)* are consistent *with which* propositions *(i. – v.)? Which* propositions *(a. – e.)* imply *which* propositions *(i. – v.)? And which* propositions *(a. – e.)* are equivalent *to which* propositions *(i. – v.)?*

a. There are 8,098,789,243 stars.	i. All triangles have three sides.
b. All squares have four sides.	ii. There are fewer than 17,561,224,389 stars.
c. Some squares have six sides.	
d. There are 8,098,789,243 stars or it is not the case that there are 8,098,789,243 stars.	iii. There are more than 8,098,789,242 stars and fewer than 8,098,789,244 stars.
	iv. There are 124,759,332,511 stars.
e. The U.S. entered World War I in 1917.	v. The U.S. entered World War I after 1912.

   (Partial answer: a.   *is inconsistent with iv.*
                         c.   *is inconsistent with i., ii., iii., iv., and v.*
                         a.   *is consistent with i., ii., iii., and v.)*

2. a. Is proposition A, defined below, consistent or inconsistent with proposition B?

      "A" = *Bill is exactly 6′ tall.*
      "B" = *Bill is exactly 6′ 2″ tall.*

    b.   Is proposition C, defined below, consistent or inconsistent with proposition D?

          "C" = Someone is exactly 6′ tall.
          "D" = Someone is exactly 6′ 2″ tall.

    c.   Is proposition E, defined below, self-consistent or self-inconsistent?

          "E" = Someone is exactly 6′ tall and 6′ 2″ tall.

3.   Explain why it is misleading *to say such things as:*

    "In the actual world, Canada's being north of Mexico is inconsistent with Mexico's being north of Canada";

or

    "In the world of Time Enough for Love, *the proposition that Lazarus falls in love with two of his daughters implies the proposition that Lazarus is a father."*

*   *   *   *   *

Symbolization

Our repertoire of symbols can now be extended to encompass not only the modal properties represented by "□", "◇", "▽", and "△", but also the modal relations of consistency, inconsistency, implication, and equivalence. They are standardly represented in symbols as follows:

    (1) The concept of consistency: "○"

    (2) The concept of inconsistency: "φ"

    (3) The concept of implication: "→" [called *arrow*]

    (4) The concept of equivalence: "↔" [called *double-arrow*][29]

Each of these symbols may be written between symbols which stand for propositions to yield further propositional symbols (e.g., "P○Q", "P→Q").

    Each of these symbols may be defined contextually as follows:

"P ○ Q"	$=_{df}$	"P is consistent with Q"
"P φ Q"	$=_{df}$	"P is inconsistent with Q"
"P→Q"	$=_{df}$	"P implies Q"
"P↔Q"	$=_{df}$	"P is equivalent to Q"

    29. These latter two symbols are not to be confused with the two symbols "⊃" and "≡" with which some readers may already be familiar. The two symbols "⊃" (called *hook* or *horseshoe*) and "≡" (called *triple-bar*) will be introduced later in this book and will there be used to stand for the relations of material conditionality and material biconditionality respectively. At that time we shall take some pains to argue that the relations of material conditionality and material biconditionality are distinctly different from any relations which have been introduced in this first chapter; in particular, that they are distinct from implication and equivalence.

EXERCISE

Refer to question 1 in the preceding exercise. Let the letters "A" – "E" stand for propositions a. – e. and the letters "J" – "N" for the propositions i. – v. Re-do question 1 expressing all your answers in the symbolism just introduced.

(Partial answer: A φ M

C φ J,   C φ K,   C φ L,   C φ M and C φ N

A ○ J,   A ○ K,   A ○ L,   A ○ N)

5.   SETS OF PROPOSITIONS

The truth-values, modal properties, and the modal relations which may be ascribed to individual propositions and to pairs of propositions, may, with equal propriety, be ascribed to *sets* of propositions and to pairs of sets of propositions.

Truth-values of proposition-sets

A set of propositions will be said to be *true* if every member of that set is true. And a set of propositions will be said to be *false* if not every member of that set is true, i.e., if at least one member of that set is false. Note carefully: a set of propositions may be false even though not every member of that set is false. A single false member in a set of propositions is sufficient to render the set false. And of course it follows from this that if a set is false, we are not entitled to infer of any particular member of that set that it is false; we are entitled to infer only that at least one member is false.

> *Example 1:   A true set of propositions*
>
> *(1.26)*   {Snow is white, The U.S. entered World War I in 1917}.[30]
>
> *Example 2:   A false set of propositions*
>
> *(1.27)*   {Snow is white, The U.S. entered World War I in 1914}.

It should be clear that the two expressions (1) "a set of false propositions" and (2) "a false set of propositions", do *not* mean the same thing. A set of false propositions is a set *all* of whose members are false; a false set of propositions is a set *at least one of whose* members is false.

Modal properties of proposition-sets

A set of propositions will be said to be *possibly true* or *self-consistent* if and only if there exists a possible world in which every member of that set is true.

Self-consistency is a 'fragile' property. It is easily and often unwittingly lost (see chapter 6, section 7). Consider the following example:

---

30. Here and subsequently in this book we use a pair of braces (i.e., "{" and "}") as a means to designate a set.

> {April is taller than Betty,
> Betty is taller than Carol,
> Carol is taller than Dawn,
> Dawn is taller than Edith,
> Edith is taller than Frances,
> Frances is taller than April}.

Notice how every subset consisting of *any* five of these propositions is self-consistent. Remove the first, *or* the second, *or* the third, etc., and the *remaining* set is self-consistent (which of course is *not* to say that it is true). But in reintroducing the removed proposition and consequently enlarging the set to what it was, self-consistency is lost. And once self-consistency is lost, in this set as in any other, it can never be regained by *adding* more propositions. Some persons think that self-consistency can be restored by inserting a proposition of the following kind into a self-inconsistent set: The immediately preceding proposition is false. But this device can *never* restore self-consistency. (See the exercises on p. 44.)

A set of propositions is *possibly false* if and only if there exists a possible world in which at least one member of that set is false.

A set of propositions is *necessarily true* if and only if every member of that set is necessarily true, i.e., if in every possible world every member of that set is true.

A set of propositions is *necessarily false* or *self-inconsistent* if and only if there does not exist any possible world in which that set is true, i.e., if in every possible world at least one proposition or another in that set is false.

And finally, a set of propositions is *contingent* if and only if that set is neither necessarily true nor necessarily false, i.e., if and only if there exists some possible world in which every member of that set is true and there exists some possible world in which at least one member of that set is false.

EXERCISES

Part A

For each set below tell whether that set is (1) possibly true and/or possibly false; and (2) necessarily true, necessarily false or contingent.

i.   {*Canada is north of Mexico, Hawaii is in the Pacific Ocean, Copper conducts electricity*}

ii.   {*Snow is white, Pine is a softwood, Coal is red*}

iii. {*There were exactly twelve tribes of Israel, There were exactly fourteen tribes of Israel*}

iv.   {*All sisters are female, All triangles have three sides, All squares have four sides*}

v.   {*Some coffee cups are blue, Some coffee cups are green, Some coffee cups are yellow*}

vi.   {*Some triangular hats are blue, All triangles have three sides, Some squares have five sides*}

vii. {*All triangles have three sides, Some triangular hats are blue*}

viii. {*Someone believes that today is Monday, Someone believes that today is Wednesday*}

ix.   {*Grass is green, Someone believes that grass is green*}

x.   {*All sisters are females, All females are sisters*}

Part B

1. *Explain why self-consistency can never be restored to a self-inconsistent set of propositions by the device of inserting into that set a proposition of the sort: The immediately preceding proposition is false.*

2. *The example used above which reports the relative heights of April and Betty, etc., can be made self-consistent by the removal of the last proposition. What argument is to be used against the claim that it is the last proposition in the above set which 'induces' the self-inconsistency and hence is false?*

3. *A self-inconsistent set of three propositions of which every proper non-empty subset is self-consistent is called an* antilogism. *An example would be:*

> {*Lorna has three brothers,*
> *Sylvia has two brothers,*
> *Sylvia has twice as many brothers as Lorna*}.

   Find three examples of antilogisms.

4. **Find a set of three** contingent *propositions such that each pair of propositions drawn from that set constitutes a self-inconsistent set. Example:*

> {*Norman is shorter than Paul,*
> *Norman is the same height as Paul,*
> *Norman is taller than Paul*}.

5. *Explain why one should* not *adopt the following definition of "necessary falsehood" for a set of propositions: A set of propositions is necessarily false if and only if every member of that set is necessarily false.*

* * * * *

Modal relations between proposition-sets

Two sets of propositions will be said to stand in the relation of *consistency* if and only if there exists some possible world in which all the propositions in both sets are jointly true.

Two sets of propositions stand in the relation of *inconsistency* if and only if there does not exist a possible world in which all the propositions of both sets are jointly true.

One set of propositions stands in the relation of *implication* to another set of propositions if and only if all the propositions of the latter set are true in every possible world, if any, in which all the propositions of the former set are true.

And two sets of propositions stand in the relation of *equivalence* if and only if all the propositions in one set are true in all and just those possible worlds, if any, in which all the propositions of the other set are true.

To illustrate these definitions, we cite the following examples.

> *Example 1:*

> The set of propositions

> > *(1.28)* {Ottawa is the capital of Canada, All men are mortal}

> is *consistent* with the set of propositions

> > *(1.29)* {Snow is white, Today is Tuesday, Some dogs meow}.

Example 2:

The set of propositions

(1.30)   {April is older than Betty, Betty is older than Carol, Carol is older
         than Diane}

is *inconsistent* with the set of propositions

(1.31)   {Diane is older than Edith, Edith is older than April}.

Example 3:

The set of propositions

(1.32)   {Mary invited Brett to act in the play, Gresham invited Sylvia to act in
         the play}

implies the set of propositions

(1.33)   {Sylvia was invited to act in the play, Mary invited someone to act in
         the play}.

Example 4:

The set of propositions

(1.34)   {Today is Wednesday}

is *equivalent* to the set of propositions

(1.35)   {It is later in the week than Tuesday, It is earlier in the week than
         Thursday}.

As we can see, some, although not all, of these sets of propositions contain more than one member, i.e., more than one proposition. Does this mean that the relations of consistency, inconsistency, etc., are not always dyadic, or two-placed relations? Not at all. For a dyadic relation is a relation which holds between two *items* and each of the above sets may be counted as a single item even if some of them have two or more members. Hence a relation which holds between two *sets* of propositions is still a dyadic relation even if there is more than one proposition in either or both sets.[31]

Insofar as modal relations can obtain between sets of propositions as well as between single, individual propositions, certain consequences follow which we would do well to explore.

---

31. Note that although *(1.35)* is *equivalent* to *(1.34)*, the set *(1.35)* does not itself constitute an equivalence-class, i.e., not all its members are equivalent to one another. One should be careful not to suppose that the relation of equivalence can hold only between equivalence-classes.

It needs to be pointed out that whenever a modal relation R holds between two individual propositions, P and Q,[32] there will always be an infinity of non-identical propositions belonging to the same equivalence-class as P, and an infinity of non-identical propositions belonging to the same equivalence-class as Q, and that *any* proposition belonging to the former class will stand in the relation R to *any* proposition belonging to the latter class. This is easy to prove.

Remember, first, that for any proposition P, whether contingent or noncontingent, there is a set of propositions each of which is true in precisely the same set of possible worlds as P; that is to say, any proposition P, of whatever modal status, is a member of an equivalence-class.

Secondly, the equivalence-class to which any given proposition P belongs is a set of propositions with an infinite number of members. How may we establish this latter claim? For a start, we may note that the set of natural numbers is a set with an infinite number of members. Now for each of these natural numbers there exists a proposition which asserts that the number has a successor. Hence the number of such propositions is itself infinite. Moreover, each of these propositions is not only true, but necessarily true. It follows that there is an infinite number of necessary truths. Now, as we saw before, since every necessary truth is true in precisely the same set of possible worlds as every other necessary truth, the set of necessary truths forms an equivalence-class. And, as we have just seen, this equivalence-class must have an infinite number of members. In short, every necessarily true proposition belongs to an equivalence-class which has an infinite number of members. But if this is so, then the same must be true also of every necessarily false proposition. For it is obvious that there must be an infinite number of necessarily false propositions: to each natural number there can be paired off a necessarily false proposition, e.g., the proposition that that number has no successor, and it is equally obvious that this infinite set of propositions constitutes an equivalence-class with all other propositions which are necessarily false. Hence every necessarily false proposition belongs to an equivalence-class which has an infinite number of members.

How about contingent propositions? The same result holds for them too. As we saw before (p. 37), for any contingent proposition whatever, there exists another non-identical but equivalent proposition which asserts the joint truth of both that proposition and some necessarily true proposition. But there is an infinite number of necessarily true propositions any one of which may be asserted to be true conjointly with a given contingent proposition. Hence for any contingent proposition whatever there exists an infinite number of non-identical but equivalent propositions each of which asserts the joint truth of that proposition and some necessarily true proposition. Hence every contingent proposition belongs to an equivalence-class which has an infinite number of members.

Consider, in the light of all this, two individual propositions, A and B, which stand in some modal relation R. For instance, let us suppose that A is the contingent proposition

(1.3)   The U.S. entered World War I in 1914

and B is the contingent proposition

(1.21)   The U.S. entered World War I before 1920.

There is an infinite number of non-identical propositions which are equivalent to A, and an infinite number of non-identical propositions which are equivalent to B. Thus it follows from the fact that *(1.3)* (i.e., A) implies *(1.21)* (i.e., B) that there is an infinitely large number of propositions equivalent to A each of which implies an infinitely large number of propositions equivalent to B.

---

32. Or, we might equally say, "between two unit sets {P} and {Q}. . . . "

Parallel conclusions follow for each of the other modal relations of consistency, inconsistency, and equivalence.

In sum, the point may be put this way: Whenever two propositions, P and Q, stand in any modal relation R, all those propositions which are equivalent to P, of which there is necessarily an infinite number, will similarly stand in the modal relation R to each of the infinite number of propositions which are equivalent to Q.

An interesting, neglected corollary may be drawn from this principle. In section 4 we argued that there are only two species of the modal relation of inconsistency: either two inconsistent propositions (and now we would add "proposition-sets") are contraries or they are contradictories. Now while it has long been acknowledged, indeed insisted upon, that no proposition has a unique (i.e., one and only one) contrary, it has often been as strenuously insisted that every proposition does have a unique contradictory, i.e., that there is one and only one proposition which stands in the relation of contradiction to a given proposition. But in light of the distinction between propositional-identity and propositional-equivalence and in light of the fact that modal relations hold equally well between sets of propositions as between propositions themselves, these claims need to be re-examined. Let us begin with some examples. Consider the proposition

(1.36)   Today is Wednesday.

Among its contraries are

(1.37)   Today is Monday;

(1.38)   Today is Saturday.

Now let's look at some of its contradictories. These will include

(1.39)   Today is not Wednesday;

(1.40)   Today is not the day after Tuesday;

(1.41)   Today is not the day before Thursday, etc.

What *difference* can we detect between the contraries of the proposition (1.36) and the contradictories of that same proposition? Just this: the contradictories of a given proposition form an equivalence-class (e.g., (1.39), (1.40), and (1.41) are all equivalent to one another), while the contraries of a given proposition are not all equivalent to one another. Thus while the claim that every proposition has a unique contradictory cannot be supported, it can be superseded by the true claim that all the contradictories of a proposition are logically equivalent to one another, i.e., that the set of contradictories of a proposition is itself an equivalence-class. No such claim can be made for the contraries of a proposition. The set consisting of all the contraries of a given proposition is *not* a set of equivalent propositions.

Minding our "P"s and "Q"s

Insofar as the kinds of properties and relations we are concerned to ascribe to single propositions may, as we have just seen, be ascribed to sets of propositions, we would do well to point out that both propositions and sets of propositions may equally well be represented by the same sorts of symbols in the conceptual notation we use. More specifically, when we write such things as "P stands in the relation R to Q if and only if . . . ", etc., we should be understood to be referring, indiscriminately, by our use of "P" and "Q", both to single propositions and to sets of propositions.

In the next section we shall introduce what we call "worlds-diagrams" and will label parts of them with "P"s and "Q"s. For convenience and brevity we often treat these symbols as if they referred to single propositions. In fact they ought to be thought to refer either to single propositions or to proposition-sets.

EXERCISES

1. *Which proposition-sets (a. – e.) are inconsistent with which proposition-sets (i. – v.)? Which proposition-sets (a. – e.) are consistent with which proposition-sets (i. – v.)? Which proposition-sets (a. – e.) imply which proposition-sets (i. – v.)? And which proposition-sets (a. – e.) are equivalent to which proposition-sets (i. – v.)?*

   a. *{Today is Tuesday, Bill has missed the bus, Bill is late for work}*

   i. *{Bill has missed the bus}*

   b. *{Someone returned the wallet, Someone lost his keys}*

   ii. *{Someone who lost his keys returned the wallet}*

   c. *{The Prime Minister is 6′ tall, The Prime Minister is exactly 5′ 2″ tall}*

   iii. *{Mushroom omelets are not poisonous, No mushroom omelet is poisonous}*

   d. *{Some mushrooms are poisonous, Some mushrooms are not poisonous}*

   iv. *{John is 15 years old, John is 5′ 3″ tall}*

   e. *{John is 15 years old and is 5′ 3″ tall}*

   v. *{Although Bill has missed the bus, he is not late for work}*

2. *Which one of the ten sets of propositions in exercise 1 is a set of equivalent propositions?*

3. *Construct an equivalence-class of three propositions one of which is the proposition that Sylvia is Diane's mother.*

4. *Construct an equivalence-class of three propositions one of which is the proposition that two plus two equals four.*

6.   MODAL PROPERTIES AND RELATIONS PICTURED ON WORLDS-DIAGRAMS

Worlds-diagrams have already been used: figure *(1.b)* introduced our basic conventions for representing an infinite number of possible worlds, actual and non-actual; and figures *(1.d)*, *(1.e)*, and *(1.f)* gave graphic significance to our talk of the different sorts of modal status that propositions have according to whether they are contingent, necessarily true or necessarily false, respectively. So far we have given these diagrams merely an *illustrative* role: our *talk* of possible worlds could have sufficed by itself. However, these diagrams can also be given an important *heuristic* role: they can facilitate our discovery and proof of logical truths which might otherwise elude us.

In order that we may better be able to use them heuristically we adopt the following two simplifying conventions:

(a) We usually omit from our diagrams any representation of the distinction between the actual world and other (non-actual) possible worlds. When the need arises to investigate the consequences of supposing some proposition to be actually true or actually false, that distinction can, of course, be reintroduced in the manner displayed in figures *(1.d)*, *(1.e)*, and *(1.f)*, or as we shall see soon, more perspicuously, simply by placing an "×" on the diagram to mark the location of the actual world among the set of all possible worlds. But, for the most part, we shall be concerned primarily with investigating the relationships between propositions independently of their truth-status in the actual world, and so shall have infrequent need to invoke the distinction between actual and non-actual worlds.

(b) We omit from our diagrams any bracketing spanning those possible worlds, if any, in which a given proposition or proposition-set[33] is false. This means that every bracket that we use is to be interpreted as spanning those possible worlds only in which a given proposition (or proposition-set) is true. In the event that a given proposition is not true in any possible world, i.e., is false in all possible worlds, we 'locate' that proposition by means of a point placed outside (and to the right of) the rectangle representing the set of all possible worlds. In effect we thus 'locate' any necessarily false proposition among the impossible worlds.

In light of these simplifying conventions, let us first reconstruct the three basic worlds-diagrams depicting the modal properties of contingency, necessary truth, and necessary falsity (figures *(1.d)*, *(1.e)*, and *(1.f)*), and then consider how they might be supplemented in order to depict modal relations.

Worlds-diagrams for modal properties

A single proposition (or proposition-set) P, may be true in all possible worlds, just some, or none. There are no other possibilities. If, then, we depict the set of all possible worlds by a single box, it follows that we have need of three and only three basic worlds-diagrams for the modal properties of a proposition (or proposition-set) P. They are:

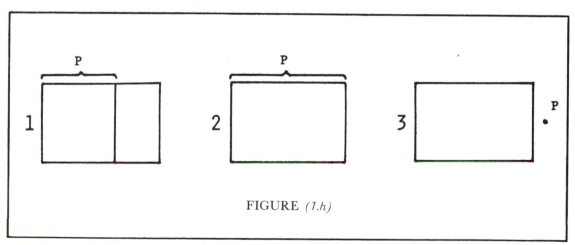

FIGURE *(1.h)*

33. See the subsection "Minding our 'P's and 'Q's", pp. 47–48.

Diagram 1 in figure *(1.h)*, p. 49, depicts the contingency of a single proposition (or proposition-set) P. The proposition P is contingent because it is true in some possible worlds but false in all the others. In effect, diagram 1 is a reconstruction of figure *(1.d)* made in accordance with the two simplifying conventions specified above. Our diagram gives the modal status of P but says nothing about its actual truth-status (i.e., truth-value in the actual world).

Diagram 2 depicts the necessary truth of a single proposition P. The proposition P is necessarily true, since it is true in all possible worlds. In effect, diagram 2 is a reconstruction of figure *(1.e)* made in accordance with our simplifying conventions.

Diagram 3 depicts the necessary falsity of a single proposition P. Here P is necessarily false since it is false in all possible worlds. In effect, diagram 3 is a simplification of figure *(1.f)*.

Worlds-diagrams for modal relations

In order to depict modal relations between two propositions (or two proposition-sets) P and Q, we need exactly fifteen worlds-diagrams. In these worlds-diagrams (see figure *(1.i)* on p. 51), no significance is to be attached to the relative *sizes* of the various segments. For our present purposes all we need attend to is the relative *placement* of the segments, or as mathematicians might say, to their topology. For the purposes of the present discussion our diagrams need only be qualitative, not quantitative.[34]

EXERCISE

Reproduce figure (1.i) *and add brackets for "∼P" and for "∼Q" to each of the fifteen worlds-diagrams.*

*   *   *   *   *

Interpretation of worlds-diagrams

Diagrams 1 to 4 depict cases where both propositions are noncontingent. Diagrams 5 to 8 depict cases where one proposition is noncontingent and the other is contingent. The final seven diagrams (9 to 15) depict cases where both propositions are contingent.

Now each of these fifteen diagrams locates two propositions, P and Q, with respect to the set of all possible worlds, and thence with respect to one another, in such a way that we can determine what modal relations one proposition has to the other. How can we do this?

The modal relations we have singled out for consideration so far are those of inconsistency, consistency, implication, and equivalence. Recall, then, how each of these four relations was defined: P is *inconsistent* with Q if and only if there is no possible world in which both are true; P is *consistent* with Q if and only if there is a possible world in which both are true; P *implies* Q if and only if [definition (b)] there is no possible world in which P is true and Q is false; and P is *equivalent* to Q if and only if in each of all possible worlds P has the same truth-value as Q. Recall, further, that our device for depicting a proposition as true in a possible world is to span that world by means of a bracket labeled with a symbol signifying that proposition.

34. Later, when we come to discuss the concept of "the contingent content" of a proposition, we shall suggest how one might want to reinterpret these worlds-diagrams so that the sizes of the segments do take on significance. (See chapter 6, section 11.)

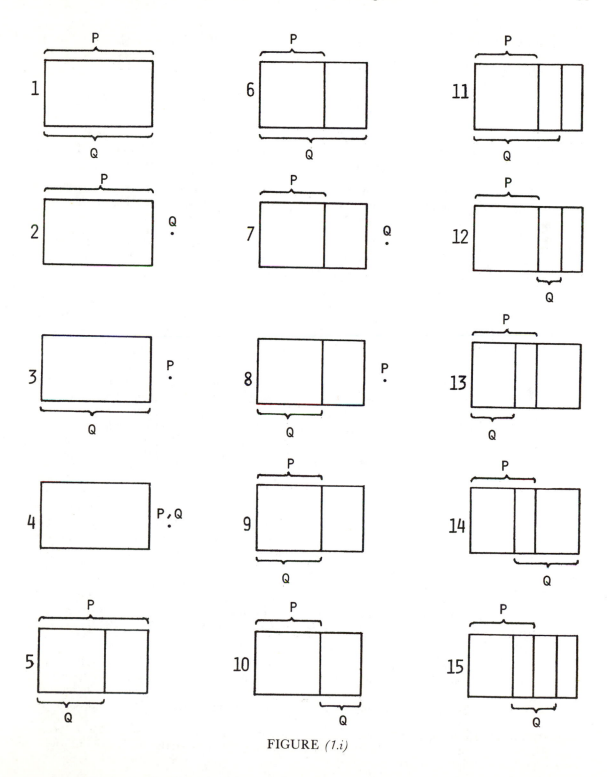

FIGURE *(1.i)*

The requisite rules for the interpretation of our worlds-diagrams follow immediately:

Rule 1:   P is *inconsistent* with Q if and only if there does not exist any set of possible worlds which is spanned both by a bracket for P and by a bracket for Q;

Rule 2:   P is *consistent* with Q if and only if there does exist a set of possible worlds which is spanned both by a bracket for P and by a bracket for Q;

Rule 3:   P *implies* Q if and only if there does not exist any set of possible worlds which is spanned by a bracket for P and which is not spanned by a bracket for Q (i.e., if and only if any set of possible worlds spanned by a bracket for P is also spanned by a bracket for Q);[35]

Rule 4:   P is *equivalent* to Q if and only if there does not exist any set of possible worlds which is spanned by the bracket for one and which is not spanned by the bracket for the other (i.e., the brackets for P and for Q span precisely the same set of worlds).

It is the addition of these rules of interpretation that gives our worlds-diagram the heuristic value that we earlier claimed for them. By applying them we can prove a large number of logical truths in a simple and straightforward way. Consider some examples:

(i)   Diagrams 2, 3, 4, 7, and 8 comprise all the cases in which one or both of the propositions P and Q is necessarily false. In none of these cases is there any set of possible worlds spanned both by a bracket for P and by a bracket for Q. Hence, by Rule 1, we may validly infer that in all of these cases P is inconsistent with Q. In short, *if one or both of a pair of propositions is necessarily false then those propositions are inconsistent with one another.*

(ii)   Diagrams 1, 2, 3, 5, and 6 comprise all the cases in which one or both of the propositions P and Q is necessarily true. In each of these cases, except 2 and 3, there is a set of possible worlds spanned both by a bracket for P and by a bracket for Q. Hence, by Rule 2, we may validly infer that in each of these cases, except 2 and 3, P is consistent with Q. But diagrams 2 and 3 are cases in which one or other of the two propositions is necessarily false. We may conclude, therefore, that *a necessarily true proposition is consistent with any proposition whatever except a necessarily false one.*

(iii)   Diagrams 3, 4, and 8 comprise all the cases in which a proposition P is necessarily false. In none of these cases is there a set of possible worlds spanned by a bracket for P. Hence in none of these cases is there a set of possible worlds which is spanned by a bracket for P and not spanned by a bracket for Q. Hence, by Rule 3, we may validly infer that in each case in which P is necessarily false, P implies Q no matter whether Q is necessarily true (as in 3), necessarily false (as in 4), or contingent (as in 8). By analogous reasoning concerning diagrams 2, 4, and 7 — all the cases in which a proposition Q is necessarily false — we can show that in each case in which Q is necessarily false, Q implies P no matter whether P is necessarily true (as in 2), necessarily false (as in 4), or contingent (as in 7). In short, we may conclude that *a necessarily false proposition implies any and every proposition no matter what the modal status of that proposition.*

(iv)   Diagrams 1, 3, and 6 comprise all the cases in which a proposition Q is necessarily true. In none of these cases is there a set of possible worlds which is *not* spanned by a bracket for Q. Hence, by Rule 3, we may validly infer that in each case in which Q is necessarily true, Q is implied by a proposition P no matter whether P is necessarily true (as in 1), necessarily false

35. This means that P implies Q in three cases: (i) where the bracket for P spans no possible worlds at all (i.e., P is necessarily false); (ii) where the bracket for P is included within the bracket for Q; and (iii) where the bracket for P is coextensive with the bracket for Q.

(as in 3), or contingent (as in 6). By analogous reasoning concerning diagrams 1, 2, and 5 — all the cases in which a proposition P is necessarily true — we can show that in each case in which P is necessarily true, P is implied by a proposition Q no matter whether Q is necessarily true (as in 1), necessarily false (as in 2), or contingent (as in 5). In short, we may conclude that *a necessarily true proposition is implied by any and every proposition no matter what the modal status of that proposition.*

The special heuristic appeal of these worlds-diagrams lies in the fact that, taken together with certain rules for their interpretation, we can literally *see* immediately the truth of these and of many other propositions about the modal relations which propositions have to one another. The addition of still further definitions and rules of interpretation later in this book will enable us to provide more perspicuous proofs of important logical truths — including some which are not as well-known as those so far mentioned.

A note on history and nomenclature

So far we have given names to only a few of the modal relations which can obtain between two propositions. We have spoken of *inconsistency* (and its two species, contradiction and contrariety), of *consistency*, of *implication*, and of *equivalence*. Within the philosophical tradition, however, we find logicians talking also of modal relations which they call "superimplication" (sometimes called "superalternation"), "subimplication" (sometimes called "subalternation"), "subcontrariety", and "independence" (sometimes called "indifference").

By "superimplication" and "subimplication" (or their terminological alternates), traditional logicians meant simply the relations of *implication* and of *following from* respectively. To say that P stands in the relation of *superimplication* to Q is simply to say that P *implies* Q, while to say that P stands in the relation of *subimplication* to Q is simply to say that P *follows from* Q (or that Q *implies* P). In short, subimplication is the converse of superimplication, i.e., of implication.

By "subcontrariety" we mean the relation which holds between P and Q when P and Q *can both be true together but cannot both be false.* That is to say, *subcontrariety* is the relation which holds between P and Q when there is at least one possible world in which both are true (P and Q are consistent) but there is no possible world in which both are false ($\sim$P and $\sim$Q are inconsistent).[36]

By "independence" we mean the relation which holds between P and Q when *no relation other than consistency holds between the two.* That is to say, *independence* is the relation which holds between P and Q when there is at least one possible world in which both are true (P and Q are consistent), there is at least one possible world in which both are false ($\sim$P and $\sim$Q are also consistent), there is at least one possible world in which P is true and Q is false, and there is at least one possible world in which P is false and Q is true.

Of the various modal relations we have distinguished, only one is uniquely depicted by a single worlds-diagram. This is the relation of independence. Independence is depicted by diagram 15 and by that diagram alone. Each of the other modal relations is exemplified by two or more of the fifteen worlds-diagrams. Historically, this fact has not always been recognized. Within traditional logic,[37]

---

36. The term "subcontrariety" reflects the fact, well known to traditional logicians, that subcontrary propositions are contradictories of propositions which are contraries and stand in the relation of *subimplication* to these contrary propositions. Thus P is a subcontrary of Q if and only if (a) $\sim$P and $\sim$Q are contraries, and (b) the contrary propositions, $\sim$P and $\sim$Q, imply Q and P respectively.

37. By "traditional logic" we mean the logic which was founded by Aristotle (384–322 B.C.), enriched by the Stoics and Megarians, and effectively canonized by sixteenth- and seventeenth-century logicians.

the terms "equivalence", "contradiction", "superimplication", "contrariety", "subimplication", and "subcontrariety" were often used *as if* each of them, too, were relations which, in terms of our worlds-diagrams, we would uniquely depict by a single diagram. Traditional logicians tended to think of equivalence as that relation which we can reconstruct, by means of our worlds-diagrams, as holding in diagram 9 alone; of contradiction as if it could be depicted in diagram 10 alone; of superimplication (and hence of implication) as if it could be depicted in diagram 11 alone; of contrariety as if it could be depicted in diagram 12 alone; of subimplication as if it could be depicted in diagram 13 alone; and of subcontrariety as if it could be depicted in diagram 14 alone. That is to say, they tended to think of these relations as if they could hold only between propositions both of which are contingent. (It is easy to see, by simple inspection, that diagrams 9 through 15 depict the only cases in which both propositions are contingent.) One consequence of the traditional preoccupation with relations between contingent propositions was, and sometimes still is, that someone brought up in that tradition, if asked what logical relation holds between a pair of *contingent* propositions (any of those depicted by diagrams 9 through 15), had little difficulty in invoking one of the standard repertoire of "equivalence", "contradiction", "superimplication", "contrariety", "subimplication", "subcontrariety", or "independence"; but if asked what logical relation holds between a pair of propositions one or both of which is *noncontingent* (any of those depicted by diagrams 1 through 8), simply would not know what to say.[38]

A second and more significant consequence of this preoccupation with relations between contingent propositions was, and still is, that the "intuitions" of some (but not, of course, all) persons under the influence of this tradition are not well attuned to the analyses, in terms of possible worlds, of relations like equivalence and implication; they tend to consider these analyses as "counter-intuitive", and certain consequence of these analyses as "paradoxical".[39]

Capsule descriptions of modal relations

It may be helpful to gather together the descriptions we have given in various places of those modal relations which are our principle concern.

P is *inconsistent* with Q:	there is no possible world in which both are true
P is a *contradictory* of Q:	there is no possible world in which both are true and no possible world in which both are false
P is a *contrary* of Q:	there is no possible world in which both are true but there is a possible world in which both are false
P is *consistent* with Q:	there is a possible world in which both are true
P *implies (superimplies)* Q:	there is no possible world in which P is true and Q is false
P *follows from (subimplies)* Q:	there is no possible world in which Q is true and P is false

38. Answers can, however, be given. Worlds-diagram 8, for example, depicts a relation which satisfies the descriptions given of *two* modal relations, viz., implication and contrariety. That is, two propositions, P and Q, which stand in the relation depicted in diagram 8, are such that (1) P implies Q and (2) P and Q are contraries.

39. In chapter 4 we develop this point further and suggest also that some resistence to these analyses has its source in a failure to distinguish between valid inference and demonstrability.

P is *equivalent* to Q: in each possible world, P and Q have matching truth-values

P is a *subcontrary* of Q: there is a possible world in which both are true but there is no possible world in which both are false

P is *independent* of Q: there is a possible world in which both are true, a possible world in which both are false, a possible world in which P is true and Q is false, and a possible world in which P is false and Q is true

EXERCISES

Part A

1. Which worlds-diagrams (in figure (1.i)) represent cases in which P is necessarily true (i.e., in which □P obtains)?

2. Which worlds-diagrams represent cases in which Q is necessarily true? [□Q]

3. Which worlds-diagrams represent cases in which P is contingent? [∇P]

4. Which worlds-diagrams represent cases in which Q is contingent? [∇Q]

5. Which three worlds-diagrams represent cases in which we may validly infer that P is actually true (i.e., true in the actual world)?

6. Which seven worlds-diagrams represent cases in which P implies Q? [P→Q]

7. Which seven worlds-diagrams represent cases in which Q implies P? [Q→P]

8. Which eight worlds-diagrams represent cases in which P is consistent with Q? [P ∘ Q]

9. Which seven worlds-diagrams represent cases in which P is inconsistent with Q? [P ϕ Q]

10. Which three worlds-diagrams represent cases in which P and Q are contradictories?

11. Which four worlds-diagrams represent cases in which P and Q are contraries?

12. Which four worlds-diagrams represent cases in which P and Q are subcontraries?

13. Which three worlds-diagrams represent cases in which P and Q are equivalent? [P↔Q]

14. Which worlds-diagrams represent cases in which P is possible and in which Q is possible? [◇P and ◇Q]

15. Which worlds-diagrams represent cases in which P is possible, Q is possible, and in which P is inconsistent with Q? [◇P and ◇Q and (P ϕ Q)]

16. Which worlds-diagrams represent cases in which neither P implies Q nor Q implies P? [∼ (P→Q) and ∼ (Q→P)]

17. Which worlds-diagrams represent cases in which both P implies Q and P is consistent with Q? [(P→Q) and (P ∘ Q)]

18. *Which worlds-diagrams represent cases in which both P implies Q and P is inconsistent with Q?* [(P→Q) and (P ⧄ Q)]

19. *Which worlds-diagrams represent cases in which both P implies Q and Q does not imply P?* [(P→Q) and ~ (Q→P)]

20. *Which worlds-diagrams represent cases in which P and Q are consistent with one another but in which P does not imply Q?* [(P ○ Q) and ~ (P→Q)]

21. *Which worlds-diagrams represent cases in which P and Q are inconsistent with one another and in which P does not imply Q?* [(P ⧄ Q) and ~ (P→Q)]

22. *Which worlds-diagrams represent cases in which P implies P?* [P→P]

23. *Which worlds-diagrams represent cases in which P is contingent, Q is necessarily true, and in which P implies Q?* [∇P, □Q, and (P→Q)]

24. *Which worlds-diagrams represent cases in which P is necessarily true, Q is contingent, and in which P implies Q?* [□P, ∇Q, and (P→Q)]

25. *Which worlds-diagrams represent cases in which P is equivalent to Q and in which P and Q are inconsistent with one another?* [(P↔Q) and (P ⧄ Q)]

26. *Which worlds-diagrams represent cases in which P implies ~ P?* [P→ ~ P]

27. *Which worlds-diagrams represent cases in which ~ P implies P?* [~ P→P]

28. *Which worlds-diagrams represent cases in which P is consistent with ~ P?* [P○ ~ P]

29. *Which worlds-diagrams represent cases in which both P implies ~ Q and P is consistent with Q?* [P→ ~ Q and P○Q]

30. *Which worlds-diagrams represent cases in which P is contingent and ~ P is necessarily true?* [∇P and □ ~ P]

31 – 45. *For each of the fifteen worlds-diagrams in figure (1.i) find any two propositions which stand in the relation depicted by that diagram.*

Example: diagram 14

> *Let "P" = There are fewer than 30,000 galaxies.*
> *Let "Q" = There are more than 10,000 galaxies.*

Part B

The expression "It is false that P implies Q" is ambiguous between saying "P does not imply Q" and "P's being false implies Q" which may be symbolized unambiguously as "~ (P→Q)" and "(~ P→Q)" respectively.

46. *Which worlds-diagrams represent cases in which P does not imply Q?* [~ (P→Q)]

47. *Which worlds-diagrams represent cases in which P's being false implies Q?* [~ P→Q]

48. *Which worlds-diagrams represent cases in which both P's being true implies Q and P's being false implies Q?* [(P→Q) and (~ P→Q)]

Part C

The expression "Q is a false implication of P" means "Q is false and Q is an implication of P." In order to represent this relation on a set of worlds-diagrams we shall have to have a device for depicting the actual world (i.e., for depicting that Q is false). Rather than persisting with the convention of figures (1.d), (1.e), and (1.f), we shall hereinafter adopt the simpler convention of representing the location of the actual world among the set of possible worlds by "×". In worlds-diagrams 1 through 4, the "×" may be placed indiscriminately anywhere within the rectangle. But when we come to diagrams 5 through 15 we are faced with a number of alternatives. To show these alternatives we will label each of the internal segments of the rectangle from left to right beginning with the letter "a". Thus, for example, worlds-diagram 11 containing an "×" in the central segment would be designated "11b". A worlds-diagram on which the location of the actual world is explicitly marked by an "×", we shall call a "reality-locating worlds-diagram".

49. Taking account of all the different ways the actual world may be depicted on a worlds-diagram, how many distinct reality-locating worlds-diagrams are there for two propositions?

50. Using the convention just discussed for describing a worlds-diagram on which the actual world is depicted, which worlds-diagrams represent cases in which Q is a false implication of P? [(P→Q) and ~Q]

51. Assume P to be the true proposition that there are exactly 130 persons in some particular room, 2B. Let Q be the proposition that there are fewer than 140 persons in room 2B. Draw a reality-locating worlds-diagram representing the modal relation between these two propositions.

(For questions 52–55) Assume that there are exactly 130 persons in room 2B. Let P be the proposition that there are exactly 135 persons in room 2B, and Q the proposition that there are at least 133 persons in room 2B.

52. Is Q implied by P?

53. Is Q true?

54. Is P true?

55. Draw a reality-locating worlds-diagram representing the modal relation between the propositions, P and Q.

* * * * *

Appendix to section 6

It is an interesting question to ask, "How many different ways may *three* arbitrarily chosen propositions be arranged on a worlds-diagram?" The answer is "255".

It is possible to give a general formula for the number (W_n) of worlds-diagrams required to depict all the possible ways of arranging any arbitrary number (n) of propositions. That formula is[40]

$$W_n = 2^{2^n} - 1$$

40. Alternatively, the formula may be given recursively, i.e.,

$$W_1 = 3, \text{ and}$$

$$W_{n+1} = (W_n + 1)^2 - 1$$

Using this latter formula it is easy to show that the next entry in table *(1.j)*, i.e., W_7, would be 39 digits in length.

We may calculate the value of W_n for the first few values of n.

n	W_n
1	3
2	15
3	255
4	65,535
5	4,294,967,295
6	18,446,744,073,709,551,615

TABLE *(1.j)*

7. IS A SINGLE THEORY OF TRUTH ADEQUATE FOR BOTH CONTINGENT AND NONCONTINGENT PROPOSITIONS?

In this chapter we have introduced one theory of truth, the so-called Correspondence Theory of Truth which has it that a proposition P, which ascribes attributes **F** to an item a, is true if and only if a has the attributes **F**. Sometimes this theory is summed up epigrammatically by saying that a proposition P is true if and only if 'it fits the facts'.

Now some philosophers who are perfectly willing to accept this theory as the correct account of the way the truth-values of contingent propositions come about, have felt this same theory to be inadequate or inappropriate in the case of noncontingent propositions. We would do well to review the sort of thinking which might lead one to this opinion.

Suppose one were to choose as one's first example a contingent proposition, let us say the proposition

(1.42)   Canada is north of Mexico.

When one asks what makes *(1.42)* actually true, the answer is obvious enough: this particular proposition is actually true because of certain peculiar geographical features of the actual world, features which are shared by some other possible worlds but definitely not by all.

Following along in this vein, we can ask a similar question about noncontingent propositions. Let us take as an example the noncontingent proposition

(1.43)   Either Booth assassinated Abraham Lincoln or it is not the case that Booth assassinated Abraham Lincoln.

If we now ask what makes this proposition true, some persons have felt that the answer cannot be of the same sort as that just given in the case of the example of a contingent proposition. For these persons rightly note that whereas the truth-value of *(1.42)* varies from possible world to possible world, the truth-value of *(1.43)* does not. No matter how another possible world may differ from the actual world, no matter how outlandish and farfetched that world might seem to us in the actual world, the truth-value of *(1.43)* will be the same in that world as in the actual world. In the actual world, Booth did assassinate Lincoln and *(1.43)* is true. But there are other possible worlds in which Lincoln did not go to Ford's Theater on April 14, 1865, and lived to be re-elected to a third term; yet in those worlds, *(1.43)* is true. Then, too, there are those possible worlds in which Booth did shoot Lincoln, but the wound was a superficial one and Lincoln recovered; yet in those worlds, too, *(1.43)* is true.

In the eyes of some philosophers these latter sorts of facts challenge the correspondence theory of truth. In effect these philosophers argue that the truth of noncontingent propositions cannot be accounted for by saying that 'they fit the facts' since they remain true whatever the facts happen to be. How could the truth of *(1.43)* in one possible world be explained in terms of one set of facts and its truth in another possible world in terms of a different set of facts? The very suggestion has seemed to these philosophers to constitute a fatal weakness in the correspondence theory of truth. In their view there just doesn't seem to be any proper set of facts to which true noncontingent propositions 'correspond'. And so, they have been led to propose *additional* theories of truth, theories to account for the truth-values of noncontingent propositions.

One of the oldest supplemental theories invoked to account for the truth of necessary truths holds that their truth depends upon what were traditionally called "The Laws of Thought", or what most philosophers nowadays prefer to call "The Laws of Logic". Precisely what is encompassed within these so-called laws of thought has been an issue of long dispute among philosophers. Nevertheless, it seems fairly clear that whatever else is to be included, the laws of thought do include the 'Laws' of Identity, of The Excluded Middle, and of Noncontradiction: roughly, the 'laws' that an item is what it is, that either an item has a certain attribute or it does not, and that an item cannot both have a certain attribute and fail to have it.

But this supplemental theory turns out, on examination, to be wholly lacking in explanatory power. For if there is controversy over the matter of what is to be included among the laws of thought, there has been even greater controversy, with more far-reaching implications, over the matter of what sorts of things these so-called "laws of thought" *are*. The account which seems to work best in explaining what the laws of thought are, is that which says of them that they are themselves nothing other than noncontingently true propositions. But if this account is adopted — and it is by most contemporary philosophers — then it is very hard to see how the laws of thought can serve as an explanation of what it is that the truth-values of noncontingent propositions depend on. The trouble is that if a certain class of noncontingently true propositions, the honored "laws of thought", are to account for the truth (or falsity) of other (the run-of-the-mill) noncontingent propositions, then some further, presumably still more honored propositions must account for *their* truth, and so on and on without end. In short, invoking some propositions to account for the truth or falsity of others leads one to an infinite regress or lands one in a circularity.

A second supplemental theory, which we shall call "the linguistic theory of necessary truth", holds that the truth-values of noncontingent propositions come about, not through correspondence with the facts, but rather as a result of certain 'rules of language'. Capitalizing on the very word "contingent", this theory is sometimes expressed in the following way: The truth-values of contingent propositions are *contingent* upon the facts, while the truth-values of noncontingent propositions are *not* contingent upon the facts but are determined by rules of language. Or put still another way: contingent truths (and falsehoods) are factual; noncontingent truths (and falsehoods) are linguistic.

The linguistic theory of necessary truth does not belong only to the preserve of philosophers. It is enshrined also in commonplace talk of certain propositions being true (or false) "by definition". Thus, it might be said, the proposition

(1.44)   All rectangles have four sides

owes its truth to the fact that we human beings have resolved to *define* the term "rectangle" as "plane closed figure with four straight sides all of whose angles are equal". For, given such a stipulative definition, the truth of *(1.44)* follows immediately.

This talk of "definitional truths", and similar talk of "verbal truths", suggests that necessary truths are not grounded — as are contingent truths — in correspondence between propositions and states of affairs, but are grounded rather in some sort of correspondence between propositions and the arbitrary conventions or rules for the use of words which we language users happen to adopt.

Yet, despite its initial plausibility, this theory seems to us defective.

Its plausibility, we suggest, derives — at least in part — from a confusion. Let us concede that when we introduce a new term into our language by defining it (explicitly or implicitly) in terms of already available expressions, we make available to ourselves *new ways of expressing* truths. But this does not mean that we thereby make available to ourselves new truths.

Once we have introduced the term "rectangle" by definition in the manner sketched above, the sentence

(1.45)   "All rectangles have four sides"

will express a necessary truth in a way in which we could not have expressed it earlier. But the necessary truth which it expresses is just the necessary truth

(1.46)   All plane closed figures with four sides all of whose
          angles are equal have four sides

and this is a proposition whose truth is far less plausibly attributable to definition. For this proposition, one is more inclined to say, would be true even if human beings had never existed and had there never been any language whatever in the world.

Talk about necessary truths being "true by definition" may also derive some plausibility from the fact that our *knowledge* that certain propositions are true sometimes stems from our *knowledge* of the meanings, or definitions, of the terms in which they are expressed. Thus a person who comes to know that the expression "triac" *means the same as* the expression "bidirectional triode thyristor" may thereby (even without knowing independently what either means) know that the sentence

(1.47)   "All triacs are bidirectional triode thyristors"

expresses a necessarily true proposition. But this does not mean that the necessary truth of the proposition so expressed is itself something that stems from the meanings of these expressions.

Perhaps the gravest defect in the linguistic theory of necessary truth has to do with its inability to explain how it is that necessary truths, such as those of logic and mathematics, can have significant practical applications in the real world. In such applied sciences as aeronautics, engineering, and the like, arithmetical truths may be applied in ways which yield important new inferential truths about the world around us: about the stress tolerances of bridges, the efficiency of airplane propellers, etc. But if these necessary truths are merely the result of arbitrary human conventions for the use of mathematical symbols, all this becomes a seeming miracle. Why should the world conform so felicitiously to the consequences of our linguistic stipulations?

The explanation of the success of logic and mathematics in their applications to the world, we suggest, lies elsewhere: in the possible-worlds analysis of necessary truth. Necessary truths, such as those of mathematics, apply to the world because they are true in all possible worlds; and since the actual world is a possible world, it *follows* that they are true in (i.e., apply to) the actual world. This account of the matter, it should be noted, does not require a different theory of truth from that which we have given for contingent propositions. To say that a proposition is true in the actual world is, we have claimed, to say that it fits the facts in the actual world, i.e., that states of affairs in the actual world are as the proposition asserts them to be. And likewise, to say that a proposition is true in some other possible world — or, for that matter, in all possible worlds — is just to say that in that other world — or all possible worlds — states of affairs are as the proposition asserts them to be. One and the same theory of truth suffices for all cases: the case when a proposition is true in all possible worlds and the case when it is true in just some (perhaps the actual one included).

In order to see how this single account of truth suffices for all cases, let us return to the example of the noncontingent proposition *(1.43)* to see how this theory might be invoked to explain its truth.

But first, let us reflect for a moment on another proposition, viz., the *contingent* proposition

> *(1.48)*   Either George Washington was the first president of the United States or Benjamin Franklin was the first president of the United States.

This proposition, being contingent, is true in some possible worlds and false in all the others. What feature is it, in those possible worlds in which *(1.48)* is true, which accounts for its truth? The answer is obvious: *(1.48)* is true in all and only those possible worlds in which either Washington or Franklin was the first president of the United States. But note — as in the case of the noncontingent proposition *(1.43)* — how much variation occurs between the worlds in which the proposition is true. In the actual world, for example, Washington, not Franklin, was the first president of the United States. Thus in the actual world, *(1.48)* is true. But in some other possible worlds, Franklin, not Washington, was the first president of the United States. But in that world, too, *(1.48)* fits the facts, i.e., is true.

Here, then, we have a parallel to the situation we discovered in the case of the noncontingent proposition *(1.43);* that is, we have already noted that *(1.43)* is true in some possible world in which Booth assassinated Lincoln and is true in some possible world in which he did not. The relevant difference, in the present context, between these two cases — the noncontingent proposition *(1.43)* and the contingent proposition *(1.48)* — lies in the fact that the former proposition is true in every possible world in which Booth did not assassinate Lincoln, while the latter is true in only some of the possible worlds in which Washington was not the first president. But this difference clearly has only to do with whether the set of possible worlds in which each proposition fits the facts comprises all, only some, or none of the totality of possible worlds. It in no way challenges the claim that the truth of both *(1.43)* and *(1.48)* is to be accounted for in the same way, viz., in their fitting the facts.

Summing up, we may say that there is no *special* problem about the truth-values of noncontingent propositions. They are true or false *in exactly the same sort of way* that contingent propositions are true or false; i.e., depending on whether or not they fit the facts. The supposition that there are two kinds of truth, or that there is a need for two theories of truth, is misconceived. *Propositions* are true or false; also they are contingent or noncontingent. And these various properties of propositions (two for truth-status and two for modal-status) can combine in various ways (four, to be exact). But it should not be thought that in saying of a proposition that it is, for example, noncontingently true, we are saying that it exemplifies one of two types of *truth*. Rather, this expression ought to be construed as "noncontingent *and* true". Viewing the matter in this fashion, it is easy to see that the question about the special way in which the truth (or falsity) of noncontingent propositions is supposed to come about *does not even arise.* Logic does not require more than one theory of truth.

8.   THE "POSSIBLE-WORLDS" IDIOM

Throughout this book we speak often of other possible worlds. Why have we, in common with many other philosophers and logicians, adopted this idiom? The answer lies in its enormous heuristic value.

Many contemporary philosophers believe that the possible-worlds idiom provides a single theoretical framework powerful enough to illuminate and resolve many of the philosophical problems surrounding such matters as

1.   The logical notions of necessity, contingency, possibility, implication, validity, and the like

2.   The distinction between logical necessity and physical necessity

3.   The adequacy of a single theory of truth

4.   The identity conditions of propositions and of concepts

5.   The disambiguation of sentences

6.   The link between the meaning of a sentence and the truth-conditions of the proposition(s) it expresses

7.   The technique of refutation by imaginary counterexamples

8.   The epistemic concept of that which is humanly knowable

9.   The distinction between accidental and essential properties

10.   The concept of the contingent content of a proposition

11.   The concept of probabilification

Each of these is dealt with, in the order given, in this book. But the list goes beyond the confines of this book. Recent work couched within the possible-worlds idiom includes work in

12.   Ethics

13.   Counterfactuals

14.   Epistemic logic

15.   Propositional attitudes

and much more besides. To cite some examples: C.B. Daniels in *The Evaluation of Ethical Theories:*

> For the purposes of this book, an ethical theory is simply a determination of a unique set of ideal worlds. An ideal world, relative to a theory that determines it as ideal, is a possible world, a fairy world perhaps, in which everything the theory says is ideally true is in fact true. An ideal world relative to an ethical theory is a world in which everything the theory says ought to be the case is the case.[41]

41. Halifax, Nova Scotia, Dalhousie University Press, 1975, p. 1.

David Lewis, in *Counterfactuals:*

> *'If kangaroos had no tails, they would topple over'* seems to me to mean something like this: in any possible state of affairs in which kangaroos have no tails, and which resembles our actual state of affairs as much as kangaroos having no tails permits it to, the kangaroos topple over. I shall give a general analysis of counterfactual conditions along these lines.
>
> My methods are those of much recent work in possible-world semantics for intensional logic.[42]

And Jaakko Hintikka, in "On the Logic of Perception":

> **When does *a* know (believe, wish, perceive) more than *b*? The only reasonable general answer seems to be that *a* knows more than *b* if and only if the class of possible worlds compatible with what he knows is smaller than the class of possible worlds compatible with what *b* knows.[43]**

The extraordinary success, and the veritable explosion of research adopting the possible-worlds idiom was not the motivation or even the expectation in its adoption. As a matter of fact, the idiom is not especially new; only its widespread adoption is. Talk of possible worlds can be found throughout the writings of the great German mathematician and philosopher, Gottfried Leibniz (1646–1716). Leibniz was quite at home in the possible-worlds idiom. He liked to philosophize in terms of that idiom, asking such questions as, "Is this the best of all possible worlds?" and "Why did God create this particular world rather than some other possible world?" And writing of those truths which we (and he on occasion) have called "necessary", he penned these germinal lines:

> These are the eternal truths. They did not obtain only while the world existed, but they would also obtain if GOD had created a world with a different plan. But from these, existential or contingent truths differ entirely.[44]

Leibniz's style and idiom were in advance of their time. Other logicians, and perhaps Leibniz too, saw no particular *advantage* in this way of talking, merely an alternative. It was not until the early 1960s that philosophers such as Kripke and Hintikka returned to Leibniz's idiom and used it both to illuminate the philosophical bases of logic and to push the frontiers of logic and many other areas of philosophy in new directions.

Nonetheless, it is important to keep this talk of 'other possible worlds' in its proper philosophical perspective. We must never allow ourselves to regard this manner of talk as if it were talk about actually existing parts of this world. Whoever supposes that other possible worlds are basic entities of the physical universe has failed to appreciate the point of our earlier insistence that other possible worlds are not 'out there' in physical space. Other possible worlds are *abstract* entities like numbers

---

42. Cambridge, Mass., Harvard University Press, 1973, p. 1.

43. *Models for Modalities: Selected Essays,* Dordrecht, D. Reidel, 1969, p. 157.

44. "Necessary and Contingent Truths" translated from *Opuscules et fragments inédits de Leibniz,* ed. Courturat, Paris, Félix Alcan, 1903, pp. 16–22, reprinted in *From Descartes to Locke* ed. T.V. Smith and M. Grene, Chicago, The University of Chicago Press, 1957, pp. 306–312. We are grateful to our colleague, David Copp, for calling this passage to our attention.

and propositions.[45] We feel driven to posit them because we seem unable to make ultimate sense of logic without them. Positing the existence of these abstract entities allows us to unify logic, to rigorize it, to expand it, and most importantly in our eyes to *understand* it.

45. This distinction between abstract and non-abstract (i.e., concrete) entities will be examined at greater length in the next chapter.

2

Propositions

1. INTRODUCTION

In chapter 1 we undertook three main tasks: to introduce the concept of possible worlds; to introduce the concept of propositions and their truth or falsity; and to show how various logically important properties and relations of propositions can be explicated in terms of the ways in which the truth-values of propositions are distributed across the set of all possible worlds.

In this chapter we invoke the concept of possible worlds in order to give an analysis of what propositions *are;* to give an explanation as to why they need to be distinguished from the sentences which may be used to express them; and to provide a method for identifying and referring to particular propositions.

2. THE BEARERS OF TRUTH-VALUES

When we first introduced propositions as the items which are the bearers of truth-values, we said that propositions must be distinguished from the sentences which may be used to express them in much the same way as numbers must be distinguished from the numerals which may be used to express them (chapter 1, p. 10, footnote 8). But *why* must they be so distinguished? And what *are* propositions if they are not to be identified with sentences? These are the questions which we wish to answer in this section.

First, however, let us explore briefly the analogy we have drawn between propositions and numbers. Why should we want to distinguish between numbers and numerals? The following reasons have seemed to most mathematicians and philosophers to be compelling:[1] (i) — Numerals have physical existence as marks on paper, on blackboards, etc., as patterns of sound, distributions of molecules on magnetic tape, or the like. Numbers do not. It makes sense, for instance, to speak of a numeral being written in blue ink or white chalk, being large or small, decipherable or indecipherable. None of these

---

1. Exceptions are those who espouse the *nominalist* thesis that there are no abstract entities. See, for instance, W.V.O. Quine and Nelson Goodman, "Steps Toward a Constructive Nominalism", *Journal of Symbolic Logic,* vol. 12 (1947), pp. 105–122. Not surprisingly, Quine and Goodman are foremost among the proponents of the equally nominalist thesis that sentences, not propositions, are the fundamental entities required by logic. For a spirited criticism of nominalism in mathematics, logic, and physics see Hilary Putnam's short and eminently readable *Philosophy of Logic,* New York, Harper Torchbooks, 1971.

properties, by way of contrast, can sensibly be attributed to numbers. For numbers are abstract items,[2] expressible by those physical items which we call numerals, but not identical with them. We can erase a numeral — render it nonexistent as a physical entity — but in so doing we do nothing to render the number which that numeral expresses nonexistent. (ii) — Numerals do not stand in a one-to-one correspondence to numbers. On the one hand, for any given unique number — for example, the number two — there are different numerals which may be used to express it. Corresponding to the number two is not only the Arabic numeral "2" but also the Roman numeral "II". The numerals "2" and "II" are items in different languages. But the number two is not. If it were an item in a language then we should have to say, absurdly, that it belonged to one particular language, say Arabic, to the exclusion of any other. (iii) — Numbers have arithmetical properties and stand in arithmetical relations. Numerals do not. Mathematical operations of addition, subtraction, multiplication and division can be carried out on numbers, but not on numerals. To be sure, there are some idioms which suggest the contrary. We can and do speak of halving both numbers and concrete physical things. But it is clear that "halving" is here ambiguous between a mathematical operation and a physical one. Half the number two is the number one. Half the numeral "2" is, e.g., "ɔ" or "ς". The *mathematical* operation called "halving" can be applied to numbers but not to numerals, whereas the *physical* operation called "halving" can be applied to numerals but not to numbers.

Each of these three arguments has its analogue for the distinction between propositions and sentences. (i) — Sentences have physical existence as marks on paper, on blackboards, etc., as patterns of sound, distributions of molecules on magnetic tape, or the like.[3] Propositions do not. It makes sense, for instance, to speak of a sentence being written in blue ink or white chalk, being large or small, decipherable or indecipherable. None of these properties, by way of contrast, can sensibly be attributed to propositions. For propositions, we shall argue, are abstract items, expressible by those physical items which we call sentences, but not identical with them. We can erase a sentence — render it nonexistent as a physical entity — but in so doing we do not deprive the proposition which it expresses of existence. (ii) — Sentences do not stand in a one-to-one correspondence to propositions. On the one hand, for any given unique proposition, such as two plus two equals four, many sentences may be used to express it. Corresponding to the proposition that two plus two equals four is not only the English sentence "Two plus two equals four" but also the French sentence "Deux et deux font quatre", the German sentence "Zwei und zwei gleich vier", and so on. The sentences "Two plus two equals four" and "Deux et deux font quatre" are items in different languages. But the proposition that two plus two equals four is not. If it were an item in a language then we should have to say, absurdly, that it belonged to one particular language, say English, to the exclusion of any other. (iii) — Propositions have logically significant attributes: they have truth-values, have modal properties, and stand in modal relations. Sentences do not. Logical operations, such as those of conjunction, disjunction, negation, and the like, can be carried out on propositions but not on sentences. To be sure, some idioms suggest the contrary. We can and do speak of conjoining propositions and of conjoining sentences. But it is clear that "conjoining" is here ambiguous between a logical operation and a grammatical one. The logical conjunction of the proposition that two plus two equals four with the proposition that two plus two

2. This claim is compatible both with *conceptualism* — the view that such abstract entities exist insofar as they are created by the activity of human thinking — and with *Platonic realism* — the view that such abstract entities exist in their own right, independently of human thinking. The philosopher Kant and the mathematician L.E.J. Brouwer are foremost among the representatives of conceptualism regarding numbers. Plato, Frege, and Russell are notable exponents of this sort of realism. As will become obvious in this section, the present authors believe that such realism is the only ultimately defensible theory regarding the fundamental items both of arithmetic, viz., numbers, and of logic, viz., propositions.

3. In arguments (i) and (ii) we use the word "sentence" to refer to what we shall later call a "token" (as distinct from a "type"). We did this also in the parallel arguments (i) and (ii) regarding numerals. For more on the type/token distinction see p. 71ff.

equals four is logically equivalent to the proposition that two plus two equals four. The grammatical conjunction of the sentence "Two plus two equals four" with the sentence "Two plus two equals four" is the *non*equivalent (because double-length) sentence "Two plus two equals four and two plus two equals four." The logical operation can be applied to propositions but not sentences, whereas the grammatical operation can be applied to sentences but not to propositions.

In terms of the analogy between numbers and propositions and of the attendant arguments for distinguishing these items from numerals and sentences, respectively, we foreshadow some of the main conclusions of the present section. But not all of them. In order to do justice to some of the other arguments for identifying propositions as the bearers of truth-values — and, incidentally, in order to do at least partial justice to some of the arguments *against* such an identification — we propose to set these conclusions aside, provisionally at least, and pursue the question "What sorts of items have truth-values?" with open minds.

Our approach in what follows is the time-honored one of dialectical enquiry. We advance a tentative thesis, subject it to critical examination, repair its shortcomings by offering a new thesis, subject it in turn to critical examination; and so on until we produce a thesis which, hopefully, is found viable.

EXERCISES

Fill in the blanks with either "numeral" or "number" so as to allow the sentence to express a true proposition.

1.   *Twice four is the* _____ *eight.*

2.   *I just repainted the* _____*s on my mailbox.*

3.   *The* _____ *"25" is constructed by placing the* _____ *"5" to the right of the* _____ *"2".*

4.   *Twelve* _____*s appear on the face of a clock.*

5.   *"Two" and "2" are two different symbols which may be used to refer to the* _____ *which is twice one.*

Fill in the blanks with "sentence" or "proposition" so as to make the following claims true.

6.   *"Two plus two equals four" is a* _____ *of English.*

7.   *"Two plus two equals four" expresses a necessarily true* _____.

8.   *The* _____ *"Today is Monday" means the same as "Today is the day before Tuesday."*

9.   *The* _____ *that today is Monday is equivalent to the* _____ *that today is the day after Sunday.*

10. *It is possible to erase a* _____; *it is not possible to erase a* _____.

*   *   *   *   *

*Thesis 1:   Such things as beliefs, statements, assertions, remarks, hypotheses, and theories are the
             bearers of truth and falsity.*

Objection to Thesis 1:   Each of the terms, "belief", "statement", etc., is ambiguous.

Now it is absolutely clear that we do, on occasion, attribute truth and falsity to beliefs, statements,
assertions, remarks, hypotheses, and theories. And it may plausibly be argued that each of these kinds
of things is a genuine bearer of truth-values. What is not quite so clear, however, is just what is meant
by "belief", "statement", "assertion", "remark", "hypothesis", and "theory" when truth and falsity
are at issue.
    Each of these expressions is ambiguous. Each is ambiguous, in the first place, between:

> (a)   the state, act, or disposition of believing, stating, asserting, remarking,
>   hypothesizing, or theorizing;

and

> (b)   that which is believed, stated, asserted, remarked, hypothesized, or theorized.

Let us illustrate this distinction by considering a case of belief.
    Suppose John Doe believes himself to be ill. Then there are two quite different sorts of questions —
corresponding to (a) and (b) above — that we might want to ask about this belief. On the one hand,
we might want to ask a question like "What brought about this belief of his?" or "When did he start
believing that?" In such a case we would be asking about John Doe's state of belief (or, as some would
say, his *act* of believing"). His belief, in this sense of the word (that of (a) above), is something which
may arise at a specific moment of time and persist through time; it may be brought about or caused by
some other event or state of affairs, e.g., by his having eaten too much; and it may in turn bring about
or cause another event or state of affairs, e.g., his calling for the doctor.
    On the other hand we may distinguish the *content* of his belief, that which he believes. It is this
latter feature which may occur in other persons' beliefs as well. Although no other persons can have
John Doe's belief in the sense that their *acts* of believing cannot be the same act as John Doe's, *what*
they believe, viz., that John Doe is ill, may be shared both by them and John Doe. In this second sense
of "belief", the sense in which we talk of *what* is believed (the sense (b) above), a belief may be shared
by many persons.

Thesis 2:   Acts of believing (stating, asserting, etc.) are the bearers of truth-values.

*Objections to Thesis 2:   First, the class of truths and falsehoods vastly outnumbers the class of
                 belief-acts. Secondly, under this proposal some truths and falsehoods would be without
                 contradictories.*

Acts of belief (assertion, etc.) are temporal entities. They begin at some point in time and end at some
later time. For example, when we were young many of us thought that the moon traveled along with
our moving car at night, but as adults we no longer believe this. Over the course of our lifetimes, we
will each entertain thousands, maybe even millions or billions of beliefs. For present purposes,
however, the exact number is of no importance. What is of importance is whether or not the total
number of belief-acts for all mankind is sufficiently large for them to be identified as the bearers of
truth and falsity.
    Earlier, in chapter 1, we proved that the number of truths is infinite and that the number of
falsehoods is infinite: to each number within the infinite set of natural numbers there corresponds the
truth that that number has a successor, and to each natural number there corresponds the falsehood

that that number has no successor. It now needs to be observed that the number of truths and falsehoods exceeds the number of natural numbers, i.e., is *nondenumerably* infinite. For the class of *real* numbers is larger than the class of natural numbers and to each of the real numbers there corresponds at least one unique truth and at least one unique falsehood about that real number. The full import of this fact is not always appreciated. It is all too easy to conceive of an infinite class as being just a very large finite class. But to say that the number of truths and falsehoods is infinite (let alone nondenumerably infinite) is not just to make a claim of the sort that the number is a trillion or a centillion[4] or the like. It isn't even to say that a centillion is just a minute fraction of the number of truths and falsehoods. So vast is the class of noncontingent truths and falsehoods that a centillion truths or falsehoods — or any other finite number — does not constitute *any* fraction whatever of the whole class.

And not only is the class of noncontingent propositions nondenumerably infinite. So, too, is the class of contingent propositions. The number of points of physical space is nondenumerably infinite, and to each of these points may be paired off, as the case may be, the contingent truth or falsehood which ascribes the presence of physical matter to that place.

With this background, we now come to the critical question: Is the class of belief-acts large enough for them to be identified with the nondenumerably infinite number of members of the class of truths and falsehoods? As a matter of fact, there does *not* seem to be even an infinite number of belief-acts (let alone a nondenumerably infinite number). This is not to say that there could not be, that in some possible world there isn't an infinite number of belief-acts; but it is to say that in this, the actual world, there seem to be far too few belief-acts for them to be reasonably identified as those things which are true and false. Just reflect on how many possible beliefs about the actual world are never entertained by us. Who, for example, has had or ever will have beliefs about the exact position of each atom of the sun's interior at exactly 6:01 A.M. on June 18, 1893, etc. etc.? Is it reasonable to argue that although no one has yet had any such beliefs, someday someone will? We think not.

If we are right in thinking that the number of belief-acts is smaller than the number of truths and falsehoods, have we not found a fatal objection to the theory that belief-acts are those things which are true and false? Obviously we have. For it is logically impossible that truths and falsehoods should be belief-acts if there are more truths and falsehoods than there are belief-acts.

However, the matter does not quite end here. For it is open to the proposer of the thesis that belief-acts are those things which are true and false to take objection to the idea that we have some independent way of ascertaining the number of truths and falsehoods. We can imagine him arguing in this way:

> You seem to know that there are an infinite number of truths and an
> infinite number of falsehoods. But this is question-begging; your belief is
> a result of your theory that truths and falsehoods are propositions. If you
> put that theory out of your mind, and assume nothing about the number
> of truths and falsehoods, the proposal that belief-acts are those things
> which are true and false, works.

But does it? Let us see.

Presumably the person who argues that belief-acts are those things which are true and false will allow the possibility, indeed the actuality, of mankind's having neglected collectively to believe everything there is to believe. But this concession has odd implications. Imagine a person walking along in a forest one day. He glances at a tree and believes (correctly) that it is a birch. Suppose, however, that he is the only person ever to have seen that tree and that a forest fire destroys it that

---

4. One (British) centillion = 10^{600}.

night without anyone else ever taking any notice of it. Suppose, further, that no one ever entertains the belief that it is false that that tree is a birch. It will then follow that if the class of bearers of truth-values were to be identified with acts of belief, a certain act would be true but would have no contradictory, since no person ever believes that it is false that that tree is a birch. In short, if we were to identify the class of truths and falsehoods with the class of belief-acts we would have to give up the claim that to every truth there corresponds a non-empty class of falsehoods each of which is a contradictory of that truth. Under this proposal, some truths and some falsehoods would be without contradictories. Not only would this make a shambles of logic; it is thoroughly counterintuitive as well. We have a strong disposition to insist that even if no one were to believe of the birch tree that it is not a birch, then were anyone to believe it, what he would believe is false.

Note carefully how we just expressed ourselves. In effect we said that it is possible that even though no one believes some particular thing, that thing which could be believed *is* false. We did not say that that thing which could be believed *would be* false if it *were to be* believed. That is, our common, hard-won conception of truth and falsehood has it that truth and falsehood may exist independent of human belief, that truth and falsehood do not as it were 'come into existence' with correct or mistaken human belief.

In short, it is not our holding to the theory that propositions are the bearers of truth and falsity which prompts our belief in an infinite number of truths and of falsehoods; it is quite the other way around. It is the widespread and strong belief that there are unexpressed and unbelieved truths and falsehoods which prompts us to look for a truth-value vehicle of prodigious number.[5]

It follows that insofar as a belief can properly be said to be true or false, we must understand that we are using the term "belief" in sense (b), not in sense (a). And by similar reasoning we may conclude that it is only in sense (b), not sense (a), that statements, assertions, remarks, hypotheses, and theories can be the bearers of truth-values. We may put it like this: beliefs, statements, etc., are true or false just when that which is believed, stated, etc., is true or false.

EXERCISES

For each of the following, explain in which sense of "belief" (act of belief or object of belief) the claim could be true.

1. *His belief that it was raining was fleeting; he glanced again out the window and saw that it was sleeting.*

2. *The belief that it is raining is inconsistent with the belief that it is not.*

3. *That a person believes that it is raining is consistent with his also believing that it is not.*

4. *Her belief that she was prime minister was induced by a mushroom omelet.*

5. *Her belief that she was prime minister was false.*

6. *No one's beliefs antecede his birth (or at least the moment of his conception).*

*   *   *   *   *

5. When we come to Thesis 5 we will discover that Quine, who eschews propositions, does not abandon the thesis that the number of truth-value bearers must be infinite. In arguing that the number of truth-value bearers is infinite, Quine is in arrgement with us.

Thesis 3:   That which is believed, stated, etc., is what is true or false.

Objection to Thesis 3:   Talk about 'that which is believed' is unclear. What sorts of things can be believed? In particular, are these things sentences or propositions?

The distinction we have just made between acts, statements, or dispositions of believing, asserting, etc., and that which is believed or asserted is important and valuable. But the matter can hardly end there. **The trouble is that our talk — in the manner of (b) — of that which is believed, stated, asserted, remarked, hypothesized, and theorized is itself ambiguous. Consider the so-called theory that the earth is flat, and call it E. Plainly we may not only speak of the theory that E, but also of the belief that E,** the statement that E, the assertion that E, the remark that E, and the hypothesis that E. But what exactly is the status of E itself? Here philosophical opinion divides between those who say that "E" is the name of a *sentence*, viz., "The earth is flat", and those who say that "E" is the name of what they call a *proposition*, viz., the proposition that the earth is flat — a proposition which is typically *expressed* in English by the sentence "The earth is flat" but which is not to be identified with that or any other sentence. Accordingly, our talk of those things which are believed, stated, etc., and which can be bearers of truth-values, is equivocal between: (b′) talk of sentences; and (b″) talk of propositions. Let us examine the case for each.

Thesis 4:   Sentences are the bearers of truth-values.

Objections to Thesis 4:   Only certain kinds of sentences are plausible candidates for the bearers of truth-values. In addition there is an ambiguity in the notion of "sentence". It is necessary to distinguish between sentence-tokens and sentence-types.

Much of the impetus for saying — in the manner of (b′) — that it is sentences which have truth-values (whether or not these sentences are believed, stated, etc., by anyone), comes from an aversion to talk about propositions. It is not that talk of sentences' being true or false is any more natural than the rival piece of philosophers' jargon; for it may well be argued that when, on occasion, persons speak of a sentence as true or false they are merely speaking elliptically of the truth or falsity of that which is expressed by the sentence (of that which, on the rival theory, is to be called a proposition). Rather it is claimed that propositions, unlike sentences, cannot easily, if at all, be individuated (distinguished from one another and from other things in such a way that we can identify one and the same individual); or again it is claimed that there is simply no need to populate the universe with such obscure entities when all our practical and philosophical purposes are as well, if not better, served by talk of sentences.

Let us see, then, how well the thesis that sentences can be thought to be the bearers of truth and falsity fares under a careful examination.

All is not plain sailing for those who prefer sentences. For a start, a number of refinements are needed. We might begin, for instance, by pointing out that not all sentences, but only those which we call declarative — as opposed to, say, interrogative and imperative sentences — can on any ordinary interpretation, be said to be true or false. But even this restriction of the class of truth-valued sentences will not suffice. In *extra*ordinary circumstances a declarative sentence may be used in such a way that neither truth nor falsity is attributable to it (as, for example, if members of a secret society were to use "John Doe is ill now" as a password); and in quite ordinary circumstances something true or false may be conveyed by a nondeclarative sentence or even by something other than a sentence (as, for example, when John Doe utters the word "Yes" in answer to the interrogative "Are you ill?" or when he merely nods his head). Moreover, it is clear that John Doe can have a true or false belief, e.g., that he is ill, without his either uttering or inscribing any sentence at all. The answer that would be given, however, is that although John Doe may not engage in any verbal performance of utterance at all, he must, insofar as he has the belief that he is ill, be either disposed to engage in the utterance of the sentence "I am ill now" or at least disposed to accept the sentence "I am ill now" as true of himself. Such refinements of the sentence-theory can be, and have been made. But we will not pursue them, since as we shall soon see, other more serious difficulties have yet to be faced.

Before turning to these more serious difficulties in the sentence-theory, however, let us pause to recognize an ambiguity in the very term "sentence".

The ambiguity can be brought to light by asking how many sentences occur in the box below:

John Doe is ill on Christmas Day 1973.

John Doe is ill on Christmas Day 1973.

Two answers could be given, with equal plausibility.

(i)   We might say that there is only *one sentence* in the box, and that it has there been inscribed twice; or

(ii)   We might say that there are *two sentences* — albeit of the same type — inscribed in the box.

If we choose to answer in the manner of (i), we are thinking in terms of what philosophers call "sentence-types"; while if we choose to answer in the manner of (ii), we are thinking in terms of what philosophers call "sentence-tokens". This distinction between *sentence-types* and *sentence-tokens* may be illuminated by asking, somewhat analogously, how many colors occur in the box below:

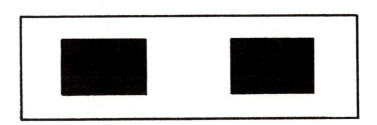

Again, two answers could be given with equal plausibility. (i′) We might say that there is *one color* in the box, viz., the color black. (ii′) Alternatively, we might say that there are *two color patches* in the box, both black. If we choose to answer in the manner of (i′), we are thinking in terms of what philosophers call *universals;* while if we choose to answer in the manner of (ii′), we are thinking in terms of what philosophers call *instances.* Plainly, sentence-tokens stand to sentence-types in much the same way as color-patches stand to colors: they are instances of universals.

Which is it, then, that are to count as vehicles of truth-values: sentence-tokens or sentence-types?

EXERCISES

1.   *The rectangle below*

> *Some athletes are students.*
>
> *Some students are athletes.*

contains

     A.   two sentence-tokens of the same type;

     B.   two sentence-types of the same token;

     C.   two sentence-tokens of different types;

     D.   two sentence-types of different tokens;

     E.   none of the above.

2.   *The rectangle in question 1 above contains*

     A.   two logically consistent sentences;

     B.   8 word-tokens instancing 4 word-types;

     C.   8 word-tokens instancing 8 word-types;

     D.   4 word-tokens instancing 8 word-types;

     E.   4 word-tokens instancing 4 word-types;

     F.   8 word-types instancing 4 word-tokens;

     G.   4 word-types instancing 8 word-tokens.

3.   *As well as distinguishing sentence-tokens from sentence-types, as was done in the preceding discussion, and word-tokens from word-types, as was done implicitly in question 2, do we also have to distinguish numeral-tokens from numeral-types? Explain.*

*   *   *   *   *

Thesis 5:   Sentence-tokens *are the bearers of truth-values.*

Objection to thesis 5:   The same difficulty arises as with Thesis 2, viz., there are more truths than there are sentence-tokens.

Anyone who abjures the abstract and takes comfort in the concrete will be likely to opt for the thesis that it is sentence-*tokens* which are truth-valued. For the criteria for individuating sentence-tokens are reassuringly straightforward: whether they take the form of written inscriptions or speech episodes, they can be individuated in the standard ways appropriate to physical objects and physical events (sound-producing movements), respectively. So there are no problems on this score. But how about their credentials as truth-vehicles? Is it really the case that for every truth there actually exists a sentence-token?

Although the number of actual sentence-tokens is staggeringly large, it is nonetheless far, far smaller than the number of truths. It is reasonable to suppose that the class of truths extends well beyond the sentential expression of these truths. There are many truths of mathematics and logic, for instance, which neither have been, nor (we may suppose) ever will be, encapsulated in sentential form. As just one instance recall our earlier example (Objection to Thesis 2) of the infinitude of noncontingent truths which ascribe the property of having a successor to each of the natural numbers. Then, too, there are vast numbers of contingent truths about the physical universe which have not yet, and possibly never will be, discovered. As a practical matter, just consider how many contingent truths there are about the actual world, truths which no one has asserted, is now asserting, or ever will assert. Just reflect on the series of sentences which begins: "(1) There is more than one atom of oxygen in the Atlantic Ocean; (2) There are more than two atoms of oxygen in the Atlantic Ocean; (3) There are more than three atoms of oxygen in the Atlantic Ocean; etc., etc., etc." We have good reason to believe that even if every person in the entire history and future of the world were to spend his lifetime adding more sentences to this *one* set, the set would never be completed in the anticipated lifespan of the physical universe. And this is just one set; there are countless others sets of this sort besides.

One of the chief contemporary sponsors of the sentence-theory, Quine, argues explicitly that there are quite enough sentence-tokens for them to be identified as the bearers of truth and falsity.[6] His argument is that the class of sentence-tokens need not be thought of as restricted merely to a subset of the class of word strings which persons may happen to inscribe or utter. If, instead, we conceive of sentence-tokens as *mathematical sequences* of those word-tokens which are inscribed or uttered at some time or other, then we may conclude that there are as many sentence-tokens as there are truths and falsities.

Against this ingenious theory we offer two main objections. First, there is something highly implausible about the suggestion that actual sentence-tokens are merely *mathematical* sequences of word-tokens. Ought they not rather to be identified with *temporally and/or spatially* ordered sequences of word-tokens? Suppose — contrary to fact — that the only words ever to be uttered or inscribed occurred in the utterance or inscription of the sentences "The cat is on the mat" and "Henry stood in front of the door." Then it would seem to be just plain false to say that the world numbers among its items the sentence-token "The mat is in front of the door." Yet this is what Quine's theory commits us to. Secondly, Quine's theory makes the existence of any truths dependent upon an historical accident, viz., the invention of language. It leads directly to the uncomfortable conclusion that had words never been invented there never would have been any truths. We shall return to this objection later, when dealing with Thesis 9, in our dialectical argument.

It seems clear, then, that *actual* sentence-tokens simply do not exist in the profusion that the theory calls for, and that we must therefore — if intent on preserving the theory — allow that it is either actual or *possible* sentence-tokens which carry truth and falsity. But once we say this, the advantages of this version of the sentence-theory over the rival proposition-theory have been narrowed almost to the point of nonexistence. For sentence-tokens which exist only as *possibilia* lack that concreteness and ease of individuation which first recommended them to us. *Possibilia* are just as abstract as propositions and admit of no easier individuation.

Thesis 6:   Sentence-types *are the bearers of truth-values.*

Objection to Thesis 6:   This thesis leads to ascribing contradictory assertions to persons who have not contradicted themselves.

---

6. W.V.O. Quine, *Word and Object,* M.I.T., Technology Press, and New York, Wiley, 1960, pp. 194–195.

It will not do to say simply that a sentence-*type*, such as that which corresponds to "I am ill now", is that which is true or false. For suppose that a token of this type were to be uttered by John Doe, while a token of its grammatical denial, viz., "I am not ill now", were to be uttered by his sister, Jill Doe. Then, if it were the sentence-*type* which was true or false, we should, in accordance with the dictates of logic and commonsense alike, be obliged to say that John and Jill were contradicting each other and that only one of them could be saying what is true. Or again, suppose the sentence-token "I am ill now" were uttered by John Doe immediately after overindulging his appetite at Christmas, and that the grammatical denial of the latter, the sentence "I am not ill now", were to be uttered by him after he has recovered from all illness. Then, if it were the sentence-type corresponding to "I am ill now" which is true (or false as the case may be), we should, once more in accordance with the dictates of logic and commonsense, have to conclude that he was contradicting himself and that only one of his utterances was true. After all, two people contradict each other if one says that something is true and the other says that the very same thing is false; and likewise a single person contradicts himself if he says both that something is true and that the very same thing is false.

Plainly something has gone wrong here. The simple fact of the matter is that what John Doe said, when he uttered the sentence "I am ill now", and what Jill Doe said, when she uttered the sentence "I am not ill now", were both true; and again that what John Doe said at Christmas and what he said some time later were both true. There must be something seriously amiss with a theory which commits us to imputing inconsistency where none exists. At the very least an amendment is called for.

Thesis 7:   Context-free sentences are the bearers of truth-values.

Objection to thesis 7:   It is necessary to distinguish context-free sentence-types from context-free sentence-tokens.

The amendment which sentence-theorists tend to favor is that of saying that the sentences, or utterances of sentences, of which truth and falsity are best predicated are what they call *context-free sentences*.[7] The basic idea of a context-free sentence is really very simple. If we consider a sentence like, "At one atmosphere of pressure, water freezes at 32°F.", we are not at all tempted to suppose — as we might in the case of "I am ill now" — that its truth-value varies with the special circumstances of its utterance or inscription: with who uttered it, or when he uttered it, or the like. No matter who utters it, or when he utters it, the sentence "At one atmosphere of pressure, water freezes at 32°F." has a constant truth-value, viz., truth. It is context-free in the way that the sentences of mathematics, physics, and the sciences generally are. Plainly enough context-free sentences cannot generate inconsistencies in the same way as do sentences like "I am ill now". If, then, some way could be found of transforming context-dependent sentences into context-free ones, the theory that sentences are the primary bearers of truth-values would have some chance of salvation. How might such a transformation be effected? The proposal is that pronouns like "I" are to be replaced by names, temporal references like "now" are replaced by dates, and tenses are cancelled altogether. Thus a context-dependent sentence such as "I am ill now", when uttered by John Doe on Christmas Day 1973, is transformed into the context-free sentence "John Doe is [in a tenseless sense] ill on Christmas Day 1973"; while the denial of this context-dependent sentence, when uttered by John Doe a week later, is rendered by the context-free sentence "John Doe is not ill on January 1, 1974." These context-free paraphrases of the two utterances of the context-dependent sentences "I am ill now" and "I am not ill now" not only express more precisely what it was that John Doe took himself to be asserting on each of the occasions when he uttered them, but also reveal — what we knew all along —

---

7. Quine and some others, somewhat less perspicuously, call context-free sentences "eternal sentences".

that he wasn't really contradicting himself at all when he first uttered the one and then, at a different time, uttered the other.

But with the concept of a context-free sentence now in hand, we must ask whether it is context-free sentence-*types* or context-free sentence-*tokens* which are supposed to be the bearers of truth and falsity.

EXERCISE

Read the following sentence aloud: "I started reading this page five minutes ago." Now paraphrase what you have just said so as to generate a context-free sentence.

*   *   *   *   *

*Thesis 8:   Context-free sentence-*tokens *are those things to which truth and falsity may be attributed.*

Objection to Thesis 8:   Again, there are more truths than there are sentence-tokens, context-free or otherwise.

Context-free sentence-tokens form a proper subclass of the class of sentence-tokens. And if there are too few sentence-tokens to satisfy the theory that sentence-tokens are to be identified as the bearers of truth and falsity, then a fortiori, there must be too few *context-free* sentence-tokens to do the job. In the whole history of mankind there have probably been only a few thousand, a few million at most, context-free sentence-tokens offered as reconstructions of context-dependent ones.

EXERCISE

One of the objections to Thesis 2 was that a consequence of holding that actual belief acts are the bearers of truth-values is that this makes the claim that every proposition has a contradictory both contingent and actually false. Show how this same criticism can be brought to bear both on Thesis 5 and on Thesis 8.

*   *   *   *   *

*Thesis 9:   Context-free sentence-*types *are those things to which truth and falsity may be attributed.*

Objections to Thesis 9:   First, the criteria for the individuation of context-free sentence-types are obscure. Secondly, because persons sometimes use words with different meanings, they will express different things even though the context-free sentence-types associated with their utterances are identical. Thirdly, this account cannot do justice to the fact that persons lacking a language can, nonetheless, hold true beliefs.

How about the supposition that it is context-free sentence-*types* which are truth-valued? Note that this proposal does not fall victim to the objection leveled against its immediate predecessor. Context-free sentence-types, unlike context-free sentence-tokens, *do* exist in the profusion required by the theory. For a sentence-type exists even when no token of that type exists. And one can plausibly argue that to every truth (and falsehood) there 'corresponds' a context-free sentence-type. But this is not to say that these context-free sentence-types ought to be identified as the bearers of truth-values. There are difficulties in such a hypothesis.

In the first place, if we adopt this view we immediately abandon whatever advantages actual sentence-tokens have over propositions. For sentence-types — context-free or otherwise — are quite unlike sentence-tokens in that they are not physical objects or events locatable in space and time; and they cannot therefore be individuated in the way that inscriptions and utterances can. Strictly speaking, the answer to our earlier question as to how many sentences there were in the box cannot be — if we are thinking of sentence-types — that there is one. For sentence-types, as distinct from sentence-tokens, are not the sorts of things which can be *in* a box, or *on* a page, or *on* the tip of someone's tongue, or anywhere else. There could have been one or two, or *more*, sentence-tokens in the box; but there could not be any sentence-types *in* the box.

More precisely, we should say rather that one sentence-type was *instanced* by the two sentence-tokens in the box.

The box example, however, turns out to be a fairly simple one. For the two sentence-tokens which, we said, were instances of one and the same sentence-type were typographically identical. But suppose they had not been typographically identical. Suppose, for instance, that one were to be italicized (e.g., "*John Doe is ill on Christmas Day 1973*") and the other not; or that one were to be written in capital letters (e.g., "JOHN DOE IS ILL ON CHRISTMAS DAY 1973") and the other in a mixture of capital and lowercase letters (e.g., "John Doe is ill on Christmas Day 1973"). Would we still want to say of these typographically different sentence-tokens that they were instances of the *same* sentence-type? Probably we would; for it seems reasonable to lay down as a sufficient condition of two sentence-tokens being of the same type that they be composed of the same words in the same order. But now suppose that one or more words in one or more of the sentence-tokens were to be misspelled. Would we still want to say that they were tokens of the same type? Our criteria for being of the same type now begin to look fuzzy. After all, the change of just one letter (or digit) might convert a sentence-token instancing one sentence-type into a sentence-token instancing another. Consider:

> John Doe is ill on Christmas Day 1973.
>
> John Doe is ill on Christmas Day 1975.

And finally consider this case:

> John Doe is honored on Christmas Day 1973.
>
> John Doe is honoured on Christmas Day 1973.

How many sentence-types are instanced by the two sentence-tokens in this last box?

From what has already been said it is apparent not only that sentence-types — context-free ones included — are abstract entities, but also that the criteria for their individuation are troublesome.

Yet so far we have considered only those context-free sentence-types of which context-free sentence-token instances actually exist. How about those which are instanced by the non-actual, merely possible, context-free sentence-tokens which we earlier felt obliged to postulate in order to accommodate unexpressed and undiscovered truths about logic, mathematics, and the universe at large? If the context-free sentence-types which are instanced by actual context-free sentence-tokens are abstract in the first degree, those which are instanced only by *possible* (and hence abstract) ones must be abstract in the second degree; and the criteria for their individuation must be correspondingly even more elusive.

Problems of abstractness and of the elusiveness of identity-conditions for context-free sentence-types are not the end of it: there are problems about their truth and falsity as well. These latter problems are not unique to the context-free sentence-type account. They arise for *any* version of the theory that it is sentences which are the primary bearers of truth-values, whether these sentences are context-free or context-dependent, types or tokens, or any combination of these. For this reason we shall state them in quite general terms.

In the first place, one and the same sentence (of whatever kind) is subject to different semantic construals by different people or at different times: the same sentence may — as we commonly say — "*mean* different things". Change of meaning, of words or lengthier expressions, is a familiar-enough fact of comparative linguistics. Thus, for example, one might observe that many North American speakers of English are disposed to use "disinterested" and its cognates to mean what English speakers throughout most of the rest of the world mean by "uninterested". Suppose, then, that speakers from each of these two classes of language-users are asked to consider the sentence "John Doe shows complete disinterest over the question of who was responsible for the oil spill" and to say whether it is true or false. Members of one class of speakers may say it is true, on the grounds that John Doe, though very interested in ecological issues, is able to treat questions about responsibility for ecological disturbance with the full impartiality that becomes one who is a judge; while members of the other class of speakers may say it is false simply on the grounds that John Doe, though of undoubted impartiality, is far from showing lack of interest in issues of ecology. Are they contradicting each other? If it were precisely the same thing which members of the one class asserted and members of the other class denied, we should have to say that they are, and hence that only members of one class could be saying what is true. Yet plainly, since the members of these two different classes mean different things by "disinterested", what some are asserting is quite different from what the others are denying. So there is no inconsistency after all. The case reminds one of the apparent conflict, discussed earlier, between John Doe and his sister Jill. However, in this case, unlike the earlier one, we cannot resolve the seeming conflict by resorting to the notion of a context-free sentence and saying that the context-free sentence asserted by one is different from the context-free sentence denied by the other. For this time the conflict has arisen over what is itself already a context-free sentence. So differences in meaning — for different people or even for the same people at different times — must be taken into account; and we can avoid inconsistency only by allowing that it is not, after all, context-free sentences *simpliciter* (whether tokens or types) which are the trouble-free bearers of truth and falsity; but rather that it is sentences *along with their meanings* which are the bearers of truth and falsity. But once we start talking thus about the *meanings* of sentences (context-free or context-dependent, types or tokens), we are well into the realm of abstractions which sentence-theorists tend to regard as forbidden territory.

In the second place, *any* version of the sentence-theory — type, token, context-free, context-dependent — must run into difficulties over prelinguistic times. For even if there is no clear sense in which our grunting forebears can be said to have made statements, assertions, or the like to each other, nonetheless we must surely allow that they had beliefs and that certain of their beliefs were true while others were false. But if, *ex hypothesi,* these were prelinguistic times, then these believers lacked a grammar and a semantics. But for a sentence to be intelligible, to be a content of a belief, the would-be believer must comprehend the grammar and semantics of that sentence, i.e. that sentence must belong to a language which the believer has mastered, or must be translatable into a language which the believer knows. But if the would-be believer lacks *all* language, then there is *no* sentence which he believes. Nor will it do to argue in this case, in the sort of way that we did earlier when we tried to accomodate the sentence-theory to John Doe's unexpressed belief that he was ill, that although our forebears did not actually either utter or inscribe sentences like "That animal is dangerous", they must, nevertheless, if they believed that a particular animal was dangerous, have been *disposed* to assent to such a sentence. For the logic of the case we are envisaging is that our forebears on occasion believed that a particular animal was dangerous when it was indeed dangerous; so that what they believed was true; and yet that there was no sentence expressing this belief which they could — given their complete lack of familiarity with verbal expressions — have even been disposed to assent to, let alone to have uttered or inscribed. Of course, the problem we are posing presumes that it is at least possible to have a belief in the absence of any linguistic means for expressing that belief. But surely that presumption is warranted. Why else would our early ancestors have come to utter or inscribe sentences in some now-forgotten language (sentences which if preserved we would translate into English as "That animal is dangerous"), unless they believed that certain animals were dangerous? It seems wholly implausible to suppose that the use of sentences, or words, for that matter, antedated man's thought and belief. And it seems hardly, if at all, more plausible to suppose that by some cosmic coincidence or pre-established harmony, word and thought, sentence and belief, paragraph and reasoning, sprang into existence together. So the Gospel of John, chapter 1, verse 1, needs to be rewritten: we cannot say "In the beginning was the Word", but must say rather "In the beginning was the Thought" (where the word "thought" is taken as encompassing also belief, reasoning, and the like). To be sure, without words and sentences at our disposal our thinking, believing, and reasoning can reach no great heights. But if we say that language is a precondition of all thinking, believing, and reasoning, then we must not only countersay, for instance, Kohler's descriptions of the thinking capabilities of the apes, but also deny to our own forebears certain of those capacities and dispositions which, there is reason to suppose, aided them in the evolutionary struggle for survival: the capacity or disposition to believe, and believe truly, that certain animals were dangerous, that they had to forage or hunt if they were to eat, and so on. Yet if they could entertain such beliefs, and what they believed could be true or false, and there were at the time no sentences or other linguistic devices at their disposal, then we can only conclude that what they believed truly or falsely could neither have been a sentence nor have been analyzable in terms of sentences. Sentences, context-free or context-dependent, types or tokens, may help *us* to express the truths that they believed; but they did not help them. Once more the class of truths has failed to be exhausted by the class of sentences.

So what exactly is it that is true or false? Right at the outset, it will be remembered, we drew a distinction between: (a) the state or act of saying, believing, etc., that something is the case; and (b) that which is said, believed, etc., to be the case. And we found good reason to reject (a) altogether. Then we turned to (b) and saw the need to draw another distinction; this time between: (b′) the sense in which what is said, believed, etc., is a sentence; and (b″) the sense in which what is said, believed, etc., is what is called a proposition, something expressible by a sentence but by no means identifiable with a sentence. And after a fairly lengthy investigation we have found serious difficulties with (b′), in each of its various guises. It is time to see how (b″) can fare.

Thesis 10:   Propositions are those things to which truth and falsity may be attributed.

Objection to Thesis 10:   It is unclear what sorts of things propositions are.

The move away from sentences *simpliciter* to specially constructed context-free sentences as bearers of truth-values removes much of the initial motivation of the original sentence-theory. Context-free sentences — involving as they do substitutions for pronouns, temporal references, and tenses, made in the light of our *understanding* of what a person takes himself to be asserting when he utters a context-dependent sentence — begin to look rather like what the proposition-theorist calls "the proposition expressed by" such context-dependent sentences. Like propositions they are not themselves to be identified with context-dependent sentences, but may be said to be what these sentences express or convey. And like propositions, if true they are always true and if false they are always false; or rather, like propositions, they are omnitemporally true or omnitemporally false.[8]

---

8. For a discussion of the thesis that propositions bear their truth-values omnitemporally, see section 5, this chapter.

Given that the sentence-theory seems to be coming to resemble more and more the proposition-theory, and given the several difficulties which we have seen are attendant upon *any* version of the sentence-theory, it would now be appropriate to turn our attention to the proposition-theory.

Perhaps the first thing to note about propositions is that one reason philosophers have talked about them is that they have seen the need to speak compendiously about that which is true or false without identifying what is true or false with any of the candidates so far considered. They have observed that one and the same thing which is true, such as that the earth is round, can be believed, stated, asserted, supposed, doubted, hypothesized, theorized, etc.; that the truth that the earth is round can be expressed in many different ways within different natural languages or even within one and the same natural language; that there are truths, such as that lions can kill men, which at a certain stage in human prehistory could not be expressed in any language whatever; and that there are still other truths which it is reasonable to suppose that nobody will even discover let alone express. They have said, in effect: "Let us call items like this which are true — or for that matter, false — 'propositions'; then we can avoid more circumlocuitous expressions like 'That which was said (believed, etc.) to be true'." In short, one reason the term "proposition", in its technical philosophical sense, has been introduced is to effect a certain economy of language.

Does this mean that talk of propositions has been introduced solely as a manner of speaking — that propositions are mere fictions? Not at all. To be sure, the term "proposition" does facilitate our talk about whatever is true or false. But we must recognize that philosophers who opt for the proposition-theory regard such talk as referential talk; they maintain that there are nonphysical things which are true or false, and that the term "proposition" can be used when we want to refer to them.

But if propositions are neither physical entities nor fictional ones, what sort of entities are they?

Thesis 11:   Propositions are to be identified with the meanings of sentences.

Objections to Thesis 11:   First, the criteria for individuating propositions and for individuating the meanings of sentences are different. Secondly, sentence meanings can be identical even though the propositions expressed are different. Thirdly, meanings are not expressed by sentences; propositions are.

Having rejected all kinds of sentences, both sentence-types and sentence-tokens, as the bearers of truth-values, and having said that propositions are neither physical nor fictional entities, what else is there with which propositions might be identified? One answer that deserves attention is that propositions are the *meanings* of sentences.

The view that propositions are the meanings of sentences derives some plausibility from one of the standard arguments for saying that it is propositions, not sentences, which are true or false: namely that truth-bearers cannot be identified with anything which is unique to one or another language — that the bearers of truth must be things which "transcend" any particular language and are the sort of things which can be shared by several languages. Suppose an English-speaker utters the sentence, "The earth is round", while a French-speaker utters the sentence, "La terre est ronde." Then, the argument goes, there is a sense in which both speakers assert the same thing and assert it truly. If you like, they both assert the same truth. Yet the truth which both of them assert cannot be identified with the words which either of them utters, for one utters an English sentence while the other utters a French one. Hence, although each of these sentences may be said to "express" the same truth, that which they both express is not a sentence in either English or French or, for that matter, in any other language. Rather it is, in the proposed terminology, a proposition. The argument seems a good one so far as it goes. But it leaves unanswered the question concerning the status of these proposed entities, propositions. And so it has come about that some philosophers, seeking to settle this question, and reflecting on the fact that one thing which is common to both speakers is that the sentence that one utters *means the same as* the sentence the other utters, have concluded that the true proposition which both assert should be identified with the common meaning of these two sentences.

However, despite its initial attractiveness, this answer does not stand up to careful probing. To begin, the criteria for individuating propositions and for individuating the meanings of sentences are different. The sentence-meanings of two sentences can be identical even though the expressed propositions are different. And conversely, the propositions expressed by two sentences can be identical on occasions when the respective sentence-meanings are different.

In the first instance, we can point to sentences which have the same meaning but which express different propositions: as when John Doe utters the sentence "I am ill" and Jean d'Eau utters the sentence which means the same in French, viz., "Je suis malade." The sentences which they utter are correct translations of one another and so, on any ordinary reckoning, have the same meaning; yet one person expresses the proposition that John Doe (an Englishman) is ill while the other person expresses the different proposition that Jean d'Eau (a Frenchman) is ill. Plainly the proposition that one person expresses may be true while the proposition that the other person expresses may be false; yet their sentences have the same meaning.

And, in the second instance, looking at the converse, there are cases where we would want to say that the same proposition can be expressed by sentences having different meanings: as when John Doe says "I am ill" while his sister Jill says "My brother John is ill." If John is in fact ill, then each is expressing the same true proposition; yet the meanings of the sentences which they use to express this truth are different.

Further, this way of conceiving of propositions cannot do justice to their role as the bearers of truth and falsity.

In the first place, we do not as a matter of fact ordinarily attribute truth or falsity to sentence-meanings. It makes little if any sense to say "The meaning of your sentence is true." To be sure, we do sometimes say "What you meant to say was true" where a person has expressed himself clumsily or incorrectly. But since "what you meant to say" is here synonymous with "what you intended to say" this usage lends no support whatever to the thesis that truth is attributable to sentence-meanings.

Secondly, and more importantly, the suggested identification of propositions with sentence-meanings cannot accommodate those facts of natural history which we earlier took to be counter-instances to any version of the sentence-theory whatever: the fact that our nonspeaking forebears and some speechless creatures may reasonably be supposed to have entertained beliefs which were true or false in the absence of any sentences which might have expressed those true or false beliefs. The suggestion that it is sentence-meanings which are true or false is simply a version of the sentence-theory in general and suffers the fate of all such theories.

However, it might be said that there is another way of construing the sentence-meaning account which enables it to evade these difficulties: viz., that speaking of sentence-meanings is simply a way of speaking of meanings which are customarily — but not invariably — the meanings of sentences, and that it is these meanings, considered quite independently of the sentences with which they are usually associated, which should be identified with propositions, i.e., which should be identified as the bearers of truth and falsity. Those philosophers who like to think of meanings as abstract entities on a par with propositions might thus be tempted to effect an economy in their ontology by the simple expedient of identifying the two. But, for a start, the two cannot be identical. For the kind of association which meanings have with sentences is different from that which propositions have. Meanings, when they are associated with sentences, are meanings *of* those sentences; they are not expressed by them. Propositions, when they are associated with sentences, are *expressed by* those sentences; they are not propositions *of* those sentences. And in any case, meanings — as we have already seen — just are not the sorts of things which can play the role for which propositions have been cast: they just are not the sorts of things which can be true or false. Propositions cannot be identified with meanings *simpliciter* any more than they can be identified with meanings of sentences.

EXERCISES

1. *Find an example of two sentences which differ in meaning and which it would be natural to use to express one and the same proposition. Are the sentences in your example context-free or context-dependent?*

2. *Find an example of two sentences which are alike in meaning but which it would be natural to use to express two different propositions. Are the sentences in your example context-free or context-dependent?*

3. *What arguments can be brought to bear against the thesis that it is the meanings of* context-free *sentences which are the bearers of truth-values?*

*   *   *   *   *

Thesis 12:   Propositions are to be identified with sets of possible worlds.

Objections to Thesis 12:   First, sets of possible worlds do not seem to be the right sort of things to be the objects of belief, doubt, etc. Secondly, this account would entail that there is only one necessarily true proposition and only one necessarily false proposition.

One proposal which has been promoted in recent years is that propositions are to be identified with sets of possible worlds; that is, it has been claimed that each proposition just *is* a set of possible worlds.

For every proposition there exists a set of possible worlds in which that proposition is true.[9] This being so, some philosophers have suggested that it may be profitable to identify each proposition with that set of possible worlds in which it is true. Of course, the point could not be put just this way; we should have to change our manner of describing the situation. Instead of saying that a proposition, P, is true in some set or other of possible worlds, W, we would say, "The proposition, P, *is* the set of possible worlds, W."

Several considerations favor this proposal.

For one, adopting it would markedly reduce our ontology; that is, would reduce the number of *kinds* of entities we require to make sense of our conceptual scheme. Instead of having to talk about both propositions and sets of possible worlds, we could make do just with sets of possible worlds. We would thereby avoid postulating the existence of an additional kind of abstract entity.

Secondly, in much work in formal semantics and in certain areas in formal logic, epistemology, and ethics, no distinction need be made between propositions and sets of possible worlds. For certain purposes it makes no difference whether propositions are *paired off* with sets of possible worlds or, in a stronger sense, are *identified* with sets of possible worlds.

Thirdly, there is the very attractive feature that sets have certain properties which lend themselves admirably to our purposes of explaining the logical attributes of propositions. For example, recall the modal relation of implication. Implication, we said, is that relation which one proposition bears to another when the latter is true in all possible worlds in which the former is true. If, however, propositions were to be identified with sets of possible worlds, the relation of implication could be

---

9. In the case of necessarily false propositions, the relevant set of possible worlds is empty, i.e., has no members. But no matter; a set having no members is every bit as much a genuine set as is a set having one or more members.

explicated more simply still: "P implies Q if and only if P is a subset of Q." Similarly all the other modal attributes of propositions could be explicated in set-theoretical terms: a necessarily true proposition would be simply the universal set (of possible worlds); a necessarily false proposition, the null (or empty) set; and a contingent proposition, a nonempty proper subset of the universal set.

Shall we, then, finally conclude that propositions are nothing other than sets of possible worlds?

The choice is not altogether easy or straightforward; for in spite of all the benefits to be gained by adopting such a proposal, there are some powerful objections. Although there are certain properties which sets possess which make sets attractive for identifying them with propositions, sets possess some properties and lack some others which would seem to make them unsuitable for identifying them with propositions.

In the first place we must remember that propositions are not only the bearers of truth-values; they are also, and importantly, the objects of belief, doubt, assertion, speculation, remembering, forgetting, etc. For not only is it proper to say, "P is true", where "P" names a proposition; it is equally appropriate to say such things as, "He believed P", or "He believed the proposition which she had expressed." Now while we seem to speak easily and naturally of one's believing a proposition (or a set of propositions), there is no corresponding idiom in which we would naturally talk of believing a possible world or a set of possible worlds. We do not normally think of possible worlds or sets of possible worlds as the proper *kinds* of thing either to be believed or to be disbelieved. At first impulse, our inclinations would probably be to say that sets of possible worlds are just not the right sort of thing to be an object of belief, doubt, assertion, etc. We probably would be inclined to say that while we can believe a proposition, we do not even understand what it would mean to say that we believe a certain set of possible worlds.

This first alleged difficulty with the proposal that propositions literally *are* sets of possible worlds may not be as damaging as it initially appears to be. For although we do not normally think of ourselves as believing sets of possible worlds, and indeed have not assigned any viable meaning to the expression, "He believes such-and-such a set of possible worlds", this is not to show that the notion is forever doomed to be regarded as a nonsensical one, or that we might not in time come to regard the latter way of talking as perfectly natural. At present the notion seems strange, but that is not the same as saying, even less showing, that the notion is intrinsically unsatisfactory. But what this first argument does is to alert us to the fact that the proposal, if adopted, will involve our making some significant adjustments or extensions to our naive, or prephilosophical, concept of a proposition.

If the foregoing were the only objection one had to identifying propositions with sets of possible worlds, quite probably we would judge the positive benefits to outweigh the oddity just mentioned, and we would adopt the proposal. But the choice is made less attractive by the presence of another problem.

If propositions were nothing other than sets of possible worlds, there could be no distinction between propositional-equivalence and propositional-identity, or in other words, we would be forced to conclude that any two propositions which were *equivalent* (i.e., true in just the same set of possible worlds) were also identical. As we have already seen in chapter 1, this result is counterintuitive. One hardly wishes to say, e.g., that the proposition that all sisters are female is the very same proposition as the proposition that two plus two is four. Yet the adoption of the thesis that propositions are nothing other than sets of possible worlds immediately forces us to this counterintuitive and objectionable conclusion. It is easy to see why. Sets are completely determined (i.e., individuated) by their members. There is no possibility of distinguishing two sets having identical members. If set S_1 has the same members as set S_2, then S_1 is the *very same set* as S_2. If, then, we were to identify propositions with sets of possible worlds, all necessarily true propositions would turn out to be identically the same set, viz., the universal set of possible worlds, and hence there would be but *one* necessarily true proposition. Similarly there would be but one necessarily false proposition, viz., the empty set. And all equivalent contingent propositions, e.g., (1) that Tom is ten years old and that all sisters are female and (2) that

Tom is ten years old and that two plus two is four, would turn out to be one and the same proposition, i.e., would turn out to be identical.

It is just because sets are completely determined by their membership that the second objection to the proposal that propositions literally are sets of possible worlds cannot easily be accommodated. The first objection we leveled was not altogether decisive, just because it was open to a supporter of the thesis to argue that one could simply 'stretch' the concept of what a proposition is so as to allow that a person could believe a set of possible worlds. But the second objection cannot be met in this way. One can adopt the proposal and avoid the sting of its consequences, viz., that there is exactly one necessarily true proposition, that there is exactly one necessarily false proposition, and that all equivalent contingent propositions are identical, only by changing the very concept of what a set is or by giving up the thesis that equivalent propositions need not be identical.

If, however, we wish as we do to retain both our current conception of sets and our intuition that not all equivalent propositions are identical, we are logically forced to abandon the proposal that propositions literally are sets of possible worlds. Taken together, the two objections to Thesis 12 show that the conceptual price which would have to be paid for adopting it is too great.

Thesis 13:   Propositions are abstract entities in their own right; that is, they are sui generis, *they are not to be identified with any other kind of abstract entity.*

Objection to Thesis 13:   None, provided one can tolerate other such abstract entities as sets and numbers, etc.

Having argued that propositions cannot be identified either with the meanings of sentences or with sets of possible worlds, we must now ask with what, if anything, they are to be identified.

Perhaps the time has come for us to look with suspicion on the suggestion that they should be identified with anything — if "being identified with anything" means being identified with anything *else*. Why should not propositions be *sui generis?* That is to say, why should they not be abstract entities in their own right?

There is, of course, an objection which is to be expected at this point, viz., "If propositions are abstract entities, then they are wholly inaccessible to human experience." This sort of objection is frequently voiced by those philosophers who, like Quine, demand that there be behavioral criteria for identifying objects of belief and who claim that these behavioral criteria are more easily satisfied if we identify the objects of belief with (concrete) sentences rather than with (abstract) propositions. In reply, we could, of course, rehearse once more the dialectic that we have already gone through in attempting to clarify this claim that sentences are the bearers of truth-values (are they sentence-types? sentence-tokens? context-free types? context-free tokens? etc.). Or we could point to the fact that in trying to get clear about precisely what proposition it is that a person believes, we can invite him to consider various counterfactual possibilities — various alternative possible worlds, as we have called them — and pose hypothetical questions of the form "If such and such were to happen, would you still want to assert your belief in P?" so as to elicit reactions, of a straightforwardly *behavioral* kind, to these other possible worlds.[10] Or, meeting the objection head-on, we might simply point out that if propositions are abstract entities then at least they seem to be in good company. After all, many mathematicians as well as philosophers have come to the conclusion that sets are abstract entities — not to be identified with collections of physical objects — and that numbers are abstract entities — not to be identified with numerals — and that sentence-types are abstract entities — not to be identified with any actual utterances or inscriptions. Why not allow propositions the same sort of ontological status as these?

10. See, further, section 7 ("Sentential Ambiguity and Possible-Worlds Testing") of the present chapter.

The strongest argument for the existence of propositions as abstract entities is that along with sets and numbers — and, for that matter, along with sentence-types, attributes, arguments, and the like — an appeal to them seems indispensable to any sophisticated attempt to understand the world of our experience. An appeal to something other than sentences and other than states or acts of believing, stating, asserting, remarking, hypothesizing, theorizing, and the like, is needed if we are to make ultimate sense of our ascriptions of truth and falsity. Propositions, conceived of as abstract entities in their own right, seem to do the trick. So conceived, they play the roles which have traditionally been assigned to them: they may be considered in abstraction from any sentences which are used to express them and for that matter, from any language whatsoever; they are suitable for being the objects of belief, doubt, etc.; and they are suitable for being the bearers of truth and falsity.

In saying that propositions are abstract, nontangible, timeless entities, our claim may be likened in several important respects to Bertrand Russell's claim put forward at the turn of the century that numbers are classes (or sets).[11] In reaching his conclusion Russell capitalized on the then little-known but important writings of Gottlob Frege.[12] A few years earlier Frege had undertaken to review all the most plausible theses available to him concerning the ontological status of numbers. One by one he showed that none of these theses, e.g., that numbers are numerals (inscriptions), that numbers are sensible things, that numbers are something subjective, etc., was adequate. In the end, his own solution, viz., that numbers are concepts, was to meet the same fate in the hands of Russell. Russell, acknowledging his indebtedness to Frege, rejected Frege's solution in favor of his own solution which has proved more satisfactory, viz., that numbers are classes. On at least one standard account of what classes are, it immediately follows that numbers are abstract, nontangible, timeless entities. Could *these* have been the things to which persons had (unknowingly) been referring for millennia when they did arithmetic, and to which English-speaking persons for the previous several centuries had (unsuspectingly) been referring when they used the words "one", "two", and "three"? The answer which Russell championed — an answer which has come to be widely accepted — is an unequivocal "Yes." Similarly we — along with many other philosophers — want to promote the thesis that the things referred to by such expressions as "What he denied" and "What she believed," are *propositions*, even though most persons who use these expressions have little if any idea what the actual referents of these expressions are. Insofar as persons could for centuries, and indeed some persons still continue to, use successfully the terms "one", "two", and "three", without knowing what the referents of these terms are, we argue that it is no objection to our solution to say that persons who use such expressions as "What he denied" and "What she believes" do not suspect that they are referring to abstract, timeless entities. As far as we can tell, no other account of the ontological status of the bearers of truth-values is adequate to fit the many things we *do* wish to say about such entities, and no other account is also free of attributing to such entities properties we wish *not* to ascribe to them. In sum, our answer to the question which began this section, viz., "What are the bearers of truth-values?" is: "propositions".

In the light of all this, what are we now to say about the thesis with which we began — the thesis according to which items other than propositions, e.g., beliefs, statements, assertions, remarks, hypotheses, theories, etc., may also be bearers of truth-values? Is this earlier thesis to be abandoned as superficial and/or just plain wrong-headed? Such a verdict would be altogether too harsh. The account we have eventually given is a *theoretical* one which serves to make coherent sense of the various attributions of truth and falsity which we make to these other items. To be sure, we do, in ordinary or casual contexts, attribute truth and falsity to beliefs, assertions, remarks, hypotheses,

11. Bertrand Russell, *Principles of Mathematics,* Cambridge, University Press, 1903.

12. Gottlob Frege, *Die Grundlagen der Arithmetik,* Breslau, 1884. Translated by J.L. Austin as *The Foundations of Arithmetic,* Oxford, Blackwell & Mott, Ltd., 1950. 2nd. revised edition, New York, Harper Torchbooks, 1959.

theories, and the like. But as we saw early on, when discussing that first thesis, our attributions of truth-values to these items is fraught with ambiguity. The upshot of our subsequent discussion of the succeeding theses is, in effect, that this ambiguity may be resolved in a theoretically sound way by regarding these attributions as expedient ellipses. That is, we can *reconstruct* these attributions in the following sort of way. We may allow that a belief is true or false just when the proposition believed is true or false; that a statement is true or false just when the proposition stated is true or false; that a remark is true or false just when the proposition remarked is true or false; and so on. From this hard-won, theoretical vantage point we can even reconstruct talk of a sentence's being true or false: true when the proposition which the sentence is understood to express is true, false when the proposition which the sentence is understood to express is false.

Categorial differences between sentences and propositions

It may be profitable at this point to pause briefly to catalog some of the differences between sentences and propositions.

There are certain descriptive categories which apply only to sentences and others which apply only to propositions.

For example, the categories of "meaningful" and "meaningless" apply only to sentences, not to propositions. Although a sentence may be meaningless, no proposition is. But this is not to say that every proposition is meaningful. Rather, propositions are neither meaningful nor meaningless. The categories "meaningful" and "meaningless" simply do not apply to propositions — any more than do the terms "red" and "blue". In denying that propositions are red, we do not want to be understood as implying that they are some other color. Rather the point is that the entire family of color predicates simply *does not apply* to propositions. The same holds for the family of predicates consisting of "meaningful" and "meaningless".

Similarly sentences, but not propositions, are grammatical or ungrammatical; sentences are in a language, propositions not; sentences may be translated or paraphrased, propositions not; sentence(-tokens) are physical states of affairs, propositions are not; sentences may be ambiguous or vague, propositions not.

On the other hand, we have taken some pains to argue that propositions, but not sentences, are strictly speaking the bearers of truth and falsity. Whenever truth or falsity is attributed to sentences, it is done so either mistakenly or through expediency. Similarly it is propositions, not sentences, which possess modal properties (e.g., necessary truth, necessary falsity, contingency, etc.) and which stand in the various modal relations (e.g., consistency, inconsistency, implication, equivalence, etc.) one to another.

One final note

Our sponsorship of propositions as the bearers of truth-values and, for that matter, as the items between which logical relations hold, arises out of our concern to make sound *philosophical* sense of logic. We readily admit that much, if not all, of the purely formal business of logic — the calculations, the derivations, the proofs — can be conducted without even raising the issues which divide proposition-theorists from sentence-theorists. Stockbrokers can make their daily transactions without settling fundamental issues in economics. And mathematicians can agree about the theorems of arithmetic without having a commonly shared view about the nature or "ontology" of numbers. Likewise, logicians can agree about the *results* of logic without agreeing about logical theory and, in particular, without agreeing about the nature or ontology of the bearers of truth-values. Not all logicians wish to pursue the philosophy of logic. But those who do are invited to consider carefully our arguments for saying that talk of propositions is philosophically indispensable.

3.   THE STRUCTURE OF PROPOSITIONS: A SPECULATIVE THEORY

As a result of a lengthy dialectical argument we have reached the conclusion that the bearers of truth and falsity are abstract entities which are not to be identified with any of the other abstract entities ready at hand in our ontology, e.g., they are neither sets, sentence-types, sentence-meanings, nor possible worlds.

Yet this is not to say that they are unstructured or that they do not number among their *components* one or more of these or some other abstract entities.

That propositions are structured entities, that they have components, is clear from a variety of considerations.

One thing which attests to the internal complexity of propositions is the fact that we use sentences, rather than mere words, to express them. Moreover, if it were not for the complexity of propositions it is very hard to see how we could possibly understand which proposition it is which is being expressed when we hear and understand a sentence we have never heard before. If, somehow or other, the structure of sentences didn't 'reflect' the structure of propositions, then the (rough) mapping which exists between the two would be a phenomenon of monumental coincidence.

Secondly is the fact that we can, and do, *analyze* propositions. We can reflect on the proposition that Mary and John came to the party together and 'see' that this proposition *implies* that Mary came to the party. Again, if propositions were without structure, but were instead atomic entities incapable of analysis, then it is incomprehensible how we might ascertain the presence of this implication, or indeed, of any other logical attribute.

Philosophers have struggled for a long time trying to adduce a viable theory of the structure of propositions. Doubtless the best-known attempt in this century is that of Ludwig Wittgenstein in his landmark *Tractatus Logico-Philosophicus*.[13] In the end, his attempt did not work, and he along with everyone else abandoned that particular theory. But the quest continues. Several persons today are engaged in trying to construct such a theory. Perhaps the most notable among them is Peter Strawson.[14]

In this section we will offer the first tentative suggestions for a theory of our own. It is hardly fully developed, but we have some reason to believe that it might, at least, be 'in the right direction'. But whether it is or not, it should be emphasized that very few of the *other* things we wish to say about propositions require that this theory be true. For example, in subsequent sections of this chapter we examine ways to *refer* to propositions, to *individuate* them, etc. These latter sorts of investigations do *not* require that we have a settled view as to the nature of the internal structure of propositions; indeed, quite the contrary is the case: the sorts of investigations just mentioned can proceed entirely in the absence of any theory as to the structure of propositions.

With these caveats expressed, then, let us turn to our speculations.

The theory we are to consider holds, briefly, that a proposition is identical with a set of concepts-in-truth-valued-combination. This calls for some elaboration.

Concepts

The term "concept" is one of the oldest items in the vocabulary of philosophy and has been given especially wide currency in the writings of twentieth century philosophers. Yet although talk of concepts is common, accounts of what concepts *are*, or of what it is to have a concept, are rarely given.

13. Translated by D.F. Pears and B.F. McGuinness, London, Routledge & Kegan Paul, 1961 (original edition published in German, 1921, under the title *Logisch-philosophische Abhandlung*).

14. *Subject and Predicate in Logic and Grammar*, London, Methuen & Co. Ltd., 1974.

Without pausing to consider rival accounts that have been, or might be, given of what concepts are,[15] let us say forthwith what *we* mean by "concept".

For a start, like Frege and many others we wish to distinguish concepts from *conceptions* or *ideas*.[16] The latter are psychological entities which come into being and pass away from time to time during the lifetimes of conceiving beings. Concepts, as we shall speak of them, do not. Thus we want to be able to speak of a concept, such as that of number, having application to the world independently of the existence of persons' psyches.

Secondly, like Moore and many others we want to distinguish concepts from *words* or other *linguistic items*.[17] Words, like sentences, belong to specific languages. Concepts, like propositions, do not. Plato's analysis of what knowledge is, for instance, was not an analysis of a word in Greek but — we want to say — an analysis of a concept which is independent of Greek or any other language.

Nevertheless, although concepts are not to be identified with verbal expressions they may, we suggest, be *expressed* by verbal expressions which are used to designate certain kinds of items: items of reference (names and descriptions); properties (one-place predicates); and relations (two-or-more-place predicates). Words, when used in certain ways, may *express* concepts just as sentences, when used in certain ways, may *express* propositions.

But *which* words, it will be asked, are the ones which express concepts? Our suggestion is that concepts are expressible by those words which feature in a kind of *open sentence*. An open sentence, in general, is a sentence which contains a gap such that, when the gap is filled with an appropriate expression, the resulting *closed sentence* expresses something true or false.[18] The particular kind of open sentence which can express a concept is that in which the gap is to be filled either (1) *by a referring expression* of some kind (whether it be an indeterminately referring expression like "something" or "everything" or a determinately referring expression such as a name or a description) or (2) *by a sentence expressing a proposition.* For instance, the open sentences

> " . . . is a bachelor"
>
> " . . . is older than . . . "
>
> " . . . is older than the Sphinx"
>
> " . . . believes that . . . "
>
> " . . . and . . . "

are all concept-expressing by these criteria, whereas the open sentences,

15. For a survey of some of these, see P.L. Heath, "Concept", in *The Encyclopedia of Philosophy*, ed. P. Edwards, New York, Macmillan, 1967.

16. See his "Concept and Object" in *Translations from the Philosophical Writings of Gottlob Frege*, ed. Peter Geach and Max Black, Oxford, Blackwell, 2nd. revised edition, 1959, pp. 42–55, and *The Foundations of Arithmetic*, trans. J.L. Austin, esp. pp. 33–37.

17. See "A Reply to My Critics" in *The Philosophy of G.E. Moore*, ed. P.A. Schilpp, La Salle, Open Court, 1968, vol. 2, p. 664.

18. Open sentences are sometimes called *propositional functions*. Russell defines a propositional function as "any expression containing an undetermined constituent, or several undetermined constituents, and becoming [we would say "expressing"] a proposition as soon as the undetermined constituents are determined." "The Philosophy of Logical Atomism" reprinted in *Logic and Knowledge,* ed. R.C. Marsh, London, George Allen & Unwin Ltd., 1956, p. 230.

"Henry . . . a bachelor"

"Henry is . . . James"

"Someone believes that all men . . . "

are *not* concept-expressing.[19] Thus the concept of being a bachelor (the concept of a particular *property*) is expressible in English by the words "is a bachelor", that of being older than (the concept of a particular *relation*) by the words "is older than", that of being older than the Sphinx (the concept of a particular *relational property*) by the words "is older than the Sphinx", the concept of belief (the concept of what is called a propositional attitude) by the words "believes that", and the concept of conjunction (the concept of a particular relation) by the word "and".

Note that, on this account of what a concept is, it makes perfectly good sense to talk of concepts of the items referred to by names or descriptions. For even though names and descriptions standardly fill the gaps in concept-expressing open sentences like those displayed above, this does not preclude names and descriptions from featuring *elsewhere* in concept-expressing open sentences. As Quine has pointed out,[20] closed sentences like

"Henry is a bachelor"

"Pegasus is a winged horse"

can give rise to open sentences like

"x is Henry and is a bachelor"

"x is Pegasus and is a winged horse"

respectively, by the simple although artificial device of forming the verb-expressions "is Henry" and "is Pegasus" from the corresponding nouns. In this way we can allow ourselves to talk, legitimately, of the concepts of being Henry, of being Pegasus, and so on. We can have the concept of being such-and-such an item just as we can have concepts of properties and concepts of relations.[21]

Logicians often emphasize that open sentences — unlike closed ones — do not express anything true or false. Clearly, therefore, if concepts are identified with what open sentences (of the above specified kind) express, concepts — unlike propositions — are neither true nor false. Nevertheless, it seems natural to speak of concepts being "true of" or "false of " certain items; or again, to speak of concepts

19. Hereinafter we shall write concept-expressing open sentences with variables in place of the gaps. In place of expressions which are referring expressions, we will use the lowercase English letters "p" through "z". These variables are to be known as *individual variables*. In place of sentences which express propositions, we will use the uppercase English letters "P" through "Z". These variables are to be known as *sentential variables*.

20. W.V.O. Quine, *From a Logical Point of View,* Cambridge, Harvard University Press, 1961, p. 8.

21. Note that we speak here of concepts *of* properties and *of* relations. Many philosophers treat concepts as if they themselves *were* properties. See, for instance: Frege, "Concept and Object", p. 51; P.F. Strawson, *Subject and Predicate in Logic and Grammar,* pp. 13–20; and A. Pap, *Semantics and Necessary Truth,* New Haven, Yale University Press, 1958, p. 435. And some of these — Strawson, for instance— also treat concepts as if they were constituents of, or — as he puts it — "figure in", propositions. But insofar as concepts figure in propositions they cannot be identical with properties. The property of being a winged horse is no more a constituent of the proposition that Pegasus is a winged horse than is Pegasus. To be sure, we speak equally of the property of being a winged horse and the concept of being a winged horse. But identity of mode of expression does not confer identity on that which is expressed.

as "having application to" or "lacking application to" certain items; or, conversely (following Frege), to speak of items "falling under" concepts. Thus we shall say that a concept, C, is *true of* or *applies to* an item, *a*, (or, conversely, that item, *a*, *falls under* concept, C) if and only if *a* has the attribute of which C is the concept, e.g., the concept of *being green* is true of (applies to) your eyes if and only if your eyes are green.[22]

Attributes of concepts

This talk of concepts being true of or applying to items allows us to give an account of the fact — often acknowledged but seldom explained — that concepts can stand to one another in the same sorts of modal relations as can propositions. Once more we invoke possible worlds. Thus:

> concept C_1 is *inconsistent* with concept C_2 if and only if there is no possible world in which both concepts apply to the same item (e.g., the concepts of being a sister and being a male)[23];
>
> concept C_1 is *consistent* with concept C_2 if and only if there is at least one possible world in which both concepts apply to the same item (e.g., the concepts of being a sister and being wise);
>
> concept C_1 *implies* concept C_2 if and only if any possible world in which C_1 applies to an item C_2 also applies to that item (e.g., the concepts of being a sister and being female); and
>
> concept C_1 is *equivalent* to concept C_2 if and only if there is no possible world in which either concept has application to an item without the other concept having application to the very same item (e.g., the concepts of being a sister and being a female sibling).

And other modal relations, from the total range depicted by the fifteen worlds-diagrams of figure *(1.i)*, may likewise hold between concepts.

In similar fashion we can give an account of the fact that concepts can have different modal properties. Thus, we shall say that

> concept C is *necessarily applicable* if and only if in every possible world C has application to some item or other (e.g., the concept of being a prime number);
>
> concept C is *necessarily nonapplicable* (a self-contradictory concept, as we usually say) if and only if there is no possible world in which C has application to some item or other (e.g., the concept of being both round and not round); and
>
> concept C is *contingently applicable* if and only if there is at least one

---

22. Plainly this account, which gives the applicability conditions for concepts of properties, can easily be extended to yield applicability conditions for concepts of relations, etc.

23. Similarly the concept expressed by "either . . . or . . ." on the one hand and the concept expressed by "neither . . . nor . . ." on the other are inconsistent, indeed contradictories, since there is no possible world in which both concepts apply to the same pair of propositions and in every possible world one of them does.

possible world in which C has application to some item or other and at least one possible world in which C does not have application to any item whatever (e.g., the concept of being red).[24]

It is evident that these three kinds of modal property for concepts are analogous to the three kinds of modal property for propositions, viz., necessary truth, necessary falsity, and contingency respectively.

One qualification is necessary, however. We have defined necessarily applicable concepts merely as concepts which in every possible world are true of *at least one item*. Are there, it is then natural to ask, any concepts which are necessarily applicable in the stronger sense of applying in every possible world to *every* (not just at least one) item? It seems there are. The apparently simple concepts of being a thing (item, object), of being self-identical (identical with itself), and of being an existent[25] (existence) are all cases in point. So, too, are such patently complex concepts as those of being red or not red, being intelligent or not intelligent — indeed any concepts comprising the disjunction of a given concept C and its complement not-C.[26] Such concepts, we shall say, are *universally* as well as necessarily applicable.

By way of contrast, some necessarily applicable concepts will not be universally applicable. We shall say that they are *non-universally* as well as necessarily applicable. Such concepts are applicable in all possible worlds to some item or other but in some possible worlds do not apply to everything. As examples we might cite the concepts of all those items which philosophers have traditionally described as "necessary existents" (meaning that they exist in all possible worlds), e.g., numbers, sets, and propositions. Thus it might plausibly be argued: (i) that the number eight, for instance, exists in all possible worlds since in all possible worlds there exists a number which is twice four; (ii) that the *concept* of the number eight is therefore necessarily applicable; but nevertheless, (iii) that the concept of the number eight, unlike the concept of self-identity, is not universally as well as necessarily applicable since that concept is not true of every item (i.e., since some items do not have the property of being eight).

EXERCISES

1.   *For each of the following concepts say what its modal property is, and for each of the 15 possible pairs say whether the relation of consistency holds between the members of the pair:*

   (a)   is a parent

24. Strawson is getting at much the same point when he writes: "every general concept occupies a position in *logical* space (or in *a* logical space), a position which it can wholly share with no other" (*Subject and Predicate in Logic and Grammar*, p. 17). The metaphor of logical space is, of course, one we have employed already when talking about the set of all possible worlds.

25. Note that by "the concept of existence" we do *not* mean "the concept of actual existence". The concept of existence has application in non-actual possible worlds to all these non-actual possible items which exist therein; but the concept of actual existence clearly does not. We need to distinguish existence from actual existence in much the same way as we earlier distinguished truth from actual truth.

26. In saying that not-C is the complement of the concept C we mean that not-C has application to all those items to which C does not have application. Note that, for example, the concept of being meaningful is *not* the complement of the concept of being meaningless, since there are some things, e.g., propositions, to which neither concept is applicable.

(b)   is someone's offspring

(c)   is a daughter

(d)   is a prime number

(e)   is red and colorless

2.   *Which of the above concepts imply which of the others?*

*   *   *   *   *

Identity conditions for concepts

Some equivalent concepts seem, intuitively, to be identical as well. Most of us would say, for instance, that the concept of being a sister is not only equivalent to the concept of being a female sibling but is identical to it. They are equivalent, of course, because there is no possible world in which one has application to a thing without the other having application to the very same thing. And they are identical, we would want to say, because anything that can truly be ascribed to one can truly be ascribed to the other; because, in a word, they have no differentiating attributes.[27] To be sure, the verbal expressions "sister" and "female sibling" are different (as, again, are the French word "soeur" and the German word "schwester"). And this might dispose us to say that the concepts are different. But they are not. These expressions are simply different ways of expressing one and the same concept; there is no attribute which can truly be ascribed to the concept expressed by one of these terms which cannot truly be ascribed to the concept expressed by each of the others.

Other equivalent concepts seem, intuitively, not to be identical. To cite just one sort of case: the concept of being red or not red is equivalent to the concept of being intelligent or not intelligent. They satisfy our definition of equivalence, as do all concepts which are universally-cum-necessarily applicable. Yet they are not identical, we feel, insofar as certain attributes of one are different from attributes of the other, e.g., they have different constituents. What account, if any, is to be given of this stronger notion of concept-identity?

There are five sorts of case that we will need to consider:

(1)   Among the set of concepts which are universally-cum-necessarily applicable are some which do not involve disjunctions of complementaries. These are the seemingly simple concepts of thinghood, of self-identity and of existence. Our first task must be to determine whether these concepts are identical as well as equivalent. Are there, then, any differentiating attributes which would render these concepts nonidentical? Provided we remember that by "the concept of existence" we mean the concept which applies in each possible world — not just the actual one — to all the items which exist therein, it seems that there are no attributes of the concept of existence which differentiate it from the concept of thinghood or, for that matter, from the concept of self-identity. It seems that to have the concept of a possible existent just *is* to have the concept of a possible thing and just *is*, again, to have the concept of a self-identical thing. In any case, many philosophers have treated these concepts, pairwise at least, as if they are identical. Thus Kant, for instance, claims "we do not make the least addition to the thing when we further declare that this thing *is*", which amounts to saying that the concepts of thinghood and existence

27. For the concept of a differentiating attribute see chapter 1, section 4, p. 39.

are identical.[28] And Salmon and Nakhnikian have shown that the concept of existence — standardly expressed in logic by "Ex" — can be defined as nothing more nor less than the concept of identity — standardly expressed by "x = x" — without disturbing any of the accepted results of logic.[29]   There seem, more generally, to be no untoward philosophical, or logical, consequences of presuming the identity of these 'three' concepts.

(2)   By way of contrast, there are many other universally-cum-necessarily applicable concepts of which we would want to say that, though equivalent, they are *not* identical. As already noted, the concept of being red or not red is equivalent but not identical to the concept of being intelligent or not intelligent. And we can elaborate on the reasons why. For among the simpler concepts which are the constituents of one there are some which are not even equivalent to those which are constituents of the other. The concept of being red has application in some possible worlds to items to which the concept of being intelligent does not. Hence these two concepts are not even equivalent; a fortiori they are not identical. But if they are not identical then neither, of course, are the complex disjunctions (of complementaries) of which they are constituents.

(3)   Among the set of concepts which are necessarily nonapplicable we must include the complementaries of the universally-cum-necessarily applicable concepts in category (1) above, viz., the concepts of whatever is non-self-identical, of whatever is not a possible thing, and of whatever is not a possible existent. These concepts plainly satisfy our definition of equivalence. And, if our earlier arguments about their complementaries are sound, these will be identical as well.

(4)   The matter stands otherwise for those necessarily nonapplicable concepts which consist of the *conjunctions* of complementary concepts: for instance, the concepts of being red *and* not red and of being intelligent *and* not intelligent. For these cases, concept-equivalence sometimes fails to carry with it concept-identity. And the reasoning given for cases in category (2) explains, mutatis mutandis, why. They will be nonidentical just when any of their constituent concepts are nonequivalent.

(5)   Consider finally those cases which involve either (a) the disjunction of a contingently applicable concept with a concept belonging to categories (1) through (4), or (b) the conjunction of a contingently applicable concept with a (1) – (4) concept. As examples of (a) we have: the concept of being a sister or red or not red, and the concept of being a sister or intelligent or not intelligent. Clearly both these concepts will be equivalent to one another and equivalent, moreover, to the simple concept of being a sister (tout court). Yet, for the reasons already given, they will not be identical. As examples of (b) we have: the concept of being a sister and either red or not red, and the concept of being a sister and either intelligent or not intelligent. Here, too, for the reasons given, we can explain why such concepts are equivalent without being identical.

Indeed, if we review the three categories of cases in which equivalence may hold but identity fail to hold, viz., categories (2), (4) and (5), it should now be evident that the same explanation holds for each sort of case. Concepts are nonidentical just when at least one of the constituents of one is not equivalent to at least one of the constituents of the other.

28. *Critique of Pure Reason,* p. 628.

29. " 'Exists' as a Predicate", *Philosophical Review,* vol. 66 (1950), p. 539.

Turning this around, we obtain the following *identity-conditions for concepts:*

> Concepts are identical if and only if they are equivalent and there is no consituent of one which is not equivalent to one of the constituents of the other.

Since equivalence of concepts has already been explicated in terms of their applicability-conditions across the set of all possible worlds, it follows that the identity of concepts is likewise explicable.

Analysis of propositions

We started out to give a theory of the nature of propositions and found it necessary first to give a theory of the nature of concepts. It is time we connected the two.

A long-standing tradition in philosophy has it that one of the chief aims of philosophy is to *analyze* (and thus gain a clearer understanding of what is involved in) propositions and concepts. The tradition enjoyed (and in some ways is still enjoying) its heyday in the work of so-called "Analytic Philosophers" within the present century. But it had its roots in the work of Plato and Aristotle, and has been exemplified in the work of all great philosophers since then. There is another tradition according to which propositions have concepts as their constituents. It forms a keystone in the philosophical writings of Kant.[30] But it, too, is traceable back to the Greeks and still lives on in the work of many contemporary philosophers.[31] These two traditions come together in the view, perhaps most clearly articulated by G. E. Moore, that sooner or later, in the analysis of a proposition, one comes across a set of concepts which are its constituents and these, if complex, may be analyzed into still simpler concepts.[32] It is this view which we must now explore.

By "analysis", in general, we mean the examination of a complex of some kind with a view to determining what are its constituents and what are the relations between these constituents. Now it seems clear that on *any* view of what propositions are — whether they are identified with sentences, meanings, sets of possible worlds, or whatnot — it would be agreed that they are *complex, structured* items and hence subject to analysis. But what *are* the constituents of propositions? And in what relations do they stand to one another?

On the theory we are here offering the ultimate constituents of propositions are concepts.[33] For example: the constituents of the (false) property-ascribing proposition

(2.1)   Muhammed Ali is an Olympic skier

---

30. For Kant *every* proposition is either such that the concept of the predicate is "contained" in the concept of the subject (i.e., is analytic) or such that the concept of the predicate lies "outside" the concept of the subject (i.e., is synthetic). See his *Critique of Pure Reason,* Introduction, B10.

31. Peter Strawson, for example, talks of "the concepts which figure in a proposition". See his editorial introduction to *Philosophical Logic,* London, Oxford University Press, 1967, p. 10.

32. See, especially, "A Reply to My Critics", in *The Philosophy of G.E. Moore,* ed. P.A. Schilpp, vol. 2, p. 664.

33. We say that the *ultimate* constituents of propositions are concepts since some propositions, viz., so-called compound propositions, have other (simpler) propositions as *their* constituents. The point is, however, that the *simplest* propositions in a compound propositions have concepts as *their* constituents. In order to avoid unnecessary complications we will proceed for the present by largely ignoring compound propositions. We show how they can be handled in chapter 4, section 2.

are the contingently applicable concepts of being Muhammed Ali and being an Olympic skier; the constituents of the (false) relational proposition

>   *(2.2)*   Canada is south of Mexico

are the contingently applicable concepts of being Canada, being Mexico, and being south of.

   Propositions, however, are not just *collections* (unordered sets) of their constituent concepts. A proposition is what it is by virtue of the fact that its constituents stand to one another in certain *ordered* ways. Wittgenstein made this sort of point when he wrote, in his *Tractatus Logico-Philosophicus:*

>   A proposition is not a medley of words. — (Just as a theme in music is not a medley of notes.) A proposition is articulated. *(3.141)*

And G. E. Moore made the same point, more fully, when he wrote:

>   The fact which we express by saying that Edward VII was father of George V, obviously does not simply consist in Edward, George, *and* the relation of fatherhood. In order that the fact may be, it is obviously not sufficient that there should merely be George and Edward and the relation of fatherhood; it is further necessary that the relation should *relate* Edward to George, and not only so, but also that it should relate them in the particular way which we express by saying that Edward was father of George.[34]

Whatever account we are to give of the proposition-yielding relation, it is clear that this relation must be sensitive to the order in which the conceptual constituents of a proposition occur within that proposition. This becomes clear when we consider the proposition

>   *(2.2)*   Canada is south of Mexico

and its converse

>   *(2.3)*   Mexico is south of Canada.

If *(2.2)* and *(2.3)* were constituted merely by the sets of their conceptual constituents, viz., {being Canada, being Mexico, being south of}, we should have to conclude that they were equivalent, and indeed identical.

   It will not do to describe the ordering relation which holds between the conceptual constituents of a proposition as if it were itself another constituent of that proposition. For then we should need to specify still another ordering relation by means of which the set of constituents, when thus expanded, is ordered. In short, we would be embarked on an infinite regress.

   Moreover, the ordering relation is not simply one which ascribes certain conceptual constituents to some others. Consider, for example, the proposition

>   *(2.1)*   Muhammed Ali is an Olympic skier

whose conceptual components are the members of

>   {*being Muhammed Ali, being an Olympic skier*}

   34. G.E. Moore, "External and Internal Relations", in *Philosophical Studies*, London, Routledge & Kegan Paul, 1965 (copyright 1922), pp. 277–278.

Clearly proposition *(2.1)* does not ascribe the *concept of being an Olympic skier* to the *concept of being Muhammed Ali*. Rather it ascribes (the *property* of) being an Olympic skier to (the *item*) Muhammed Ali himself.

The proposition-yielding relation, then, must be one which assigns attributes of which certain constituents are the concepts to items of which other constituents are the concepts. In the case of proposition *(2.1)*, this relation may be expressed by saying:

> the item of which *being Muhammed Ali* is the concept has the attribute
> of which *being an Olympic skier* is the concept

or, in the locution of modern logic:

> there is an item, x, such that x falls under the concept of *being Muhammed Ali* and x falls under the concept of *being an Olympic skier.*

And, in the case of proposition *(2.2)*, the proposition-yielding relation may be expressed by saying:

> The item of which *being Canada* is the concept stands in the relation of
> which *being south of* is the concept to the item of which *being Mexico* is
> the concept

or, in the locution of modern logic:

> there is an item, x, such that x falls under the concept of *being Canada,*
> and there is an item, y, such that y falls under the concept of *being
> Mexico,* and x and y (in that order) fall under the concept of *being south of.*

In spite of the differences between these two cases a generalization can be made. Let us, borrowing from Strawson,[35] write

> "*ass* {   }"

to represent the *proposition-yielding relation*. Then we can say that the structure, *ass* {being Muhammed Ali, being an Olympic skier}, just *is* the proposition *(2.1)*; that the structure, *ass* {being Canada, being south of, being Mexico}, just *is* the proposition *(2.2)*; and so on. More generally, we can say that a proposition just *is* its constituent concepts standing in the proposition-yielding relation. Or, equivalently, we may say — with less appearance of circularity — that a proposition just *is* a truth-valued combination of concepts.[36]

Identity conditions for propositions

In chapter 1 (pp. 39–40) we argued that propositions are nonidentical if there are any attributes of one which are not attributes of the other. The fact that one proposition involves concepts different from those involved in another is sufficient to differentiate them. We now see that propositions may also

35. P.F. Strawson, *Subject and Predicate in Logic and Grammar*. Strawson gives a much more detailed and sophisticated account of the proposition-yielding relation. See especially pp. 20–35 and 84–92. ("*ass*" is his abbreviation of "assignment".)

36. For more on the relation between propositions and concepts, see chapter 4, section 2.

be differentiated from one another by having their conceptual components ordered differently within the proposition-yielding relation. This taken together with the account above of the identity-conditions for concepts provides a solution to the problem of giving identity-conditions for propositions:

> a proposition P is identical to a proposition Q if and only if P and Q have identical conceptual constituents, standing in the same order, in the proposition-yielding relation.

This account of what propositions *are* answers a question about their ontological status. It says nothing about how we might refer to them or individuate them in practice. To these matters we now turn.

4.   ON REFERRING TO SENTENCES AND TO PROPOSITIONS

Techniques for referring to sentences

Sentence-tokens of some sentence-types can be asserted and thus come to express propositions. But there are things other than asserting that can be done with a sentence-token of a type the tokens of which are typically used to assert a proposition. We might, for example, count the words in it, translate it, paraphrase it (which is of course a case of translating within one language), parse it, or examine its phonetic structure, etc. In such cases the sentence-token is not a vehicle for communication but an object of study. And in such cases we want a device by which we can refer to the sentence without also asserting it. One device is to enclose the entire sentence-token in quotation marks.

Example

"John loves Mary" means the same as "Mary is loved by John."

Sometimes, for the sake of emphasis in exposition, we add the redundant terms "the sentence" before the quoted sentence and place commas to the left and right of the quotation marks.

Example

The sentence, "John loves Mary", means the same as the sentence, "Mary is loved by John."

A sentence along with surrounding quotation marks is the *conventional name* of the sentence within the quotation marks. Thus one way of referring to a sentence is by its conventional name.

A second way to refer to a sentence is by the use of an assigned name rather than the conventional name. The conventional names of long sentences are themselves even longer. Thus when referring to some sentences it becomes cumbersome to use their conventional names. We can assign a nonconventional name by stipulation. There is a variety of devices in common use to effect such an assignment, and there is a variety of different kinds of symbols used for such names. The most common symbols are those that use capital letters of the English alphabet, numerals, or combinations of letters and numerals. In these pages we shall use all three kinds of symbols. The actual assignment may be effected as shown in the following examples:

Examples

Let "A" = "John loves Mary."

(B2) "Mary is loved by John."

Using these shorter, assigned names, we can reiterate our former claim in a more compact form, viz., "A means the same as B2." A related device which we will use on occasion to assign a name to a sentence is to set that sentence off from the body of the text, indent it, place quotation marks around it, and finally to preface it with a set of parentheses containing two numerals separated by a point.

Example

(13.6)   "Someone reported the accident."

The role of the *"13"* in the above example is to indicate the chapter in which the sentence was first labeled, and the role of the *"6"* is to indicate which numbered example in the chapter this sentence happened to be. Subsequently, if we wished to refer to this sentence we would do so by using the symbol *"(13.6)"* as the name of the sentence; for example, we might write: *"(13.6)* contains four words."

A third way of referring to sentences is by describing them. Thus, for example, we might say that the first sentence of this paragraph consists of eleven English words. The descriptive expression "the first sentence of this paragraph" refers to the sentence "A third way of referring to sentences is by describing them." This method of description gives us the ability to refer to certain sentences even when we do not know their conventional names. Thus, although I don't know what words you uttered when you uttered your first sentence after waking today and am consequently unable to refer to that sentence by its conventional name, I can refer to it, nonetheless, simply by describing it as: "the first sentence you uttered after waking today".

This device of describing sentences rather than naming them is extremely useful. Without it we could not, for example, ask a person to repeat the last sentence he just uttered but which we failed to catch. If we were required to name the sentence in order to ask him to repeat it, we would, of course, be unable to do so. It makes sense to say, "I did not hear what you just said", but it is very peculiar (to say the least) to say, "I did not hear you just say 'Hello, I am Alfred E. Neuman.'"

Basic techniques for referring to propositions

There are at least three different ways to refer to sentences. How shall we refer to propositions? Just as we might wish not to utter a sentence assertively but rather to say something about it, so too we might wish not to express a proposition but to say something about it. For example, we might wish to say that one proposition in particular logically follows from another specified one, but not wish to express either one. In such a case we will need a device by means of which we can refer to a proposition.

One such device uses the English word, "that". Prefacing a sentence with the word "that" generates the *name* of the proposition which that sentence would express if asserted.

Example

Incorrect: John was late logically follows from John and Mary were late.

Incorrect: "John was late" logically follows from "John and Mary were late."

Correct: That John was late logically follows from that John and Mary were late.

The last example above, although grammatically correct, grates on our ear. Thus sometimes for the sake of euphonics and sometimes for the sake of emphasis we add the redundant term "the proposition" before the "that".

Example

The proposition that John was late logically follows from the proposition that John and Mary were late.

A second way in which we can refer to propositions is to place a sentence in quotation marks and preface the resulting sentence-name with the words, "the proposition expressed by the sentence", or more often, its abbreviation, "the proposition expressed by".

Example

The proposition expressed by "John was late" logically follows from the proposition expressed by "John and Mary were late."

Just as in the case of sentences, so too in the case of propositions we can refer to propositions by assigning them numerical names by stipulation. We have already used this device in chapter 1. There we indented a sentence-token, which expressed the proposition under consideration, and assigned a numerical label. That we were naming a proposition, and not a sentence, is conveyed by the fact that the sentence-token appears without quotation marks. The accompanying numerical label (e.g., "*(1.3)*") constructed after the fashion for sentence-names as described above, serves as a nonconventional name for the proposition expressed by the indented sentence. In short, labels attached to indented sentences which appear *with* quotation marks are the names of *sentences* [see, e.g., *(2.4)*, p. 101]; labels attached to indented sentences which appear *without* quotation marks are the names of *propositions* [see, e.g., *(1.3)*, p. 16].

On occasion we shall also use English letters and combinations of letters and numerals (e.g., "P1") as the names of propositions. We will assign such names in any of three ways. First we may depend on the context of the discussion to make it clear that a given symbol stands for a particular proposition (or for a sentence, as the case may be). Or we may state explicitly that we are assigning some symbol to be the name of a particular proposition. For example, we could if we pleased, state explicitly that the letter "Q" will name the proposition expressed by the sentence "John was late", and that the letter "R" will name the proposition expressed by the sentence "John and Mary were late." Thus using "Q" and "R" as the names of propositions, it would be perfectly proper to write "Q logically follows from R." Quotation marks would *not* be needed around the names of the propositions, nor would those names need to be prefaced with "that". Finally we shall sometimes use an explicit shorthand device, viz., that of using the equals-sign ("=") to make the assignment.

Example

Let "P2" = Today is Monday.

This is to be read as saying: "Let the symbol 'P2' be the name of the proposition expressed by the sentence 'Today is Monday'." Alternatively, this may be read as "P2 is the proposition that today is Monday." The fact that the sentence which occurs to the right of the equals-sign appears *without* quotation marks indicates that we are here constructing the name of a *proposition* and not of a sentence.

Fourthly, again as in the case of sentences, we can refer to propositions by describing them. The expression "the first proposition you expressed after waking today" certainly refers to a proposition, although admittedly, you might not recall which one it is.

There is yet a fifth way of referring to propositions. It is by constructing the gerund phrase corresponding to the indicative sentence which expresses the proposition. Thus the following two sentences mean the same thing:

"The proposition that John walked down the street logically follows from the proposition that John and his dog walked down the street."

"John's having walked down the street logically follows from John and his dog's having walked down the street."

Advanced technique for referring to propositions: context-free references

The technique of prefacing a sentence with the word "that" in order to refer to a proposition is by far the most common technique at our disposal. It is not, it should be pointed out, a technical device invented by logicians. Quite the contrary, it is a device which originates in workaday prose. Everyone, logician and nonlogician alike, uses it countless times every day. Just consider how many times a day we say and hear such things as "The prime minister said that the foreign minister will make a trip abroad in September", "Someone once said that to err is human", and "Let me remind you that I told you that you should call ahead if you are going to be late."

For most purposes, this simple technique of prefacing a sentence with the word "that" succeeds in securing reference to the proposition intended. But it doesn't always. There are some circumstances, both in ordinary affairs and in the more specialized concerns of logic, in which it becomes necessary to resort to somewhat more sophisticated techniques.

For example, imagine that on Dec. 25, 1973, Jane Smith were to have said, "John is not feeling well", and sometime later, in different circumstances on Jan. 1, 1974, in reply to a routine inquiry about John's health, she were to have said, "John is feeling fine." If we were to try to report both things that Jane Smith said, restricting ourselves to the simple device of merely repeating the sentences she uttered prefacing them by "that", we would find ourselves saying something of this sort:

> *(2.4)*   "Jane Smith said that John is not feeling well and that John is feeling fine."

This way of putting it would make it appear that Jane Smith had contradicted herself. But clearly she had not done so.

Or consider the case in which three persons, Albert, Beatrice, and Constance, are talking together. Albert says, "I remember the first time I met Beatrice." Constance, who is momentarily distracted, doesn't catch this remark, and asks Beatrice what Albert said. Beatrice can hardly adopt the naive 'that'-construction. If she did, she would find herself saying, "He said that I remember the first time I met Beatrice"; that is, she would find herself claiming that Albert said she remembers the first time she met herself. Instead she should (and would) say something of this sort: "He said that he remembers the first time he met me."

Obviously, for some cases, we shall require a more sophisticated technique for referring to a proposition than the simple one of prefacing with "that" the sentence which happened on an occasion to express that proposition. Many techniques are used in commonplace prose. We will not, and probably cannot, catalog them all. Instead we shall outline a single strong technique which works in all cases, a technique which, admittedly, were it to be adopted widely in workaday prose, would lead to stilted talk. But the latter is no real objection; the technique is designed to satisfy the technical requirements of logic, and is not intended for adoption in ordinary speech and writing.

The sorts of difficulties which we have just reviewed, viz., the appearance of contradiction in the case of the report of what Jane Smith said, and the mistake in reference in what Beatrice might have said, can both be corrected by making context-free references to the propositions expressed.

For many sentences, the matter of which proposition that sentence happens to express will depend importantly on the *context* of the uttering or the writing of that sentence. Consider, for example, the sentence-type corresponding to

> *(2.5)*   "She purchased a new home yesterday."

What proposition would be expressed by the uttering of a sentence-token of this type? Obviously there is no single answer. Which proposition happens to be expressed on a given occasion of utterance or inscription of a token of this type will depend crucially on the particular circumstances of that utterance or inscription, i.e., on the context. It will depend on who is being referred to by "she" and will likewise depend on which day is being referred to by "yesterday", and this latter, of course, will be determined by the matter of when the sentence-token is written or uttered.

One technique for making a context-free reference to a proposition involves, first, applying that technique adopted by the sentence-theorists to construct context-free sentences, viz., paraphrasing the original utterance in the following way:

> All pronouns which refer to particular persons, places, times, things, events, etc., are to be replaced by nouns or descriptive phrases which denote just those items; and all tacit references in an assertion, whether to persons, places, times, things, events, etc., are to be made explicit.

Then, secondly, the context-free sentence resulting from the paraphrase is to be prefaced by "that".

Note, of course, that the first step, the paraphrasing, is not a mechanical procedure. It involves *understanding* what proposition is being expressed.[37]

Let's take two examples. Suppose that someone were to say, "I was here yesterday." What proposition are we to say that that person had expressed? To begin we would have to know *who* the speaker was (i.e., the referent of the pronoun "I"). Let us suppose it was Bertrand Russell. Secondly we would have to know *when* the sentence was uttered; this would be required in order that we should know what day was being referred to by "yesterday". Let us suppose that the sentence was uttered on Nov. 2, 1958. And thirdly, we would have to know *where* the sentence was uttered. Suppose that it was uttered on the steps of Royal Albert Hall in London. Knowing these three things, but only then, we are in a position to make a *context-free* reference to the proposition expressed. And it is, simply, the proposition that Bertrand Russell was on the steps of the Royal Albert Hall in London on Nov. 1, 1958.

For our second example, let us return to *(2.4)*, i.e., the problematic report of what Jane Smith said about John's health. By making context-free references to the propositions she expressed, all appearance of her having contradicted herself disappears:

> *(2.6)*   "Jane Smith said that John was not feeling well on Dec 25, 1973 and that John was feeling fine on Jan. 1, 1974."

Of course, not all sentences need to be repaired in this fashion before they are suitable for prefacing with "that". Many will be quite correct just as they stand. For example, no such repair or modification would be required for the sentence "Copper conducts electricity", nor for the sentence "Two plus two equals four", nor for the sentence "Canada's Centennial Year was 1967." But for any sentence in which there is either a tacit reference to a place or to a time or an occurrence of a pronoun whose referent is a particular person, place, thing, time, event, etc., that sentence must be paraphrased to make all such references explicit if that sentence is to be used in a context-free 'that'-construction.[38]

EXERCISES

Add quotation marks in the following in all, and only those, places where they are required so as to render the claim being made true. If a sentence is correct as it stands, mark it as correct.

37. Sometimes a sentence is ambiguous and hence more than one proposition may be understood as being expressed by it. For such cases, the above technique does not suffice. Techniques for handling ambiguous sentences will be discussed in section 7.

38. For present purposes this final summing up of the technique for generating context-free references to propositions will have to suffice. The inclusion of the qualification "particular" is intended to exclude such cases as: "If any oxygen remains in a light bulb after manufacture, then it will cause that bulb to burn out prematurely." Here the terms "it" and "that" do not refer to particulars thing — in the vocabulary of the Logic of Analysed Propositions we would want to say that these terms are bound by quantifiers — and they would not have to be "paraphrased-away". But this still leaves the following case: "If Bertrand Russell was one of the authors of *Principia Mathematica,* then he was a collaborator of Alfred North Whitehead's." According to our rule, we should have to replace "he" in this sentence (since "he" refers to a particular) with "Bertrand Russell". While no harm will result if we do, it is not, it is clear, strictly required in this case. But it is easier to make the rule slightly stronger than need be, than to make it more complicated just in order that it should be only as strong as absolutely necessary.

1. *Today is Monday contains three words-tokens.*

2. *That today is Monday implies that tomorrow is Tuesday.*

3. *The name of the proposition that you are twenty-one years old is that you are twenty-one years old.*

4. *That two plus two equals four is true.*

5. *Two plus two equals four is neither true nor false.*

6. *Whatever is true is not also false.*

7. *Two plus two equals four contains the same number of word-tokens as four plus four equals eight.*

8. *The sentence-type instanced by the cat is on the mat is a context-dependent sentence-type.*

9. *The context-free sentence copper conducts electricity expresses a possibly true proposition.*

10. *That today is Monday is the name of a proposition which implies that tomorrow is Tuesday.*

*   *   *   *   *

Untensed verbs in context-free references

The great Scottish philosopher, David Hume, was born in 1711. Suppose that in 1719 his mother had said,

> *(2.7)* "David will be ten years old in two years."

Suppose also that David Hume himself said in 1721,

> *(2.8)* "I am ten years old this year."

And finally, suppose that three years later a friend of his had said to him,

> *(2.9)* "You were ten years old three years ago."

Clearly, all three speakers would have expressed the *same* proposition; but one would have used a future tense verb, one a present tense, and one a past tense. Thus, obviously, a single proposition can be expressed by a variety of sentences using verbs of different tenses. How, then, shall we refer to the proposition expressed by *(2.7)*, *(2.8)* and *(2.9)*? Shall we use a future tense verb, a present tense one, or a past tense one? Of course we can do any of these; we need only take recourse to the device of saying: "the proposition expressed by the sentence, '......', when spoken by so-and-so at such-and-such a time in this-or-that place". But suppose we wish to refer to the proposition expressed without taking recourse to quoting a specific utterance. Suppose, more particularly, that we wish to avail ourselves of a context-free 'that'-construction.

If we refer to a proposition by means of a context-free 'that'-construction, then any time which is referred to by that proposition will be explicitly expressed. But if this is so, then the verb we use need not be tensed; the explicit reference to a specific time will carry the temporal information.

How shall we express an untensed verb? The convention adopted is to use symbols which are typographically or phonemically indistinguishable from present tense verbs but to use them to represent untensed verbs. Thus, for example, a context-free reference to the proposition expressed by *(2.7)*, *(2.8)*, and *(2.9)* using an untensed verb would be,

> *(2.10)*   "the proposition that David Hume is ten years old in 1721".

The "is" which occurs in *(2.10)* is not, appearances notwithstanding, a present tense verb; it is an untensed one. It is being used here in the same way in which the verb "conducts" is being used in the sentence,

> *(2.11)*   "Copper conducts electricity."

In this latter sentence, although the verb "conducts" is typographically indistinguishable from a present tense verb, it is not a present tense verb. Rather, it is an untensed verb, and what is being expressed by *(2.11)* is not the proposition that copper conducts electricity at present; it is the proposition that copper conducts electricity at all times — past, present, and future.

5.   THE OMNITEMPORALITY OF TRUTH

We have said that noncontingent propositions have the same truth-values in all possible worlds, and have said that contingent propositions have different truth-values in different possible worlds. But these claims leave a particular question unanswered, viz., "Can propositions *change* their truth-values?" If a proposition is true (or false) at one time in a possible world, does it have that truth-value in that possible world at all times, or might it change in truth-value from time to time?[39]

Consider the proposition that John Doe is ill on Dec. 25, 1973. Let us call this proposition "J". Suppose now that John Doe was in fact suffering grievously from influenza on Dec. 25, 1973. Clearly the proposition J is *now* (several years later) true. But was J true *before* Dec. 25, 1973? Was it true, for example, a month earlier, on Nov. 25, 1973? Was it true a year earlier? Was it true ten thousand years earlier?

To all these latter questions we wish to reply: yes. We wish to argue that all propositions are omnitemporally true or false; that they do not "become" true or false; that those which are true always have been and ever will be true, and those which are false always have been and ever will be false.

How shall we justify this answer?

We begin by noting that the question "When did it become true?" cannot even intelligibly be raised for a vast number of propositions. Are we seriously to ask when it became true that four is twice two, or when it became false that all squares have eleven interior angles? Of course, there may well have been, and probably were, specific times when these noncontingent propositions first became *known*. But surely we would want to insist that in coming to have their truth-values known, these propositions did not thereby *become* true or false. They had been, as it were, true or false all along; that is, the proposition that four is twice two was true even before anyone knew it; more specifically

---

39. In this section we shall concern ourselves only with the question of the *temporal* changeability of truth-values. We leave the question of the *spatial* changeability of truth-values, that is, the question whether propositions can change in truth-value from place to place, to be explored in the exercises at the end of this section.

it always has been true, is now, and ever will be; it is, in a word, omnitemporally true; there never was a time when it was anything other than true; it never 'became' true.

Or consider the contingent proposition, the natural law that pure water freezes (at standard atmospheric pressure) at 32°F. Again it strikes us peculiar to ask, "When did this proposition become true?" Surely not when it was discovered to be true. Water had been freezing at 32°F. millions of years before anyone discovered that fact and will (presumably) continue to freeze at 32°F. long after human beings have disappeared from the universe. Can we, then, identify the moment of this proposition's becoming true with the moment when some water first froze at someplace or other in the dark recesses of prehistory? This answer doesn't sit any more comfortably. For we should surely want to say of a still earlier epoch that it was true of water then that it was the sort of stuff which would freeze at 32°F., even if none of it happened yet to have frozen. All in all, there just doesn't seem to be any time, any specific moment of history, of which it can reasonably be said that it was at that moment that the proposition that water freezes at 32°F. 'became' true.

For a truly prodigious number of propositions the question "When did it become true (or false)?" does not even intelligibly arise. But is this the case for *all* propositions? Could the question be significant for some special class of propositions? Are there some propositions which we would want to say did 'become' true (or false) at some particular time? Clearly the proposition-theory would be both tidier and simpler if *all* propositions were to turn out to be omnitemporally true or false. But can such a thesis be maintained? Are there any untoward consequences in our saying that every proposition bears its truth-value (in each possible world) omnitemporally?

Some philosophers have thought that there are. In particular they have argued that it must be allowed that at least some propositions are not omnitemporally true or false. And they have been led to this position because they have thought that to maintain otherwise is to commit oneself to a belief in fatalism, i.e., the doctrine that all our actions are beyond our control, that they are in some sense predestined. What might lead a person to such a belief? The reasoning is something of this sort:

> If it is true now that I will do A tomorrow, then tomorrow I will do A.
> But if it is true now that I will do A tomorrow, then tomorrow, when I
> do A, I am not choosing to do it; I am not responsible for doing it; I am
> doing it because it was destined that I should do it.

But this argument commits a serious logical blunder. It puts the cart before the horse, so to speak. It is not a proposition's being true which makes us do something tomorrow. It is rather that our doing something tomorrow accounts for a certain proposition's being true, namely the proposition which ascribes that particular action to us tomorrow. It may well be true today that you will sneeze four times tomorrow. But it is not the truth of this proposition which makes you sneeze. Rather it is that you do sneeze four times tomorrow which 'makes' or accounts for this particular proposition's truth. What makes you sneeze is an irritation in your nose, not the truth-value of a proposition. Truth-values of propositions are not causal agents. They don't cause anything, sneezes, murders, acts of generosity, or extreme contrition. They are just not the *sorts* of things which make us *do* anything at all. But if this is so, then there is no cause for concern in allowing a proposition about the future to be conceived of as being true even now. That a proposition about the future is even now true does not, it is clear, entail fatalism. And consequently there is no objection on this score to saying that what happens in the future, including those things which are within our capacity to bring about, accounts for certain propositions (viz., all those about the future) being true (or false) today, yesterday, and a million years ago.[40]

40. For a more detailed discussion of fatalism, see R.D. Bradley's "Must the future be what it is going to be?" *Mind,* vol. 68 (1959), reprinted in *The Philosophy of Time,* ed. R.M. Gale, Garden City, N.Y., Anchor Books, Doubleday & Co. Inc., 1967, pp. 232–251.

There is yet another, very different sort of argument which has sometimes been advanced in support of the position that some propositions 'become' true at a certain time. It is an argument which trades on the well-known fact that words often vary in meaning over a period of time.[41] For example, by the then-current definition of "obscene", public nudity was considered to be obscene in Victorian times; by today's (or tomorrow's) definition, public nudity is not considered to be in and of itself obscene. Reflecting on these facts, some persons have been tempted to put the matter this way:

> The proposition expressed by "Public nudity is obscene" was true in the late nineteenth century, but it is no longer true, i.e., it has changed its truth-value, it has become false, in the latter half of the twentieth century.

If one adopts the sentence/proposition distinction, then it is easy to see that this way of putting the matter rests on an elementary muddle. The point properly should be put this way:

> The sentence "Public nudity is obscene" in the late nineteenth century expressed a proposition which is true, and that same sentence (or more exactly, a sentence-token of that same type) when uttered in the late twentieth century expresses a (different) proposition which is false.

What we have here is not a case of one proposition which has a changing truth-value, but rather one sentence-type whose tokens over a period of time express different propositions. What changes over the course of the century mentioned is not the truth-value of a proposition, but which proposition a particular sentence-type happens to express. If "obscene" changes in meaning, then "Public nudity is obscene" might very well, and probably will, express a different proposition. The case may be likened to a change in the referent of the expression "the king" in the sentence "The king is bald." Suppose a country, let us say Upper Sylvania, has a succession of kings. Then, through the years when various persons in that country, speaking of their own king, utter the sentence "The king is bald" it will happen that some will speak truly and others falsely. But it is not that one proposition switches its truth-value from time to time. Quite the contrary, as various kings come and go, the sentence "The king is bald" expresses a number of different propositions. Spoken in 1834, the sentence "The king is bald" would have expressed a proposition about the then-current king, Modernus XIV; and the same sentence spoken in 1947 would have expressed a proposition about the then-current king (the great-great grandson of Modernus XIV), Reactus I.

By taking advantage of the technique of constructing context-free references to propositions, we can readily dispel the appearance that there is but a single proposition involved in this latter case. There is not one proposition involved, but several, e.g., the proposition that Upper Sylvania's king in 1834, Modernus XIV, is bald; the proposition that Upper Sylvania's king in 1947, Reactus I, is bald; etc.

Once again we see that an attempt to argue that some propositions 'become' true or false rests on a confusion and fails to make a good case for adopting such a thesis.

In at least two instances, then, those who would argue that some propositions ought to be thought of as not being omnitemporally true (or false) fail to make their case. This is not to say, of course, that there might not exist better arguments which would support their contention. But we do not

---

41. And, we might add, from place to place. Recall the discussion, earlier in this chapter, of the term "disinterested." (See p. 78.)

know of any, and, clearly, the onus is on those who would so maintain to support their position with better arguments. Until those arguments are forthcoming, the desire for simplicity and tidiness would demand that we assume that all propositions are omnitemporally true or omnitemporally false.

There is yet another reason for our wanting to say that propositions are omnitemporally true or false, and it is that to deny it would render logic itself vastly more complicated. For one thing we would require (at least) a third 'truth-value', which is to say we would have to abandon the Law of the Excluded Middle. For whatever considerations demand that we maintain that propositions about the future are not now true also demand that propositions about the future are not now false. Whatever argument leads to the conclusion that the proposition that you will sneeze four times tomorrow is not now true, must *mutatis mutandis* apply to the *falsehood* of that proposition's *contradictories,* e.g., that it is not the case that you will sneeze four times tomorrow. One cannot, with consistency, deny truth to the former and assert the falsehood of the latter. Thus the theory that propositions about the future cannot be true now, implies the stronger thesis that propositions about the future lack any truth-value whatever, i.e., are neither true nor false. But *this* consequence would effectively destroy the account we have given of the relations of contradiction, equivalence, etc. For all these accounts are premised on the supposition that in every possible world every proposition has either one or the other truth-value. Our accounts of these relations, then, would have to be made considerably more complicated.

In sum, our reasons for postulating that propositions — noncontingent and contingent alike — are omnitemporally true or false are twofold: (1) so assuming does not seem to have any undesirable consequences; and (2) failing to so assume, has profoundly complicating effects on logic.[42]

For our purposes, then, we shall assume throughout this book that propositions are omnitemporally (and for that matter, omnispatially) true or false. This assumption seems to us to be warranted and fruitful. We have no need of the notion, indeed we explicitly eschew the notion, of a proposition's 'becoming' true or false.

EXERCISES

1. *What argument can be brought to bear against the claim that the proposition that water freezes at 32°F. became true at that moment in deep antiquity when the first molecule of water was formed?*

2. *Can a proposition vary in modality? Could a proposition, for example, be contingent at one time and noncontingent at another? Explain your answer.*

42. Some logicians have set out to explore in detail the complicating effects, on logic, of denying the omnitemporality of truth and falsity. Their explorations have gone in two main directions. Some have developed what are called *tense logics:* they have worked out the consequences of allowing tensed verbs to remain in proposition-expressing sentences so that what they call "propositions" about the future may *change* their truth-values with the passage of time. Others have developed so-called *multi-valued logics:* in these logics, they have worked out, among other things, the consequences of saying that 'propositions' about the future are *neither true nor false,* although they may become so when, in the fullness of time, events make them so. Both sorts of logics find a place for close relatives of the modal notions of contingency, noncontingency, inconsistency, implication, and the like. But neither operates with precisely the same notions that we explicated in chapter 1. Moreover, from our vantage point it looks as if both are trying to do logic in terms of sentences rather than, as we are doing, in terms of propositions.

3.   What reasons can you give in support of the claim that propositions do not vary in truth-value from place to place?

6.   PROPOSITIONS, SENTENCES, AND POSSIBLE WORLDS

Consider the contents of the following three boxes:

Box 1 | The cat is on the mat. |

Box 2 | "The cat is on the mat." |

Box 3 | The proposition that the cat is on the mat |

Box 1 contains an undistinguished English sentence. Box 2 contains the name of that sentence constructed in accordance with the standard convention described in section 4. And Box 3 contains the name of the proposition expressed by the sentence in Box 1.

Both Boxes 2 and 3 contain names, of a sentence in the earlier case and of a proposition in the latter. The former of these names was constructed by our taking a sentence-token of the type instanced in Box 1 and surrounding it with quotation marks; the latter was also constructed by taking a sentence-token of the type instanced in Box 1, but then prefacing it with the words "the proposition that".

In spite of the fact that both the names occurring in Boxes 2 and 3 are constructed out of (physical) tokens of the same type, there are important differences between them.

One does not have to *understand* the sentence in Box 1 in order to know which sentence-type is being referred to by the name in Box 2. But one does have to understand the sentence in Box 1 in order to know which proposition is being referred to by the name in Box 3. For example, suppose someone did not know what the word "cat" means. As a consequence that person would not understand the sentence in Box 1; yet he might perfectly well know that the name in Box 2 is the name of that sentence-type, a token of which can be seen in Box 1. We can name sentence-types easily, even when we do not understand them. But suppose that same person were to consider the name in Box 3. Would he know which proposition was being referred to? Of course, somebody might tell him in words which he did understand, but barring that, he would not be able to tell, in reading through the contents of Box 3, which proposition was being referred to.

In short, the matter of determining the referent of a sentential name (e.g., the contents of Box 2) is *not* dependent on a knowledge of the meanings of the terms in the sentence which has been placed in quotation marks. On the other hand, the matter of determining the referent of a propositional name (e.g., the contents of Box 3) *is* dependent on a knowledge of the meanings of the terms in the sentence which has been prefaced with the expression "the proposition that" or simply "that".

If a person were to ask us, "What is the referent of the name in Box 2?", we could simply point to the contents of Box 1 and say, "It is a sentence-type of which this is a token." But what shall we say to the person who asks us, "What is the referent of the name in Box 3?" Our first inclination would be to reply, "It is the proposition that the cat is on the mat." But immediately we feel the unhelpfulness of this answer. It is as if someone were to ask us, "Who was it who was named

'Lester Pearson'?", and we were to reply, "It was Lester Pearson." While this answer is true, it is not very helpful. It would be more helpful to a person who wanted to know, "Who was it who was named 'Lester Pearson'?", to reply with something of this sort: "It was the prime minister of Canada from April 1963 to April 1968" or "It was the seventh president of the United Nations General Assembly." In short, what we would like to do in response to such a question is to give a *description* of the thing being asked about.

Is this really a problem? Could a propositional name, such as the one in Box 3, fail to pick out a single proposition? Could it, perchance, pick out more than one?

Clearly it could designate any number of completely different propositions. For example, it would designate one proposition if the word "cat" were being used to refer to cats; it would designate quite different propositions if the word "cat" were being used to refer to dogs or to wristwatches or to footprints. Similarly, it would designate one proposition if the word "on" were being used to mean one thing's being on another; it would refer to quite different propositions if the word "on" were being used to mean one thing's being beside another or one thing's being in debt to another, etc.

It is clear, then, that the matter of which proposition we refer to by using a propositional name will depend importantly on the meanings and references of the words in the sentence which we preface by a "that". This raises some problems when we come to invoke talk of propositions in the context of a discussion of possible worlds.

It is easy to refer to a sentence-token which occurs in another possible world. We can say of a fictitious world, for example, that someone in it wrote the sentence, "The cat is on the mat." And our ability to refer to his inscription is in no way dependent upon our knowing what proposition that person might have intended to express by writing what he did.

But now a serious problem presents itself. When it comes to referring to the proposition which our fictional utterer expressed, how precisely are we to refer to it? After all, those very same words may be used in *other* possible worlds by *other* fictional utterers to express still *other* propositions. There is no single proposition which the sentence "The cat is on the mat" expresses in all the possible worlds in which it is uttered. More generally, whatever sentence we utter, there is always someone, somewhere, either in the actual world or in some other possible world, who uses the very same sentence to express an altogether different proposition. If their using our words and sentences in a different sense affected what *we* say, then everything we say would be completely indeterminate as to meaning.

How can this intolerable range of indeterminacy be narrowed? Posed in these general theoretical terms the problem may seem insoluble. Yet the solution — or at least a partial one — is at hand; we need only attend to some of the conventions implicit in our actual linguistic practice.

The same sort of problem presents itself, on a reduced scale, when we consider the different meanings which words and sentences may have in the actual world. For instance, in the actual world, English speakers use the letter-sequence "p"-"a"-"i"-"n" to refer to a certain kind of sensation, while French speakers use that same letter-sequence to refer to bread. How, then, it might be asked, can we determine what is being referred to on a particular occasion of utterance of that letter-sequence? How is it that we, as English speakers, have no difficulty whatever in saying truly of French-speaking persons that they feel pain, not bread, when they injure themselves? How is it that French speakers have no difficulty whatever in saying truly of English-speaking persons that they eat bread, not pain, when they sit down to breakfast? The answer is obvious. In using the letter-sequence "p"-"a"-"i"-"n", each set of speakers takes for granted two interpretative provisos: (1) that the letter-sequences and the word-sequences which they utter (or inscribe) are to be understood in terms of the conventions of a *single* language (we shall call this the *uni-linguo proviso*); and (2) that that language is their *own* (we shall call this the *linguo-centric proviso*).

Now these two provisos amount to unstated but universal conventions not only for the interpretation of those letter-sequences which we call words, but also for the interpretation of those word-sequences which we call sentences. They are implicit in our linguistic behavior. We shall try to make them explicit.

The uni-linguo proviso

Whenever we wish to say anything at all, it is necessary that we operate under the *uni-linguo proviso:* the proviso that the various sentences we utter or write are each items in *one* language. This is not to say that a bilingual speaker could not utter, for example, some sentences in French and others in English. The uni-linguo proviso certainly allows for this possibility. What it does not allow, however, is that a speaker could meaningfully use a sentence in the absence of any conventions whatever — implicit or explicit — for assigning it to some one language or other.

The uni-linguo proviso is so natural and so effortlessly satisfied that it might seem as if it is never violated. But it sometimes is violated inadvertently and occasionally is violated intentionally. We can see an example of the violation of the uni-linguo proviso in the perplexities in which some persons land themselves and their listeners when they try to compare the decimal system of arithmetical notation with the binary. Such persons have failed to realize that, in such a case, they are in fact operating with two *languages.* Consider, for example, the symbol "10". What *number* does this symbol represent? In the decimal system of notation, this symbol represents the number ten, while in the binary system of notation this symbol represents the number two. In the decimal system of notation the sum of the numbers represented by the symbols "10" and "10" is represented by the symbol "20", while in the binary system of notation the sum of the numbers represented by the symbols "10" and "10" is represented by the symbol "100". But many persons, especially when they are newly introduced to the binary system, are likely to become confused about these points and to try to express them in the following way:

> "In the decimal system, ten plus ten is twenty, while in the binary system, ten plus ten is one hundred."

This way of putting it makes it seem as if the sum of ten plus ten is variable, that changing the so-called 'base' of one's arithmetic changes the sum of pairs of numbers. But the sum of numbers is invariable. Ten added to ten has the *same* result whether one is adding in the decimal system or the binary. Ten plus ten is twenty in *any* arithmetic system. The confusion arises in thinking that the symbol "10" in both the decimal system and the binary system refers to the number ten. It does in the former but not in the latter. Consider the following sentence:

$$\text{"10} + 10 = 100\text{"}$$

Does this sentence express something true or false? If it is construed as a sentence of the decimal system, it expresses a falsehood; if of the binary system, a truth. Taken by itself, with no stipulation or understanding as to which language it is a member of, it does not express any proposition. But once it is stipulated, for example, that it is a sentence in the decimal system of expression, then the fact that it might also be used to express a true proposition in the binary system does not alter or even affect the fact that what it expresses is false.

The lesson to be learned from this example can be generalized. It does not apply only to the case of languages of arithmetic. The point to be learned is that until a sentence is assigned to a specific language it is a meaningless string of noises or marks which expresses no proposition whatever. And unless a proposition-expressing sentence is assigned to a single language, the matter of which proposition it expresses will be indeterminate.

The linguo-centric proviso

For practical purposes it is not sufficient merely to operate under the uni-linguo proviso. Theoretically, a person uttering sentences which customarily would be thought to belong to one particular language, could, if he were both clever enough and so inclined, use those sentences with meanings determined by another language. Thus, for example, a person could theoretically use the sentence "Today is Sunday", to express what you and I would express by saying, "The light bulb in the lamp in the den has burned out." And similarly, every other sentence he uttered could also be assigned a non-ordinary meaning. In short, one could speak in a secret code and still observe the uni-linguo proviso. But it is clear what the cost would be: virtually no one who was not privy to his 'game' and its specific details (that is, the 'dictionary' for translating between two languages, the grammar of the other language, etc.), would have any idea which proposition he was trying to express. If we are to have a maximum of intelligibility and ease of understanding, it will not do to have the meanings of our utterances veiled in this way. Rather, practical necessity demands that we adopt a stronger proviso than the unadorned uni-linguo proviso. As a practical matter we insist that the propositions expressed by our utterances be determined not by what *someone* could express by making such an utterance, but rather by what propositions *we and others like us* typically express by making such an utterance. (We presuppose ourselves and others with whom we converse to belong to a community of speakers of a common language.) To operate under this stronger proviso is to adopt the *linguo-centric proviso*.

The linguo-centric proviso will, then, require that — when we use English words and sentences either to express a proposition, or in conjunction with a convention for naming, to refer to a proposition — we be understood as using those words and sentences with the meanings and references which *our* linguistic community gives them in this, the actual, world.

The linguo-centric proviso is not a piece of cultural conceit nor is it a piece of local parochialism, but quite the contrary. It is a practical necessity for any person's speaking intelligibly that he operate under his own community's version of the linguo-centric proviso. The linguo-centric proviso is not required solely by English speakers. It is as much a practical precondition of a Frenchman's, a German's, or a Maori's speaking intelligibly as it is of our speaking intelligibly. Likewise, it is a precondition for the successful communication between persons in a non-actual possible world. Unless a Frenchman (German, Maori, or for that matter a Martian, etc.) and his listeners can assume that their words have their *customary* meanings, the things they utter, if not of indeterminate meaning, will at the very least be unintelligible to the other members of the same linguistic community.

Securing reference to propositions

As we have seen, theoretically the sentence

> *(2.12)* "The cat is on the mat"

could be used to *express* any proposition whatsoever. And as a consequence, the propositional name

> *(2.13)* "that the cat is on the mat"

could *refer* to any proposition whatsoever. But by using the sentence *(2.12)* and the name *(2.13)* in contexts which presuppose our own version of the linguo-centric proviso, we can confidently use one to express a specific proposition, and the other to refer to it. That proposition is, simply, the one which is *standardly expressed* by the sentence *(2.12)* when that sentence is taken to be a sentence of the *English* language in the *actual* world, *here* and *now*.

The resolve to operate under this proviso answers a worry some persons have about the possibility of any proposition's being true (or false) in all possible worlds. The worry may be expressed in this way:

> It has been claimed that the proposition that all rectangles have four sides is true in all possible worlds. But there is no unique proposition which is referred to by the propositional name "that all rectangles have four sides". The propositional name "that all rectangles have four sides" will refer to different propositions in different possible worlds according as the words in the sentence, "All rectangles have four sides", have different meanings in those various possible worlds. There is no *one* proposition named by the expression "that all rectangles have four sides", and a fortiori no proposition which is true in all possible worlds. For every series of words whatsoever, there is some possible world in which those words are used to express a false proposition. Hence the class of necessary truths, the class of propositions which are true in all possible worlds, is empty. There are no necessary truths. And by similar reasoning we can show that there are no necessary falsehoods. In short, there are no noncontingent propositions.

To this worry we may now reply:

> It does not matter that the name *we* use to refer to a specific proposition may also be used in a different possible world to refer to another proposition. The proposition to which *we* are ascribing necessary truth is the one *we* are referring to, using the standard meaning-conventions for English in the actual world here and now. When we say that the proposition that all rectangles have four sides is true in all possible worlds, it is simply irrelevant to object that our words may be used by the inhabitants of a different possible world to refer to something else.

In short, it must be understood that when we ascribe necessary truth to the proposition expressed by the sentence "All rectangles have four sides", we are ascribing necessary truth to that proposition only which contemporary speakers of English ordinarily express in the actual world by means of that sentence. It matters not at all that speakers of another language, in this or any other possible world, might use that same *sentence* to express other propositions and that some of these other propositions will have modal properties different from the modal properties of the proposition we express. The possibility of such other uses of the physical item the *sentence* "All rectangles have four sides", in no way militates against the fact that the *proposition* which we express in our language in the actual world (through our use of that sentence), is not only true in the actual world, but is true in all possible worlds.[43]

43. It should be clear that the requirement of operating under the linguo-centric proviso is *not* a requirement which arises out of one's having adopted the theory that it is propositions, not sentences, which are the bearers of truth-values. Sentence-theorists, too, will want to insist on the need for this proviso. No sentence-theorist would want to attribute the property of truth (or falsity) to a specific sentence unless he was assured that the words in that sentence were being used in their customary sense and that the grammar of the sentence was standard or 'normal'. For example, when a sentence-theorist claims that the sentence-token "All rectangles have four sides" is true, he does so under the cloak of the linguo-centric proviso. He intends and

7. SENTENTIAL AMBIGUITY AND POSSIBLE-WORLDS TESTING

Sentential ambiguity

In section 6 we saw how the linguo-centric proviso can help us to secure reference to a particular proposition despite the fact that one and the same propositional name can be used, i.e., is used in other possible worlds, to refer to countless different propositions. Ipso facto we have seen how that same proviso can help us to determine what proposition a particular sentence *expresses* despite the fact that one and the same sentence can be used to express countless different propositions.

But the linguo-centric proviso does not enable us to secure reference to a particular proposition when, in a single linguistic community in the actual world, one and the same propositional name is used to refer to *more* than one proposition. Ipso facto that proviso does not help us to determine what proposition a particular sentence *expresses* when, in the actual world, it is used to express more than one proposition. In short, the linguo-centric proviso does little to solve the problems posed by sentential ambiguity. Let us explain.

Sentences can be ambiguous, in the actual world, in any or all of several different ways.

Sometimes a sentence is ambiguous because it contains an ambiguous word or phrase; for example,

(2.14)   "Now I can see what you were talking about"

which is ambiguous between

(2.15)   "Now I understand what you were talking about"

and

(2.16)   "Now I have caught sight of what you were talking about."

Sometimes a sentence is ambiguous because of its grammatical structure; for example,

(2.17)   "Flying planes can be dangerous"

which is ambiguous between

(2.18)   "Flying planes are sometimes dangerous"

and

(2.19)   "It can be dangerous to fly a plane."[44]

And sometimes a sentence is ambiguous because of the different roles it can be given in communication; for example,

(2.20)   "In the evolutionary struggle for existence just the fittest species survive"

---

expects that we will take his words in their customary sense. The proposition-theorist will say that it is the proposition which the sentence "All rectangles have four sides" expresses which is true, while the sentence-theorist will say that it is the sentence itself; but each will insist that his own claim is conditional upon the words "all" "rectangles" "have" "four" "sides" being used in their customary sense and is conditional upon the grammar of the sentence being normal.

44. Sentences like *(2.17)*, which are ambiguous because of their grammatical structure, are said to be amphibolous (pronounced am · phib · o · lous).

which is sometimes used in such a way that it is ambiguous between the truism

> (2.21)   "In the evolutionary struggle for existence just the surviving species survive"

and the dubious generalization which may be expressed as

> (2.22)   "In the evolutionary struggle for existence just the physically strongest species survive."

In the presence of any of these kinds of sentential ambiguity it would be inappropriate to speak — as we often have done of nonambiguous sentences in preceding sections — of *the* proposition which is "standardly" or "customarily" expressed by the sentence. For there is, in these latter cases, no such proposition; that is, there is no such *single* proposition. We cannot, in the presence of these sorts of ambiguity, confidently rely upon the linguo-centric proviso to make it clear what proposition a given sentence expresses or what proposition a given propositional name refers to. For in cases of these kinds, the conventions of the language we speak allow for a sentence to express *more than one* proposition.

How then, in cases of sentential ambiguity, can we determine which particular proposition is being expressed, or referred to, on a particular occasion of sentential utterance?

In some circumstances the answer is easily supplied: We can disambiguate the ambiguous sentence by attending to the *context* of its utterance — the immediate linguistic context, perhaps, or, more broadly, the sociogeographic context.[45] In each of the cases of ambiguity cited above it is not too hard to imagine contexts of utterance in which disambiguation can easily be effected. For instance, it may be that the sentence "Now I can see what you were talking about" is uttered in circumstances where it is obvious that the item which was being talked about is not (perhaps even could not be) something in anyone's visual field, so that "see" is patently to be interpreted in the sense of "understand"; or it may be that the sentence "Flying planes can be dangerous" is sandwiched in someone's discourse immediately after the sentence "Your father and I wish that you wouldn't take flying lessons" and immediately before the sentence "And it is especially dangerous for someone who, like yourself, is poorly coordinated", so that "flying" is patently to be interpreted as a verb, not an adjective; or again, it may be that the sentence "In the evolutionary struggle for existence just the fittest species survive" is uttered in the context of a discussion of the alleged virtues of body-building, of jogging, and of cardiovascular fitness, so that it is clear that the speaker's claim is most aptly expressed by (2.22).

But although attention to context sometimes suffices for disambiguation, it does not always suffice. Ambiguous sentences are sometimes uttered in contexts which leave their interpretation open; and sometimes they are uttered in virtual isolation from any context whatever. How can disambiguation be effected then?

The method of possible-worlds testing

Fortunately, there is available to us a more general and more powerful method than that of appealing to context: what we shall call *the method of possible-worlds testing*. What the method amounts to is simply this: we confront the utterer of a given ambiguous sentence with the descriptions of various sets of possible worlds and ask the utterer to say in which sets, if any, the proposition he or she is asserting is true and in which sets, if any, it is false.

---

45. Recall, once again, our earlier discussion of the adjective "disinterested".

There is nothing particularly esoteric or difficult involved in applying the method of possible-worlds testing. It is implicit in our commonplace strategy for getting clear about what someone is asserting when we ask a question of the form: "Do you mean (are you asserting) ..., or ..., or ...?" followed (when necessary) by asking a further question or series of questions of the form: "If none of these, then do you mean (are you asserting) ..., or ..., or ...?", where the blanks are filled in by descriptions of possible states of affairs (sets of possible worlds) one or more of which, we begin by presuming, the speaker 'has in mind'.

The object of the method of possible-worlds testing is to match an unknown proposition to a specific set of possible worlds, and thereby to distinguish it from other propositions. In this respect it may aptly be likened to the party game called "Twenty Questions", whose object it is to figure out, by posing questions which can be answered either by "yes" or "no", exactly what thing the person being questioned has in mind. In practice, however, the method of possible-worlds testing usually is not as protracted as the game of Twenty Questions. This is because it is typically used as a *supplement* to the linguo-centric proviso: it is used to pick out one proposition from among a small number of stipulated alternatives; that is, it is called into use in the face of sentential ambiguity where the alternative interpretations are generally known and few.[46]

By a series of carefully chosen descriptions of various sets of possible worlds, we try to isolate just that set of possible worlds, if any, in which the intended proposition is true, and just that set of possible worlds, if any, in which it is false. To each description of a set of possible worlds which we ask the utterer of an ambiguous sentence to consider, we may envisage any of three sorts of responses: the person questioned may reply that the proposition he means to express is true in some, but not all, of the possible worlds we have described; that it is true in none of them; or that it is true in all.[47] If

46. Theoretically, but impractically, the method of possible-worlds testing *could* be used in circumstances in which we had no idea whatever what proposition a person intended to express by uttering a certain sentence. Perhaps such a person is speaking in code, or in a foreign or unknown language. In such a case, where the speaker and listener do not share the *same* linguo-centric proviso, the method of possible-worlds testing, through laborious application, just *might* reveal what proposition the speaker had in mind; or, more probably, if it worked at all, would reveal an equivalence-class of propositions, one of which the speaker intended to express.

Admittedly, however, this may be an overly sanguine point of view. Quine has argued [*Word and Object*, chapter 2] that there is always a residual, in principle ineliminable, indeterminacy in translation, i.e., that however much evidence one has that one has translated correctly, the evidence always underdetermines the hypothesis. If Quine is right in this, then the method of possible-worlds testing will be similarly limited in its efficacy: it may be used to narrow appreciably the range of possible propositions from which to choose the one intended by an utterer of some problematic sentence, but will be unable to narrow that range to a unique proposition or even to an equivalence-class of propositions.

47. We are presuming, of course, that the person being questioned is both willing and able to cooperate with us in our pursuit of clarity. However, not everyone is like this. Some are unwilling to cooperate: their sentences remain ambiguous and unclear and the propositions, if any, which they use their sentences to express, remain hidden from all but themselves. The method of possible-worlds testing is no answer to human intransigence. Others are unable to cooperate: their sentences remain ambiguous and unclear and it is uncertain whether they are using these sentences to express any propositions at all. People can and do mouth words without any idea of what they are trying to say. The method of possible-worlds testing is no cure for mindlessness.

Perhaps more importantly, we are also in our description of the method of possible-worlds testing disregarding the problem posed by sentential vagueness. For simplicity, we are pretending that the person we are interrogating answers all our questions unequivocally and with no ambivalence. But this is a somewhat idealized situation. More realistically we can well imagine that for descriptions of some sets of possible worlds,

we continue our questioning to the point where our descriptions have exhausted all possible worlds (and this is easy to do, since it is a trivial matter to construct 'complementary' sets of descriptions — one description need only be a contradictory of another description), there are three and only three possible outcomes to the application of this method. The person questioned may in the end: (1) opt for some set of possible worlds and reject all others; (2) opt for none; or (3) opt for all. Let us consider examples of each of these outcomes.

An Example of Case (1)

Suppose someone were to say "Human conduct is subject to moral rule", and that we were unclear as to precisely what proposition, if any, is being asserted. We describe a set of possible worlds, the worlds of Judeo-Christian belief, in which there is a personal deity who issues moral edicts. Are these the worlds in which what is being asserted is true? The answer we receive is "Not exactly; some of them are and some of them are not." But we wish to know exactly which ones are and which ones are not. So we try again. We describe a different set of possible worlds, the worlds of Greek mythology, in which several gods and goddesses subject us to their whims, some of them moral and some not so moral. Are these the worlds in which what is being asserted is true? Again the answer is "Not exactly; some of them are and some of them are not." So we try again. And again. Eventually by judicious trial and error we discover that what is being asserted is true in just those possible worlds in which acting morally brings its own reward, while acting immorally brings its own punishment. And now, whether or not we agree with what is being asserted, we at least know what it is; we know that what has been asserted is a contingent proposition, true in some possible worlds, false in all the others; and we have distinguished that proposition from other propositions which might plausibly have been, but were not in fact, asserted by the utterance of the ambiguous sentence.

Note that the method of possible-worlds testing involves asking whether the proposition we are trying to isolate is *true* in each member of a stipulated set of possible worlds, not the deceptively 'similar' question whether the proposition in question is *consistent* with the description of that set of possible worlds. After all, the proposition that acting morally brings its own reward while acting immorally brings its own punishment is consistent with our description of the possible worlds of Judeo-Christian theology (this was the point of the answer "Not exactly; some of them are [worlds in which the proposition is true] and some of them are not"); and that proposition is consistent, too, with our description of the possible worlds of Greek mythology. Yet both of these sets of worlds, we are supposing, are ones which the speaker says are not encompassed by the truth of what he is asserting. Of course, our story might have been different. Among the sets of possible worlds which the speaker accepts there might have been worlds in which the Judeo-Christian God issues edicts

---

our respondent will be ambivalent or confused as to what he wishes his answer to be; in addition to being ambiguous, his utterance is vague: he himself is not clear as to *precisely* which proposition he intends to express. The existence of vagueness in a sentential utterance is illustrated in the following situation. A person says, "John is tall." We wish to know precisely what proposition is being expressed. We ask the utterer, "Would what you have expressed be true in a possible world in which John is 7′ 4″ in height?" The utterer replies, "Yes." We then ask, "Would what you have expressed be true in a possible world in which John is 5′ 11″?" In the face of this latter question, the respondent may hesitate, and finally say, "I'm not sure." Given such a response, we would have to say that his initial utterance was somewhat vague. It was vague because the utterer himself was vague, i.e., uncertain, as to precisely which proposition he wanted to express. Vagueness, then, is a property which attaches to utterances, i.e., sentences, when their utterers are vague.

and worlds in which Zeus and his cohorts manipulate human conduct as well as worlds in which there is an apt coincidence between certain types of actions (viz., moral and immoral ones) and certain types of consequences (viz., rewards and punishments). If that had been the case, then we should have concluded that the proposition which our speaker asserted encompassed *all* of these possibilities — that he was asserting that either God issues edicts *or* the gods subject us to moral rules *or* there is a cosmic coincidence between act and consequence. If the speaker allows that *any* of these sets of possible worlds are ones in which what he asserted is true, he is asserting something less specific (something with less contingent content as we shall say later [chapter 6, section 11]) than if he allows only one of these sets of possibilities. But he is nonetheless asserting something quite *definite*. Being true in a greater number of worlds does not make a proposition less definite or more vague. It only makes it less specific.

An Example of Case (2)

Suppose someone is telling us a story about his walking trip in the mountains of Austria and of how he came across a charming village in which there lived what he describes as "an old man who is a particularly zealous barber". Without explaining or elaborating he goes on with his story and we are left wondering what he meant by "zealous" —what he was asserting when he said that the barber was zealous. Later we question him. We describe a set of possible worlds — those in which the barber is a dedicated churchgoer, defender of the faith, and so on — and ask him if these are the possible worlds in which what he was asserting is true. No, we are told; the barber is not a religious zealot; he is just zealous in his job. But what does that mean? It turns out that the barber is described as zealous because he insists on shaving *all* those in the village who do not shave themselves, and because, further, he insists on shaving *only* those in the village who do not shave themselves. At first this state of affairs may seem to us eminently reasonable: there are two classes of men in the village, those who shave themselves and are therefore (according to the barber's policy) not shaved by the barber, and those who do not shave themselves and are therefore (according to the barber's policy) shaved by the barber. Yet on rethinking the situation, something puzzles and eludes us. What does the story-teller mean by "all" the men in the village? Does this include the barber? Without waiting for an answer we press ahead with our questions. Is what the story-teller is asserting true in those possible worlds in which the barber shaves himself? The story-teller, after a little thought, says, "No, of course not, for the barber shaves only those men who do *not* shave themselves." Very well, then, we ask, "Is what the story-teller is asserting true in those possible worlds in which the barber does not shave himself?" Once more the story-teller pauses. Then, with considerable chagrin, he admits, "No, for according to the story the barber shaves all those men who don't shave themselves." At this point no more need be said. There *cannot* be a barber in Austria or, for that matter, in any possible world, who is 'zealous' in the story-teller's sense of the word. For all the possible worlds in which there is a barber are either worlds in which the barber shaves himself or worlds in which the barber does not shave himself. Yet the proposition which the story-teller was asserting is, on his own admission, *false* in both these sets of possible worlds. There are no possible worlds, then, in which a barber exists who satisfies what the story-teller means by 'zealous'. In short, the proposition which the story-teller was asserting when he said that he met a particularly zealous barber on his walking tour cannot possibly be true, i.e., is necessarily false.[48]

48. The story of the zealous barber is adapted from the so-called 'Barber's Paradox' of Bertrand Russell.

Note that in case (2), as in all others in which we come to suspect that a speaker is saying something necessarily false, our best strategy is to divide the set of *all* possible worlds into exhaustive subsets and see in which, if any, of these subsets the speaker wishes to maintain his claim. This is what we did in dealing with the story of the zealous barber. Implicitly we subdivided the set of all possible worlds into those in which a barber exists and those in which no barber exists. Tacitly, we dismissed the latter, since they are worlds in which the story-teller's assertion is patently false, and offered for consideration the two remaining sets of possible worlds: those in which there is a barber who shaves himself and those in which there is a barber who does not shave himself. These three sets of worlds exhaust all possibilities. And since the story-teller's assertion is false in all three, it plainly *cannot* be true.

An Example of Case (3)

Consider, once more, the sentence *(2.20)*, viz., "In the evolutionary struggle for existence just the fittest species survive." As already observed, this sentence may be used to express a contingent proposition about the survival-value of physical fitness and strength. But, equally, it may be used to express the proposition that only the surviving species survive, viz., the kind of necessary truth expressed by those sentences which we sometimes call *tautologies*. How does it come about that persons sometimes use *(2.20)* in this latter way? The following sort of occurrence is probably familiar to us all. Someone starts a discussion by telling us that in the evolutionary struggle for survival just the "fittest" species survive. And it immediately occurs to us that if by "fittest" we are supposed to understand "physically strongest", then the claim being made is highly contentious and probably false. Counterexamples crowd into our minds. How about dinosaurs? Surely, by any ordinary criterion of physical strength and fitness, they must count among the fittest species that have ever populated the earth. Yet, patently, they did not survive. And how about, on the other hand, the delicate butterfly? Its physical fitness is at a minimum — certainly in comparison with that of dinosaurs — yet it survived when they did not. Faced with such counterexamples as these, the proponent of the original claim may, of course, retract and admit that he was wrong. But, equally, he may try to save face by redefining "fittest" for us. By "fittest species", he tells us, he didn't really mean "physically strongest": rather he meant something like "best adjusted to the environment". Thus amended, his claim is perhaps less vulnerable to *prima facie* counterexamples. But not wholly. Were not dinosaurs extremely well adjusted to the environment of their times? Or if not, then we need to have the notion of being well adjusted to the environment explicated for us. What is to count as the test or criterion of this sort of fitness (i.e., adjustment to environment)? Pressed for an answer, the proponent of the original claim may reply that the criterion of adjustment to the environment is obvious: we look to see which species have in fact survived. But if this is his answer — if, that is, he cannot give an *independent* criterion of "fitness" or "adjustment", i.e., a criterion which is not parasitic upon the notion of survival itself — then his claim turns out to be absolutely *invulnerable to any possible counterexample*. It turns out, in other words, to be true in all possible worlds, i.e., to be necessarily true, since it is then nothing more than the truism that the surviving species survive.[49]

---

49. If a sentence is so used that the proposition it expresses is invulnerable to all *possible* counterexamples, it loses its credentials as a pronouncement of genuine science. As Michael Scriven puts it: "One could go a step further and define 'the fittest' as 'those which survive'; that is not stretching but breaking the concept, and this step would be fatal to all scientific claims of the theory." ["Explanation and Prediction in Evolutionary

Philosophers sometimes use a variation of the method of possible-worlds testing in order to establish not that what someone said is truistic, but the weaker conclusion that what someone said cannot mean what it ordinarily means. For instance, consider the sentence, often asserted by religious persons,

> *(2.23)*   "God loves us as if we were His own children."

What, exactly, is being expressed by such a sentence? First of all, apart from some theologians, most persons believe that God's existence is a contingent matter, i.e., that God exists in some possible worlds and not in others. This being so, most persons would use *(2.23)* to express a contingent proposition; the proposition expressed by *(2.23)* would be false in all those possible worlds in which God does not exist. But in which subset of all possible worlds is the proposition expressed by *(2.23)* true? It is here that substantial disagreement may exist between persons. Suppose we were to describe a possible world in which God allows truly calamitous misfortunes to befall mankind, and the religious-minded utterer of *(2.23)* insists that the proposition he is expressing is true in such a world. Suppose, even, that he would insist that the proposition expressed is true in every possible world in which both God and persons exist no matter how extreme the suffering of those human beings. Under such circumstances we would be forced to the conclusion that he must mean something different by his use of the word "love" from what we ordinarily mean in using that term. For clearly we would not describe a parent as one who "loved his children", who had it in his power to prevent, yet allowed, truly calamitous misfortunes to befall his children. Loving parents simply do not behave in this fashion. Of course this argument will work only if the believer also holds that God is omnipotent and that he has complete power over the course of events. But given that presupposition, it seems fair to conclude, at the very least, that the 'love' which is being ascribed to our Heavenly Father must be very different (qualitatively) from that of any earthly father.[50]

Note that we can conclude that the proposition which a person expresses is necessarily true only if there is no possible *set of circumstances* which would make it false i.e., no possible world in which it is false. It does not suffice merely for there to be no conceivable *experiences* which would falsify it. Thus it may well be that, as some philosophers have argued, no set of human experiences could ever falsify the proposition that sea serpents exist somewhere or other. But this would not show that sea serpents necessarily exist. Similarly, it may well be that, as some philosophers have argued, no set of human experiences could ever falsify the so-called "causal principle", viz., that every event has a cause. But this would not show that the causal principle is necessarily true. The set of possible human experiences is very different from the set of possible worlds.

Janus-faced sentences

The method of possible-worlds testing is not only an invaluable aid towards resolving ambiguity; it is also an effective weapon against a particular form of linguistic sophistry.

Thinkers often deceive themselves and others into supposing that they have discovered a profound truth about the universe when all they have done is utter what we shall call a "Janus-faced

---

Theory", *Science*, vol. 130 (Aug. 28, 1959), pp. 477–482, reprinted in *Man and Nature*, ed. R. Munson, New York, Dell, 1971.] A related point has been made by Morton Beckner: "No discredit is cast upon selection theory by showing that it is in fact compatible with all available evidence. On the contrary, discredit would accrue only if it were shown to be compatible with all possible evidence." [*The Biological Way of Thought*, Berkeley, University of California Press, 1968, p. 164.]

50. This is the sort of argument which is developed by Anthony Flew in "Theology and Falsification" in *New Essays in Philosophical Theology*, ed. A. Flew and A.C. MacIntyre, New York, Macmillan, 1964, pp. 96–130.

sentence". Janus, according to Roman mythology, was a god with two faces who was therefore able to 'face' in two directions at once. Thus, by a "Janus-faced sentence" we mean a sentence which, like "In the evolutionary struggle for existence just the fittest species survive", faces in two directions. It is ambiguous insofar as it may be used to express a noncontingent proposition, e.g., that in the struggle for existence just the surviving species survive, and may also be used to express a contingent proposition, e.g., the generalization that just the physically strongest species survive.

If a token of such a sentence-type is used to express a noncontingently true proposition then, of course, the truth of that proposition is indisputable; but since, in that case, it is true in *all* possible worlds, it does not tell us anything distinctive about the actual world. If, on the other hand, a token of such a sentence-type is used to express a contingent proposition, then of course that proposition does tell us something quite distinctive about the actual world; but in that case its truth is far from indisputable. The sophistry lies in supposing that the indisputable credentials of the one proposition can be transferred to the other just by virtue of the fact that one sentence-token might be used to express one of these propositions and a different sentence-token of one and the same sentence-type might be used to express the other of these propositions. For by virtue of the necessary truth of one of these propositions, the truth of the other — the contingent one — can be made to seem indisputable, can be made to seem, that is, as if it "stands to reason" that it should be true.

Among the more common examples of sentences which are often used in a Janus-faced manner is the sentence

(2.24)   "Everyone acts selfishly all the time."

It may be used to express the proposition

(2.25)   No one's acts are ever altruistic

in which case — on any ordinary understanding of what "altruistic" means — the claim being made is contingent but false. Or it may be used to express the proposition

(2.26)   Every person's acts are always performed by those persons themselves

in which case the proposition is undoubtedly true — because necessarily true — but is no longer an interesting topic for debate. The trouble is, of course, that someone may utter (2.24) with the intent of making a significant psychological claim about the sources and motives of human action — as in the manner of (2.25) — but, when challenged, try to save face by taking refuge in a tautology — such as (2.26). Not only is such a move on a par with crasser forms of prevarication; it may tempt us, if we do not keep our wits about us, to attribute to the contingent psychological claim the kind of indisputability which belongs only to necessary truths.

It should be evident how the method of possible-worlds testing can guard against sophistries of this kind. We need only ask the utterer of a token of a Janus-faced sentence-type whether there is any possible state of affairs in which the proposition being asserted is false. If the answer is "No", then the proposition being asserted will undoubtedly be true, even though it may not strike us as very informative. But if the answer is "Yes", then we shall want to enquire as to whether the set of circumstances in which it is false happens to include the actual world. All too often the contingent propositions which Janus-faced sentences may be used to express turn out not only to be *possibly* false but to be *actually* false as well.

Utterers of tokens of Janus-faced sentence-types may, of course, be quite unclear as to which kind of propositions they intend to express. Janus-faced sentences can beguile us all, speakers as well as hearers. But this much is clear: we cannot have it both ways; we cannot, that is, on one and the same occasion of the utterance of a token of a Janus-faced sentence-type claim *both* that it expresses a proposition possessing the indisputable credentials of a necessary truth *and* that it expresses a proposition which is distinctively true of the world in which we live. For no proposition is both contingent and noncontingent even though one and the same sentence-type may be instanced sometimes by tokens used to express a contingent proposition and sometimes by tokens used to express a noncontingent one.

EXERCISES

For each of the following Janus-faced sentences explain how, on one interpretation, it may be used to express something indisputable (perhaps necessarily true), while, on another interpretation, it may be used to express something dubious (perhaps contingent and false).

1.   *"One cannot be certain of the truth of any contingent proposition."*

2.   *"Sounds exist only when they are heard."*

3.   *"All persons are born equal."*

4.   *"I can never have your thoughts."*

5.   *"The future must be what it is going to be."*

6.   *"Everyone is entitled to his/her own beliefs."*

7.   *"Tomorrow never comes."*

8.   POSSIBLE-WORLDS PARABLES

Sometimes a theory to the effect that a certain proposition, A, implies another proposition, B, (or, equivalently, that it is impossible for A to be true without B being true) becomes so deeply entrenched in our thinking that it takes on the status of a virtual dogma. The reasons for its entrenchment may be many and varied. It may be that some currently favored theory, T, taken together with A, does imply B. Or it may be that the supposed connection has been laid down by authority or merely been taken for granted and never adequately subjected to critical examination. The reasons themselves may be of interest to the intellectual historian, the sociologist, or even the psychologist. But they are not our present concern. What does concern us are the methods by which such a theory may be assailed. And one of the most effective of these is the telling of a possible-worlds parable.

By "a possible-worlds parable" we mean a story, directed against a theory of the above kind, which purports to describe a possible world in which A is true and B is false — a world, the possibility of which would show that, contrary to the theory, A does not imply B.

The method of telling possible-worlds parables, it should be noted, is different from the method of possible-worlds testing. It is different in intent and different in execution. The method of possible-worlds testing aims at disambiguating sentence-utterances; and it does this, when successful, by conducting a conceptual survey — in principle if not in practice — of the set of all possible worlds and determining in which, if any, the proposition expressed is true. The method of possible-worlds parables, by way of contrast, aims at refuting a philosophical theory; and, when successful, it does so by conceptually constructing at least one possible world which is a counter-example to the theory and which shows the theory to be false. In fact, the method of possible-worlds parables is simply a special case of the more general method of testing a theory by looking for counter-examples. Consider *any* theory T — scientific or philosophical, highly speculative or utterly mundane — which asserts that all things of a certain kind, i.e., all things having one certain property, are also things of a second kind, i.e., are things having another property. Such a theory, T, might be about crows (e.g., saying that all things which are crows are also things which are black) or it might be about possible worlds (e.g., saying that all possible worlds in which the proposition A is true are also worlds in which the proposition B is true). One of the tests of T's acceptability is that it withstand a determined search for counter-examples — a determined search, that is, for an instance of a thing which is of the first kind mentioned and which is not also of the second kind. If the theory is a scientific one, asserting that in the actual world all things which have the property **F** are things which have the property **G**, we shall have to look for an *actual* counter-example, something that has the property **F** and which does not also have the property **G**. For example, if the theory is the simple one that all (actual) crows are black, we would look to see whether we could find anywhere in the actual world a crow which is not black. But if the theory is a purely philosophical one, asserting that A implies B, or equivalently, that every possible world in which A is true is also a possible world in which B is true, we need not restrict our search for counter-examples to just one possible world, the actual world. Since the theory makes a claim about *all* possible worlds, the scope of our inquiry may be extended to possible worlds other than the actual one. Such a theory will be refuted if we can find *any* possible world, actual or non-actual, in which A is true and B is false.

In order to see how the telling of a possible-worlds parable can refute a philosophical dogma, consider, once more, the theory that only creatures with a language can entertain beliefs. This is a theory which we examined earlier (this chapter, section 2, Thesis 9) when disputing the view that it is sentences, rather than propositions, which are the bearers of truth-values. Our counter to it, remember, was that there is good reason for saying that *in the actual world,* in prelinguistic times, our own ancestors entertained beliefs some of which were true and some of which were false. And in like manner, it has been argued by Norman Malcolm[51] that there is good reason for saying, again, that *in the actual world* languageless creatures such as dogs can think or believe that such and such is the case, e.g., that a cat has gone up a tree.

Now it is clear that if, as both we and Malcolm have argued, there are circumstances in the actual world in which a languageless creature thinks or believes a proposition to be true, then the theory, which has gone virtually unchallenged since the days of Descartes — that the ability to think or believe implies possession of a language in which that thinking or believing can be expressed — is thereby refuted. Nevertheless both we and Malcolm are, in a sense, indulging in overkill. We are both producing actual counter-examples when all that is called for is a possible one. Let us, then, consider how a similar theory might be refuted by means of a story of circumstances which, so far as we know, never were or will be actualized. And in order to extract a new philosophical lesson, let us consider a slightly weaker version of the No-Beliefs-Without-Language Theory.

Case Study 1:   The thesis that persons (creatures) who lack a language cannot have reflective beliefs

The theory that we are to consider maintains that it is impossible for a creature to have reflective beliefs unless that creature possesses a language, or in other words, that lacking a language *implies*

51. "Thoughtless Brutes", a presidential address published in the *Proceedings and Addresses* of the American Philosophical Association, vol. 46 (1973), pp. 5–20.

the absence of reflective beliefs. By "reflective beliefs" we mean beliefs issuing from one's reflecting on one's beliefs, rather than issuing from, for example, external stimuli. Let us call the theory that it is impossible to have reflective beliefs in the absence of language the "No-Reflective-Beliefs-Without-Language Theory". It is not hard to see that a philosopher could consistently reject the No-Beliefs-Without-Language Theory while subscribing to the No-Reflective-Beliefs-Without-Language Theory. Indeed, this is Malcolm's own position. He argues that there is more than enough nonlinguistic behavior exhibited by languageless creatures to justify our ascribing to them beliefs founded upon their *direct* awareness of their environment, but he denies that any amount of nonlinguistic behavior exhibited by languageless creatures could ever justify us in ascribing to them beliefs founded upon *reflective* awareness.[52]

One way of assailing the theory that reflective awareness implies possession of a language would be to attack the argument that Malcolm presents for it. And perhaps the best way of doing that would be to point out that even if it were a fact that no amount of nonlinguistic evidence could ever *justify* the ascription of reflective awareness to languageless creatures, it still would not *follow* that languageless creatures do not have the ability to be reflectively aware of their beliefs. The non-existence of evidence for a state of affairs does not imply the non-existence of that state of affairs itself.

However, by the same token, refuting this or any other argument for the No-Reflection-Without-Language Theory is not the same as showing the theory itself to be false. In order to show that the theory itself is false — in order to show, that is, that reflective awareness does not imply possession of a language — a different strategy of frontal attack is required: we need to show that it *is* possible for a languageless creature to reflect upon its own beliefs. And one of the best ways of showing this is to construct a possible-worlds parable.

The following possible-worlds parable — adapted from Donald Weiss' article "Professor Malcolm on Animal Intelligence"[53] — sets out to do just this. Imagine that on some fictitious planet we come across an animal (hereinafter called "Arthur") that has emerged from an egg that was long before abandoned by its mother. Let us further suppose that although we (hidden behind the reflective glass portholes of our spaceship) can observe Arthur, Arthur cannot observe us. Arthur, we note, never comes across any other animate creature and, not surprisingly, never learns a language. Nevertheless, as the months go by (while we prepare our spaceship to conduct a long-planned astronomical experiment) we observe Arthur learning to cope with his environment in increasingly sophisticated ways. He invents and masters the use of tools, and by trial and error develops complex techniques for securing food, shelter, and even some of the comforts of life. Among other things, he learns to make tools out of metal. He does this, as did our forebears, by heating bits of metal in a forge and hammering them into shape while they are hot. It soon becomes apparent to all of us, including the behavioral scientists on our intergalactic expedition — that Arthur believes that metals become malleable when heated. Then one day Arthur chances upon a piece of metal, left by earlier visitors, which seems not to conform to the general rule: although heated to the same degree as other pieces of metal he has found, this piece is hardly more malleable than it was when cold. The experience presents a challenge to his beliefs. What will Arthur do? Fascinated, we watch as Arthur becomes agitated, paces this way and that, then sits down and stares fixedly into space. Fifteen minutes pass. Then he leaps to his feet, brings in more fuel, rigs up a second set of bellows and sees his strenuous efforts rewarded with success: the recalcitrant metal at last becomes malleable. We, the privileged

---

52. The distinction between direct awareness of a state of affairs and reflective awareness that one is aware of that state of affairs, is one which Malcolm marks — somewhat oddly — by distinguishing between "mere thinking", on the one hand, and "having thoughts", on the other hand.

53. Donald Weiss, "Professor Malcolm on Animal Intelligence", *Philosophical Review,* vol. 84 (1975), pp. 88–95.

observers of all this, are tempted to say that Arthur has reflected upon his belief in the malleability of all metals, hypothesized that a more intense heat may make even the most recalcitrant metals malleable, and put his hypothesis to the test of experience. And when, in subsequent months, we observe further instances of such behavior in response to other challenges to his beliefs, we all — including the behavioral scientists among us — conclude that without a doubt Arthur *was* indulging in reflective awareness and evaluation of his beliefs. It therefore comes as no surprise when, after an untimely accident brings about Arthur's death, we learn from a postmortem examination that Arthur's central nervous system was at least as highly developed as our own. If he could display such reflective intelligence without knowing any language, we speculate, what might he have achieved had he known one?

Is this parable a conclusive one? Does it establish unequivocally that it is possible for a languageless creature to have reflective beliefs? A residual doubt might trouble us: in our parable we have said that no one *taught* Arthur a language, and we certainly haven't ascribed one to him; but can we be assured that he doesn't in fact *have* a language? Couldn't Arthur *have* a language even if he never *exhibits* any linguistic behavior, e.g., never converses with anyone, never speaks, writes, reads, etc.? In short, can we be assured that we really have told a parable in which a person both lacks a language and, nevertheless, has reflective beliefs?

How can we meet this worry? In this way: by asking anyone who seriously thinks that Arthur might, under the conditions described, nonetheless have a language, to continue the parable in such a way as to describe the additional facts which would support that attribution. Given that Arthur has never been taught a language, has never conversed with anyone, has never spoken, has never written anything, nor has ever read anything, it is rather hard to see what else might be true of him which would make our attributing to him the having of a language a reasonable hypothesis. Our rebuttal may be put this way: What more might reasonably be required to show that a person does *not* have a language than our showing that he has never been taught one, has never spoken one, has never heard one, has never written one and has never read one?

But suppose that the proponent of the No-Reflective-Beliefs-Without-Language Theory is undeterred. Suppose he counters with one of our very own arguments. Suppose he reminds us that the absence of evidence for the existence of something does not imply that the thing does not exist. Couldn't it be argued that although we have said that there is no evidence whatsoever for Arthur's having a language, this is not to show that he in fact does not have one?

How serious is this objection? How shall we meet it?

We can meet it by asking the critic just what it is supposed to show. Is it supposed to show that in the absence of our finding any evidence for Arthur's having a language it is nonetheless *possible* that he has one? If this is what it is supposed to establish — and it does look as if this is the strongest contention the critic would be likely to maintain — we can reply in two ways. In the first place, we could point out that the absence of evidence for a thing's existence does not imply the possibility of that thing's existence. If, for example, we were to set out to look for a round square we would fail to find any evidence for the existence of one. Yet we should hardly want to conclude from this lack of evidence that it is nonetheless possible that round squares exist. They do not, of course; they are impossible objects. In short, the critic's claim that it is *possible* that Arthur has a language is problematic, and is not seen to be established by our parable. But all this may be put aside. There is a much more telling objection to be leveled. For in the second place we can point out that even if it were to be allowed that it is possible that Arthur has a language, this is too weak a claim to support the original thesis. The original thesis maintains that if Arthur has reflective beliefs, then it is *necessary* that he have a language. And this original, stronger thesis does seem to be undercut (i.e., rendered implausible) by our possible-worlds parable. What the parable does not challenge is the weaker thesis that it is *possible* that a creature having reflective beliefs possesses a language. But this is as it should be, since this weaker thesis is patently true.

Neither, of course, will it do to object to the moral of the parable by arguing that the world described in our parable does not actually exist, that it is purely a fanciful product of our imagination. That much may be conceded without affecting the point at issue. For all that is required in order to refute the theory that there cannot be reflective beliefs without language, it must be remembered, is that we find a *possible* counter-example, i.e., a counter-example in which there is no inconsistency. That the counter-example of our choice happens to be non-actual is wholly beside the point. The purported connection between reflective awareness and language may hold in the actual world, but since it does not hold in all possible worlds, the connection is only a contingent one, not the logical one of implication.

Case Study 2:   The thesis that persons (creatures) who lack a language cannot believe necessary truths

For a second case study, let us consider still another theory which asserts the primacy of language within the structure of knowledge and belief. A philosopher might well allow that a languageless creature may believe certain contingent propositions on the basis of direct awareness of his environment, or even that a languageless creature may believe certain contingent propositions on the basis of reflecting upon his own beliefs, and yet deny that a languageless creature could ever come to believe (in the truth of) propositions which are necessarily true. That is to say, a philosopher might consistently reject both the No-Beliefs-Without-Language Theory and the No-Reflective-Beliefs-Without-Language Theory while at the same time subscribing to what we may call the No-Belief-In-Necessity-Without-Language Theory.

It is not hard to understand why someone might want to adopt this third position. In the first place, it might be argued that there is a radical difference between belief in contingent propositions, e.g., that the cat went up the tree, or that there is some temperature above which every metal melts, and belief in a necessary proposition, e.g., that if one thing is heavier than a second and that second is heavier than a third, then the first is heavier than a third. The difference, it would be said, is that although a languageless creature could come to believe in the truth of a contingent proposition on the basis of its direct awareness of its environment, i.e., states of affairs in its own world, no languageless creature could come to believe in the truth of a necessary proposition on the basis of such direct awareness. Since necessarily true propositions — the argument would continue — are true in all possible worlds and since no creature has *direct* awareness of any situation in any other possible world than its own, no creature could have direct awareness of the truth of a necessary proposition. And in the second place, it might be argued that *we* could never have behavioral evidence, of the kind appealed to in connection with our prelinguistic ancestors and languageless Arthur, which would warrant our ascribing belief in a necessary truth to a languageless creature, since belief in a necessary truth would be compatible with any behavior whatever that a languageless creature displayed. Hence, there could never be any *distinctive* behavior pattern the presence of which would establish belief in such a truth.

However, regardless of what arguments are advanced for the theory[54] there is a strong argument against it: one which takes the form of a possible-worlds parable.

Let us imagine that in some world the science of neurophysiology is developed to the point where invariable correlations are discovered between certain so-called 'mental states', e.g., of belief, of supposition, etc., and certain states of the central nervous system. And let us suppose, further, that

---

54. Note than an argument akin to the first one just cited — an argument to the effect that it is impossible through experience to gain knowledge of necessary truths — is dealt with in chapter 3 (pp. 168–169), while an argument akin to the second has already been dealt with by pointing out that the non-existence of evidence for a state of affairs does not imply the non-existence of that state of affairs.

neurophysiologists have discovered not only the specific locus within the brain of those neural states which are the correlates of certain *kinds* of belief but also what kinds of electrochemical reactions take place within these highly localized neurons when *particular* beliefs of these various kinds are being consciously entertained. In particular, let us suppose that whenever a language-possessing creature actively (or as philosophers would say, "occurrently") believes that if one thing is heavier than a second and the second heavier than a third, then the first is heavier than the third, then during this sort of belief-episode and during no others, particular neurons of type K are in excitation state α. Moreover, let us assume that this invariable correlation is found to hold for all language users, whether they happen to speak English, German, Russian, or whatever. This particular correlation is observed to be exceptionless in the case of all language-possessing creatures; indeed, it is constantly verified by readings from the neuron-scanners which are implanted in the brains of all language-speakers in our imagined world.

Now it so happens that the philosophers in this world are all firm adherents of the theory that belief in a necessary proposition implies possession of a language. The neurophysiologists, however, are somewhat sceptical and resolve to put this theory to the test. They contrive an ingenious, although somewhat inhuman, experiment. A newly-born child to whom they give the name "Henry" is put into a specially equipped laboratory where he is nurtured, raised and — in a manner of speaking — 'educated' in complete ignorance of the existence of other animate creatures. Henry is exposed to all sorts of shapes, colors, textures, sounds, weights, and the like, but never to a language. He plays games with a set of six balls of different weights and is rewarded when he learns to arrange them from left to right in order of increasing weights. He does this, the experimenters observe, by picking them up in pairs, judging their comparative weights, and then arranging or rearranging them in the correct order. Just from watching Henry's behavior, the experimenters are tempted to conclude that Henry believes the necessary truth that if one thing is heavier than a second and the second heavier than a third, then the first is heavier than the third. Excitedly, they turn to the readings from the neuron-scanner implanted in Henry's brain. And there, as they had anticipated, they see that Henry's K-type neurons are indeed in excitation-state α. They are tempted to rush to the Academy of Philosophy with their findings. But caution prevails. It is only after they have repeated the experiment a number of times with the same result, then duplicated it for other necessary truths which they suppose Henry to believe, and have tested their findings with other unfortunate languageless subjects, that they announce the demise of the No-Belief-in-Necessity-Without-Language Theory.

Case Study 3:   *The thesis that a justified belief in a true proposition constitutes knowledge*

Possible-worlds parables need not always draw as much on fantasy as does the one just considered. It sometimes suffices, in order to refute a philosophical theory, to draw attention to possibilities much closer at hand, as it were, i.e., to possible worlds not much different from the actual one.

One philosophical thesis in epistemology, or the theory of knowledge, which may be traced back to Greek Antiquity,[55] is the theory that a justified belief in a proposition which is true constitutes knowledge. Yet only recently, in 1963 to be exact, was the first refutation of this thesis published. In a short but remarkably incisive article, Edmund Gettier produced two telling counter-examples.[56] In our idiom, we would say that he told some possible-worlds parables. With the insight his paper has given us, we can offer a possible-worlds parable which is somewhat simpler even than the ones he told.

55. Plato, *Theaetetus* 201 and *Meno* 98.

56. "Is Justified True Belief Knowledge?", *Analysis,* vol. 23 (1963), pp. 121–3.

The thesis which we are challenging may be stated, equivalently, in this fashion: A person's justifiably believing a true proposition P implies that person's knowing P. This thesis, of course, is readily paraphrased into a possible-world's idiom, viz., "Any possible world in which both P is true and a person, *a,* justifiably believes that P is also a world in which *a knows* that P." Given this latter paraphrase, the strategy of attack becomes clear: we must try to describe a possible world in which (1) a person justifiably believes a true proposition, and (2) that person does not know that that proposition is true. Can we tell such a parable? Although examples eluded philosophers for centuries, it is now a trivial matter for tyros in philosophy to construct them with ease. Here is but one case.

We imagine a possible world in which a secretary has relied for years on the electric clock hanging on his office wall. For all the forty years he has worked in that office, the clock has never once been wrong. One morning a client walks in the door below the clock. Since her back is to the clock she doesn't see it, and wishing to know what time it is, she asks the secretary. He glances at the clock for the first time that day, reads it correctly, and reports "It is ten minutes past nine." Now as it happens, unknown to him, the hitherto trusty clock expired exactly twelve hours earlier. He happened to glance at it at just the one moment during the morning when its unmoving hands were pointing at the right time. Three conditions are satisfied: (1) the proposition that the time is ten minutes past nine, is true; (2) he believes that proposition to be true; and (3) he is justified in believing that proposition to be true — after all, the clock has been unerringly reliable for forty years. But does he *know* that it is ten minutes past nine? We would hardly want to say so. Rather we would say that his was a merely fortuitous belief, and this for the reason that one cannot know what time it is by reading a stopped clock.

In sum, then, we have our counter-example. There is a possible world in which a person justifiably believes a proposition which is true and yet does not know it. From a proposition's being true and being justifiably believed, *it does not follow* that that proposition is known to be true. Knowledge, in short, requires something more than mere justified true belief. And what this something *more* might be is a question which has occupied many philosophers in recent years.

EXERCISES

Part A

Try to refute each of the following claims by telling a brief possible-worlds parable.

1.   *It is impossible to share another person's pain.*

2.   *Body-swapping is logically impossible. No one person could possibly have successively two different bodies; if the bodies are different, then the persons are different.*

3.   *That God is good is incompatible with there being evil in the world.*

4.   *It is a necessary condition of something's being a physical object that it be visible.*

5.   *It is impossible to determine whether two persons with normal vision, viz., who pass all the standard tests for colorblindness, really do in fact perceive colors in the same way.*

Part B

Now try to assess how successful each of your attempted refutations was.

Knowledge

1. THE SUBJECT MATTER AND THE SCIENCE OF LOGIC

Each of the first two chapters has been devoted to one of two fundamental kinds of entity which we have posited in order to make philosophical sense of logic: possible worlds and propositions, respectively. Given these two kinds of entities it is easy to characterize the *subject matter* of logic. The subject matter of logic, we may now say, comprises the modal properties and relations which propositions have as determined by the ways in which their truth-values are distributed across the set of all possible worlds. Propositions *about* these modal properties and relations may, with obvious propriety, be called *propositions of logic* or, more briefly, *logical propositions.*

Now it is clear from the account we have given of propositions that, in a perfectly straightforward sense, the subject matter of logic exists independently of whether or not anyone ever studies it. The facts, or true propositions, of logic await our discovery in just the same sort of way as do the propositions which make up the subject matter of physics, chemistry, biology, psychology, history, and the like.

Propositions have certain modal properties and stand in certain modal relations whether or not human beings ever come to know that they do. (Compare this with the claim that copper can conduct electricity. This was a fact of physics before human beings discovered it.) In short, the subject matter of logic may be — and has here been — described without invoking any concepts concerning the nature and scope of human knowledge (i.e., without invoking any *epistemic* concepts). In this regard it differs not at all from the subject matter of physics, chemistry, and the like.

But the subject matter of logic no more constitutes a *science* of logic than the subject matter of physics constitutes a science of physics. When we talk about any sort of science we are talking about an organized body of known propositions, or, at the very least, well-confirmed believed propositions, *and* a distinctive methodology for obtaining knowledge of the subject matter of that science. It is by virtue of this latter fact — that the methodology it adopts is a part of the very characterization of a science — that we can say, for example, that modern physics is importantly different from ancient or scholastic physics. It is not so much the subject matter which has changed (although it certainly has) but, more important, its methodology.

If we wish to talk about the science of logic we shall have to talk about our knowledge of the subject matter of logic and about how it is possible to have, and how we do have, knowledge of the modal attributes of propositions. We shall have to see how we can, and how we do in practice, have knowledge of the ways in which the truth-values of propositions are distributed across the set of all possible worlds.[1] This we shall do in chapter 4.

In this chapter we prepare the way by asking the preliminary questions: What, exactly, is it to have knowledge? What is the scope of human knowledge? In what way or ways, can knowledge be acquired? And, finally: Is our knowledge of the subject matter of logic obtainable by methods which are in any way distinctly different from those employed in such sciences as physics and chemistry?

2.   THE NATURE OF KNOWLEDGE

There are many uses of the verb "to know" and its cognates. We can speak of knowing a person (a tune, a city, etc.); knowing *of* a good doctor (of the answer to a question, etc.); knowing *why* the unemployment rate is rising (why the landslide occurred, etc.); knowing *where* to go for a good meal (where the capital of British Columbia is situated, etc.); knowing *how to* ski (how to get an "A" in Philosophy, etc.); knowing *how* a clock works (how it is possible that the engine stalled, etc.); knowing *that* snow is white (that $2 + 2 = 4$, etc.); and so on.

Of these different uses, some but not all can fairly be explicated in terms of the last mentioned, viz. the one in which the verb "knows" takes as its grammatical object an expression referring to a proposition.[2] Sometimes this is conveniently called "knowing that", but it should be clear that so-called "knowing that" is not confined to cases where the English verb "knows" is followed by a 'that'-construction referring to a proposition. Each of the following counts as a case of "knowing that":

(3.1)   She knows that it is 2:30 P.M.

(3.2)   He knows what she told him.

(3.3)   They know whether it is raining in Chicago.

A more apt description of this sort of knowledge is "propositional knowledge". It is more apt since it does not make appeal to the vagaries of English usage; indeed, it does not make appeal to any linguistic items at all. We prefer, then, to speak of "propositional knowledge" rather than of "knowing that". (It was, of course, propositional knowledge that we were talking about when — at the very end of chapter 2 — we discussed a Gettier-type possible-worlds parable which could be brought to bear on the traditional analysis of knowledge.)

Our concern in this chapter is solely with propositional knowledge or, as it is sometimes put, our knowledge of propositions.

Unfortunately both the expressions "propositional knowledge" and "knowledge of propositions" suffer a certain ambiguity. Consider the following two sentences:

(3.4)   "They know all the axioms of Euclidean geometry",

and

(3.5)   "He knows the proposition expressed by '$2 + 2 = 4$'."

---

1. Our conception of the subject matter and science of logic differs little, if at all, from that of Strawson. In his introduction to *Philosophical Logic* (Oxford, Oxford University Press, 1967, p. 1), he describes logic itself (what we have called the *science* of logic) as "the general theory of the proposition" and speaks of the subject matter of logic as "relations of deducibility and implication between propositions".

2. It is not at all clear for the case of *knowing how to*. Indeed Gilbert Ryle has even suggested that some cases of *knowing that* are just as plausibly explicated in terms of *knowing how to* as vice versa. See *The Concept of Mind*, London, Hutchinson, 1949, chap. 2.

These sentences are ambiguous between reporting that certain persons (1) are acquainted with certain propositions, and (2) know the truth-values of those propositions. Similarly, if we were to ask the question, "How do we come to have knowledge of propositions in general and of the propositions which are the subject matter of logic in particular?", our question would be open to two different interpretations.

The interrogative sentence "How do we have knowledge of such and such a proposition?" may be construed in either of two ways: (i) as asking how we come to be acquainted with, or to entertain in our minds, a given proposition; and (ii) as asking how we come to have knowledge of the *truth-value* of a given proposition. Construed in the manner of (i), most persons are likely to answer the question by saying that they had heard the proposition discussed, seen it expressed in writing, or in some other way been prompted by their sense-experience to entertain it. Construed in the manner of (ii), however, the question needs to be answered in a very different sort of way. In order to "have knowledge of a proposition" in sense (ii) it is necessary that one have knowledge of that proposition in sense (i). But it is by no means sufficient. Hence, even if it were the case (as some would hold) that it is only through experience that we can come to be acquainted with propositions, it by no means follows that our knowledge of the truth-values of propositions is possible only through experience.[3] As we shall see later, it is not only conceivable but also seems to be true that some propositions which we come to entertain as a result of experience are *known* to be true not as a result of experience but by reflection or what some philosophers have called "unaided reason". When, hereinafter, we ask about our knowledge of propositions we are to be understood as asking question (ii). That is, we shall be asking how we can, on occasion, know a proposition to be true (or false). Or, in still other words, we shall be asking how we can, on occasion, know *that* a proposition is true (or false).

Before pursuing that question, however, we need to be a little clearer about the analysis of the notion of propositional knowledge itself. What does it mean to say that a person, *a*, knows that P?

Gettier[4] has shown that the traditional analysis of propositional knowledge as justified true belief falls short of providing a set of sufficient conditions. But does it not at least provide a set of necessary conditions?

Even that has been disputed by some philosophers. Let us consider briefly some of the objections that have been raised: first, to the claim that what is known must be true; second, to the claim that what is known must be believed; and third, to the claim that the belief in what is known must be justified.

1.   Is it a necessary condition of the truth of a's *knowing that* P, *that* P *should be true?*

It is sometimes pointed out that knowledge-claims are often made about propositions which turn out to be false. In the Middle Ages, for instance, most persons claimed to know — on the basis of their own observation and the authority of the Holy Scriptures — that the earth is flat. Do not examples like this show that the truth of a proposition is not after all a necessary condition of knowledge of that proposition? Hardly. What they show is that the truth of a proposition P is not a necessary condition of the truth of the proposition that someone has *claimed* to know that P. But that is very different from showing that the truth of P is not a necessary condition of the truth of the proposition that someone has *claimed truly* to know that P, where by "claimed truly to know that P" we do *not* mean "claimed

---

3. Kant was making somewhat the same point when he wrote: " . . . though all our knowledge begins with experience, it does not follow that it all arises out of experience." *Critique of Pure Reason,* Introduction, B1, Kemp Smith translation, London, Macmillan, 1950.

4. Recall our discussion of Gettier's paper "Is Justified True Belief Knowledge?" at the end of the section on possible-worlds parables, in chapter 2.

sincerely to know that P" but rather "claimed to know that P where the claim to know is itself a true claim (i.e., it is true that one knows that P)". If the proposition which *a* claims to know is false, we want to say, then *a*'s claim to know, i.e., the proposition that *a* knows that P, is also false.

It will not do to object that persons in the Middle Ages were nevertheless *justified* in believing, on the evidence then available to them, that the earth is flat. For even if this were so — even if, as we sometimes say, "to the best of their knowledge" the earth is flat — there is a gulf between being justified in claiming to know P and its being true that one knows P. And that gulf can only be bridged by the condition that P actually be true.

Nor will it do to point out that many of the knowledge-claims that *we* make might possibly turn out to be false. In the first place, the claim that one cannot have knowledge that P unless P is true must not be construed as implying that P could not possibly be false if it is known to be true. Contingent propositions (all of which are possibly false), as well as necessary ones, may be true — and may be *known* to be true. And secondly, if it does turn out that a proposition which we claim to know to be true is not true but false, then we — like our forebears — are logically obliged to give up the claim to know it. Knowledge-claims are perfectly compatible with human fallibility. If, contrary to everything that we now with justification believe to be the case, it were to turn out that the earth is flat after all, then we, not our forebears, would have to give up one of our knowledge-claims.

But, it may be said, if we allow that certain of our claims to know may be mistaken, does it not follow that we can never *know* that we know anything? The suggestion that it does follow has lured many thinkers — including some contemporary philosophers — into the radically sceptical position of doubting that we can ever know anything at all. But does it follow? In the first place, it may help to remind ourselves that not all our knowledge-claims are as susceptible to doubt as are those on which the sceptic tends to concentrate attention. We can allow that many, or even all, the knowledge-claims made in contemporary physics, for instance, may turn out to be in need of correction. If so, then as they stand they are mistaken. And if what is claimed to be true is not true but false then it does follow that we do not know it to be true. But there is no need to suppose with the sceptic that *all* the propositions that we currently claim to know are false. Why should we not equally suppose some of them to be true? If it is possible that a contingent proposition is false, it is also possible that it is true. And if a proposition *is* true then — provided, of course, that the other necessary conditions for knowing are satisfied — the sceptic's objection to our claim that we know that proposition to be true deserves to fall on deaf ears. Secondly, even if we were to allow that any given proposition which we claim to know might turn out to be false, it still would not follow that *all* our knowledge-claims might be mistaken. If this latter proposition — that all our knowledge claims might be mistaken — were true, and the sceptic not only believed it to be true but also claimed that he was justified in believing it to be true, then this very proposition would itself constitute a counterexample to the sceptic's thesis.[5] For it would itself be a proposition which the sceptic knew to be true. In short, if the sceptic tries to press his case by saying that his thesis is true and that he knows it to be true, he refutes himself.

One cannot without self-contradiction claim to know that nothing can be known. The worry about how one can ever *know* that one knows anything turns out to be no more threatening than the original worry about whether one can ever know a proposition to be true. If we claim to know that P and P turns out to be false then it is false that we know that P and false also that we know that we know that P. But it is demonstrable that some of the propositions that people claim to know are *not* false. The proposition that one *cannot* know that nothing can be known is a case in point. And there are many others besides.

One last point deserves mention. How, it might be asked, can the thesis that if *a* knows that P then P is true be reconciled with the fact that we sometimes claim — and claim truly — to know that a

---

5. Of course, a sceptic may well resist being lured into making this further claim and thus avoid the charge of self-refutation. Sophisticated scepticism is not as easily refuted as the more naive version presented above.

proposition P is false? This worry, though it deserves mention, hardly deserves serious attention. For it stems from a simple confusion. Consider the claim that *a* knows that the proposition

(3.6)   Canada is south of Mexico

is false. Then the proposition which *a* knows when *a* knows that *(3.6)* is false is not the false proposition that Canada is south of Mexico but rather the true proposition that *(3.6)* is false. That is to say, what *a* knows when *a* knows that *(3.6)* is false is not *(3.6)* but

(3.7)   The proposition that Canada is south of Mexico is false

which is, of course, true. The traditional analysis which holds that knowledge that P implies the truth of P has nothing to fear from objections like these.

The relation between the proposition that *a* knows that P and the proposition that P is true may be depicted on a worlds-diagram. If we let "P" represent a contingent (knowable)[6] proposition, and let "K" represent the proposition that *a* knows that P, we will have:

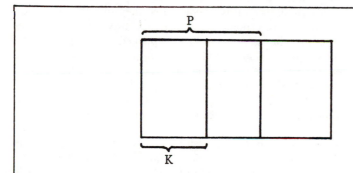

FIGURE *(3.a)*

In this figure, P is represented as being a contingent proposition. The diagrams appropriate for the cases where P is necessarily true and where P is necessarily false are left as exercises at the end of this section.

Every possible world in which *a* knows that P (i.e., in which K is true) is a world in which P is true; but the converse does not hold. There are possible worlds in which P is true but in which *a* does not know that it is so.

2.   Is it a necessary condition of a's *knowing that* P, *that* a *believe that* P?

One argument that has sometimes been advanced against the claim that knowledge implies belief stems from the fact that persons sometimes utter, quite sincerely, sentences such as: "I know it's true; but I just can't believe it" or "I know it's true; but it will take me some time to believe it." Sentences like these may well be uttered in the face of some unexpected momentous or shocking event, e.g., the winning of a large lottery, the outbreak of war, the assassination of a political figure, the death of a

6. We do not assume that all propositions are knowable. See the next section.

close friend or relative. Does that not mean that there are, after all, possible worlds — the actual one among them — in which a person may know that P and yet not believe that P? At least two answers may be given.

One answer is simply to point out that merely saying that something is so does not make it so. Thus, it might be said, from the fact that persons sometimes *claim* to know what they do not believe, it does not follow that what they claim is true or even that what they claim is self-consistent. Indeed, if — as the traditional analysis holds — knowledge does imply belief, then it is no more possible to know what one does not believe than it is possible to square the circle. Some persons have claimed the latter just as some persons have claimed the former. But neither is *really* possible; hence, both these claims are mistaken.

The trouble with this first rejoinder is that it appears to beg the question by simply assuming the truth of that which is being disputed. Further, it is too harsh — because too literalistic — in its construal of what proposition a person asserts when uttering one of the sentences in dispute. The second rejoinder is not subject to these criticisms.

The second rejoinder begins from the recognition that the proposition someone asserts when uttering such a sentence as "I know it; but I just can't believe it", is not at all paradoxical or self-contradictory. Are such persons *really* claiming that they don't believe what they know? A more charitable interpretation is that of supposing that they are indulging in hyperbole when they say " . . . but I just can't believe it" and that what they are really asserting might more perspicuously be expressed by saying something like: " . . . but I find it astounding that this should have happened", " . . . but I find it hard to imagine what things will be like now" or " . . . but I find it hard to adjust my thought and action to fit the facts", or some combination of these or similar expressions. But if this is what is being said, then these putative counterexamples to the thesis that knowing implies believing lose their sting. They are not genuine counterexamples at all. On this interpretation, a person who knows that P also believes that P no matter how difficult he finds it to readjust his expectations and to get his emotions in order.

This second line of defence of the traditional analysis that knowledge implies belief is sometimes itself challenged. Certain persons have argued that both the first objection and the two replies thereto take it for granted that the claim that *a* knows that P is consistent with the claim that *a* believes that P. "But," these latter persons would object, "careful attention to how we actually *use* the two expressions 'I know' and 'I believe' would reveal that, far from its being the case that *a*'s knowing that P implies *a*'s believing that P, the claim that *a* knows that P implies that *a* does *not* believe that P." After all, it would be said, if *a* knows that P then it is wrong for *a*, or anyone else, to say merely that *a* believes that P since this would suggest that *a* does not know it. What are we to make of this objection?

The first point to note is that even if, as is alleged, we do not ordinarily say that we believe that P when we feel entitled to make the stronger claim that we know that P, it by no means follows that believing that P *implies* not knowing that P. It may be true that if *a* merely claims to believe that P other persons will *infer* that *a* doesn't know that P. But this proves nothing. Inference is not always geared to implication. Not all inference is valid inference. My saying "I believe that P" may *suggest* that I do not know that P; and others may be led to infer the latter. But my saying "I believe that P" does not *imply* that I do not know that P; and anyone who infers the latter from the former has made a deductively invalid inference.

That brings us to a second rejoinder. The objection derives much of its plausibility from failure to distinguish between a person's merely claiming to believe that P and that person's claiming to merely believe that P.[7] Now it is clear that if a person, *a*, claims to merely believe that P then what *a* is

7. Failure to make the distinction may be engendered in part by the fact that one and the same ambiguous sentence, viz., "*a* claimed merely to believe that P", may be used sometimes to express one proposition, sometimes to express the other.

claiming is inconsistent with *a*'s knowing that P. Knowledge that P is incompatible with *mere* belief that P since by "mere belief" we mean "belief which does not qualify as knowledge". *Mere* belief that P is belief which falls short of being knowledge insofar as at least one of the other conditions besides belief which is required for knowledge is not satisfied, e.g., *a* may believe P in the case where P is false; or *a* may believe P, but not be justified in believing P, etc. If, then, *a*'s merely claiming to believe that P implied *a*'s merely believing that P, it would follow that what *a* claims when *a* merely claims to believe that P, viz., that *a* believes that P, would also be inconsistent with *a*'s knowing that P. And if this were the case then the proposition that *a* knows that P would not imply the proposition that *a* believes that P.[8] But does the proposition

> *(3.8)*   *a* believes that P

imply the proposition

> *(3.9)*   *a* merely believes that P?

Plainly not. To be sure, *(3.9)* implies *(3.8)*; but that is another matter. We can allow that knowledge does not imply, and indeed is incompatible with, *mere* belief. But we cannot conclude from this that knowledge does not imply, or that it is incompatible with, belief *tout court*.

Much of what we have been saying about the relations between knowledge, belief, and mere belief may profitably be depicted on one worlds-diagram.

> Let   "K" = *a* knows that P;
>
>   "B" = *a* believes that P;
>
>   "M" = *a* has a mere belief that P.

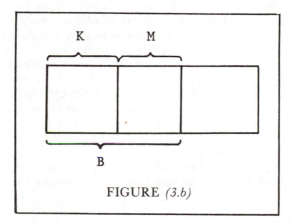

FIGURE *(3.b)*

---

8. Unless, of course, all propositions which assert that someone, *a*, knows a proposition, P, were self-contradictory. But they are not.

3.   Is it a necessary condition of a*'s knowing that* P, *that* a *be justified in believing that* P?

One objection to the third condition stipulated in the classical analysis of knowledge stems from the fact that persons sometimes make knowledge-claims about their lucky guesses. For instance, a person *a* may feel quite certain that he will win the next lottery and, when he does win it, say "I just knew I would." The objection to the classical analysis is that here we have a case where a person knows that P but where nevertheless only the first two conditions are satisfied while the third is not. How seriously should we take this alleged counterexample?

Once again, not everything that a person says must be taken at face value. Do persons whose hunches or intuitions about the outcomes of lotteries turn out right really mean to claim that they had antecedent *knowledge* of those outcomes? Put the question to such persons and it is likely that their answer will be in the negative and that what they intended was simply that they had a strong or even overpowering conviction about the outcome. Or, if this answer does not emerge at first we might further ask *how* they knew — on what *grounds* their claim to knowledge was being made — and, in all probability, they will then drop the claim to knowledge and settle for an avowal of subjective conviction instead. But subjective conviction is not the same as justification. Once the distinction has been pointed out, most persons will accept the correction. Of course, they didn't *really* know, although the strength of their belief was the same as if they had known. Or if they do not admit this, we feel that they do not fully understand what knowledge is.[9]

More serious difficulties arise when we try to say what it is for a belief to be justified.

What is it for a belief to be justified? Some philosophers have thought that the relation of justification is a relation which can hold only between propositions. Accordingly, they have said that the belief in P can be justified only if P is either implied by, or is evidentially supported (i.e., probabilified)[10] by, some *other* proposition, Q. But if this is one's view of what the relation of justification consists, one is easily led into circularity or an infinite regress. For the very same question about justification which we asked in connection with P may also be asked in connection with Q. What justifies us in believing Q? On the analysis just reported, it can only be some other proposition, R. But if R is identical with P, then our attempt at justification ends in circularity. And if R is not identical with P then we are embarked on a search for further justifying propositions — a search which must either end in circularity or regress to infinity. In our search for ultimate justification we seem trapped within the infinite domain of propositions with no chance of making a satisfactory independent appeal.

There are two main ways out of this difficulty. One is to point out that the notion of justification need not, indeed should not (on pain of circularity or infinite regress), be identified with that of *ultimate* justification. It is obvious that *a*'s true belief that P is not justified by appeal to Q, where Q either implies or evidentially supports P, if *a* believes Q to be false, i.e., *a* must believe Q to be true if *a* is to justify his belief in P by appeal to Q. But must the belief that Q be itself justified in order that the belief that P be justified? Ordinarily, it might be said, we would count the true belief that P as a justified true belief provided that it is supported by some other true proposition Q — whether or not belief in Q is itself justified. Admittedly, the question about Q's justification can in turn be raised. But, it would be insisted, that is *another* question.

Another, more fruitful, approach is to be found in offering an alternative analysis of the relation of justification. Let it be admitted that on many occasions when we ask for the justification of a proposi-

---

9. This comment is not quite as question-begging as it seems. If a high percentage of English-speakers were to insist that knowledge was nothing more than true belief, we might want to say that the expression "*a* knows that P" was ambiguous or that there are *two* senses of "knowledge" according to only one of which is it correct to analyze knowledge as involving justification.

10. A possible-worlds analysis of probability is sketched in chapter 6, section 11.

tion, P, our answer consists in appealing to some other proposition, Q. But must all propositional justification be itself propositional? If we were to allow, for instance, that experience itself — not just propositions about experience — could justify belief in the truth of a proposition, the bonds of propositional justification would be broken. Or again if we were to allow that the exercise of reason — not just propositions about the exercise of reason — could justify belief in the truth of a proposition, once more we could evade both circularity and infinite regression.

When, in sections 4 and 5 of this chapter, we investigate various *modes* of knowledge — experiential and ratiocinative, empirical and a priori — we will in effect be adopting this second rejoinder to the objection that justification is in principle impossible to achieve and consequently cannot be a necessary condition of knowledge. For the present, however, we have said enough to defend the traditional view that a person, *a*, can truly be said to know that P only if P is true, *a* believes that P and *a*'s belief that P is justified.

The relation between a person's knowing a proposition P and a person's having a justified true belief that P may easily be depicted on a worlds-diagram.

Let   "K" = *a* knows that P,

"C" = *a* has a justified true belief that P.

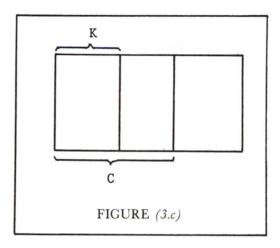

FIGURE *(3.c)*

Before Gettier produced his telling counterexamples (see section 8 in the previous chapter), it was thought that K and C are logically equivalent. Now we know differently: C may be true (i.e., a person may have a justified true belief that P) without K being true (i.e., without that person knowing P). C, it turns out, is 'broader' than K, i.e., C is true in all possible worlds in which K is true and is true in more besides.

In the period since Gettier's paper appeared, philosophers have sought some further condition to conjoin to the classical three so as to make the new analysis narrower; to contract it so that the possible worlds in which it is true are precisely those worlds in which *a* knows that P is true.

4.   *What might the missing fourth necessary condition for a's knowing that P be?*

One of the most promising answers — and the one which we shall adopt here if only for the sake of getting on with the main business of this chapter — is to be found in treating the concept of knowledge as in part a *defeasible* concept. By "a defeasible concept" we mean a concept for which the conditions of application can be stated only by including at least some *negative* clauses. For instance, it has been argued that the concept of responsibility is a defeasible concept since the ascription of responsibility for an act to a person, *a*, who otherwise satisfies the standardly recognized conditions for being responsible may be 'defeated' by evidence that, for example, *a* was *not* of age, was *not* acting freely, was *not* sane at the time, and so on.[11] In like manner, it has been suggested,[12] the concept of knowledge is defeasible since the ascription of knowledge to a person, *a*, who otherwise satisfies the standardly recognized conditions for knowing that P, may be defeated by evidence of a certain kind.

More particularly, the suggestion is that we should ascribe the property of knowing that P to a person, *a*, at a specific time *t* provided that (i) P is true; (ii) *a* believes at *t* that P; (iii) *a*'s belief that P is justified at *t*; and further, provided that (iv) *it is not the case* that there is some true disqualifying proposition, Q, such that if *a* had believed at *t* that Q then *a* would not at *t* have been justified in believing that P. When these latter two conditions, (iii) and (iv), are jointly satisfied, we may say that *a*'s belief in P is *indefeasibly justified.*

By means of the addition of the fourth, negative, condition we seem to be able to cater for Gettier-type examples. Consider, in its light, the case of the secretary who not only believes and says truly that the time is ten minutes past nine but also is justified in his belief since the clock at which he glances has never been wrong in forty years and gives that time. The Gettier-type objection arises if it happens that, at that precise time on that particular morning, the hitherto trustworthy clock — unbeknown to the secretary — has been at a standstill for twelve hours. For then, we want to say, the secretary's true belief that it is ten past nine is a merely fortuitous one and hence does not qualify as knowledge. It is, we should want to say, a *mere belief.* The inclusion of the fourth condition explains why. The secretary's justified and true belief that the time is ten past nine does not count as knowledge that it is ten past nine because there does exist a true proposition, viz., that the clock has been stopped for some time, such that, were he then to believe *it* to be true, he would not be justified in believing that the time is ten past nine.

On this account, the traditional analysis does provide a set of three necessary conditions for knowledge; and these conditions, when supplemented by the fourth, negative, condition constitute also a set of sufficient conditions. On this account, then, knowledge is to be analyzed as *indefeasibly justified true belief.* Taken together, these four conditions are logically equivalent to *a*'s knowing that P.

EXERCISES

Let "P" represent a contingent proposition which is known in some but not all of the possible worlds in which it is true, and

let   *"B"* = a *believes that P*

"M" = a *has a mere belief that P*

"J" = a *has a justified belief that P*

"T" = a *has a true belief that P*

"C" = a *has a justified true belief that P.*

11. See H.L.A. Hart's paper "The Ascription of Responsibilities and Rights", in *Logic and Language*, edited by A. Flew, Series I, Oxford, Blackwell, 1951.

12. Peter D. Klein, "A Proposed Definition of Propositional Knowledge", *The Journal of Philosophy*, LXVIII, no. 16 (August 1971), pp. 471–482.

1.   *On one worlds-diagram, place the three propositions, B, M, and J.*

2.   *On one worlds-diagram, place the three propositions, B, T, and J.*

3.   *On one worlds-diagram, place the three propositions, B, M, and T.*

4.   *On one worlds-diagram, place the three propositions, P, J, and T.*

5.   *On one worlds-diagram, place the three propositions, P, B, and M.*

6.   *On one worlds-diagram, place the three propositions, C, T, and M.*

7.   *If we let "P" now represent a noncontingent true proposition which is known in some but not all possible worlds, which, if any, of the preceding worlds-diagrams will have to be redrawn?*

8.   *If we let "P" now represent a noncontingent false proposition, which, if any, of the worlds-diagrams in exercises 1 – 6 will have to be redrawn?*

3.   THE LIMITS OF HUMAN KNOWLEDGE

One of the incidental conclusions that we tried to establish in section 2 was that, contrary to what the sceptic would have us believe, knowledge of the truth of at least some propositions really is possible. We demonstrated this for the case of the noncontingent proposition that it cannot be known that no one knows nothing: and we suggested that there are countless other propositions, too, some noncontingent and some contingent, which we do in fact know to be true. All of us — even the sceptics — in the conduct of our daily lives, cannot but act upon the presupposition that a great many of the propositions that we *believe* we know to be true are ones that we do in fact *know* to be true: that the words on this page are written in English, that no one can live for long without oxygen, that $2 + 2 = 4$, and so on. Suppose, now, that this presupposition is correct. Are there, we may then wish to ask, any *limits* to our knowledge?

The known and the unknown

One kind of answer would be to draw attention to the distinction between those propositions which are known to be true and those which are not and to say that the boundary between the two fixes the limits of our knowledge.

That there is such a distinction goes without saying. But it would be vacuous and of little interest unless we could further say which propositions are actually known and which are not actually known.

Yet any attempt to say this runs into difficulties. For to say that a proposition is known to be true is ordinarily to say that *at some particular time* it is known to be true. A proposition which is not known to be true at t_1 may come to be known at t_2. And a proposition which is known at t_1 may be forgotten at t_2. So we need to specify a temporal parameter and say for what time the limits of the known are supposed to be determined.

This faces us with a dilemma. If we decide on some *particular* time — even the present moment — to the exclusion of any other, then an element of arbitrariness is introduced and the exercise loses any of the *philosophical* interest that it might otherwise have had. It may be interesting from a sociological point of view to know that at such and such a time the limits of human knowledge were so and so. But it is hardly of enduring philosophical significance. For the boundary between the known and the unknown, thus conceived, is wholly subject to the vagaries of human history, and shifts with the passage of time.

If, on the other hand, we try to answer the question by giving an encyclopedic catalogue of all the true propositions which *at some time or other* are known by someone or other, we run into other difficulties. To be sure, the limits of human knowledge, so conceived, would be permanent and unchanging. But, unless there comes a time later than which no new truths are discovered, the epistemic Eldorado which is here envisaged seems likely forever to elude us. For consider what it would be like to achieve it. We should have to include in our encyclopedia not only all those true propositions which once were and currently are known to be true but also those which, at the time of compiling the encyclopedia, no one yet knew. Suppose, then, that there is some proposition, P, whose truth someone, e.g., an inventor, will first discover at a time, t_2, which is later than the time, t_1, at which the encyclopedia is prepared. If P is included in the encyclopedia of propositions known at t_1 then its truth, contrary to our hypothesis, is *not* first discovered at t_2. And if P is *not* included in the encyclopedia at t_1, then, contrary to another of our hypotheses, the encyclopedia of all the propositions which are known by someone or other at some time or other is not·complete.

How else might the question about the limits of human knowledge be answered?

The knowable and the unknowable

A second kind of answer might be given by invoking a distinction between what is knowable and what is unknowable. Such a distinction, if there is one, would not depend, for its philosophical significance, upon our being able to specify which true propositions are in fact knowable and which are unknowable at this particular time or that, or at some time or other. That there should be such a distinction at all, some limit to what it is *possible* for human beings to know, would in itself be a matter of note.

But is there such a distinction? We have already argued that there are at least some true propositions which are in fact known and which are therefore capable of being known. But are there any true propositions which not only are not in fact known — now or at any other time — but also are in principle unknowable? This is the question which we must now face.

There is one way of construing this question according to which the answer is clearly negative. It is clear, for a start, that to ask whether or not a true proposition, P, is know*able* is to ask whether or not it is *possible* that P be known. But what do we mean here by "possible"? If we give it a straightforward possible-worlds analysis the question becomes: Is there any possible world in which P is known (by someone or other)? And then, provided that we do not place any restriction on *how* P might come to be known, the answer seems obvious. For any true proposition P, whatever, there is at least one possible world in which someone knows that P. After all, if we place no restrictions on how P may be known, we must allow among our possible worlds ones in which some omniscient god simply *reveals* the truth of P to some human being, *a*, in such circumstances that all the necessary and sufficient conditions for *a*'s knowing that P are satisfied. In this case there can be no proposition which cannot possibly be known, no proposition which is in principle unknowable, and hence no distinction to be drawn between knowable and unknowable propositions.

The trouble with this way of construing the question, however, is that it does not take seriously enough the restrictions under which human beings labor, in the actual world, in their attempts to acquire propositional knowledge. Allowing the possibility that human beings should know any proposition that an omniscient being might know not only destroys any chance of a distinction between what is knowable and what is unknowable but also renders void any distinction between what is knowable and what is simply true. That which it is possible in some purely logical sense for us to know, plainly, ought not to be identified with that which it is *humanly* possible to know.

The objection is a good one. Yet it leaves us with a problem. What account can we give of this notion of humanly possible knowledge?

Let us start again with the notion of a possible world. But this time let us take seriously the facts that in the actual world we human beings possess certain capacities for knowledge-acquisition and lack others; that our ability successfully to exercise these capacities is at least partly a function of what the world is like; and that any knowledge which merely happens to be bestowed upon us by some god, angel, demon, or whatnot, cannot properly be counted as distinctively human. Then we can say that it is humanly possible for P to be known if and only if there is at least one logically possible world in which (1) P has the same truth-value as P does in the actual world, i.e., P is true; (2) all the laws of nature are identical with those which hold in the actual world; (3) there is a sentient being, *a*, with the very same capacities for knowledge-acquisition as humans have in the actual world; and (4) *a* acquires knowledge that P is true by the unaided exercise of those capacities. In other words, a proposition P will be knowable if either (a) it is known in the actual world by a person exercising ordinary human capacities, or (b) it is known in some other possible world which is very like the actual world in that P is true in both that world and the actual world, and the knower in that world labors under the same physical constraints as are imposed on all of us by the natural laws of the actual world.

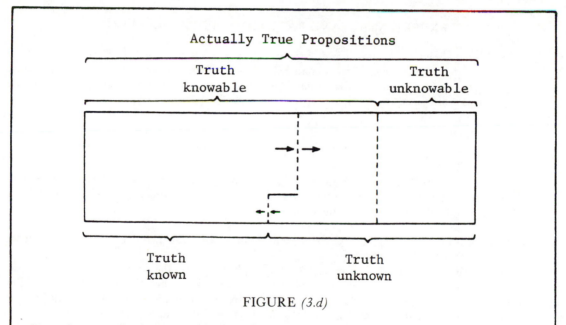

FIGURE *(3.d)*

Some, but not all, true propositions are knowable, i.e., are such that it is possible for human beings to know them to be true. Of these, some, but not all, are actually known to be true. The boundary between the knowable and the unknowable cannot change. The boundary between the known and the unknown is constantly changing as more and more unknown but knowable propositions become known and as a few known propositions are lost to us. This applies to contingent and noncontingent propositions alike.

This account can be further simplified. As we noted in chapter 1 (pp. 6–7), to talk about a logically possible world in which the laws of nature are identical with those which hold in the actual world is to talk about a *physically* possible world. So we might, alternatively, choose to say that it is humanly possible for P to be known if and only if there is at least one physically possible world in which conditions (1), (3), and (4) obtain.

In the next section we will explore what capacities human beings actually have for knowledge-acquisition. But for the moment it suffices to point out that, on this account of what it is for it to be humanly possible to know P, the distinction between what is humanly knowable and what is not humanly knowable is easily preserved and does not collapse into the distinction between what is true and what is false. On the present account there will, of course, be some actually true propositions which will be known to be true in the actual world or in some other possible world which is very similar to the actual world in the ways just described. These propositions will comprise the class of the humanly knowable true propositions. But in addition (as we shall see later in this chapter), there will be some actually true propositions which are not known to be true, either in the actual world or, again, in other possible worlds of the relevant kind. These propositions will comprise the class of humanly unknowable true propositions. The boundary between these two classes of actually true propositions constitutes, in a philosophically interesting way, the limits of human knowledge.

4. EXPERIENTIAL AND RATIOCINATIVE KNOWLEDGE

What capacities for knowledge-acquisition do human beings actually possess? Most philosophers have said that, as a matter of contingent fact, human beings — as distinct from other conceivable beings such as Martians, angels, gods, and devils — have the capacity to acquire knowledge in only two sorts of way: by some sort of appeal to experience, or by some sort of appeal to reason.

Experiential knowledge

Experience, we sometimes say, is a great teacher. Kant put it like this:

> Experience is therefore our first instruction, and in its progress is so inexhaustible in new information, that in the interconnected lives of all future generations there will never be any lack of new knowledge that can be thus ingathered.[13]

Whether by appeal to our own experience, or to that of others, it seems the pool of human knowledge may be much increased.

But what do we mean here by "experience"? Many philosophers, the so-called Empiricists chief among them, would say that they mean *sense-experience,* i.e., experience through the senses. Now admittedly our senses of sight, hearing, touch, taste, smell, temperature, pain, etc., play a major role in providing us with information about the world around us. But it is surely an open question as to whether there can be other modes of awareness — other modes of experience — besides sense-experience. Telepathy and other forms of so-called extrasensory perception, for instance, cannot be ruled out in advance as possible means of acquiring knowledge even if their credentials have not yet been established. Nor can introspection, meditation, instinct, or even 'tripping out', no matter how suspect they have seemed to some. Might not the Yaqui Indians of Mexico have their own way of knowing, as Carlos Castaneda claims in his book *The Teachings of Don Juan: A Yaqui Way of Knowledge?*[14] These are fascinating questions. But we need not delay for their answers here. We can afford to be fairly liberal as to which of these we call a mode of experience. For *whatever* we allow to count as a mode of experience, it still remains a question as to whether, and under what conditions, appeal to that mode of experience justifies our claim to propositional knowledge. Appeals to sense-experience have no guarantee of privileged status in this regard. As philosophers have long

13. *Critique of Pure Reason,* Introduction, A1.

14. Berkeley, University of California Press, 1968.

pointed out, such appeals are by no means infallible guides to knowledge. The deliverances of sense-experience need to be subjected to all sorts of checks before we can justifiably claim that what our senses tell us is the case really is the case. It remains to be seen whether some other mode of experience might on occasion also provide justifying conditions for knowledge-claims. When, therefore, we speak of employing an appeal to experience as a means of acquiring knowledge, we shall leave it open as to which *kinds* of experience may give us knowledge, and in what circumstances.

Nevertheless, appeal to sense-experience provides us with a paradigm. Consider, for instance, our knowledge of the truth of the proposition

(3.10)   Krakatoa Island was annihilated by a volcanic eruption in 1883.

How might we come to know the truth of such a proposition? For most of us today the answer will be that we read about it in a history or geography book, or perhaps a treatise on geology; that we were taught about it at school; that we heard about it from someone else; that we came across reports of it in old newspapers; that we heard about it on a radio or television program. For those of an earlier generation the answer might be that they read about it in newspapers of the time; that they heard about it from eyewitnesses; that they had seen for themselves the physical evidence of its aftermath as for year after year high-altitude dust caused brilliant sunsets around the world; or even that they themselves had witnessed the gigantic eruption from a ship far out at sea. Now all these answers, philosophers have said, reduce to one: *experience*. They reduce to experience in the sense that the evidential support for the truth of *(3.10)* is sooner or later traceable back to what someone or other experienced or became aware of. If we ourselves had seen the flash, heard the blast, felt the surge of the onrushing tidal wave, smelt the acrid fumes, and sailed into a sea of floating pumice and searing lava toward what had once been a luxuriant tropical island, then our evidence for the truth of *(3.10)* would have been *direct*. But if, by way of contrast, we had merely read in the newspaper about the eruption, listened to the testimony of reliable witnesses, or noted the condition of the stratosphere, then our evidence for the truth of *(3.10)* would not have been direct but *inferential*. In either case, however, the source and warrant for our claims to know that *(3.10)* is true would be — we shall say — *experiential*.

The notion of experiential knowledge, then, may be defined thus:

> "P is knowable experientially" $=_{df}$ "It is humanly possible to know P either by direct appeal to experience or by valid inference from propositions one or more of which is known experientially."[15]

Just as we can afford to be undogmatic about what is to count as experience, so too we can be liberal over the question as to precisely where, if at all, to draw the line between direct experience and inference from experience. *Prima facie* there is need for such a distinction. It seems natural to mark it, as we have done in the Krakatoa case, by counting as direct the experiences of so-called "eyewitnesses" and as inferential the experiences of those others whose grounds for claiming to know that *(3.10)* is true include reliance on the trustworthiness of eyewitnesses, assumptions about stratospheric conditions, geological evidence, and whatnot. But one might want to draw the line elsewhere. Some would want to say that direct experience is limited to how things look, sound, feel, etc. (in a word, how things 'seem') to be, and that any claim about how things really are, which goes beyond direct experience, relies on inference. For present purposes, however, we can leave room for philosophical maneuver on this point. And, for that matter, we can even accommodate those who would deny that there is any distinction to be drawn at all. In defining experiential knowledge as knowledge gained

15. In chapter 4, section 4, we distinguish between two kinds of valid inference: deductively valid and inductively valid inference. The above definition encompasses both kinds.

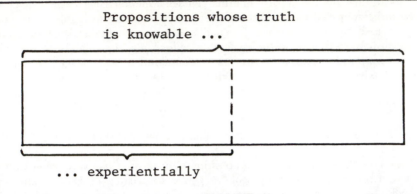

FIGURE *(3.e)*

Of the propositions which it is humanly possible to know some may be known either by direct appeal to experience or by inference therefrom. Such propositions are knowable experientially. But experiential knowledge is not the only mode of knowledge. Another mode, as we shall see, is ratiocinative.

either by direct appeal to experience *or* by inference from experience, we are not committing ourselves as to whether *both* need be involved. We think it natural to say that both sometimes are involved. But that is a point that need not be pressed.

Ratiocinative knowledge

With but a few exceptions, most philosophers have agreed that experience is not our sole teacher.[16] Our own capacity for understanding and reasoning seems, when it is exercised, to be another.

It is easy to give examples of propositional knowledge which is apparently acquired in this other way. Consider, for instance, the proposition

> *(3.11)*   Either Krakatoa Island was annihilated by a volcanic eruption in 1883 or it is not the case that Krakatoa Island was annihilated by a volcanic eruption in 1883.

Now *(3.11)*, like proposition *(1.5)* considered earlier, is a proposition which is expressed by asserting of two contradictories,

> *(3.10)*   Krakatoa Island was annihilated by a volcanic eruption in 1883,

and

> *(3.12)*   It is not the case that Krakatoa Island was annihilated by a volcanic eruption in 1883,

that one or the other is true. And hence proposition *(3.11)*, like proposition *(1.5)*, is necessarily true. How do we know? Well, we have only to reflect on the sort of reasoning we went through in

16. John Stuart Mill is one of the exceptions. He was an Empiricist insofar as he insisted that we can have knowledge of the actual world only by appeal to experience. But whereas many other Empiricists allowed that some knowledge, e.g., of mathematical and logical truths, is possible independent of experience, Mill did not. He was, we may say, a Radical Empiricist.

connection with *(1.5)*. We saw then (on pp. 16–17) that since one member of a contradictory pair is true in all those possible worlds in which the other is false, and the other member of the contradictory pair is true in all the remaining possible worlds, then in each possible world one or other of the contradictory pair is true; so that any proposition — such as *(1.5)* or *(3.11)* — which is expressed by our asserting that one or the other of a contradictory pair of propositions is true cannot itself fail to be true. Now the interesting thing about all such propositions is that we can show, and hence know, them to be true, indeed to be necessarily true, solely by reasoning them out for ourselves. We do not need at any point to appeal to that sort of experiential evidence that seemed to be needed in the case of proposition *(3.10)*. It does not matter for the purposes of our determining the truth-value of *(3.11)* whether *(3.10)* is true or false, or whether *(3.12)* is true or false, let alone whether *(3.10)* and *(3.12)* are individually *known* to be true or false by experience or by any other means. For we can know that *(3.11)* is true, and know that it must be true, without knowing of *(3.10)* and *(3.12)* which is true and which is false. The source and warrant for our knowledge of the truth of *(3.11)* is not experiential, but, as we shall say, *ratiocinative*. It is to be found within ourselves, in our own powers of understanding and reasoning.

There was a time when philosophers were wont to try to explain our ratiocinative knowledge of propositions like *(3.11)* by invoking the notion of *self-evidence*. But such an approach is notoriously unhelpful. If a person says that the truth of a proposition is self-evident, and means simply that the truth of that proposition is evident to him or herself, we are being told more about the person than about the proposition. Self-evidence, if it is taken to be a mere measure of subjective certainty, can vary from person to person and hence affords no explanation of how knowledge-claims are to be justified. Yet if, on the other hand, a person says that the truth of a proposition is self-evident, and means simply that the truth of that proposition is evident from the nature of the proposition itself, we are being told very little — except perhaps that knowledge-claims about its truth stand in no need of appeal to experience. We are not being told *how* knowledge-claims about its truth are to be supported. Talk of self-evidence, thus construed, is itself in need of explanation.

What, then, is involved when we acquire knowledge by the exercise of our own powers of understanding and reasoning? Once more Kant comes to our aid when he points out

> A great, perhaps the greatest, part of the business of our reason consists in the analysis of the concepts which we already have. . . . [17]

Note that Kant does not say that the *only* business of reason consists in analysis of concepts. He certainly would want to insist that at least part of the business of reason consists in making deductively valid *inferences* from the results of conceptual analysis. For instance, he explains that in giving a demonstration of the properties of the isosceles triangle, a mathematician uses reason "not to inspect what he discerned either in the figure, or in the bare concept of it . . . but to bring out what was necessarily implied in the concepts that he himself had formed [of the isosceles triangle] . . . "[18]

This talk of analyzing concepts and of making inferences therefrom certainly seems more informative than mere talk of self-evidence. And it seems especially apt when we try to explain how our reasoning concerning the proposition *(3.11)* yielded knowledge of that proposition's truth. For a start, we analyzed that proposition itself and noted that it asserts of a pair of contradictories that one or the other is true. Now the concept involved when we say of one or other of a pair of propositions that at least one is true is — as we saw earlier (chapter 1, section 3) — the concept of *disjunction*. In short, we analyzed the proposition as involving the disjunction of contradictories. Next, we analyzed these

17. *Critique of Pure Reason*, Introduction, B9.

18. *Critique of Pure Reason*, Preface to 2nd edition, Bxii.

concepts themselves and the way in which they are articulated in proposition *(3.11)*. And then, reflecting upon the results of this simple analysis, we inferred that the proposition is true — indeed that it is necessarily true.

In the light of this we propose the following definition of ratiocinative knowledge:

> "P is knowable ratiocinatively" =$_{df}$ "It is humanly possible to know P by appeal to reason (e.g., by analysis of concepts) or by valid inference from propositions which themselves are known by appeal to reason."

Note that we do not here commit ourselves to the view that knowledge acquired by analysis of concepts or by inference therefrom exhausts all modes of ratiocinative knowledge. We cite them only as examples — paradigm examples — of what it is to appeal to reason. Thus we leave open the question whether there might not be some other modes of ratiocinative reasoning. Again we cite the examples of alleged ESP, intuition, etc. If they were to count as genuine modes of knowledge, it would still be unclear whether they were experiential, ratiocinative, or something else. In due course we will examine two further kinds of reasoning which some philosophers have suggested are also modes of ratiocinative reasoning: transcendental argumentation and baptismal reference-fixing. For the present it will simplify our discussion if we restrict it to the paradigm cases of ratiocination, viz., analysis of concepts and inference therefrom. And just as we can afford to be liberal about where to draw the line between direct experience and inference therefrom, so, too, we can allow ourselves to be liberal about where to draw the line between analysis of concepts and inference from the results of such analysis.

Sometimes — we are inclined to say — we can know a proposition to be true by analysis of the concepts involved with little or no inference therefrom. To take one of Kant's examples, the proposition

(3.13)   All bodies are extended

is one which we can know to be true — indeed know to be *analytically true*,[19] as Kant put it — simply by virtue of the fact that in analyzing the concept of *body* we come across the concept of extension as covertly contained therein. Do we, in such a case, *infer* that the proposition, the constituent concepts of which we have analyzed, is true? If so, the inference is of the most trivial kind. It is, as Kant put it, "thought through identity";[20] or, as we shall later describe it, it is an inference which may be justified by appeal to the rule of inference known as that of Simplification.[21]

In other cases the inferential element seems to be more at a premium. Consider, for example, the proposition

(3.14)   There are as many even numbers as there are both even and odd numbers.

19. In this book we shall make little use — except in chapter 4 — of the notion of analytically true (or analytically false) propositions. Such a notion involves an amalgamation of the purely logical (or modal) notion of necessarily true (or necessarily false) propositions with the epistemic notion of how we can acquire knowledge of the truth (or falsity) of certain propositions.

20. *Critique of Pure Reason,* Introduction, B10.

21. See chapter 4, section 4. Essentially the point is that the proposition, P1, that something is a body, implies the proposition, P2, that that thing is extended and . . . and . . . , etc., (where the blanks are to be filled in by predicates naming other properties the concepts of which are involved in the analysis of the concept of *body*), and that the proposition, P3, that that thing is extended, may be validly inferred in accordance with the Rule of Simplification from the proposition P2.

We do in fact know this proposition to be true. But how? Talk of self-evidence is distinctly unhelpful here, especially if it is construed as mere subjective conviction. For, far from seeming to be self-evidently true, this proposition, upon first acquaintance, strikes most persons as self-evidently false. Nor does simple analysis of concepts seem to suffice to establish its truth. The truth of *(3.14)* can be established ratiocinatively, but only by analysis of the concepts involved — those of *even number, odd number,* and *as many as,* in particular — together with a good deal of inferential reasoning. In simplified form that inferential reasoning consists in the demonstration that each member of the series of all integers can be put into a one-to-one correspondence with each member of the series of even integers in the following way:

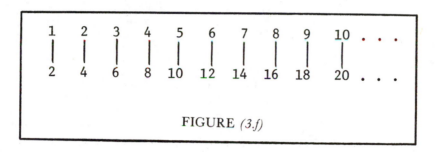

FIGURE *(3.f)*

(3.15)   To every number, even or odd, there corresponds a unique even number, its double; to each even number there corresponds a unique number in the series of all integers, viz., its half. But this is just to say that there are exactly as many even numbers as there are even and odd numbers together.

The conclusion we have just reached was by way of ratiocination. We made no appeal to experience whatever in determining that *(3.14)* is, after all, true.[22] Our reasoning involved both analysis of concepts and inference therefrom.

There are, it should be noted, some propositions the knowledge of whose truth, if it is humanly possible at all, can be acquired only by an enormous investment in inferential reasoning. The proofs of many theorems in formal logic and pure mathematics certainly call for a great deal more than simple analytical understanding of the concepts involved. And in some cases the amount of investment in analysis and inference that seems to be called for, in order that we should know whether a proposition is true or false, may turn out to be entirely beyond the intellectual resources of mere human beings. As a case in point consider the famous, but as yet unproved, proposition of arithmetic known as Goldbach's Conjecture, viz.,

(3.16)   Every even number greater than two is the sum of two primes.

Most persons know what "even number" means (that is, they understand the concept of being-an-even-number). And most persons know what "prime number" means (they understand the

---

22. It is important to recognize that establishing the conclusion that there are as many even numbers as even and odd numbers together was via the argument of *(3.15)* and not via the figure *(3.f)*. The function of the figure is purely heuristic; insofar as it is incomplete it cannot establish the conclusion we have reached. It serves merely to illustrate some, but not all, of what is being asserted in the ensuing argument *(3.15)*.

concept of what it is for a number to be prime): a number is prime if it is divisible without remainder only by the number one and by itself. Goldbach's Conjecture is easily understood. In fact we understand it well enough to be able to test it on the first few of an infinite number of cases, thus:

Four is the sum of two and two.

Six is the sum of three and three.

Eight is the sum of three and five.

Ten is the sum of three and seven.
      (Also, ten is the sum of five and five.)

Twelve is the sum of five and seven.

(and so on and on and on)

In this case, it is clear that we know what proposition is being expressed by the sentence, "Every even number greater than two is the sum of two primes." And in virtue of knowing this, we know what concepts are involved. But our familiarity with these concepts, and our ability to apply them in the above five examples, does not (apparently) suffice to allow us to know whether the Conjecture is true or false. For, as we have observed, proposition *(3.16)* is — at the time of writing — unproved. Moreover, for all we know, it may turn out to be unprovable by any being having the capacities for knowledge-acquisition which we human beings have. Of course, we do not *now* know whether or not it will eventually succumb to our attempts to prove it. Maybe it will. In this case it will be known

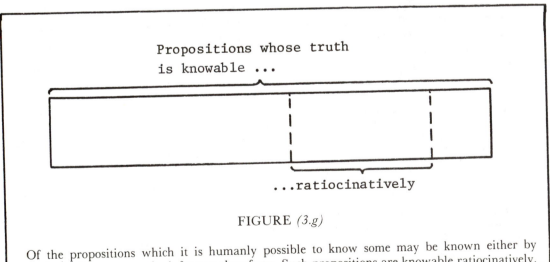

Propositions whose truth
is knowable ...

...ratiocinatively

FIGURE *(3.g)*

Of the propositions which it is humanly possible to know some may be known either by analysis of concepts or by inference therefrom. Such propositions are knowable ratiocinatively. As previously noted some propositions are knowable experientially.

ratiocinatively. But then, again, maybe it will not. In that case it may well be one of those propositions whose truth is not known because its truth is *unknowable*. At present we simply do not know which.

Appendix to Section 4

Finally we might ask ourselves about the status of traditional so-called 'pencil and paper' operations and, in modern times, the use of computational aids such as electronic calculators and the like. How do they figure in the scheme of things? Is the knowledge they furnish to be construed as experiential or ratiocinative? To answer this question, let's back up a bit.

Clearly if a person adds together a series of numbers 'in his head', as it were, then surely we must construe his knowledge as ratiocinative. But what if he were to do just the same thing but write the appropriate numerals on a sheet of paper as he proceeded? That simple fact hardly ought to cause us to want to change our account of the *kind* of knowledge obtained. His markings on the paper are most naturally construed as just the expression, or public display, of his ratiocinative reasoning. They should be regarded, clearly, as simply an extension or an aid to his reasoning; they should hardly be considered 'an appeal to experience'. Should our account, however, change when a person comes to rely on a self-running calculator to perform calculations which obviously transcend his ability to 'do in his head'? For example, no one is capable of calculating in his head the twenty-two thousandth digit in the decimal expansion of π. A person must use several pencils and a great deal of paper, and expend many hours in the task, or he must rely on a computer. If he does the latter, shall we say that he has appealed to experience? Even in this latter case we shall not do so. A person who learns the twenty-two thousandth digit in the decimal expansion of π by reading the printout of a computer is entitled to claim that his knowledge is obtained ratiocinatively. Why? Because computers are designed to carry through mathematical computations in a mechanical fashion each of whose steps is a mechanical (or electrical) analogue of a computational step which is sanctioned by a ratiocinatively warranted rule of inference. The computer, in calculating the twenty-two thousandth digit in the decimal expansion of π, does nothing that a human being *could* not do ratiocinatively using pencil and paper and given enough time and enough helpers to detect any errors he might make. In short, the conclusion may be put this way: in the twentieth century we have arrived at a state of technology sufficiently advanced that we are able to have our machines carry on some of our ratiocinative reasoning for us. And the knowledge they furnish us, when it proceeds from ratiocinatively known truths in accordance with ratiocinatively warranted inference rules,[23] may itself properly be termed "ratiocinative".

5.   EMPIRICAL AND A PRIORI KNOWLEDGE

In their discussions of the possible modes of human knowledge many philosophers have felt the need for a further distinction: that between *a priori* knowledge and *empirical* knowledge.

Kant was one of these. Indeed it is his use of the terms "a priori" and "empirical" which most philosophers today take themselves to be following. Now Kant thought that the ratiocinative/experiential distinction was an important one. He drew it along the same sorts of lines as we have: indeed, his talk of knowledge "through reason's own resources" and of knowledge "a posteriori" conforms precisely to the definitions we have given of "ratiocinative knowledge" and "experiential knowledge", respectively. But he also thought it important to draw a distinction between a priori and empirical knowledge.

---

23. For a discussion of the justifying of inference rules, see chapter 4, section 4.

Definitions of "empirical" and "a priori"

Kant's definition runs as follows:

> We shall understand by *a priori* knowledge, not knowledge independent of this or that experience, but knowledge absolutely independent of all experience. Opposed to it is empirical knowledge, which is knowledge possible only *a posteriori,* that is, through experience.[24]

Note that empirical knowledge is here, and elsewhere, defined — *not* as knowledge which is possible a posteriori — but rather, as knowledge which is possible *only* a posteriori, i.e., *only* experientially.[25] That is to say, it is defined as knowledge which it is not humanly possible to acquire without appeal to experience. A priori knowledge, by way of contrast, is defined as knowledge which is absolutely independent of all experience; that is to say, it is defined as knowledge which it *is* humanly possible to acquire without appeal to experience.

Following Kant, and sharpening up his definitions so as to highlight the contrast between the empirical/a priori distinction and the experiential/ratiocinative distinction, let us say:

> "P is knowable empirically" $=_{df}$ "It is humanly possible to know P *only* experientially",

and let us also say:

> "P is knowable a priori" $=_{df}$ "It is humanly possible to know P *other than* experientially."

What is essential to our (and Kant's) definition of "empirical" is that a proposition may be said to be knowable empirically only if an appeal to experience is *necessary* in order for us to acquire knowledge of its truth. And what is essential to our (and Kant's) definition of "a priori" is that a proposition may be said to be knowable a priori if an appeal to experience is *not* necessary in order for us to acquire knowledge of its truth. By way of contrast, our definition of "experiential" (and Kant's of "a posteriori") merely picks out a way in which it is *possible* for us to acquire knowledge of a proposition's truth. And our definition of "ratiocinative" (like Kant's expression "through reason's own resources") merely picks out another way in which it is *possible* for us to acquire knowledge of a proposition's truth. The latter definitions, unlike the former, have nothing whatever to say about what is necessary or not necessary for human knowledge.

Unfortunately, the difference between these two sets of definitions is rather subtle. Indeed, it is so subtle that sometimes philosophers who subscribe to the above explicit definitions of "empirical knowledge" slip into using the term "empirical" when they should use the term "experiential". They slip into saying that something is knowable empirically when it can be known by appeal to experience, i.e., is knowable experientially. If we remember that something is knowable empirically when it can be known *only* by appeal to experience, i.e., when it can be known *only* experientially, we should be able to avoid this mistake. It might also help if we remember that the terms "experiential" and "ratio-

---

24. *Critique of Pure Reason,* Introduction, B2–3.

25. Kantian scholars might like to note that, throughout the *Critique of Pure Reason,* Kant preserves the distinction between the empirical and the a posteriori — in the way we are drawing it — with complete scrupulousness.

cinative" are definable independently of one another, in terms of whether it is experience or reason (respectively) which makes knowledge possible, whereas the terms "empirical" and "a priori" are *inter*definable: a priori knowledge is knowledge for which experience is *not* necessary, i.e., a priori knowledge is *non*empirical knowledge, while empirical knowledge is knowledge for which experience *is* necessary, i.e., empirical knowledge is knowledge which is *not* a priori.

We have here two epistemic distinctions: two distinctions between ways of acquiring knowledge of what is knowable — two distinctions having to do with the *epistemic status* of those items which are knowable, viz., propositions.

But why, it may be asked, have we, like Kant and many other philosophers, thought it *important* to introduce the second classification of modes of knowledge? Why should we not remain content with the first and try to say everything we want to say in terms of it? The answer has to do with the standard requirements of philosophical taxonomy.

There are two properties that we usually demand of a satisfactory classificatory scheme, viz., (1) that it be exhaustive in the sense of covering all the cases to be classified and (2) that it be exclusive in the sense of covering each case only once. The taxonomic scheme used by biologists, for instance, is drawn up in such a way as to satisfy both these requirements. It is, or aims to be, exhaustive insofar as it includes all species so far known. And it is, or aims to be, exclusive insofar as no individual is counted as belonging to more than one species. Admittedly, the job of the taxonomist in biology seems never to be complete. But that is because the frontiers of biological knowledge are forever expanding. A new species is discovered and the classificatory scheme is expanded to include it; exhaustiveness is thus preserved. Or a borderline case between two recognized species is discovered and the boundaries between species are adjusted to avoid overlap: the problematic individuals are assigned to one species or the other, or an entirely new species is defined; exclusiveness is thus preserved.

Changes in the taxonomy of what is known might be expected so long as our knowledge is increasing. But changes in the taxonomy of what is humanly know*able* can hardly be expected on these grounds. Indeed, since the humanly knowable comprises the totality of what is known at any time by the exercise of human capacities in all physically possible worlds, its boundaries can neither increase nor decrease but timelessly remain the same. Any classificatory scheme for talking about the humanly knowable might be expected, therefore, to satisfy both the requirements of exhaustiveness and exclusiveness.

This is where the first of our two epistemic distinctions — that between experiential and ratiocinative ways of knowing what is knowable — lets us down. It is only dubiously exhaustive and certainly is not exclusive.

The nonexhaustiveness and nonexclusiveness of the experiential/ratiocinative distinction

In the first place it is highly questionable whether it is exhaustive. Might there not be other ways for human beings to acquire knowledge besides experience and reason? We have already seen that unless we define "experience" extremely broadly, cases of alleged telepathy, precognition, meditation, inspiration, and whatnot, will demand a hearing as apparent exceptions. And there is no guarantee against other counterexamples, apparent or real, being produced in the future.

In the second place the distinction is certainly not an exclusive one. The truth-value of some propositions can be known both experientially and ratiocinatively. Consider the proposition,

> (3.17)   There is no route by which one can cross over all seven bridges of Königsberg without recrossing at least one bridge.

The seven bridges of Königsberg (now Kaliningrad) posed a unique problem to the burghers. There were two islands in the river which passed through the town. Seven bridges connected the islands and the banks of the river in the fashion shown in the following illustration.

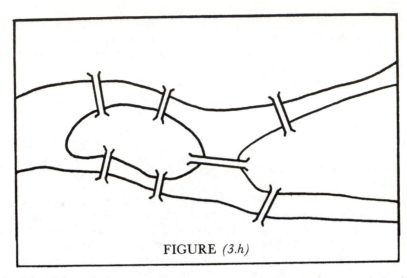

FIGURE *(3.h)*

The question arose whether there is a route by which one can cross each of the bridges without crossing any bridge twice. It doesn't take very long to convince oneself that there is no such route. Presumably the burghers tried the test with their feet. The townspeople of Königsberg, having actually tried numerous times to cross all the bridges just once, could be said to have *experiential* knowledge that proposition *(3.17)* is true.

In the early eighteenth century, the mathematician Leonhard Euler, in a famous paper,[26] was able to prove mathematically that proposition *(3.17)* is true. With Euler we have come to have *ratiocinative* knowledge of the truth of *(3.17)*. What was first learned experientially outdoors by tramping around the banks of the river Pregel (Pregolya) was later relearned by the powers of pure reason (presumably) in the comfort of Euler's study where he merely carefully and ingeniously thought about the problem.

It thus emerges that some truths, that about the bridges of Königsberg being one, are knowable both experientially *and* ratiocinatively. We have already said that the experiential/ratiocinative distinction is (probably) not exhaustive. And now we have just shown that it surely is not exclusive. It thus lacks both the properties we would like in a classificatory scheme: exhaustiveness and exclusiveness.

The exhaustiveness and exclusiveness of the empirical/a priori distinction

By way of contrast, the empirical/a priori distinction has both properties. In the first place, it is exhaustive for the class of knowable propositions. To be sure there are probably infinitely many propositions whose truth cannot be known by any finite sentient being. (And remember [section 3], the knowledge possessed by an omniscient God is hardly relevant in an examination of *human* knowledge.) But for any proposition which is or can be known through human faculties, we can confidently assert that it is empirical, since it is necessary to appeal to experience in order to know it, or a priori, since it is *not* necessary to appeal to experience in order to know it.

The proposition which asserts of a given knowable proposition, P, that it is empirical is a contradictory of the proposition which asserts of that very same knowable proposition, viz., P, that it is a priori. Little wonder, then, that the empirical/a priori distinction is exhaustive for the class of

26. Leonhard Euler, "The Seven Bridges of Königsberg", in *The World of Mathematics,* ed. James R. Newman, New York, Simon and Schuster, 1956, vol. I, pp. 573–580. This paper is easy reading and is enthusiastically recommended.

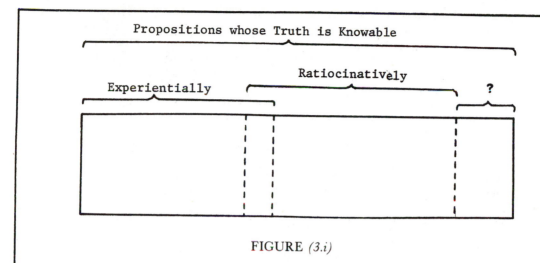

FIGURE *(3.i)*

The experiential/ratiocinative distinction is neither guaranteed to be exhaustive (as the question mark is intended to show it seems an open question whether there are still other ways of obtaining knowledge[27]) nor is it guaranteed to be exclusive (the area of overlap shows that there are propositions which can be known in both ways).

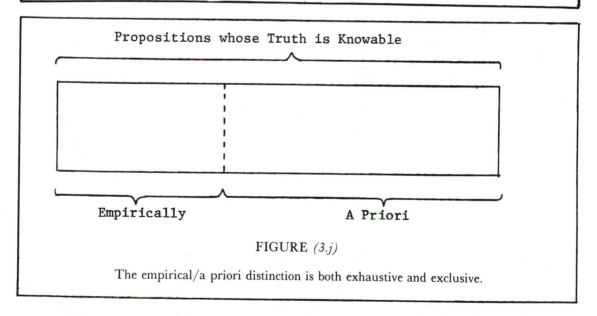

FIGURE *(3.j)*

The empirical/a priori distinction is both exhaustive and exclusive.

27. For the purposes of simplifying both our discussions and various subsequent figures, we will proceed as if propositions knowable by some means other than experience or reason could not also be known in one (or both) of these more familiar ways. Of course, strictly speaking, we are not entitled to this assumption. In figure *(3.i)*, the area enclosed by the bracket bearing the question mark as a label should overlap *each* of the areas bearing the labels "experientially" and "ratiocinatively". This refinement, or correction, will be made later in figure *(3.m)*. Here we shall ignore it, but do not wish to suggest that it cannot nor need not eventually be made.

knowable propositions. For contradictory propositions, it will be remembered, are exhaustive in the sense that in each of all possible worlds it must be the case that one or the other is true. Hence it is that in each of all possible worlds it must be true of each knowable proposition either that it is knowable only by appeal to experience (empirically) or that it is knowable without appeal to experience (a priori). It is not possible that there should be some knowable proposition which is not one or the other.

In the second place, the empirical/a priori distinction is exclusive. Although certain knowable propositions, as we have seen, are knowable both experientially and ratiocinatively, no knowable proposition can be both empirical and a priori. We have the same logical guarantee of its exclusiveness as we have of its exhaustiveness. For contradictory propositions are not only exhaustive but also exclusive in the sense that there is no possible world in which both are true; hence there can be no possible world in which it is true both that a knowable proposition is empirical and that it is a priori.

Consider again the proposition *(3.17)*. We agreed that the proposition

(3.17)   There is no route by which one can cross over all seven bridges of Königsberg without recrossing at least one bridge

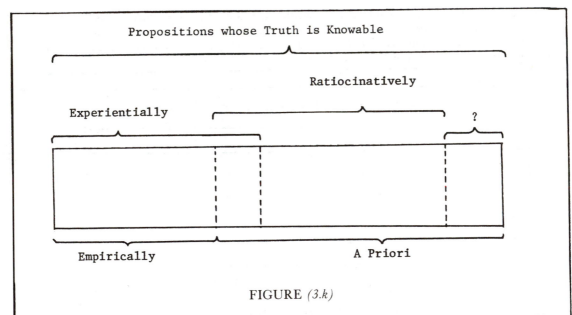

FIGURE *(3.k)*

The class of propositions whose truth can be known *only* through appeal to experience (the empirically knowable propositions) is contained within the class of propositions whose truth can be known through appeal to experience (the experientially knowable propositions). That is to say, all empirical knowledge is experiential knowledge; but the converse does not hold. Again, the class of propositions whose truth can be known by unaided reason (the ratiocinatively knowable propositions) is contained within the class of propositions whose truth is knowable without appeal to experience (the a priori knowable propositions). That is to say, all ratiocinative knowledge is a priori knowledge; but, if there happen to be still other ways of gaining knowledge than through experience and reason, the converse will not hold.

could be known both experientially and ratiocinatively. But this does not mean that it can be known empirically. For this proposition would be knowable empirically only if it were *necessary* to appeal to experience in order to know it to be true. But if, as is the case, it can also be known by ratiocinative means, it follows that it is not knowable *only* by appeal to experience, and hence it is not knowable empirically, but rather is knowable a priori. In short, if a proposition can be known to be true by ratiocinative means then, whether or not it can also be known experientially, it is knowable a priori and is *not* knowable empirically.

It follows from what we have said that the two epistemic distinctions are related to one another as in figure *(3.k)*.

Is a priori knowledge certain?

There is a widespread custom of referring to a priori knowledge as "certain". But is this correct? Is a priori knowledge certain? Is it more certain than empirical knowledge?

Before we can answer these questions we must become aware that they are ambiguous. What exactly is being asserted when someone says "a priori knowledge is certain"? This claim could be understood in either of two very different ways: (1) it could mean that all propositions which are knowable a priori are themselves certain, in the sense of being noncontingently true; or (2) it could mean that a priori reasoning — one of the *ways* in which *we come to know* some truths — is itself certain, in the sense of being infallible. We must be very careful not to run together these two different claims and, more especially, not to think that subscribing to one of them logically commits us to subscribing to the other.[28]

In the next section of this chapter we devote some considerable time to answering the first question. That is, we shall ask whether a priori reasoning can ever suffice to give us knowledge of contingent as well as — as we have already seen — at least some noncontingent propositions.

But in the present subsection, let us examine the other proposition which someone might be asserting in saying "a priori reasoning is certain", viz., that a priori reasoning is infallible.

Is a priori reasoning infallible? The answer is obvious: No. In order to show this one need look no further than the fact that two persons, each reasoning a priori from the same set of propositions, may come to different answers to a problem. It is all too common to find persons getting different results when, for example, they add up long columns of figures, or when they try to prove theorems in algebra and geometry.

In short, to seek an answer to a problem a priori, or to try to ascertain the truth-value of a proposition a priori, is merely to adopt a way of trying to find an answer. It is simply a way of seeking knowledge, a way which need take no recourse to experience. But it is not an invariably *reliable* path to knowledge; it is not infallible. Persons can be mistaken in their a priori reasoning just as they can be mistaken in an empirical approach to finding out the truth-values of propositions. Not only do we sometimes misperceive the physical world and get some of our beliefs about contingent matters wrong; we may also falter in our reasoning and get some of our beliefs about noncontingent matters wrong. For example, many persons have believed that they have found a priori proofs of Goldbach's Conjecture. But none of these proofs has withstood careful scrutiny. Other persons, also adopting a priori methods, have always managed to find fatal flaws in the proofs so-far advanced.

Does the possibility that one can falter in one's a priori reasoning discredit it? Not at all — no more

---

28. The particular kind of ambiguity being examined here has been called by some philosophers "the product/process ambiguity". John Hospers (*An Introduction to Philosophical Analysis,* second edition, Englewood Cliffs, N.J., Prentice–Hall, 1967, p. 15) illustrates it with the sentence, "They went to look at the construction." The sentence is ambiguous between expressing the propositions (1) that they went to look at the *thing* being constructed, and (2) that they went to watch the *activity* of constructing that thing. In like manner we are distinguishing knowledge as product and process.

so than the fact that one can falter in the application of empirical methods invalidates them. The possibility of making an error, of being confused or of misremembering, infects both of our ways of knowing, the empirical and the a priori alike. But this is not to say that these methods cannot yield knowledge. It is only to say that they are not infallible guides to truth. The possibility of making errors — perceptual, ratiocinative, or whatever — ought not to deter us from the pursuit of knowledge. Although we have no guarantee that either empirical methods or a priori methods will furnish us knowledge, we can be quite sure that knowledge will elude us if we ignore them.

Once one understands that the a priori mode of seeking knowledge is not infallible, how, we might ask, does one go about checking for mistakes on a given occasion of its use? The answer is: in just the same sorts of ways we try to find whatever mistakes there might be in a particular instance of the use of empirical methods. First and foremost, we recheck the process carefully. Then, if we wish still further corroboration, we might repeat the process, i.e., do it over again from the beginning. Also we might enlist the aid of other persons, asking them to go through the process themselves, and then comparing our results with theirs. And finally, we might make our results public, holding them up for scrutiny to a wider audience, and hoping that if there is a mistake, the joint effort of many persons will reveal it.

How many of these additional tests we will in fact invoke will depend on a variety of extra-logical matters, e.g., such things as the intrinsic difficulty of the reasoning and its importance to us. It is not, after all, a difficult chain of reasoning which allows persons to figure out that every square has the same number of interior angles as it does sides. One hardly needs the corroboration of other persons for this piece of reasoning, and it would be absurd to think that because a priori methods are fallible that this particular result of their application is in any way doubtful. To point out that a priori modes of reasoning are fallible is *not* to endorse scepticism or in any way to suggest that everything which we believe ourselves to know a priori is doubtful. If by no other means, then by *experience* we have learned that much of our a priori reasoning is corroborated by further testing. As a result, even in advance of testing, we are entitled to be confident that on many occasions when we reason a priori we do it correctly.

6.   EPISTEMIC AND MODAL STATUS CONSIDERED TOGETHER

In the course of introducing each of the two sets of epistemic distinctions we have had occasion to refer to propositions — some of them contingent, the others noncontingent — which are paradigmatic examples of items of knowledge that can be known in one way or another: experientially, empirically (only experientially), ratiocinatively, or a priori. Thus, for instance, we cited the contingent proposition *(3.10)* as a typical example of something that can be known to be true experientially, and the noncontingent propositions *(3.11)*, *(3.13)*, and *(3.14)* as typical examples of something that can be known to be true ratiocinatively. But it by no means follows from anything we have said that *all* contingent propositions are knowable *only* experientially (i.e., empirically). Nor does it follow from anything we have said that *all* noncontingent propositions are knowable ratiocinatively, let alone that they are knowable *only* ratiocinatively, hence *only* nonexperientially. Might there not be some contingent propositions belonging to epistemic categories other than the experientially knowable? And might there not be some noncontingent propositions belonging to epistemic categories other than the ratiocinatively knowable? So far we have left these and related questions largely unexamined. It is time for us now to explore, in a quite systematic way, how each of the four *epistemic* categories can be combined with the two *modal* categories of contingency and noncontingency.

Having sorted out the various combinations and interrelations possible among the four epistemic categories, and having pictured these various interrelations on figure *(3.k)*, we must now proceed to add to that figure the modal distinction between the contingent and the noncontingent. (At the same time we will re-introduce the category of unknowable propositions.) Doing so will give us figure *(3.l)*.[29] On it we notice that there is a total of *ten* different classifications of propositions. This is not to say, however, that propositions of each of these ten different kinds actually exist. It is an important philosophical question to see just how many, and which, of these categories are in fact instanced by propositions.

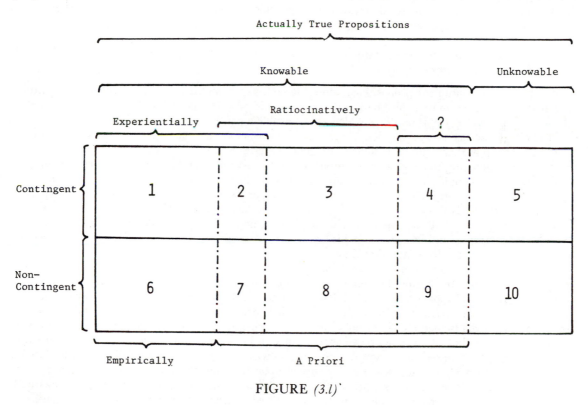

FIGURE *(3.l)*

1.   Are there any contingent propositions which are knowable empirically?

It is quite uncontroversial that there are numerous contingent propositions which are knowable experientially. For example, *(1.3)* and *(3.10)* clearly are such. But the question arises whether these, or any other contingent propositions which are knowable experientially are knowable *only* experientially. The question comes down to this: Is there any contingent proposition which is knowable experientially and which is *not* knowable by any other means? The received opinion by the vast majority of philosophers is that among the contingent propositions which are knowable experientially, at least some are *not* knowable by any other means. (The question whether perhaps none is knowable by any other means is treated below [questions, 2, 3, and 4]. In the meantime we will examine the widely held thesis that at least some are knowable exclusively, or solely, by experiential means.) The aforementioned propositions, *(1.3)* and *(3.10)*, seem to be of just this sort. We know that the U.S. entered World War I in 1917 (i.e., we know *(1.3)*); we know that Krakatoa

29. Remember, we made a simplifying assumption in figure *(3.i)* regarding the area labeled with the question mark.

Island was annihilated by a volcanic eruption in 1883 (i.e., we know *(3.10)*). In each case our knowledge is experiential. Moreover it seems to be unavoidably experiential. It is very hard to see how it would be possible to have ratiocinative knowledge or any other kind of knowledge of facts such as these. How, for example, in our having mastered the concepts which figure in propositions *(1.3)* and *(3.10)* could we come to know specific facts of world history? How indeed? The conclusion we seem driven to is that there is a class of contingent propositions which are knowable only by an appeal to experience, that is, empirically.

2. *Are there any contingent propositions which are knowable both experientially and ratiocinatively (and* ipso facto, *a priori*)?

Category 2, viz., contingent propositions knowable both experientially and ratiocinatively, constitutes the first of the three most problematic categories in this scheme, specifically, all those categories (2 through 4) of *contingent* propositions which are knowable a priori.

It is a logically necessary condition of there being any members of Category 2 (and of Categories 3 and 4 as well) that there should be some contingent propositions which are knowable a priori.

Are there, then, any contingent propositions whose truth-values are knowable a priori? Although it looks harmless enough, the answer to this question is far from uncontroversial. Indeed it is no exaggeration to say that it effectively divides most philosophers into two camps — those who say "Yes" and those who say "No" — and that controversy still rages between them.[30]

In these pages we shall not align ourselves with one camp or the other. We shall content ourselves merely with a report of the debate. If history is a good guide in these matters, we can expect the controversy to continue for quite some time.

During the past two hundred years or so, the question whether there are any contingent propositions knowable a priori has often (indeed fashionably) been expressed in Kant's terms: Are there any synthetic a priori judgments?[31] By "synthetic" Kant meant roughly what we mean by "contingent": in any event, he contrasted synthetic judgments with analytic ones and plainly thought that the latter exhausted the class of noncontingent propositions, "analytic" being the term which he chose to explicate the notion of noncontingency. But well before Kant adopted this near-standard way of formulating it, the question — however couched — was seen to be of vital significance: the viability of a whole method of philosophical inquiry turned upon it. After all, ancient Greek mathematicians (such as Euclid) and philosophers (such as Plato and Aristotle) had argued that ratiocinative methods, well suited to the armchair or the ivory tower, sufficed to give us knowledge of certain truths of mathematics and logic: such truths, they claimed, can be known a priori. But the truths of mathematics and logic — on the account we are giving— are all noncontingent. They are true in the actual world, to be sure; but so too are they true in all possible worlds. Consequently these a priori knowable truths tell us nothing *distinctive* about the actual world. They give us no information which would enable us to distinguish our world, the actual world, from possible but non-actual worlds. And so the question naturally enough arises as to whether armchair methods or ivory-tower modes of inquiry can ever suffice to establish the truth or falsity of propositions which might be thought to lie within a natural science — physics or chemistry or biology, for example — propositions which would tell us something about the actual world as distinct from other possible worlds: in a word, contingent propositions. This is what has traditionally been at issue when philosophers have asked, "Are there any synthetic a priori

---

30. Some, like W.V.O. Quine, belong to neither camp since they would deny the very distinctions between contingent and noncontingent propositions, on the one hand, and between empirical and a priori knowledge, on the other. They reject the very terms of the dispute as confused.

31. *Critique of Pure Reason,* Introduction, B19.

propositions?" Or, as we might more aptly put it, "Are there any contingent propositions *knowable* a priori?"[32]

Few philosophers of repute have ever seriously maintained that we can have a priori knowledge of such contingent matters as the structure of the heavens, or the shape of the earth, or the natural history of ungulates — matters which plainly have to do with distinctive features of the actual world and, for that matter, with highly localized features of that part of the actual world which we happen to occupy.[33] Knowledge of matters such as these, it has usually been allowed, can be achieved only by someone or other getting up and about in the world and experiencing, through observation, experiment, or whatnot, the distinctive features which it happens to have.

However, many reputable philosophers have argued at length that there nevertheless do exist some propositions of a highly general kind — metaphysical propositions, as they are usually called — which, by pure unaided reason, can be known to be true; propositions which, by virtue of the fact that they need not be true in other possible worlds, are contingent; and which, by virtue of the fact that we can argue for their truth without ever stirring from our armchairs or abandoning the seclusion of our ivory towers, can be known a priori.

If there are such propositions, then — as Kant pointed out — a genuine science of metaphysics is possible. For metaphysics, on his conception, is just that field of inquiry which seeks by a priori means to discover the most general truths about the nature of the universe — truths so general and profound as to lie beyond the purview of physics or any other such experientially based science. According to Kant, there are such propositions and a science of metaphysics is thereby shown to be possible. Thus, for instance, he constructed what he called a "transcendental argument" (roughly an argument which transcends, because it does not require any appeal to, experience) for saying that the proposition,

(3.18)   Every event has a cause

is both synthetic [contingent] and knowable a priori. It is synthetic, he claimed, because unlike the analytic [noncontingent] mathematical proposition,

(3.19) $(a+b) > a$ [which he reads as "the whole is greater than its part"]

no amount of analysis of concepts could show (3.18) to be true.[34] And even though (3.18) is avowedly not knowable analytically, it is nonetheless knowable a priori, he claimed, since his transcendental argument establishes a priori that the universality of causal connections in the actual world is a necessary condition of our having any experiential knowledge of this world. In other words, Kant

32. It is misleading to talk of propositions being a priori or empirical. Strictly speaking, it is the modes of *knowing* propositions, not the propositions themselves, which may be spoken of as being a priori or empirical.

33. History is replete, however, with cases of obscurantists who have thought that their astronomical or geographical theories, for instance, could be justified, a priori, on the grounds that they 'stood to reason' or could be validly inferred from 'revealed truth'; and the story (probably apocryphal) still persists of the medieval churchmen who excommunicated a priest for challenging their belief that the number of teeth in a jackass' mouth should be determined piously and (in a manner of speaking) a priori by consulting the Church's 'infallible' teachings rather than impiously and experientially by opening its mouth and counting.

34. Kant discusses these examples in the *Critique of Pure Reason*, Introduction, B5 and B17 respectively. He seems to be saying that (3.18) is contingent by virtue of its being not analytically knowable. This account of contingency does not jibe with the one we offered earlier. We should prefer to say that (3.18) is contingent, not because it cannot be known analytically, but rather because it is true in some possible worlds and false in all the others. Simply put, we define "contingency" as a logical property and not as an epistemological one. Be that as it may, it remains just as real a problem for us as for Kant whether (3.18) is contingent and knowable a priori.

argued that one couldn't have knowledge of anything unless proposition *(3.18)* were true; and since we do have knowledge of at least some things, he concluded both that *(3.18)* is true and that it can be known to be true without appeal to experience.

Other philosophers, before Kant and since, have also argued for the respectability of metaphysics as a genuine mode of inquiry, and many have put forward their own candidates for the status of contingent a priori truths. Indeed a number of prominent philosophers today, of whom Peter Strawson is perhaps the foremost example, have employed arguments strikingly like Kant's to similar ends.[35] Transcendental arguments are enjoying a current vogue; and defenders of the thesis that there are contingent propositions which are knowable a priori are not hard to find.

Ranged against them, however, are hosts of philosophers who deny that a priori knowledge of contingent propositions is possible. They believe that those contingent propositions which can be known are knowable only by an appeal to experience, and that there is no a priori knowledge of contingent truths. To the extent that a priori knowledge is possible, it is alleged to be restricted exclusively to noncontingent propositions.[36] Hence, they maintain, a science of a priori metaphysics of the kind Kant envisaged is impossible in principle. Far from being the grandest of all forms of human inquiry, metaphysics — they would say — is a conceptual fraud foisted on us by those who cannot get their thinking straight.

An antimetaphysical bent of mind characterizes many of those philosophers who, aptly, have come to be called "Empiricists". The Empiricist tradition in philosophy includes among its foremost representatives persons such as the eighteenth-century Scottish philosopher David Hume (in reaction to whose antimetaphysical diatribes Kant was provoked to write his *Critique of Pure Reason*), and the contemporary English philosopher Sir Alfred Ayer (who became one of the principal spokesmen in the 1930s in the English-speaking world of the philosophy known as Logical Positivism or Logical Empiricism).[37]

In line with their contention that there are no contingent propositions which are knowable a priori, it is characteristic of Empiricists, whenever confronted with a proposition which is putatively both contingent and knowable a priori, to argue that either that proposition is not contingent or it is not knowable a priori. Thus, for example, when confronted with Kant's claim that the proposition

(3.18)   Every event has a cause

is both contingent and knowable a priori, some Empiricists, as we might expect, have replied that it is not contingent, while others have preferred to argue that it is not knowable a priori. Or again, against those philosophers who would argue that Euclidean geometry provides us a priori with contingent information about the actual world, typically Empiricists have replied that to the extent that Euclidean

35. See, for instance, Strawson's *Individuals: An Essay in Descriptive Metaphysics*, London, Methuen, 1959.

36. A few philosophers of this persuasion take an even more radical stance: they allege that no proposition, regardless of its modal status, can be known a priori. The principal expositor of this stronger thesis was the English philosopher, John Stuart Mill. For Mill, all knowledge was empirical. It should be clear, however, from what has already been said in this book, that we have rejected Mill's thesis. We have already given examples, e.g., *(3.11)* and *(3.13)*, of propositions which can be known a priori. See Mill's *A System of Logic, Ratiocinative and Inductive*, (1843), 8th ed., London, Longmans Green, 1965, and *Examination of Sir William Hamilton's Philosophy*, London, Longmans Green, 1865.

37. See especially Hume's *A Treatise of Human Nature* (1739), ed. L.A. Selby-Bigge, Oxford, Clarendon Press, 1964; *An Enquiry Concerning Human Understanding* (1745), ed. Eric Steinberg, Indianapolis, Hackett Publishing Company, 1977; Ayer's *Language, Truth and Logic*, London, 1936, 2nd ed., 1946; *The Foundations of Empirical Knowledge*, London, Macmillan, 1940; and *The Problem of Knowledge*, London, Macmillan, 1956.

geometry provides knowledge a priori, all its results are noncontingent, and to the extent that it provides any contingent information, that information can be known only by appeal to experience, i.e., empirically.[38]

In more recent years the dispute over the question whether there are any contingent propositions which are knowable a priori has taken on renewed interest and vitality as a result of the contemporary renaissance in logic itself which we reported in chapter 1. Lately there have appeared arguments in support of the existence of a priori knowledge of contingent propositions, arguments which, however, do not also defend the existence of an a priori metaphysics of the Kantian, or even of the Strawsonian kind.

Using the phrase "stick S" as a description of the well-known glass-encased platinum-iridium bar in Paris which originally served as the standard by means of which meter lengths were conventionally determined, Saul Kripke has argued that the proposition

(3.20)   The length of stick S at time t_0 is one meter

is both contingent and knowable independently of experience, i.e., is knowable a priori.[39] Kripke's claim turns in part on a distinction which he, in effect, draws between two kinds of definition: those which fix the *meaning* by giving synonyms and those which fix *reference;* but it can be understood well enough without going deeply into that.[40] Thus, in the case of *(3.20)*, for instance, he argues first that the proposition is contingent: it is contingent, he claims, because although the length that we call "one meter" is the same in all possible worlds, the length of stick S, which happened to be one meter at t_0 in the actual world, could have been different (i.e., is different in at least some other possible worlds), so that the proposition *(3.20)*, although true, is contingent; nonetheless, it is capable of being known a priori, he argues secondly, because those persons who laid it down as a reference-fixing definition that the term "one meter" should refer to whatever length it was which stick S had at time t_0 would not need to get out any measuring tapes or in any other way try experientially to determine S's length, but rather, simply as a consequence of their own stipulations, could know *(3.20)* to be true.

38. For detailed discussions of these controversies see R.D. Bradley's (1) "The Causal Principle", *Canadian Journal of Philosophy*, vol. IV, no.1 (Sept. 1974); and (2) "Geometry and Necessary Truth", *Philosophical Review*, vol. 73 (1964). The latter paper is available in the *Bobbs-Merrill Reprint Series in Philosophy*.

39. Saul A. Kripke, "Naming and Necessity", in Harman and Davidson, eds., *Semantics of Natural Language*, Dordrecht, D. Reidel, 1972; especially pp. 274–5, 279, and 346–7.

40. Suffice it to say that, if Kripke is right, not all propositions which are knowable a priori are necessarily true. The proposition

(3.21)   All sisters are female,

which is expressed by the sentence,

(3.22)   "All sisters are female",

all of whose terms are 'meaning-defined' is necessarily true and knowable a priori. But the true proposition expressed by the sentence,

(3.23)   "The length of stick S at time t_0 is one meter"

where "one meter" is, as we might say, 'referentially-defined', which is (allegedly) also knowable a priori, is not necessary: it is contingent.

Whether Kripke's contributions to the perennial debate can survive criticism remains to be seen. But this much is already clear about his arguments: they offer little if any solace (and were not intended to offer solace) to those who have staked the possibility of a Kantian-type metaphysics on the outcome to the question whether any contingent propositions exist which are knowable a priori. For there is nothing at all grand, but on the contrary something rather trite, about the examples which Kripke espouses. If there are such contingent propositions whose truth-values can be known a priori as it were — that is, as a result of our having stipulated references for certain of the words we use — such propositions would hardly seem to be on a par with the profundities that metaphysicians have traditionally aspired to promote.

Keeping in mind this broad background of debate concerning the existence of contingent propositions knowable a priori, let us now return to its first instance, that concerning Category 2. Note that even if one were to argue that there are some contingent propositions which are knowable a priori, it would not follow that there are any contingent propositions which are knowable ratiocinatively, and still less that there are any contingent propositions knowable both ratiocinatively and experientially.

To argue that some contingent propositions are knowable ratiocinatively requires a stronger argument than one which purports to establish that some contingent propositions are knowable a priori. For ratiocinative knowledge may be but one mode of a priori knowledge. So the question whether there are any contingent propositions knowable ratiocinatively must be independently addressed.

Note that neither Kant nor Kripke argues that one could have knowledge of contingent propositions by means of the *paradigm* kinds of ratiocination, viz., analysis of concepts and inference therefrom. Philosophers like Kant and Kripke, who wish to maintain the possibility of a priori knowledge of contingent propositions, have been driven to propose *exotic* kinds of aprioricity: transcendental arguments in the case of Kant, and baptismal reference-fixing definitions in the case of Kripke. (In this section we have merely presented these other alleged modes of aprioricity. Question 4 will give us the opportunity to evaluate these candidates by pursuing the questions whether there are any nonratiocinative but a priori means of gaining knowledge. There we shall examine the credentials of Kant's and Kripke's candidates to see whether they might be better classified as nonratiocinative a priori modes. Our conclusion there will be that not only are they not ratiocinative; they are not a priori, either. But this is to anticipate.)

If one were to construe either Kant's *(3.18)* or Kripke's *(3.20)* as being examples of contingent propositions knowable by ratiocination (albeit exotic ratiocination), might either of these two propositions also serve as an example of Category 2, i.e., a contingent proposition knowable both ratiocinatively and experientially?

Kripke's example *(3.20)* would seem to be the more promising of the two.[41] Indeed

> *(3.20)*   The length of stick S at time t_o is one meter

would appear to be about as good a candidate for Category 2 as one is likely to find.

Now there seems to be no good reason whatever to deny that *(3.20)* could be known to be true experientially. We have only to suppose that accurate records were kept of the temperature of S at t_o (they were); that people subsequent to t_o adopted other means of determining whether something is a meter long (they did); and that the laws of nature pertaining to the relationship between length and temperature have been invariant since t_o (we have good reason to suppose that they have been). It then becomes easy to envisage someone finding out, *by appeal to the actual experience* of measuring S today, that *(3.20)* is true, i.e., that S had a certain length at some particular previous time. It would then

---

41. It has proven notoriously difficult to argue convincingly that *(3.18)* can be *known* experientially.

follow, that *if (3.20)* is not only, as Kripke claims, knowable a priori, but is, more specifically, knowable ratiocinatively, then at least some contingent propositions are knowable both ratiocinatively *and* experientially.

None of this, of course, answers the question whether there *are* any contingent propositions which are knowable both ratiocinatively and experientially. If Kripke's examples can be correctly construed as instances of ratiocinatively knowable propositions, then there are; but before concluding that they can be, one would do well to bear in mind that an entire school of philosophy, the Empiricist, adamantly denies the existence of such a class of propositions. Going even further, the Empiricists deny that there are any contingent propositions knowable a priori, whether by ratiocination in its most familiar forms, whether by exotic kinds of ratiocination, or whether by nonexperiential, nonratiocinative means. Empiricists, that is, insist that not only Category 2 but also the subsequent Categories, 3 and 4, are empty.

3.   *Are there any contingent propositions which are knowable ratiocinatively (and* ipso facto *a priori) but which are not knowable experientially?*

Like Question 2, this one turns partly on the answer we give to the logically prior question, viz., whether there are any contingent propositions knowable a priori. If there are no contingent propositions which are knowable a priori then it follows immediately that there are no contingent propositions which are knowable *only* ratiocinatively and not experientially.

But suppose that there are at least some propositions which are contingent and knowable ratiocinatively. Might not some of them be knowable *only* in ways which make no appeal to experience?

Some of the claims made within classical metaphysics would seem to be likely candidates. Many of these propositions do *not* seem to be knowable experientially. If, then, one were to accept the claim that they are contingent and knowable ratiocinatively, one would be satisfied that there are contingent propositions which are knowable only a priori. What might some of the candidates be for such a classification? The following stand out.

(3.24)   Nothing can be created out of nothing.

(3.25)   There is nothing in an effect which was not present in its cause.

(3.26)   Physical things are composed of invisible, weightless, intangible substrata in which the properties of things inhere and cohere.

(3.27)   Only those physical things exist which are perceived.

(3.28)   There is only one physical space.

(3.29)   If a property were universal (e.g., if every physical thing had *precisely* the same temperature), then that feature of the world would be undetectable.

It is characteristic of all these propositions that, at one time or another, metaphysicians have taken some pains to argue that they are *not* knowable experientially. Indeed, it is a principal tenet of metaphysics that its findings should 'transcend' experience, that knowledge of their truth-values should lie outside the capabilities of mere experience.

Again, as with Category 2, immediately preceding, Empiricists will take issue. Empiricists, we can be sure, will claim that none of these propositions is both contingent and knowable a priori, and consequently that none can be both contingent and knowable only ratiocinatively.

4.   Are there any contingent propositions which are knowable by other than experiential or ratiocinative means?

As we said before, when discussing the nonexhaustiveness of the experiential/ratiocinative distinction, unless we define "experience" and "ratiocination" so as to cover every conceivable alleged case of knowledge being acquired by telepathy, precognition, meditation, intuition, etc., it will remain an open question whether there might not be modes of knowledge-acquisition other than the experiential and the ratiocinative.

Fortunately we have no need here to debate any exotic questions about the credentials of ESP and the like, let alone to decide whether any of the propositions supposedly known by such means fall outside the provinces of experience and reason. For there are other candidates, already better known to us, whose credentials we have still to examine. One is the proposition

(3.18)   Every event has a cause

which, according to Kant, can be known a priori, hence without any appeal to experience, but which at the same time cannot be known by analysis of concepts or inference therefrom. The other is the proposition

(3.20)   The length of stick S at time t_0 is one meter

which, according to Kripke, also can be known a priori, but again not by analysis of concepts or inference therefrom. The former is said, by Kant and some others, to be knowable by transcendental argument; the latter is said, by Kripke and some others, to be knowable by a means which we earlier described as baptismal reference-fixing.

Let us start with Kant. In raising the question whether

(3.18)   Every event has a cause

might be knowable by transcendental argument one presupposes that it is knowable. Yet this presupposition has not passed unchallenged. Some philosophers — especially Logical Positivists — have argued that it is both unverifiable and unfalsifiable by any means whatever and, in the light of their theory, have concluded that it is unknowable. Other philosophers have directed their attacks on the very idea of a transcendental argument, arguing: (1) that transcendental arguments do not do what they are supposed to do since they are either invalid or unsound; or (2) that such arguments make a covert appeal to a now-suspect principle of meaningfulness — the so-called Verificationist Principle which was favored by Logical Positivists and which still infects the arguments of many nonpositivist thinkers.[42]

The criticism which we would urge against the claim that (3.18) is knowable a priori by a transcendental argument is that, even if transcendental arguments were acceptable in other respects, they still would not show that their conclusions can be known a priori since the premises from which

42. For more on the Verificationist Principle see the following discussion of Question 5. For more on the claim that transcendental arguments involve an appeal to verificationism, see: Barry Stroud, "Transcendental Arguments", *Journal of Philosophy*, vol. LXV, no. 9 (May 2, 1968), pp. 241–254; W.B. Stine, "Transcendental Arguments", *Metaphilosophy*, vol. 3, no. 1 (Jan. 1972), pp. 43–52; R. Rorty, Symposium: "Verificationism and Transcendental Arguments", *Nous*, vol. 5, no. 1 (Feb. 1971), pp. 3–14.

they begin can only be known experientially. Let us suppose, for instance, that Kant's transcendental 'proof' of *(3.18)* does indeed show that the truth of *(3.18)* is a necessary condition of our having the knowledge and experience which we do in fact have. Even so, we cannot conclude that *(3.18)* can be known a priori to be true. For the proposition that we have both knowledge and experience is something which itself is known not a priori but only by experience. Accordingly, on both Kant's and our own account of what it is for knowledge to be gained empirically, it follows that *(3.18)* can be known (if at all) *only* experientially, i.e., empirically, not a priori. We must not be led into supposing that the conclusion to an argument is knowable a priori just because the reasoning from premises to conclusion is purely a matter of a priori ratiocination. The issue, in such a case, is rather whether the premises themselves are knowable a priori or empirically. And in the case before us — as, we suggest, in all other purported examples of conclusions established by transcendental arguments — the premises are plainly empirical. Seen in this perspective the claim of propositions like *(3.18)* to fill the gap envisaged by Question 4 seems wholly mistaken.

The situation is not altogether different in the case of Kripke's example, *(3.20)*. Kripke claims that *(3.20)* is knowable a priori by "someone who has fixed the metric sytem by reference to stick S". Of any person who institutes the convention (or set of conventions) embodied in the metric system by stipulating that the term "meter" shall designate rigidly, i.e., in all possible worlds, the length which S happens contingently to have at t_0 in the actual world, Kripke claims that "he knows automatically, without further investigation, that S is one meter long."[43]

It is clear that the very same argument can be pressed into service for saying that any and every baptismal act of reference-fixing provides the baptiser with a priori knowledge. Not only is a priori knowledge automatically at the command of those who set up the metric system of length or, changing the example to another of Kripke's, to those who set up the Celsius system of temperature by stipulating that "100°" should refer to the temperature at which water boils at sea level; it is automatically provided to all those who give names to their children, their cheeses, or their chickens. Indeed, according to this argument, a priori knowledge can be created by fiat — by the simple device of naming anything at all. In assigning a name, say "Zsa Zsa", to an item, x, one automatically (and hence, according to Kripke, a priori) knows that the contingent proposition that x is Zsa Zsa is true.

It is interesting to note how Kripke's suggestion fits into the philosophical tradition.

In one respect Kripke, like all philosophers of genius, is bucking the tradition. Whereas earlier philosophers — especially the Rationalists — thought of a priori knowledge as the proper preserve of persons of intellect, reasoning power, and insight, Kripke has argued that it is within the grasp of anyone who can name anything — presumably even the babe in his cot systematically naming his toys.[44] This does not mean that Kripke is wrong. But it does mean that if Kripke is right then Kant in his quest for an answer to the question "How are synthetic (contingent) a priori judgments possible?", overlooked the obvious. He had no need for the elaborate and difficult transcendental arguments by which he sought, in his *Critique of Pure Reason*, to determine what are the "pure concepts of understanding" which are presupposed by experience and hence not "given" in experience. He needed only, like Kripke, to observe what goes on in any act of naming.

---

43. "Naming and Necessity", p. 275.

44. Presumably, also, it was within the grasp of our prelinguistic forebears at the moment when — according to most theories — they laid the foundations of language by assigning names to things. If so, Kripke's claim can be recruited in favor of our earlier contention that our prelinguistic ancestors could believe certain propositions to be true even though there were, by hypothesis, no sentences to express them. If, by the single act of assigning names, they came to have a priori knowledge, then *a fortiori* they had beliefs. See chapter 2, pp. 78–79.

In another respect, Kripke is within the tradition. Like Kant and many others he views a priori knowledge — at least insofar as it is of contingent propositions — as 'maker's' knowledge, knowledge which we in a sense make or create. In effect he gives a new twist to the theory — once popular with the Logical Positivists and early so-called Linguistic Philosophers — that truth of certain kinds can literally be created by convention. The twist lies in the fact that whereas conventionalists like Ayer, Carnap, Hahn, and the early Strawson[45] tried to explain the apriority of *necessary* propositions in terms of "definitions of symbols", "rules of language", or "conventions of meaning", Kripke tries to explain the alleged apriority of certain *contingent* propositions in terms of reference-fixing definitions, acts of baptism, or conventions of naming.

But can the mere act of naming ever really create a priori knowledge? Admittedly, the proud parents who name (whether in a baptismal ceremony or less formally) their first-born daughter "Zsa Zsa" know "automatically, without further investigation", the truth of the proposition that their first-born daughter is Zsa Zsa. But does that mean that they have a priori knowledge in the sense of "a priori" that we have been discussing? The question is by no means a simple or clear one and perhaps must await developments in the semantic theory of naming and in philosophy of psychology before it can be settled definitively. Nevertheless we venture a few simple remarks by way of furthering the present discussion.

Consider, more closely, cases in which it seems natural to say, with Kripke, that in bestowing a name on an object one knows automatically, without further investigation, what the object is (i.e., is named). The parents say, "Let's call her 'Zsa Zsa' "; or the French academicians say, "We hereby call the length of this stick 'one meter' " (in French, of course). *How* do they, at the time of so saying, know the truth of the relevant propositions? Some philosophers would be inclined to object that the question doesn't properly arise since the word "name", like the words "promise", "guarantee", and "apologize" — all of which may sensibly be prefixed by "I hereby . . ." — functions in sentences like the above, not to report *that* one is doing something, e.g., that one is naming, but merely to do or perform that very thing, e.g., perform the act of naming.[46] The objection, however, is misconceived. The fact that one is not, in performing the act of naming, *asserting* that one is so doing, let alone asserting that one *knows* that one is so doing, does not preclude us from asking whether, at that time, one in fact knows what one is doing. Nor does it preclude us from asking *how* one knows what one is doing, or what *follows* from the fact that one knows what one is doing.

But if these questions are permissible, their answers are obvious. Zsa Zsa's parents know the truth of the proposition that their daughter is Zsa Zsa because that proposition is inferred "automatically" from another proposition which they know to be true, viz., that they gave her that very name. And they know the latter proposition to be true because *they attended to to what they were doing at the time.* Likewise with the French academicians. On this analysis, however, the propositions which were supposed to be known a priori turn out to have their "source and warrant" (as Kant would put it) in experience — the experience of attending to what one is doing in the very act of naming and,

45. See A.J. Ayer, *Language, Truth and Logic*, 1st edition, London, Gollancz, 1936; Rudolf Carnap, *The Logical Syntax of Language*, New York, Harcourt, Brace & World, 1937; Hans Hahn, "Logic, Mathematics and Knowledge of Nature", 1933, trans. and published in Ayer, ed., *Logical Positivism*, Glencoe, Ill., Free Press, 1959; P.F. Strawson, "Necessary Propositions and Entailment Statements", *Mind*, vol. 57 (1948), pp. 184–200. For trenchant criticisms see W.C. Kneale, "Are Necessary Truths True by Convention?" *Proceedings of the Aristotelian Society*, Suppl. vol. 21 (1947); Arthur Pap, *Semantics and Necessary Truth*, New Haven, Yale University Press, 1958, chap. 7; and W.V.O. Quine, "Truth by Convention", reprinted in *Readings in Philosophical Analysis*, ed. Feigl and Sellars, New York, Appleton-Century-Crofts, 1949.

46. These expressions, when so used, are usually called "performatives" following J.L. Austin. See his "Other Minds", reprinted in A.G.N. Flew, ed., *Logic and Language*, 2nd series, Oxford, Blackwell, 1953, pp. 123–158.

moreover, having experiential cognizance of the very thing named. To restate the point we made earlier in connection with Kant's claim that *(3.18)* can be known a priori, we must not conclude that a proposition is knowable a priori just because it can be shown to follow, by a piece of a priori reasoning, from some other proposition.

In conclusion, then, we can agree with Kripke that those who fix the reference of the term "meter" could, at the time of fixing it, know the truth of

(3.20)   The length of stick S at t_0 is one meter

"automatically, without further investigation". But we should want to insist that this does not mean that *(3.20)* is knowable a priori. We might allow, perhaps, that the *inference* from the fact that they bestowed the name "meter" on the length which the stick had at that time was made "automatically". And we might allow, too, that once this inference has been made no "*further* investigation" — no further appeal to experience — is needed. But this is only because, on the account we are suggesting, all the requisite appeal to experience has already been made.

If we are right, neither the Kantian nor the Kripkean examples permit us confidently to assert that there are propositions which are knowable by means other than experience or ratiocination. Indeed, in retrospect, our analysis suggests that the prospects of finding any genuine examples of contingent a priori propositions are even more forlorn than we earlier — in our discussion of Questions 2 and 3 — were prepared to allow.

5.   *Are there any contingent propositions which are unknowable?*

This question has an interesting history in modern philosophy. In the 1930s and 40s the Logical Positivists argued that the claim that there are contingent propositions which are unknowable is nonsense. They took the hallmark of a contingent proposition to be its testability, and rejected as meaningless any sentence which did not express something testable. This was the very point of their Verificationist Principle.[47]

Now there are many objections that can be made to the Positivists' thesis. One is that it confuses sentences with what sentences express. Although sentences might be nonsensical, propositions never are. But more to the point is the fact that on the account given in these pages of what a contingent proposition is, namely a proposition which is true in some possible worlds and false in some others, there is good reason to think that some contingent propositions are unknowable. Indeed we can even give an example of a contingent proposition which is in principle unknowable, e.g., the proposition expressed by the sentence,

(3.30)   "On April 13, 1974, an extraterrestrial being, who has the ability, and who always exercises it, to thwart our attempts to detect him, stood on the tower of the Empire State Building."

47. Verificationist theories of meaning were formulated in different ways at different times (See Carl Hempel, "Problems and Changes in the Empiricist Criterion of Meaning", reprinted in A.J. Ayer, ed., *Logical Positivism*, Glencoe, Illinois, Free Press, 1959). Most sophisticated formulations allowed that noncontingent propositions did not need empirical backing and claimed only that this was essential only to contingent propositions if they were to be meaningful [sic].

For a contemporary exposition of Verificationism, see Michael Dummett's *Frege: Philosophy of Language*, London, Duckworth, 1973, esp. pp. 463–470. Dummett's account "dispenses altogether with the conception of objective truth-values, determined independently of our knowledge or means of knowledge, by a reality external to us" (p. 470). It is clear that this involves, among other things, a rejection of the correspondence theory of truth adopted in this book, and, as he recognizes, a rejection of classical two-valued logic. He concedes, however, that the consequences of his account "have never been systematically worked out" (p. 468).

In saying that the proposition expressed by *(3.30)* is unknow*able,* we are of course, saying that it is unknown; but we are also saying more. Remember that we are here examining the limits of *human* knowledge. And although there will be some possible worlds in which something or other (God, perhaps) knows the truth-value of the proposition expressed by *(3.30)*, that fact is simply irrelevant to our claim.

To say that the proposition expressed by *(3.30)* is unknowable is merely to say that it is unknown by any sentient beings who have the same set of sensory modes and reasoning abilities as we human beings have and who find themselves in possible worlds which have the same physical laws as our actual world has. An extraterrestrial being who is undetectable by any human modes of experience and who is also undetectable by any physically constructible instrument is an extraterrestrial being whose existence must forever lie beyond human ken.

To be sure, the Positivists would claim that insofar as *(3.30)* does not assert anything which can be known to be true or known to be false, it does not express a proposition at all. But this seems to be little more than a piece of dogma rendered plausible, to some, by a faulty theory of meaning. It may be admitted, with the Positivists, that in the absence of evidence for the existence of an undetectable extraterrestrial being we have no good reason to believe that such a being really exists. We may even agree that *(3.30)* is a sentence the utterance of which need hardly be taken very seriously. But this is a far cry from saying that what *(3.30)* expresses cannot possibly be true, or false, let alone that *(3.30)* is literally meaningless.

There was a time when the verificationist theory of meaning seemed plausible not only to some philosophers but also to some scientists. It was often invoked in early formulations of the theories of relativity and quantum mechanics. But today it no longer seems plausible. Thus for example we find contemporary astrophysicists arguing with respect to black holes that "there are parts of the universe from which, in principle, we cannot get any information."[48] To be sure, it seems on current theory to be physically impossible for us ever to obtain information about the internal states of black holes. Nonetheless, serious speculation abounds about what those internal states might in fact be. This speculation is not unbridled. It is seen by physicists to be subject to the constraint of consistency with currently well attested physical and cosmological theories. But of course the very question of consistency or inconsistency can arise only on the presumption that the speculative theory — even if unverifiable and unfalsifiable — nevertheless really *is* true or false.

6. *Are there any noncontingent propositions knowable empirically, that is, knowable experientially but not a priori?*

To begin, we must put to rest an argument which would attempt to prove that *experiential* knowledge of noncontingent truths is impossible. The flawed argument goes like this:

> If a proposition is noncontingently true, i.e., is necessarily true, then it is true in all possible worlds. But our experience of how things are is of only one among this infinity of possible worlds; that is, it is restricted to the actual world. How, then, could we have *experience* which would show that a proposition is true in all possible worlds? Our experience is limited to the actual world and does not extend to non-actual ones. It could hardly suffice, therefore, to establish truths about non-actual but possible worlds. In short, it is not possible to have experiential knowledge of noncontingent truths.

48. Larry Smarr, quoted in "Those Baffling Black Holes", in *Time,* vol. 112, no. 10 (Sept. 4, 1978), p. 58.

In spite of its initial plausibility, this argument is, in the final analysis, unsound.

The alleged difficulty which the argument purports to expose evaporates as soon as we distinguish between (1) knowing that a proposition is true, and (2) knowing that a proposition is necessarily true.

Since necessary truths are true in all possible worlds, and the actual world is a possible one, they are also true in the actual world. And hence our experience of how things are in the actual world may very well suffice to establish the truth (in the actual world) of a proposition which is true both in the actual world and in all other possible (but non-actual) worlds as well. That is to say, experience can sometimes suffice to show that a necessarily true proposition is true *simpliciter*. What experience cannot suffice to establish is that a necessarily true proposition is necessary; but it may show that it is true. As Kant put it: "Experience teaches us that a thing is so and so, but not that it cannot be otherwise."[49]

Having effectively rejected the argument which claims to show that experiential knowledge of noncontingent truths is impossible, we can now proceed to look for examples of such truths. They are easy to find. We need only cite the example of the necessarily true proposition

> *(3.31)*   It is raining or it is not raining.

The easiest way to come to know that *(3.31)* is true is by ratiocinative reasoning. But, nevertheless, one *could* determine its truth-value by looking out the window and seeing that it is raining, from which one could ascertain by valid inference that the proposition in question is true.

It cannot, then, be doubted that there is *experiential* knowledge of noncontingent truths.

But all this is just by way of scene-setting. Question 6, is not, after all, whether there is experiential knowledge of noncontingent propositions, but whether there are any noncontingent propositions which are knowable empirically, that is, knowable *only* experientially. And it is at this point that our answer must become somewhat lame.

We are quite unable to cite any examples of noncontingent propositions which we can confidently say are unknowable by any other than experiential means. We find ourselves in the situation in which the townspeople of Königsberg were in before Euler succeeded in producing his proof. Even before his proof, they already knew that there was no route of the stipulated sort which connected the seven bridges; but they did not know, nor is it easy to see how they could have known, that this conclusion could also be arrived at ratiocinatively. As it later happened, the problem did succumb to ratiocinative reasoning; but until it did, there was no way of knowing that what they knew experientially was also knowable ratiocinatively.[50] There do not seem to be any guarantees whatever in this matter. Although some noncontingent propositions may come to be known experientially, this does not imply that they may not, after all, be demonstrable ratiocinatively.

---

49. *Critique of Pure Reason*, Introduction, B3.

50. It is interesting to note that the case study of the Königsberg problem furnishes us with an example of a point we made in rebuttal to the specious argument which began this answer to Question 6. Before Euler's proof, the townspeople of Königsberg knew the truth-value of proposition *(3.17)*. What they did not know was whether *(3.17)* was contingent or not; whether the fact that there was no route of the described kind was due to an idiosyncratic feature of the local landscape or whether it was more wide-ranging. The answer to the latter question came in Euler's proof. What he showed was that it was *impossible* that there should be such a route, effectively showing that the obstacle to such a route was not an idiosyncratic feature of the local landscape but a feature which would be found in any possible world whatever which contained seven bridges deployed as they were in Königsberg.

Summing up, our answer seems to be this: various noncontingent propositions are knowable experientially. Whether they are knowable *solely* experientially, that is, knowable empirically, we simply do not know. But, equally, we do not know of any good argument whatever which would suggest that there are no such propositions. There may be; there may not be. We have no reason here to prefer one answer to the other.

7. *Are there any noncontingent propositions which are knowable both experientially and ratiocinatively?*

Yes. We have just cited two examples: *(3.31)*, the proposition that it is raining or it is not raining, and *(3.17)*, the one dealing with the bridges of Königsberg.

8. *Are there any noncontingent propositions which are knowable ratiocinatively (and* ipso facto *a priori) but which are not knowable experientially?*

As a step towards finding the proper answer to this question, let us begin by considering the proposition,

$$(3.32) \quad 1 + 1 = 2$$

Let it be understood ("stipulated" if you prefer), that we are talking about the sum of two numbers 1 and 1, not about the consequences of putting one thing alongside another thing. So considered, the sentence "1 + 1 = 2" expresses a noncontingently true proposition. Although the consequence of putting one thing alongside another may well be that there is nothing at all (in the case where sufficient quantities of uranium are put together to form a critical mass), or only one thing (in the case where one raindrop coalesces with another), or three or more (in the typical case where a male rabbit is put into a hutch with a female) —the *sum* of the *numbers* 1 and 1 cannot possibly be other than 2. Now this noncontingently true proposition (like *(3.31)*) can be known to be true both ratiocinatively and experientially. On the one hand, we can know the truth of *(3.32)* simply by virtue of understanding the *concepts* of oneness, addition, equality, and twoness. We can, therefore, know it to be true ratiocinatively. On the other hand, we can know *(3.32)* to be true simply by discovering, as a matter of general experience, that whenever there is one thing and another thing there are two things. A whole method of teaching children so-called mathematical "skills" is based on the presupposition that mathematical truths can be learned by generalization from experience.

But are *all* noncontingent truths which are knowable ratiocinatively, like the proposition that one plus one equals two, also knowable experientially? Or, are there some noncontingent truths which are knowable ratiocinatively, but which are *not* knowable experientially?

Although there seems to be no doubt that such simple truths of arithmetic as *(3.32)* can be learned experientially, it is hard to see how experience can suffice when it comes to dealing with large numbers or complicated calculations.[51] What sort of *experience* could it be which teaches us that proposition

$$(3.33) \quad 347091 \times 6038 = 2{,}095{,}735{,}458$$

51. It is interesting to note that John Stuart Mill argued in *A System of Logic, Ratiocinative and Inductive* [1843] that *all* mathematical truths have to be established by inductive generalization from experience rather than ratiocinatively. By way of reply, Gottlob Frege, in *The Foundations of Arithmetic* [1884] (translated by J.L. Austin, New York, Harper, 1960), pointed out that this would mean that we would not be entitled to assert that $1{,}000{,}000 = 999{,}999 + 1$ unless we had observed a collection of a million things split up in exactly this way (pp. 10–11).

is true? Although proposition *(3.32)* can reasonably be claimed to be knowable both experientially and ratiocinatively (that is, to belong to Category 7), it is very implausible to make a similar claim for proposition *(3.33)*. It seems that for all but the simplest mathematical propositions, experience could never suffice to give us knowledge of their truth-values and that we must instead have recourse to ratiocinative methods.

Or, consider the fact that we know, for example, that the mathematical constant π is a nonrepeating, nonterminating decimal. How could we possibly know this experientially? We could not, of course. The constant π is the ratio of the circumference of a (perfect) circle to its diameter. No matter how carefully we construct and measure a circle we can never get more than roughly ten decimal places of accuracy — that is, we can physically measure π only to about ten decimal places. But so doing would never show what we already know, namely, that the decimal expression for π runs on to an infinity of digits after the decimal point. It is clear in this case, again, that we have an instance of knowledge of a noncontingent truth which is quite unknowable experientially.

Thus the answer to this eighth question, whether there are any noncontingent propositions which are knowable ratiocinatively but not experientially, would seem to be: Yes.

9.   *Are there any noncontingent propositions which are knowable a priori but by means other than ratiocination?*

Earlier in this section we asked the comparable question about contingent propositions. Our answer, it may be remembered, was that neither of the serious candidates considered — those put forward by Kant and Kripke — could confidently be accepted. And that left only the forlorn possibility that more exotic examples of ESP, meditation, and so on, might fill the gap. The present case seems little different. No philosopher, so far as we know, has ever suggested that necessarily true propositions might be known a priori by transcendental argument. So even if transcendental arguments *were* to prove their worth as ways of providing wholly a priori knowledge, it seems unlikely that they would ever be invoked in support of a positive answer to Question 9. Again, although Kripke's claim that a priori knowledge of contingent propositions is made possible by reference-fixing definitions is paralleled by the standard conventionalist claim that a priori knowledge of noncontingent propositions is made possible by meaning-assigning definitions, the conventionalists would hasten to add that any knowledge so acquired arises through *analysis* of the meaning so assigned or by inference therefrom. In other words, the comparable conventionalist view about a priori knowledge of noncontingent propositions attributes this knowledge to a paradigm form of ratiocination. Finally, so far as the exotic cases are concerned, it seems safe to say that no one at all — philosopher or otherwise — has ever supposed that ESP or the like could yield *a priori* knowledge of *non*contingent truths.

The only case that seems worth discussing is that of intuition. Mathematicians, in particular, and sometimes logicians as well, are prone to ascribe their discoveries of new truths in mathematics and logic to "sheer intuition". We have already — in section 4 — discussed the near cousin of intuition, viz., self-evidence, and have found it wanting. But whereas those who talked of self-evidence would almost certainly have counted it as a form of ratiocinative knowledge, those who talk of intuition tend not to. The appeal to intuition is often made in such a way as to suggest that intuited propositions are neither known by experience nor known by ratiocination.

But are such propositions really known at all? Once more we need to remind ourselves of the difference between coming to believe a proposition which is true and knowing that that proposition is true. We might well allow that a person can come to believe — by intuition or whatnot — that a proposition is true when it is in fact true and yet deny, on the grounds that the justificatory condition of knowledge is not satisfied, that that person has *knowledge* of the truth of that proposition. Intuition, though it may be a means of discovery, can hardly count as a genuine mode of knowledge and a fortiori can hardly count as a mode of a priori knowledge.

Frege saw that very clearly in *The Foundations of Arithmetic* when he bemoaned the fact that

> We are all too ready to invoke inner intuition, whenever we cannot produce any other ground of knowledge.[52]

He claimed, correctly, that when we judge a proposition to be a priori or empirical,

> this is not a judgement about the conditions, psychological, physiological and physical, which have made it possible to form the content of the proposition in our consciousness; nor is it a judgement about the way in which some other man has come, perhaps erroneously, to believe it true; rather, it is a judgement about the ultimate ground upon which rests the justification for holding it to be true.[53]

And for this reason he sought, in his own investigations of mathematics and logic, never to invoke an appeal to intuition but always to give rigorous proofs of the propositions which he took to be true. Then, and only then, was he satisfied that he *knew* the proposition to be true.

Frege seems clearly to be correct in all this. But if so then intuition can hardly be counted as a nonratiocinative means of acquiring genuine knowledge of noncontingent propositions.

True, there *may* be still other ways of knowing such propositions than those we have considered. And it must be admitted that we know of no good argument which demonstrates the impossibility of nonratiocinative knowledge of noncontingent propositions. But it is surely safe to conclude that the prospects for finding any cases of such knowledge look very bleak indeed.

10.   *Are there any noncontingent propositions which are unknowable?*

We begin by asking ourselves, "What conditions would have to be satisfied in order that *all* noncontingent propositions could be known?" For, if it turns out that no such set of conditions is satisfiable, then there will exist some noncontingent propositions which are unknowable. What might such a set of necessary conditions be?

The number of noncontingent propositions is infinite. To see this, one need only recall that every proposition of arithmetic (whether true or false) is noncontingent, and that clearly there must be an infinity of these since there is an infinity of numbers and there is an infinity of true propositions about *each* number and an infinity of false propositions about *each* number. Thus there are as many false noncontingent propositions (viz., an infinite number) as there are true noncontingent propositions (viz., an infinite number).

Given the immensity of the class of noncontingent true propositions, in what ways can we expect to know them? Experiential means will do for some of them. We have already seen this in the case of proposition *(3.32)*, the proposition that one plus one is two. Experience, we said, could teach us that this proposition is true. But the numbers referred to by our hypotheses need not be too large before experiential methods fail us. This was illustrated in the case of proposition *(3.33)*. So although some noncontingent truths are knowable experientially, others, indeed an infinite number of others, would seem to be knowable, if at all, only ratiocinatively.

Now what conditions would have to be satisfied for these remaining propositions to be knowable ratiocinatively? Some of them, of course, can be known analytically, i.e., can be known directly by conceptual analysis. But again, the vast bulk of them cannot be known by these methods. The

---

52. G. Frege, *The Foundations of Arithmetic,* Oxford, Blackwell (2nd revised ed.), 1959, p. 19.

53. *Ibid.,* p. 3.

Goldbach Conjecture would seem to be a case in point. Of the infinitely many noncontingent propositions which cannot be known experientially or analytically, there would appear to be only one means remaining for knowing their truth, viz., inferring them from analytical truths already established. This is the way most mathematicians have come to view the problem. The limits of the knowable among noncontingent propositions have come to be regarded as virtually coinciding with the limits of the validly inferable.

Is the method of inference up to the task? By taking recourse to inferential methods can we hope to be able to establish (at least in principle) the truth-value of every noncontingent proposition?

In the first half of this century the question was seriously pursued for a special class of noncontingent propositions, viz., arithmetical propositions. Although this class hardly exhausts the class of noncontingent propositions, a negative answer about the class of arithmetical propositions would obviously require a negative answer concerning the larger class of which it is a part. That is, it is a necessary condition for all noncontingent propositions being knowable, that all arithmetical propositions be knowable, and the latter class is knowable only if inferential methods can suffice to establish all those among them which are not knowable by other means.

A serious limit on the power of inferential methods was established in a famous paper published in 1931 by the mathematician-logician, Kurt Gödel.[54] In this paper Gödel showed that not *all* true propositions of arithmetic can be inferred from a finite set of consistent axioms.

But to say that not *all* true propositions may be derived from a finite set of true axioms is *not* to say that there exists *any one* true proposition which could not so be deduced. For every finite consistent set[55] of axioms there will always exist some propositions which cannot be inferred from that set, but this still allows that any of those propositions could be inferred from another or from an enlarged set of axioms. Any proposition one chooses could always be inferred from one set or other; the only point is that not *all* propositions could be inferred from any *one* finite set no matter how large.

But what exactly does this imply in regard to the question we are pursuing? Does Gödel's Proof show that there are some noncontingent propositions which are unknowable?

Gödel's Proof shows us that in order to know greater and greater numbers of noncontingent propositions, we should have to use larger and still larger sets of axioms: a small finite set of axioms is demonstrably inadequate to the task. With this said, our answer would seem to be near at hand.

Ever-larger sets of axioms can be used to *establish* the truth of their implications only if those axioms are themselves *known* to be true. (Although any axiom can, of course, be derived from itself, this does nothing to show that that axiom is true. To show that an axiom is true, it is necessary to demonstrate the truth of the axiom extrasystematically, i.e., by some means other than by derivation from itself or from other axioms in the axiom-set.) Can we establish the truth of the members of ever-increasing axiom-sets without falling into a vicious infinite regress? Experiential means are obviously inadequate to the task; similarly, conceptual analysis would also seem to be inadequate. This leaves inference. But if we are to rely on inference, from which propositions are we to infer the problematic axioms? Presumably more powerful axioms. But if this is so, then the epistemic problem — far from being solved — is compounded, and our hope for a solution skirting the problem of a vicious regress is confounded.

The two means we have available to gain knowledge — experience and ratiocination — taken singly or in concert with inference appear to be inadequate to the magnitude of the task which Gödel has

---

54. Kurt Gödel, *On Formally Undecidable Propositions*, translated by J. van Heijenoort, in *From Frege to Gödel: A Source Book in Mathematical Logic, 1879–1931*, ed. by J. van Heijenoort, Cambridge, Mass., Harvard University Press, 1967, pp. 596–616. For a popularized exposition of this important but difficult paper, see *Gödel's Proof* by Ernest Nagel and James R. Newman, New York, New York University Press, 1958.

55. Or more exactly, for every recursively generable consistent set of axioms, finite or infinite.

shown confronts us. Faced as we are with an infinitely large set of arithmetical propositions which are not derivable within any arithmetic having a finite number of axioms, we seem driven to the conclusion that some (indeed an infinite number) of these unknown propositions must remain unknowable.

For all we know, Goldbach's Conjecture might be just such a proposition. We do not have experiential knowledge of its truth in advance of a mathematical demonstration of its truth, as we had in dealing with the Königsberg Problem. Perhaps Goldbach's Conjecture is unprovable. We will come to know that it is *not*, only if someone should happen (by inferential means) to prove it true or prove it false. Until then, it remains unknown, and for all we know, unknowable.

Appendix to section 6: a complete classificatory scheme for the epistemic and modal distinctions

At the expense of complicating figure *(3.l)* somewhat, we can drop the simplifying assumption we made earlier concerning that part of the figure labeled with the question mark.

It is clear that the three categories, (1) *knowable experientially,* (2) *knowable ratiocinatively,* and (3) *knowable by some other means,* can combine in *seven* ways, not merely four as depicted in figure *(3.l)*. The three additional ways, not represented, are:

(a)   knowable experientially and by some other, nonratiocinative means;

(b)   knowable experientially, ratiocinatively, and by some other means as well; and

(c)   knowable ratiocinatively and by some other, nonexperiential means.

These three additional categories can all be represented by subdividing that section on figure *(3.l)* labeled with the question mark. Doing so will give us the following figure:

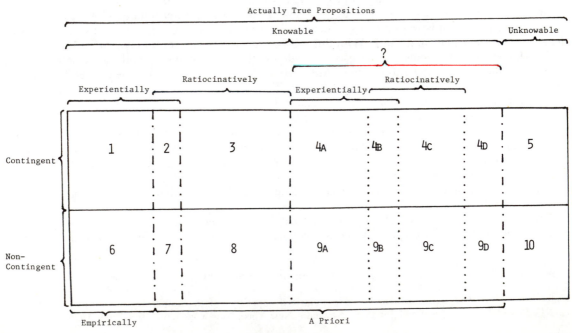

FIGURE *(3.m)*

Now, then, we must ask, "Which of these eight categories, viz., 4a through 4d and 9a through 9d, are empty and which have members?" The answers we give to each of these eight questions will depend on the answers we have given to the original questions, 1 through 4 and 6 through 9. Let us take one example. Consider the first of this new set of questions, viz., "Are there any contingent propositions which are knowable experientially and by some other, nonratiocinative means?" That is, "Is category 4a empty or not?" The answer to this question will depend on the answers we have given for the original questions 1 and 4, viz., [in (1)] whether there are any contingent propositions knowable experientially and not ratiocinatively, [in (4)] whether there are any contingent propositions knowable by other than experiential or ratiocinative means. We replied that undoubtedly there *are* contingent propositions knowable experientially which are not knowable ratiocinatively, and that there *may* be contingent propositions which are knowable by other than experiential or ratiocinative means. In *combining* these two answers, the answer to the question whether there are any propositions in category 4a becomes: We simply do not know; there may be.

If one goes through all the categories, 4a through 4d and 9a through 9d, the strongest claim that can be made in any case, is that the category *may* have some members. In none of these cases can we say with any good reason that there *is* a proposition in that category.

EXERCISE

Try to argue for each of the categories 4b through 4d and 9a through 9d whether that category is empty or not.

7.   THE EPISTEMOLOGY OF LOGIC

We began this chapter by asking how knowledge of the subject matter of logic is possible and whether that knowledge is obtained in a way different from knowledge in physics and chemistry. To help answer these questions we have spent much time discussing some fundamental epistemological distinctions and have just completed a classificatory scheme containing no fewer than ten major categories of propositions.

The scene is now set for us to ask where exactly in this elaborate scheme the subject matter of logic is to be placed.

Let us begin with the exhaustive and exclusive classification comprising the horizontal division on figure *(3.m)*: the contingent/noncontingent classification. Are the propositions which make up the subject matter of logic contingent or noncontingent? Let us remind ourselves just which propositions these are. They are those propositions which ascribe to other propositions modal attributes. They are not propositions which ascribe attributes to physical things in the actual world or in any other world; and they are not propositions which ascribe truth-values (simpliciter) to other propositions. They are a very specific set of propositions. They are propositions *about* propositions, and more specifically about a certain set of attributes (viz., modal attributes) of propositions.

Now what about these propositions? Are they contingent or noncontingent? Or, perhaps, are some of them contingent and some noncontingent? At this point we will merely assert an answer: they are all of them noncontingent. Although a proof for this claim could be given now, we have chosen to reserve it for later in this book. A nonformal *proof* that all the propositions of logic are noncontingent is given in chapter 6.

This means that the subject matter of logic is to be found distributed somewhere across categories 6 through 10, and that the *science* of logic will be restricted to at most these five categories. As a matter of fact, however, it turns out the science of logic is concerned with no more than *two* of these categories, viz., 7 and 8. Let us see why.

Immediately we can see that the science of logic can have no commerce with propositions in category 10. It is logically impossible to have a science of unknowable propositions. For all we know, there may be some logical propositions which are humanly unknowable. But if there are any, they lie beyond the reach of human science.

This leaves four categories, viz., categories 6 through 9, as possible categories of logical propositions which are subject to investigation by the science of logic. But two of these, viz., categories 6 and 9, are, as we have already seen, problematic. We have no way of knowing whether either of them has *any* members. And if it is difficult to say, in the first instance, whether there are *any* noncontingent truths knowable empirically (category 6) or knowable other than experientially or ratiocinatively (category 9), then it is doubly difficult to say whether there are any truths of logic in these categories, for truths of logic form a proper subset of the class of noncontingent truths. Even if we could be assured that categories 6 and 9 do have members, it would require further argumentation to establish that among these members are some propositions of logic.

Having utterly no guarantee, then, that any of its subject matter lies outside of categories 7 and 8, it is hardly any wonder that the science of logic is concerned exclusively with propositions knowable ratiocinatively.

Whether it is a case of the subject matter dictating the methodology (i.e., ratiocination), or the methodology dictating the subject matter, is a question which is idle and profitless to pursue. For the fact of the matter is that by a long series of historical adjustments the subject matter of logic and the methodology of logic have been adapted to fit one another.

The natural sciences (e.g., physics, chemistry, astronomy), the life sciences (e.g., botany, zoology, medicine) and the social sciences (e.g., history and economics) are all *empirical* sciences. Their subject matter is concerned with but one possible world, the actual one. The science of logic (and the science of mathematics, too, for that matter) is an *a priori* science. Not only is its subject matter different from the other sciences in that it is concerned with all possible worlds; its methodology differs too in that it adopts exclusively the ratiocinative method of gaining knowledge.

It has not always been this way. The natural sciences and the science of logic have not always been characterized by such different methodologies. If we look into ancient texts in mathematics and physics we discover that their methodologies were often confused amalgams of both ratiocinative and empirical methods. In Euclid's geometry, for instance, we find his attempt to prove the congruence of a certain pair of triangles by the expedient of moving one of them (in imagination) in space on top of the other. But this is now commonly seen as an unwitting intrusion of an empirical method into what we now regard as an a priori science. What happens to the shape of a thing when it moves about in space cannot be known a priori but can be known only by appeal to experience. Similarly, on the other side, we can find the inappropriate intrusion of a priori methodologies in the physical sciences. An example is the ancient physical theory that objects of unequal weight fall at speeds proportional to their weights. The justification of this theory was that '*it stood to reason* that heavy things fall faster than light things.' It was only in the seventeenth century that a man of extraordinary genius, Galileo, realized that this 'obvious truth' was a contingent matter and in need of experimental verification. And in actually performing the test he discovered that this seeming 'truth of reason' was in fact false. The a priori method in physics was thereby struck a blow from which it never recovered. And over the course of subsequent centuries, scientists and philosophers alike have tried to remove all vestiges of apriorism in physics.

The conscious attempt to purge unwitting appeals in a priori sciences to natural phenomena knowable empirically came later. It is only in the nineteenth century that such illicit methods as the one of Euclid's just mentioned were purged from geometry and other mathematical and logical sciences. Here the credit, in part, goes to such persons as Riemann, Gauss, and especially David Hilbert.

Universal agreement that logic is, or should be, a ratiocinative science has, however, never been achieved. For a variety of reasons, some philosophers have asserted the contrary. Mill, we have already seen, argued against this view of logic on the basis of his belief that the only knowledge possible was empirical knowledge, that there was no such thing, ultimately, as a priori knowledge. Logic, as conceived by him, is just a high-order set of generalizations knowable empirically.

That there should be some controversy regarding the epistemology of logic is not surprising. Indeed it would be surprising if there were not. For the controversy surrounding its epistemology is a ramification of the controversy surrounding its ontology. To each of the ontologies discussed in chapter 2, there corresponds a distinctive epistemology. We have argued for an ontology which makes the subject matter of logic noncontingent *propositions*, and we have opted for the corresponding epistemology which, in our view, is that of ratiocination. In our view, logic is an a priori science.

Our answer, then, to the question "How is knowledge in logic possible?" is: by a priori reasoning, or more specifically, by ratiocinative reasoning. It remains now, in our next chapter, to examine how ratiocinative reasoning might assume different degrees of sophistication — how, in effect, the propositions of logic might be subjected to minimal degrees of analysis or to maximal degrees.

4

The Science of Logic: An Overview

1. INTRODUCTION[1]

Our discussions in chapter 3 of the nature, scope, and modes of human knowledge have helped prepare the way for an overview, in the present chapter, of the science of logic. Here we shall give an account, in deliberately general terms, both of *what* we know of the subject matter of logic and of *how* we know it.

Logic, as a science, has much in common with the other special sciences — mathematics, physics, chemistry, and the rest. Like each of them it is no mere collection of known propositions, but is rather an *organized* body of knowledge with its own highly general principles and laws. And like each of them it has its own *methods* of inquiry, its own distinctive ways of expanding knowledge.

Yet logic also has a special status among the sciences. In the first place, it is the most general science insofar as all propositions whatsoever fall within its compass, whereas each of the other sciences treats of relatively restricted sets of propositions — propositions about numbers, about material particles, about chemical properties, and so on. This fact has led some logicians to claim, somewhat paradoxically, that logic has no subject matter at all and that it is the science of pure form. (We shall try to put this claim into perspective later in this chapter.) In the second place, logic shares with mathematics the distinction of relying on methods which are purely a priori, whereas each of the remaining sciences relies on methods which are largely empirical.[2] This fact has led some thinkers to claim that arithmetic is but an extension of logic. Whether or not there is any line of demarcation between the two and, if so, where it should be drawn is still an issue much in dispute within the philosophy of mathematics. We will make no further comment upon it. Whatever the outcome, it would generally be agreed — except by Radical Empiricists like Mill — that the methods of logic (and probably those of mathematics) are wholly ratiocinative and hence a priori.

1. The material in this chapter provides a natural bridge between chapters 3 and 5; however, it is both complex and condensed. Teachers may wish to make judicious selections from among its six sections.

2. But not wholly. Each of the so-called "empirical sciences" makes use as well of the a priori principles and findings of logic (and in many cases, of mathematics). This is not surprising in the light of our definition of "empirical". For, it will be remembered, to say that a proposition is knowable empirically is to say that it is knowable only experientially, while to say that a proposition is knowable only experientially is just to say that the only way in which it can be known is by direct appeal to experience *or by inference therefrom*. And this is where the a priori science of logic (and, in many cases, of mathematics) plays a role. For an inference that is made from a proposition which is known by appeal to experience will be known to be a *valid* inference if and only if it accords with the a priori principles and findings of logic.

We shall start our overview of the science of logic by saying something more about these methods.

Since there are two main ways of acquiring ratiocinative knowledge — by analysis and by inference therefrom — it follows that, to the extent that our knowledge of logical propositions is a priori, it too is gained by analysis or inference. To be sure, it is possible to acquire knowledge of some necessary truths, including some truths of logic, experientially. But experience, we have seen (following Kant), cannot give us knowledge of the modal status of these propositions. Nor does it offer us any surety as a method for systematically expanding our knowledge of the subject matter of logic. On the contrary, such knowledge as it gives us arises, as it were, adventitiously. The a priori methods of analysis and inference offer us the best prospect for building a *science* of logic.

2.   THE METHOD OF ANALYSIS

The method of analysis has always been employed in the sciences of mathematics and logic — and, for that matter, philosophy. Euclid employed it when, in his *Elements,* he analyzed the concepts of being a point, being a straight line, triangle, etc. In this way he laid the foundations of geometry. Plato employed it when, in his *Theatetus,* he analyzed the concept of knowledge, and again, in his *Republic,* when he analyzed the concept of justice. In this way, Plato laid the foundations of two important subdisciplines of philosophy: epistemology (i.e., theory of knowledge) and philosophy of politics, respectively. Aristotle employed it when, in his *Organon,* he analyzed syllogistic reasoning and the modal concept of necessity; the Megarian logicians employed it when, in miscellaneous inquiries, they analyzed conditional propositions. Between them, Aristotle and the Megarians laid the foundations of logic.[3] In all these as well as other fields, analysis is still fundamental.

But what does analysis, in philosophy and logic, consist of? What are its objects? And what are its results?

Analysis, in general, as we pointed out in chapter 2, consists in the examination of a complex item of some sort with a view to determining what constituents make it up and how they are related to one another. This is evident in fields such as chemistry, grammar, and the like. Philosophical analysis differs from these and other analytical enterprises primarily in the nature of the complex items it examines. In chemistry one analyzes chemical compounds. In grammar one analyzes sentences. What does one analyze in philosophy, in general, and in logic, in particular?

The objects of philosophical analysis

That propositions and concepts, insofar as they are complex, are *among* the items which we analyze when doing philosophy, was noted when — in chapter 2 — we developed the theory that propositions are truth-valued combinations of concepts. G. E. Moore, in his classic answer to the question, wrote as if they were the *only* objects of analysis,

> In my usage [of the term 'analysis'] both *analysandum* and *analysans* must be concepts or propositions.[4]

3. For more on the contributions of the Megarians, see W. and M. Kneale, *The Development of Logic,* Oxford, Clarendon Press, 1962, chapter 3, esp. pp. 113–138.

4. See "A Reply to My Critics", in *The Philosophy of G.E. Moore,* ed. P.A. Schilpp, La Salle, Open Court, 1968, vol. 2, p. 664. By the term "analysandum" we mean the expression of the object of analysis; by the term "analysans" we mean the expression of the result of analysis. Compare the parallel accounts of the terms "definiendum" and "definiens" given in footnote 18, p. 26, chapter 1. Definitions are (usually) of verbal

One might object that Moore's answer is too restrictive since it seems to preclude our giving analyses of *arguments* which are surely among the prime objects of analysis in logic. Then again, it seems to preclude our giving analyses of *questions* and *commands,* items to which philosophers, especially recently, have devoted a good deal of close analytical scrutiny.

But these are quibbles. An argument, from the point of view of analysis, is just a pair of proposition-sets standing in relation to one another as premises to conclusion. And questions and commands, although they are not themselves propositions or concepts, are analyzable (just as propositions are) into conceptual constituents — albeit ones which stand in non-truth-valued types of combination. In any case, so far as our present interest is concerned — that of describing the method of analysis as it applies within the science of logic — Moore's answer is entirely adequate. We can afford to ignore questions, commands, requests, prayers, and the like. For the preoccupation of the science of logic is, as we might have expected, a restricted one: it is concerned almost solely[5] with the analysis of propositions, of concepts (insofar as they feature in propositions) — and, as an aside, of arguments (insofar as propositions feature in them).

Three levels of analysis

There seem to be three main forms which analysis can take in logic:

1.   that in which the analysandum is a proposition while the analysans features, as the constituents of that proposition, a simpler proposition (or set of propositions) together with a simpler concept (or set of concepts);

2.   that in which the analysandum is a proposition while the analysans features, as the constituents of that proposition, a set of concepts; and

3.   that in which analysandum is a concept while the analysans features, as the constituents of that concept, a set of simpler concepts.

We shall consider one or two examples of each form of analysis.

Examples of form 1:

Consider, first, the proposition

> *(4.1)*   Either it is necessarily true that sisters are female or it is not.

Plainly *(4.1)* is admissible as an object of analysis. For it is a complex which has other *propositions* among its constituents, viz.,

> *(4.2)*   It is necessarily true that sisters are female

and

> *(4.3)*   It is not necessarily true that sisters are female.

---

expressions; analyses, as Moore would insist, are never of verbal expressions but always and only of what verbal expressions express, viz., concepts or propositions.

5. We say "almost solely" in order to allow for the fact that some philosophers have tried to construct what they call logics of nonpropositional kinds. See, for instance: Charles L. Hamblin "Questions", *Australasian Journal of Philosophy,* vol. 36 (1958), pp. 159–168; and David Harrah, "A Logic of Questions and Answers", *Philosophy of Science,* vol. 28 (1961), pp 40–46. Attempts have also been made to construct logics of imperatives.

Any proposition which has other propositions among its constituents is what we call a *compound proposition*. Hence, *(4.2)* is a compound proposition. By way of contrast,

(4.4)   Sisters are female

is *not* a compound proposition since it does not have any other propositions among its constituents. Such a proposition we call a *simple proposition*. Note that the propositions *(4.2)* and *(4.3)*, which are constituents of the compound proposition *(4.1)*, are themselves compound propositions. Though they are *simpler* than *(4.1)* they are nevertheless not *simple* propositions since each has the even simpler proposition *(4.4)* as one of its constituents. In short, *(4.1)* may be regarded as having *(4.2)* and *(4.3)* among its constituents even though each of the latter is itself susceptible to being analyzed into still simpler constituents. Another constituent of *(4.1)* is the concept of *disjunction,* i.e., the concept of that relation which holds between two (or more) propositions in all those possible worlds (if any) in which at least one of them is true or between two (or more) concepts in all those possible worlds (if any) in which at least one of them has application. In short, the constituents of *(4.1)* are the two propositions, *(4.2)* and *(4.3)*, plus the concept of disjunction; and, within *(4.1)* these constituents stand in propositional combination.

As a second example of analysis of the first form consider the proposition

(4.2)   It is necessarily true that sisters are female.

We have already noted that *(4.2)* features as a propositional constituent in the analysans of *(4.1)*. Yet it, too, may be analyzed since, it, too, is a complex which has simpler constituents. One of these constituents, we have seen, is the simple proposition *(4.4)*. Another is the concept of necessary truth. And within *(4.2)* these two constituents — one a proposition, the other a concept — stand in propositional combination insofar as the property of necessary truth is predicated of, or ascribed to, the proposition *(4.4)*.

Before proceeding to examples of analyses of the second and third forms, we would do well to note a common feature of analyses of the first form. In each case, the analysandum is shown by analysis to have, among its constituents, propositions which, though they themselves are susceptible to analysis, are nevertheless *at this level of analysis* left *unanalyzed*. For this reason we shall refer to that part of the science of logic which deals with propositions at this level of analysis as *The Logic of Unanalyzed Propositions*.

Example of Form 2:

(4.4)   Sisters are female.

As already noted, *(4.4)* features as a propositional constituent in the analysans of *(4.2)*. Yet it, too, may be analyzed. Although it is a simple proposition, with no other propositions among its constituents, it is nevertheless complex insofar as it has concepts as its constituents, viz., the concepts of being a sister and of being female. And, within *(4.4)*, these two constituent concepts stand in propositional combination insofar as the property, of which being female is the concept, is predicated of, or ascribed to, the items to which the concept of being a sister applies.

A common feature of all analyses of the second form is that each has as its analysandum a proposition which is shown by analysis to have, among its constituents, concepts which, though they themselves are susceptible to analysis, are nevertheless *at this level of analysis* left *unanalyzed*. For this reason we shall refer to that part of the science of logic which deals with propositions at this level of analysis as *The Logic of Unanalyzed Concepts* (often known as The Logic of Predicates).

Example of Form 3:

> *(4.5)*   being a sister

Although the concept of being a sister features as a conceptual constituent in the analysans of *(4.4)*, it itself is subject to analysis. For it, too, is complex. Among the simpler concepts which are its constituents are the concepts of being female and of being a sibling. Another constituent is the concept of *conjunction,* i.e., the concept of that relation which holds between two (or more) propositions in all those possible worlds (if any) in which both of them are true, or — as in the present case — between two (or more) concepts in all those possible worlds (if any) in which both of them have application to the same item. In short, the constituents of *(4.5)* are the concepts of being female, being a sibling, and conjunction.

A common feature of all analyses of the third form is that each has as its analysandum a concept which is shown to be analyzable into simpler (though not necessarily simple) concepts. For this reason we shall refer to that part of the science of logic which deals with concepts at this level of analysis as *The Logic of Analyzed Concepts.*

The idea of a complete analysis

Now it is clear, upon review, that each successive form of analysis considered is, in a fairly precise sense of the word, a *deeper* analysis than that of the preceding form. That which features as a constituent in the analysans corresponding to a given analysandum may in turn be analyzed into even simpler constituents. This fact in no way precludes the possibility of our giving an analysis of a certain form — or, as we have otherwise put it, "at a certain level" — which is a *complete analysis relative to that level.* But it has led some philosophers to entertain the ideal of an *absolutely complete analysis* — the ideal of a type of analysis which would involve breaking down a proposition or concept into constituents which are *ultimately simple* insofar as they do not themselves have any simpler constituents and so do not admit of any further analysis. The early Wittgenstein thought in this way. He argued, in his *Tractatus Logico-Philosophicus,* that if any propositions or concepts are to be determinate, then complex propositions must be analyzable into ultimately simple propositions and these in turn must be analyzable into those ultimately simple constituents for which he reserved the word "names".[6] And Moore, although he seems not to have committed himself to the extremes of Wittgenstein's position, thought that there are *in fact* some concepts which are ultimately simple and unanalyzable. In his *Principia Ethica,* for example, he came to this conclusion about the concept of goodness.[7] Fortunately, we do not have to settle here the question whether there are any ultimate simples of analysis, let alone whether there *must* be such. It suffices for us to learn the lesson which both these philosophers and their contemporary, Bertrand Russell, never tired of teaching, viz., that a proposition or concept, the grammar of whose expression appears simple, may well turn out, on analysis, to be logically complex. Indeed Russell's analysis[8] of the seemingly simple proposition

---

6. Ludwig Wittgenstein, *Tractatus Logico-Philosophicus,* trans. D.F. Pears and B.F. McGuinness, London, Routledge & Kegan Paul, 1961; especially theses 3.23, 3.25, 3.201, and 3.202. See also his *Notebooks 1914–16,* ed. G.H. von Wright and G.E.M. Anscombe, trans. G.E.M. Anscombe, New York, Harper & Brothers, 1961, p. 46.

7. G.E. Moore, *Principia Ethica,* Cambridge, Cambridge University Press, 1962 (copyright 1903).

8. B. Russell, "On Denoting", *Mind,* vol. 14 (1905), pp. 479–493.

(4.6)   The present King of France is bald

into the conjunction of three simpler propositions, viz.,

(4.7)   There is some item which is King of France,

(4.8)   At most one item is King of France,

and

(4.9)   Any item which is King of France is bald,

is widely, and deservedly, regarded as one of the classics of analytical philosophy. To be sure, each of these three propositions which feature in the analysans of (4.6) is itself susceptible to analysis at a *deeper* level. But at the level at which Russell's analysis is given, (viz., the Logic of Analyzed Propositions), it counts as a *complete* analysis.

The need for a further kind of analysis

Analysis, at any of the three levels distinguished, and whether complete or partial, can make it possible for us to obtain knowledge a priori of the *relations* between the propositions or concepts which feature as the objects of analysis and other propositions or concepts.

In the first place, it yields knowledge of the relation between the analysandum and the analysans. For, if the analysis is sound and complete, it shows that the analysandum is *equivalent* to the analysans. And, if the analysis is sound but only partial or incomplete, it shows that the analysandum *implies* the analysans. For instance, the analysis offered above of the concept of being a sister is a complete analysis and hence, if sound, shows that this concept is *equivalent* to the concept of being both female and a sibling. By way of comparison, Kant's analysis of the concept of body, discussed in chapter 3, purports to be only a partial analysis and hence, if sound, shows only that the concept of body *implies* the concept of extension. The knowledge acquired in each case is, of course, acquired without any need of appeal to experience. It is acquired by virtue of, as Kant would put it, "reason's own resources", and hence is acquired a priori.

In the second place, the types of analysis so far considered may prepare the ground for discovering previously undiscovered relations between the proposition or concept featured in the analysandum and some proposition or concept which does *not* feature in its analysans. For instance, Russell's analysis of the proposition (4.6), that the present King of France is bald, gives us grounds for inferring that this proposition is inconsistent with any proposition which is inconsistent with any of the propositions featured in its analysans. For example, it would be inconsistent with the proposition that there are at present several Kings of France.

Now it is all very well to learn, by analysis, that a proposition, P_1, is equivalent to or implies a proposition, P_2; or, again, that a concept, C_1, is equivalent to or implies a concept, C_2. But this in itself does not tell us whether P_1 is a true proposition; nor does it tell us whether concept C_1 has application in this or any other possible world. Analysis which merely tells us what are the constituents of a proposition can tell us that (4.1) is equivalent to the disjunction of (4.2) and its negation, viz., (4.3), but — by itself — it cannot tell us anything about the truth-value or modal status of (4.1). Again, analysis which merely tells us what are the constituents of a concept can tell us that the concept of a greatest prime number is equivalent to the concept of a number which has no factors except itself and one, and which has no successor which is a prime, but — by itself — it cannot tell us whether the concept of a greatest prime number has application in this or any other possible world.

Yet have we not spoken hitherto of analysis as a means whereby one might in certain cases ascertain the *truth-value* of a proposition — in an a priori manner — *by analyzing that very proposition?* How can this be possible?

The answer is that if, at any of the three levels of analysis distinguished — that of the logic of Unanalyzed Propositions, that of the Logic of Unanalyzed Concepts, or that of the Logic of Analyzed Concepts — we wish to ascertain the truth-value of the proposition analyzed or the applicability of the concept analyzed, we must supplement analysis into constituents by what is commonly called "truth-condition analysis", or what we prefer to call "possible-worlds analysis".[9] It is only when "analysis" is so understood that we can make sense of the notion of analytically determined truths.

Possible-worlds analysis

By "possible-worlds analysis" we mean the investigation of the conditions under which a proposition is true or the conditions under which a concept has application — where, by "conditions", we do not mean conditions in the actual world but mean, rather, conditions in any possible world. In other words, possible-worlds analysis is the investigation which sets out to determine whether a proposition is true or a concept has application in all, in none, or in some but not all possible worlds. It is the sort of analysis which *can* tell us, for instance, that the concept of the greatest prime number has no possible application — that it is (as we put it in chapter 2) a necessarily non-applicable concept. And it is the sort of analysis which *can* tell us, for instance, that proposition *(4.1)* is true in this as well as all other possible worlds — that it is a necessarily true proposition.

That analysis of propositions and concepts should — in the last resort — involve reference to possible worlds is only to be expected, since (as we argued in chapter 2) the explication of concepts involves reference to sets of possible worlds, and propositions just *are* truth-valued combinations of concepts. But quite independently of that, the link with possible worlds remains. It has been made, implicitly at least, and explicitly in many cases, ever since the dawn of analytical philosophy, even though many analysts would not have thought of so describing it.

Consider, once more, Kant's treatment of the proposition

(3.13)   All bodies are extended.

Kant's analysis of *(3.13)* is, in effect, an amalgam of analysis into constituents and of possible-worlds analysis. He calls *(3.13)* an analytic judgment on the grounds (a) that it has among its constituents the concepts of body and of extension, and (b) that the concept of extension is "bound up with" the concept of body. Elsewhere, in characterizing analytic propositions more generally, he speaks of these as propositions in which the concept of the subject covertly "contains" the concept of the predicate. Now it is clear that what Kant means by his "binding" and "containment" metaphors is simply this: that in the case of an analytic proposition it is not *possible* for the concept of the subject to apply without the concept of the predicate also applying. In particular, he may be understood as saying of *(3.13)* that it is not possible for the concept of body to have application to a particular item unless the concept of extension also has application to the same item. But, as we have already seen — in our own earlier analyses of the modal concepts of possibility, necessity, etc. — this is just to say that there is no *possible world* in which the concept of the body applies to an item when the concept of extension does not;[10] which is to say that the concept of body *implies* the concept of

9. We prefer talk of "possible-worlds analysis" not only because it links the notion of analysis firmly with much else that we have said in this book, but also because it is less restrictive than talk of "truth-condition analysis". The latter sort of talk is appropriate only in connection with propositions, not in connection with concepts. Concepts have *applicability* conditions but not *truth* conditions.

10. Note that, on this account, to say — with Kant — that concept C_1 "contains" concept C_2 is to say that

extension; which is to say that it is *necessarily true* that if something is a body then it is extended. Thus it is that analysis into constituents, combined with possible-worlds analysis, can lead to knowledge of the contingency or noncontingency of a proposition and sometimes also of its truth-value.

Significantly, the analysis, at level 3, of a concept such as those of being a body or of being a sister can — when supplemented by analyses of other concepts — yield knowledge of the modal status and truth-value not only of the proposition within whose analysans that concept, at level 2, features as a constituent, but can also sometimes help us acquire knowledge of the modal status and truth-value of propositions at level 1. To illustrate, let us revert once more to the series of propositions *(4.1)*, *(4.2)*, *(4.3)*, and *(4.4)* within each of which the concept *(4.5)*, of being a sister, features as a constituent.

In analyzing

> *(4.5)*   being a sister

we are, in effect, attempting to say *what it is* to be a sister by determining in which possible worlds *(4.5)* has application. And our answer is that *(4.5)* has application in a certain set of possible worlds, viz., that which may summarily be described by saying that it is the set in which both the simpler concepts, of being female and of being a sibling, have application to the same item. This means, of course, that the analysans is *equivalent* to the analysandum. For, on the account we gave (in chapter 2) of the equivalence of concepts, concepts are equivalent if and only if in any possible world in which one has application to a given item, the other has application to the same item. It means, too, that the concept of being a sister *implies* each of the concepts featured in the analysans, separately and jointly: it implies being female; it implies being a sibling; and it implies being both female and a sibling. And that, in turn, means that it is *necessarily true* that if something is a sister then it is female; that it is *necessarily true* that if something is a sister then it is a sibling; and that it is *necessarily true* that if something is a sister then it is both female and a sibling.

It is evident that one of the consequences of our determining the applicability conditions of the concept *(4.5)* is that we have thereby also determined both the truth-value and modal status of the proposition

> *(4.4)*   Sisters are female

within which *(4.5)* occurs as a constituent. For to conclude, as we just did, that it is necessarily true that if something is a sister then it is female, *just is* to conclude that *(4.4)* is both true and necessarily so. Thus, by a process of reasoning analogous to Kant's, we have established that *(4.4)* is analytically and *a fortiori* necessarily true.[11]

Once this has been established it is, of course, a relatively straightforward matter — involving only an additional understanding, through analysis, of the concept of necessity — to determine both the modal status and the truth-value of

---

the set of possible worlds in which C_2 has application includes or contains the set of possible worlds in which C_1 has application — not, as might have been supposed, the other way around. This curious 'reverse' mapping of propositions onto sets or classes is not unique to this one occasion. It is a universal phenomenon. Consider the proposition expressed by the sentence "A thing's being both red and square implies that it is red." The first class just referred to is the class of red and square things, and the second, the class of red things. Which of these two classes 'contains' the other? Clearly, the *latter* contains the *former*.

11. Recall from chapter 3, p. 146, that an analytically true proposition is one which is known a priori *by analysis* to be necessarily true.

(4.2) It is necessarily true that sisters are female.

For *(4.2)* simply asserts of *(4.4)* that *(4.4)* has the property of necessary truth which our analysis of *(4.4)* shows it to have. In other words, since analysis of *(4.2)* shows it to predicate of *(4.4)* the very property which *(4.4)* has been shown, by analysis, to have, *(4.2)*, like *(4.4)*, can be known to be true analytically; and hence *(4.2)*, like *(4.4)*, is necessarily true.[12]

It then becomes a straightforward matter — involving only the additional understanding, through analysis, of the concept of negation — to determine both the modal status and the truth-value of

(4.3) It is not necessarily true that sisters are female.

For since *(4.3)* is the negation of *(4.2)*, it will be false in all those possible worlds in which *(4.2)* is true. And since *(4.2)* has been shown to be true in *all* possible worlds, we can conclude that *(4.3)* is false in all possible worlds, i.e., that it is necessarily false.

Moreover, once we have established, by reasoning of the kind just displayed, that *(4.2)* is true, and indeed that it is necessarily true, it is but a small step — involving only an additional understanding through analysis, of the concept of disjunction — to determine the truth-value, and indeed the modal status, of

(4.1) Either it is necessarily true that sisters are female or it is not.

Degrees of analytical knowledge

Exactly how much we can come to know about *(4.1)* is a function of how much analytical knowledge of its constituents we take into account. If we take into account merely the fact that *(4.2)* is true, and leave out of account the fact that analysis can show it to be necessarily true, we can — by invoking the analysis of the concept of disjunction — show *(4.1)* to be true. For the concept of disjunction is the concept of a relation which holds between propositions (and derivatively between concepts) when at least one of those propositions is true (or, in the case of concepts, when at least one of those concepts has application to a given item). Thus, since *(4.1)* involves the disjunction of two propositions, *(4.2)* and *(4.3)*, of which we know *(4.2)* to be true, *(4.1)* must itself be true. Clearly, then, knowledge of the analysis of the concept of disjunction, taken together with knowledge of the truth of one of the propositions disjoined in *(4.1)*, suffice to give us knowledge of the *truth-value* of *(4.1)*. But it tells us nothing of its modal status. We can, however, determine the modal status of *(4.1)* in either of two ways. (a) We can tell that *(4.1)* is *necessarily* true, if we take into account the additional fact — already ascertained by analysis — that one of the disjuncts in *(4.1)* is the negation of the other. Thus, since *(4.3)* is the negation of *(4.2)*, and hence (as we have already seen) is false in all those possible worlds in which *(4.2)* is true (and *ipso facto* is true in all those possible worlds in which *(4.2)* is false), these two disjuncts exhaust the set of all possible worlds in the sense that in all possible worlds one or other of them is true. But this is just to say that in all possible worlds either *(4.2)* or *(4.3)* is true; which is to say that *(4.1)* — which asserts that

---

12. The reasoning can be generalized. Given any proposition, P_1, whatever, if analysis of P_1 shows P_1 to be necessarily true, then any proposition, P_2, which asserts that P_1 is necessarily true, is itself knowable by analysis and hence is necessarily true; likewise for any proposition, P_3, which asserts of P_2 that it is necessarily true; and so on *ad infinitum*. Here we have proof of the thesis $\Box P \rightarrow \Box \Box P$ — a thesis which, taken together with the converse thesis $\Box \Box P \rightarrow \Box P$, yields one of the so-called "reduction laws", viz., $\Box P \leftrightarrow \Box \Box P$, of the systems S4 and S5 of modal logic. (See pp. 220–224, for more on reduction laws.)

either *(4.2)* or *(4.3)* is true — is necessarily true. (b) Again, we can tell that *(4.1)* is *necessarily* true, if we take into account the fact — already ascertained by analysis — that one of its disjuncts, viz., *(4.2)*, is necessarily true. For the analysis of the concept of disjunction shows that the disjunction of any two propositions is true in all those possible worlds in which either disjunct is true. If, therefore, as we have already ascertained by analysis, *(4.2)* is not only a disjunct in *(4.1)* but also is necessarily true, then *(4.1)* will be true in all those possible worlds in which *(4.2)* is true, viz., in all possible worlds. Once more, then, *(4.1)* may be shown, by analysis, to be necessarily true.

Plainly, the analysis of a concept at the deepest level, viz., level 3, may, when supplemented by possible-worlds analyses, at levels 2 and 1, of other concepts, yield knowledge a priori of the modal status of a wide range of propositions and of the truth-value of some of them. At each level one has only to incorporate the results of conceptual analysis at the deeper level in order to acquire this knowledge. (Perhaps it is for this reason that many philosophers refer to *all* analysis as *conceptual analysis* even when the ostensible analysandum is not a concept but a proposition.)

By the same token, if we *neglect* to take into account knowledge acquired by analysis at a deeper level, we can preclude ourselves from acquiring certain sorts of knowledge about the propositions analyzed. This holds even *within* a given level. For instance, within level 1 — the level which leaves certain constituent propositions unanalyzed — if we analyze *(4.1)* merely to the point of recognizing it as the disjunction of two simpler propositions, we cannot thereby determine its modal status and hence cannot determine its truth-value either. If, however, we analyze it more deeply as involving the disjunction of two propositions one of which is the negation of the other, then we *can* — by analyzing the concepts of disjunction and negation — determine both its truth-value and its modal status. Likewise, if we analyze *(4.2)* merely to the point of recognizing it as a proposition which attributes the property of being necessarily true to the simpler proposition *(4.4)*, we can determine *(4.2)*'s modal status but not its truth-value: we can tell that it is noncontingent but not whether it is noncontingently true (necessarily true) or noncontingently false (necessarily false).[13] If, however, we analyze *(4.2)* more deeply, as involving the attribution of necessary truth to a proposition which itself is shown, by analysis, to be necessarily true, then we can tell its truth-value as well as its modal status: we can tell that it is necessarily true, not just that it is noncontingent. And again, if we analyze *(4.4)* in turn merely to the point of recognizing it as a proposition which attributes the property of being female to those items which have the property of being sisters, we cannot determine either its truth-value or its modal status. If, however, we analyze *(4.4)* more deeply, so as to reveal that the set of possible worlds in which the concept of being a sister has application to a given item is included within the set of possible worlds in which the concept of being female has application to the same item, we can then tell that *(4.4)* is — as we saw before — not just true but necessarily so.

The point we are making may be put more generally by saying that although analysis at the level of the Logic of Unanalyzed Propositions can reveal the modal status, or the modal status and the truth-value of certain propositions, these propositions are a proper subset of those whose modal status, or modal status and truth-value, can be determined by analysis at the level of the Logic of Unanalyzed Concepts (the Logic of Predicates); and the latter propositions are a proper subset of those whose modal status, or modal status and truth-value, can be determined by analysis at the level of the Logic of Analyzed Concepts.

The method of analysis, it is clear, is capable of yielding knowledge of the modal status of propositions, and in the case of noncontingent propositions often of the truth-value as well, wholly a priori, i.e., without need of any recourse to experience of how things stand in the actual world.

---

13. We show this in chapter 6 when we argue that possible-worlds analyses show that *all* attributions of modal status to propositions are noncontingent, i.e., either necessarily true or necessarily false. See pp. 333–36.

3.   THE PARADOX OF ANALYSIS

Despite what we have just said, it has seemed to some philosophers that analysis can *never* yield knowledge of anything that we do not already know. Indeed it is very easy to be beguiled by the so-called "Paradox of Analysis" into concluding that the method of analysis is either superfluous or productive of conceptual error.

Moore's problem

The paradox received its classic formulation in C. H. Langford's essay, "The Notion of Analysis in Moore's Philosophy":[14]

> Let us call what is to be analyzed the analysandum, and let us call that which does the analyzing the analysans. The analysis then states an appropriate relation of equivalence between the analysandum and the analysans. And the paradox of analysis is to the effect that, if the verbal expression representing the analysandum has the same meaning as the verbal expression representing the analysans, the analysis states a bare identity and is trivial; but if the two verbal expressions do not have the same meaning, the analysis is incorrect.

For instance — changing examples to one discussed by Moore — the analysis of the concept

(4.10)   being a brother

may be stated in some such way as the following:

(i)   "The concept of being a brother is identical with the concept of being a male sibling";

(ii)   "The propositional function 'x is a brother' is identical with the propositional function 'x is a male sibling' ";

or

(iii)   "To say that a person is a brother is the same thing as to say that that person is a male sibling."[15]

But no matter in which way one states the analysis — no matter what verbal expression one gives of the analysandum and the analysans — the paradox presents itself. If the proposition expressed by any of the sentences, (i), (ii), or (iii), is true, then it seems that the very same proposition may be expressed by saying

(iv)   "The concept of being a brother is identical with the concept of being a brother."

That is to say, if the analysis is correct then the proposition expressed by any of (i), (ii), or (iii) is identical with the proposition expressed by (iv). But (iv) — it is said — is "trivial" in the sense that it gives no information. Hence if any analysis of (4.10) is correct, it is trivial. And equally, of course, if it is not trivial then it is not correct.

14. Published in *The Philosophy of G.E. Moore*, pp. 321–41, esp. p. 323.

15. These three alternative ways of expressing the analysis are suggested by Moore in his "Reply to My Critics", *The Philosophy of G.E. Moore*, pp. 535–687n. Note that mode (ii) makes it clear that Moore, too, regards a concept as what is expressed by certain sorts of propositional function (i.e., "open sentence" as we earlier put it in chapter 2).

A Moorean solution

The paradox, it has been pointed out,[16] is a special case of the paradox of identity. How can *any* statement of identity, if true, be informative and non-trivial? Since the number 9 is identical with the number 3^2, how can the equation "$9 = 3^2$" be more informative than the trivial equation "$9 = 9$"?

A good many suggestions have been made as to how the paradox can be avoided.[17] Many of these are too lengthy for us to consider here. In any case our own preference is to follow up on some suggestions made by Moore in his "Reply" — suggestions which he himself did not quite see how to carry through:

> I think that, in order to explain the fact that, even if "To be a brother is the same thing as to be a male sibling" is true, yet nevertheless this statement is *not* the same as the statement "To be a brother is to be a brother", one *must* suppose that both statements are in *some* sense about the expressions used as well as about the concept of being a brother. But in *what* sense they are about the expressions used I cannot see clearly; and therefore I cannot give any clear solution to the puzzle. The two plain facts about the matter which it seems to me one must hold fast to are these: That if in making a given statement one is to be properly said to be "giving an analysis" of a *concept,* then (a) both *analysandum* and *analysans* must be *concepts,* and, if the analysis is a *correct* one, must, in some sense, be *the same concept,* and (b) that the *expression* used for the *analysandum* must be a different *expression* from that used for the *analysans* ... and a third may be added: namely this: (c) that the *expression* used for the *analysandum* must not only be *different* from that used for the *analysans,* but that they must differ in this way, namely. that the expression used for the *analysans* must *explicitly mention* concepts which are not explicitly mentioned by the expression used for the analysandum. ... And that the *method of combination* should be explicitly mentioned by the expression used for the *analysans* is, I think, also a necessary condition for the giving of an analysis.[18]

Now it seems to us that Moore is on the right track in insisting on conditions (a), (b), and (c) — and, of course, in adding as a fourth condition a specification of the method of combination (what we have called "propositional combination"). Where he went wrong, we suggest, was in his attempt to give these conditions a summary description by saying, at the outset, that "one must suppose that both statements [the informative one and the noninformative one] are in some sense *about* the expressions used as well as *about* the concept of being a brother" [our italics]. For once he had put it this way, the puzzle was for him — as indeed it would be for us — insoluble. He had already rejected the view — as we have — that a statement of analysis is about verbal expressions: "both *analysandum* and *analysans* must be concepts or propositions, *not* mere verbal expressions."[19] Little wonder that he could not see clearly in *what* sense the analysans is "about" the verbal expressions used. It is not "about" them in any sense whatever.

---

16. Arthur Pap, *Semantics and Necessary Truth,* New Haven, Yale University Press, 1958, p. 275.

17. Among the most interesting are those of Alonzo Church, "The Paradox of Analysis", *Journal of Symbolic Logic* (1946) pp. 132–3 (discussed critically by Pap in *Semantics and Necessary Truth,* pp. 276–279); Pap himself, *op. cit.;* and John L. Mackie, *Truth, Probability and Paradox,* Oxford, Clarendon Press, 1973, pp. 1–16.

18. *The Philosophy of G.E. Moore,* p. 666.

19. *Ibid,* p. 664.

The desiderata we have to keep in mind, if a solution is to be found, emerge more clearly when we compare the following three sentences:

> *(4.11)*   "The expression 'being a brother' expresses the same concept as (means the same as) the expression 'being a male sibling'."

> *(4.12)*   "Being a brother is identical with being a male sibling."

> *(4.13)*   "Being a brother is identical with being a brother."

The first thing to note is that these sentences are *not* all "about" the same thing. *(4.11)* is about the verbal expressions "being a brother" and "being a male sibling": it says of them that they express the same concept (or, as it is sometimes put, "mean the same"). *(4.12)* and *(4.13)*, however, are not about verbal expressions but about concepts. On this score, then, *(4.11)* fails to meet Moore's condition (a), whereas both *(4.12)* and *(4.13)* satisfy it. The second thing to note is that these sentences do *not* all express analyses. *(4.11)* fails again because, as Moore points out, it merely tells us that two expressions express the same concept without telling us what that concept is: it "could be completely understood by a person who had not the least idea of what either expression meant".[20] And *(4.13)* fails because it does not meet either of Moore's conditions (b) or (c). Sentence *(4.12)*, it is clear, is the only sentence which satisfies all three conditions, (a), (b), and (c) — and, for that matter, the fourth condition which concerns the method of combination as well. The third point to note is that these sentences do *not* all seem equally informative. Sentence *(4.11)* certainly gives us information, even though it is informative about words not about concepts. Sentence *(4.12) seems* to be equally informative; but the trouble is to see how it can be since, on the one hand, it is not about words but concepts, and on the other hand, it expresses the very same proposition as does *(4.13)* which plainly is not informative about anything at all.

The solution which eluded Moore, though he came very close to finding it, is really quite simple. It lies in recognizing that *a sentence can be informative about something which that sentence is not about* — or more particularly, that a sentence can give information about a verbal expression even when it is not *about* that verbal expression (does not *mention* it) but simply *uses* that verbal expression to say something about a concept. Thus although the sentence

> *(4.12)*   "Being a brother is identical with being a male sibling"

is about the concepts of being a brother and being a male sibling (it truly asserts their identity) and not about the verbal expressions "being a brother" and "being a male sibling" (which plainly are *not* identical), nonetheless this sentence *contains* the expressions "being a brother" and "being a male sibling" among its constituents; it *uses* these expressions to say something about the concepts of being a brother and being a male sibling; and, *in using them, it conveys information about the use of these expressions*, viz., the information that they may be used to express one and the same concept. If this is correct, we can then explain why it is that *(4.12)* seems just as informative as *(4.11)* even though it is not about what *(4.11)* is about. *(4.12)* is as informative as *(4.11)* because *(4.12) conveys* (or *shows*) what *(4.11) says*.[21] And we can also explain why it is that *(4.13)* seems totally

---

20. *The Philosophy of G.E. Moore*, p. 662.

21. The distinction between what sentence expresses (i.e., says) and what it conveys (i.e., shows) should be easily grasped at the intuitive level. It can, however, be explicated in strictly logical terms. To say that *(4.12) shows* that the expression "being a brother" expresses the same concept as the expression "being a male

uninformative even though it expresses exactly the same proposition as does *(4.12)*. For what *(4.13)* shows is *not* the same as what *(4.12)* shows. It conveys only that the expressions "being a brother" and "being a brother" may be used to express one and the same concept — which is not to convey any information at all. In short, *(4.12)* says what *(4.13)* says but does not show what *(4.13)* shows; and at the same time, *(4.12)* shows what *(4.11)* says but does not say what *(4.11)* says.[22] By virtue of what *(4.12)* says, it expresses identity; by virtue of what it shows, it is informative.

The above solution seems to be perfectly general insofar as it applies not only to the paradox of analysis but also to the wider paradoxes of identity. If the number 9 is identical with the number 3^2, how can the equation "$9 = 3^2$" be more informative than the trivial equation "$9 = 9$"? It would be informative, of course, to say that the numeral "9" expresses the very same number as does the expression "3^2". But, the equation "$9 = 3^2$" does not say this: it says something about numbers, not about the numerals or other devices which express them. Our solution applies straightforwardly. The equation "$9 = 3^2$" says just what the equation "$9 = 9$" says but does not show what "$9 = 9$" shows (viz., something uninformative). And at the same time, the equation "$9 = 3^2$" shows what is said when we utter the sentence "The numeral '9' expresses the very same number as does the expression '3^2'", but it does not say what this sentence says.

A correct statement of analysis (i.e., a sentence expressing a correct analysis), like any correct statement of identity, *can* tell us something which we do not already know: it can tell us that certain expressions express the same concept (number, proposition, or whatnot), not indeed by *saying* anything about them, but by *showing,* by the way we use them in the sentence expressing the analysis, that they express the same concept (number, proposition, or whatnot). The method of analysis has nothing to fear from the so-called "Paradox of Analysis". It is not a genuine paradox at all but a solved puzzle.

4.   THE METHOD OF INFERENCE

Inference, it may be recalled, may play a role both in the acquisition of experiential knowledge and in the acquisition of ratiocinative knowledge. Thus, we saw (in chapter 3) that experiential knowledge is knowledge gained either by direct appeal to experience or *by inference therefrom* while ratiocinative knowledge is knowledge gained by appeal to reason, e.g., by analysis of concepts or *by inference therefrom.* In each case, inference serves as a means whereby knowledge which has already been gained may be *expanded.*

But what exactly is inference? Does all inference yield knowledge? How can we be sure that any particular inference will yield knowledge rather than mere true belief, or, worse still, false belief? Only when we have answered these and other related questions will we be able fully to understand the role which inference plays in the science of logic.

---

sibling" is to say that the proposition (1), that a person who in uttering the sentence *(4.12)* expresses the necessary truth that being a brother is identical with being a male sibling, *implies* the proposition (2), that the expressions "being a brother" and "being a male sibling" express the same concept.

22. Students of Frege and the early Wittgenstein will recognize that this solution owes something to Frege's distinction between sense and reference and to Wittgenstein's distinction between what can be said and what can be shown. Nevertheless, Frege's distinction (which was, incidentally, invoked by Church in his attempt to solve the paradox) is not ours. Neither is Wittgenstein's. For Wittgenstein, what is said is always something contingent, what is shown is always something noncontingent, and what is said can never be shown. For us, by way of contrast, one can show something contingent and one can say it too. To repeat: *(4.12)* shows what *(4.11)* says, viz., something contingent about the uses of the expressions "being a brother" and "being a male sibling".

The nature of inference

We would do well, for a start, to get clear as to what we mean by "inference". Even so usually reliable a source as *Webster's New Collegiate Dictionary*[23] can get it wrong. One of the definitions offered there of "inference" is

> the act of passing from one proposition, statement or judgment considered
> as true to another whose truth is believed to follow from that of the former.

This will not do. In the first place, an act of inference need not be performed on a proposition which is "considered true".[24] It may be performed on a proposition whose truth-value is quite *unknown* to us; as, for example, when we test a hypothesis by drawing inferences from it and then checking to see whether the propositions inferred are true or false. And it may also be performed on a proposition which is considered, or even known, by us to be *false*; as, for example, when — in cross-examination — we demonstrate that a certain piece of testimony which we already believe or know to be false, really is false by showing that certain patently false propositions can validly be inferred from that testimony. The source of *New Collegiate*'s error is not too hard to diagnose. Ordinary usage, in most contexts, sanctions the insertion of the expression "the truth of" before the expression "the proposition that" (and equally before such expressions as "the statement that", "the belief that", etc.). Equally it sanctions the deletion of this expression. Strictly speaking, in most cases the presence of "the truth of" is redundant — except perhaps for emphasis or stylistic flourish — and also quite innocuous.[25] Thus, the two expressions "infer Q from P" and "infer *the truth of* Q from *the truth of* P" are synonymous. This allows us to say, for example, that the inference from the proposition that the moon is made of green cheese to the proposition that the moon is edible *is the very same inference* as the inference from *the truth of* the proposition that the moon is made of green cheese to *the truth of* the proposition that the moon is edible. The latter use of the expression "the truth of" loses its innocuousness only if, as was done in the *New Collegiate*, we not only suppose — as we should — that all cases of drawing an inference from a proposition P are cases of drawing an inference from the truth of a proposition P but take the further step of supposing — as we should not — that all such cases are cases of drawing an inference from a proposition P "considered as true". This further (inferential) step is quite unwarranted. If it is made, it obscures the important fact that inferences can be, and are, validly made from propositions regardless of their truth-values and regardless, too, of the beliefs, if any, that we happen to have about their truth-values. What is true is not that when one infers Q from P one believes P and, on that basis, believes Q, but rather that when one infers Q from P, then *if* one believes that P *then* one believes that Q. The first amendment that is called for, then, is the deletion of the words "considered as true".

The second amendment needed is the deletion of the word "another". Must the proposition inferred be different from the proposition from which it is inferred? Consider the inference from the proposition

---

23. Springfield, Mass., G. & C. Merriam Co., 1974.

24. *Webster's New Collegiate Dictionary* is not alone in making this first mistake. Philosophers have often made it, too. For instance, Peter Strawson tells us that in inferring or drawing conclusions "you know some facts or truths already, and are concerned to see what further information can be derived from them". (*Introduction to Logical Theory*, London, Methuen, 1952, p. 13.) Similarly, Stephen Barker defines it thus: "*Inference* is the mental act of reaching a conclusion from one's premises, the achievement of coming to believe the conclusion because one comes to see, or think one sees, that it follows logically from premises already accepted as true." (*The Elements of Logic*, New York, McGraw-Hill, 1965, p. 8.)

25. Note that the two sentences, "The book is on the table" and "It is true that there is a book on the table", express logically equivalent propositions. This case is generalizable for all sentences which express propositions.

> *(4.14)*   There are at least 10 marbles in the bag,

to the proposition,

> *(4.15)*   There are no fewer than 10 marbles in the bag.

Most of us would regard the inference from *(4.14)* to *(4.15)* as a valid one despite the fact that *(4.14)* is *the very same proposition* as *(4.15)*. Yet, if we were to take the *New Collegiate* definition seriously, we should have to deny that this is a valid inference on the grounds that it is not an inference at all. This time the source of error is likely to be found in custom, or metaphor, or both. It is undoubtedly true that the inferences we customarily draw lead us from one proposition, or set of propositions, to another (non-identical) proposition or set of propositions. And it is undoubtedly true that the seemingly apt metaphor of "passing from" — as it is employed in the above definition — encourages the belief that where there is inference there is passage, movement, or at least difference. But that which is customary need not — as the inference from *(4.14)* to *(4.15)* makes clear — be universal. And metaphor, when it is misleading, should be abandoned. In the present instance, neither custom nor metaphor should deter us from allowing the propriety of saying that a proposition may be inferred from itself.

The *New Collegiate* definition of "inference" can withstand the first of our suggested amendments. But with the attempt to make the second its syntax falls apart. We therefore offer the following preliminary definitions of "inference":

> "inference" = $_{df}$ "an act or a series of acts of reasoning which persons perform when, from the truth of a proposition or set of propositions, P, they conclude the truth of a proposition or set of propositions, Q".

Or again, capitalizing on the redundancy of "the truth of" in both of its occurrences in the above, more simply:

> "inference" = $_{df}$ "an act or a series of acts of reasoning which persons perform when, from a proposition or set of propositions, P, they conclude a proposition or set of propositions, Q".

Several points about our repaired definition deserve comment.

On the one hand, the repaired definition avoids the errors of the *New Collegiate*'s definition. The question is left open, as it should be, as to whether in any given inferece the proposition P, from which inference is made, is true (let alone considered, believed, or known to be true). And the question is also left open as to whether in any given inference, the proposition Q, which is inferred from some proposition P, is the same as or different from P. (Consistently, throughout this book, we use the letters "P" and "Q" as propositonal *variables* to stand for any propositions whatever, even one and the same proposition.)

On the other hand, our definition preserves the merits of that in the *New Collegiate*. It endorses, indeed further emphasizes, the fact that inference is a human act (or at least is an act of a conscious, reasoning creature). This fact is important insofar as, like any human act, the act of inference is subject to evaluation: in particular — and this is a point which we will develop shortly — it is an act which is sometimes performed well and sometimes performed badly.

In spite of these improvements, our preliminary definition is not wholly satisfactory. It neglects the fact that inference may properly be made from, and to, concepts as well as propositions. For example, we should want to say that we can make an inference from the concept of being a brother to the concept of being a male. To get it quite right, the definition of "inference" should be expanded by adding:

"or when, from a concept C_1 they conclude a concept C_2."

It should be emphasized that it is propositions and concepts from which, and to which, inferences are made. To be sure, it is perfectly proper to speak of inferring that someone is angry from his raised voice, red face, and violent gesticulations. But, on analysis, we should want to say that the inference in such a case still takes propositions or concepts as its point of departure — that, strictly speaking, it is not the raised voice, the red face, and violent gesticulations from which we make the inference but rather from the person's voice being raised, his face being red, his gesticulations being violent, etc. And a similar construction, we suggest, is to be placed upon such talk as that of "inferring from the evidence", "inferring from the silence", and so on. Indeed, our own earlier accounts of experiential and ratiocinative knowledge likewise admit of propositional reconstrual. When we say that experiential knowledge is knowledge gained either by direct experience or by inference therefrom, we mean that it is knowledge gained by experience either by direct experience or from *propositions* known thereby. And similarly, when we say that ratiocinative knowledge is knowledge gained, for example, by analysis of concepts or by inference therefrom, we mean it is knowledge gained, for example, by analysis of concepts or by inference from *propositions* known thereby.

We are all probably aware of the fact — to which our definition of "inference" gives due recognition — that inference is a practical human activity, that some of us are better at it than others, and that even the most skillful inferrers do not always draw their inferences unerringly. In short, we recognize that some inferences are "good" (or, as we shall prefer to say, *valid*) while others are "bad" (or, as we shall prefer to say, *invalid*).

But what is it for an inference to be valid as opposed to invalid? How can we be sure that any given inference is valid rather than invalid? And how, in practice, can we proceed so as to maximize inferential acuity and minimize inferential error?

Valid and invalid propositional inferences

The question as to how valid inferences differ from invalid ones is primarily a logical one. Not surprisingly, its answer may be obtained, ratiocinatively, by reflecting on the very definition of "inference". Since propositional inferences are acts which persons perform when from a proposition or set of propositions P, they conclude a proposition, or set of propositions Q, any inference from P to Q will be a valid one only if Q follows from P, and will be an invalid one only if Q does *not* follow from P (chapter 1, p. 32). Sharpening up this answer in definitional form we have:

> "The immediate inference from P to Q is valid" $=_{df}$ "Q is inferred solely from P and Q follows from P"

and

> "the immediate inference from P to Q is invalid" $=_{df}$ "Q is inferred solely from P and Q does not follow from P".

Some inferences, however, are not immediate: one infers P from Q, not solely from P, but through the mediation of some other proposition or propositions. Thus we have:

> "The mediate inference from P to Q is valid" $=_{df}$ "Q is inferred from P through a *sequence* of immediate inferences each of which is valid"

and

> "the mediate inference from P to Q is invalid" $=_{df}$ "Q is inferred from P through a *sequence* of immediate inferences one or more of which is invalid".

Now it is important to note that there is not just one notion of what it is for Q to follow from P: there is a broad notion and there is a narrow one. In the narrow sense of the word, when we say that Q follows from P we mean that Q *follows necessarily* from P. In the broad sense of the word, when we say that Q follows from P we mean that Q *follows probably* from P. And according to whether we choose to interpret the expression "follows from" in one way or the other, the expressions "valid" and "invalid", as they occur in the above definitions of valid and invalid inference, may themselves be construed either narrowly or broadly.

The inference from P to Q is said to be *deductively valid* when Q follows in the narrow sense, i.e., necessarily, from P. It is in this narrow sense of "follows from" that we were using the expression when, in chapter 1 (p. 31), we said that the relation of following from is the converse of the relation of implication. Thus the inference from P to Q is deductively valid just when P *implies* Q.

The inference from P to Q is said to be *inductively valid* when Q follows in the broad sense, i.e., follows probably, from P (or, conversely, when P *probabilifies* Q).

Hitherto we have not had occasion to use the expressions "follows from" and "valid" in any but their narrow, deductive senses. The broader, inductive senses of these words will be discussed more fully in chapter 6. There we shall see that these broader notions, like their narrower counterparts, can be defined in terms of the notion of *possible worlds* and hence that the inductive relation of *probabilification*, like its deductive cousin, *implication*, is a *modal* notion.[26] For the most part, however, our concern in this book is with deductive logic, with deductive validity, with following necessarily and its converse, implication. Accordingly, unless express notice is given to the contrary, we shall *continue* to use words like "logic", "validity", and "follows from" in their narrow, deductive senses while occasionally adding the qualifier "deductive" by way of reminder.

Now it is all very well to be told what logical properties an inference must have in order for that inference to be valid. It is quite another matter to be able to *ascertain* whether any particular inference has those logical properties. How can this be done?

Determining the validity of inferences: the problem of justification

Many philosophers who would unhesitatingly answer the logical question about the nature of validity as we have express puzzlement — even concern — about how this further epistemic question should be answered.

The problem of justifying any claim that an inference is *inductively* valid is notoriously difficult. Ever since it received its classic formulation in the writings of David Hume,[27] the problem of induction has perplexed many and even haunted some. It comes in many guises. How can we be sure that the so-called 'laws of probability' will not change? Why, if at all, is it reasonable to employ certain inductive rules of inference? And so on. There seems not yet to be any generally accepted solution to this problem (or rather, this nest of problems).[28]

---

26. Roughly, P *probabilifies* Q if *most* of the possible worlds in which P is true (if any) are worlds in which Q is true. By way of contrast, of course, P *implies* Q if and only if *all* of the possible worlds in which P is true (if any) are also worlds in which Q is true.

27. See David Hume, *A Treatise of Human Nature,* ed. L.A. Selby-Bigge, Oxford, Clarendon Press, 1888, book I, part 3, and *An Enquiry Concerning Human Understanding,* ed. Eric Steinberg, Indianapolis, Hackett Publishing Co., 1977, especially sect. 4. A recent restatement is to be found in Nelson Goodman's *Fact, Fiction, and Forecast,* 3rd ed., Indianapolis, Hackett Publishing Co., 1979, chapters 3 and 4.

28. For a succinct review of the problem and various attempts at its solution, see Max Black's article, "Induction", in the *Encyclopedia of Philosophy,* ed. Paul Edwards, London, Macmillan, 1967, vol. 4, pp. 169–181.

Likewise, the problem of how we can ever justify the claim that an inference is *deductively* valid has seemed to some both a problem and a source of potential philosophical embarrassment. The range of proffered solutions to a large extent parallels that for the problem of induction. Thus, as Nelson Goodman has pointed out in his *Fact, Fiction, and Forecast*,[29] some philosophers have thought that rules of deductive logic can be justified by appeal to higher-order rules, principles or axioms; some have thought that they are grounded in the very nature of the human mind; and some, Goodman among them, have thought that they can be justified pragmatically, as it were, in terms of their efficacy in leading us to conclusions which we find acceptable.

The solution seems, in principle at least, to be fairly straightforward. If, as we have said, an inference from P to Q is deductively valid just when P implies Q, we can *justify* the claim that an inference from P to Q is deductively valid simply by *justifying* the claim that P implies Q. And that is something which, so far as we know, can be done in one way and one way only, viz., a priori, by *analyzing* the conditions for the application of the concepts involved in the propositions concerned. For instance, we can justify the so-called Rule of Simplification, which says that from the assertion of P and Q one may validly infer P, by showing that the corresponding statement of implication, viz., that the proposition that P and Q are true *implies* the proposition that P is true, is analytically true. To be sure, analysis does have its limits. Some noncontingent propositions, including statements of implication, seem to resist all attempts at analytical justification; and even in cases where analytical knowledge can be gained it is by no means always gained easily. To the extent that there are limits to our ability to determine, by analysis, whether or not a proposition P implies a proposition Q, there will be limits also to our ability to determine whether the inference from P to Q is deductively valid. But — and this is the important point — the limits to the latter do not exceed the limits to the former. The problem of justifying inference is not endemic: it does not apply to inferences per se but to those only for which the corresponding statements of implication cannot be justified by analysis.[30] Of course, the question can always be raised as to how recourse to the method of analysis is itself to be justified. But that, it is clear, is another question. In any case, the fact is that, despite any deep doubts that may linger about the ultimate justification of inference, analysis, or whatnot, there is a large measure of agreement over which inferences are deductively valid and which are not; and, when pressed to justify these logical appraisals, persons standardly take recourse to analytical methods.

Let us, then, agree that we can and do often justify claims that our inferences are deductively valid and that we can do this in the last resort, by analyzing the propositions from which and to which our inferences are made to see whether the logical relation of implication really does hold between them.

Even so, a problem remains. Although analysis is the ultimate guarantor of inferential validity, it does not serve as a *practical* guide whereby we can direct our inferential activity. Compare the predicament of a would-be mountain climber who knows what it is to be atop a mountain, and who knows how — if called upon — he would justify his claim to have climbed it, but who still wants to know: How do I get there from here (without a slip)? The problem remaining for a would-be inferrer, after he has been told what it is for an inference to be valid and how — if called upon — he might justify his claim to have performed a valid inference, may be expressed in the same way: How do I get there from here (without a slip)? What is required, in each case, is a set of principles or rules for achieving the desired end. In the case of the would-be mountain climber, the rules are rules of climbing and will be treated under such headings as "Belaying", "Rappelling", and the like.

---

29. pp. 63–64.

30. Note that it does not follow from anything which we have said that a similar solution can be found for the problem of justifying claims that certain inferences are inductively valid. On this question the controversy is too large for us to pursue.

In the case of the would-be inferrer, the rules are rules of inference and go by such names as "Simplification", "Modus Ponens", and the like.

Rules of inference

The formulation of deductively valid rules of inference has long been a standard occupation of logicians. Needless to say, sound inferential practice did not have to await the formulation of such rules. Well before Aristotle first formulated the rules of syllogistic reasoning, persons constructed valid syllogisms. And even today, countless persons perform countless valid inferences each day in complete ignorance of the rules that contemporary logic affords. The essential point about rules of inference is not that we must *know* them in order that we might perform our inferences validly, but only that when we do perform our inferences they must accord with these rules if they are to be valid. Moreover, if we *do* know them, our inferential performances are — like those of the mountain climber who knows the rules for belaying, rapelling, etc. — likely to be improved. Knowledge of the rules of valid inference helps — as we put it earlier — to maximize inferential acuity and minimize inferential error. Knowledge of rules of valid inference can help us to infer from a given proposition only what follows from that proposition.

Now it is a common feature of all rules — rules of inference included — that they admit of universal application. By this we do not mean that rules necessarily have more than one actual instance of application; we mean only that rules necessarily have more than one *possible* instance of application. It makes no sense to speak of a rule which *can* apply to one case only.

It is, of course, just because rules are universal, and admit of application to indefinitely many instances, that they have the pragmatic value which logically minded persons have always cherished from Aristotle to the present day. In order to ascertain whether any *particular* inference that we want to make or have already made is valid or not, we need not undertake the painstaking and often difficult business of deeply *analyzing* the particular premises and conclusion that feature in that inference, checking to see whether there are any possible worlds in which those premises are true while that conclusion is false, so as to determine whether those particular premises imply that particular conclusion. We need to analyze the propositions only to the extent that we can ascertain whether or not that particular inference is an instance which accords with one of those general rules of inference which logicians have *antecedently certified*, by analysis, as valid.

As examples of some of the most commonly invoked rules of inference we cite a handful from the Logic of Unanalyzed Propositions.

Conjunction:

From the proposition P and the proposition Q, one may validly infer the conjunction of P and Q.

[Example of application: Nixon knew about Watergate. Agnew knew about Watergate.   ∴ Nixon knew about Watergate and Agnew knew about Watergate.]

Simplification:

From the conjunction of P and Q, one may validly infer the proposition P.

[Example of application: Mao Tse-Tung was an opponent of Chiang-Kai-Shek and Chou-En-Lai was an opponent of Chiang-Kai-Shek.   ∴ Mao Tse-Tung was an opponent of Chiang-Kai-Shek.]

Identity:

> From the proposition P, one may validly infer the proposition P.[31]

> [Example of application: It is going to rain.   ∴ It is going to rain.]

Addition:

> From the proposition P, one may validly infer the disjunction of P with Q.

> [Example of application: John Doe will have heard the news.   ∴ Either John Doe will have heard the news or Sue will have heard the news.]

Transposition (sometimes known as *Contraposition*):

> From the proposition that if P then Q, one may validly infer that if it is not the case that Q then it is not the case that P.

> [Example of application: If John is married to Sue then John is Sue's husband. ∴ If it is not the case that John is Sue's husband, then it is not the case that John is married to Sue.]

Modus Ponens:

> From the proposition that if P then Q and the proposition P, one may validly infer the proposition Q.

> [Example of application: If all caged animals are neurotic then Felix is neurotic. All caged animals *are* neurotic.   ∴ Felix is neurotic.]

Modus Tollens:

> From the proposition that if P then Q and the proposition that Q is false, one may validly infer the proposition that P is false.

> [Example of application: If all caged animals are neurotic then Felix is neurotic. Felix is *not* neurotic.   . . Not all caged animals are neurotic.]

Hypothetical Syllogism (also known as the *Chain Rule*):

> From the proposition that if P then Q and the proposition that if Q then R, one may validly infer the proposition that if P then R.

> [Example of application: If it rains the snow will melt. If the snow melts the World Cup slalom will be cancelled.   ∴ If it rains the World Cup slalom will be cancelled.]

Disjunctive Syllogism:

> From the proposition that either P or Q and the proposition that P is false, one may validly infer Q.

---

31. The recognition that Identity is a valid rule of inference should dispel any lingering doubts about our criticism of the definition given of "inference" in *Webster's New Collegiate Dictionary.*

[Example of application: Either John Doe will have heard the news or Sue will have heard the news. ·John Doe will not have heard the news.   ∴ Sue will have heard the news.]

Constructive Dilemma:

From the three propositions, that if P then Q, that if R then S, and that either P or R, one may validly infer the proposition that either Q or S.

[Example of application: If Thoeni wins the slalom an Italian will win the World Cup. If Stenmark wins the slalom a Swede will win the World Cup. Either Thoeni or Stenmark will win the slalom.   ∴ Either an Italian or a Swede will win the World Cup.]

What kind of rule is a rule of inference?

The class of rules, of whatever kind, can be subdivided into two mutually exclusive and jointly exhaustive subclasses: the class of rules which are propositions and the class of rules which are **nonpropositions. The class of nonpropositional rules includes such rules as "Keep off the grass" and "Do not drink and drive." Of such rules, it makes no sense to ask whether they are true or false. The concepts of truth and falsity do not apply to such entities.**[32] The class of propositional rules includes rules such as "All residents earning a gross annual income in excess of $1,500 are required to file an income tax return." Of this latter rule, it *is* perfectly proper to ask whether it is true or not.

Are rules of inference propositional or nonpropositional ones? Both what we have already said of inference rules and a perusal of the examples just given should make the answer clear. Inference rules are *propositions,* and it is proper to ask of alleged or proffered inference rules whether they are true or false. Consider, for example, the Rule of Simplification: from P and Q one may validly infer P. Whatever else one might wish to say of this rule, one thing which cannot be gainsaid is that it is *true.*

Although inference rules are undoubtedly *useful,* the justification of a particular inference rule does not lie in citing its utility; it lies *only* in an a priori demonstration of its *truth.*

To say that valid inference rules are *true* is to say something about their logical status. It is not to describe the manner in which they may be *used* in making inferences. This latter matter requires that we look at another way of classifying rules.

The class of all rules, of whatever kind, may be subdivided into a second set of mutually exclusively and jointly exhaustive subclasses: the class of rules which are directives and the class of rules which are nondirectives. Among the directive propositional rules are to be found such rules as "To multiply a number by eleven, first multiply that number by ten and then add the product to the original number." Among the nondirective propositional rules are to be found such rules as "On the anniversary date of the mortgage, the mortgagor may make payments in multiples of $1,000 against the principal balance." Of both of these kinds of propositional rules we can properly inquire as to their truth-values. But there is a difference between them: the former may be viewed as a 'recipe'; the latter not. The former kind of rule tells us explicitly how to proceed in a given circumstance; it outlines an explicit series of steps to be followed. The latter is not a recipe; it merely tells us what *may* be done, i.e., what is permitted, in a certain circumstance.

---

32. This is not to say, of course, that there might not be propositions which 'correspond' to these rules, such propositions as, e.g., that the city's bylaws forbid one's walking on the grass, or that there is a $1,000 fine for drinking and driving, etc.

Now which of these two kinds of rules are rules of inference? Are they recipes, or do they merely state what it is logically permissible to do?

A brief examination of the foregoing list of inference rules provides an answer. Inference rules are not recipes; each tell us only that some particular inference is permitted; none tells us which particular inference we should make.

Thus it turns out that talk of 'following' an inference rule is entirely inappropriate. One can 'follow' a set of recipes; but inference rules are not recipes.

One cannot 'follow' a set of inference rules in order to make a valid inference. Rather it is that one reasons and makes inferences, and if the inferences are valid, then they are properly said to *accord with* valid rules of inference.

To every valid inference there corresponds a valid rule of inference with which that inference accords. But this is not to say that to every valid inference there corresponds a *known* valid rule of inference. Inferences may be valid without our knowing that they are and without our being able to cite a known valid inference rule with which they accord.

Inference and the expansion of knowledge

That the making of a valid inference may lead us to knowledge of propositions which we did not previously know is fairly obvious. What is not obvious, however, is precisely *why* this is so, under what *conditions* it is so, and what *sort* of knowledge valid inference-making can yield.

The class of all cases in which we make a valid inference from a proposition P to a proposition Q may be divided into two subclasses:

> (1)   the cases in which we make the inference and *know* that the proposition P is true;

> (2)   the cases in which we make the inference and do *not* know that the proposition P is true.

Consider, first, the cases in which we validly infer Q from P and know P to be true. Now we have already seen, from our discussion of the nature of knowledge (chapter 3, section 2), that if a proposition P is known to be true then it *is* true. And we have also seen, from our discussion of the nature of valid inference (earlier in this section), that if we validly infer Q from P where P is true, then Q is true. It follows, then, that if we validly infer Q from P where P is known to be true, Q is *true.* But does it also follow, in these circumstances, that Q will be *known* to be true? And if not, what further conditions need to be satisfied in order for Q to be known?

First let us remind ourselves of the four conditions which we found, by analysis, to be separately necessary and jointly sufficient for the application of the concept of knowledge: we can be said to know P if and only if P is *true,* we *believe* that P is true, our belief that P is true is *justified,* and this justified true belief is *indefeasible.* It will help, for illustrative purposes, if we pursue our inquiry in terms of an example.

Let P be the (compound) proposition

> *(4.16)*   If it rains the snow will melt, and if the snow melts the World Cup slalom will be cancelled

and let Q be the (compound) proposition

> *(4.17)*   If it rains, the World Cup slalom will be cancelled.

Clearly, the immediate inference from *(4.16)* is (deductively) valid. It accords with the rule of inference which we called Hypothetical Syllogism. Suppose that we *know (4.16)* is true. Does it follow, when we validly infer *(4.17)* from *(4.16)*, that we *know (4.17)* to be true?

Well, in the first place, it is easy to show that *(4.17)* satisfies the first condition for its being known, viz., that *(4.17)* is *true*. This follows from the fact that since, by hypothesis, *(4.16)* is known to be true, *(4.16)* is true, together with the fact that if *(4.16)* is true and *(4.17)* is validly inferred from *(4.16)* — as it is — then *(4.17)* is true. Secondly, *(4.17)* will be *believed* to be true. Two conditions suffice for our believing *(4.17)*: one, that we infer *(4.17)* from a proposition P; two, that we believe P to be true. Both these conditions are satisfied when we infer *(4.17)* from *(4.16)*. As may be recalled, although we disagreed with the view that inference is always from believed propositions to believed propositions, we subscribe to the view that when inference *is* made from a proposition which is believed to be true, then this inferred proposition is also believed to be true. Thirdly, our true belief in *(4.17)* will be *justified*. It is justified insofar as it accords with the antecedently certified rule of Hypothetical Syllogism. Logical appeal of this kind counts as a paradigm of justification.

Up to this point we have shown that the first three of the four necessary conditions for knowing Q are satisfied. But is the indefeasibility condition also satisfied? One thing that is clear is this: that since *(4.17)* follows from *(4.16)* and *(4.17)* is true, there cannot be any true proposition R, belief in which would equally justify our concluding that *(4.17)* is false. For in order that we should be equally justified in concluding that *(4.17)* is false on the basis of a belief in R, R would not only have to be true but be such that the falsity of *(4.17)* follows from R. But this is impossible. There cannot be any two *true* propositions, from one of which it follows that *(4.17)* is true while from the other of which it follows that *(4.17)* is false. However, this does not entitle us to conclude that the indefeasibility condition is satisfied. In order that it should be satisfied there must not be any true proposition R, belief in which would even *undermine* the belief that *(4.17)* is true. Suppose, then, that R is the proposition that we came to make the valid inference from *(4.16)* to *(4.17)*, not on the grounds that it accords with the Rule of Hypothetical Syllogism, but on the mistaken grounds of a belief that it accords with the Rule of Modus Ponens. And suppose, further, that R is true. Then, if we were to *believe* that R is true, i.e., were to believe that our inference from *(4.16)* to *(4.17)* has been made on mistaken grounds, our belief in the truth of *(4.17)* *would* be undermined. Hence, the defeasibility condition would not, in the circumstances envisaged, be automatically satisfied.

Plainly, then, we are not entitled to conclude that in the case where we make a valid inference from P to Q and know P to be true we will also know Q to be true. But we *are* entitled to conclude that in such a case we will know Q to be true *provided that* the defeasibility condition happens also to be satisfied.

The conclusion we have just established about all cases of kind (1) is, of course, perfectly general. It matters not *how* we obtained knowledge of P in the first instance, whether experientially or ratiocinatively. It is worth noting, however, that from our earlier definitions of "experiential knowledge" and "ratiocinative knowledge" it follows that if we know Q by validly inferring it from P where P is known experientially then Q will also be known experientially; whereas if we know Q by validly inferring it from P where P is known ratiocinatively, then Q will also be known ratiocinatively.[33]

Before turning to the examination of cases of kind (2) — cases in which we validly infer Q from P and do *not* know that P is true — in order to determine what sort of knowledge, if any, such

---

33. This is not to suggest, however, that Q (like P) might not be known in both ways. Our argument, of chapter 3, pp. 168–170, showed that some noncontingent propositions can be known in both ways.

inference may yield, it is worth observing that this kind of case covers a variety of possibilities. In saying that we do not know that P is true we are allowing the possibility of our merely believing, but not knowing, that P is true; the possibility of our not having the faintest idea whether P is true or not; the possibility of our believing, but not knowing, that P is false; the possibility of our knowing that P is false; and even the possibility of our knowing that P is necessarily false. The question before us is simply whether in any of these cases, our validly inferring Q from P can yield knowledge, and, if so, knowledge of what.

On first hearing the question we may be inclined to answer: No — that mere inference by itself cannot yield knowledge, i.e., that inference cannot yield knowledge unless it is inference from a proposition, or propositions, which are already known. But this, we shall now try to show, would be a mistake.

Our answer will be, to the contrary, that in cases of kind (2), valid inference may indeed yield knowledge: knowledge not, perhaps, of the truth of Q; but knowledge, rather, of the conditional proposition that if P is true then Q is true.[34]

Once more, for illustrative purposes, we shall argue the case in terms of a particular (arbitrarily chosen) example. This time, for the sake of variety, let P be the (compound) proposition

> (4.18) If all caged animals are neurotic then Felix is neurotic; and all caged animals are neurotic

and let Q be the (simple) proposition

> (4.19) Felix is neurotic.

Clearly, the immediate inference from (4.18) to (4.19) is (deductively) valid. It accords with the rule of inference which we called Modus Ponens. Suppose that the truth of (4.18) is not known (perhaps because we do not know the truth of one of its conjuncts, viz., that all caged animals are neurotic). Under what conditions, when we validly infer (4.19) from (4.18), does it follow that we *know* the truth of the proposition that if (4.18) is true then (4.19) is true?

Our discussion goes along the same broad lines as that given for cases of kind (1). In the first place, the proposition that if (4.18) is true then (4.19) is true is a *true* proposition. This, as already noted, follows trivially from the fact that (4.19) may validly be inferred from (4.18). Secondly, the proposition that if (4.18) is true then (4.19) is true, will be *believed* to be true. This follows from the fact that when we infer (4.19) from (4.18) we *conclude* that (4.19) is true if (4.18) is true, which is — *inter alia* — to *believe* that (4.19) is true if (4.18) is true. Thirdly, our true belief that if (4.18) is true then (4.19) is true will be *justified*. It is justified by appeal to a valid rule, viz., Modus Ponens, with which the inference accords. But will the inference be indefeasibly justified? It may be, but it need not. Suppose someone who makes this inference by appeal to Modus Ponens does so fortuitously — e.g., not out of an understanding that this rule sanctions this particular inference, but purely out of a habit to invoke this particular rule, a habit which is exercised more often incorrectly than correctly. In such circumstances the indefeasibility condition would not be satisfied and we would want to say that one's justified true belief in the conditional proposition that if (4.18) then (4.19) ·was *not* knowledge. Nonetheless, in cases of kind (2), the indefeasibility condition may, equally well, *be* satisfied. One's inference may well proceed, not from mere habit of

---

34. Note that we are not saying that where Q is validly inferred from P then, independently of whether or not we know P to be true, it follows that if P is true then Q is true. To say that is to say something true but — in the light of the intimate connection between the notions of validity and of implication — it is also rather trivial. Our thesis is the stronger one that (subject to one proviso) where Q is validly inferred from P then, independently of whether or not we know P to be true, it follows that we *know* that if P is true then Q is true.

thought, but from genuine understanding — and if so, then it is possible that one should gain knowledge.

More generally, we may conclude, from our examination of this case, that our validly making an immediate inference to a proposition Q, from a proposition P, in circumstances in which it is possible to cite an antecedently certified rule of inference, is by itself sufficient — provided the defeasibility condition is satisfied — to give us knowledge of the truth of the conditional proposition that if P is true then Q is true. This conclusion, it should be noted, also holds for inferences of kind (1).

The *sort* of knowledge obtained in cases of kind (2) is importantly different from that obtained in cases of kind (1). Whereas in cases of kind (1) the knowledge obtained of Q may be *either* experiential (where P is known experientially) *or* ratiocinative (where P is known ratiocinatively), and the knowledge of the conditional proposition that if P is true then Q is true is likewise ratiocinative, the knowledge obtained in cases of kind (2) is *always ratiocinative,* i.e., is always obtained solely by the exercise of one's own powers of reason, and hence is *always* a priori.[35]

But whichever kind of valid inference is involved, one thing is clear: the making of a valid inference may lead us to knowledge of the truth of propositions which we did not previously know to be true; and it can do this with respect to any field of human knowledge whatever, or with respect to propositions belonging to any subject matter whatever.[36]

EXERCISES

For each of the following say with which rule of inference it accords.

1. *Eva is a bank director. Joseph is a lawyer. ∴ Eva is a bank director and Joseph is a lawyer.*

2. *Harry is a judge. ∴ Harry is a judge or Harry is a former district attorney.*

3. *If Paul is older than Lorna then Lorna isn't ahead of him in school. Paul is older than Lorna. ∴ Lorna isn't ahead of Paul in school.*

---

35. It may be wondered, at this point, why we have assigned inference a subsidiary role in our account of how ratiocinative (and hence a priori) knowledge can be gained. Recall that we defined ratiocinative knowledge as knowledge obtainable "by appeal to reason, e.g., by analysis of concepts or by inference therefrom". Why, it may be asked, the word "therefrom"? Have we not just shown that the making of a deductively valid inference can, all by itself, yield knowledge of certain propositions? Why, then, do we not count inference and analysis as *two,* independent, means to ratiocinative knowledge? The answer lies in the fact that we wish to accord analysis a certain *epistemic primacy* which — on our view — inference does not possess. By this we mean that, if our earlier arguments are sound, it is sound analysis which is the ultimate guarantor of the validity of inferences, not the validity of inferences which is the ultimate guarantor of sound analysis. To be sure, we must, in the course of analyzing a concept or proposition, make inferences; and these inferences, if the analysis is to be sound, must be valid. To that extent, analysis and inference go hand-in-hand and will stand or fall together (as sources of ratiocinative knowledge). But it seems to us that there is a very good sense in which, when it comes to matters of justification, the method of analysis serves to justify the method of inference, not the other way around. If we are wrong about this, our definition of ratiocinative knowledge can easily be repaired by the simple expedient of dropping the word "therefrom".

36. Although the arguments have been conducted by means of examples of immediate inferences, our conclusions can be generalized to the case of mediate inferences as well.

4. *If Martin is older than Jennifer, then Jennifer is older than Jonathan. If Jennifer is older than Jonathan, then Jonathan is older than Diane. ∴. If Martin is older than Jennifer, then Jonathan is older than Diane.*

5. *If it is necessary that all aunts are females then it is possible that all aunts are females. It is necessary that all aunts are females.   ∴. It is possible that all aunts are females.*

5.   INFERENCE WITHIN THE SCIENCE OF LOGIC

Among the various uses of rules of inference are their uses in *deductive systems*. By a "deductive system" we mean a body of proposition-expressing sentences or formulae which is systematized by means of certified deductively valid rules of inference in such a way as to display logical interconnections between its various items. Although deductive systems can be constructed within fields other than logic — notably mathematics (Euclid's *Elements* provides the first known example of a deductive system) and parts of physics — it is within the science of logic (sometimes called "the science of inference") that they have their purest form. Most commonly, deductive systems are either *axiomatic systems* or *natural deduction systems*. Our aim, in what follows, will be first to show how these two kinds of deductive systems may be employed within *logic* and then to show how their employment therein can lead to the systematic expansion of *logical knowledge*.

Axiomatic systems for truth-functional propositional logic[37] and predicate logic were first constructed by Frege in his *Begriffsschrift* (1879) and developed more fully by Whitehead and Russell in their *Principia Mathematica* (3 vols., 1910–1913). The construction of axiomatic systems for modal propositional logic was first essayed by C. I. Lewis in his *Survey of Symbolic Logic* (1918) and then developed more fully in his *Symbolic Logic* (coauthored with C. H. Langford, 1932). It is to one of the systems offered in the latter book, the system known as S5, that we turn for illustrative purposes. We have chosen the axiomatization of a *modal* logic for reasons of principle, having to do with the philosophical standpoint of this book. Since logic is the study of modal properties and relations, only a *modal* logic can be expected to do philosophical justice to the subject of logic. We have chosen S5, from among the several systems which Lewis developed (and the numerous systems which others have developed), because it seems to us, as to many others, that it is the 'strongest' philosophically defensible system of propositional modal logic, insofar as every other modal logic which subsumes S5 contains theses which seem to us philosophically indefensible as explications of implication, consistency, possibility, necessity, etc.[38]

Inference within axiomatic systems: the example of S5

Perhaps the first thing to note is that although S5, like any other axiomatic system, could in principle be constructed solely with the use of expressions in a *natural language* such as English, no axiomatic system ever is thus constructed. Rather, in S5, as in all other axiomatic systems, recourse is taken to a *symbolic language*[39] in terms of which the truths belonging to the subject matter

---

37. What it is for a logic to be truth-functional will be explained in detail in chapter 5. Roughly, a propositional logic is truth-functional if the truth-values of its compound propositions are determined by, or a function of, the truth-values of its unanalyzed constituent propositions.

38. For a lengthy discussion of its defensibility, see W. and M. Kneale, *The Development of Logic*, Oxford, Clarendon Press, 1962, pp. 548–568.

39. There are several reasons why recourse is invariably taken to symbolism. One is precisely that which

concerned may be expressed, while the use of natural language is restricted to our descriptions of how the truths of that subject matter may initially be expressed and subsequently generated. We call the symbolic language in terms of which the truths of the system are expressed the *object-language* of the system, and the language, in terms of which we talk about expressions in the symbolic object-language, the *meta-language* of the system.

We commence our sketch of S5 by using English as our meta-language in order to describe the *axiomatic basis* of that system. An axiomatic basis for S5[40] comprises:

(a)   A list of the *symbolic vocabulary* to be employed in the object-language. Some of the symbols are taken as undefined or "primitive" while others are defined. Thus we may list as our primitive symbols:

"P", "Q", "R", etc. (propositional symbols)

"$\sim$", "$\cdot$" (symbols for the concepts of negation and conjunction, respectively)

"$\Diamond$" (symbol for the concept of logical possibility)

and go on to define further symbols thus:

"$(P \vee Q)$" $=_{df}$ "$\sim(\sim P \cdot \sim Q)$"

"$(P \supset Q)$" $=_{df}$ "$\sim(P \cdot \sim Q)$"

"$(P \equiv Q)$" $=_{df}$ "$((P \supset Q) \cdot (Q \supset P))$"

"$\square P$" $=_{df}$ "$\sim \Diamond \sim P$"

"$(P \rightarrow Q)$" $=_{df}$ "$\sim \Diamond(P \cdot \sim Q)$"

"$(P \leftrightarrow Q)$" $=_{df}$ "$((P \rightarrow Q) \cdot (Q \rightarrow P))$"[41]

---

has led us, increasingly throughout this book, to use symbols. What one wants to say may thereby be expressed more succinctly and unambiguously. Another is that artificially introduced symbols are usually free from the disease of association-of-ideas — the disease which usually infects our uses of expressions in natural languages and bedevils the inferences which we try to make in terms of them.

40. We here take some liberties with Lewis' account by simplifying and employing — in some cases — different symbols and terminology.

41. The symbols "$\cdot$" (for conjunction), "$\vee$" (for disjunction), "$\supset$" (for material conditionality), and "$\equiv$" (for material biconditionality) deserve comment. Together with the symbol "$\sim$" (for negation) they compromise the standard repertoire of truth-functional symbols. The concepts of negation, conjunction, and disjunction have already been defined; but a brief reminder is in order. The *negation* of a given proposition is true in all those possible worlds (if any) in which that proposition is false, and false in all those possible worlds (if any) in which that proposition is true. The relation of *conjunction* hold between two propositions in all those possible worlds (if any) in which both are true. The relation of *disjunction* holds between two propositions in all those possible worlds (if any) in which at least one of them is true. The concepts of material conditionality and material biconditionality are readily definable along the lines of Lewis' definitions. Thus we shall say that the relation of *material conditionality* holds between P and Q in all those possible worlds (if any) in which it is

(b)   A set of *formation rules*. These are, in effect, rules of grammar for the symbolic language being constructed — rules, that is, which determine which formulae constructed out of the symbolic vocabulary are to count as grammatical, i.e., *well-formed formulae* (wffs), and which are to count as ungrammatical, i.e., *not well-formed*. The formation rules of the system S5 are:

R1:   Any propositional symbol standing alone is a wff.

R2:   If α is a wff, so is $\sim\alpha$.[42]

R3:   If α is a wff, so is $\Diamond\alpha$.

R4:   If α and β are wffs, so is $(\alpha \cdot \beta)$.

(We do not need to give formation-rules for wffs involving the defined symbols since these are effectively provided by the definitions for the introduction of these symbols.) By successive applications of these rules we can generate all and only the well-formed formulae of our symbolic language.

(c)   A selected set of wffs, known as *axioms*. A great deal of care usually goes into selecting, from among the infinitely many wffs which the formation rules allow us to construct, the relative handful which are to be accorded the privileged status of axioms. For purposes of constructing S5, Lewis selected A1 to A6 plus A10 out of the following list:

A1: $(P \cdot Q) \rightarrow (Q \cdot P)$

A2: $(P \cdot Q) \rightarrow P$

A3: $P \rightarrow (P \cdot P)$

A4: $((P \cdot Q) \cdot R) \rightarrow (P \cdot (Q \cdot R))$

A5: $((P \rightarrow Q) \cdot (Q \rightarrow R)) \rightarrow (P \rightarrow R)$

A6: $P \rightarrow \Diamond P$

A7: $\Diamond (P \cdot Q) \rightarrow \Diamond P$

A8: $(P \rightarrow Q) \rightarrow (\Diamond P \rightarrow \Diamond Q)$

---

not the case that P is true and Q false, while the relation of *material biconditionality* holds between P and Q in all those possible worlds (if any) in which both are true or both are false. Subject to the qualifications discussed in chapter 5, section 2, "$\sim$P" may be read as "not P", "P·Q" as "both P and Q", "P∨Q" "either P or Q", "P ⊃ Q" as "if P then Q", and "P≡Q" as "P if and only if Q".

42. Note that the Greek letters "α", "β", etc. do not belong to the object-language but to the meta-language. They are used to supplement the meta-language, English, and are known as *meta-logical variables*. "α", "β", etc. stand indiscriminately for any wffs whatever.

A9: $\diamond\diamond P \rightarrow \diamond P$

A10: $\diamond P \rightarrow \square \diamond P$

(A1 to A6, he showed, suffice to construct a very weak system which he called S1. Progressively stronger systems are constructible by adding further axioms to those for S1. Thus S2 = A1 to A6 + A7; S3 = A1 to A6 + A8; S4 = A1 to A6 + A9; and S5 = A1 to A6 + A10. Although A7, A8, and A9 do not feature as *axioms* in S5 they are provable as theorems therein.)

(d)   A set of rules of inference, known as *transformation rules*. The transformation rules of a system enable us to transform the axiom-wffs into new wffs, and these in turn into still further wffs. Any wff obtained in this way is known as a *theorem* of the system. (Together with the axioms, the theorems make up the *theses* of the system.) It is usual to be as parsimonious as possible in selecting one's transformation rules. Thus, for the purposes of deriving the theorems of S5 we can get along nicely with:

TR1:   [Conjunction] if α is a thesis and β is a thesis, then $(\alpha \cdot \beta)$ is a thesis.

TR2:   [Modus Ponens] If α is a thesis and $(\alpha \rightarrow \beta)$ is a thesis, then β is a thesis.

TR3:   [Uniform Substitution] If α is a thesis and β is the result of substituting some wff for a propositional symbol uniformly throughout α, then β is a thesis.

TR4:   [Substitution of Equivalents] If α is a thesis in which β occurs, and $(\beta \leftrightarrow \gamma)$ is a thesis, and one substitutes γ for some occurrence of β in α, then the result of that substitution is a thesis.

Of these, TR1 and TR2 are already familiar (though we earlier stated them slightly differently). TR3 and TR4 are unfamiliar, but may easily be understood in terms of examples of their application. Thus TR3 licences us to make such inferences as those from

A6: $P \rightarrow \diamond P$

to each of the following:

T1: $Q \rightarrow \diamond Q$

T2: $(P \cdot Q) \rightarrow \diamond(P \cdot Q)$

and so on. In effect, TR3 reflects the fact that since a propositional variable is simply a wff which is arbitrarily chosen to stand for any proposition whatever, we can substitute for it any other arbitrarily chosen proposition-expressing wff whatever, provided that we do so consistently, i.e., uniformly. TR3, unlike TR4, does not require of any two wffs, one of which is to be substituted for the other, that they be equivalent. On the other hand, TR4, unlike TR3, does not require of a wff which is to be substituted for another, that it be substituted uniformly. Thus, for instance, supposing that we have already established, as a thesis, the equivalence

T3: $P \leftrightarrow \sim \sim P$,

TR4 licences us to make the inferences from T3 and

A6: $P \rightarrow \Diamond P$

to

T4: $\sim \sim P \rightarrow \Diamond \sim \sim P$

(in which the substitution of " $\sim \sim P$ " for "P" *is* carried out uniformly), or to

T5: $\sim \sim P \rightarrow \Diamond P$

(in which the substitution is *not* carried out uniformly).

From the above axiomatic basis for S5 the rest of the system may be generated by repeated applications of one or more of the rules of inference listed in (d) to one or more of the axioms listed in (c) or to one or more of the theorems previously so generated.

The general concept of *proof* may be given the following rigorous definition for the special case of S5: a finite sequence of formulas (A through T), each of which either (i) is an axiom of S5, or (ii) is a theorem derived from one or more previous members of the sequence in accord with a stated transformation rule of S5, is said to be a *proof of* T *in S5*.[43]

There are infinitely many theorems derivable in S5. We list just a few of special interest.

T6: $\Box P \rightarrow P$

T7: $(P \rightarrow Q) \rightarrow (\Box P \rightarrow \Box Q)$

T8: $\Diamond (P \cdot Q) \rightarrow (\Diamond P \cdot \Diamond Q)$

T9: $(\Box P \vee \Box Q) \rightarrow \Box (P \vee Q)$

T10: $\sim \Diamond P \rightarrow (P \rightarrow Q)$

T11: $\Box P \rightarrow (Q \rightarrow P)$

T12: $(\Box P \cdot \Box Q) \rightarrow (P \leftrightarrow Q)$

T13: $\Box P \leftrightarrow \Box \Box P$

T14: $\Diamond P \leftrightarrow \Box \Diamond P$

T15: $\Box P \leftrightarrow \Diamond \Box P$

Questions involving the understanding of T6 to T12 will be posed as an exercise. T13 and T14 are

43. For illustrations of S5 proofs see p. 221ff.

singled out because of their role as so-called "reduction principles". Their philosophical significance will be discussed later.

It is worth noting that corresponding to each of the above theses of S5 there is what is called a "derived inference rule of the system". Roughly, a derived rule (or "derived transformation rule", as it is sometimes called) is a rule of inference which does not occur in the original set but which corresponds to an axiom or to an already established theorem and hence can be derived from the original set. Since to every theorem there corresponds a derivable rule of inference and there is an unlimited number of theorems, we may conclude that there is an unlimited number of derived rules of inference to be obtained if one wishes. Of course, nobody ever so wishes. A system encumbered by as many derived rules of inference as theorems would be ridiculously redundant. In practice, one makes use of a relatively small number of derived rules.

Inference within natural deduction systems

Turning now to deductive systems of the second kind, viz., natural deduction systems, it will suffice for our purposes if we concentrate mainly on the description of how such systems operate.

Natural deduction systems were first constructed independently by Gerhard Gentzen and Stanisław Jaśkowski in 1934. The employment of such systems in various branches of formal logic — propositional and predicate logics, modal, and nonmodal — is now well established. Indeed, for a variety of reasons, they are now regarded by many logicians with more favor than axiomatic systems. The troublesome task of selecting just the 'right' axioms as the starting point for our deductions is circumvented. Both the kinds of inference rules employed,[44] and the manner of their employment are much more natural (as the term "natural deduction" is intended to betoken) than in the case of axiomatic systems. And they do not tempt us so strongly to suppose that the subject matter of logic is on a par with that of, e.g., Euclidean geometry or classical mechanics, by virtue of being likewise axiomatizable — a supposition which fails to recognize that logic has a special status as the science which provides rules of inference for the systematic investigation of these other sciences whereas they provide none for it.

Although we have no need here to give an illustration of how a full system of natural deduction is set up it will help if we illustrate how the rules of such a system operate by applying such rules to an example expressed first in natural language and then subsequently in the symbolism of truth-functional propositional logic.

Consider the argument of someone who asserts all three of the following propositions:

(4.20) If Stenmark did not win the slalom then he did not race

(4.21) But either he raced or the snow conditions must have been dangerous and he withdrew

(4.22) Stenmark did not win

and goes on to conclude

(4.23) The snow conditions must have been dangerous.

---

44. The rules usually are not selected so austerely and usually are not as seemingly artificial as, e.g., the rule of Uniform Substitution.

Most of us can 'see' that the argument is valid. But how do we *know?* How could we *demonstrate* that the conclusion follows from the premises? An appeal to axiomatics is obviously not going to be much help. No premise is an instance of any axiom, nor is the conclusion an instance of any theorem of any axiomatic system of logic. To be sure, the conditional proposition that if the premises are true then the conclusion is true will, if the argument is valid, be an instance of a theorem of an axiomatic system of logic. But to show that it is would be a lengthy and difficult matter and a quite unnatural thing to do in the circumstances. How much more natural it would be for us to reason as follows:

From the premises *(4.20)* and *(4.22)* it follows that

   (4.24)   Stenmark did not race.

But from *(4.24)* and the other premise, *(4.21)*, it follows that

   (4.25)   The snow conditions must have been dangerous and Stenmark withdrew

from which it obviously follows that

   (4.23)   The snow conditions must have been dangerous.

What we are doing in this piece of natural deduction is implicitly invoking various familiar rules of inference in order to bridge the gap from premises to conclusion by constructing a *series of steps,* each of which follows from one or more of the preceding steps or premises, and the last step of which is the conclusion. We could, if we wished, make it quite explicit as to which rules of inference we are invoking. If so, we could point out that the rule which gets us from the conjunction of *(4.20)* and *(4.22)* to *(4.24)* is the rule of *Modus Ponens;* that the rule which gets us from the conjunction of *(4.24)* and *(4.21)* to *(4.25)* is the rule of *Disjunctive Syllogism;* and that the rule which gets us from *(4.25)* to the conclusion *(4.23)* is that of *Simplification*. In so doing, we would be demonstrating the validity of the argument and the necessary truth of the corresponding conditional, by showing, in step-by-step fashion, that the conclusion follows from (may be derived from, may validly be inferred from) the premises.

The example just given does not strictly belong to any natural deduction system since it is not expressed in a purely symbolic language and, as we have pointed out, no deductive systems — axiomatic or otherwise — are ever expressed in anything but symbolic notation. On the other hand, it is clear that the example just given *could* have been expressed in some set of symbols for propositional logic and that, when so expressed, the derivations involved *could* have been made in a quite mechanical way. If it had been so expressed the argument would look as follows:

$$
\begin{array}{lll}
(4.20a) & \sim P \supset \sim Q & \\
(4.21a) & Q \lor (R \cdot S) & \left.\right\} \quad \text{Premises} \\
(4.22a) & \sim P & \\
\end{array}
$$

$$
\therefore \quad (4.23a) \quad R \qquad \text{Conclusion}
$$

Our *proof* that *(4.23a)* follows from the conjunction of the premises would then be set out thus:

$(4.24a)$	$\sim Q$	From $(4.20a)$ and $(4.22a)$ by Modus Ponens
$(4.25a)$	$R \cdot S$	From $(4.21a)$ and $(4.24a)$ by Disjunctive Syllogism
$\therefore$ $(4.23a)$	R	From $(4.25a)$ by Simplification,

where the explicit justification for each step in the proof is set out on the right-hand side by citing both the rule of inference which warrants the step and the previous steps (either premises or subsequent steps or a combination of the two) from which the inference is made.

The crucial difference between natural deduction systems and axiomatic systems can now be brought out. In an axiomatic system we begin with theses (the axioms) and we end with theses (the theorems), and all the intermediate steps are theses (viz., theorems). Every single step in the proof of a thesis must itself be a thesis. In a system of natural deduction this need not be the case. We *may* begin with a thesis (i.e., a thesis of an axiomatic system); but we *need not*. And, even when we begin with a thesis and end with a thesis, some of the intermediate steps need not be theses.

It is noteworthy that, in our descriptions of these two kinds of deductive system we have not needed to invoke any talk of the *truth* of the theses they generate, let alone talk of our *knowledge* of the truth of such theses. This reflects the important fact, noted earlier (p. 205, fn. 39), that both kinds of deductive system are invariably constructed with the help of a symbolic notation within which derivations of theses may be constructed without any potentially misleading distractions of the kind that so often plague our inferences when we have a particular interpretation in mind. Although deductive systems are usually *constructed* with some interpretation of the symbols in mind, they may be *considered* independently of any such interpretation. When so considered, a deductive system is said to be an *uninterpreted system*.

Now it is clear that within an uninterpreted system it is *pointless* to ask of any given thesis whether that thesis expresses a truth, let alone whether what it expresses is known to be true. Such questions simply do not arise. Nevertheless they can be *made* to arise — can be made pointful — provided that certain sorts of interpretations are assigned to the symbols, i.e., just as soon as the system is made an *interpreted system*. Strictly speaking, from a formal point of view an uninterpreted axiom is nothing other than a string of marks on a paper or a string of sounds. These marks or noises can be made to express propositions by our interpreting them, i.e., by our specifying for each of their constituent symbols what meaningful interpretation it is to have. Consider for example, the string of symbols "(P $ Q) # (P ! Q)". We stipulate that "$", "#", and "!" are dyadic operators, that "(" and ")" are disambiguating punctuation, and that "P" and "Q" are variables. Beyond this, nothing more is specified. What does this axiom express? Literally, nothing. But it can be *made* to express an indefinitely large range of propositions. We will illustrate just two.

First, the string of symbols may be given a fairly obvious interpretation which would have it express a truth of physics, viz., that the value of the resultant force brought about by two independent forces, P and Q, acting in the same direction on a point [i.e., "(P $ Q)"] is numerically equal to [i.e., "#"] the arithmetic sum of the two individual forces [i.e., "(P ! Q)"].

Alternatively, the string may be given quite a different interpretation, this time, however, yielding a false proposition of physiological audiometrics, viz., that the perceived pitch of the complex sound consisting of two notes sounding in immediate succession [i.e., "(P $ Q)"] is indistinguishable from [i.e., "#"] the perceived pitch of those same two notes sounding in unison [i.e., "(P ! Q)"].

Thus it is that, for any theses of suitably interpreted systems, we can ask the questions which we have hitherto so studiously shunned. We can ask: Do the theses (or sentences which are their substitution-instances[45]) express true propositions? And further: Can we *know* that the

---

45. The parenthetical qualification is needed in order to cater for deductive systems whose theses are not themselves proposition-expressing sentences but rather are *sentence-forms* all of whose *substitution-instances* are

theses (or sentences which are their substitution-instances) express true propositions?

These questions can be asked of a thesis of an interpreted deductive system no matter what interpretation is given — whether the interpretation given is the *intended interpretation,* i.e., the interpretation which it was intended that the symbolism should bear when the system was constructed, or some *non-intended interpretation,* i.e., an interpretation which it was not intended that the symbolism should bear but which it can be given. The symbolism of truth-functional propositional logic was first constructed with a logical interpretation in mind: an interpretation according to which the letters "P", "Q", "R", etc. were to be interpreted as *propositional* variables, the symbols "∼", "·", and "∨", etc., as expressing the *truth-functional* concepts of negation, conjunction, and disjunction, etc., and so on. It so happens, however, that the symbolism may also be given a different interpretation — an interpretation according to which it does not present a systematization of propositional logic but a systematization of the theory of electrical switching circuits. And other unintended interpretations are also possible.

In what follows we will set aside these unintended, nonlogical, interpretations and concentrate solely on the intended, logical, interpretations which systems such as those for propositional logic and predicate logic are standardly given. We will concentrate, that is, solely on questions about the truth, and our knowledge of the truth, of the logical propositions which, on the intended interpretation, the theses of various deductive systems express.

Consider the case of axiomatic systems. A wff is not usually designated as a thesis unless it has at least a prima facie case for being *considered* true on the intended interpretation. We know that *if* the axioms of a system S are true, i.e., true on the intended interpretation (this is a qualification which we hereinafter take for granted when speaking of the truth of wffs), and the rules of inference are valid, i.e., truth-preserving in all possible worlds, then the theorems will be true. Moreover, we know that if the axioms of S are *necessarily* true, not just contingently so, and the rules of inference are valid, then the theorems will be necessarily true. (This can easily be verified by inspection of the fifteen worlds-diagrams which make it clear that from a necessary truth only necessary truths follow [See chapter 1, p. 51].) But how do we *know* whether the axioms of S are true? This plainly cannot be settled within S itself (even when S is interpreted). After all, among the considerations which dictate our initial choice of the axioms is the requirement that the axioms be *independent* of one another in the sense that, although the theorems are derivable from them in accordance with the rules of inference of the system[46] none of them is itself derivable in this way from the *other*

---

proposition-expressing sentences. The distinction between sentence-forms and the sentences which are their instances is drawn with some care in chapter 5, section 6. Strictly speaking, it makes no sense to ask questions about the truth-value or modal status of the propositions expressed by theses which have the status of sentence-forms rather than sentences. For there are no such propositions. On the other hand, we *can* ask about the truth-value and modal states of the propositions expressed by the sentences which are *substitution-instances* of such theses. A sentence-form all of whose instances express necessarily true propositions will be said to be *valid;* one all of whose instances express necessarily false propositions will be said to be *contravalid;* and one which is neither valid nor contravalid will be said to be *indeterminate.* (See chapter 5, section 7.) Although the distinction will be observed scrupulously throughout chapters 5 and 6, it will render our present discussion simpler if we leave it to be *understood* here that talk of the truth-value or modal status of a thesis is subject to the parenthetical qualification.

46. Note the *special* sense in which it is required that the axioms be "independent". This is a different sense of "independence" from that involved when we said, in chapter 1, that two propositions are *logically independent* if and only if from the truth or falsity of one we cannot validly infer the truth or falsity of the other. Within an axiomatic system two axioms are *inferentially independent* if and only if from the truth or falsity of one we cannot validly infer, *by means of the transformation rules of that system,* the truth or falsity

axioms. If, then, the axioms of S are independent, it is not possible to establish their truth by derivation within S. It follows that the only way in which the truth or necessary truth of the axioms of S can be established is *extrasystematically*. And that, it is clear, is where recourse must be taken to what we have called "the method of analysis".

In the case of truth-functional propositional logic, this is standardly done by giving the sort of truth-condition analysis which is to be found in so-called *truth-tables*.[47] In the case of modal propositional logic, this is standardly done by constructing *semantic tableaux;* or, alternatively, it can be done more intuitively by appeal to *worlds-diagrams* in the manner already sketched in chapter 1 and subsequently developed more fully in chapter 6. Truth-tables, on the one hand, and semantic tableaux and worlds-diagrams, on the other hand, provide *decision procedures* for deciding on the truth-value (and, indeed modal status) of theses within truth-functional propositional logic and modal propositional logic, respectively. Between them, these analytical methods suffice to determine, for any thesis of propositional logic standardly interpreted, whether or not that thesis expresses something true or false, together with the modal status of what that thesis expresses.

In the case of predicate logic, i.e., logic of unanalyzed concepts, the scene is somewhat different. Not only is there no decision procedure for predicate logic (truth-functional or otherwise) *as a whole;* it is provable that there cannot be one.[48] Certain substantial fragments of predicate logic, however, do submit to appraisal by these, or similar, analytical methods.[49] In short, for all those cases in which it is possible to determine the truth-value or modal status of theses of axiomatic systems for propositional and predicate logics, it is possible to do so by recourse to what we have broadly described as the methods of analysis.

How about the theses of natural deduction systems for these logics? These generate no special problem. A natural deduction system for a given branch of logic does not contain different theses from those within an axiomatic system for that branch, but uses rules of inference to organize, or

---

of the other. Theses of an interpreted system may be inferentially independent even when they are not logically independent.

This fact is particularly pertinent to the controversy which surrounds the so-called paradoxes of implication: that a necessarily false proposition implies any proposition, that a necessarily true proposition is implied by any proposition, and that any two necessarily true propositions are equivalent. These theses, which we will discuss at greater length in section 6, pp. 224–230, have sometimes been construed as asserting respectively that any proposition may be demonstrated to follow from a necessarily false proposition, that any necessarily true proposition may be demonstrated to follow from any proposition whatever, and so on. Consequently, it has often been claimed, these theses, if they were true, would make the matter of the demonstration of noncontingent truths in logic and mathematics a trivial matter. For instance, it would mean that in order to prove the necessarily true proposition that the square root of two is not the quotient of any two whole numbers, we need only derive it from the contingent proposition that it is raining by appeal to the fact that the former is a necessarily true proposition and hence is implied by any proposition whatever. But this worry about the potential for trivializing mathematics and logic is unwarranted. For to say that a necessarily true proposition is implied by any other proposition is not to say or to imply that a necessarily true proposition may be validly inferred *by means of the transformation rules of a certain system* from any proposition whatever. Within any non-trivial, epistemically productive, logical system such pairs of propositions as that the square root of two is not the quotient of any two integers and that it is raining will be inferentially independent with respect to the rules of that system even though they are not logically independent.

47. Recall that a truth-condition analysis is what we prefer to call a "possible-worlds analysis". Truth-tables are simply one form of possible worlds analysis. We introduce them in chapter 5.

48. See G.J. Massey, *Understanding Symbolic Logic,* New York, Harper & Row, 1970, pp. 338–9, for a discussion of what he calls "Church's thesis theorem".

49. For an excellent introduction to the use of such methods for two important fragments of predicate logic, see Hughes and Londey, *The Elements of Formal Logic,* London, Methuen, 1965.

systematize, the theses in a different way. So whatever analytical method suffices to give us knowledge of the truth-value or modal status of theses within an axiomatic system will suffice also to give us knowledge of the truth-value or modal status of theses in the corresponding natural deduction system. They are the very same theses.

Our questions about the truth, the modal status, and our knowledge of the truth and modal status, of the propositions which, on standard interpretations, the theses of various deductive systems of logic express, can now be answered straightforwardly. In the first place, to the extent that, by the employment of analytical methods such as those described, we are able to know of a proposition P (expressed by a thesis of an interpreted deductive system) that it is true, we are also able to know of any proposition Q (expressed by a thesis of an interpreted deductive system) which we validly infer from P, that it also is true. Secondly, to the extent that, by the employment of analytical methods, we are able to know of a proposition P (expressed by a thesis) that it is *necessarily true,* we are also able to know of any proposition Q (expressed by a thesis) which we validly infer from P, that it also is *necessarily true.*

The conclusions just reached can, of course, be generalized. They apply not only to propositions expressed by theses within interpreted deductive systems but to propositions expressed in any way whatever. The making of valid inferences within deductive systems is one way of expanding our knowledge of the subject matter of logic. But it is not the only way. Valid inference made outside the compass of deductive systems also leads to the expansion of logical knowledge.

EXERCISES

1. *By using the method of counterexamples, as outlined in the section on* Possible Worlds Parables *in chapter 2, try to show why the converses of T6, T7, T8, and T9 do not hold.*

2. *Reread chapter 1, pp. 50–53. Which worlds-diagrams are illustrations of T11? Which are illustrations of T12?*

3. *Find two different interpretations of "(P $ Q) # (P ! Q)" which yield truths, and two different interpretations which yield falsehoods.*

*   *   *   *   *

The theoretical warrant of the method of direct proof

The distinction drawn earlier between mediate and immediate inference (p. 195) is paralleled by a distinction between mediate and immediate proofs. A mediate proof will have a sequence of steps between the premises and the conclusion; an immediate one will not. Each of the preceding proofs has been a mediate one; later will we cite several examples of immediate (one-step) proofs.

All immediate proofs, and some mediate ones, are direct proofs; that is, are proofs in which every step is derived solely from the premises or by a sequence of steps from the premises. By way of contrast, some mediate proofs are indirect (otherwise known as conditional proofs); that is, are proofs in which additional assumptions, not included within the original premise-set, are introduced (see. for example, step (3) in the proof in footnote 63 on p. 227). In what follows we will be concerned solely with direct proofs.

What logical principles justify the construction of mediate direct proofs?[50]

---

50. We shall not concern ourselves with the corresponding question for indirect proofs.

It may seem obvious that since the rules of inference employed in constructing each of these intermediate steps are valid, the final step in the construction of the proof, viz., the conclusion, must follow from the premises. But can we prove this? In order to do so we need to invoke two metalogical principles, the Augmentation Principle and the Collapse Principle.

It might be thought that the only metalogical principle involved is that of the Transitivity of Implication, viz., that if P implies Q and if Q implies R, then P implies R. It may seem, that is, that if the premise-set of an argument implies some proposition, and if that proposition in turn implies another, then the premise-set implies the latter proposition, and so on. But this principle does not suffice. For the intermediate steps in a mediate proof are often inferred, not from an immediately preceding step, but from more remote earlier steps; moreover intermediate steps are often inferred not from single antecedent steps but from two or more such steps or premises (see, for example, step *(4.25a)* in the proof on p. 212).

A mediate direct proof consists of a set of premises, A_1 through A_m (whose conjunction we shall call "A"), a number of intermediate steps, B_1 through B_n, and a conclusion C. Schematically, a mediate direct proof looks like this:

A_1

·

·   } Premises

A_m

B_1

·   } Intermediate steps

·

B_n

C   }   Conclusion

Each step, beginning with B_1 and proceeding through and including the last, the conclusion C, is inferred from some one or more premises or antecedent steps.

The two meta-logical principles involved are:

THE AUGMENTATION PRINCIPLE:

If P implies Q, then the conjunction of P with any other proposition, R, also implies Q.

Symbolically we would have: $(P \rightarrow Q) \rightarrow [(P \cdot R) \rightarrow Q]$

THE COLLAPSE PRINCIPLE:

If P implies Q, then the conjunction of P and Q, viz., $P \cdot Q$, is logically equivalent to P.

Symbolically we would have: $(P \rightarrow Q) \rightarrow [(P \cdot Q) \leftrightarrow P]$

(The proof of these principles is left as an exercise in chapter 6, section 9.)

Let us now see how these two principles can be invoked to solve our current problem. Consider the first of the intermediate steps, i.e., B_1, in the schema for mediate direct proofs. Since it is the first step, no intermediate step precedes it and it must be inferred from some one or more propositions among the premise-set A. Provided that it is inferred in accord with a valid inference rule, then by the very definition of "valid" we are assured that B_1 logically follows from those premises which are cited in its derivation. Now by the Augmentation Principle we know that if B_1 logically follows from *some* of the premises, then it follows from them *all* (that is, from them all taken together). And by the Collapse Principle we know that if B_1 follows from the premise-set A, then the set of propositions consisting of all the premises along with B_1 is logically equivalent to the original set of premises. In effect, then, we can regard B_1 as just another premise, and the proof can now be regarded as looking like this:

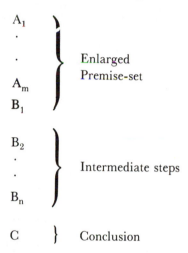

A_1

.

.

A_m

B_1
⎫ Enlarged Premise-set

B_2

.

.

B_n
⎫ Intermediate steps

C ⎫ Conclusion

We now proceed to repeat the same sort of reasoning in the case of the next intermediate step, B_2. In so doing we show that regarding B_2 as just another premise will leave the validity of the argument quite intact: the set of propositions consisting of A_1 through B_2 is logically equivalent to the set consisting of A_1 through A_m. We continue in this stepwise fashion until we have shown that the entire set of propositions A_1 through B_n is logically equivalent to the original premise-set A. Finally we are in a position to infer C. C, like any other step in the proof, will be inferred from some one or more antecedent propositions in the proof. Again we invoke the Augmentation Principle. Insofar as C logically follows from some propositions in the set A_1 through B_n, it also logically follows from the entire set, A_1 through B_n. But we have already shown that the set A_1 through B_n is logically equivalent to the original set, A_1 through A_m. Thus, in inferring C in this fashion, we have shown that C logically follows from the original premise-set.[51]

In sum, by constructing a proof in which a proposition is validly inferred from a set of propositions which are themselves validly inferred from a premise-set, we show that that proposition is implied by that premise-set, and that the corresponding argument (that is, the proof without its intermediate steps) is *deductively valid*.

---

51. Whatever logically follows from one of two logically equivalent proposition-sets logically follows from the other also. In symbols: $[(P \leftrightarrow Q) \cdot (P \rightarrow R)] \rightarrow (Q \rightarrow R)$.

EXERCISE

Verify the principle of the Transitivity of Implication by the following procedure:

Select from the fifteen worlds-diagrams (figure (1.i)*) all those in which P implies Q. From each of these, construct additional diagrams in which Q implies R (for example, diagram 9 will give rise to three additional diagrams, i.e., those in which Q is equivalent to R, in which Q implies the contingent proposition R, and in which R is necessarily true). Check to see that in every case where P implies Q and Q implies R, P implies R.*

6.   A PHILOSOPHICAL PERSPECTIVE ON LOGIC AS A WHOLE

Our discussion of the fruits of analysis led us to adopt a threefold division of logic into

(1)   the Logic of Unanalyzed Propositions (Propositional Logic, as we are now calling it);

(2)   the Logic of Unanalyzed Concepts (Predicate Logic);

and

(3)   the Logic of Analyzed Concepts (Concept Logic).

Of these, (1) and (2) are standardly recognized and well developed— in no small measure because they lend themselves to systematic exploration by means of deductive systems. By way of contrast, (3) is certainly not well developed and is only rarely accorded recognition as a proper part of logic. One of our aims, in this section, is to give a philosophical defence of its inclusion within the science of logic. Our other main aim is also philosophical. We wish to argue for the centrality within logic as a whole (and a fortiori within each of its three main parts) of the so-called "branch" called Modal Logic, and for the centrality, within that "branch", of the truths expressed by the theses of Lewis' system S5. We concentrate on the role which modality plays in Propositional Logic and make only a few remarks about its role within Predicate Logic or Concept Logic (parts of logic which largely fall outside the compass of this book).

The indispensability of modal concepts within propositional logics

A broad view of propositional logic must allow that propositional logic is a genus within which may be found several species and many subspecies. Two of the main species, *truth-functional* logic and *modal* logic, have attracted principal attention. But there are others, chief among which are *epistemic* logic (dealing with relations between such epistemic concepts as those of knowledge and belief), *deontic* logic (dealing with relations between such ethical concepts as those of obligation and permission), and *tense* logics (dealing with relations between concepts such as those of past, present, and future). And within certain of these it must further be allowed that insofar as different axiomatizations of the same sets of theses, or even axiomatizations of different sets of theses, have been constructed, there are — so to speak — many subspecies.

Now it has long been customary, within introductory presentations of propositional logic, to accord truth-functional logic pride of place either by neglecting these other logics altogether or by representing each of these as a mere "accretion" upon the "central core" of truth-functional logic. There have been several reasons for this, some of them good, some of them not so good. Among the good reasons we must cite the facts that the truth-functional concepts of negation, conjunction, disjunction, etc., lend themselves to simple analysis in terms of the conditions for their application; that these concepts play a more *obvious* role in ordinary argumentation and inference than do modal, epistemic, deontic, and temporal concepts; that a propositional logic which avoids non-truth-functional notions lends itself to the construction of extremely *simple* decision procedures; and that a certain pedagogical elegance is achieved if we first present some axiomatic basis for truth-functional logic and then *add* to it the special axioms and rules which are needed in order to handle these non-truth-functional concepts. The not-so-good reasons include the all-too-common belief that the truth-functional concepts which some uses of the words "not", "and", "or", "if . . . then", and "if and only if" express[52] are the only strictly logical concepts, whereas non-truth-functional concepts such as those standardly expressed by phrases such as "it is necessary that", "it is known that", and "it is obligatory that" are all tainted with extralogical impurities; that logic has no need of non-truth-functional-concepts; and that the non-truth-functional concepts — especially the modal ones — are somehow philosophically suspect. But whatever the reasons, this mode of presentation has encouraged, if not generated, the view that modal logic is just one of many accretions on the central, pure, truth-functional core of logic, and that modal logic merely examines the relationships between the modal concepts of necessity, possibility, impossibility, etc. in the same sort of way as, e.g., deontic logic examines the relationships between the deontic concepts of being obligatory, being permitted, being forbidden, etc.

On our view all this is topsy-turvy. Given that logic is concerned — as, since its founding days, it has universally been agreed to be — with formulating principles of *valid* inference and determining which propositions *imply* which, and given that the concepts of validity and implication are themselves modal concepts, it is modal logic rather than truth-functional logic which deserves to be seen as central to the science of logic itself. We do not deny for a moment that logicians can and usually do pursue the task of determining which principles or rules of inference are valid, and which theses of logic may be derived in accordance with these rules, without giving any thought to modal logic or giving explicit recognition to modal concepts in their symbolism. We deny only that they can give a *philosophically* satisfactory account of the notions of validity and derivation without appeal to those modal concepts which it is the province of modal logic to investigate. From a philosophical point of view, we submit, it is much sounder to view modal logic as the indispensible core of logic, to view truth-functional logic as one of its fragments, and to view "other" logics — epistemic, deontic, temporal, and the like — as accretions either upon modal logic (a fairly standard view, as it happens) or upon its truth-functional component.[53]

Now, for anyone who shares this perspective on the matter, the question immediately arises as to *which* modal logic gives the most philosophically adequate account of the set of modal relations of which the relation of implication is a member. For the trouble is that we are seemingly faced with an embarrassment of riches. Even if we restrict ourselves to the "classical" presentation of modal logic by C. I. Lewis we find no fewer than eight distinct systems or logics: five in the series S1 to S5,

---

52. It is universally agreed that only some uses of these words can be construed truth-functionally. We spend a good bit of time in chapter 5 saying which uses they are.

53. Our view of the matter is shared, it seems, by W. and M. Kneale. In the section of their book *The Development of Logic* which they devote to modal logic, they try to give a "proper appreciation of the status which modal logic has among deductive theories" (p. 557) by presenting logic in a new way. Essentially, that new way (which they admit is "less easy to understand at first encounter" [p. 558]) involves presenting logic as a set of second-order propositions concerning the relation of implication. Compare our account of the subject matter of logic as second-order propositions which ascribe modal properties and relations to other propositions (chapter 3, pp. 129, 175).

and three in the distinct series S6 to S8. Subsequently, other logicians have constructed many more, some lying as it were 'between' members of the Lewis series, others lying 'outside' those series. There are now so many modal logics that the author of a recent book reports, in his Introduction, that he will discuss "literally hundreds" of them.[54] Fortunately, not many of these demand scrutiny for our purposes. Many have been constructed expressly as instruments for the analysis of specific sorts of verbal contexts in which modal expressions are used, and others investigate the consequences of incorporating special assumptions along with more familiar modal laws. Only a relative handful compete for attention as systematic explanations of the concepts of logical implication, of logical necessity, logical possibility, and the like. And, of these, the best candidate, in the view of many philosophers, is Lewis' system S5.[55]

Probably the most serious objections to the view that S5 gives a philosophically defensible account of the most fundamental concepts of logic are those which stem from the presence within it of the formulae which we listed earlier as

$$T10: \quad \sim \Diamond P \rightarrow (P \rightarrow Q)$$

$$T11: \quad \Box P \rightarrow (Q \rightarrow P)$$

$$T12: \quad (\Box P \cdot \Box Q) \rightarrow (P \leftrightarrow Q)$$

$$T13: \quad \Box P \leftrightarrow \Box \Box P$$

$$T14: \quad \Diamond P \leftrightarrow \Box \Diamond P$$

T10, T11, and T12 are commonly referred to as "paradoxes of (strict) implication". They are not unique to S5 but are to be found in a number of weaker systems as well, i.e., systems whose axiomatic bases suffice for the proof of proper subsets of the theorems in S5. Indeed, they are found in systems as weak as S2. T13 and T14 are known as the Weak and Strong Reduction Principles, respectively. We will discuss the Reduction Principles first, and then come back to the so-called paradoxes.

Problems about the reduction principles

Even before we consider the problems that are supposed to arise about T13 and T14, it is possible to explain why the former is said to be "weak" and the latter "strong", and to explain, further, why they are jointly called "Reduction Principles". Significantly enough, we can do this without so much as considering for a moment what these wffs might mean, or, what interpretation they might be given.

In saying that T14 is stronger than T13 we mean not only that S5, within which T14 is provable, is stronger than S4, within which T13 is provable, but also that once we have proved T14, it is a fairly straightforward matter to prove T13. We *show* this by constructing a series of three proofs.

First we prove that the Strong Reduction Principle, T14, is a theorem of S5. The distinctive

54. D. Paul Snyder, *Modal Logic and its Applications*, New York, Van Nostrand Reinhold, 1971.

55. See, for instance, W. and M. Kneale, *The Development of Logic*, pp. 559–566. They claim that S5, when generalized in a system which takes implication as fundamental, suffices "for the reconstruction of the whole of logic as that is commonly understood" (p. 563). See also Jaakko Hintikka's conclusion: "The system S5, then, seems to be the best formalisation of our logic of *logical* necessity and *logical* possibility." ["The Modes of Modality" in *Acta Philosophica Fennica*, vol. 16 (1963).]

axiom of S5, viz., ◊P→□ ◊P, (A10), uses the symbol "→". By way of contrast, T14, viz., ◊P↔□ ◊P, uses the symbol "↔". How do we get from the former to the latter? It will help simplify our proof of T14 if, instead of using Lewis' axiom A6, viz., P→ ◊P, we use another formula, viz., □P→P, which suffices for the generation of precisely the same set of theses as A6. Let us call this formula A6*.[56] Our proof of T14 employs the axiomatic basis of S5, viz., the rules TR1, TR2, TR3, and TR4 together with the axioms A1 to A6 + A10 (or the equivalent set A1 to A6* + A10). We obtain T14 from this axiomatic basis by means of a proof set out thus:

(1)   □P→P   [A6*]

(2)   □ ◊P→ ◊P   [(1) × TR3 (◊P/P)]

(3)   ◊P→□ ◊P   [A10]

(4)   (□ ◊P→ ◊P)·(◊P→□ ◊P)   [(2), (3) × TR1]

(5)   ◊P↔□ ◊P   [(4) × Def. ↔]

[A brief explanation is in order. On each line of the proof we write a numbered wff which is either an axiom — e.g., wffs (1) and (3) — or a theorem — e.g., wffs (2), (4), and (5). To the right of the wff, in square brackets, we write the *justification* for writing that wff. In the case of axioms, merely citing them as such suffices. In the case of theorems, however, we justify our writing them down by citing a transformation rule or a definition which entitles us to derive them from previously numbered wffs, i.e., from wffs which are axioms or wffs which are previously derived theorems. The abbreviation "[(1) × TR3 (◊P/P)]" written after wff (2), for instance, tells us that we obtain (2) from (1) by substituting ◊P for P in accordance with the Rule of Uniform Substitution.] The wff which appears as a theorem on the last line of the proof is, of course, the Strong Reduction Principle. Q.E.D.

Next, we prove that the distinctive axiom (A9) of S4, viz., ◊◊P→ ◊P, is provable as a theorem in S5. Once more it will help us simplify our proof if, instead of using Lewis' formulation of A9, we use another formula, viz., □P→□□P, which is interchangeable with it, and call it A9*. The proof of A9* (= A9) within S5 then runs thus:

(1)   P→ ◊P   [A6]

(2)   □P→ ◊□P   [(1) × TR3 (□P/P)]

(3)   ◊P↔□ ◊P   [T14]

(4)   ◊□P↔□ ◊□P   [(3) × TR3 (□P/P)]

(5)   □P→□ ◊□P   [(2), (4) × TR4 (□ ◊□P/ ◊□P)]

(6)   □P↔ ◊□P   [T15]

(7)   □P→□□P   [(5), (6) × TR4 (□P/ ◊□P)]

56. It may be of interest to note that Gödel's axiomatization of S5 employs a weakened version of A6* rather than A6. See chapter 6, p. 356.

[The abbreviations of the justifications given for (5) and (7), both of which cite TR4, call for comment. On expansion, the justification given for (5) tells us that since, in (4), $\Diamond\Box P$ and $\Box\Diamond\Box P$ have been proved equivalent, we can obtain (5) from (2) by substituting $\Box\Diamond\Box P$ for $\Diamond\Box P$ where the latter occurs in (2), in accordance with TR4, i.e., the Rule for Substitution of Equivalents. Similarly, the justification given for (7) tells us that since, in (6), $\Box P$ and $\Diamond\Box P$ have been proved equivalent, we can obtain (7) from (5) by substituting $\Box P$ for $\Diamond\Box P$ where the latter occurs in (5), in accordance with TR4.] The wff which appears as a theorem on the last line of this proof is, as already noted, interchangeable with the distinctive axiom of S4. Moreover, the proof is an S5 proof since it utilizes the Strong Reduction Principle, T14, in the proof of which we previously utilized the distinctive axiom of S5, viz., A10. Thus we can conclude, at this point, that S5 contains S4.

Finally, we can show that the Weak Reduction Principle, T13, is provable in S4. Its proof utilizes the distinctive axiom of S4, viz., A9* (= A9), as the following demonstrates:

(1) $\Box P \rightarrow P$ [A6*]

(2) $\Box\Box P \rightarrow \Box P$ [(1) × TR3 ($\Box P/P$)]

(3) $\Box P \rightarrow \Box\Box P$ [A9*]

(4) $(\Box\Box P \rightarrow \Box P) \cdot (\Box P \rightarrow \Box\Box P)$ [(2), (3) × TR1]

(5) $\Box P \leftrightarrow \Box\Box P$ [(4) × Def.$\leftrightarrow$]

A little reflection on these proofs shows not only that S5 'contains' S4, since the axiomatic basis of S4 is provable therein (see the second proof), but also that once we have proved T14 within S5 (see the first proof), we can easily prove T13. Thus our second proof used T14, at line (3), together with A6, to prove $\Box P \rightarrow \Box\Box P$, at line (7). And our third proof used this result, together with A6* (= A6), to prove T13. It remains only to add the well-known fact that T14 is *not* provable in S4, but *is* in S5[57], in order to conclude that whereas T13 is derivable from T14, T14 is not derivable from T13. Ipso facto, T14 is the stronger and T13 the weaker of the two Principles.

But why are either T13 or T14 called "Reduction Principles"? Once more we can answer the question without recourse to matters of interpretation. T13 says that $\Box P$ is provably equivalent to $\Box\Box P$. Now according to TR4 (the Rule for Substitution of Equivalents), if two wffs are provably equivalent then one may be substituted for the other wherever it occurs. It follows that in any wff in which there is a double occurrence (an iteration) of the symbol $\Box$ — or, for that matter, in any wff which is equivalent to one in which there is a double occurrence of $\Box$ — we can always delete the left-hand occurrence of $\Box$ and so *reduce* the number of its occurrences. When we do this systematically in the way that T13 indicates, we are left in S4 with just twelve distinct, i.e., non-equivalent, irreducible modalities; viz.,

$\Box P,$	$\Box\Diamond P,$	$\Box\Diamond\Box P$
$\sim\Box P,$	$\sim\Box\Diamond P,$	$\sim\Box\Diamond\Box P$
$\Diamond P,$	$\Diamond\Box P,$	$\Diamond\Box\Diamond P$
$\sim\Diamond P,$	$\sim\Diamond\Box P,$	$\sim\Diamond\Box\Diamond P$

57. This can easily be *seen* although its proof is a difficult matter. After all, if $\Diamond P \leftrightarrow \Box\Diamond P$ were provable in S4 then $\Diamond P \rightarrow \Box\Diamond P$ would be also. But if the latter were provable in S4, there would be no difference between S5 and S4 since $\Diamond P \rightarrow \Box\Diamond P$, as we have seen, is the distinctive axiom of S5.

T14 effects a further reduction so that we are left, in S5, with only the first on each of the above four rows, viz.,

$$\Box P, \qquad \sim \Box P, \qquad \Diamond P, \qquad \sim \Diamond P.$$

T13 and T14 are called "Reduction Principles", then, because T13 reduces all wffs containing combinations of the symbols $\Box$ and $\Diamond$ to wffs containing at the most *three* such symbols, while T14 reduces them to wffs containing at most *one* such symbol.[58] In each case, longer strings are permitted but are dispensable.

Now it is one thing to show, as we have, that T14 (and hence also T13) is provable in S5. It is quite another thing to show that these Reduction Principles, on interpretation, are philosophically defensible. That is our next task.

The interpretation which we have been giving the symbolism of S5 should by now be sufficiently familiar. Nevertheless, it bears summarizing. The letters "P", "Q", "R", etc. are taken to stand for propositions; the symbols "$\sim$" and "$\cdot$" are taken to stand for the truth-functional concepts of negation and conjunction, respectively; "$\Diamond$" and "$\Box$" are taken to stand for the modal concepts of logical possibility (truth in at least one possible world) and logical necessity (truth in all possible worlds), respectively; and "$\rightarrow$" and "$\leftrightarrow$" are taken to stand for the modal relations of implication and equivalence, respectively. The question before us, then, is whether, *on this interpretation* of the symbols, T13 and T14 are true.

Consider T13 first. T13 asserts an equivalence or two-way relation of implication, viz., (a) that $\Box P$ implies $\Box\Box P$, and (b) that $\Box\Box P$ implies $\Box P$. There can hardly be any doubt about the truth of (b), for (b) is simply a substitution-instance of the obvious truth that if P is necessarily true then it follows that P is true (expressed in symbols as $\Box P \rightarrow P$).[59] The only question that can seriously be raised is about (a). But (a)'s truth, on reflection, is similarly obvious. For (a) simply tells us that if P is true in all possible worlds, then the proposition *that* it is true in all possible worlds will itself be true in all possible worlds.

T14 yields to the same sort of analysis. It, too asserts a two-way relation of implication, viz., (a) that $\Diamond P$ implies $\Box\Diamond P$, and (b) that $\Box\Diamond P$ implies $\Diamond P$. Once more (b) must be accepted on pain of denying that necessary truths are true. And (a) simply tells us that if P is true in at least one possible world then the proposition *that* it is true in at least one possible world will be true in all possible worlds. If the obviousness of (a) seems elusive, the following argument may help. To deny the truth of (a) would be to assert that P may have the property of being true in at least one possible world even though the assertion that it has this property is not true in every possible world, i.e., is false in at least one possible world. But this seems obviously false if we think in terms of examples. Let P be the proposition

(4.26)   We are at the beginning of a new Ice Age.

Then, whether or not P is true, it is at least *possibly* true. So the antecedent of (a) is true for this substitution-instance of P. Might there, then, be a possible world in which it is false that *(4.26)* is logically possible, i.e., a possible world in which *(4.26)* is logically impossible? Hardly. It now seems obvious that a world in which *(4.26)* is logically impossible, i.e., self-contradictory, is not a

---

58. On a different account of what is to count as a modality, some logicians count both P and $\sim P$ as additional modalities, and hence S4 and S5 have respectively, 14 and 6 irreducible modalities.

59. Obviously, if we allow the truth of $\Box P \rightarrow P$ then we must allow the truth of $\Box\Box P \rightarrow \Box P$ since the latter follows from the former in accordance with the Rule of Uniform Substitution (substituting $\Box P$ for P).

possible world but an impossible one. It follows that one cannot consistently assert the antecedent of (a) and deny its consequent. In brief, on our interpretation, (a) can be seen — on reflection and analysis — to be just as incontrovertibly true as (b).

Why, it may then be asked, have T13 and T14 seemed to some philosophers to be obviously false or even meaningless? An explanation is called for.

The charge of meaninglessness, though it is often enough heard, does not deserve to be taken very seriously. To the rhetorical question, "What could it possibly *mean* to say such things as that it is true in all possible worlds that it is true in all possible worlds that P?", one can only reply that one ought not to let one's mind be boggled by complex strings of words (or symbols) but ought, rather, to set oneself the task of thinking through — as we did above — what they *do* mean.

By way of contrast, the objection which has it that T13 and T14 are obviously false is of considerable philosophical interest since it usually stems from a subtle assimilation of the notions of necessary truth and provability. Suppose, for instance, that instead of interpreting □P in T14 to mean that P is necessarily true, we interpret it to mean that P is provable by appeal to a specified set of inference rules, e.g., within a deductive system. Then, since ◇P is definitionally equivalent to ~ □ ~ P, we should have to interpret ◇P as meaning that P cannot be disproved by appeal to that set of rules. And then the formula ◇P↔□◇P will be read as asserting that if (and only if) P cannot be disproved by invoking certain rules, then the fact that it cannot be disproved by invoking these rules can itself be *proved* by invoking them. But this, for most cases, turns out to be false. On this interpretation, then, the Strong Reduction Principle of S5, and hence S5 itself, turns out not to be philosophically defensible. The answer that is called for in this case is that the concepts of necessary truth and provability are not at all the same; that the former is a purely logical concept while the latter is an epistemic one; and that unless one takes pains to keep the two distinct — as we have done at length in chapter 3 and again in this chapter — wholesale philosophical confusion is likely to ensure. The objection itself is a case in point. More particularly, we should point out that although being proved to be necessarily true is a sufficient condition of being necessarily true, it is not a necessary condition since there may be — and probably are, if our arguments in chapter 3 are sound — many necessary truths which are neither proved nor provable.

The objections to the Reduction Principles of S5 center around the interpretation, or misinterpretation, of the symbols "□" and "◇". The objections to the so-called paradoxes, T10, T11, and T12, center around the interpretation, or misinterpretation, of the symbol "→". It is to these that we now turn.

Problems about the paradoxes

Recall, for a start, the interpretations which we have given of T10 through T12.

> T10:   ~◇P→(P→Q)

is to mean that if P is necessarily false or self-contradictory then it follows that P implies any proposition Q whatever; i.e., that a necessarily false proposition implies any and every proposition.

> T11:   □P→(Q→P)

is to mean that if P is necessarily true then it follows that P is implied by any proposition Q whatever; i.e., that a necessarily true proposition is implied by any and every proposition. And

> T12:   (□P · □Q)→(P↔Q)

is to mean that if P and Q are both necessarily true then they mutually imply one another; i.e., that necessary truths are equivalent to one another. Since the usual criticisms concentrate on T10 and T11, we will deal first with them and then come back to T12.

One of the commonest complaints about T10 and T11, and hence also about all the Lewis systems, including S5, which contain them, is that they reflect a "highly artificial", "specialized", "purely formal" concept of implication, a concept which bears only a remote resemblance to our 'ordinary' notion of implication. It may help a little, then, if we briefly set the Lewis systems into historical perspective and then say why he thought his systems captured the essential features of the ordinary concept. Right at the outset, let it be admitted that Lewis' own terminology may have contributed, at least in part, to the supposition that there is a 'gap' between ordinary implication and the notion that features in his systems. He called the relation which we have symbolized by "$\rightarrow$", and which he symbolized by the so-called fish-hook "$\prec$", the relation of *strict* implication. In so naming it, he may well have made it sound, to untutored ears, as if strict implication is indeed far removed from ordinary implication. The fact is, however, that he used the name "strict implication" in order to differentiate between the kind of implication which functions in his systems, and which he thought to be *identical* with ordinary implication, and the relation for which Whitehead and Russell, in their epoch-making *Principia Mathematica* (1910–13), had co-opted the expression "implication" (nowadays called "material implication"). In any case, the kind of implication which features in his systems has it in common with ordinary implication that in both cases it is a necessary condition of P implying Q that it should *not be possible* for P to be true and Q to be false. By way of contrast, the "implication" of *Principia Mathematica* was a merely truth-functional relation which held between P and Q whenever *as a matter of fact* it is not the case that P is true when Q is false. It was *this* account of implication, Lewis felt, which was artificial, specialized, and purely formal. The use of the word "strict", in his characterization of the kind of implication found in his systems, was introduced to effect a contrast with Whitehead and Russell's use of the term "implication". In short, his use of the term "strict" in "strict implication" was occasioned by a mere quirk of history. It needs to be remembered, then, that when Lewis defined strict implication as the relation which holds between P and Q when it is not *possible* that P be true and Q be false, he took himself to be defining ordinary implication.[60] Interestingly enough, ancient and medieval logicians had taken themselves to be doing exactly the same thing when they, too, had defined implication in the same way. Thus, for instance, we find that in the fourth century B.C., Diodorus Cronus offered the same modal analysis as Lewis and contrasted it with what Diodorus regarded as the eviscerated truth-functional account offered by his gifted pupil, Philo of Megara. Plainly, the dispute about implication had a precursor twenty-four centuries before Lewis took issue with Whitehead and Russell. And it also had a precursor in the medieval period when the Schoolmen contrasted the very same modal account as Lewis gave with the truth-functional one of Philo.

That Lewis was right about the *necessary* conditions for P being said, in the ordinary sense, to "imply" Q, is seldom disputed. But was he right in claiming further that the impossibility of P being true while Q is false, is a *sufficient* condition of P implying Q? This is where we encounter the objection based on the "paradoxes" T10 and T11. For T10 and T11 are generated only if we take the impossibility of P being true and Q false to be a sufficient condition.

Lewis' main reply was that the so-called paradoxes are not really paradoxical at all and that, to see that they are not, we need only reflect on the fact that our ordinary intuitions about what implication is, and about what implies what, commit us to them. He therefore gave two *independent* proofs of theses which are special cases of T10 and T11, respectively — proofs which do not depend

---

60. See C.I. Lewis, *A Survey of Symbolic Logic,* Berkeley, University of California Press, 1918, esp. p. 324.

upon any alleged artificialities in his axiomatic systems S2 to S5, but depend only upon what we would ordinary agree to be valid rules of inference in any context or sphere of discourse. We give the first proof (for a special case of T10) only. It requires merely that we subscribe to each of the inference rules, Simplification, Addition, and Disjunctive Syllogism.

Consider, first, some necessarily false proposition which asserts

(a) $P \cdot \sim P$

From (a), by Simplification, we may validly infer

(b)   P

From (b), by Addition, we may validly infer

(c)   ·P or Q

From (a), by Simplification, we may validly infer

(d) $\sim P$

But from (c) and (d), by Disjunctive Syllogism, we may validly infer

(e)   Q

where Q, of course, may be any proposition at all. It is clear that by a series of steps — each warranted in the manner of natural deduction systems by a rule of valid inference — we can deduce any proposition whatever from a necessarily false proposition of the form $P \cdot \sim P$. And since, as we saw earlier, an inference (or series of inferences) from one proposition to another is valid if and only if the former *implies* the latter, we have here a proof that a necessarily false proposition of the form $P \cdot \sim P$ implies any proposition whatever. That is, we have here a proof of a special case of the so-called "paradox" T10.[61]

It is sometimes suggested that "all one has to do" in order to avoid the conclusion of this independent argument is to give up one of the rules of inference cited. But the situation is nowhere near as simple as that. The conclusion can be avoided only at the cost of giving up *at least one more* of the ordinarily accepted rules of inference. For, without using *any* of the above-mentioned rules, we can give *another* proof for a special case of T10 (viz., for $[P \cdot \sim P] \rightarrow \sim Q$), and a proof for a special case of T11. The proof of the former requires only that we agree to a proposition which is ordinarily agreed to state a fact of implication, viz.,

T16: $(P \cdot Q) \rightarrow P$[62]

---

61. The proof is a proof of $(P \cdot \sim P) \rightarrow Q$. We call this a "special case" of T10 because it does not have the full generality of T10. Thus T10 does not require that the necessarily false (impossible) proposition from which any proposition follows be in the form of an explicit contradiction. It claims that *any* necessarily false proposition — whether or not of this form — implies any proposition. (Similar remarks apply, mutatis mutandis, to our remarks about the special case that is provable for T11.)

62. $(P \cdot Q) \rightarrow P$, of course, is the 'fact' about implication which corresponds to the Rule of Simplification.

and agree, further, to a rule of inference which, ever since Aristotle, has been recognized as valid, viz.,

Antilogism:

> From the claim that two propositions imply a third we may validly infer that either of them together with the negation of the third implies the negation of the other.

From T16, in one step, by Antilogism, we may make a valid immediate inference to

T17: $(P \cdot \sim P) \longrightarrow \sim Q$

Yet T17 is simply a special case of T10 since it asserts that any necessarily false proposition of the form $P \cdot \sim P$ implies any proposition whatever.[63]

The other proof requires only that we accept the proof just given as valid and agree, further, to the already familiar rule of inference known as

Transposition:

> From the claim that one proposition implies another, one may validly infer that the negation of the latter implies the negation of the former.

From T17, in one step, by Transposition, we may validly infer

T18: $Q \longrightarrow \sim (P \cdot \sim P)$

Yet T18 is simply a special case of T11 since it asserts that any necessarily true proposition of the form $\sim (P \cdot \sim P)$ [necessarily true because it asserts the negation of the necessarily false $(P \cdot \sim P)$] is implied by any proposition whatever. Clearly, in order to avoid the "paradoxical" T17 we should have to give up either T16 or the rule of Antilogism. And in order to avoid the "paradoxical" T18 we should have to give up at least one of these or the rule of Transposition. What these two proofs, together with those of Lewis, show is that cases of the alleged paradoxes can be avoided only at the cost of *more than one* of our ordinary intuitions about what implies what and what may validly be inferred from what.

63. As a matter of fact, this proof can be extended to establish that *every* necessarily false proposition — not only those of the form "$(P \cdot \sim P)$" — implies every proposition whatever. One need only invoke the truth that every necessarily false proposition implies both itself and its negation, i.e., the principle $[\Box \sim P \rightarrow (P \rightarrow [P \cdot \sim P])]$, and the proof — using the method of mediate conditional proof (abbreviated "C.P.") of natural deduction — is straightforward:

(1) $\Box \sim P \rightarrow (P \rightarrow [P \cdot \sim P])$

(2) $(P \cdot \sim P) \rightarrow \sim Q$ [T17]

(3) $\Box \sim P$ [Assumption]

(4) $P \rightarrow (P \cdot \sim P)$ [(1), (3) × Modus Ponens]

(5) $P \rightarrow \sim Q$ [(4), (2) × Hypothetical Syllogism]

(6) $\Box \sim P \rightarrow (P \rightarrow \sim Q)$ [(3)–(5) × C.P.]   Q.E.D.

EXERCISE

It is sometimes supposed that the 'paradoxes' of strict implication, i.e., the proposition that a necessarily true proposition is implied by any proposition and the proposition that a necessarily false proposition implies any proposition, may be expressed in this way:

$$"Q \rightarrow \Box P";$$

$$"\Box \sim P \rightarrow Q".$$

Try to explain why these are incorrect *paraphrases of the prose claims and do* not *express those propositions.*

*   *   *   *   *

Relevance logics

Now some logicians say they are prepared to pay this cost in order to avoid the paradoxes. As proof of their willingness, some have actually constructed deductive systems within which many of our ordinary intuitions about implication are preserved but the paradoxical theorems are not. For instance, the System E of Alan Ross Anderson and Nuel D. Belnap[64] manages to avoid the paradoxes at the cost of rejecting the rule of Disjunctive Syllogism. And a good many other logicians have worked at constructing so-called *Relevance Logics* which it is hoped will achieve the same end by other similar means. Their dissatisfaction with any account (such as Lewis') which holds it to be a sufficient as well as necessary condition of P implying Q that it should be impossible for P to be true and Q false, plainly runs very deep. It cannot be dismissed as stemming from any superficial misunderstanding of Lewis' term "strict implication". Neither does it stem merely from reaction to the unexpectedness of the consequences (T10 and T11) which his account generates.[65] It stems rather from a deep conviction that *more* is required for the relation of implication to hold between P and Q, where the "more" is seen as being some "inner connection", some "identity of content", or "connection of meaning" between P and Q. This is what is meant when, in discussions of Relevance Logics, it is said that *relevance* is also a necessary condition of P implying Q. The complaint leveled against the Lewis-type definition of implication is that it commits us to the view that implication can hold between two propositions in a purely "external" way. The paradoxes, it would be said, are merely *symptoms* of the defect to which they are reacting: they are not the principal defect itself.

A detailed examination of the pros and cons of Relevance Logics cannot be undertaken here. We will venture just a few brief remarks to help set the issue into perspective.

What Relevance Logicians are getting at can be made clear if we consider a particular substitution-instance of one of the paradoxes; e.g., T11: $\Box P \rightarrow (Q \rightarrow P)$. Let P be the proposition

$$(4.27) \quad 9 = 3^2$$

and let Q be the proposition

---

64. Anderson and Belnap, "The Pure Calculus of Entailment", *Journal of Symbolic Logic*, vol. 27 (March 1962) pp. 19–52.

65. If it did, Lewis' claim that they are "paradoxical only in the sense of expressing logical truths which are easily overlooked" should suffice as an answer. See C.I. Lewis and C.M. Langford, *Symbolic Logic*, The Century Co., 1932; second edition, New York, Dover, 1959, p. 248.

> *(4.28)*   The mists are hanging low today.

Let us agree that *(4.27)* is necessarily true; i.e., let us assume the truth of

> *(4.29)* $\square(9 = 3^2)$

Then, since the rule of inference corresponding to T11 says that if a proposition is necessarily true we may validly infer that it is implied by any proposition whatever, we may validly infer from *(4.28)* the proposition

> *(4.30)*   (The mists are hanging low today)$\rightarrow$($9 = 3^2$)

But *(4.30)*, the Relevance Logician points out, is counterintuitive. And it is counterintuitive, he further tells us, just because the truth of *(4.28)* is *irrelevant* to the truth of *(4.27)*. *This*, he concludes, is what is paradoxical about the Lewis-type definitions: they lead us to hold that propositions imply one another when the relevance-condition is not satisfied.

Their complaint is obviously connected closely with that which we discussed, in chapter 1, about the paradoxicality of the claim that any two necessarily true propositions are logically equivalent to one another. That claim, it should be obvious, is precisely what is asserted in systems S2 to S5 by the thesis

> T12: $(\square P \cdot \square Q)\rightarrow(P\leftrightarrow Q)$

Its apparent paradoxicality, it will be remembered, stemmed from our disinclination to say of the necessarily true propositions

> *(1.5)*   Either the U.S. entered World War I in 1917 or it did not

and

> *(1.23)* Either Canada is south of Mexico or it is not

that they are *really* equivalent even though our definition of "equivalence" forced this conclusion upon us. They have nothing to do with one another, we were inclined to say; so how *could* they be equivalent? It seems clear in retrospect that the qualms thus expressed about equivalence were rooted in the same sort of qualms which Relevance Logicians have expressed about implication. If two propositions have nothing to do with one another, how can one imply the other (as is claimed by T10 and T11) let alone be equivalent to the other (as claimed by T12)?

Our way of handling the earlier problem about equivalence suggests a way of dealing with, or at least of throwing some light on, the related problems about implication. We then suggested that the air of paradox involved in the claim that *(1.5)* is equivalent to *(1.23)* could be removed by recognizing that propositional identity is merely a special case of propositional equivalence so that, although all cases where an identity-relation obtains will be cases where an equivalence-relation obtains, we should not expect the converse to hold. We have a similar suggestion to offer about implication. Let us allow that whenever certain sorts of "inner connection" or "identity of content" obtain between two propositions, as in the cases of proposition-pairs such as

> *(4.31)*   Pat is someone's sister

and

> *(4.32)*   Pat is female

or again

> *(4.16)*   If it rains the snow will melt, and if the snow melts the World Cup slalom
>   will be cancelled

and

> *(4.17)*   If it rains, the World Cup slalom will be cancelled

then the relation of implication will obtain between these propositions. But let us not expect that the converse will also hold in every case. In other words, we suggest that although the finding of the right sort of identity of content is sufficient ground for concluding that an implication relation holds, it is a mistake to suppose it also to be necessary.

It is easy to see how the demand for relevance or inner connection arises. The relevance-condition is *automatically* satisfied in so many of the 'ordinary' cases of implication that come before us: it is satisfied in all cases of implication between contingently applicable concepts; it is satisfied in all cases of implication relations between contingent propositions;[66] and it is even satisfied in many cases of implication relations between noncontingent concepts as well as propositions. Little wonder, then, that the expectation is generated that the relevance condition should be satisfied in *every* case of implication, and a fortiori in *every* case of equivalence.

It is tempting to dismiss the Relevance Logicians' demands for inner connections, and their consequent criticisms of systems like S5 (which accept the impossibility of P being true and Q false as a sufficient condition for P implying Q), by saying that these demands and criticisms are to be attributed to what Wittgenstein once called "a main cause of philosophical disease", viz., "a one-sided diet: one nourishes one's thinking with only one kind of example" (*Philosophical Investigations,* § 593). But that would be too cavalier. For although the proponents of Relevance Logic seem, up to this point, to have had little or no success in defining the concept of *relevant implication*, there can be little doubt but that such a concept is worth defining. We can characterize such a concept broadly by saying that it has application to a proper subset of the cases in which the relation of strict or logical implication holds; and we can say that it stands to the concept of logical implication (definable in terms of possible worlds) in much the same sort of way as the concept of propositional identity stands to the concept of propositional equivalence. The difficulty is to characterize the finer-grained concept of relevant implication more precisely than that.

One thing is clear, however. Nothing is gained by saying that strict or logical implication isn't *really* a case of implication at all. And nothing is gained — but on the contrary much is lost — by insisting that certain standard rules of inference which intuitively strike us as valid are really not so. In rejecting, as invalid, rules such as those of Addition and Disjunctive Syllogism we would be committed also to rejecting each of the analytical methods whereby those rules are customarily justified.[67] And if we give up these, we seem left with no recourse to reason as a way of providing backing for any of our logical intuitions. The cost, in brief, seems prohibitive — prohibitive of reason itself.

The move to predicate logic

Whether or not the following of one proposition from another is *always* dependent (as Relevance Logicians believe) upon the existence of an internal connection between them, there can be no doubt

---

66. Recall our suggestion (in chapter 1, p. 54) that much of the air of paradox generated by possible-worlds analyses of implication is due to a preoccupation with contingent propositions.

67. Among the analytical methods that would have to be abandoned are those of truth-table analysis, given in chapter 5, and the reductio technique, given in chapters 5 and 6. Needless to say, our use of worlds-diagrams as a decision-procedure for truth-functional and modal propositional logic — demonstrated in chapters 5 and 6 — would also go by the board.

that our ability to *show* that one proposition follows from another is *often* dependent upon our ability to *show* that there is a certain sort of internal connection between them. Analysis of the kind which is achieved within the logic of propositions — the logic of unanalyzed propositions, that is — may fail to show that one proposition follows from (or, conversely, implies) another just because it neglects all matters to do with the internal structure of simple propositions and hence neglects all matters to do with the internal connections between simple propositions.

To be sure, propositional logics do not neglect the internal structure of *compound* propositions such as

> *(4.1)*   Either it is necessarily true that sisters are female or it is not

and

> *(4.2)*   It is necessarily true that sisters are female.

Truth-functional propositional logic can tell us that *(4.1)* is to be analyzed as having the structure of a compound proposition which is the disjunction of two contradictories; and it will exhibit this structure by saying that *(4.1)* has the form $P \lor \sim P$. Likewise, modal propositional logic can tell us that *(4.2)* is to be analyzed as having the structure of a compound proposition which ascribes necessary truth to a simpler proposition; and it will exhibit this structure by saying that *(4.2)* has the form $\Box P$. Moreover, by virtue of thus analyzing these compound propositions, these two kinds of propositional logic can reveal a great deal about the internal (logical) connections between these compound propositions and other propositions. But neither logic tells us anything about the internal structure of the *simple* propositions which they involve. And as a consequence neither can tell us anything about any internal, logical, connections which these simple propositions may bear to one another.

In order to show that certain propositions imply others, or that certain corresponding inferences are valid, we often (though not, of course always) must take recourse to such details of the structure of simple propositions as is revealed by analysis at a deeper level: that provided by the logic of predicates — of unanalyzed concepts, that is.

Consider, for example, the argument from the propositions

> *(4.33)*   All politically enlightened persons are sympathetic to socialism

and

> *(4.34)*   All women's liberationists are politically enlightened

to the proposition

> *(4.35)*   All women's liberationists are sympathetic to socialism.

No matter what one thinks of the truth of either of the premises or of the conclusion of this argument, there can be no doubt of its *validity:* the conclusion follows from the premises; the premises imply the conclusion. But how can this be *shown?* Here the logic of propositions cannot help us. By employing the meager analytical and notational resources of propositional logics we can show that the argument has a certain structure or form, one which we might record by writing

$$P$$
$$Q$$
$$\overline{}$$
$$\therefore \quad R$$

But there is nothing about the analyzed structure of the argument as thus exhibited which entitles us to conclude that the argument is valid. The argument

> *(4.34)*   All women's liberationists are politically enlightened
>
> *(4.36)*   All persons sympathetic to socialism are politically enlightened
> ───
> *(4.37)*   ∴ All persons sympathetic to socialism are women's liberationists

has precisely the same form, as revealed at that level of analysis, and yet it is patently *invalid.* After all, there are probably many persons who believe both *(4.34)* and *(4.36)* to be true and yet would strenuously deny *(4.37);* and even if their beliefs are mistaken, it is clear that they cannot fairly be charged with inconsistency as can anyone who asserts the premises but denies the conclusion of a *valid* argument.

   Nevertheless, the validity of the first argument can be shown. It can be shown once we employ the richer analytical and notational resources of predicate logic.

Traditional syllogistic

Aristotle was the first known logician to put any of these requisite resources at our disposal. He put the science of formal logic on its feet by formulating the rules whereby the validity of arguments of this sort — *syllogistic* arguments, as they are called — may be determined. Within the traditional syllogistic logic which he established, the first argument may be analyzed as having the form:

> All M are P
>
> All S are M
> ─────────
> ∴   All S are P

and the second as having the form

> All P are M
>
> All S are M
> ─────────
> ∴   All S are P

where the form of the argument is determined by (a) the internal structure of each proposition and (b) the connection between these internal structures. As to (a), traditional logic analyzed propositions (of the kind that occur in syllogisms) as having one or other of four possible forms:

> A: All ... are ...   (Universal affirmative)
>
> E: No ... are ...   (Universal negative)
>
> I: Some ... are ...   (Particular affirmative)
>
> O: Some ... are not ...   (Particular negative)

where the blanks are filled by so-called "terms". (A term may be regarded, from the point of view of modern logic, as an expression which stands for a property which can be predicated of some item or other, e.g., being a women's liberationist, being politically enlightened, being sympathetic to socialism, etc.) As to (b), traditional logic recognized that the terms which occur within the premises and conclusion can occur within the *argument* in one or other of four possible ways known as "*Figures* of Syllogism". Thus, where "S" stands for the term which occurs as *subject* of the conclusion as well as in one of the premises, "P" stands for the term which occurs as *predicate* of the conclusion as well as in one of the premises, and "M" stands for the so-called *middle term*, i.e., the term which occurs twice in the premises, the four figures of syllogism are:

I	II	III	IV
M P	P M	M P	P M
S M	S M	M S	M S
∴ S P	∴ S P	∴ S P	∴ S P

It can easily be seen that, provided one abides by the convention of always writing the premise which contains the predicate of the conclusion (the *major term,* as it is called) first, and the premise which contains the subject of the conclusion (the *minor term,* it is called) second, these are the only ways in which the major, minor, and middle terms can occur. It can also be seen that since, on this analysis, each of the three propositions involved in each figure may itself have any one of four internal structures or forms (those cited in (a)), there are altogether 4×4^3 (= 256) distinct ways in which the internal structures of the propositions in a syllogism may be connected. Thus there are 256 possible *forms of syllogism.* Needless to say, of the 256 only a relative handful exhibit modes of connection all of whose instances are valid arguments. One of Aristotle's great achievements was to list all the valid forms and provide a set of rules by means of which to distinguish them from the others.

The details of traditional syllogistic analysis need not concern us here. The main point to note is that the validity of many arguments can be determined simply by analyzing them to the level made possible within that tradition and checking to see whether the form which, on analysis, that argument is found to have, is one of the certifiably valid ones. *We do not have to analyze the terms themselves or even understand what concepts they express* in order to show that certain arguments are valid. For instance, the form of the argument from the conjunction of *(4.33)* and *(4.34)* to *(4.35)* turns out to be one of the valid ones. By way of contrast, the form of the argument from the conjunction of *(4.34)* and *(4.36)* to *(4.37)* turns out *not* to be one of the valid ones. Note that we do not say that any argument whose form is not certifiably valid is an argument which can be certified as invalid. Plainly, that would be a mistake. As we have already seen, in passing from the logic of unanalyzed propositions to the logic of unanalyzed concepts, an argument whose form at one level of analysis is not certifiably valid may turn out, at a deeper level of analysis, to be valid nonetheless. Having a certifiably valid form is a sufficient condition of the validity of an argument but it is not a necessary condition. (We will make more of this point in chapter 5.)

Modern predicate logic

The analytical and notational resources of modern predicate logic are much richer than those of traditional syllogistic. Accordingly, many more arguments yield to its treatment. Like traditional syllogistic, it recognizes that so-called *quantifier-words,* like "all" and "some", express concepts which feature in the internal structure of a proposition in such a way as to determine that proposition's logical connections with other propositions independently of what other concepts feature in that proposition, and independently, too, of the analysis of those concepts. But unlike traditional syllogistic it utilizes a symbolism which blends with that of propositional logic to provide a much more versatile means of exhibiting the internal structure of propositions. Consider, for instance, the way in which modern predicate logic enables us to validate the argument from *(4.33)* and *(4.34)* to *(4.35)*.

First let us analyze the propositions themselves. The proposition

>   *(4.33)*   All politically enlightened persons are sympathetic to socialism

is analyzed as asserting that if any items have the property of being a politically enlightened person then those items have the property of being sympathetic to socialism. Using the individual variable "x" to stand for any item whatever,[68] and the predicate letters "**P**" and "**S**" to stand for the properties of being politically enlightened and being sympathetic to socialism, we can then render this analysis in symbols as

> $(x)\ (\mathbf{P}x \supset \mathbf{S}x)$

to be read as "For any x, if x has the property **P** then x has the property **S**". Similarly, the proposition

>   *(4.34)*   All women's liberationists are politically enlightened

is analyzed as having the form

> $(x)\ (\mathbf{W}x \supset \mathbf{P}x)$

where "**W**x" bears the obvious interpretation "x has the property of being a women's liberationist". And the conclusion

>   *(4.35)*   All women's liberationists are sympathetic to socialism

is analyzed as having the form

> $(x)\ (\mathbf{W}x \supset \mathbf{S}x)$.

The argument can then be set out thus:

$$(x)\ (\mathbf{P}x \supset \mathbf{S}x)$$
$$\underline{(x)\ (\mathbf{W}x \supset \mathbf{P}x)}$$
$$\therefore (x)\ (\mathbf{W}x \supset \mathbf{S}x)$$

68. The lowercase letters at the end of the alphabet are standardly used as *individual variables*, i.e., so as to refer indiscriminately to any individuals whatever. Since individual variables are used not to refer to any particular items but indiscriminately to any items whatever, it follows that two or more distinct variables (e.g. "x" and "y") may have one and the same item as their referents.

Now we could, at this point, simply appeal to the educated logical intuitions of anyone who understands the symbolism to validate the argument. And for the purpose of this exercise it would obviously not matter whether one understood what the predicate letters "**P**", "**S**", or "**W**" stood for (what properties they denoted or what concepts they expressed). But intuition is not always reliable. And in any case, the rich resources of predicate logic are at hand.

In order to *show* that the argument is valid we appeal to the already familiar rule of Hypothetical Syllogism along with two rules which belong to predicate logic, viz., the rules of Universal Instantiation (U.I.) and Universal Generalization (U.G.). U.I. tells us that whatever is true of every item is also true of any given item. And U.G. in effect tells us that we can infer a truth about every item from a truth about an arbitrarily selected item.[69] We can then prove that the conclusion follows from the premises by constructing a series of steps from premises to conclusion, each step being justified by appeal to a valid rule of inference. The proof goes as follows:

(1)   (x) (**P**x ⊃ **S**x)   [Premise]

(2)   (x) (**W**x ⊃ **P**x)   [Premise]

(3)   **P**x ⊃ **S**x   [(1) × U.I.]

(4)   **W**x ⊃ **P**x   [(2) × U.I.]

(5)   **W**x ⊃ **S**x   [(4), (3) × Hypothetical Syllogism]

(6)   (x) (**W**x ⊃ **S**x)   [(5) × U.G.]

The proof offered is constructed in the style of natural deduction rather than axiomatics. But needless to say, a proof of the validity of the argument could equally well, though with a good deal more difficulty, be given in an axiomatization of predicate logic, i.e., in the so-called Predicate Calculus.

So far, the only quantifier we have used is the universal quantifier "(x)". With its help we can analyze and render into symbolic form propositions which make assertions about *all* items having a certain property. But not all propositions make universal claims. Sometimes we merely want to make the lesser claim that there is *at least one* item which has a certain property. In order to give straightforward expression to such claims, modern predicate logic uses the *existential quantifier* "(∃x)" — to be read as "There is at least one item such that. . . ." Thus if we wanted to analyze the proposition

(4.32)   Some persons sympathetic to socialism are women's liberationists

we could write

(∃x) (**S**x · **W**x)

and read it as "There is at least one x such that x is an **S** and x is a **W**". Strictly speaking, any formula containing an existential quantifier can be rewritten in the form of one containing a universal quantifier, and vice versa, as the following equivalences make clear:

69. More perspicuously, U.G. could be stated this way: If a property holds of a member of a set irrespective of which member it is, then that property holds of every member of that set.

$$\text{``(x) (}\mathbf{S}x \supset \mathbf{W}x\text{)''} =_{df} \text{``}{\sim}(\exists x)\ (\mathbf{S}x \cdot {\sim}\mathbf{W}x)\text{''}$$

$$\text{``(}\exists x)\ (\mathbf{S}x \cdot \mathbf{W}x\text{)''} =_{df} \text{``}{\sim}(x)\ (\mathbf{S}x \supset {\sim}\mathbf{W}x)\text{''}$$

Nevertheless, the symbolism is a lot easier to read and to work with if we allow this small redundancy.

Modal notions in predicate logic

Our purposes in giving the foregoing sketches of the symbolism of traditional and modern predicate logic have been twofold. First, we have wanted to illustrate the fact that in the case of many valid inferences, the analytical and notational resources of *propositional* logic do not suffice to show us why these inferences are valid. For such cases, we need a deeper analysis such as that provided by *predicate* logic. Secondly, we have wanted to prepare the ground for an intelligible discussion of the role which modal concepts play at this deeper level of analysis. We are now ready for that discussion.

Although the object-languages of traditional syllogistic and modern predicate calculus contain no symbols for the modal properties of necessity, possibility, etc., or the modal relations of implication, equivalence, etc., it is clear that insofar as these systems are taken to establish the logical truth of certain theses or the validity of certain argument-forms, modal concepts are *implicitly* invoked.

They are *explicitly* invoked in modal predicate logic. Once more, it was Aristotle who did the pioneering work. His treatment of modal syllogistic, it has been conjectured, was his last major contribution to logic. That treatment, however, although it motivated much medieval interest in modal concepts, was far from satisfactory. It was not until the 1940s that Ruth C. Barcan (later Ruth Barcan Marcus) investigated ways of blending modal logic with modern theory about the quantifiers "(x)" and "(∃x)" and so founded modal predicate logic as it is usually understood.[70]

Many of the most interesting, and also many of the most controversial, questions about modal predicate logic concern the formula by means of which Barcan tried to effect the 'mixing' of the two kinds of logic. The formula, which has come to be known as "the Barcan Formula" (BF) may be symbolized in two forms:

$$\text{BF1:} \quad \Diamond(\exists x)\mathbf{F}x \rightarrow (\exists x)\Diamond\mathbf{F}x$$

(the form in which she originally propounded it); or as

$$\text{BF2:} \quad (x)\ \Box\mathbf{F}x \rightarrow \Box(x)\mathbf{F}x$$

(which can easily be shown to be equivalent to BF1, and which is the form which has most often attracted attention). BF1 may be read as asserting: From the proposition that it is possible that there exists an item which has the property **F** it follows that there exists an item which possibly has **F**. And BF2 may be read as asserting: From the proposition that every item necessarily has the property **F** it follows that it is necessary that everything has the property **F**.

There is nothing surprising nor controversial about the presence in BF1 and BF2, respectively, of the wffs $\Diamond(\exists x)\mathbf{F}x$ and $\Box(x)\mathbf{F}x$. The wff $\Diamond(\exists x)\mathbf{F}x$ is easily recognizable as a substitution-instance of the wff $\Diamond P$ of modal propositional logic; and $\Box(x)\mathbf{F}x$ is easily recognizable as a substitution-instance of the wff $\Box P$ of modal propositional logic. The surprises, and the puzzles, are to be found in the rest of each of these formulae: (a) in the mere presence of the wffs $(\exists x)\Diamond\mathbf{F}x$ and $(x)\Box\mathbf{F}x$ in BF1 and BF2, respectively; and (b) in the asserted implications whereby $(\exists x)\Diamond\mathbf{F}x$ is claimed to follow from $\Diamond(\exists x)\mathbf{F}x$ and $(x)\Box\mathbf{F}x$ is claimed to imply $\Box(x)\mathbf{F}x$.

70. Independently and concurrently, Carnap developed foundations for modal predicate logic.

Modalities de dicto and de re

The mere presence of the wffs $(\exists x)\Diamond\mathbf{F}x$ and $(x)\Box\mathbf{F}x$ seems to some philosophers to be philosophically suspect, for it reminds them of a distinction which medieval logicians made much of: that between modalities *de dicto* and modalities *de re*. By a *de dicto* modality, as Thomas Aquinas explained it, is meant the attribution of a modal property to a *proposition* as in the proposition

> *(4.39)*   It is possible that Socrates is running

whereas by a *de re* modality is meant the attribution of a modal property to an *individual* as in the proposition

> *(4.40)*   Socrates is possibly running.

The distinction itself, it would be admitted, is not particularly troublesome; indeed it reflects accurately enough the two main uses of modal expressions in natural languages such as Latin and English. What is troublesome, 'they would say, is what some philosophers have *said* about the distinction. Some philosophers have said that *de re* modalities are irreducibly different from *de dicto* ones and that, accordingly, it makes sense to revive the Aristotelian doctrine of *essentialism,* i.e., the doctrine that some properties inhere essentially or necessarily in the individuals which have those properties. As against this, many philosophers, such as Quine, regard essentialism as an anachronism which deserves no place in a scientific view of the world. Accordingly, philosophers of Quine's conviction find expressions like $(x)\Box\mathbf{F}x$ and $(\exists x)\Diamond\mathbf{F}x$, in which the modal symbols appear in *de re* position, thoroughly misleading. If these wffs are merely notational variants on the corresponding wffs *de dicto,* viz., $\Box(x)\mathbf{F}x$ and $\Diamond(\exists x)\mathbf{F}x$, then — they would say — quantified modal logic is an unnecessary complication. But if they are taken to be irreducibly different from their *de dicto* counterparts, then — they would say — quantified modal logic is metaphysically objectionable.

This first objection to BF1 and BF2 can, of course, be met by arguing that there is nothing at all wrong with essentialism and that the contrary view, expressed by John Stuart Mill in the words "Individuals have no essences", is itself insupportable. There has in fact been a revival in recent years of interest in, and support for, the doctrine of essentialism. Unfortunately we cannot pursue the issue here.[71]

A second objection to BF1 and BF2 is that each of the asserted implications seems to be exposed to obvious counterexamples. As an instance of

> BF1: $\Diamond(\exists x)\mathbf{F}x \longrightarrow (\exists x)\Diamond\mathbf{F}x$

consider the case where $\mathbf{F}x$ expresses the concept of being someone who landed in Kansas in 1916 from a space-yacht called "Dora". Then BF1 commits us to saying that the proposition

> *(4.41)*   It is possible that there exists someone who landed in Kansas in 1916 from a space-yacht called "Dora"

implies the proposition

> *(4.42)*   There exists someone who possibly landed in Kansas in 1916 from a space-yacht called "Dora".

71. For a readable defence of essentialism and discussion of some of the issues surrounding it, see Baruch A. Brody, "Why Settle for Anything Less than Good Old-Fashioned Aristotelian Essentialism?" *Nous,* vol. 7 (1973), pp. 351–365.

Suppose, however, that what makes *(4.41)* true is the fact that in the possible world of Heinlein's novel *Time Enough For Love* the chief character, Lazarus Long, has the property of landing from a space-yacht, etc. Does it follow from this that there really *is* someone (someone in the actual world) who possibly has that property? Surely not. Although Lazarus may exist in the possible world of *Time Enough For Love,* he may well not exist in the actual world — and, for that matter, neither may anyone else of whom it is true to say that he might have landed in a space-yacht in 1916. *(4.42)* cannot follow from *(4.41)* since it may be false when *(4.41)* is true. Again, as an instance of

$$\text{BF2:} \quad (x) \, \square \, \mathbf{F}x \longrightarrow \square \, (x)\mathbf{F}x$$

consider the case where **F**x expresses the concept of being something that exists. Then BF2 commits us to saying that the proposition

> *(4.43)*   Everything necessarily exists

implies the proposition

> *(4.44)*   It is necessarily true that everything exists.

Suppose, however, that we hold *(4.43)* to be true because, like some essentialists, we hold that existence is an essential property of everything that *actually* exists.[72] Does it follow from this that, as *(4.44)* asserts, in the case of every possible world everything that exists in the actual world exists there also? Hardly. Although Nixon exists in the actual world and hence, according to some essentialists, essentially exists therein, he surely does not exist in all the possible but nonactual worlds which, in our more fanciful moments, we conceive of.

All this is very puzzling. Not only have many astute thinkers accepted the Barcan formulae as obvious truths of logic; it also turns out that these formulae are derivable as theorems in certain axiomatizations of modal predicate logic, viz., in certain axiom systems which combine the truth-functional predicate calculus with S5. On the face of it, then, if we were to accept the purported counterexamples given above then we should have to reject either the truth-functional predicate calculus or the modal system S5. Neither seems a palatable alternative. But, then, too, the counterexamples to the Barcan formulae also seem very persuasive.

There is a way out of this logical bind. It turns out that the Barcan formulae are not derivable in *all* axiomatizations of predicate logic but only in some. They are derivable only in axiomatizations which yield, as theorems, formulae some of which contain what are called *free variables*. They are not derivable in axiomatizations which yield, as theorems, formulae all of which are said to be universally closed.[73] This means that the choice before us is not quite as painful as it might have seemed. We can continue to accept the counterexamples as genuine, and continue to accept S5, simply by deciding to accept as theorems only those formulae of predicate logic which are universally closed. Quantified S5, thus presented, does not contain either of the Barcan formulae.[74]

72. Brody, *op. cit.,* holds this. **F** is an essential property of an object, O, on his view, just when O has that property and would go out of existence if it lost it. Since nothing can continue to exist if it loses the property of existence, existence — on his view — is an essential property. On his view, that is, *(4.43)* is true.

73. Roughly, a formula contains a free variable if it contains a variable which is not subject to quantification. Thus, in $(x)(\mathbf{F}x \supset \mathbf{G}y)$, y is free since it is not "bound" by, or subject to, the quantifier (x). The formula $(x)(\mathbf{F}x \supset \mathbf{G}y)$ is not universally closed. We can make it into a universally closed formula, however, by subjecting the free variable y to universal quantification as in $(y)(x)(\mathbf{F}x \supset \mathbf{G}y)$.

74. This important result was first proved by Saul Kripke, "Semantical Considerations on Modal Logic", *Acta Philosophica Fennica,* vol. 16 (1963), especially pp. 57–90. As Kripke points out, the acceptance, as theorems, of

We are still left with the puzzle that, quite independently of the alleged derivability of the Barcan formulae within quantified S5, many philosophers have found these formulae intuitively acceptable. Why should this be? We might be tempted, at this point, to invoke the hypothesis that these philosophers simply have not subjected their beliefs in the Barcan formulae to that kind of strenuous search for counterexamples which, in chapter 2, we described as the Method of Possible-Worlds Parables.[75] If so, we are inclined to say, they would surely have turned up the counterexamples cited. and accordingly have abandoned these beliefs. But this hypothesis would not do justice to the situation. The fact is that the sponsors of the Barcan formulae accept these formulae not out of ignorance of the existence of purported counterexamples, but because they have a view of what possible worlds are which does not allow us, without inconsistency, even to construct these supposed counterexamples. Let us explain.

Heterogeneous and homogeneous possible worlds

It is clear, on reflection, that in offering these counterexamples we were presupposing that an object which exists in one possible world might not exist in another. Thus our counterexample to BF1 depended upon the assumption that Lazarus Long exists in some nonactual possible worlds even though he does not exist in the actual one. And our counterexample to BF2 depended upon the assumption that even though Nixon does exist in the actual world he does not exist in some non-actual possible world. In other words, we have been supposing that possible worlds are *heterogeneous* in respect of which objects they contain: that some objects which do not exist in the actual world do exist in other possible worlds, and that some objects which do exist in the actual world do not exist in other possible worlds.

But suppose we were to take the view that possible worlds are *homogeneous* in respect of which objects they contain: that all and only those objects which exist in the actual world can intelligibly be supposed to exist in other possible worlds. Then other possible worlds will differ from ours only in respect of the differing properties which these objects have and in respect of the differing relations in which these objects stand to one another. But since Lazarus does not exist in the actual world, there will not be any possible worlds in which he does exist; and since Nixon exists in the actual world, there will not be any possible worlds in which he fails to exist. On this *homogeneous-worlds* view, the counterexamples simply cannot be envisaged and the Barcan formulae express obvious truths. [76]

At this point it is tempting to ask: Which of these views about possible worlds is the correct one? Tempting, perhaps; but not a question to be pursued here. Our own view of the matter should be evident from the fact that we chose to introduce possible worlds, in chapter 1, p. 1, by reference to Lazarus Long and the 'world' of Heinlein's novel. We find it highly implausible to suppose that

---

formulae containing free variables is "at best a convenience". He might well have added that at worst it puts us into the logical bind sketched above. For some pertinent cautionary morals about the construction and interpretation of axiomatic systems see Hughes and Cresswell, *An Introduction to Modal Logic*, 2nd ed., London, Methuen, 1968, p. 182.

75. Chapter 2, section 8. A possible-worlds parable is a story which presents a counterexample to some thesis of the form A → B by describing a possible world in which A is true and B is false.

76. The homogeneous-worlds view, it is worth noting, is one to which quite a number of philosophers are drawn for reasons which have nothing to do with a defence of the Barcan formulae. Wittgenstein seems to have adopted it in his *Tractatus Logico-Philosophicus* (see, especially, 2.002 and 2.023). And others, like A.N. Prior, seem drawn to it because of views they hold about naming. See his *Objects of Thought*, Oxford, Clarendon Press, 1971, pp. 169–170.

everything which does exist exists necessarily and that nothing could even possibly exist except what does exist. But whichever view one adopts, this much is clear. Possible worlds — talk about which, we have argued, plays a fundamental role within propositional logic in explicating the notions of implication, validity, and the like — *continues* to play the same sort of role within predicate logic even though, at that level of analysis, the concept of a possible world itself becomes a prime object for further analysis.

That said, we turn to a question even more vexed than any we have considered hitherto, viz.,

Is there really a logic of concepts?

The case for saying that the science of logic needs to be pursued, on occasion, to a deeper level of analysis than that provided for within Predicate Logic — the Logic of Unanalyzed Concepts, as we have called it — stems from three seemingly undeniable facts: (1) that philosophers find it natural to speak of certain concepts, e.g., that of being a sister, standing in the relation of *implication* to others, e.g., that of being female; standing in this relation of *inconsistency* to others, e.g., that of being male; and so on; (2) that relations such as those of implication and inconsistency are paradigms of *logical* relations; and (3) that the analytical and notational resources of Predicate Logic (and a fortiori also those of Propositional Logic) do not suffice as ways of *justifying* our beliefs that these logical relations do in fact obtain.

Prima facie, the case is a strong one. It can be made even stronger if we turn from the now-hackneyed examples of being a sister and being female to other examples which seemingly also demonstrate the inadequacy of Predicate Logic to certify the full range of logical relations. Here is a handful of illustrative concept-pairs:

> (a)   *(4.45)*   knowing that P
>   and *(4.46)*   believing that P;
>
> (b)   *(4.47)*   being red
>   and *(4.48)*   being colored;
>
> (c)   *(4.49)*   being an event
>   and *(4.50)*   occurring at some time or other;
>
> (d)   *(4.51)*   being taller than
>   and *(4.52)*   being at least as tall as;
>
> (e)   *(4.53)*   being more than 20 in number
>   and *(4.54)*   being at least 19 in number.

Each of the implication relations obtaining in (a), (b), (c), (d), and (e) is representative of a whole set of similar implication relations: that in (a), of the sorts of implications which have been recognized in traditional epistemology and are nowadays enshrined in epistemic logics; that in (b), of the sorts of implications which hold between *determinate* properties and the more general *determinable* properties under which they fall; that in (c), of the sorts of implications which hold between *categories* of things and the various determinable properties which are among their essential properties; that in (d), of the sorts of implications which can hold between relational concepts; and that of (e), of the sorts of implications which can hold between quantitative and number concepts. And it would not be hard to cite examples of other pairs of concepts the members of which stand to one another in still other logical relations (drawn from the set of fifteen depicted by the worlds-diagrams of figure *(1.i)*) which fall outside the certificatory competence of Predicate Logic.

Nor can this failure be excused by saying that Predicate Logic is designed only to display logical relations between (whole) propositions rather than those between conceptual constituents of propositions. This is no excuse; it is part of the complaint. In any case, the failure is equally evident within the field of propositions. We need only consider certain propositions within which the concepts cited in (a) through (e) feature in order to see that valid inferences may be drawn from propositions, as well as concepts, in ways which Predicate Logic seemingly cannot explain. There seems no doubt, for instance, of the validity of each of the following inferences:

(a*)   from *(4.45*)*   The Pope knows that P
     to   *(4.46*)*   The Pope believes that P;

(b*)   from *(4.47*)*   This liquid is red
     to   *(4.48*)*   This liquid is colored;

(c*)   from *(4.49*)*   John described the event
     to   *(4.50*)*   John described something that happened at
                some time or other;

(d*)   from *(4.51*)*   Molly is taller than Judi
     to   *(4.52*)*   Molly is at least as tall as Judi;

(e*)   from *(4.53*)*   There are more than 20 apples in the basket
     to   *(4.54*)*   There are at least 19 apples in the basket.

Yet, on the face of it, the validity of each of these inferences can be certified only by analyzing concepts which Predicate Logic must perforce leave unanalyzed.

Thus it is that the very same sorts of considerations which led us to make the move from Propositional Logic to Predicate Logic seem to impel us to make a further move from Predicate Logic, within which the logical powers of many concepts go unrecognized, to a still deeper level of logical analysis — that of a Logic of Concepts. Not surprisingly, therefore, many philosophers — especially over the past twenty years or so — have thought it wholly proper to entitle, or subtitle, their analytical inquiries "The Logic of . . ." (where the gap is filled in with a description of a concept or set of concepts, e.g., " . . . Decision", " . . . Preference", " . . . Pleasure", " . . . Religion", " . . . Moral Discourse", etc.). For instance, Jaakko Hintikka subtitles his book *Knowledge and Belief* — one of the foundational works in epistemic logic — *An Introduction to the Logic of the Two Notions,* and takes pains to insist: "The word 'logic' which occurs in the subtitle of this work is to be taken seriously."[77] He goes on to show that logical relations of consistency, inconsistency, implication, and the like, hold between various epistemic notions ("concepts" as we have called them) in ways of which formal logic takes no cognizance.

Yet there are many logicians for whom this talk of a Logic of Concepts is, at best, to be taken in jest. At worst, they would say, such talk betrays an ignorance of the true nature of logic. The science of logic, as they see it, is a purely formal one, akin to pure mathematics, and hence has nothing to do with the properties of, or relations between, such substantive concepts as those of knowledge and belief, being red and being colored, or the like. It is concerned solely with formulating the principles or rules of valid inference which warrant certain patterns or forms of argument independently of any

77. J. Hintikka, *Knowledge and Belief: An Introduction to the Logic of the Two Notions,* Ithaca, Cornell University Press, 1962, p. 3.

special attributes of the substantive concepts which feature therein. Concepts such as those of knowledge and belief may well feature within valid arguments; but not in ways which are relevant to those arguments' validity. If an argument is valid, it is valid solely by virtue of its form. Against those who, like ourselves, are convinced that the inference

> (a*)   from   *(4.45*)* The Pope knows that P
>   to   *(4.46*)* The Pope believes that P

as it stands, is valid, those who believe in the omnicompetence of formal logic to deal with all matters of validity would argue: (1) that this inference is *not* valid as it stands, since it is not warranted by any rules of formally valid inference; (2) that our conviction to the contrary stems from the fact that we are taking for granted the truth of the further premise

> *(4.55)*   If any person knows that P then that person believes that P;

and (3) that when this further premise is explicitly invoked, the strictly invalid inference in (a*) is transformed into an inference whose validity Predicate Logic can easily demonstrate. For then, the two premises *(4.45*)* and *(4.55)* can be seen to exhibit the forms

> **K**a

[where the letter "a" is an individual constant[78] standing for the Pope, and the predicate letter "**K**" stands for the property of being a person who knows that P] and

> (x)(**K**x ⊃ **B**x)

[to be read as "For any x, if x has the property **K** then x has the property **B**"], respectively. And the validity of the inference from these two premises to the conclusion *(4.46*)* — symbolized as "**B**a" [where "a" stands for the Pope, as before, and "**B**" for the property of being a person who believes that P] — can then be demonstrated as follows:

> (1)   **K**a   [Premise]
> (2)   (x)(**K**x ⊃ **B**x)   [Unstated Premise]
> (3)   **K**a ⊃ **B**a   [(2) × U.I.]
> (4)   **B**a   [(3), (1) × Modus Ponens]

But within the argument, as thus laid out, the concepts of knowledge and belief — on whose internal connections the validity of the inference was initially supposed to hinge — have dropped out of sight and out of mind. The predicate letters "**K**" and "**B**" could stand for any properties whatever and the individual constant "a" for any item whatever, and the argument would still be valid, i.e., formally valid. Moreover, it would be claimed, the same sort of treatment suffices to bring *all* cases of allegedly nonformally valid inferences within the compass of formal logic.

Now it must be admitted that the formalist's stratagem does work, in the sense that it is always possible, in the case of any example that we might cite of a nonformally valid inference, to cite some further premise or premises the addition of which will transform the inference into a formally valid one. However, this does not in itself settle the issue. For the nonformalist will be quick to point out

---

78. The first few lowercase letters of the alphabet are standardly used as names of particular items or individuals. They are known as *individual constants* since they are taken to have constant reference to the individuals of which they are the assigned names.

that these additional premises, which the formalist claims are needed if the inference is to be validated, are not really needed at all. After all, when we take a look at these additional, allegedly needed premises, we find that they invariably have the character of so-called analytic propositions, i.e., propositions which can be certified by analysis as necessarily true. Plainly, the additional premise, viz., *(4.55)*, which is supposedly required for the formal validation of (a*), is analytic (and hence necessarily true). And so, too, are those which are supposedly required for the formal validation of (b*) through (e*), viz., respectively,

> *(4.56)*   If anything is red then it is colored;
> *(4.57)*   If anything is an event then it happens at some time or other;
> *(4.58)*   If x is taller than y, then x is at least as tall as y;

and

> *(4.59)*   If there are more than 20 items then there are at least 19.

But it is easily shown — the nonformalist continues — that necessarily true propositions can always be dispensed with (or deleted) in the case of a valid inference.[79] Hence, if — as the formalist allows — the inferences in (a*) through (e*) are valid in the presence of these necessarily true propositions, they must also be valid in their absence.

What does the formalist have to say to all this? He will not contest the claim that if a valid inference contains a necessarily true premise, then that premise may be dispensed with without affecting the validity of the inference. For this result is one whose truth he recognizes from having examined formal systems containing formally certifiable necessary propositions. But what he will contest is the claim that propositions *(4.55)* through *(4.59)* are genuine examples of necessarily true propositions. He will allow that, within the long-standing tradition founded by Kant, they are paradigm examples of analytic propositions. But he will deny that they meet the requisite conditions for saying that they are necessarily true. For, he will now insist, a proposition can no more be said to be necessarily true unless it is formally true than an argument can be said to be valid unless it is formally valid.

At this point the dispute begins to sound as though it has come full circle, or close to it. Or rather, it begins to sound as though it is bedeviled by a large measure of verbal disagreement. What one party counts as a valid inference the other does not, since it does not meet certain formal criteria of validity; what one party counts as a necessarily true proposition the other does not since, again, it does not meet certain formal criteria — this time of necessary truth. In short, what one party counts as a logical property or a logical relation, the other does not.

The disagreement, although verbal, is not trivial. It stems from the presence, within the logical tradition established by Aristotle, of two different though related strands of concern: concern, on the one hand, with the *semantic* questions as to what it is for an argument to be valid or for a proposition to be necessarily true; and concern, on the other hand, with discovering formal or *syntactic* marks, the presence of which offers assurance of an argument's validity or a proposition's necessary truth.

There can be little doubt that, throughout much of the history of logic, the second sort of concern has been predominant. To be sure, Aristotle wrestled for some time with semantic questions about the notions of validity and necessary truth. But he did not advance much beyond the point of seeing that the first can be explicated in terms of the second — that an argument is valid when its conclusion

79. The argument is a simple one. To say that the conjunction of a proposition P with an "additional" proposition R implies a proposition Q is just to say that all the possible worlds in which P and R are true together are worlds in which Q is true. But in the case where R is necessarily true, the set of possible worlds in which P and R are true together is precisely the same set of worlds in which P is true alone. (This is easily verified by considering figure *(5.d)* in chapter 5.) Hence, if P and R imply Q, and R is necessarily true, P by itself implies Q.

follows "of necessity" from its premises — and that the second can be explicated in terms of the notion of possibility — that which is necessarily true is that which is not possibly false. His greatest achievements came with the discovery of certain formal marks of validity and his formulation of formal principles or rules which can guarantee the validity of syllogistic inferences. It was these achievements which his latter-day successors, Boole, Frege, Russell, and company, followed up so brilliantly in order to establish formal logic as a science comparable in rigor, power, and abstractness to the science of mathematics. Indeed, so preoccupied have some logicians become with the development of formal systems and techniques that, in the idiom of many, talk of logic is taken to be synonymous with talk of formal logic, or even of mathematical logic.

Too strong a predilection for the formal, however, tends to obscure the fact of the continuing presence throughout the history of philosophy of the other set of concerns: concerns with the semantic analysis of our preformal intuitions about validity, necessity, and other related logical concepts. Aristotle, we have suggested, was motivated to undertake his formal inquiries just because of the light which he thought they could throw on these concepts. And medieval logicians undertook their studies of modal logic partly for the same sort of reason. But it is only recently — since the early 1960s, in fact — that the imbalance of the formal over the semantical has begun to be redressed. It is being redressed, of course, by the development — in the hands of philosopher-logicians like Saul Kripke and Jaakko Hintikka — of so-called *possible worlds semantics*.

The merits of the possible worlds approach to logic are becoming increasingly clear to philosophers and logicians alike. It makes possible a semantical explication of the concepts of validity, necessary truth, and so on, which is free of the constraints of formal logic as hitherto conceived. As we have seen, it tells us that a proposition is necessarily true if and only if it is true in all possible worlds — an explication which accords well with Aristotle's view that necessary propositions are such that it is not possible that they should be false; and it tells us that an argument is valid if and only if in all possible worlds, if any, in which its premises are true its conclusion is true — an explication which accords well, again, with Aristotle's view that an argument is valid when its conclusion follows "of necessity" from its premises. It allows, of course, that satisfying certain formal conditions is a *sufficient* condition of an argument's validity or a proposition's necessary truth. But it does not allow the formalist's claim that these formal conditions are *necessary* ones. Thus it enables us to make good sense, for instance, of talk about knowledge implying belief without resorting to the formalist's ad hocery of invoking 'additional' premises. And it enables us to make good sense of talk about the necessary truth of propositions such as *(4.55)* through *(4.59)*, despite the fact that they are neither among the recognized truths of formal logic nor even instantiations of such truths. The explications of logical concepts offered by possible worlds semantics allow room for our belief that there is, after all, a legitimate field of logical inquiry which, for want of a better description, may be called The Logic of Concepts.

It must not be thought, however, that the possible worlds approach to the science of logic turns its back on the hard-won achievements of formal, 'mathematical' logic. On the contrary; it takes the results of formal logic for granted, gives them a semantical underpinning, and tries to supplement these results with results of its own — results which allow for the development along semantical-cum-formal lines of logics for concepts such as those of knowledge and belief, preference, decision, and so on. In short, the possible worlds approach to logic — replete as it is with modal talk — brings together the two main strands of logical inquiry in such a way that justice is done both to the achievements of the formalists and to the nonformal analyses which philosophers have traditionally given of the substantive concepts which figure centrally in our thinking about this and other possible worlds.

From the vantage point of this perspective it can be seen that, although our own terminological preferences are clear, it does not really matter how one uses the word "logic" — whether in such a way that the "formal" in "formal logic" becomes redundant or in such a way as to allow the possibility of nonformal logical attributes. What matters is only that one recognizes that concepts and propositions can have properties and stand in relations which are explicable in terms of their application or truth in the set of all possible worlds, even when those properties and relations are not recognized within established formal logics. Failure to recognize this fact can only be a stumbling block in the way of future logico-philosophical inquiry.

5

Truth-Functional Propositional Logic

1. INTRODUCTION

In this chapter, and the remaining chapter 6, we turn from the vista of logic as a whole and concentrate solely on the Logic of Unanalyzed Propositions. Even then, our focus is a limited one. We say nothing more about the method of inference and concern ourselves mainly with how the method of analysis can lead to knowledge of logical truth.

The present chapter takes a closer look at the truth-functional fragment of propositional logic. We try to show: (1) how the truth-functional concepts of negation, conjunction, disjunction, material conditionality, and material biconditionality may be expressed in English as well as in symbols; (2) how these concepts may be explicated in terms of the possible worlds in which they have application; and (3) how the modal attributes of propositions expressed by compound truth-functional sentences may be ascertained by considering worlds-diagrams, truth-tables, and other related methods. In effect, we try to make good our claim that modal concepts are indispensable for an understanding of logic as a whole, including those truth-functional parts within which they seemingly do not feature.

2. TRUTH-FUNCTIONAL OPERATORS

The expressions "not", "and", "or", "if . . . then . . . ", and "if and only if" may be said to be *sentential operators* just insofar as each may be used in ordinary language and logic alike to 'operate' on a sentence or sentences in such a way as to form *compound* sentences.

The sentences on which such operators operate are called the *arguments* of those operators. When such an operator operates on a *single* argument (i.e., when it operates on a single sentence, whether simple or compound), to form a more complex one, we shall say that it is a *monadic operator*. Thus the expressions "not" and "it is not the case that" are monadic operators insofar as we may take a simple sentence like

> *(5.1)* "Jack will go up the hill"

and form from it the compound sentence

> *(5.2)* "Jack will not go up the hill"

247

or (more transparently)

> *(5.3)*   "It is not the case that Jack will go up the hill."

Or we may take a compound sentence like

> *(5.4)*   "Jack will go up the hill and Jill will go up the hill"

and form from it a still more complex sentence such as

> *(5.5)*   "It is not the case that Jack will go up the hill and Jill will go up the hill."[1]

When an expression takes as its arguments *two* sentences and operates on them to form a more complex sentence we shall say that it is a *dyadic operator*. Thus, the expression "and" is a dyadic operator insofar as we may take two simple sentences like

> *(5.1)*   "Jack will go up the hill"

and

> *(5.6)*   "Jill will go up the hill"

and form from them a compound sentence such as

> *(5.7)*   "Jack and Jill will go up the hill"

or (more transparently)

> *(5.8)*   "Jack will go up the hill and Jill will go up the hill."

Or we may take two compound sentences like

> *(5.2)*   "Jack will not go up the hill"

and

> *(5.9)*   "Jill will not go up the hill"

and form from them a still more complex sentence such as

> *(5.10)*   "Jack will not go up the hill and Jill will not go up the hill."

The expressions "or", "if . . . then . . . ", and "if and only if" are also dyadic operators. Dyadic operators are sometimes called sentential *connectives* since they connect simpler sentences to form more complex ones.[2]

---

1. Note that this sentence is ambiguous between "It is not the case that Jack will go up the hill and it is the case that Jill will go up the hill" and "It is not the case both that Jack will go up the hill and Jill will go up the hill." This ambiguity, along with many others, is easily removed in the conceptual notation of symbolic logic, as we shall shortly see.

2. Some authors like to regard "it is not the case that" as a sort of degenerate or limiting case of a connective — a case where it 'connects' just one sentence. We, however, will reserve the term "connective" for dyadic operators only.

Now each of the sentential operators cited above is commonly said to be *truth-functional* in the sense that each generates compound sentences out of simpler ones in such a way that the truth-values of the propositions expressed by the compound sentences are determined by, or are a function of, the truth-values of the propositions expressed by the simpler sentential components. Thus it is commonly said that "it is not the case that" is truth-functional since the compound sentence "It is not the case that Jack will go up the hill" expresses a proposition which is true in just those possible worlds in which the proposition expressed by its simple sentential component "Jack will go up the hill" is false, and expresses a proposition which is false in just those possible worlds in which the proposition expressed by the latter sentence is true; that "and" is truth-functional since the compound sentence "Jack will go up the hill and Jill will go up the hill" expresses a proposition which is true in just those possible worlds in which the propositions expressed by the sentential components "Jack will go up the hill" and "Jill will go up the hill", are both true, and expresses a proposition which is false in all other possible worlds; that "or" is truth-functional since the compound sentence "Jack will go up the hill or Jill will go up the hill" expresses a proposition which is true in all those possible worlds in which at least one of the propositions expressed by the sentential components is true, and expresses a proposition which is false in all other possible worlds; and so on.

This common way of putting it gives us a fairly good grip on the notion of truth-functionality. But it is seriously misleading nonetheless. For it is just plain false to say of each of these sentential operators that it *is* truth-functional in the sense explained. We should say rather that each *may be used* truth-functionally while allowing that some at least may also be used non-truth-functionally. Let us explain case by case.

The uses of "not" and "it is not the case that"

It is easy enough to find cases in which the word "not" operates truth-functionally. When, for instance, we start with a simple sentence like

> *(5.11)*   "God does exist"

and insert the word "not" so as to form the compound sentence

> *(5.12)*   "God does not exist"

we are using "not" truth-functionally. The proposition expressed by the compound sentence *(5.12)* will be true in all those possible worlds in which the proposition expressed by the simple sentential component of that sentence is false, and will be false in all those possible worlds in which the latter is true. But suppose now that we start with a simple sentence,

> *(5.13)*   "All the children are going up the hill"

and insert the word "not" so as to form the compound sentence

> *(5.14)*   "All the children are not going up the hill."

This latter sentence is ambiguous. And the answer to the question whether the operator "not" is being used truth-functionally on *(5.13)* depends on which of two propositions *(5.14)* is being used to express. On the one hand, *(5.14)* could be used by someone to express what could better, that is, unambiguously, be expressed by the sentence

> *(5.15)*   "It is not the case that all the children are going up the hill."

In such a circumstance we would say that the "not" in *(5.14)* is being used (even though infelicitously) truth-functionally. But if, on the other hand, *(5.14)* were to be used to express the proposition which would be expressed by the sentence

(5.16)   "None of the children is going up the hill"

then we would want to say that the "not" in *(5.14)* would be used non-truth-functionally. In this latter case, the truth-value of the proposition expressed by *(5.16)* viz., the proposition,

(5.17)   None of the children is going up the hill

is not determined by, is not a truth-function of, the proposition expressed by the simple sentence *(5.13)*, viz., the proposition

(5.18)   All the children are going up the hill.

The two disambiguations of the sentence *(5.14)*, viz., the sentences *(5.15)* and *(5.16)*, express propositions which are logically non-equivalent. Only the former of these propositions is a truth-function of the proposition expressed by the simple sentential component of *(5.14)*, viz., the simple sentence *(5.13)*, "All the children are going up the hill"; the other is not. Why is the proposition expressed by the sentence *(5.16)* — i.e., the proposition *(5.17)*, that none of the children is going up the hill — *not* a truth-function of the proposition *(5.18)*, viz., that all the children are going up the hill? The answer is simply that the truth-value of *(5.17)* is not determined by, i.e., is not a function of, the truth-value of *(5.18)*. It would suffice for *(5.17)*'s not being a truth-function of *(5.18)* if either the truth of *(5.18)* did not determine the truth-value of *(5.17)* or the falsity of *(5.18)* did not determine the truth-value of *(5.17)*. As it turns out, however, both these conditions obtain: *neither* the truth *nor* the falsity of *(5.18)* determines the truth-value of *(5.17)*. For there are possible worlds in which *(5.18)* is true and in which *(5.17)* is false, e.g., worlds in which there are children and they all are going up the hill. But in addition, there are possible worlds in which *(5.18)* is true, but so is *(5.17)*, e.g., worlds in which there are no children (see chapter 1, p. 19, footnote 12). Then, too, there are possible worlds in which *(5.18)* is false, and in which *(5.17)* is true, e.g., worlds in which there are children, but none of them is going up the hill. And finally there are possible worlds in which *(5.18)* is false and *(5.17)* is likewise, e.g., worlds in which some, but not all, of the children are going up the hill. In short, the truth-value of *(5.17)* is undetermined by the truth-value of *(5.18)*. Not so, however, with the proposition expressed by the sentence *(5.15)*. This proposition is a truth-function of the proposition *(5.18)*. In any possible world in which *(5.18)* is true, the proposition expressed by *(5.15)* is false; and in any possible world in which *(5.18)* is false, the proposition expressed by *(5.15)* is true.

By way of contrast with the word "not", the expression "it is not the case that" (which we used in *(5.15)*) seems always to operate truth-functionally. Prefix it to any proposition-expressing sentence, whether simple or compound, and the resultant compound sentence will express a proposition which is true in all those possible worlds in which the proposition expressed by its sentential component is false; and vice versa. Thus it is that an effective test for determining whether "not" is being used truth-functionally in a compound sentence is to see whether the proposition being expressed by that sentence can equally well be expressed by a compound sentence using "it is not the case that" instead. If it can be so expressed then "not" is being used truth-functionally; if it cannot then "not" is being used non-truth-functionally.

But why this preoccupation with the truth-functional sense of "not", the sense that is best brought out by the more pedantic "it is not the case that"? We earlier said (pp. 14–15) that any proposition which is true in all those possible worlds in which a given proposition is false and which is false in all those possible worlds in which a given proposition is true, is a *contradictory* of that proposition. When therefore we now say that in its truth-functional uses "not" generates a compound sentence out of a simpler one in such a way that the proposition expressed by the compound sentence will be true in all those possible worlds in which the proposition expressed by the simpler one is false, and will be false in all those possible worlds in which the latter is true, we are simply saying that in its truth-functional uses "not" expresses the *concept* of negation and that the proposition expressed by either one of these sentences is a contradictory of the proposition expressed by the other. Hence the significance, for logic, of the truth-functional uses of "not". For between them, it will be remembered, a proposition and any of its contradictories are *exclusive* in the sense that there is no possible world in which both are true, and *exhaustive* in the sense that in each of all possible worlds it must be that one or the other of them is true.

We have earlier introduced a simple piece of *conceptual notation* for the truth-functional uses of the monadic sentence-forming operators "not" and "it is not the case that", i.e., for those uses of these expressions in which they express the concept of negation. Recall that we write the symbol " $\sim$ " (called *tilde*) in front of the symbol for any proposition-expressing sentence "P", just when we want to express the negation of that proposition. Then " $\sim$ P" expresses the negation of P. We read " $\sim$ P" as "it is not the case that P" or, more briefly, as "not-P". Alternatively, " $\sim$ P", can be read as, "It is false that P", or as "P is false".

It is important to note that tilde is not to be regarded simply as a piece of shorthand for an expression in some natural language such as English. For the reasons already given it should not be regarded, for instance, simply as a shorthand way of writing whatever we would write in English by the word "not". Rather it is to be regarded as a piece of notation for that which certain expressions in natural languages such as English may, on occasion, be used to express, viz., the *concept* of negation.

The truth-functional properties of the concept of negation can be displayed in the simple sort of chart which logicians call a *truth-table*. The truth-table for negation may be set out thus:

	P	$\sim$ P
(row 1)	T	F
(row 2)	F	T

TABLE *(5.a)*

In effect, a truth-table is an abbreviated *worlds-diagram*.[3] In the (vertical) column, to the left of the double line, under the letter "P", we write a "T" and an "F" to indicate, respectively, all those possible worlds in which the proposition P is *true*, and all those possible worlds in which the proposition P is *false*. "T" represents the set of all possible worlds (if any) in which P is true; "F" represents the set of all possible worlds (if any) in which P is false. Together these two subsets of possible worlds exhaust the set of all possible worlds. Each possible world is to be thought of as being included either in the (horizontal) row marked by the "T" in the left-hand column of table *(5.a)* or in the (horizontal) row marked by the "F" in that column. In short, the rows of the left-hand column together represent an exhaustive classification of all possible worlds.

3. More exactly, it is a schematic collapsed set of worlds-diagrams. Note how table *(5.a)* captures some, but not all, of the information in figure *(5.b)*.

Obviously, however, for some instantiations of "P", one or other of these rows will represent an *empty* set of possible worlds. In the case where P is contingent, both rows of the truth-table will represent *non*-empty sets of possible worlds. But if P is *non*contingent, then one or the other row of the truth-table will represent an empty set of possible worlds. Thus, for example, if P is necessarily true, then the first row of the truth-table will represent the set of *all* possible worlds, and the second row will represent an empty set of possible worlds. On the other hand, if P is necessarily false, the latter pattern will be reversed. If P is necessarily false, then the first row of the truth-table represents an empty set of possible worlds and the second row represents the set of all possible worlds. This fact will be seen to have important consequences when we try to use truth-tables to ascertain the modal attributes of propositions.

In the right-hand column of the truth-table, under the symbol " ∼ P", we write down the truth-value ∼ P will have in each of the two sets of possible worlds defined by the rows of the left-hand column. Thus, reading across the first row of the table, we can see that in those possible worlds (if any) in which P is true, ∼ P is false; and reading across the second row, we can see that in those possible worlds (if any) in which P is false, ∼ P is true.

It is easy to see that truth-functional negation is an operation which 'reverses' the truth-value of any proposition on which it 'operates', i.e., which is its argument. That is to say, ∼ P has the opposite truth-value to P, whatever the truth-value of P happens to be. It follows, too, that ∼ ∼ P has the *same* truth-value as P in all possible cases. This latter fact is usually referred to as the *Law of Double Negation*. It is in this sense, and this sense only, that one may correctly say "two negatives make a positive".

Table *(5.a)* enables us to introduce a rule for the depiction of the negation of a proposition on a worlds-diagram. The rule is this:

Represent the negation of a proposition by a bracket spanning all the possible worlds, if any, which are not spanned by a bracket representing the proposition itself.

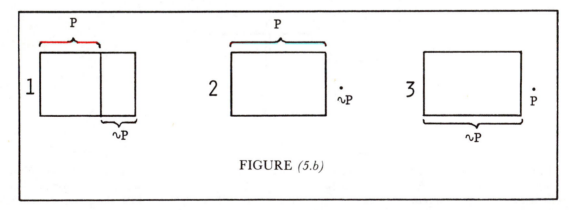

FIGURE *(5.b)*

Later in this chapter (section 9), we shall use this rule, together with rules for the depiction of other truth-functional operators, in order to devise a procedure for ascertaining the modal attributes of certain propositions.

The uses of "and"

In its truth-functional uses, "and" is a dyadic sentence-forming operator on sentences, i.e., a sentence-forming connective, which expresses the concept of *conjunction*. We symbolize conjunction in our conceptual notation by writing the symbol " · " (to be called *dot*) between the symbols for the sentences conjoined. Thus where "P" is the symbol for a proposition-expressing sentence (whether simple or compound) and "Q" is the symbol for a proposition-expressing sentence (again whether simple or compound), then "P · Q" expresses the conjunction of "P" and "Q". The truth-table for conjunction is

P	Q		P · Q
T	T		T
T	F		F
F	T		F
F	F		F

TABLE *(5.c)*

As with all truth-tables it is helpful to regard this one also as an abbreviated worlds-diagram. The four horizontal rows constitute a mutually exclusive and jointly exhaustive classification of all possible worlds. The first two rows (i.e., the rows bearing "T"s under the single "P") together represent all those worlds in which P is true. This subset of worlds in which P is true is in turn subdivided into that set in which Q is also true (represented on the truth-table by row 1 and marked by the "T" in column 2 under the "Q"), and into that set in which Q is false (row 2). And the set of possible worlds in which P is false is, in turn, subdivided into two smaller sets, that in which Q is true (row 3) and that in which Q is false (row 4). Together these four rows represent every possible distribution of truth-values for P and for Q among all possible worlds. Every possible world must be a world in which either (1) P and Q are both true, (2) P is true and Q is false, (3) P is false and Q is true, or (4) P is false and Q is false. There can be no other combination. Thus every possible world is represented by one or another row of our truth-table.

Again, as on table *(5.a)* (the truth-table for negation), we point out that for some instantiations of the symbols on the left-hand side, some of the various rows of the truth-table will represent an empty set of possible worlds. Thus, for example, if P is necessarily true and Q is contingent, both the third and the fourth rows of table *(5.c)* will represent empty sets of possible worlds. For in both these sets, P has the value "F", and there are, of course, no possible worlds in which a necessarily true proposition is false. Other combinations of modal status for P and for Q will, of course, affect the table in other, easily ascertainable, ways. We investigate the consequences of this in section 5.

To the right of the double line in the truth-table for conjunction we are able to read the truth-value of the proposition expressed by "P · Q" for each of the four specified sets of possible worlds. Only in those worlds in which both P and Q are true, is P · Q true. In all other cases (worlds), P · Q is false.

Table *(5.c)* enables us to introduce a rule for the depiction of conjunction on our worlds-diagrams. It is this:

> Represent the conjunction of two (or more) propositions by a bracket spanning the set of possible worlds, if any, in which both propositions are true.

The fifteen diagrams are:

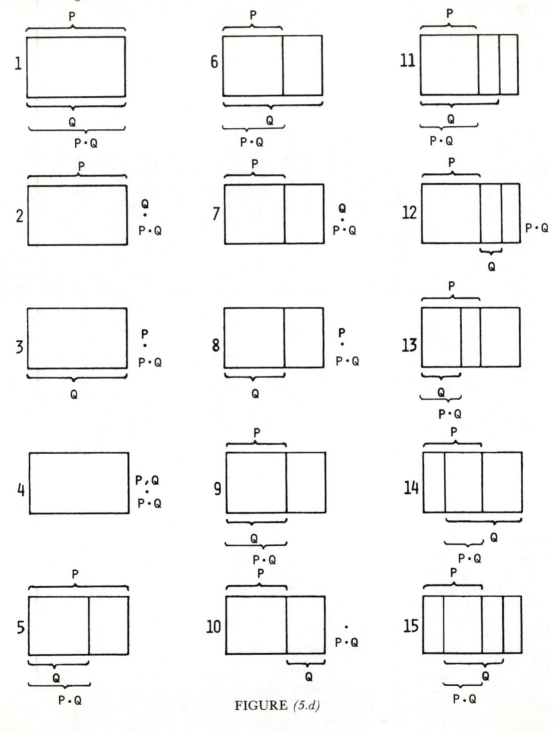

FIGURE *(5.d)*

It can be seen that if P and Q are inconsistent with one another (as in 2, 3, 4, 7, 8, 10, and 12), then there will not be any set of *possible* worlds in which both are true, and hence there will be no area on the rectangle which is common to the segments representing those propositions. In such a case the bracket representing the conjunction (P · Q) is relegated to a point, external to the rectangle, which represents the set of impossible worlds. But if the propositions involved are consistent with one another (as in 1, 5, 6, 9, 11, 13, 14, and 15), then there *will* be a set of possible worlds in which those propositions are both true, and hence there will be an area on the rectangle which is common to the segments representing those propositions. After all, to say that two propositions are consistent is *just to say* that it is possible that they should both be true together, i.e., that there is a possible world in which both are true. Not surprisingly then, the segment on our rectangle which represents the conjunction of two propositions is just that segment whose presence is indicative of the fact that those propositions are consistent with one another. In other words, two propositions are consistent with one another if and only if their conjunction is possibly true.

Note that the symbol " · " (dot) should no more be regarded merely as a shorthand abbreviation for "and" than " ~ " (tilde) should be regarded as a shorthand abbreviation for "not". Three main considerations lead us to say that it is an item of *conceptual* notation.

In the first place, there are other ways, in English, of expressing the concept of conjunction. Suppose we want to assert the conjunction of the proposition that there are five oranges in the basket and the proposition that there are six apples in the bowl. One way of expressing their conjunction would be to use the sentence "There are five oranges in the basket *and* six apples in the bowl." But the conjunction of these two propositions might be expressed in other ways as well. We might use the sentence "There are five oranges in the basket *but* six apples in the bowl." Or we might say, "There are five oranges in the basket; *however,* there are six apples in the bowl." Or, again, we might say, "*Although* there are five oranges in the basket, there are six apples in the bowl." The words "but", "however", and "although", just as much as the word "and", may be used in truth-functional ways to express the concept of conjunction. When these words are so used, the truth-conditions for the propositions expressed by the sentences they yield are precisely the same as those for the propositions expressed by the sentences which, in its truth-functional uses, "and" may be used to construct. The truth-conditions for the propositions they then express are those specified in the truth-table for " · ".

In the second place, the concept of conjunction can be conveyed without using any sentence-connective whatever. One way — indeed one of the commonest of all ways — of expressing the conjunction of two propositions is simply to use first the sentence expressing one and then the sentence expressing the other. If we want to assert both that there are five oranges in the basket and that there are six apples in the bowl, then we need only utter, one after the other, the two separate sentences: "There are five oranges in the basket" and "There are six apples in the bowl." We will then be taken, correctly, to have asserted both that there are five oranges in the basket and that there are six apples in the bowl. The fact that someone who asserts first one proposition and then another has thereby asserted both of them, licenses the *Rule of Conjunction* (see chapter 4, section 4). Here again we find no one-to-one correspondence between uses of "and" and the concept of conjunction. The concept of conjunction can be expressed by connectives other than "and" and can even be expressed in the absence of any sentence-connective at all.

In the third place, the sentence-connective "and" admits of uses in which it is *not* truth-functional — uses in which the compound sentences which it helps to form express propositions whose truth-values are not determined solely by the truth-values of the propositions expressed by the simple sentences which "and" connects. This can easily be seen if we reflect on the fact that conjunction, which "and" expresses in its truth-functional uses, is *commutative,* in the sense that the order of the conjuncts makes no difference to the truth-value of their conjunction. We have only to inspect the truth-table for conjunction to see that the truth-conditions for P · Q are precisely the same as the truth-conditions for Q · P. But consider the case where "and" is used to conjoin the two sentences and

> *(5.19)* "John mowed the lawn"

> *(5.20)* "John sharpened the lawn mower."

Sentences *(5.19)* and *(5.20)* can be conjoined in either of two ways to yield, respectively,

> *(5.21)* "John mowed the lawn and John sharpened the lawn mower"[4]

and

> *(5.22)* "John sharpened the lawn mower and mowed the lawn."

Are the truth-conditions for the proposition expressed by *(5.21)* the same as the truth-conditions for the proposition expressed by *(5.22)*? Hardly. The proposition which would ordinarily be expressed by *(5.21)* could well be true while that ordinarily expressed by *(5.22)* might be false. In cases such as these, the *order* in which the sentential components occur when they are connected by "and" makes a great deal of difference to the truth-values of the propositions expressed by the resulting compound sentences. For the order in which the simple sentences, "John mowed the lawn" and "John sharpened the lawn mower", occur is taken to convey a certain temporal ordering of the events which these sentences assert to have occurred. The most natural reading of *(5.21)* would be to read it as asserting that John sharpened the mower *after* he mowed the lawn; while the most natural reading of *(5.22)* would have this latter sentence asserting that John sharpened the mower *before* he mowed the lawn. In short, as used in *(5.21)* and *(5.22)*, "and" can be taken to mean "and *then*". In these cases the compound sentences formed through the use of "and" are not commutative as are those sentences resulting from using "and" in a purely truth-functional way. The meaning of "and" in such sentences is not exhausted. as it is in its truth-functional uses, by the truth-conditions for conjunction.

How, if at all, can our conceptual notation for conjunction capture the 'extra' meaning which "and" has in its non-truth-functional, noncommutative uses? How, for instance, can we convey in our conceptual notation the idea of temporal ordering which is intrinsic to our understandng of sentences such as *(5.21)* and *(5.22)*?[5] The answer lies, not in tampering with the meaning of "·", but in modifying the sentences conjoined. The simplest way of doing this is to use temporal indices such as "... at time 1" (abbreviated "at t_1") or "... at time 2" (abbreviated "at t_2"). We can express what we mean in sentences *(5.21)* and *(5.22)* in other sentences which use "and" truth-functionally, if we treat the components of *(5.21)* and *(5.22)* as context-dependent sentences (chapter 2, p. 75ff) — sentences which have to be made context-free by the use of some temporal index if we are to know what proposition each expresses. Thus we can make explicit the meaning of *(5.21)*, and at the same time use "and" truth-functionally, by saying

> *(5.23)* "John mowed the lawn at t_1 and sharpened the mower at t_2."

Here the temporal indices do the job of conveying the fact that the first-mentioned event occurred before the latter-mentioned one. And similarly we could convey the sense of *(5.22)* by saying

> *(5.24)* "John sharpened the mower at t_1 and mowed the lawn at t_2."

---

4. To comply with ordinary English style, we delete the reiteration of the grammatical subject, i.e., "John" in the second conjunct of the conjunctions below, specifically in *(5.22)* – *(5.25)*.

5. The particular non-truth-functional use of "and" here being examined should not be thought to be the only non-truth-functional use of "and." There are others. For example, "and" is also sometimes used to convey *causal* relations, as when we might say, "He fell on the ski slopes and broke his ankle."

These latter two sentences, in which the temporal indices occur explicitly, *are* commutative. Thus the truth-conditions are *identical* for the following two assertions:

(5.23)   "John mowed the lawn at t_1 and sharpened the mower at t_2."

(5.25)   "John sharpened the mower at t_2 and mowed the lawn at t_1."

Not only do these latter reformulations of (5.21) make explicit what that original sentence implicitly asserts, but they substitute truth-functional uses of "and" for a non-truth-functional one and thus render the original sentence susceptible to treatment within our conceptual notation.

The uses of "or"

First, some reminders. A compound sentence consisting of two proposition-expressing sentences joined by "or" is said to be a *disjunction*. The two component sentences in the disjunction are said to be its *disjuncts*. And the operation of putting together two proposition-expressing sentences by means of the dyadic operator "or" is called the *disjoining* of those two sentences.

   The dyadic sentence connective "or", like "and", is often used truth-functionally. But, unlike "and", "or" has two distinct truth-functional uses. Sometimes it is used to mean that, of the two propositions expressed by the sentences it connects, *at least one* is true; sometimes it is used to mean that, of the two propositions expressed by the sentences it connects, *one and only one* is true. Let us distinguish between these two uses by speaking of *weak* or *inclusive disjunction* in the first case, and of *strong* or *exclusive disjunction* in the second case.

   The concept of weak disjunction is captured in our conceptual notation by the symbol "∨" (to be called *vel* or *wedge* or *vee*). Its truth-conditions are given in the following truth-table:

P	Q	P ∨ Q
T	T	T
T	F	T
F	T	T
F	F	F

TABLE *(5.e)*

   Table *(5.e)* enables us to introduce a rule for the depiction of (weak) disjunction on a worlds-diagram. It is this:

> Represent the (weak) disjunction of two propositions by a bracket spanning the set of possible worlds, if any, in which at least one of the two propositions is true.

It can now be seen that unless both the propositions disjoined are necessarily false (as in 4) there will

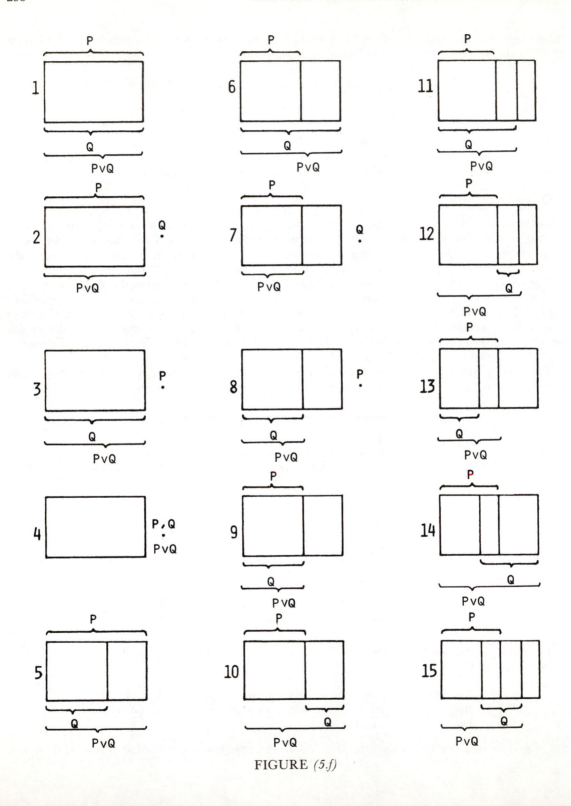

FIGURE *(5.f)*

always be at least some possible worlds in which their disjunction is true. That is to say, the proposition expressed by a disjunctive sentence is *possibly true* unless both the propositions expressed by its disjuncts are necessarily false.

Many, if not most, of our ordinary uses of "or" are weakly disjunctive and hence are captured by the truth-table for "∨". If, for example, we were to explain John's absence from an examination which we knew he was intent on writing by saying

> *(5.26)*   "John is ill or he missed the bus"

we would be saying something whose truth is compatible with the possible state of affairs of John's being ill *and* his missing the bus. That is, if it should turn out both that John was ill and that he missed the bus, we should hardly want to say that what *(5.26)* expresses is false. Quite the contrary: if John both was ill and missed the bus, then what *(5.26)* expresses would be true.

But other uses of "or" are strongly disjunctive and are not captured by the truth-table for "∨". Consider the following example:

> *(5.27)*   "The origin of the *Trumpet Voluntary*, traditionally attributed to Henry Purcell, has been the subject of much recent dispute. This piece of music was composed by Purcell or it was composed by Jeremiah Clarke."

In this latter instance, the connective "or" is almost certainly intended by the speaker to represent the 'stronger' species of truth-functional disjunction. The most natural reading of this example would be that in which the speaker is asserting that either Purcell or Clarke, *but not both of them,* composed the *Trumpet Voluntary*. The symbol we use for the stronger, exclusive, sense of "or" is " $\underline{\vee}$ " (to be called *vee-bar*). Its truth-table is this:

P	Q	P $\underline{\vee}$ Q
T	T	F
T	F	T
F	T	T
F	F	F

TABLE *(5.g)*

If "or" is interpreted in its stronger sense in *(5.27)*, then the second sentence of *(5.27)* will express a falsehood if Purcell and Clarke both composed the *Trumpet Voluntary* — see row 1 of table *(5.g)*. (Both would have composed it if each had independently composed the identical piece of music.)

There are, then, two senses of "or", each of which is truth-functional. However, in our conceptual notation we shall make use of only one of them: the inclusive sense represented by the symbol "∨". The exclusive sense occurs less frequently, and when it does it can easily be defined in terms of concepts already at our disposal: specifically, the concept of negation, represented by " ∼ "; the concept of conjunction, represented by " · "; and the concept of inclusive disjunction, represented by "∨". (We shall see precisely how to state this definition later in this chapter [p. 309].)

We have been speaking so far of weak and strong (i.e., inclusive and exclusive) disjunction.

Hereinafter when we use the term "disjunction" without qualification we shall mean "weak" or "inclusive disjunction" which may be symbolized by the use of "∨".

We have given examples in which the English operators, "not" and "and", are used non-truth-functionally. Are there similar examples in which "or" also is used non-truth-functionally? There are, indeed, some such examples, but they are relatively more rare than the corresponding non-truth-functional uses of "not" and "and". That is to say, although "or" is sometimes used to connect proposition-expressing sentences in a non-truth-functional fashion, its uses in this role are very much less frequent than the uses of "not" and "and" in non-truth-functional roles. Let us examine an instance. Consider:

> *(5.28)* "Any solution is acidic which will turn litmus paper red, or, nothing but an acidic solution will turn litmus paper red."

The occurrence of "or" in *(5.28)* is non-truth-functional. It is insufficient for the truth of what this sentence expresses, that the two disjuncts express truths. What more is required is that both sentences express equivalent propositions. In effect, the "or" in this instance is being used with the same sense as "i.e." to mean "that is". In effect, only if the two disjuncts express equivalent, as well as true propositions, is what the disjunction expresses true. And clearly, two disjuncts can both express true propositions without those propositions being equivalent. Just consider: the proposition that litmus paper is purple is true; but had the sentence, "litmus paper is purple", replaced the like-valued second conjunct of *(5.28)*, we should hardly want to say that the resulting sentence still asserted something true. For *(5.28)* would then become

> *(5.29)* "Any solution is acidic which will turn litmus paper red, or, litmus paper is purple."

Although both disjuncts of *(5.29)* express truths, that sentence itself expresses a false proposition. Since substituting another sentence expressing a different true proposition for the second disjunct in *(5.28)* yielded (in *(5.29)*) a disjunctive sentence expressing a false proposition, the use of "or" in *(5.28)* is *not* truth-functional.[6]

Since the operators in the conceptual notation we are introducing represent only truth-functional operators, it is clear that we cannot capture the whole sense of *(5.28)* through the use of these operators alone. Nonetheless these truth-functional operators can, and need to, be called upon to express *part* of the sense of that sentence. When we were explaining, just above, the truth-conditions of the proposition expressed by *(5.28)* we said that it would be true if (1) the disjuncts of *(5.28)* express equivalent propositions, and (2) those propositions are true. But notice: in saying this, we have just invoked the truth-functional use of "and". And what this means is that the non-truth-functional use of "or" in *(5.28)* is to be explicated in terms of, among other things, a truth-functional operator. This particular result is not exceptional. Virtually all non-truth-functional operators have, we might say, a truth-functional 'component' or 'core'.

EXERCISE

For each of the following cases, construct a worlds-diagram and bracket that portion of the diagram representing P ⊻ Q:

---

6. The authors wish to express their thanks to their colleague, Raymond Jennings, for calling their attention to this non-truth-functional use of "or".

  a. *P is necessarily true; Q is contingent*

  b. *P is necessarily true; Q is necessarily true*

  c. *P is contingent; Q is a contradictory of P*

  d. *P is contingent; Q is necessarily false*

*   *   *   *   *

Interlude: compound sentences containing two or more sentential operators

As long as a sentence — for example, "A · B" — in our conceptual notation contains only a single operator, there is no opportunity for that sentence to be ambiguous. But when a sentence contains two or more operators, generally that sentence will be ambiguous unless measures are taken to correct it. Before we give an example of such an ambiguity in our conceptual notation, let us examine a parallel case in arithmetic. Consider the sentence

  (5.30) "X = 3 + 5 × 2"

What is the value of "X"? There is no clear answer to this question, for the expression "3 + 5 × 2" is obviously ambiguous. This expression could mean either (1) that X is equal to the sum of three and five (which is of course eight), which in turn is multiplied by two, yielding a value of sixteen for X; or (2) that three is to be added to the product of five and two, which would then yield a value of thirteen for X. Such an ambiguity is, of course, intolerable and must be corrected. The easiest way to correct it (but not the only way) is to introduce bracketing, using parentheses, to group the parts into unambiguous components. Thus the two ways of reading *(5.30)* can be distinguished clearly from one another in the following fashion:

  (5.31) "X = (3 + 5) × 2"

  (5.32) "X = 3 + (5 × 2)"

  Now let us examine a parallel ambiguity in an English sentence which uses two operators. Let us return to one of the examples which introduced our discussion of "and".

  (5.5) "It is not the case that Jack will go up the hill and Jill will go up the hill."

At the time we introduced this sentence we mentioned that it is ambiguous. In our conceptual notation it is a simple matter to resolve the ambiguity. Letting "B" stand for "Jack will go up the hill", and "G" stand for "Jill go up the hill", we may express the two different propositions which may be expressed by *(5.5)* in the following two different, unambiguous, sentences:

  (5.33) "(∼B) · G"[7]

  (5.34) "∼(B · G)"

-----

7. As we shall see in a moment, the parentheses around the first conjunct of *(5.33)* are not essential. However, at this point, since we lack the explicit rules which would allow us to read *(5.33)* unambiguously if the parentheses were to be deleted, we require them.

In English, each of these two sentences may be expressed this way:

>   *(5.35)*   "It is not the case that Jack will go up the hill, and [or "but" if you prefer] it
>   is the case that Jill will."

>   *(5.36)*   "It is not the case both that Jack will go up the hill and that Jill will go up
>   the hill."

Notice that if *(5.33)* and *(5.34)* had been written without the parentheses, they would be indistinguishable from one another and would be ambiguous in exactly the same sort of way that *(5.5)* is.

Clearly our conceptual notation stands in need of some device to enable us to disambiguate otherwise ambiguous sentences. Bracketing (i.e., the use of parentheses) is one such device. We shall adopt it here.[8]

The formation rules in a logic are designed to yield only those unambiguous strings of symbols which we earlier (chapter 4, section 5) called *wffs* (well-formed formulae). Truth-functional Propositional Logic allows for the construction of two kinds of well-formed formulae, those called "sentences" and those called "sentence-forms". The difference between the two (which we will see in due course is an important difference) is determined by the fact that the former contain no sentence-variables and the latter contain at least one sentence-variable.[9]

The formation rules for securing well-formedness in formulae (i.e., in sentences and in sentence-forms) in Truth-functional Propositional Logic are:

>   R1:   Any capital letter of the English alphabet standing alone is a wff.

>   R2:   Any wff prefixed by a tilde is a wff.

>   R3:   Any two wffs written with a dyadic truth-functional connective between them
>   and the whole surrounded by parentheses is a wff.

Examples: The following are well-formed formulae (wffs) according to the rules R1 – R3:

>   A
>
> $\sim$ P
>
>   (P $\vee$ B)
>
>   ($\sim$ (P $\cdot$ Q) $\vee$ (R $\cdot$ $\sim$ S))

(Of these, the first is a sentence; the other three are sentence-forms.)

>   The following are *not* wffs:

>   A $\sim$
>
>   P $\vee$

8. For an exposition of a parentheses-free notation, see I.M. Copi, *Symbolic Logic*, fourth edition, New York, Macmillan, 1973, pp. 231–2.

9. The English letters "A" through "O" are designated as being sentence-constants; the letters "P" through "Z", sentence-variables. For the significance of this distinction, see section 6, pp. 301ff.

$$P \cdot B \vee C$$

$$(A \cdot B \vee C)$$

We also adopt the following *conventions:*

A: *We may, if we like, drop the outermost pair of parentheses on a well-formed formula.*

Example: "$(P \vee B)$" may be rewritten as "$P \vee B$".

[Note, however, that if a wff has had its outermost parentheses deleted, those parentheses must be restored if that formula is to be used as a component in another formula.]

B1:   *We may, if we like, drop the parentheses around any conjunct which is itself a conjunction.*

Example 1:   "$(A \cdot ((B \vee C) \cdot D))$" may be rewritten as "$(A \cdot (B \vee C) \cdot D)$".

Example 2:   By two successive applications of this convention, we may rewrite "$(A \cdot ((B \vee C) \cdot (D \cdot E)))$" as "$(A \cdot (B \vee C) \cdot D \cdot E)$".

B2:   *We may, if we like, drop the parentheses around any disjunct which is itself a disjunction.*

Example: "$(A \vee ((B \cdot C) \vee D))$" may be rewritten as "$(A \vee (B \cdot C) \vee D)$".

The uses of "if . . . then . . . "

Sometimes we want to assert that a proposition P isn't true unless a proposition Q is also true; i.e., that it is not the case both that P is true and that Q is false. A natural way of saying this in English is to utter a sentence of the form "If P then Q" (or sometimes, more simply, "If P, Q"). We shall call any sentence of this form a *conditional* sentence. A conditional sentence, then, is a compound sentence formed out of two simpler ones by means of the dyadic sentence-connective "if . . . then . . . " (or, sometimes, "if" where the "then" is unexpressed but understood). The simpler sentence which occurs in the if-clause we shall call the *antecedent;* the one which occurs in the then-clause we shall call the *consequent.*

It is obvious enough that in those instances when a conditional of the form "If P then Q" is used *simply* to assert that it is not the case both that P is true and that Q is false, the connective "if . . . then . . . " is functioning in a purely truth-functional way. For in a sentence of the form "It is not the case both that P is true and that Q is false" both the operators "it is not the case that"(a monadic operator, it will be remembered) and "and" (a dyadic operator) are functioning purely truth-functionally. Hence the compound sentence "It is not the case both that P is true and that Q is false" is a truth-functional sentence. Indeed, it can be recorded in the conceptual notation already at our disposal by writing "$\sim (P \cdot \sim Q)$". It follows that in those instances when "If P then Q" is used to assert no more than "It is not the case both that P is true and that Q is false", the conditional "If P then Q" is itself truth-functional and can be recorded as "$\sim (P \cdot \sim Q)$". The proposition, If P then Q, will then have the *same* truth-conditions as $\sim (P \cdot \sim Q)$: it will be true in all those possible worlds in which it is not the case both that P is true and that Q is false, i.e., true in all those possible worlds in which $\sim(P \cdot \sim Q)$ is true; and it will be false in all and only those possible worlds in which the negation of $\sim(P \cdot \sim Q)$ is true, i.e., false in all and only those possible worlds in which $(P \cdot \sim Q)$ is true, i.e., false in all and only those possible worlds in which P is true and Q is false.

We call any sentence expressing a proposition which has these truth-conditions, a *material conditional;* and we call the relation which holds between the proposition expressed by the antecedent and the proposition expressed by the consequent of such a conditional the relation of *material conditionality.*

The relation of material conditionality is rendered in our conceptual notation by writing the symbol "⊃" (to be called *hook* or *horseshoe*) between the symbols for the sentences it connects. Thus where "P" is the symbol for a proposition-expressing sentence and "Q" is the symbol for a proposition-expressing sentence, "P⊃Q" is the symbol for the material conditional within which "P" occurs as antecedent and "Q" occurs as consequent.

As we have just shown, the relation of material conditionality will hold between any two propositions P and Q (in that order) in every possible world except in those possible worlds in which P is true and Q is false. Hence the truth-table for material conditionality is:

P	Q	P ⊃ Q
T	T	T
T	F	F
F	T	T
F	F	T

TABLE *(5.h)*

Table *(5.h)* allows us to introduce a rule for the depiction of material conditionality on a worlds-diagram:

> Represent the relation of material conditionality obtaining between two propositions by a bracket spanning all those possible worlds, if any, in which it is not the case that the first is true and the second is false.

This rule may be easier to grasp if we break it down into two stages:

1. Find all the possible worlds in which P is true and Q is false.

2. Draw the bracket for P⊃Q so as to span all the possible worlds, if any, which remain.

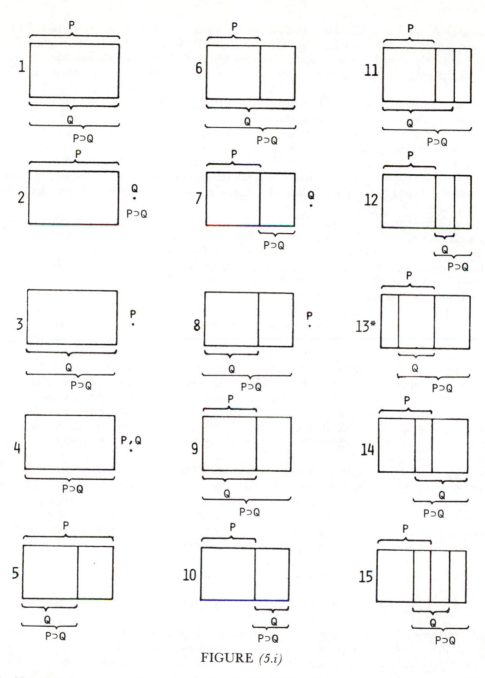

FIGURE *(5.i)*

*   Note that for ease in placing the bracket for "P⊃Q" on diagram 13, we have moved the segment for Q to the right-hand side of the segment for P. No logical relations are disturbed by our doing this.

Figure *(5.i)* shows that in all those worlds-diagrams which depict an instance in which P implies Q (viz., 1, 3, 4, 6, 8, 9, and 11), we find that the bracket for P⊃Q spans all possible worlds. That is to say, in all and only those cases in which P implies Q, P⊃Q is true in all possible worlds. (Note carefully: this latter fact is reflected in our definition (c) of "implication" which appears in chapter 1, p. 31.)

Further, we can see that unless P is necessarily true and Q is necessarily false (as in 2), there will always be some possible worlds in which the relation of material conditionality holds between P and Q. That is to say, any proposition asserting that the relation of material conditionality holds between two propositions, P and Q, is *possibly true* unless P is necessarily true and Q is necessarily false. Of course such a proposition will not be *true in fact* unless the possible worlds in which it is true include the *actual world*. A proposition which asserts that the relation of material conditionality holds between two propositions, P and Q, is true in fact only when in the actual world it is not the case both that P is true and that Q is false.

In discussing the sentential operators, "it is not the case that", "and", and "or" we had little difficulty in citing examples of their uses which were purely truth-functional — uses, that is, in which they simply expressed the truth-functional concepts of negation, conjunction and (weak or inclusive) disjunction, respectively. In this respect the sentence connective "if . . . then . . . " is somewhat different. Only rarely do we ever assert in ordinary discourse a conditional sentence which is purely truth-functional. An example would be:

(5.37)   "If he wrote that without any help, then I am a monkey's uncle."

Here the truth-functional property of the connective "if . . . then . . . " is relied upon, together with our knowledge that the proposition expressed by the consequent is blatantly false, in order to assert the falsity of the proposition expressed by the antecedent. For the only condition under which P⊃Q may be true while Q is false, is for P also to be false. On nearly every occasion when we use a conditional sentence in a strictly truth-functional way, we are using it in the facetious manner of *(5.37);* we are adopting a style of speech which allows us colorfully to deny a proposition (that expressed by the antecedent of the conditional) without uttering the words "not", "it is not the case that", or "I deny that", etc.

Apart from the just-mentioned curious use of a conditional sentence, there do not seem to be any other sorts of examples in which the use of the "if . . . then . . . " connective is *purely* truth-functional — examples in which that connective is used to express the (truth-functional) concept of material conditionality and that concept alone. For as philosophers of language have often pointed out, sentences of the form "If P then Q" usually express much *more* than a mere truth-functional relation. Usually such sentences assert or presuppose more of a connection between P and Q than that which holds when it is not the case both that P is true and Q false. For instance, the connection may be the logical relation of implication, as is expressed by the sentence

(5.38)   "If the Queen's husband has children, then he is someone's father."

(We might call this a *logical* conditional. The proposition expressed by a logical conditional is true if and only if the proposition expressed by the antecedent of that conditional *logically implies* the proposition expressed by the consequent.) Or, the connection may be a causal one, as it is in the case of the sentence

(5.39)   "If the vacuum cleaner motor short-circuits, the fuse in the electrical box in the basement will blow."

(We might call this a *causal* conditional. The proposition expressed by a causal conditional is true if and only if the proposition expressed by the antecedent of that conditional *causally implies* the proposition expressed by the consequent.) Or, the connection may be the sort of connection which involves explicit or implicit statistical correlations as in the case of the sentence,

(5.40)   "If there are six plates on the table, then there are six persons expected for dinner."

(We might call this a *stochastic* or *statistical* conditional. The proposition expressed by a stochastic conditional is true if and only if the proposition expressed by the antecedent of that conditional *probabilifies* (i.e., raises the probability of) the proposition expressed by the consequent.)

Each one of these sentences, *(5.38)*, *(5.39)*, and *(5.40)*, being of the form, "If P then Q", is a conditional sentence, but the connections asserted between the propositions expressed by their respective antecedents and their respective consequents are *stronger* than the purely truth-functional relation of material conditionality.

A puzzle arises. If virtually none of the conditional sentences we utter in ordinary discourse are to be construed as material conditionals, why, then, have logicians been concerned to define the relation of material conditionality in their conceptual notation? For we must admit that it seems hardly likely that logic should be much concerned with propositions of the sort expressed by *(5.37)*. Much could be written by way of an answer. But for present purposes three points will have to suffice.

In the first place, it is important to point out that it is a *necessary* condition for the truth of any proposition which is expressed by a conditional sentence — of any sort whatever, including the non-truth-functional ones — that it should not be the case that the proposition expressed by the antecedent of that sentence be true while the proposition expressed by the consequent be false. But this is just to say that no proposition expressed by any sort of conditional sentence is true unless the proposition expressed by the corresponding material conditional sentence is true. This fact can be put to advantage. Suppose we have a non-truth-functional sentence such as *(5.39)*, and we are intent on discovering the truth-value of the proposition it expresses. The specification of the truth-conditions of non-truth-functional sentences is very much more difficult than of truth-functional ones, and *(5.39)* is no exception. To say precisely under what conditions *(5.39)* expresses a truth and precisely under what conditions it expresses a falsehood is no easy matter and has been an object of perennial interest and investigation. Clearly the truth-conditions of *(5.39)* cannot be the same as the truth-conditions of the corresponding material conditional: *(5.39)* need not express a true proposition even though its antecedent and consequent both express true propositions. For example, we can imagine a situation in which the vacuum cleaner motor did short-circuit and the fuse did blow and yet the proposition expressed by *(5.39)* is false; the circuit for the vacuum cleaner does not pass through the fuse box in the basement; the fuse's blowing was the result of a 'coincidence'; it was not *caused* by the vacuum cleaner's malfunction. Under these circumstances, the proposition expressed by *(5.39)* would be false, even though the corresponding material conditional would express a truth. In sum, then, the truth-conditions for non-truth-functional conditionals differ from the truth-conditions for the truth-functional material conditional. Nonetheless, the material conditional has a role to play when it comes to ascertaining the truth-value (as opposed to the truth-conditions) of the proposition expressed by *(5.39)*. For this much we may confidently assert: if the *material* conditional which corresponds to *(5.39)* expresses a false proposition, that is, if the antecedent of *(5.39)* expresses a true proposition, and the consequent of *(5.39)* expresses a false proposition, then *(5.39)* expresses a false proposition. This result is perfectly general, and we may summarize by saying that the *falsity*-conditions of the material conditional constitute part of the truth-conditions (i.e., truth-value conditions) of *every* conditional.

In the second place, there are other occasions when it is useful to render certain conditionals as material ones. For example, we have said earlier that arguments are deductively valid if their premises imply their conclusions. Another way of putting this is to say that an argument is deductively valid if (and only if) a material conditional sentence, whose antecedent is the conjunction of all the premises of that argument and whose consequent is the conclusion of that argument, expresses a proposition which is necessarily true. (Later in this chapter [section 4] we will have more to say about this point, and will actually ascertain the deductive validity of some arguments by means of constructing a material conditional sentence and by looking to see what the modal status is of the proposition expressed by that sentence.)

In the third place, our conceptual notation for the material conditional lends itself to supplementation by symbolic notations which capture some of those 'extra' elements of meaning which characterize non-truth-functional conditionals. For instance, as we shall see when we consider Modal Propositional Logic in the next chapter, the non-truth-functional, modal relation of implication which holds between the proposition expressed by the antecedent and that expressed by the consequent in a logical conditional can be captured in our symbolic notation by supplementing the notation for the truth-functional material conditional in this way: "□(P⊃Q)". Similarly, the non-truth-functional relation which holds between the proposition expressed by the antecedent and that expressed by the consequent in a causal conditional may be expressed in an expanded notation in this way: "ⓒ(P⊃Q)". Here "ⓒ" is to be read as "It is causally necessary that . . ." or as "In all possible worlds in which the same causal laws hold as in the actual world, it is true that . . ."

In sum, then, there is ample reason for logicians to be interested in defining and using such a notion as material conditionality, even though this particular relation is only rarely asserted in ordinary discourse to hold between two propositions. It is, for the most part, a technical notion which plays an important and basic role in logic; in particular in the analysis of all conditionals, truth-functional and non-truth-functional alike.

Nonetheless — in spite of its genuine utility — we ought not to lose sight of the *peculiar* nature of the relation of material conditionality. Unfortunately, some logic books incautiously refer to the relation symbolized by "⊃" as the relation of "material *implication*". The trouble with this description is that it has misled countless people into supposing that, where a proposition P ⊃ Q is true, there must be some connection between the antecedent, P, and the consequent, Q, akin to that which holds when P really does imply Q, (i.e., when P logically implies Q). But this supposition leads to apparent paradox. It can easily be seen, by attending to the truth-conditions for P ⊃ Q (as captured in table *(5.h)*), that when P is false then no matter whether Q is true or false the material conditional P ⊃ Q, will be true [see rows (3) and (4)]; and again that where Q is true then no matter whether P is true or false the material conditional, P ⊃ Q will be true [see rows (1) and (3)]. Give "⊃" the description "material implication" and these truth-conditions generate the so-called "paradoxes of material implication": that a false proposition materially implies any proposition whatever, and that a true proposition is materially implied by any proposition whatever. We should have to say accordingly that a false proposition such as that Scotch whisky is nonalcoholic materially implies any and every proposition that one cares to think of — that Harding is still president of the U.S., that he is not still president of the U.S., and so on. Similarly, we should have to say that a true proposition such as that potatoes contain starch is materially implied by any and every proposition that one cares to think of — that Aristotle was a teacher of Alexander the Great, that he wasn't, and so on.

These consequences seem paradoxical because, on the one hand, they accord with our understanding of the truth-conditions for so-called material implication (and so seem to be true), while, on the other hand, they do not accord with our understanding of what the word "implication" ordinarily means (and so seem to be false). Of course, there is no real paradox here at all. We can avoid puzzlement either by constantly reminding ourselves that the term "implication", as it occurs in the description "material implication", must be stripped of all its usual associations, or (more simply and preferably) by avoiding the term "implication" altogether in this context and choosing to speak instead of "the relation of material conditionality". Likewise, instead of reading "P⊃Q" as "P materially implies Q" we may, if we wish, read it as "P materially conditionalizes Q". We have chosen the latter course. The only connection between the relation of material conditionality and the relation of implication properly so-called lies in the fact, observed a moment ago, that the relation of material conditionality will hold between P and Q in each and every possible world (i.e., □(P⊃Q) will be true) just when the relation of implication holds between P and Q (i.e., when P implies Q). But the relation of material conditionality is *not* the relation of (logical) implication, and ought to be carefully and deliberately distinguished from it.

The uses of "if and only if"

Sometimes we want to assert not only that a proposition P isn't true without a proposition Q being true but also (conversely) that a proposition Q isn't true without a proposition P being true. One way of saying this in English would be to utter a sentence of the form "P if and only if Q". We shall call any sentence of this latter form a *biconditional*. An example (albeit a non-truth-functional one) is:

(5.41)   "The motion voted on at the last meeting was passed legally if and only if at least eight members in good standing voted for it."

A biconditional sentence, then, is a compound sentence formed out of two simpler sentences by means of the dyadic sentence-connective "if and only if" (often abbreviated to "iff").

Biconditionals have many of the attributes that conditionals have. True, it makes no sense to speak of the antecedent and consequent of a biconditional, but in other respects there are obvious parallels. Like conditionals, biconditionals may be used to express simply a truth-functional relation or may be used to express any of several non-truth-functional relationships, e.g., logical, causal, or stochastic.

We shall call the truth-functional 'core' of any use of a biconditional sentence "the relation of *material biconditionality*" and will symbolize it in our conceptual notation by "≡" (to be called *triple bar*). The truth-conditions for the relation of material biconditionality may be set out as follows:

P	Q	P ≡ Q
T	T	T
T	F	F
F	T	F
F	F	T

TABLE *(5.j)*

Table *(5.j)* allows us to introduce a rule for the depiction of the relation of material biconditionality on a worlds-diagram:

Represent the relation of material biconditionality obtaining between two propositions by a bracket spanning *both* the area representing those possible worlds, if any, in which both propositions are true *and* the area representing those possible worlds, if any, in which both propositions are false.

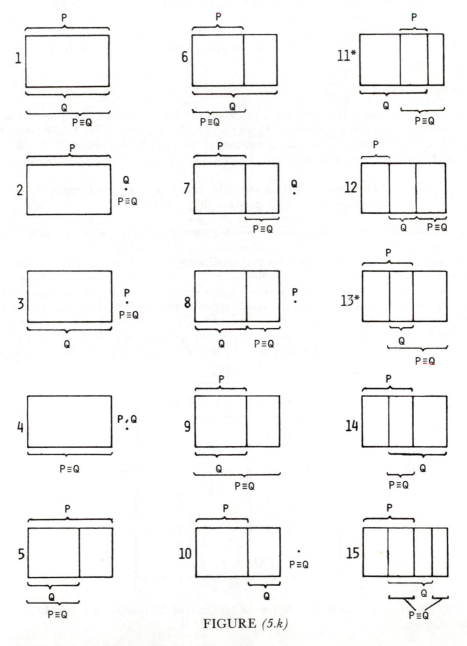

FIGURE *(5.k)*

---

*   See footnote for figure *(5.i)*.

Figure *(5.k)* shows that the relation of material biconditionality holds between two propositions in some possible world unless those propositions are contradictories of one another (see diagrams 2, 3, and 10.) That is to say, unless two propositions are contradictories of one another, there will always be some possible world in which they are both true and/or both false, and hence there will be some possible world in which the relation of material biconditionality holds between them. (Note that the relation of material biconditionality will hold in some possible world for propositions which are contraries of one another. Not all cases of inconsistency preclude the relation of material biconditionality holding.)

Examples of purely truth-functional uses of the sentence connective "if and only if" are at least as rare, and odd, as those of purely truth-functional uses of the sentence connective "if . . . then . . . ." But examples of non-truth-functional uses are easy to find. And such uses are of the same diverse sorts as are the non-truth-functional uses of "if . . . then . . . ."

The connective "if and only if" is being used to express a logical biconditional in the sentence

(5.42)   "Today is the day after Monday if and only if today is the day before Wednesday."

Here the connective "if and only if" is not being used *merely* to assert that the two propositions, (1) that today is the day after Monday and (2) that today is the day before Wednesday, have the same truth-value in the actual world. It is being used to express something stronger: namely, that in all possible worlds the two propositions have matching truth-values. In a word, what is being asserted is that the two propositions are logically equivalent.

Similarly, as was the case with the connective "if . . . then . . . ", the connective "if and only if" may be used to express a causal relation, to express what we might call a "causal biconditional".

(5.43)   "This object will continue to move in a straight line at a fixed velocity if and only if no external force is applied to it."

Again, here the connective is not being used merely to assert that the two propositions, (1) that this object will continue to move in a straight line, and (2) that no external force is applied to this object, have the same truth-value in the actual world. Something more is being asserted than just this truth-functional minimum. What more is being asserted is that in all possible worlds in which the same causal laws hold as hold in the actual world these two propositions have matching truth-values.

There are, of course, many other kinds of non-truth-functional uses of the connective "if and only if" — uses in which the relation between the propositions expressed by the connected sentences is stronger than that of material biconditionality. It is unnecessary for us to describe such uses exhaustively and, of course, we couldn't do so even if we were to try. It suffices, for our purposes, that we recognize their existence and understand the reasons why logicians, despite the overwhelming preponderance of non-truth-functional uses in everyday discourse, have tended to concentrate in their conceptual notation — until comparatively recently — on the purely truth-functional uses. The reasons parallel those given in our discussion of material conditionality.

In the first place, by virtue of the fact that it is a logically necessary (although not, of course, a sufficient) condition of the truth of a proposition expressed by non-truth-functional biconditional that the corresponding material biconditional should express a truth, it follows that if the material biconditional expresses a falsehood, then the original non-truth-functional biconditional also expresses a falsehood; i.e., the falsity of the proposition expressed by a material biconditional is a (logically) sufficient condition of the falsity of the original proposition expressed by the non-truth-functional biconditional.

Secondly, the relation of material biconditionality, like the relation of material conditionality, is truth-preserving and falsity-retributive. But unlike the relation of material conditionality, it is in addition truth-retributive and falsity-preserving. By virtue of these facts, we can easily determine the truth-value of one of two propositions which stand in the relation of material biconditionality if we are antecedently given that the relation does hold and are given the truth-value of the other proposition: if one is true, we can validly infer that the other is also; and if either is false, we can validly infer that the other is also. For purposes of making *these* sorts of inferences any 'extra', non-truth-functional, elements of meaning may safely be ignored.

Thirdly, where need arises, we can always supplement the notation for the material biconditional by other symbolic devices such as "□" and "©" so that, for example, a logical biconditional can be rendered by writing a sentence of the form "□(P ≡ Q) ". The need for such symbolic supplements to the basic notation for material biconditionality arises, for instance, when we want to record the fact (previously noted) that it is a (logically) necessary, but not a sufficient, condition for the truth of a logical biconditional that the corresponding material biconditional should be true. We can record this fact by saying that a proposition, expressible by a sentence of the form "□(P ≡ Q)" implies every proposition expressible by a sentence of the form "(P ≡ Q)", but not vice versa. This is a logical fact, entitling us to make certain inferences, which cannot be recorded symbolically without the explicit recognition, in symbols, of the non-truth-functional element of meanings which a logical biconditional has 'over and above' its purely truth-functional core.

Not surprisingly, there is still a further respect in which our discussion of material biconditionality parallels our discussion of material conditionality. We saw that the latter relation has sometimes been referred to misleadingly by the name "material implication". In much the same sort of way, the relation of material biconditionality has sometimes been referred to misleadingly by the name "material equivalence" — and with the same sort of apparent air of paradox. Read "≡" as "is materially equivalent to" and one is forced to conclude that any two true propositions are materially equivalent and that any two false propositions are materially equivalent. But, one is inclined to object, "equivalence" is too strong a description for the relation which holds, e.g., between the true proposition that Socrates was a teacher of Plato and the true proposition that Vancouver is the largest city in British Columbia, or again between the false proposition that 2 + 2 = 5 and the false proposition that painting is a recently developed art form. The air of paradox may be removed, this time, either by putting the emphasis on the word "material" as it occurs in the expression "material equivalence", or by choosing to speak of the relation of material biconditionality. We have chosen the latter course as less likely to mislead. But whichever manner of speaking is adopted, the important point to bear in mind is this: it is a sufficient condition of the relation of material biconditionality holding that two propositions be logically equivalent to one another; but the converse does *not* hold. That two propositions stand in the relation of material biconditionality (or material equivalence, if one prefers) does not suffice to ensure that they also stand in the relation of logical equivalence. The two propositions, (1) that Socrates was a teacher of Plato, and (2) that Vancouver is the largest city in British Columbia, have matching truth-values (in the actual world) — they are true — and hence stand in the relation of material biconditionality. But they certainly are not logically equivalent.

Appendix: truth-tables for wffs containing three or more letters

For cases where we wish to construct a truth-table for a compound sentence with three propositional symbols we shall require a truth-table with eight rows; for a case where there are four propositional symbols, sixteen rows. More generally, where n is the number of propositional symbols occurring, we shall require 2^n rows in our truth-table.

We adopt the following *convention* for the construction of these various rows. Let m equal the number of required rows ($m = 2^n$). We begin in the column to the immediate left of the double vertical line and alternate "T"s and "F"s until we have written down m of them. We then move one column to the left and again write down a column of "T"s and "F"s, only this time we write down two "T"s at a time, then two "F"s, etc., until (again) we have m of them. If still more columns remain to be filled in, we proceed to the left to the next column and proceed to alternate "T"s and "F"s in groups of four. We keep repeating this procedure, in each column, doubling the size of the group occurring in the immediate column to the right, until we have finished filling in the left-hand side of the truth-table. In following this mechanical procedure we will succeed in constructing a table such that the various *rows* represent every possible combination for "T" and "F". The top row will consist entirely of "T"s; the bottom row, entirely of "F"s; and every *other* combination will occur in some intermediate row.

3.   EVALUATING COMPOUND SENTENCES

Truth-functional compound sentences do not, of course, bear truth-values: no sentences do, whether they are simple or compound, truth-functional or not. Only the propositions expressed by sentences bear truth-values. Nonetheless there is a sense in which it is proper to speak of the "evaluation" of sentences. As we have seen, the truth-values of propositions expressed by truth-functional compound sentences are logically determined by the truth-values of the propositions which are expressed by the sentences which are the arguments of the truth-functional operators in those sentences. Evaluating a sentence consists in a procedure for ascertaining the truth-value of the proposition expressed by a truth-functional compound sentence given truth-value assignments for the propositions expressed by its sentential components.

Each of the examples of truth-functional compound sentences considered in the previous section featured only *one* sentential operator and at most *two* sentential arguments — one argument in the case of the monadic operator " $\sim$ ", and two arguments in the cases of the dyadic operators " $\cdot$ ", " $\vee$ ", " $\supset$ ", and " $\equiv$ ". It is time now to look at techniques for evaluating well-formed compound sentences which might feature any arbitrary number of truth-functional operators.

Although in ordinary speech and in casual writing, we have little occasion to produce sentences with more than just a few operators in them, the special concerns of logic require that we be able to construct and evaluate compound sentences of any degree whatever of complexity, short of an infinite degree of complexity. That is, we must be able to construct and to evaluate (at least in principle if not in practice) any truth-functional compound sentence having any finite number of truth-functional operators.

The Rules for Well-formedness allow us to *construct* sentences of any degree of complexity whatever. But how shall we *evaluate* intricate compound sentences? How might we evaluate a sentence such as " $\sim \sim A$ " in which there are two operators; and how might we evaluate a still more complicated sentence such as "$(A \supset \sim B) \cdot (\sim A \supset B)$" in which there are five operators?

To answer this question we shall have to see how the truth-tables of the previous section might be *used,* and this requires that we make a distinction between sentence-variables and sentence-constants.

The "P"s and "Q"s which were featured in our truth-tables for negation, conjunction, disjunction, material conditionality, and material biconditionality, as arguments of the operators, " $\sim$ ", " $\cdot$ ", " $\vee$ ", " $\supset$ " and " $\equiv$ " respectively, were *sentence-variables*. They stood indiscriminately for any proposition-expressing sentences whatever. But in addition to these kinds of symbols, we shall also want our conceptual notation to contain symbols which stand for *specific* sentences, and not — as variables do — for sentences in general. These symbols we shall call *sentential-constants* since they have a constant, fixed, or specific interpretation. We shall use capital letters from the beginning of the English alphabet — "A", "B", "C", "D", etc. — as our symbols for sentential-constants, and will reserve capital letters from the end of the alphabet — "P" through "Z" — as our symbols for sentential-variables.[10] Finally we add that any wff containing a sentential-variable is to be called a

---

10. All capital letters of the English alphabet are to be considered wffs, and hence the rules of the construction of wffs containing sentential-constants are just those already given.

sentence-form, while any wff containing only sentential-constants or containing only sentential-constants and sentence-forming operators, is to be called (simply) a *sentence.*

To see how we might use the truth-tables of the previous section to evaluate truth-functional compound sentences containing any number of operators, we must view the sentential-constants in sentences as substitution-instances of the sentential-variables (i.e., the "P"s and "Q"s) featured on those tables. If the truth-values of the propositions expressed by the sentential-constants in a truth-functional sentence are given, then — by referring to the truth-tables for the various truth-functional operators — we may evaluate the whole sentence by means of a step-by-step procedure beginning with the simplest sentential components of that sentence, evaluating then the next more complex components of that sentence, repeating the procedure — evaluating ever more complex components — until the entire sentence has been evaluated.

Consider some examples. Let us start, as it were "from scratch", with some sentences in a natural language such as English.

Example 1:

A believer and an atheist are arguing. The believer begins by enunciating the proposition that God exists. She says

> *(5.44)*   "God exists."

A little later, after advancing some of the standard arguments for atheism, the atheist concludes

> *(5.45)*   "God doesn't exist."

The believer makes the immediate rejoinder:

> *(5.46)*   "That's not the case"

and goes on to say what she thinks is wrong with the atheist's case.

Here it is evident that *(5.46)* is to be construed as expressing the negation of the proposition expressed by *(5.45)*, and that *(5.45)* is to be construed as expressing the negation of the proposition expressed by *(5.44)*. Adopting, now, our conceptual notation for sentential-constants, we may symbolize each of these three sentences respectively as

> *(5.44a)*   "A"

> *(5.45a)*   " ∼ A"

> *(5.46a)*   " ∼ ∼ A"

Now since negation is a truth-functional operation, it follows that the truth-value of the proposition expressed by " ∼ ∼ A" is a function of the proposition expressed by " ∼ A", and that the truth-value of the proposition expressed by " ∼ A" is, in turn, a function of the truth-value of the proposition expressed by "A". If, then, we could presume the truth-value of the proposition expressed by "A", it would be an easy matter to evaluate both the sentences " ∼ A" and " ∼ ∼ A", and thereby to ascertain the truth-values of the propositions expressed by these sentences. Without committing ourselves to claiming that "A" does in fact express a truth, let us consider the consequences of hypothesizing its truth. To do so, we simply *assign* "T" to the sentence "A". By treating "A" as a substitution-instance of "P" in the truth-table for negation (p. 251), we can infer that the sentence expressing the negation of A, viz., "∼A", is to bear the evaluation "F"; and then, as a further step, by treating "∼A" in turn as itself a substitution-instance of "P" in the truth-table for negation, we can infer that the sentence expressing the negation of ∼A, viz., "∼∼A", is to bear the evaluation "T". All of these steps may be combined on a single "evaluation tree".

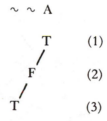

Here step (1) records our initial assignment of "T" to "A"; step (2) records the consequential assignment, made by reference to the truth-table for negation, of "F" to "∼A" (see row 1 in table *(5.a)*); and step (3) records the consequential assignment, made once more by reference to the truth-table for negation, of "T" to "∼∼A" (see row 2 in table *(5.a)*).

If, on the other hand, we had chosen as our initial assignment "F" to "A", it is an easy matter to see that we would have generated instead the following evaluation tree:

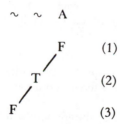

Example 2:

A partygoer says:

> *(5.47)*   "If I am out of town this weekend I won't be able to make your party. Otherwise I'll be there."

Here it is evident enough that what the partygoer has asserted might be expressed less colloquially and more perspicuously by saying:

> *(5.48)*   "If I am out of town this weekend then it is not the case that I'll be at your party. If it is not the case that I am out of town this weekend then I'll be at your party"

and that this might be expressed even more perspicuously in our conceptual notation as:

> *(5.49)*   "(B ⊃ ∼C) · (∼B ⊃ C)"

(with obvious readings for the constants "B" and "C").

Suppose now that we were given certain truth-values for the propositions expressed by the truth-functionally simple sentences "B" and "C". Suppose, for instance, that both propositions are false, i.e., that it is false that the partygoer is out of town on the weekend and false that he attends the party. Then we can evaluate the compound sentence which expresses the partygoer's claim by a number of simple steps which may be recorded thus:

$$(\; B \quad \supset \; \sim C) \quad \cdot \quad (\; \sim \; B \; \supset \; C \;)$$

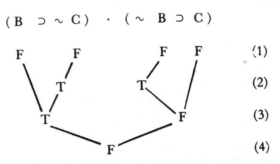

Step (1) records the initial assignment of "F" to each of "B" and "C". Step (2) records the consequential assignment of "T" to the sentences expressing the negations of B and C. Step (3) records the assignment, on the one hand, of "T" to "(B ⊃ ∼C)" (see row 3 of the truth-table for "⊃", p. 264), and, on the other hand, of "F" to "(∼B ⊃ C)" (see row 2 of the same truth-table). The final step, (4), records the assignment of "F" to the conjunction of (B ⊃ ∼C) and (∼B ⊃ C) (see row 2 of the truth-table for "·", p. 253). As we can see, each of these evaluations, after the initial assignment, is made by reference to the appropriate truth-table for the logical operator concerned.

Example 3:

Finally, by way of illustrating the technique of evaluating extended compound sentences, let us consider a sentence which is unlikely to be uttered in ordinary conversation:

(5.50)   "In view of the facts that not only will there not be a downhill race today if the rain doesn't stop and the fog doesn't clear but also that there will not be a giant slalom tomorrow if the course doesn't harden overnight, the World Cup skiers will have no opportunity to gain points unless the rain stops and the fog clears or the course hardens overnight."

Given the information that it is true that the rain stops, that the fog clears, and that the course hardens overnight, but false that the downhill race is held today, that the giant slalom is held tomorrow, and that the World Cup skiers have no opportunity to gain points, what is the truth-value of the proposition expressed by sentence *(5.50)?* To ascertain the truth-value of the proposition expressed by this extended compound sentence we need only render that sentence in the conceptual notation of symbolic logic and proceed to evaluate it. Having expressed *(5.50)* in our conceptual notation, and having written below each sentence-constant a "T" or an "F" according as that constant expresses a true or a false proposition, we may then proceed to evaluate — by reference to the truth-tables — the consequential assignments for ever larger components of that sentence.

We assign various sentential constants as follows:

We let "A" = "There will be a downhill race today";

"B" = "The rain will stop";

"C" = "The fog will clear";

"D" = "There will be a giant slalom tomorrow";

"E" = "The course will harden overnight"; and

"F" = "The World Cup skiers will have no opportunity to gain points".

Using these sentential constants we may express and evaluate *(5.50)* thus:

$$(((\sim B \cdot \sim C) \supset \sim A) \cdot (\sim E \supset \sim D)) \supset (((\sim B \cdot \sim C) \vee \sim E) \supset F)$$

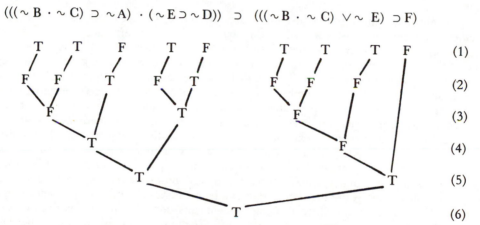

By taking recourse to the symbolism and truth-tables of formal logic we have been able to determine in a purely mechanical way, given the truth-values of the propositions expressed by "A" through "F", what the truth-value is of the proposition expressed by *(5.50)*.

This is no mean accomplishment, for it is unlikely that many of us could have done the exercise wholly in our heads. By having the means to 'break an evaluation down' into a series of completely mechanical steps, we are in a position to be able to evaluate sentences of any finite degree of complexity, whether they are sentences of ordinary conversation or the rather longer, more complex, sentences generated by the various special concerns of logic (e.g., in the testing of the validity of arguments — a matter which we shall begin to investigate shortly).

A note on two senses of "determined"

We have seen that each of the sentential operators "it is not the case that", "and", "or", "if . . . then", and "if and only if" admits of truth-functional uses — uses in which each generates compound sentences out of simpler ones in such a way that the truth-values of the propositions expressed by the compound sentences are *determined by* or are a *function of* the truth-values of propositions expressed by their simpler sentential components. In saying that the truth-values of the propositions expressed by truth-functional sentences are thus determined, we are, of course, making a purely *logical* point. We are saying, for instance, that what *makes* a proposition expressed by a compound sentence of the form "$\sim$P" true are just those conditions which account for the falsity of the proposition expressed by the simpler sentence "P", and that what *makes* a proposition expressed by a compound sentence of the form "~P" false are just those conditions which account for the truth of the proposition expressed by the simpler sentence "P"; we are saying that what *makes* a proposition expressed by a compound sentence of the form "P∨Q" false are just those conditions which account for the falsity of both "P" and "Q"; and so on. The logical point we are making holds independently of whether anyone ever comes to know the truth-value of the propositions expressed by these compound sentences by coming to know the truth-values of the propositions expressed by their simpler sentential components.

But there is another sense in which we can speak of the truth-values of propositions expressed by compound sentences in Truth-functional Propositional Logic being "determined". We may speak of the truth-values of these propositions being determined, in the sense of being ascertained, by *us* on the basis of our knowledge of the truth-values of the propositions expressed by their simpler sentential components. In saying that their truth-values may be thus determined we are, of course, making an epistemic point.

The epistemic and logical points just made are, of course, connected. It is only insofar as the truth-values of the propositions expressed by compound sentences we are considering are, so to speak, *logically* determined by the truth-values of the propositions expressed by their simpler sentential components that we can determine, *epistemically,* what their truth-values are, given initial assignments of truth-values to the propositions expressed by their simpler sentential components. How these initial assignments are made is, of course, another story. Sometimes it is on the basis of experience: we know what value-assignment to make experientially. Sometimes it is on the basis of reason or analytical thinking: we know what value-assignment to make ratiocinatively. And sometimes it is on the basis of mere supposition: we neither know experientially nor know ratiocinatively what the truth-values of these simple sentential components happen to be, but merely assume or suppose them to be such and such or so and so. But in whatever way these initial value-assignments are made, it is clear that the *consequential* assignments that we make for the propositions expressed by compound sentences of which these simple sentences are the components can be made ratiocinatively, and hence in a purely a priori way. Although the initial truth-value assignments may be made experientially or even empirically, the consequential assignments in a truth-functional propositional logic may be made a priori.[11]

EXERCISES

On the assumption that "A", "B", and "C" are each to be assigned "T", and that "D" and "E" are each to be assigned "F", evaluate each of the following.

1. $(A \cdot D) \supset (D \vee (B \cdot E))$

2. $A \equiv (\sim A \cdot B)$

3. $(C \vee B) \supset (C \vee (B \cdot A))$

4. $B \cdot (\sim A \supset B)$

5. $E \vee (D \cdot \sim (A \supset C))$

11. Recall, however, that knowledge gained by inference from experientially known truths is to be counted as experiential knowledge. When we say that consequential assignments may be made a priori, we are not claiming that the resultant knowledge is itself a priori. Whether or not it is a priori is a question whose answer depends upon whether or not it is possible to arrive at that same item of knowledge without any appeal to experience.

4.   ELEMENTARY TRUTH-TABLE TECHNIQUES FOR REVEALING MODAL STATUS AND MODAL RELATIONS[12]

Modal status

So far we have seen how the method of evaluating a truth-functional sentence may serve to reveal the truth-value of the proposition expressed by that sentence. But the real importance for Truth-functional Propositional Logic of the technique of sentential evaluation lies elsewhere. The technique assumes far greater importance when it is extended to encompass not just an evaluation for one particular assignment of "T"s and "F"s to the sentential components in a complex sentence, but a series of evaluations for every possible assignment of "T"s and "F"s to the sentential components. As a matter of fact we have already done one such complete evaluation in the previous section when we evaluated the sentence "∼ ∼ A" first with "T" having been assigned to "A" and then subsequently with "F" having been assigned to "A". In that instance nothing particularly remarkable ensued. But there are other cases in which giving an exhaustive series of evaluations may serve to reveal various modal attributes of the propositions expressed. Perhaps this is best explained by beginning with an example.

Suppose we start with the sentence

(5.51) "(A · B) ⊃ A"

Sentence *(5.51)* contains three sentential-constant *tokens* representing two sentential-constant *types*. In order to determine how many distinct assignments are possible for the sentential-constants in a sentence, we must count the types represented, not the number of tokens of those types occurring. In this instance the relevant number is two. The formula for ascertaining the number of distinct initial assignments, N, which can be made is simply, $N = 2^n$, where "n" represents the total number of sentential-constant types represented. Thus there are 2^2, i.e., *four* distinct initial assignments which might be made for *(5.51)*.

Rather than completing each evaluation in a tree-fashion as we did in the previous section, we will now write out each evaluation on the very same line as the one on which we make the initial assignment. In effect we simply compress the tree onto a single horizontal line. Thus instead of writing out the first evaluation of *(5.51)* in a tree-fashion such as

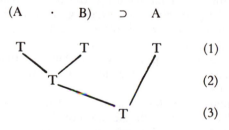

we will now write it out in this way:

$$
\begin{array}{ccccc}
\text{(A} & \cdot & \text{B)} & \supset & \text{A} \\
\text{T} & \text{T} & \text{T} & \text{T} & \text{T} \\
\text{(1)} & \text{(2)} & \text{(1)} & \text{(3)} & \text{(1)}
\end{array}
$$

---

12. Advanced truth-table techniques will be introduced in section 5.

where the numbers across the bottom correspond, as before, to the order in which the steps are performed.

Doing the evaluation on a single horizontal line allows us to perform many evaluations on a single truth-table. Indeed, we can do all possible evaluations on one truth-table. We need only set up the truth-table in the manner described earlier in section 2.

In the present instance we have

A	B	(A	·	B)	⊃	A
T	T	T	T	T	T	T
T	F	T	F	F	T	T
F	T	F	F	T	T	F
F	F	F	F	F	T	F
		(1)	(2)	(1)	(3)	(1)

TABLE *(5.l)*

Of course it may be that one or more of these rows represents a set of impossible worlds. This latter possibility arises from the fact that the initial assignments (i.e., the left-hand columns) have been made in a purely *mechanical* fashion with no regard being paid to which proposition "A" and "B" are being used to express. For example, suppose that "A" and "B" are two sentences which express logically equivalent propositions, then both the second (i.e., "T" and "F") and third assignment (i.e., "F" and "T") represent sets of *impossible* worlds. After all, there are no possible worlds in which two logically equivalent propositions have different truth-values.

Does the fact that some rows in a mechanically constructed truth-table may represent sets of impossible worlds undermine the method we are describing? Hardly. For even if some of the rows in a complete truth-table evaluation represent impossible worlds, the *remaining* rows will still represent an exhaustive classification of all *possible* worlds. Provided we do not assume that every row of a truth-table necessarily represents a set of possible worlds, but only that all of them together represent all possible worlds (and perhaps some impossible ones as well), we will be in a position to draw valid inferences from such truth-tables.[13]

Let us pay particular attention to the last column evaluated in table *(5.l)*, viz., column (3). It is a column consisting wholly of "T"s. What is the significance of this? It is simple: the proposition which is expressed by the sentence "(A · B) ⊃ A" is true in every possible world; it is, simply, a necessary truth. (Note that this conclusion follows even if some of the rows of table *(5.l)* happen to represent sets of impossible worlds. No matter, for the remaining rows represent all possible worlds.)

What we have here, then, is a case in which an exhaustive evaluation of a truth-functional compound sentence has revealed that the proposition expressed by that sentence is a necessary truth. There is no possible world in which that proposition is false. By a purely mechanical exercise we have

---

13. If there *are* any rows in a given truth-table which represent sets of impossible worlds, their elimination will put us in a position to draw *additional* information from that table. In section 5 we will explore ways of eliminating these rows and the consequences of so doing.

been able to learn in this instance that a particular proposition is necessarily true. In short, we have here a method to aid us in attempting, epistemically, to determine modal status.

Let us now consider as a second example, the sentence

(5.52)   " $\sim(\sim(A\cdot C)\vee(B\supset A))$ ".

Its truth-table is:

A	B	C	~	(	~	(A	·	C)	∨	(B	⊃	A))
T	T	T	F		F	T	T	T		T	T	T
T	T	F	F		T	T	F	F		T	T	T
T	F	T	F		F	T	T	T		T	F	T
T	F	F	F		T	T	F	F		T	F	T
F	T	T	F		T	F	F	T		T	T	F
F	T	F	F		T	F	F	F		T	T	F
F	F	T	F		T	F	F	T		T	F	T
F	F	F	F		T	F	F	F		T	F	T
			(5)		(3)	(1)	(2)	(1)		(4)	(1)	(2)(1)

TABLE (5.m)

Looking at the last column evaluated in table (5.m), viz., column (5), we can see immediately that sentence (5.52) expresses a necessary falsehood, a proposition which has the same truth-value in all possible worlds: falsity. Once again in a purely mechanical fashion we have been able epistemically to determine the modal status of a proposition expressed by a particular sentence.

How powerful is this method? It has definite limitations. It yields results only of a certain kind and only in certain circumstances. This method can never be used to demonstrate that the proposition expressed by a truth-functional compound sentence is *contingent*. This is surprising, for it is easy to think that if the final column of an exhaustive evaluation is not either all "T"s or all "F"s but is instead some combination of the two, then it would follow that the proposition expressed is contingent. But this does not follow. Suppose we have the sentence

(5.53)   "All squares have four sides and all brothers are male."

Expressed in the notation of Truth-functional Propositional Logic, this sentence might properly be translated simply as

(5.53a)   "F · M"

A complete truth-table evaluation of this latter sentence would yield

F	M	F	·	M
T	T	T	T	T
T	F	T	F	F
F	T	F	F	T
F	F	F	F	F
		(1)	(2)	(1)

TABLE (5.n)

Here, the last column to be evaluated, viz., (2), contains both "T"s and "F"s. Yet if we were to conclude that sentences *(5.53)* and *(5.53a)* express a contingent proposition, we would be wrong. The proposition expressed by these two sentences is noncontingent, and more particularly is noncontingently true.

What the method can, and cannot, show may be summarized thus:

1. If the final column in a complete truth-table evaluation of a compound sentence consists wholly of "T"s one may validly infer that the proposition expressed by that sentence is necessarily true.

2. If the final column in a complete truth-table evaluation of a compound sentence consists wholly of "F"s one may validly infer that the proposition expressed by that sentence is necessarily false.

3. If, however, the final column in a complete truth-table evaluation of a compound sentence consists of both "T"s and "F"s one is *not* entitled to infer that the proposition expressed is contingent.[14] As a test for contingency, this method is *inconclusive.*

This last point is so important, yet so often overlooked, that we can hardly emphasize it enough. The failure to take proper cognizance of it has led many persons to hold distorted views of the logical enterprise. It immediately follows from point 3 that a sentence may express a necessary truth or a necessary falsity even though a truth-tabular evaluation does not reveal it to be true in all possible worlds or to be false in all possible worlds.

The difficulty with truth-tabular methods of determining modal status is that they assign initial evaluations in a mechanical fashion and do not distinguish between assignments which designate impossible worlds and assignments which designate possible ones. (E.g., in table *(5.n)*, all of rows (2), (3), and (4) represent impossible worlds.) In short, being expressible by a sentence having a certain

14. Later, in section 5, we will explore methods to supplement the method of truth-table evaluation to make it more powerful so that it can be used as an adjunct to making an epistemic evaluation of contingency.

kind of truth-tabular evaluation (viz., a final column consisting wholly of "T"s or wholly of "F"s) is a *sufficient but not a necessary* condition for a proposition's being noncontingent. Ipso facto, being expressible by a sentence having a certain kind of truth-tabular evaluation (viz., a final column consisting of both "T"s and "F"s) is a *necessary but not a sufficient* condition for a proposition's being contingent.

EXERCISES

Part A

Translate each of the following sentences into conceptual notation using the sentential-constants specified. Then construct a truth-tabular evaluation for each translated sentence, and in each case tell what, if anything, the evaluation reveals about the modal status of the proposition expressed.

1.   *"If John and Martha are late, then John or Betty is late."*

> Let "*J*" = "*John is late*"
> "*M*" = "*Martha is late*"
> "*B*" = "*Betty is late*"

2.   *"There are fewer than two hundred stars or it is not the case that there are fewer than two hundred stars."*

> Let "*F*" = "*There are fewer than two hundred stars.*"

3.   *"There are fewer than two hundred stars or there are two hundred or more stars."*

> Let "*F*" = "*There are fewer than two hundred stars.*"
> "*E*" = "*There are (exactly) two hundred stars.*"
> "*M*" = "*There are more than two hundred stars.*"

4.   *"It is raining and it is not raining."*

> Let "*G*" = "*It is raining.*"

5.   *"If the pressure falls, it will either rain or snow."*

> Let "*F*" = "*The pressure falls.*"
> "*J*" = "*It will rain.*"
> "*K*" = "*It will snow.*"

6.   *"There are fewer than ten persons here and there are more than twenty persons here."*

> Let "*C*" = "*There are fewer than ten persons here.*"
> "*D*" = "*There are more than twenty persons here.*"

7.   *"If there are ten persons here, then there are ten or eleven persons here."*

   Let *"E"* = *"There are ten persons here."*
      "F" = *"There are eleven persons here."*

8.   *"If there are ten persons here, then there are at least six persons here."*

   Let *"E"* = *"There are ten persons here."*
      "I" = *"There are at least six persons here."*

9.   *"If a is a square, then a is a square."*

   Let *"A"* = *"a is a square."*

10.   *"If a is a square, then a has four sides."*

   Let *"A"* = *"a is a square."*
      "F" = *"a has four sides."*

Part B

11.   *For each case above in which the truth-tabular evaluation failed to reveal the modal status of the proposition expressed, say what the modal status is of that proposition.*

12.   *What is the modal relation obtaining between the propositions expressed in exercises 2 and 3 above?*

*   *   *   *   *

Modal relations

By evaluating two truth-functional sentences together on one truth-table it is sometimes possible to ascertain mechanically the modal relation obtaining between the propositions those two sentences express.

    Suppose for example that we were to evaluate the following two sentences together:

and

    (5.54) "Today is Sunday and I slept late"

    (5.55) "Today is Sunday or Monday."

We would begin by translating these into the conceptual notation of Truth-functional Propositional Logic, e.g.,

and

    (5.54a) "A · L"

    (5.55a) "A∨M"

To evaluate both these wffs on a single truth-table we will require 2^3 rows.

A	L	M	A	·	L	:	A	∨	M
T	T	T	T	T	T	:	T	T	T
T	T	F	T	T	T	:	T	T	F
T	F	T	T	F	F	:	T	T	T
T	F	F	T	F	F	:	T	T	F
F	T	T	F	F	T	:	F	T	T
F	T	F	F	F	T	:	F	F	F
F	F	T	F	F	F	:	F	T	T
F	F	F	F	F	F	:	F	F	F
			(1)	(2)	(1)		(1)	(2)	(1)

TABLE *(5.o)*

A comparison of the final column filled in under "A · L" with the final column filled in under "A∨M" is very revealing.

	A·L	A ∨ M
Row 1	T	T
Row 2	T	T
Row 3	F	T
Row 4	F	T
Row 5	F	T
Row 6	F	F
Row 7	F	T
Row 8	F	F
	(2)	(2)

FIGURE *(5.p)*

We note that there is no row in which "T" has been assigned to "A · L" and in which "F" has been assigned to "A∨M". Simply, this means that there is no possible world in which the proposition expressed by "A · L" is true and the proposition expressed by "A∨M" is false. But that this is so tells us that the first of these two propositions *implies* the second.

The method utilized in this example is perfectly general and may be stated in the following rule:

> If, in the truth-tabular evaluation of two sentences, it is found that there is no row of that table in which a sentence, α, has been assigned "T" and a sentence, β, has been assigned "F", one may validly infer that the proposition expressed by α *implies* the proposition expressed by β.

Again it is important to realize that this rule, like the rules of the previous section, states a sufficient condition but not a necessary one. Two propositions may stand in the relation of implication even though a truth-tabular evaluation of the sentences expressing those propositions fails to reveal it. One need only consider the two sentences

(5.56) "Sylvia bought a new car"

and

(5.57) "Someone bought a new car"

to see that this is so. Using "B" for *(5.56)* and "C" for *(5.57)*, the truth-tabular evaluation is:

B	C	B	C
T	T	T	T
T	F	T	F
F	T	F	T
F	F	F	F
		(1)	(1)

TABLE *(5.q)*

It is easy to see that this table fails to reveal what we already know to be the relation between the propositions expressed by "B" [or *(5.56)*] and "C" [or *(5.57)*], viz., implication.

Just as a truth-tabular evaluation may serve to reveal that two propositions stand in the relation of implication, it may also serve to reveal that two propositions stand in the modal relation of *equivalence* or the modal relation of *inconsistency*.

> If, in the truth-tabular evaluation of two sentences, it is found that in each row of the table these sentences have been assigned matching evaluations (i.e., both have been assigned "T" or both have been assigned "F"), one may validly infer that the propositions expressed by the two sentences are *logically equivalent* to one another.

If, in the truth-tabular evaluation of two sentences, it is found that there is no row in which both sentences have been assigned "T", one may validly infer that the propositions expressed by the two sentences are *logically inconsistent* with one another.

It is easy to provide illustrative cases of these rules. Let us begin with the case of equivalence. Consider the two sentences

and

(5.58) "A"

(5.59) "(A · ∿ B)∨(A · B)".

The truth-table evaluation is:

A	B	A	:	(A	•	∿	B)	∨	(A	•	B)
T	T	T	:	T	F	F	T	T	T	T	T
T	F	T	:	T	T	T	F	T	T	F	F
F	T	F	:	F	F	F	T	F	F	F	T
F	F	F	:	F	F	T	F	F	F	F	F
		(1)		(1)	(3)	(2)	(1)	(4)	(1)	(2)	(1)

TABLE *(5.r)*

A comparison of the column appearing under "A" with the final column appearing under "(A · ∿ B)∨(A · B)" reveals that the columns are identical. Such *sentences* will be said to be truth-functionally equivalent.

Truth-functionally equivalent sentences, it is clear, express propositions which have matching truth-values in all possible worlds, i.e., truth-functionally equivalent sentences express propositions which are logically equivalent to one another.

Of course two propositions may be logically equivalent even though a truth-tabular evaluation of the sentences expressing those propositions fails to reveal that they are. A case in point would be the two sentences

and

(5.60) "Iron is heavier than copper"

(5.61) "Copper is lighter than iron."

Expressed in the notation of Truth-functional Propositional Logic these two sentences might become respectively "I" and "C". A truth-tabular evaluation of the two sentence-constants "I" and "C" would not assign matching evaluations for every row of the table and hence would fail to reveal what we already know (by other means) about the two propositions expressed, viz., that they are logically equivalent.

Now let us turn to an illustration of the application of the rule for inconsistency. Suppose we take as our example

and

(5.62)   "A ≡ B"

(5.63)   " ~ (~ A ∨ B)".

The truth-tabular evaluation is

A	B	A	≡	B		~	(	~	A	∨	B)
T	T		T		•	F					
T	F		F		•	T					
F	T		F		•	F					
F	F		T		•	F					
		(1)	(2)	(1)		(4)		(2)	(1)	(3)	(1)

TABLE (5.s)

When we compare the final columns filled in under each compound sentence we find that there is no row in which both sentences have been assigned "T". Thus, in this case, where no row assigns "T" to both the first and second sentence, we may be assured that the propositions expressed by these two sentences are not both true in any possible world, i.e., that they are inconsistent with one another.

Two propositions may be inconsistent with one another even though a truth-tabular evaluation of the sentences expressing them fails to reveal it. An example is the following:

and

(5.64)   "Something is square"

(5.65)   "Nothing is square."

A mechanical truth-tabular evaluation of sentence-constants (e.g., "E" and "N") representing these sentences will assign "T", on the first row of the truth-table, to both of these constants. Hence the table will fail to show what we already know by other means, viz., that these two sentences express contradictory, and ipso facto, inconsistent propositions.

In the case of the modal relation of consistency, we find that truth-tabular methods have the same *inconclusiveness* as they were found to have in the case of our trying to use them to determine that a proposition has the modal status of contingency.

The fact that a truth-table cannot, in general, be used to reveal that two propositions stand in the relation of consistency has, once again, to do with the manner in which truth-tables are constructed. What *would* reveal that two propositions were consistent would be the existence of at least one row on a truth-table which (1) assigns "T" to both of the sentences expressing those propositions and (2) represents a set of possible worlds. The stumbling block here is the second condition, the condition which requires that one of the rows assigning "T" and "T" to the two sentences respectively be a row which represents a set of *possible* worlds. For the trouble is that in constructing truth-tables mechanically we have no way of determining from the truth-table itself which rows represent sets of *possible* worlds and which represent sets of *impossible* worlds. Provided we are looking, e.g., in the case of implication and equivalence, for the *non*-existence of a certain kind of assignment, it makes no difference whether the rows represent possible or impossible worlds. But when, e.g., in the case of consistency, we are looking for a dual assignment of "T" in a row representing a set of possible worlds, the truth-tabular method fails us.

In short, it is a necessary condition for validly inferring that two propositions are consistent that there be no truth-tabular evaluation of any sentences expressing those propositions which reveals them to be inconsistent. But this latter is by no means a sufficient condition.

EXERCISES

Part A

Translate each of the following pairs of sentences into conceptual notation using the sentential constants specified. Then construct truth-tabular evaluations for each pair of sentences, and in each case tell what, if anything, the evaluation reveals about the modal relations obtaining between the two propositions expressed.

1.   *"If I overslept, then I was late for work" and "If I was late for work, then I overslept"*

>   Let *"O"*   = *"I overslept"*
>   *"L"*   = *"I was late for work"*

2.   *"If everyone was late, then someone was late" and "Everyone was late"*

>   Let *"E"*   = *"Everyone was late"*
>   *"B"*   = *"Someone was late"*

3.   *"John has been taking lessons from his father; and he can pass his driver's test if and only if he has been taking lessons from his father" and "John can pass his driver's test"*

>   Let *"J"*   = *"John has been taking lessons from his father"*
>   *"C"*   = *"John can pass his driver's test"*

4.   *"There are fewer than two hundred stars" and "It is not the case that there are fewer than two hundred stars"*

>   Let *"H"*   = *"There are fewer than two hundred stars"*

5.   *"There are fewer than two hundred stars" and "There are two hundred or more stars"*

>   Let *"H"*   = *"There are fewer than two hundred stars"*
>   *"E"*   = *"There are (exactly) two hundred stars"*
>   *"M"*   = *"There are more than two hundred stars"*

6.   *"a is a green square tray" and "a is a square tray"*

>   Let *"B"*   = *"a is green tray"*
>   *"A"*   = *"a is a square tray"*

7. *"a is a square"* and *"a has four sides"*

>   Let *"A"* = *"a is a square"*
>   *"H"* = *"a has four sides"*

8. *"Today is Tuesday"* and *"It is earlier in the week than Wednesday and later in the week than Monday"*

>   Let *"D"* = *"Today is Tuesday"*
>   *"E"* = *"It is earlier in the week than Wednesday"*
>   *"L"* = *"It is later in the week than Monday"*

9. *"Diane and Efrem love chocolate ice cream"* and *"Efrem and Diane love chocolate ice cream"*

>   Let *"D"* = *"Diane loves chocolate ice cream"*
>   *"E"* = *"Efrem loves chocolate ice cream"*

10. *"Everything is square"* and *"Everything is square or not everything is square"*

>   Let *"E"* = *"Everything is square"*

Part B

11. *Are there any cases above in which the two propositions stand in the relation of implication but for which the truth-tabular evaluation fails to reveal that relation? Which, if any, are they?*

12. *Are there any cases above in which the two propositions stand in the relation of equivalence but for which the truth-tabular evaluation fails to reveal that relation? Which, if any, are they?*

13. *Are there any cases above in which the two propositions stand in the relation of inconsistency but for which the truth-tabular evaluation fails to reveal that relation? Which, if any, are they?*

*   *   *   *   *

Deductive validity

In chapter 1, we defined "deductive validity" in terms of "implication". Elaborating a bit, we may now offer the following definition:

>   "An argument A consisting of a premise-set S and a conclusion C is deductively valid" =$_{df}$ "The premise-set S (or alternatively the conjunction of all the propositions of S) of argument A implies the conclusion C".

In short, a necessary and sufficient condition of an argument's being deductively valid is that the premises of that argument imply the conclusion. Thus to the extent that truth-tabular methods can reveal that the relation of implication holds between two propositions (or proposition-sets), to that extent it can reveal that an argument is deductively valid.

The most obvious way of using truth-tables in an attempt to ascertain whether an argument is deductively valid is simply to conjoin all the premises and then to evaluate together on one truth-table both this compound sentence and the sentence expressing the conclusion. If no row on the truth-table assigns "T" to the first sentence and "F" to the second, we may validly infer that the argument is deductively valid.

Consider the following argument:

(5.66)

Premises $\Big\{$

If the seeds were planted in March and it rained throughout April, the flowers bloomed in June.

The seeds were planted in March but it is not the case that the flowers bloomed in June.

Conclusion $\Big\{$ It is not the case that it rained throughout April.

Translating this argument into conceptual notation, using fairly obvious interpretations for our sentential-constants, gives us:

(5.66a)

$$(M \cdot A) \supset J$$
$$\underline{M \cdot \sim J}$$
$$\therefore \sim A$$

Conjoining the sentences of the premises as our next step gives us:

(5.67)   "$((M \cdot A) \supset J) \cdot (M \cdot \sim J)$"[15]

The truth-table for (5.67) is:

A	J	M	((M	•	A)	⊃	J)	•	(M	•	∼	J)		∼	A
T	T	T						F						F	
T	T	F						F						F	
T	F	T						F						F	
T	F	F						F						F	
F	T	T						F						T	
F	T	F						F						T	
F	F	T						T						T	
F	F	F						F						T	
			(1)	(2)	(1)	(3)	(1)	(4)	(1)	(3)	(2)	(1)		(2)	(1)

TABLE (5.t)

15. It should now be obvious why we said earlier, in section 3, that we require in our logic the means to be

By comparing the final column filled in under "$((M \cdot A) \supset J) \cdot (M \cdot \sim J)$" with the final column filled in under "$\sim A$", we can see that there is no row on the truth-table which assigns "T" to the first of these sentences and "F" to the second. Thus we may validly infer that the proposition expressed by the former sentence implies the proposition expressed by the latter. But since this is so, then we may likewise infer that the original argument, from which the two compound sentences evaluated were derived, is itself deductively valid. Here, then, is an instance in which we have been able to demonstrate in a purely mechanical fashion that a certain argument, viz., *(5.66a)*, is deductively valid.[16]

In the example which we have just worked through, the results of the truth-tabular test were positive: the test revealed that the argument is deductively valid. But suppose we were to try a truth-tabular test for deductive validity in the case of some other argument and were to find that the test failed, i.e., that at least one row of the truth-table assigned "T" to the sentence formed by conjoining all the sentences expressing the premises of the argument and it assigned "F" to the sentence expressing the conclusion of the argument. Under such circumstances are we entitled to infer that the argument is *deductively invalid*, i.e., that its premises do *not* imply its conclusion? The answer is: No. And the reason parallels exactly the reason we gave earlier for saying that truth-tabular methods cannot in general be used to show that one proposition does not imply another: the row of the truth-table which assigns "T" to the first sentence and "F" to the second may represent, not a set of possible worlds, but a set of impossible worlds.

If, then, in an attempt to ascertain whether an argument is deductively valid, a truth-tabular test yields some row which assigns "T" to the sentence expressing the conjunction of the premises and an "F" to that sentence expressing the conclusion of the argument, we are not entitled to infer that the argument is deductively invalid. The test is simply *inconclusive;* and other, more sophisticated ways of determining deductive validity and invalidity, i.e., logical methods which embody a deeper conceptual analysis, will have to be adopted.

Another, but no more powerful, way to use truth-tables in an attempt to ascertain whether a given argument is deductively valid is to capitalize on the fact that "implication" (and hence "deductive validity") may be defined in terms of (1) the relation of material conditionality and (2) truth in all possible worlds.

> "P implies Q" $=_{df}$ "The relation of material conditionality holds between P and Q in all possible worlds."

In symbols, this same definition may be expressed thus:

$$\text{"P} \rightarrow \text{Q"} =_{df} \text{"}\Box(\text{P} \supset \text{Q})\text{"}$$

These definitions suggest, then, a second way to use truth-tables to ascertain validity. Because of the interdefinability of "deductive validity" and "implication" it will suffice to show that an argument is deductively valid if we show that a material conditional sentence whose antecedent expresses the conjunction of the premises of that argument and whose consequent expresses the conclusion of the argument, expresses a proposition which is true in all possible worlds.

---

able to evaulate well-formed sentences of any arbitrary length. Although we do not often *utter* sentences which contain more than five or six operators, in the testing of arguments for validity, we *manufacture* sentences which may be very long indeed and which may contain a great many operators. This will certainly be the case when the argument itself contains several premises.

16. Note, however, that the step which gets us from *(5.66)* to *(5.66a)*, i.e., the step in which we translate the original argument as stated in English into the conceptual notation of Logic, is *not* a mechanical procedure.

We will use the same example as above. This time, however, instead of evaluating the *two* sentences, "((M · A) ⊃ J) · (M · ∼ J)" and "∼A", we shall evaluate the *one* material conditional sentence "(((M · A) ⊃ J) · (M · ∼ J)) ⊃ ∼A":

A	J	M	(((M · A) ⊃ J) · (M · ∼ J)) ⊃ ∼ A
T	T	T	T
T	T	F	T
T	F	T	T
T	F	F	T
F	T	T	T
F	T	F	T
F	F	T	T
F	F	F	T

(5)

TABLE (5.u)

Here, the final column, consisting as it does entirely of "T"s, filled in under the material conditional sentence, reveals that the proposition expressed by that sentence is true in all possible worlds. Since that proposition is true in all possible worlds, the proposition expressed by the antecedent of that material conditional sentence *implies* the proposition expressed by the consequent of that same sentence. But insofar as these two propositions are just those propositions expressed by the premise-set and conclusion respectively of the original argument, we have succeeded in showing that that argument is deductively valid.

Which of these two ways of using truth-tables a person adopts in an attempt to ascertain deductive validity is purely a matter of personal taste. There is nothing as regards their efficacy to recommend one over the other. They will always yield identical results: any argument which the one reveals to be valid, the other will also; any argument which the one fails to reveal to be deductively valid, the other will also.

Even though these two ways of using truth-tables in an attempt to ascertain the deductive validity of arguments do not, and cannot, differ in their results, a word of caution ought to be sounded concerning the latter. Because the latter technique involves constructing and subsequently evaluating a material conditional, some persons have been misled into thinking that the relation one is seeking to establish when one is looking to see whether an argument is deductively valid is the relation of material conditionality. This is a totally unwarranted inference, but an all-too-common one. True enough, the latter technique, as we have described it and as it is put into practice here and in countless other books as well, does utilize a material conditional sentence. But this is not to say that we are looking to see whether simply the relation of material conditionality holds between the premises and conclusion of an argument. Rather we are looking to see whether the relation of material conditionality holds between the premises and conclusion *in all possible worlds* (not just in the actual world). For when the relation of material conditionality holds in all possible worlds between two propositions, those propositions stand in the modal relation of implication. Failure to understand this point has deceived many students of logic into thinking that deductive validity is not a *modal* property of arguments. But of course it is. Deductive validity cannot be defined simply in terms of truth and falsity and ipso facto cannot be defined in terms of the relation of material conditionality simpliciter. For an argument to be deductively valid there must be *no possible world* in which all its premises are true and its conclusion false. That is to say, for an argument to be deductively valid the relation of material conditionality must hold between its premise-set and conclusion not just in the actual world but in all possible worlds.

EXERCISES

Translate each of the following arguments into conceptual notation using the sentential constants specified. Then construct truth-tabular tests for validity, and in each case tell whether that test reveals the argument to be deductively valid.

Let "A"   = "The turntable is grounded"

    "B"   = "The hum persists"

    "C"   = "The amplifier is grounded"

    "D"   = "Diane is older than Efrem"

    "E"   = "Efrem is older than Martin"

    "F"   = "Diane is older than Martin"

1. *If the turntable is grounded and the amplifier is grounded, then it is not the case that the hum persists. But the hum persists. Therefore, either it is not the case that the amplifier is grounded or it is not the case that the turntable is grounded.*

2. *If either the turntable or the amplifier is grounded, then it is not the case that the hum persists. It is not the case that the hum persists. Therefore, the amplifier is grounded.*

3. *Diane is older than Efrem. Efrem is older than Martin. Therefore, Diane is older than Martin.*

4. *If Diane is older than Efrem, then Efrem is older than Martin. If Efrem is older than Martin, then Diane is older than Efrem. Therefore, if it is not the case that Efrem is older than Martin, then it is not the case that Diane is older than Efrem.*

5.   ADVANCED TRUTH-TABLE TECHNIQUES

Corrected truth-tables

In the previous section we have seen how the mechanical construction of truth-tables leads to certain restrictions on their interpretation, e.g., they cannot be used to demonstrate the *contingency* of a proposition expressed by a truth-functional compound sentence; they cannot be used to demonstrate the *consistency* of two propositions expressed by truth-functional compound sentences; and (in general) they cannot be used to demonstrate the deductive *invalidity* of an argument expressed by truth-functional compound sentences.

There is, however, a way to supplement Truth-functional Propositional Logic in such a way as to remove these restrictions. In effect, it involves stepping outside of the purely mechanical techniques of that Logic and supplementing them with the results of nonformal conceptual analysis. What the method amounts to is striking out all those rows on a truth-table which represent a set of impossible worlds.

Let us see how the method works. Suppose we were to start with the following two sentences

Let "G" = "There are fewer than four apples in the basket",

"H" = "There are more than ten apples in the basket",

and were to ask, "What is the logical relation obtaining between the propositions expressed by '∼(G · H)' and '∼G · H'; in particular, are these propositions consistent or inconsistent?" If we proceed to construct a truth-table in the standard way, we will discover that that table is *inconclusive:*

G	H	∼(G · H)	∼G · H
T	T	F	F
T	F	T	F
F	T	T	T
F	F	T	F

TABLE *(5.v)*

The trouble here, of course, lies in the third row. The presence of a "T" under "∼(G · H)" and a "T" under "∼G · H" would indicate the consistency of the propositions expressed by these two sentences if we could be assured that this row represents a set of possible worlds and not a set of impossible worlds. But as truth-tables are standardly constructed, no such inference may validly be made.

However, such an inference can be made if truth-tables are constructed in a nonstandard way: in a way which insures that every row of the table represents a non-empty set of possible worlds. To do this we systematically pass down through the assignments made on the left-hand side of the double vertical line and ask of each of these assignments whether it represents a set of possible worlds or a set of impossible worlds for the particular propositions expressed by the simple sentential-constants appearing at the top of the columns. When we do this, we step outside the techniques of ordinary truth-functional logic; for in doing this we are performing nonformal analysis on the propositions expressed by those simple sentential-constants.

In the present case we begin with row 1, asking ourselves whether the assignment of "T" to both "G" and "H" represents a set of possible worlds. The answer our conceptual analysis gives us is: No. By analyzing the concepts of *more than, fewer than, four, ten,* etc., which figure in these propositions we are able to ascertain analytically that there is no possible world in which it is true that there are fewer than four apples in the basket and in which it is true that there are more than ten. So we strike out row 1. By similar sorts of analysis, we also ascertain that the other three rows do represent sets of possible worlds, and consequently we allow them to remain. The truth-table which results from this process, we call, simply, a *corrected* truth-table.

G	H	$\sim$(G $\cdot$ H)	$\sim$G $\cdot$ H
~~T~~	~~T~~	~~F~~	~~F~~
T	F	T	F
F	T	T	T
F	F	T	F

TABLE *(5.w)*

From this corrected truth-table we *can* obtain the information we desire. Row 3 has survived the striking-out process, and hence the propositions expressed by " $\sim$ (G $\cdot$ H)" and " $\sim$G $\cdot$ H", respectively, are *consistent* with one another: there *is* a possible world in which these propositions are both true.

The method is perfectly general. Having performed a nonformal analysis of the modal relations obtaining between propositions expressed by *simple* sentences, we are then in a position to ascertain *mechanically* (by means of a corrected truth-table) the full range of modal attributes (including contingency, consistency, and deductive invalidity) which might be exemplified by propositions expressed by truth-functional *compound* sentences.

EXERCISES

1. *(a)   By constructing a corrected truth-table, ascertain the modal status of the proposition expressed by "I $\supset$ (K $\supset$ J)" where*

   "I" = *"There are fewer than nine apples in the basket",*
   "J" = *"There are more than three apples in the basket", and*
   "K" = *"There are (exactly) five apples in the basket".*

   (b)   Which 4 of the 8 rows of the truth-table had to be struck out in order to construct the corrected truth-table?

2.   *Using the same interpretation for "I", and "J", and "K" as in question 1, determine the modal status of the proposition expressed by "($\sim I \cdot \sim J$) $\supset K$".*

3.   *Similarly, determine the modal status of the proposition expressed by "$K \supset (I \cdot J)$".*

4.   *Using standard truth-table techniques, viz., those outlined in section 4, what can one determine about the validity of the following argument?*

$$I \supset (J \vee K)$$
$$\underline{\sim K \qquad\qquad}$$
$$\therefore \quad (I \vee J)$$

5.   *Using the nonstandard techniques of this section, and the interpretation of "I", "J", and "K" as given in question 1, what can one learn about the validity of the argument cited in question 4?*

6.   *Again, using the same interpretation for "I", "J", and "K", what does a corrected truth-table tell us about the validity of the following argument?*

$$\underline{I \cdot J \quad}$$
$$\therefore K$$

*   *   *   *   *

Reduced truth-tables

We saw in chapter 1 that if we arbitrarily choose any two propositions whatever, the two propositions must stand to one another in exactly one of the fifteen relationships depicted in the worlds-diagrams of figure *(1.i)*. This result holds even if those propositions happen to be expressed by truth-functional compound sentences containing several sentential constants.

As it turns out, there is a simple, indeed mechanical, way to get from a corrected truth-table for a pair of propositions to the one worlds-diagram among the fifteen which uniquely depicts that relationship. The method utilizes what we shall call a *reduced* truth-table.

In order to construct a reduced truth-table, one begins with a corrected truth-table and then focuses attention on the right-hand side of the double vertical line. One simply deletes all but one of those rows which happen to be alike. For example, suppose we begin with the two sentences

        "A" = "There are fewer than 100 stars" and
        "B" = "There are more than 1500 stars".

An infinity of compound sentences is constructible out of "A" and "B". Of this infinity, we choose two as examples, viz., "A≡B" and "A∨B", and ask of these, "Which one of the fifteen worlds-diagrams depicts the modal relationship obtaining between the propositions expressed by these two compound sentences?" To answer this question we begin by constructing a corrected truth-table.

Since the propositions expressed by "A" and "B" are contraries, there is no possible world in which both are true. We must strike out the first row of the truth-table.

A	B		A ≡ B		A ∨ B
T	T		T		T
T	F		F		T
F	T		F		T
F	F		T		F

TABLE *(5.x)*

Next we construct the reduced truth-table. To do this we look only at the right-hand side of the table and delete all but one of any set of rows which happen to be identical. As we can see, the second and third rows are identical: they both assign "F" to "A≡B", and "T" to "A∨B". Thus we strike out the third row. The *reduced* truth-table is thus

A ≡ B	A ∨ B
F	T
T	F

TABLE *(5.y)*

The reduced truth-table tells us two things: (1) that there are some possible worlds in which A≡B is false and A∨B is true; and (2) that there are some possible worlds in which A≡B is true and A∨B is false. By careful inspection of the fifteen worlds-diagrams for two propositions we can see that only one diagram, the tenth, depicts such a relationship. And the tenth diagram, we may recall, represents the case of contradiction holding between two contingent propositions.

There is, however, even an easier way to get from the reduced truth-table to the appropriate worlds-diagram.

A moment's reflection tells us that there is, after all, a maximum number of rows possible in a reduced truth-table: no reduced truth-table can have more than four rows, viz.,

T–T
T–F
F–T
F–F

(Any other row would have to be 'reduced' to one of these.) This fact puts an upper limit on the number of different reduced truth-tables. The only possible reduced truth-tables are those whose rows are some subset of these four. And the maximum number of ways of selecting from among four things is fifteen.[17] The fifteen possible reduced truth-tables may all be listed:

1.	T–T	5.	T–T T–F	11.	T–T F–T F–F	15.	T–F T–T F–T F–F
2.	T–F	6.	T–T F–T	12.	T–F F–T F–F		
3.	F–T	7.	T–F F–F	13.	T–T T–F F–F		
4.	F–F	8.	F–T F–F	14.	T–F T–T F–T		
		9.	T–T F–F				
		10.	T–F F–T				

FIGURE *(5.z)*

Each of these fifteen reduced truth-tables corresponds to a unique worlds-diagram. And each of these reduced truth-tables may heuristically be regarded as a 'code' or 'tabular description' of its corresponding worlds-diagram. Each of these reduced truth-tables, these *codes* so to speak, is reproduced in figure *(5.aa)* (p. 300) alongside its respective worlds-diagram and again on the very diagram itself. For example, consider reduced truth-table 11:

T–T
F–T
F–F.

We can see how this code is mapped directly onto worlds-diagram 11. The first segment of that diagram represents those possible worlds in which P is true and Q is true (T–T); the second segment, those possible worlds in which P is false and Q is true (F–T); and the third segment, those possible worlds in which P is false and Q is false (F–F).

In sum, to find the modal relation obtaining between any two propositions expressed by truth-functional compound sentences: (1) construct a corrected truth-table for those compound sentences, (2) then proceed to construct a reduced truth-table, and (3) finally match the reduced

17. The formula for the number of ways, k, of selecting from among n things is, $k = 2^n - 1$. In the present instance, $n = 4$.

truth-table to one code among the worlds-diagrams. That diagram represents the modal relation obtaining between the two propositions expressed by the compound sentences.

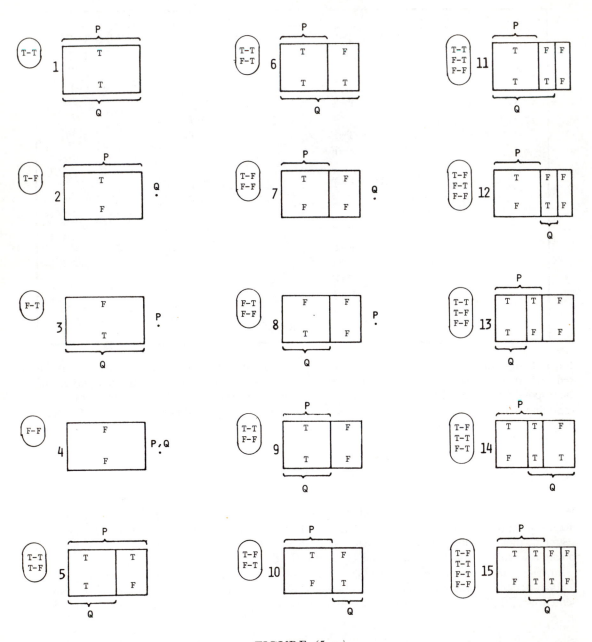

FIGURE *(5.aa)*

EXERCISES

Part A

1. Let *"A"* = *"Sylvia has (exactly) one sister"*
    "B" = *"Joseph has (exactly) four sisters"*
    "C" = *"Joseph has twice as many sisters as Sylvia".*

    Using reduced truth-tables determine which worlds-diagram depicts the modal relation obtaining between the proposition expressed by "(B · C) ⊃ A" and the proposition expressed by "(B · C)".

2. Let *"M"* = *"Al is taller than Bill"*
    "N" = *"Al is older than Bill"*
    "O" = *"Al is the same height as Bill".*

    Using reduced truth-tables determine in each case which worlds-diagram depicts the modal relation obtaining between the propositions expressed by the following pairs of compound sentences:

    a.   *"(M · N)" and "(N ⊃ O)"*

    b.   *"(M∨N)" and "∼O"*

    c.   *"(M∨O)" and "(M · O)"*

    d.   *"O" and "((M·N)∨ (N ⊃ ∼O))".*

Part B

3. *(For mathematically adept students.) Show how to derive the formula cited in chapter 1, p. 57, for the number of worlds-diagrams required to depict all the ways of arranging* n *propositions on a worlds-diagram. (Hint: how many reduced truth-tables are there in the case of three arbitarily chosen propositions?)*

6.   THE CONCEPT OF FORM

Sentences and sentential forms in a logic

We have already introduced the distinction between sentences and sentential forms, or more specifically, the distinction between sentences in Truth-functional Propositional Logic and sentence-forms in that same Logic.

A sentence (in Truth-functional Propositional Logic), we have said, is a well-formed formula which contains only sentence-*constants* (i.e., the letters "A" through "O" of the English alphabet) or only sentence-constants and truth-functional operators. A sentence-form, on the other hand, in

Truth-functional Propositional Logic, is a well-formed formula which contains at least one sentence-*variable*, i.e., one of the letters "P" through "Z".

Sentence-forms, unlike sentences, do *not* express propositions. What, then, is their role? Why do logicians concern themselves not only with sentences but with sentence-forms as well? What is the relationship between sentences and sentence-forms? Let us turn to these questions.

The relationship between sentences and sentence-forms

Sentences *instantiate* sentence-forms. Indeed, a given sentence may instantiate *several* sentential forms within a formal logic. Consider, for example, the sentence

(5.68)   "It is not the case that Henry brought the typewriter, and if Mary did, then she has put it out of sight."

Rendered in the conceptual notation of Truth-functional Propositional Logic, this sentence becomes,

(5.68a)   "$\sim A \cdot (B \supset C)$".

This latter sentence has (or instantiates) the forms:[18]

(F1)   "$\sim P \cdot (Q \supset R)$"

(F2)   "$P \cdot (Q \supset R)$"

(F3)   "$P \cdot Q$"

(F4)   "$\sim P \cdot Q$".

And — like *all* other sentences — it also instantiates the form

(F5)   "P".

(F1) through (F5) are said to be forms of the sentence *(5.68a)* because it is possible to instantiate (which is to say, to find substitution-instances of) the variables appearing in these forms so as to generate the sentence *(5.68a)*. Thus, for example, if in (F1), we were to substitute the sentential constant "A" for the sentential variable "P", "B" for "Q", and "C" for "R", we would produce the sentence "$\sim A \cdot (B \supset C)$". Similarly if, in (F3), we were to substitute "$\sim A$" for "P" and "$(B \supset C)$" for "Q", then, again, we would produce the sentence *(5.68a)*.

By way of contrast, consider the form

(F6)   "$P \cdot \sim Q$".

Is (F6) a form of *(5.68a)*? It turns out that it is not. There are no substitutions we can make for "P" and for "Q" in (F6) so as to yield the sentence *(5.68a)*. There are, of course, substitutions we can make which will yield a sentence which expresses the same *proposition* which is expressed by

---

18. In writing the forms of sentences we adopt the convention of selecting the capital letters beginning with "P" *in alphabetical order*.

(5.68a), but this is not the same as generating the very *sentence (5.68a)*. For example, we can substitute "∼A" for "P" in (F6), and "(B · ∼C)" for "Q", to yield

$$(5.69) \quad \text{"} \sim \! A \cdot \sim \! (B \cdot \sim \! C)\text{"},$$

which is truth-functionally equivalent to *(5.68a)*. Yet since (F6) cannot be instantiated to yield *(5.68a)*, (F6) is *not* a form of *(5.68a)*.

In Truth-functional Propositional Logic we may define the form of a sentence in this way:

> A sentence, S, will be said to have the form, F, if F is a well-formed formula and if the sentence S can be generated from F by substituting sentences (or sentential constants) for the sentential variables occurring in F.[19]

It is sometimes convenient to regard the forms of sentences as capsule descriptions of the logical structure of those sentences. Thus, for example, in saying of (F3) [viz., "P · Q"] that it is a form of *(5.68a)*, we may be taken to be saying that *(5.68a)* is a conjunction of two sentences. Equally well, in saying that (F2) [viz., "P · (Q ⊃ R)"] is a form of *(5.68a)* we may be taken to be saying that *(5.68a)* is a conjunction whose second conjunct is a material conditional. Both these descriptions are true of *(5.68a)*. *(5.68a)* being a fairly complex compound sentence, has *several* descriptions of its logical structure which are each true. This is not surprising since most things allow several descriptions each of which is true. For example, this page (1) is made of paper; (2) is made of white paper; (3) is rectangular; (4) has printing on it; (5) has black printing; etc., etc. Each of these descriptions is true of this page.

A common manner of speech sometimes fosters the belief that sentences typically have but a single form. Very often in reporting that such-and-such is a form of the sentence so-and-so, we express ourselves thus: "The sentence so-and-so has *the* form such-and-such." Speaking in this way, using the definite article "the", we find it easy to slip into also saying, "The form of the sentence so-and-so is such-and-such." But this is a mistake. We ought not to infer the latter from the former any more than we ought to infer the false claim that *the* attribute of a ripe banana is the attribute, yellowness, from the true claim that ripe bananas have *the* attribute of being yellow. The definite article, "the", cannot be shuttled about willy-nilly in this way. Although the sentence *(5.68a)* has the form (F2), it does not follow that (F2) is the (single) form of *(5.68a)*. In addition to saying that *(5.68a)* has the form (F2), we can also say that *(5.68a)* has the form (F1), that it has the form (F3), etc.

However, not *all* sentences instantiate more than one form in a specific logic. Although many do, not all do. Consider the two sentences

$$(5.70) \quad \text{"D"}$$

$$(5.71) \quad \text{"} \sim \! D\text{"}.$$

---

19. According to this definition, the formula "∼A · (P ⊃ Q)", where "A" is a constant and "P" and "Q" are variables, would turn out to be a form of "∼A · (B ⊃ C)". For some purposes it is helpful to regard such "mixed" formulae as forms. For example, in some cases it might be helpful to regard the sentence, "If today is Monday, then the shipment is overdue", as being of the form, "If today is Monday, then P", where "P" represents a sentential variable. However, we will have no need of such 'mixed' forms anywhere in these introductory studies, and will hereinafter usually mean by "form" a *non*-mixed formula of the sort described in the definition.

The sentence *(5.70)* instantiates exactly *one* form in Truth-functional Propositional Logic. The single form of *(5.70)* is

(F5)   "P"

while the two forms of *(5.71)* are

(F5)   "P"

(F7)   "∼ P".

The sentence *(5.70)* can be generated only from (F5) by substituting "D" for "P"; the sentence *(5.71)* can be generated either from (F5) by substituting "∼ D" for "P", or from (F7) by substituting "D" for "P". But note, the sentence *(5.70)*, viz., "D", *cannot* be generated from (F7). Although we may substitute "∼ D" for "P" in (F7) to yield

(5.72)   "∼ ∼ D",

which is of course truth-functionally equivalent to *(5.70)*, *(5.72)* is not the same *sentence* as *(5.70)*.

Any sentence which contains even a single truth-functional sentential operator will have more than one form in Truth-functional Propositional Logic. And as the number of such operators increases, the number of forms instantiated will increase as a complicated exponential function.

If there is more than one form of a sentence these forms may be arranged in order of "length". The length of a formula is determined by counting the number of letters occurring in it, the number (if any) of operators and the number (if any) of punctuation marks, viz., "(" and ")". Thus the length of (F1) is 8; while the length of (F4) is only 4. The forms of *(5.68a)* may be arranged in ascending order of length:

(F5)   "P "   (length 1)

(F3)   "P · Q"   (length 3)

(F4)   "∼ P · Q"   (length 4)

(F2)   "P · (Q ⊃ R)"   (length 7)

(F1)   "∼ P · (Q ⊃ R)"   (length 8)

Sometimes, two or more forms of a sentence may be of equal length and will have to be assigned to the same slot in the ordering thus giving rise to what is called a 'weak' ordering, not a 'complete' ordering as above.[20] For example, consider the sentence

(5.73)   "(∼ A · ∼ B) ∨ (C ⊃ C)".

Its forms, arranged in order are:

---

20. For an informal discussion of the concept of order and of three kinds of orders, see Abraham Kaplan, *The Conduct of Inquiry*, San Francisco, Chandler, 1964, pp. 178–183.

"P"	(length 1)
"P ∨ Q"	(length 3)
"(P · Q) ∨ R" "P ∨ (Q ⊃ Q)"	(length 7)
"(∿P · Q) ∨ R"	(length 8)
"(∿P · ∿Q) ∨ R"	(length 9)
"(P · Q) ∨ (R ⊃ R)" "(P · Q) ∨ (R ⊃ S)"	(length 11)
"(∿P · Q) ∨ (R ⊃ R)" "(P · ∿Q) ∨ (R ⊃ R)" "(∿P · Q) ∨ (R ⊃ S)" "(P · ∿Q) ∨ (R ⊃ S)"	(length 12)
"(∿P · ∿Q) ∨ (R ⊃ R)" "(∿P · ∿Q) ∨(R ⊃ S)"	(length 13)

FIGURE *(5.bb)*

To what extent are we able to say of two forms that one is more (or less) specific than another? Although we cannot determine the relative specificity for every pair of arbitrarily selected forms, we can often do so for some pairs. Consider, for example, the two forms,

(F2)   "P · (Q ⊃ R)"

(F3)   "P · Q".

Intuitively we should want to say that (F2) is more specific than (F3). More generally, one form may be said to be *more specific* than another when every sentence which can be generated from the former can also be generated from the latter, but not conversely. Or, putting this another way, one form will be said more specific than another if all the sentences which can be generated from the former comprise a proper subset of the sentences which can be generated from the latter. Thus (F2) is more specific than (F3). Every sentence which can be generated from (F2) can also be generated from (F3), but (F3) may be used to generate sentences not generable from (F2); for example "A · (B ∨ ∿C)".

When two forms [e.g., "P ∨ (Q ⊃ Q)" and "(∿P · Q) ∨ R",] generate sets of sentences such that neither set is a subset of the other, then the two forms are *not* comparable as to specificity — neither can be said to be more, or less, specific than the other.

The so-called *specific form* in a particular logic of a sentence is simply its *most* specific form, or that one form which is more specific than any other form of that sentence. In cases where there is a single form of greatest length, that form turns out to be the most specific form of the sentence and hence *the* specific form of the sentence. Thus (F1), viz., "∿P · (Q ⊃ R)", will be said to be the specific form of "∿A · (B ⊃ C)". (F1) is the single longest form of *(5.68a)*. In cases where two or more forms are of equal length and longer than all other forms, the one having the *fewest* number of *different* sentential variable types turns out to be the specific form. Thus although both "(∿P · ∿Q) ∨ (R ⊃ R)" and "(∿P · ∿Q) ∨ (R ⊃ S)" have the same length and together comprise the longest forms of "(∿A · ∿B) ∨ (C ⊃ C)", the former represents only three *different* sentential variable types, (viz., "P", "Q", and "R") while the latter represents four (viz., "P", "Q", "R", and "S"). Hence the former, and not the latter, is the specific form of "(∿A · ∿B) ∨ (C ⊃ C)".

The specific form in a particular logic of a sentence represents the deepest conceptual analysis possible of that sentence in that logic. Note how the specific form of the sentence, "(∿A · ∿B) ∨ (C ⊃ C)", viz., "(∿P · ∿Q) ∨ (R ⊃ R)", contains, as it were, *more* information than the form "(∿P · ∿Q) ∨ (R ⊃ S)". The former tells us something more than the latter, namely, that one of the four component sentences in the compound sentence occurs twice. The latter form also tells us that the compound sentence has four simple sentential components, but neglects to tell us that two of these sentences are tokens of the same type.

There are only three possible relationships between the class of forms of one sentence and the class of forms of another: (1) the two classes coincide; (2) the two classes overlap but do not coincide; and (3) one of the two classes is totally contained within the other but not conversely. It is logically impossible that the classes of the forms of two sentences should be disjoint, for every sentence has among its forms a form shared by every other sentence, viz., the form "P".

It is in the facts that two or more sentences may share the same form and that each and every form represents an infinity of sentence-types, that the real importance in logic of the study of sentential-forms resides. For to the extent that certain properties of sentential-forms may be correlated with the modal attributes of the propositions expressed by sentences instancing those forms, we may determine the modal attributes not just of this or that proposition but of an infinity of propositions. By attending to the forms of sentences there is the potential for us to learn (some of the) modal attributes of all of the propositions in each of many infinite classes.

EXERCISES

1. *Which forms are shared by the sentence, "$A \lor (B \cdot C)$" and "$(B \lor C) \lor (B \cdot C)$"? What is the specific form of each of these sentences? Are the specific forms identical?*

2. *Arrange all the forms of "$(A \lor \sim B) \supset (A \equiv \sim B)$" in order of length.*

7. EVALUATING SENTENCE-FORMS

Sentence-forms, as we have seen, are well-formed formulae, and as such they may be evaluated on truth-tables in exactly the same sort of way that sentences may be evaluated. However, the *interpretation* of the completed truth-table is not quite so straightforward as in the case of sentences, for sentence-forms do not, of course, express propositions. Thus we must spend a little time pursuing the matter of just what an evaluation of a sentence-form can tell us about the sentences which may instantiate that form.

The validity of sentence-forms

In addition to using the term "validity" in the context of assessing arguments and inferences, logicians also use the term with a *different* meaning. Logicians often use the term "validity" *generically* to designate a family of three properties which may be ascribed to sentence-forms.

A sentence-form will be said to be *valid* (in a particular logic) if all of its instantiations express necessary truths; it will be said to be *contravalid* if all of its instantiations express necessary falsehoods; and will be said to be *indeterminate* if it is not either valid or contravalid.[21]

21. This threefold division of sentence-forms, along with the names "valid", "contravalid", and "indeterminate", was introduced into philosophy by Rudolf Carnap in 1934 in his *Logische Syntax der Sprache*. (This book has been translated by A. Smeaton as *The Logical Syntax of Language*, London, Routledge & Kegan Paul, 1937. See pp. 173–4.)

Applying these concepts to Truth-functional Propositional Logic, we may say that a sentence-form in Truth-functional Propositional Logic is *valid* if the final column of a truth-tabular evaluation of that form contains only "T"s; is *contravalid* if the final column contains only "F"s; and is *indeterminate* if it is not either valid or contravalid, i.e., if the final column contains both "T"s and "F"s.

Valid sentence-forms in Truth-functional Propositional Logic are often called "tautological", and sentences which instantiate such forms, "tautologies". But note, a sentence-form might be valid even though it is not tautological, e.g., it might be a sentence-form in Modal Propositional Logic. Being tautological is thus a special case of a formula's being valid.

If, in Truth-functional Propositional Logic, *any* form whatever of a sentence is either valid (tautological) or contravalid, then the specific form of that sentence will also be valid or contravalid respectively. And if the specific form of a sentence is valid, then that sentence expresses a necessary truth; and if the specific form of a sentence is contravalid, then that sentence expresses a necessary falsehood. Thus finding *any* form of a sentence to be valid or contravalid is a sufficient condition for our knowing that that sentence expresses a necessary truth or necessary falsehood respectively.[22]

Having an indeterminate form is a necessary, but not a sufficient, condition for a sentence's expressing a contingency. This is a point which is often obscured in some books by their use of the term "contingency" to name indeterminate sentence-forms. This is regrettable, since it is clear that a sentence having an indeterminate form need not express a contingency. Consider again the sentence (5.53), which expresses a necessary truth:

> (5.53)   "All squares have four sides and all brothers are male."

Translated into the notation of Truth-functional Propositional Logic, this sentence, as we have seen, becomes

> (5.53a) "F · M"

whose specific form is

> (F3)   "P · Q".

(F3) clearly is an indeterminate form, not a valid one. In light of this, we state the following corollaries to our definitions:

> i)   Every sentence which has a valid form expresses a necessary truth.
>
> ii) Every sentence which has a contravalid form expresses a necessary falsehood.

But we do *not* say that every sentence which has an indeterminate form expresses a contingency. Instead, the correct statement of the third corollary is:

> iii) Only those sentences (but even then, not all of them) whose specific forms are indeterminate express contingencies.

Note that *every* sentence has at least one indeterminate form, viz., "P".

---

22. It follows immediately that it is logically impossible that one sentence should number among its forms both valid and contravalid ones.

EXERCISES

1. For each form below, determine whether it is valid, contravalid, or indeterminate.

    (a) "P ∨ ∼P"   (i) "(P ⊃ Q) ∨ (Q ⊃ P)"
    (b) "P · ∼P"   (j) "(P ⊃ Q) ∨ (R ⊃ P)"
    (c) "P · ∼Q"   (k) "P · (Q · ∼Q)"
    (d) "P ⊃ P"   (l) "(P ∨ ∼P) ⊃ (Q · ∼Q)"
    (e) "(P · Q) ⊃ P"   (m) "P ⊃ (P ⊃ Q)"
    (f) " ∼(P ⊃ P)"   (n) "(P ∨ (Q ⊃ Q)"
    (g) "P ⊃ (P∨R)"   (o) "(P ∨ R) ⊃ P"
    (h) "P ∨ (P ⊃ Q)"

2. (a) For each of the valid forms above, find an instantiation of that form which expresses a
         necessary truth.

    (b) For each of the contravalid forms above, find an instantiation of that form which expresses a
         necessary falsehood.

    (c) For each of the indeterminate forms above, (i) find an instantiation of that form which
         expresses a necessary truth; (ii) find an instantiation of that form which expresses a
         necessary falsehood; and (iii) find an instantiation of that form which expresses a
         contingency.

3. Find all the forms of the sentence, "A ⊃ (A ∨ B)". What is the specific form of this sentence?
    Are any of its forms valid?

4. Which of the forms of (5.73) [see figure (5.bb)] are valid? Which are indeterminate?

*   *   *   *   *

Modal relations

Just as we may evaluate two sentences on one truth-table, so we may also evaluate two
sentence-forms. What inferences may we validly make in light of the sorts of truth-tables we might
thereby construct? The answers parallel so closely those already given for sentences that we may
proceed to state them directly:

Implication

> If, in the truth-tabular evaluation of two sentence-forms, it is found that there is no
> row of that table in which the first sentence-form has been assigned "T" and the
> second sentence-form has been assigned "F", one may validly infer — on the
> assumption of the constancy of substitution for the various sentence-variables in the
> two forms — that any proposition expressible by a sentence of the first form *implies*
> any and every proposition expressible by a sentence of the second form.

Equivalence

If, in the truth-tabular evaluation of two sentence-forms, it is found that in each row of the truth-table these sentence-forms have been assigned matching evaluations, one may validly infer — on the assumption of constancy of substitution for the various sentence-variables in the two forms — that any proposition expressible by a sentence of the first form is *logically equivalent* to any proposition expressible by a sentence of the second form.

Inconsistency

If, in the truth-tabular evaluation of two sentence-forms, it is found that there is no row in which both sentence-forms have been assigned "T", one may validly infer — on the assumption of constancy of substitution for the various sentence-variables in the two forms — that any two propositions expressible by sentences of these forms are *logically inconsistent* with one another.

(There is, of course, as we should expect, no rule in this series for the modal relation of *consistency*.)

EXERCISES

1. For each pair of sentential forms below, determine whether the members of the pair are *truth-functionally equivalent*, i.e., are such that their instantiations express logically equivalent propositions.

    a.   "$P \supset Q$" and " $\sim (P \cdot \sim Q)$ "

    b.   "$P \supset Q$" and " $\sim P \vee Q$"

    c.   "$P \supset (Q \supset R)$" and "$(P \supset Q) \supset R$"

    d.   "$P \supset Q$" and "$(P \cdot R) \supset (Q \cdot R)$" *(Hint: use one 8-row truth-table)*

    e.   " $\sim (P \supset Q)$" and "$(P \supset \sim Q)$"

2. The operator vee-bar (i.e., "$\underline{\vee}$") may be defined contextually in terms of tilde, dot, and vel:

    "$P \underline{\vee} Q$" $=_{df}$ "$(P \vee Q) \cdot \sim (P \cdot Q)$".

    Show that the definiendum and the definiens have identical truth-conditions, i.e., that they are truth-functionally equivalent.

3. Demonstrate also the truth-functional equivalence of "$P \underline{\vee} Q$" and "$P \equiv \sim Q$".

4. Since the truth-table for "$P \supset Q$" and "$P \vee Q$" lacks the combination F–F, it is impossible to find

instantiations of these wffs which express propositions which stand in modal relations whose codes (see section 5, pp. 297–301) contain F–F, i.e., nos. 4, 7, 8, 9, 11, 12, 13, and 15.

Find those modal relations (using the numerical labels of figure (5.aa)) which cannot *obtain between two propositions having, respectively, the forms "P · ∼ Q" and "P≡Q".*

5.   *Which of the 15 relations depicted in figure (5.aa)* can *obtain among the possible instantiations of the two forms "P ⊃ Q" and "Q ⊃ P"?*

*   *   *   *   *

Argument-forms and deductive validity

An *argument-form* is, simply, an ordered set of sentence-forms which may be instantiated by a set of sentences expressing an argument.

For the sake of simplicity, however, we shall adopt a somewhat more restricted notion of an argument-form. It will suit òur purposes if we construe an argument-form as a material conditional sentence-form whose antecedent is a conjunction of sentence-forms which may be instantiated by sentences expressing the premises of an argument and whose consequent is a sentence-form which may be instantiated by a sentence expressing the conclusion of an argument. Thus the argument

$$(5.74) \quad \begin{array}{l} \text{A} \quad \cdot \quad \sim\text{B} \\ \underline{\text{A} \supset \text{C}} \\ \therefore \text{C} \equiv \sim\text{B} \end{array}$$

has among its forms

(F8)   "(P · Q) ⊃ R",

(F9)   "((P · Q) · R) ⊃ S",

(F10)   "((P · ∼ Q) · R) ⊃ (S ≡ T)",

(F11)   "((P · ∼ Q) · (P ⊃ R)) ⊃ (R ≡ ∼ Q)", etc.

Argument-forms may be evaluated on truth-tables. If an argument-form is found to be valid, then any set of sentences instancing that form, if used to express an argument, will express a deductively *valid* argument. In general most sets of sentences expressing arguments (for example *(5.74)* above) will instantiate several argument-forms. If any of these forms is valid, then the specific form (defined in parallel fashion to "the specific form of a sentence") will likewise be valid. This is why logicians, in their quest for ascertaining deductive validity by using truth-tabular methods for evaluating argument-forms, will usually attend only to the specific form of an argument. For if any lesser form is valid, the specific form will be also, and thus they can immediately learn that no lesser form is valid if they learn that the specific form is not valid.

Although there is, as we can see, an important relationship between an argument's *form* being valid, and that *argument* itself being valid, these two senses of "valid" are conceptually distinct. We should take some pains to distinguish them.

Let us remind ourselves of the very definitions of these terms. An argument is said to be valid (or more exactly, deductively valid) if its premises imply its conclusion. An argument-form, on the other hand, is said to be valid if all of its instantiations expresses deductively valid arguments.

If an argument-form is valid then we are guaranteed that every set of sentences instantiating that form expresses an argument which is deductively valid, i.e., having a valid *form* is a sufficient condition for an argument's being deductively valid. But it is not a necessary condition.

Arguments come in only two varieties: the deductively valid and the deductively invalid. Argument-forms come in three: the valid, the contravalid, and the indeterminate. All too easily, many writers in logic have argued that if an argument-form is not valid, then any argument having that form is (deductively) invalid. But this is a mistake. Only if an argument's form is *contravalid* may one validly infer, from an examination of its form, that a given argument is deductively invalid. If an argument-form is *indeterminate* (which is one of the two ways in which an argument-form may be nonvalid), nothing may be inferred from that about the deductive validity or deductive invalidity of any argument expressed by a set of sentences instantiating that form. The simple fact of the matter is that any argument-form which is indeterminate will have instantiations which express deductively valid arguments and will have instantiations which express deductively invalid arguments.

EXERCISES

Which of the following argument-forms are valid, which contravalid, and which indeterminate?

a. $P \supset Q$
$\therefore P \supset (P \cdot Q)$

b. $P \supset Q$
$\sim P$
$\therefore \sim Q$

c. $P \supset P$
$\therefore Q \cdot \sim Q$

d. $P \supset Q$
$Q \supset R$
$\therefore P \supset R$

e. $P \supset Q$
$P \supset \sim Q$
$\therefore \sim P$

f. P
$\therefore P \vee Q$

g. $P \supset Q$
$\therefore (P \vee R) \supset Q$

h. $P \supset Q$
$\therefore P \supset (Q \vee R)$

i. P
$\therefore \sim P$

j. $(P \supset Q) \vee (Q \supset R)$
$\therefore \sim(P \supset Q) \cdot \sim (Q \supset P)$

8.   FORM IN A NATURAL LANGUAGE

Consider the following sentence:

(5.75)   "Today is Monday or today is other than the day after Sunday."

Anyone who understands the disjunct, "today is other than the day after Sunday" knows that this means the same as "today is not Monday" which is to say that (5.75) expresses the very same proposition as

(5.76)   "Today is Monday or today is not Monday."

Now the question arises: When we wish to render *(5.75)* in our conceptual notation, shall we render it as

(5.77)   "A∨B",

where "A" = "today is Monday", and "B" = "today is other than the day after Sunday"; or, using the same meaning for "A", shall we render *(5.75)* as

(5.78)   "A ∨ ∼A"?

If we render *(5.75)* as *(5.77)* we shall not be able to show in Truth-functional Propositional Logic what we already know, viz., that *(5.75)* expresses a necessary truth.[23] If, however, we render *(5.75)* as *(5.78)*, we will be able to show that *(5.75)* expresses a necessary truth.

Does it follow from these considerations that the 'real' form of the English sentence *(5.75)* is "P ∨ ∼P", (i.e., the specific form of *(5.78)*), or does it follow that the 'real' form of *(5.75)* is "P∨Q" (i.e., the specific form of *(5.77)*)?

We would like to suggest that the question just posed is improper, that it has a false presupposition. Sentences in natural languages, e.g., English, French, German, etc., do not have a single or 'real' form any more than do sentences expressed in the conceptual notation of a formalized language. Typically, sentences in natural languages, like sentences in formalized languages, have several forms.

Even more to the point, however, is the question whether in speaking of the forms of a natural-language sentence, we are using the term "form" in the *same* sense in which we use it in talking of the forms of sentences which occur in our conceptual notation. This is not an easy question. Note, for example, that when we defined "form" above (p. 303), we, in effect, defined, not "form" *simpliciter,* but rather, "form in Truth-functional Propositional Logic". That is, we defined a sense of "form" which was relativized to a given language. It is not at all clear that we can cogently define a single concept of "form" which will apply to *every* language.

In our studies we do not need to ask what are the forms of the English sentence, *(5.75)*, viz., "Today is Monday or today is other than the day after Sunday." Our purposes will be satisfied if we ask instead, whether we should render *(5.75)*, whatever its forms in English might be decided to be, into our conceptual notation as *(5.77)* whose specific form is "P∨Q", or as *(5.78)* whose specific form is "P ∨ ∼P".

Our answer to this last question cannot be categorical; that is, we cannot say simply that one rendering is the right one and the other the wrong. Our answer must be conditional. We note that the specific form of "A ∨ ∼A", viz., "P ∨ ∼P", is *more specific* (in the sense previously explained) than is the specific form of "A∨B", viz., "P∨Q". It follows, then, that *(5.78)* represents a deeper conceptual analysis of the original English sentence, *(5.75)*, than does *(5.77)*. But this does not mean that *(5.78)* is *the* correct translation of *(5.75)*, nor even that *(5.78)* is 'more correct' than *(5.77)*. There is no question of right or wrong, correctness or incorrectness, in choosing between these two alternatives. Which rendering we choose will depend on the degree of nonformal analysis we perform on *(5.75)* and wish to capture in our conceptual notation. We can give only conditional answers. *If we wish simply to record the fact that (5.75) is a grammatical disjunction of two different sentences,*

---

23. Recall that the method of constructing a corrected truth-table (which would be able to show that *(5.77)* expresses a necessary truth) is a nonformal method lying outside Truth-functional Propositional Logic.

we will render it as "A∨B", and as a result will be unable to show in Truth-functional Propositional Logic that *(5.75)* expresses a necessary truth. *If*, however, we wish to record the fact that the two grammatical disjuncts of *(5.75)* express propositions which are contradictories of one another, we will render it as "A ∨ ∼A", and as a result will be able to show in Truth-functional Propositional Logic, (i.e., without recourse to corrected truth-tables) that *(5.75)* expresses a necessary truth.

There are no (known) mechanical procedures for translating from a natural language into formalized ones such as those of Truth-functional Propositional Logic: the translations come about through our understanding and analysis of the original sentences. But we would re-emphasize that analysis comes in degrees: it can be carried on quite superficially or to a greater depth and with corresponding differences in the various translations one might give for a single sentence.

The route from a sentence in a natural language to a sentence expressed in the conceptual notation of a formalized, or reconstructed language, is through nonformal logic, i.e., conceptual analysis.

Admittedly, each time we translate a sentence from a natural language into a formal one we are faced with the possibility that we may perform a nonformal analysis which is not as deep as is possible and hence we may lose certain information in the process. We have just seen such a case in the instance of sentence *(5.75)*. Does this ever-present possibility of losing information call into doubt the wisdom and efficacy of examining sentences formally?

Not in the slightest. Because formal methods have (for the most part) only a positive role to play, the possibility of losing information as one translates from a natural language into a formal one is not insidious. If the translation and subsequent formal analysis reveal something about the modal attributes of the corresponding proposition (or propositions), well and good: we are that much further ahead in our researches. But if the translation loses something important — as it might if, for example, we were to translate "Today is Monday or today is other than the day after Sunday" as "A∨B" — we are none the worse off for having tried a formal analysis. At the worst we have only wasted a bit of time; we have *not* got the *wrong* answer. In finding that "A∨B" does not have a tautologous or contravalid form we are not entitled to infer that the original English sentence expresses a contingency. Keeping our wits about us, we will recognize that in such a circumstance we are entitled to infer *nothing* about the modal status of that proposition.

In short, we adopt formal methods because in some instances they bring success; when they fail to bring success, they simply yield nothing. They do not yield wrong answers. It may be put this way: by adopting formal analyses we have a great deal to gain and nothing (except a bit of time) to lose.

9.   WORLDS-DIAGRAMS AS A DECISION PROCEDURE FOR TRUTH-FUNCTIONAL PROPOSITIONAL LOGIC

It is obvious that truth-tables provide a simple as well as *effective decision procedure* for truth-functional propositional logic. That is to say, they provide a mechanical procedure for determining the validity of any formula in that logic.

Worlds-diagrams, too, may be so used. As compared with truth-table methods they prove to be extremely cumbersome for truth-functional logic. Nevertheless we introduce them here in order to prepare the way for their use as a decision procedure in modal logic where the disparity in cumbersomeness is not so marked and the worlds-diagrams method has the virtue of intuitive transparency.

Though somewhat cumbersome, the technique of using worlds-diagrams as a decision procedure is easy to comprehend. Suppose we have a formula instancing just one variable type, "P", e.g., "(P∨P)", "(P⊃P)", "P∨(P⊃ ∼P)". In such a case we would need only the three worlds-diagrams for monadic modal properties.

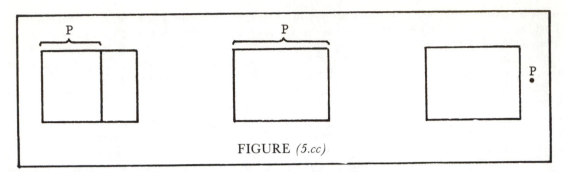

FIGURE (5.cc)

We use the rules for depiction of the various truth-functional operators in order to represent the chosen formula on each of these three worlds-diagrams. We start with the sentential components of least complexity and build up through those of greater complexity until we have depicted the whole formula. For example, in the case of the formula "P∨(P ⊃ ∼P)" we first place "P" on each of the worlds-diagrams in the set; then, in accord with the rule for placing the negation of a proposition on a worlds-diagram (section 2, p. 252), we add brackets labelled with "∼P"; at the third stage, in accord with the rule for adding brackets for material conditionals (p. 264), we add "(P⊃∼P)" to the diagrams; and finally, in accord with the rule for depicting the disjunction of two propositions (p. 257), we place the entire formula "P∨(P⊃∼P)" on each of the diagrams. The completed process, with each of the intermediate stages shown, looks like this:

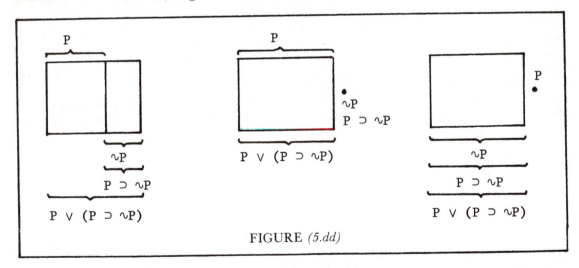

FIGURE (5.dd)

By inspection we can see that the formula "P ∨ (P ⊃ ∼P)" is *valid* since in every case its bracket spans all possible worlds, that is to say that every possible substitution-instance of this formula is necessarily true. A formula will be contravalid if its bracket in no case spans any possible world, and will be indeterminate if it is neither valid nor contravalid.

In the case of a formula instancing two variable types, "P" and "Q", e.g.,"P ⊃ (P ∨ Q)", "((P ⊃ Q) · ∼P) ⊃ ∼Q" and "(P ∨ ∼P) ⊃ (Q · ∼Q)", we need fifteen worlds-diagrams. Following the same procedure as above, we are then able to prove that the first of these formulae is valid. the second indeterminate, and the third contravalid.

EXERCISES

Use worlds-diagrams to ascertain the validity of each of the following formulae.

1. $(P \supset Q) \lor (Q \supset P)$

2. $(P \lor Q) \supset P$

3. $(P \supset Q) \supset (P \supset (P \cdot Q))$

4. $(P \cdot Q) \cdot (Q \supset {\sim}P)$

10.   A SHORTCUT FORMAL METHOD: REDUCTIO AD ABSURDUM TESTS

The method of exhaustively evaluating a wff on a truth-table and the method of depicting a wff on each diagram in a complete set of worlds-diagrams are perfectly general: they may be applied to any and every truth-functional wff to determine whether that wff is tautological, contravalid, or indeterminate. But it is clear that these methods are very cumbersome: the sizes of the required truth-tables and the size of the set of required worlds-diagrams increase exponentially with the number of propositional variable-types instanced in the formula. If as few as five propositional variable-types are instanced in one formula, we would require a truth-table of 32 rows, or a set of 4,294,967,295 worlds-diagrams; for a formula containing propositional variables of six different types, a truth-table of 64 rows; etc. Fortunately there are available other methods which sometimes yield results in far fewer computational steps.

Certain, but not all, wffs lend themselves well to a method of testing which is called "the reductio ad absurdum" or often, more simply, "the reductio test".

The general strategy in a reductio test is to try to prove that a certain sentential (or argument) form is tautological (or contravalid) by showing that the assumption that its instantiations may be used to express falsehoods (or truths respectively) leads to contradiction. For example, one might use a reductio form of proof to establish that the formula "P ∨ ∼P" is tautological by showing that to assign "F" to this formula leads to contradiction. Then, employing the principle that every contradictory of a self-contradictory proposition is necessarily true, we may validly infer that any proposition expressed by a sentence instantiating the original formula must be necessarily true.

Example 1:   Show that "P ∨ ∼P" is tautological.

Since we wish to show that a stipulated formula is tautological, we begin by making the assumption that the formula may be instantiated by a sentence expressing a false proposition. To show this assumption, we simply assign "F" to the formula "P ∨ ∼P":

$$P \lor {\sim}P$$

$$F \qquad (1)$$

From this point on, the subsequent assigments are all determined. The only way for a disjunction to be false is for both disjuncts to be false (see below, step 2). And the only way for a negation to be false is for the negated proposition to be true; thus at step 3 we must assign "T" to the second occurrence of "P". But "P" has already been assigned "F" at step 2. To complete the proof we underline the two inconsistent assignments.

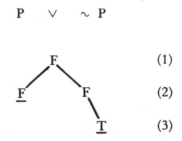

$$P \quad \lor \quad \sim P$$

What precisely does this proof tell us? It tells us that in any world in which "P $\lor$ $\sim$ P" is assigned the value "F", "P" must be assigned both the value "T" and the value "F". In short, we learn that any proposition expressed by a sentence having the form "P $\lor$ $\sim$ P" may be false only in a world in which some proposition is both true and false, i.e., in an *impossible* world. But if the only sort of world in which a proposition is false is an impossible world, then clearly, in every *possible* world that proposition is true, which is just to say that that proposition is necessarily true. Hence any and every proposition expressed by a sentence of the form "P $\lor$ $\sim$ P" is necessarily true. In other words, "P $\lor$ $\sim$ P" is tautological.

Example 2:   Show that "$\sim$ (P $\supset$ (P $\lor$ Q))" is contravalid.

To show that a stipulated formula is contravalid, we begin by making the assumption that at least one of its instantiations may express a proposition which is true. If the formula *is* contravalid, we should be able to show that a sentence instantiating this form expresses a proposition which is true only in an impossible world, i.e., expresses a proposition which is *false* in every possible world. Indeed, this is precisely what we do show:

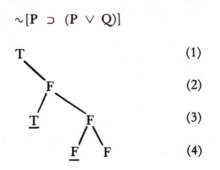

$$\sim[P \quad \supset \quad (P \quad \lor \quad Q)]$$

Example 3:   Determine whether "P $\supset$ (P $\cdot$ Q)" is tautological, contravalid, or indeterminate.

Given the presumption that we do not know whether "P $\supset$ (P $\cdot$ Q)" is tautological, contravalid, or indeterminate, our strategy will be, first, to ascertain whether it is tautological. If it is not, then, secondly, we will determine if it is contravalid. If it is neither of these, then we may validly infer that it is indeterminate. We begin, then, by trying to prove it to be tautological. To do this, we look to see whether a proposition expressed by a sentence of this form is false in any possible world. If there is such a possible world, the sentence form is not tautological.

> *Stage 1:   Is there a possible world in which "$P \supset (P \cdot Q)$", without contradiction, may be assigned "F"?*

We begin by assigning "F" to this formula. Thereafter all the subsequent assignments are logically determined, and by inspection we can see that no sentential formula is assigned both a "T" and an "F". Hence there is a possible world in which the truth-value of the proposition expressed by a sentence having this form is falsity, and hence the form is *not* tautological.

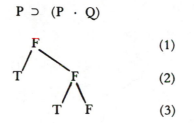

> *Stage 2:   Is there a possible world in which "$P \supset (P \cdot Q)$" may, without contradiction, be assigned "T"?*

At this second stage we begin by assigning "T" to the formula. This time, however, we find that not all the subsequent assignments are logically determined.

$$P \supset (P \cdot Q)$$

$$T \qquad (1)$$

Having assigned "T" to the material conditional, what are we to assign to the antecedent and consequent of that conditional? Any of three *different* assignments are consistent with having assigned "T" to the conditional: we may assign "T" to both antecedent and to consequent; "F" to both antecedent and consequent; or "F" to the antecedent and "T" to the consequent. Which of these three possible assignments are we to choose?

At this point we must rely on a bit of guesswork and insight. The one assignment to be avoided in this case is the last one. Let us see how it leads to inconclusive results. Suppose we were to assign "F" (at step 2) to the antecedent and "T" to the consequent. Thereafter, at step 3, the assignments would, again, be fully logically determined and we would have an inconsistent assignment.

$$P \supset (P \cdot Q)$$

T   (1)

F*   T*   (2)

T   T   (3)

What may we validly infer from this diagram? May we, for example, infer that the *only* sort of world in which "P ⊃ (P·Q)" may be assigned "T" is an impossible one? The answer is: No. And the reason is that we have not shown that there is no possible world in which "P ⊃ (P·Q)" may be consistently assigned "T". The route by which we arrived at the inconsistent assignment was not fully logically determined at every step: there was a 'choice'-point in step 2. (It will be helpful to mark assignments at choice-points with an asterisk.) Only if every possible choice were to lead to inconsistent assignments could we validly infer that the initial assignment of "T" (or "F") was a logically impossible one. At this stage (having examined only one of three choices), the results are inconclusive. So now we must examine the consequences of making a different assignment at the choice-point in step 2.

This time let us try assigning "T" to both antecedent and consequent. Again, thereafter the assignments are fully logically determined.

$$P \; \supset \; (P \; \cdot \; Q)$$

```
            T                    (1)
           / \
        T*     T*                (2)
               / \
              T   T              (3)
```

Can anything of significance for our problem be validly inferred from this diagram? Yes. We may validly infer that there *is* a possible world in which the formula "P ⊃ (P·Q)" may consistently be assigned "T", and this may be inferred from the diagram. It follows then that the form "P ⊃ (P·Q)" is not contravalid.

Together these two stages demonstrate that the form "P ⊃ (P·Q)" is *neither* tautological *nor* contravalid. It follows, then, that it is indeterminate.

Example 4:   Show that "(P ⊃ Q) ⊃ [(R ⊃ P) ⊃ (R ⊃ Q)]" is tautological.[24]

What is interesting about this example is that it includes what at first appears to be a choice-point, but turns out not to include one after all. If we apply the reductio method to this formula we will generate the following:

$$(P \; \supset \; Q) \; \supset \; [(R \; \supset \; P) \; \supset \; (R \; \supset \; Q)]$$

```
           F                     (1)
          / \
        T     F                  (2)
```

At step 2 we have written down a "T" under a material conditional. Normally, doing this would generate a choice-point; the subsequent assignments of "T"s and "F"s to the antecedent and consequent of that conditional could, as we have seen in example 3, be any of three kinds. But this is not a normal case. For if we hold off making a trial assignment at step 3, and proceed instead to examine the consequences of having placed an "F" also in step 2, we shall eventually find that the assignments appropriate for the "P" and "Q" in "(P ⊃ Q)" are logically determined.

---

24. In lengthy formulae — such as the present case — it aids readability to write some of the matching pairs of parentheses as "[" and "]".

$$(P \supset Q) \supset [(R \supset P) \supset (R \supset Q)]$$

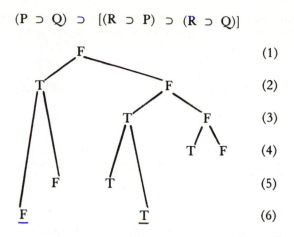

At step 2 we were forced to assign "F" to "[(R ⊃ P) ⊃ (R ⊃ Q]". This, in turn, forces us in step 3 to assign "T" to "(R ⊃ P)" and "F" to "(R ⊃ Q)". Once again, as in step 2, we have assigned "T" to a material conditional. So, again, our strategy will be to postpone making any further assignments to the antecedent and consequent of this conditional in the hope that later events will dictate the appropriate choice. Therefore we turn our attention to the "F" which we have assigned at step 3 to "(R ⊃ Q)". This of course necessitates that we assign "T" to "R" and "F" to "Q". This we do at step 4. But having assigned "T" to "R" and "F" to "Q", we are now in a position to return to the earlier apparent choice-points. At step 5, we write "F" under "Q" in "(P ⊃ Q)", and "T" under "R" in "(R ⊃ P)". This now brings us to step 6 where, again, the assignments are logically determined. Having assigned "T" to "(P ⊃ Q)" and "F" to "Q", we are forced to assign "F" to "P" in that formula; and having assigned "T" to "(R ⊃ P)" and "T" to "R", we are forced to assign "T" to "P" in "(R ⊃ P)". Finally, looking across the assignments in step 6, we can see that we have assigned both "F" and "T" to the same sentence-variable type, and hence may validly conclude that the original assignment (in step 1) was an impossible one. Since that assignment was "F", the formula is tautological.

The map of assignments in this example is fairly lengthy. As one acquires proficiency in the construction of reductio proofs one will doubtless prefer to compress the proof into a single horizontal row. The order of the steps, then, will be written along the bottom. Thus the above proof may be compressed to appear this way:

$$(P \supset Q) \supset [(R \supset P) \supset (R \supset Q)]$$

$$\underline{F}\ \ T\ \ F\qquad F\qquad T\ \ T\ \ \underline{T}\quad F\quad T\ \ F\ \ F$$

$$(6)\ (2)(5)\quad (1)\qquad (5)(3)\ (6)\quad (2)\quad (4)(3)(4)$$

Example 5:   Show that "(P ∨ ~P) · (Q ⊃ Q)" is tautological.

In accordance with the standard procedure we begin by assigning "F" to the formula. Immediately we generate a choice-point:

$$(P \lor \sim P) \cdot (Q \supset Q)$$
$$F$$
$$(1)$$

There are three different assignments which can be made to the two conjuncts of the conjunction consistent with the assignment "F" having been made to the conjunction: (a) "T" and "F" respectively; (b) "F" and "T" respectively; and (c) "F" and "F" respectively. Only if we examine all of these, by constructing additional diagrams, and find that each one leads to an inconsistent assignment may we validly infer that the original formula is tautological. As it turns out, however, two of these three assignments, the first and the second, themselves generate further choice-points. The first, in assigning "T" to a disjunction, generates three further possibilities for assignment; and the second in assigning "T" to a material conditional, also generates three further possibilities for subsequent assignments.

Clearly in such a case, the attraction of the method of reductio ad absurdum is dissipated. In this instance, the earlier truth-tabular method turns out to be the shorter one, and hence the preferred one.

Summary

The reductio ad absurdum method works in a fashion somewhat the reverse of that of the method of evaluation. In the method of evaluation, one begins with assignments of "T"s and "F"s to simple formulae and proceeds in a strictly determined fashion to assign "T"s and "F"s to longer formulae of which the original formulae are components. In the reductio method, the order of assignments is reversed. One begins by assigning "T" or "F" to a truth-functional compound sentence, and then proceeds to see what assignments of "T"s and "F"s to components of that formulae are consistent with that initial assignment. But in this latter case, one often finds that the assignments subsequent to the first are not all determined. If we assign "T" to a material conditional, we may generate a three-pronged choice-point; similarly if we assign "T" to a disjunction, or "F" to a conjunction. And no matter what we assign to a material biconditional, we may generate a two-pronged choice point. Clearly, then, the reductio ad absurdum method has its distinct limitations. The method is at its best when it is used to establish the tautologousness of a formula most of whose dyadic operators are hooks, or to establish the contravalidity of a formula most of whose dyadic operators are dots.

Whenever, in using a reductio, we run across a choice-point, we have to make various 'trial' assignments to see whether, on our initial assignment, we can find any subsequent assignment which is consistent. If it is possible, then there is nothing self-contradictory about our initial assignment. Only if it is impossible in every case whatever to make consistent assignments (and this means that we must examine every possible choice at every choice-point), may we validly conclude that the initial assignment was an impossible one for the formula.

In spite of its limitations, the reductio method is one much favored among logicians. For in many cases its application results in very short proofs. Then, too, it is often very useful in testing arguments for validity. Since showing that the form of an argument is tautological suffices for showing that argument to be deductively valid, the reductio method is often called upon by logicians to demonstrate the validity of arguments. Of course the same limitations as were just mentioned prevail in this latter context as well; but so do the same advantages.[25]

---

25. Truth-tables, worlds-diagrams, and reductio ad absurdum tests do not exhaust the logician's arsenal of techniques for ascertaining modal status, modal relations, validity of forms, deductive validity, etc. In addition, logicians make use of the method of deduction, both in Axiomatic Systems for the valid formulae of Truth-functional Propositional Logic and in so-called Natural Deduction. In this book, however, we do not develop the method of deduction any further than it was developed in chapter 4.

EXERCISES

1.   Use the Reductio ad Absurdum method to prove the following formulae to be tautologies.

   (a) $P \supset (Q \supset P)$

   (b) $P \supset (P \vee Q)$

   (c) $(P \cdot Q) \supset P$

   (d) $(P \cdot Q) \supset (P \vee R)$

   (e) $[(P \supset Q) \cdot (Q \supset R)] \supset (P \supset R)$

2.   Use the Reductio ad Absurdum method to prove the following formulae to be contravalid.

   (f) $P \cdot \sim P$

   (g) $\sim (P \supset P)$

   (h) $P \cdot (P \supset \sim P)$

3.   Use the Reductio ad Absurdum method to prove whether the following formulae are tautologous, contravalid or indeterminate.

   (i) $(P \vee Q) \supset P$

   (j) $(P \supset Q) \supset (\sim P \supset \sim Q)$

4.   Use the Reductio ad Absurdum method to prove whether the following argument-forms are valid, contravalid, or indeterminate.

   (k) $P \supset Q$
            $\underline{Q \supset \sim P}$
            $\therefore \sim P$

   (l) $P \supset (Q \vee R)$
            $\underline{Q}$
            $\therefore P \supset \sim R$

   (m) $\underline{P \supset P}$
            $\therefore Q \cdot \sim Q$

   (n) $P \supset (Q \vee R)$
            $\underline{Q}$
            $\therefore P \supset R$

   (o) $\underline{P}$
            $\therefore \sim P \supset P$

6

Modal Propositional Logic

1. INTRODUCTION

In this book we undertook — among other things — to show how metaphysical talk of possible worlds and propositions can be used to make sense of the science of deductive logic. In chapter 1, we used that talk to explicate such fundamental logical concepts as those of contingency, noncontingency, implication, consistency, inconsistency, and the like. Next, in chapter 2, while resisting the attempt to identify propositions with sets of possible worlds, we suggested that identity-conditions for the constituents of propositions (i.e., for concepts), can be explicated by making reference to possible worlds and showed, further, how appeal to possible worlds can help us both to disambiguate proposition-expressing sentences and to refute certain false theories. In chapter 3 we argued the importance of distinguishing between, on the one hand, the modal concepts of the contingent and the noncontingent (explicable in terms of possible worlds) and, on the other hand, the epistemic concepts of the empirical and the a priori (not explicable in terms of possible worlds). In chapter 4 we showed how the fundamental methods of logic — analysis and valid inference — are explicable in terms of possible worlds and argued for the centrality within logic as a whole of modal logic in general and S5 in particular. Then, in chapter 5, we tried to make good our claim that modal concepts are needed in order to make sound philosophical sense even of that kind of propositional logic — truth-functional logic — from which they seem conspicuously absent. Now in this, our last chapter, we concentrate our attention on the kind of propositional logic — modal propositional logic — within which modal concepts feature overtly. Among other things, we try to show: (1) how various modal concepts are interdefinable with one another; (2) how the validity of any formula within modal propositional logic may be determined by the method of worlds-diagrams and by related reductio methods; and finally, (3), how talk of possible worlds, when suitably elaborated, enables us to make sense of some of the central concepts of inductive logic.

2. MODAL OPERATORS

Non-truth-functionality

The rules for well-formedness in modal propositional logic may be obtained by supplementing the rules (see p. 262) for truth-functional logic by the following:

R4:   Any wff prefixed by a monadic modal sentential operator [e.g., "◇", "□", "▽", or "△"] is a wff.

R5:   Any two wffs written with a dyadic modal operator [e.g., "∘", "φ", "→", or "↔"] between them and the whole surrounded by parentheses is a wff.

In light of these rules, it is obvious that from a *formal* point of view, modal propositional logic may be regarded as an accretion upon truth-functional logic: every wff of truth-functional propositional logic is likewise a wff of modal propositional logic, although there are wffs of modal propositional logic — those containing one or more modal operators — which are not wffs of truth-functional logic. (That modal propositional logic is formally constructed by adding onto a truth-functional base ought not, however, to be taken as indicating a parallel order as regards their conceptual priority. We have argued earlier in this book (chapters 4 and 5) that although modal concepts are not symbolized within truth-functional logic, one cannot adequately *understand* that logic without presupposing these very concepts.)

Modal operators are non-truth-functional. For example, the monadic operator "◇", unlike the truth-functional operator "∼", is non-truth-functional. Given the truth-value of P, one cannot, in general, determine the truth-value of the proposition expressed by the compound sentence "◇P", as one could in the case of "∼P". Obviously if "P" expresses a true proposition, then "◇P" must likewise express a true proposition. For "◇P" says nothing more than that the proposition expressed

P	◇P	□P	▽P	△P
T	T	I	I	I
F	I	F	I	I

P	Q	P ∘ Q	P φ Q	P → Q	P ↔ Q
T	T	T	F	I	I
T	F	I	I	F	F
F	T	I	I	I	F
F	F	I	I	I	I

TABLE *(6.a)*

Beware. Do not read the "I" which appears on these tables as if it were a 'third' truth-value. There are only *two* truth-values. Clearly, for every instantiation of constants for the variables in these sentence-forms, the resulting sentences will express propositions which bear one or other of the two truth-values, truth or falsity.

by "P" is true in some possible world, and if P is true, then it is true in some possible world. But the same can not be concluded for the case in which "P" expresses a falsehood. Suppose "P" expresses a false proposition. **What, then, can we conclude about the truth-value of the proposition expressed by "◇P"?** This latter formula asserts that the proposition expressed by "P" is true in some possible world. This claim is true just in case the false proposition expressed by "P" is true in some possible world, i.e., just in case the false proposition, P, is contingent. But the proposition expressed by "◇P" is false just in case the false proposition expressed by "P" is false in every possible world, i.e., just in case the false proposition P is noncontingent. Thus whether the proposition expressed by "◇P" is false depends not simply on whether the proposition expressed by "P" is false, but in addition on whether that false proposition is contingent or noncontingent. It depends, that is, on the modality as well as the truth-value of P. This means that "◇P" has a *partial* truth-table. In the case where "P" has been assigned "T", "◇P" likewise is assigned "T"; but in the case where "P" is assigned "F", *neither* "T" *nor* "F" may be assigned to "◇P". We fill in the gap with "I", where "I" stands for "the truth-value is indeterminate on the basis of the data (i.e., truth-value) specified." Like "◇", every other modal operator will have only (at best) a partial truth-table.

It suffices for an operator to be non-truth-functional that there be a single "I" in its truth-table.

An important consequence of the fact that modal operators are non-truth-functional is that we will be unable — in contrast to the case of wffs in truth-functional logic — to ascertain the validity of modalized formulae by the truth-tabular techniques discussed in the previous chapter. How we might, instead, evaluate formulae containing modal operators is shown in sections 8 and 9.

Modal and nonmodal propositions; modalized and nonmodalized formulae

Any proposition at least one of whose constituent concepts is a modal concept is a *modal* proposition. All other propositions are *nonmodal*.

Any modal proposition can be represented in our conceptual notation by a wff containing one or more modal operators, e.g., "□", "◇", etc. But of course a modal proposition need not be so represented. A modal proposition can also be represented in our symbolism by a wff containing no modal operators, e.g., by "A", or in the case of a conditional modal proposition, by "A ⊃ B". In such a case the symbolism would fail to reveal as much as it could, viz., that a particular proposition is a modal one. But this is a characteristic of any system of symbolization. Every system of symbolization has the capacity to reveal different degrees of detail about that which it symbolizes. We have already seen, for example, how it is possible to symbolize the proposition *(5.75)*, viz., that today is Monday or today is other than the day after Sunday, as either "A ∨ ~ A" or as "A ∨ B". The latter symbolization reveals less information than the former, but neither is more or less 'correct' than the other.

A similar point can be made in the case of the symbolization of modal attributes. Consider the proposition

> *(6.1)*   It is necessarily true that all squares have four sides.

Clearly *(6.1)* is a modal proposition. Thus if we let "A" = "all squares have four sides", we can render this proposition in symbolic notation as

> *(6.2)*   "□A".

But we are not forced to do this. If for some reason we are not intent on conveying in symbols that *(6.1)* is a modal proposition, we can, if we like, represent it simply as, for example,

> *(6.3)*   "B".

Thus if we happen across a wff which does not contain a modal operator, we are not entitled to infer that the proposition represented by that wff is a nonmodal one. Being represented by a wff containing a modal operator is a sufficient condition for the proposition expressed being a modal one, but it is not a necessary condition.

A wff whose simple sentential components, i.e., capital letters, all occur as the arguments of or within the arguments of some modal operator or other will be said to be *fully modalized*. Thus, for example, the wffs

$$\text{``}\Box(P \supset Q)\text{''},$$

$$\text{``}\Diamond P \supset \Box P\text{''},$$

$$\text{``}\Diamond \Box \sim P\text{''}, \text{ and}$$

$$\text{``}\Diamond(P \cdot \Box Q)\text{''},$$

are all fully modalized.

A wff of whose simple sentential components some, but not all, occur as the arguments of or within the arguments of some modal operator or other will be said to be *partially modalized*. For example,

$$\text{``}\Diamond P \supset P\text{''},$$

$$\text{``}P \supset \Box(P \lor Q)\text{''}, \text{ and}$$

$$\text{``}\Box P \lor (\Diamond Q \supset R)\text{''},$$

are all partially modalized.

A wff of whose simple sentential components none occurs as the argument of or within the argument of a modal operator will be said to be *unmodalized*. For example,

$$\text{``}P \supset P\text{''},$$

$$\text{``}P \cdot (P \supset Q)\text{''}, \text{ and}$$

$$\text{``}P\text{''},$$

are all unmodalized.

Note that on these definitions, propositions, but not sentences, may be said to be *modal;* and sentences or sentence-forms, but not propositions, may be said to be modal*ized*.

EXERCISES

Write down all the forms of each of the following modalized formulae:

1. $\Box A \supset B$

2. $\Box(A \supset \Diamond B)$

3. $\Box(A \supset \Box A)$

4. $\Box\Box A \supset \Box A$

The interdefinability of the monadic and dyadic modal operators

We have introduced four monadic modal operators, viz., "□", "◇", "▽" and "△", and four dyadic modal operators, viz., "∘", "φ", "→" and "↔". Each of these may be defined in terms of any one of the other seven. There are, then, a total of fifty-six such definitions. Some of these we have already seen; others are new. We list them all here for the sake of completeness.

Necessary truth

"□P" = $_{df}$ "∼◇∼P"

"∼▽P · P"

"△P · P"

"∼(∼P ∘ ∼P)"

"∼P φ ∼P"

"∼P → P"

"(P ∨ ∼P) ↔ P"

Possibility

"◇P" = $_{df}$ "∼□∼P"

"▽P ∨ P"

"∼△P ∨ P"

"P ∘ P"

"∼(P φ P)"

"∼(P → ∼P)"

"∼[(P · ∼P) ↔ P]"

Contingency

"▽P" = $_{df}$ "∼□P · ∼□∼P"

"◇P · ◇∼P"

"∼△P"

"(P ∘ P) · (∼P ∘ ∼P)"

"∼(P φ P) · ∼(∼P ∘ ∼P)"

"∼(P → ∼P) · ∼(∼P → P)"

"∼[(P · ∼P) ↔ P] · ∼[(P ∨ ∼P) ↔ P]"

Noncontingency

"△P" = $_{df}$ "□P ∨ □∼P"

"∼◇P ∨ ∼◇∼P"

"∼▽P"

"∼(P ∘ P) ∨ ∼(∼P ∘ ∼P)"

"(P φ P) ∨ (∼P φ ∼P)"

"(P → ∼P) ∨ (∼P → P)"

"[(P · ∼P) ↔ P] ∨ [(P ∨ ∼P) ↔ P]"

Consistency

"P∘Q" = $_{df}$ "∼□∼(P · Q)"

"◇(P · Q)"

"▽(P · Q) ∨ (P · Q)"

"∼△(P · Q) ∨ (P · Q)"

"∼(P φ Q)"

"∼(P → ∼Q)"

"∼[(P · ∼P) ↔ (P · Q)]"

Inconsistency

"PφQ" = $_{df}$ "□∼(P · Q)"

"∼◇(P · Q)"

"∼▽(P · Q) · ∼(P · Q)"

"△(P · Q) · ∼(P · Q)"

"∼(P ∘ Q)"

"P → ∼Q"

"(P · ∼P) ↔ (P · Q)"

Implication   *Equivalence*

"P → Q" = $_{df}$ "□(P ⊃ Q)"   "P ↔ Q" = $_{df}$ "□(P ≡ Q)"

       "∼ ◇(P · ∼Q)"   "∼ ◇ ∼(P ≡ Q)"

       "∼▽ ∼(P · ∼Q) · ∼(P · ∼Q)"   "∼▽(P ≡ Q) · (P ≡ Q)"

       "△ ∼(P · ∼Q) · ∼(P · ∼Q)"   "△(P ≡ Q) · (P ≡ Q)"

       "∼(P ∘ ∼Q)"   "∼[∼(P ≡ Q) ∘ ∼(P ≡ Q)]"

       "(P φ ∼Q)"   "∼(P ≡ Q) φ ∼(P ≡ Q)"

       "(P · ∼P) ↔ (P · ∼Q)"   "(P → Q) · (Q → P)"

For every wff in which there occurs some particular modal operator, there exist other, formally equivalent wffs,[1] in which that modal operator does not occur. More particularly, for every wff in which there occur one or more *dyadic* modal operators, there exist formally equivalent wffs in which only *monadic* modal operators occur. Thus, subsequently in this chapter, when we come to examine methods for determining the validity of modalized wffs, it will suffice to give rules for handling only *monadic* modal operators. Every wff containing one or more dyadic modal operators can be replaced, for the purposes of testing validity, with a formally equivalent wff containing only monadic modal operators. The above list of equivalences gives us the means of generating these formally equivalent wffs.

     Elimination of "∘" :   every wff of the form "P ∘ Q" may be
                                 replaced by a wff of the form " ◇(P · Q)"

     Elimination of "φ":   every wff of the form "P φ Q" may be
                                 replaced by a wff of the form "∼ ◇(P · Q)"

     Elimination of "→":   every wff of the form "P → Q" may be
                                 replaced by a wff of the form "□(P ⊃ Q)"

     Elimination of "↔":   every wff of the form "P ↔ Q" may be
                                 replaced by a wff of the form "□(P ≡ Q)".

Sometimes it will be useful, too, to eliminate the two monadic modal operators "▽" and "△" in favor of "◇" and "□".

     Elimination of "▽":   every wff of the form "▽P" may be
                                 replaced by a wff of the form " ◇P · ◇∼P"

     Elimination of "△":   every wff of the form "△P" may be
                                 replaced by a wff of the form "□P ∨ □∼P"

    1. Two sentence-forms are formally equivalent if and only if, for any uniform substitution of constants for the variables therein, there result two sentences which express logically equivalent propositions. (See section 10, this chapter.)

Examples:

"P → (P ∘ Q)"	may be replaced by	"□[P ⊃ ◇(P · Q)]"
"(P ⫪ Q) ∘ R"	may be replaced by	" ◇[∼ ◇(P · Q) · R]"
"△(P ∘ Q)"	may be replaced by	"□ ◇(P · Q) ∨ □∼◇(P · Q)"

EXERCISES

For each of the following formulae, find formally equivalent wffs in which the only modal operators are "□" *and/or* "◇".

1.   P→(Q → P)

2.   P ∘ (∼Q ⫪ P)

3.   □P→(Q ⊃ P)

4.   □P→ △(P ∨ Q)

5.   (□P · □Q) → (◇P ↔ ◇Q)

3.   SOME PROBLEMATIC USES OF MODAL EXPRESSIONS

"It is possible that"

"It is possible that" has many uses in ordinary prose that one should distinguish from the use of that expression which is captured by the logical operator "◇". Two of these uses are especially worthy of note.

Most of us have viewed television dramas in which a lawyer attempts to discredit a witness by asking, "Is it possible you might be mistaken?" Witnesses who are doing their utmost to be as fair as possible(!) are likely to take this question as if it were the question, "Is it logically possible that you might be mistaken?", to which they will answer, "Yes". But an overzealous lawyer might then pounce on this admission as if it were a confession of probable error. The point is that to say of a proposition that it is *possibly* false in the logical sense (i.e., is contingent or necessarily false) is not to say that it is *probably* false. A proposition which is *possibly* false, e.g., the contingent proposition that there is salt in the Atlantic Ocean, need *not* be *probably* false; quite the contrary, this particular proposition *is* true.

Secondly, consider the use of "It is possible that" in the sentence

> *(6.4)*   "It is possible that the Goldbach Conjecture (i.e., that every even number greater than two is the sum of two prime numbers) is true."

If we do not keep our wits about us, we might be inclined to think that this sentence is being used to express the proposition that the Goldbach Conjecture is possibly true. But a person who utters *(6.4)* and who accepts a possible-worlds analysis of the concept of possibility, ought to reject such a construal of his words. For clearly, he is trying to say something true; and yet, if the Goldbach Conjecture — unknown to us — is false (which is to say that it is necessarily false), then to say that it is possibly true is (as we shall see subsequently in this chapter) to say something which is itself necessarily false. The point can be put another way: the Goldbach Conjecture is either necessarily false or necessarily true. We do not know which it is. If, however, it *is* necessarily false, then to say of it that it is possibly true is to assert a proposition which itself is necessarily false.

What a person who asserts *(6.4)* is trying to say would seem to be something of the following sort:

> *(6.5)* "To the best of our knowledge, the Goldbach Conjecture is not false."

But this sentence, too, needs careful handling. We must beware not to take this as if it were synonymous with

> *(6.6)* "It is compatible with everything which we now know that the Goldbach Conjecture is true."

Clearly this won't do. If the Goldbach Conjecture is false (and hence necessarily false) then it is *not* compatible (i.e., is not consistent) with *anything* — let alone everything — we know, and to assert that it is, would be, once again, to assert a necessary falsehood.

The proper construal of sentences *(6.4)* and *(6.5)* would seem to lie in the abandonment of the attempt to capture in terms of the logical concept of possibility (or the logical concept of consistency) whatever sense of "possible" it is which *(6.4)* invokes. What *(6.4)* attempts to express can be stated nonparadoxically in the less pretentious-sounding sentence

> *(6.7)* "We do not know whether the Goldbach Conjecture is true and we do not know whether the Goldbach Conjecture is false."

In this paraphrase all talk of 'possibility' has fallen away. To try to re-introduce such talk in such contexts is to court logical disaster (i.e., the asserting of necessary falsehoods).

Problems with the use of "it is necessary that"; the modal fallacy; absolute and relative necessity

There is a widespread practice of marking the presence of an implication relation by the use of such expressions as:

> "If . . . , then it is necessary that . . . "

> "If . . . , then it must be that . . . "

> "If . . . , then it has to be that . . . " and

> " . . . Therefore, it is necessary that . . . "

Often enough, these locutions are harmless. But sometimes they beguile persons into the mistaken belief that what is being asserted is that the consequent of the implicative proposition (or the conclusion of an argument) is itself necessarily true. Of course, some conditional propositions expressed by sentences of these types *do* have necessarily true consequents, as for example,

> *(6.8)*   "If the successor of an integer is equal to one plus that number, then it is necessary that the successor of an integer is greater than that number."

Here the expression "it is necessary that" in the consequent-clause of the sentence *(6.8)* is no cause for concern: the proposition expressed by the consequent-clause is indeed necessarily true. But often we use the very same grammatical construction in cases where the consequent-clause does *not* express a necessary truth: where the words "it is necessary that" are being used to signal the existence of an implication relation between the propositions expressed by the antecedent-clause and the consequent-clause and not being used to claim that the latter clause expresses a necessarily true proposition.

Consider the sentence

> *(6.9)*   "If Paul has three children and at most one daughter, then it is necessary that he has at least two sons."

The expression "it is necessary that" in *(6.9)* properly should be understood as marking the fact that the relation between the proposition expressed by the antecedent-clause and the proposition expressed by the consequent-clause (i.e., the relation of conditionality) holds necessarily; it should not be understood as asserting the (false) proposition that Paul's having two sons is a necessary truth.

Let "A" = "Paul has three children and at most one daughter", and "B" = "Paul has at least two sons". Using these sentential constants, the correct translation of *(6.9)* is

> *(6.10)*   "$\Box(A \supset B)$".

That is, the relation (viz., material conditionality) obtaining between the antecedent, A, and the consequent, B, holds necessarily. It would be incorrect to translate *(6.9)* as

> *(6.11)*   "$A \supset \Box B$".

To mistakenly transfer the modality of necessary truth to the consequent (as illustrated in *(6.11)*) of a true implicative proposition or to the conclusion of a deductively valid argument from the conditional relation which holds between the antecedent and consequent or between the premises and conclusion, is to commit what has come to be known as 'the' Modal Fallacy. Of course this is not the only way that one's thinking about modal concepts can go awry. There are, strictly speaking, indefinitely many modal fallacies one can commit. Yet it is this particular one which has been singled out by many writers for the title, 'the' Modal Fallacy.

We can hardly hope to reform ordinary prose so that it will accord with the niceties of our conceptual analysis. Even logicians are going to continue to say such things as

> *(6.12)*   "If today is Tuesday, then tomorrow must be Wednesday."

> *(6.13)*   "If a proposition is necessarily true, then it has to be noncontingent."

> *(6.14)*   "If Paul has three children among whom there is only one daughter, then he has to have two sons."

Let us adopt a special name for the kind of propositions expressed by the consequents of sentences utilizing this kind of construction. Let us call them "relative necessities".

A proposition, Q, then, will be said to be relatively necessary, or more exactly, to be necessary relative to the proposition P, if and only if Q is true in all possible worlds in which P is true; or, put another way, if and only if relative to all the possible worlds in which P is true, Q is true. Consider, for example, the nonmodal component of the consequent of the proposition expressed by *(6.12)*, viz., the proposition that tomorrow is Wednesday. The proposition that tomorrow is Wednesday is contingent in the *absolute* sense of "contingent", i.e., if we look at the set of all possible worlds. But this same proposition may be said to be noncontingent (specifically, necessarily true) *relative* to the set of all those possible worlds in which today is Tuesday.

There is a fallacy having no common name which is analogous to the Modal Fallacy and which sometimes arises in the use of epistemic concepts. In particular, some persons are wont to say that a proposition, P, can be known a priori if it can be validly inferred a priori from some proposition which is known to be true. This account, however, does not jibe with the explication of the concept of *aprioricity* which we gave in chapter 3. There we said that if a proposition is validly inferred from some proposition, the inferred proposition will be said to be known experientially if the proposition from which it is inferred is itself known experientially. Propositions which are known by the a priori process of inference may be said to instance the property of *relative* aprioricity; it is an open question of each of them whether it also instances the property of *absolute* aprioricity.

EXERCISES

Part A

Translate each of the following sentences into the symbolism of Modal Propositional Logic, taking care to avoid the modal fallacy.

1. *"If today is Tuesday, then tomorrow must be Wednesday."*

    > *Let "A" = "Today is Tuesday"*
    > *"B" = "Tomorrow is Wednesday"*

2. *"If today is Tuesday, then it is impossible that today is not Tuesday."*

    > *Let "A" = "Today is Tuesday"*

Part B

The modal fallacy can be very insidious. It occurs in both of the following arguments, yet some persons do not spot it. Try to see where it occurs. Then translate each of the arguments into the notation of Modal Propositional Logic in such a way that the fallacy is not committed.

3. *"If a proposition is true it can not be false. But if a proposition can not be false, then it is not only true but necessarily true. Thus if a proposition is true, it is necessarily true, and (consequently) the class of contingent truths is empty."*

4. *[It is not necessary to translate the part of this argument which is enclosed within the parentheses.]*
    "If an event is going to occur, then it cannot not occur. But if an event cannot not occur, then it must occur. Therefore if an event is going to occur, it must occur. (We are powerless to prevent

what must happen. The future is pre-ordained and our thinking that we can affect it is mere illusion.)"

Part C

Reread in chapter 1, p. 25, exercise 4, the words of Lazarus Long concerning time travel. If we let "A" = "a goes back in time" and let "B" = "a shoots his grandfather before the latter sires a's father", which, if any, of the following do you think most closely capture(s) the point of Long's claim? Which, if any, of the following, do you think he is arguing against?

(a) $\sim \Diamond A \cdot \sim \Diamond B$

(b) $\sim \Diamond (A \cdot B)$

(c) $A \longrightarrow \sim \Diamond B$

(d) $\Diamond A \cdot \Diamond B \cdot \sim \Diamond (A \cdot B)$

(e) $\sim \Diamond (A \cdot B) \longrightarrow \sim \Diamond A$

(f) $\Diamond A \supset \Box \sim B$

(g) $\sim \Diamond A$

4.   THE MODAL STATUS OF MODAL PROPOSITIONS

Every proposition is either necessarily true, necessarily false, or contingent. Since modal propositions form a proper subset of the class of propositions, every *modal* proposition must itself be either necessarily true, necessarily false, or contingent.

How shall we determine the modal status of modal propositions? So far as the methodology of Modal Propositional Logic is concerned, this question will be answered to the extent to which this logic can provide a means of ascertaining the validity of modalized formulae. A rigorous effective technique for that purpose will be presented in section 8 of this chapter. But as a step along the way toward developing that general technique, in this section we will lay the groundwork by examining only the very simplest cases, viz., those modalized formulae which consist of a single sentential variable which is the argument of (i.e., is modalized by) *one* of the operators "□", "◇", "▽", or "△". Since all of these operators are definable in terms of one another, it will suffice to examine just one of them (see section 2). The one we choose is "□". Turning our attention to "□P", we can see that there are three cases requiring our attention:

1. The modal status of □P in the case where P is contingent;

2. The modal status of □P in the case where P is necessarily true; and

3. The modal status of □P in the case where P is necessarily false.

Case 1:   What is the modal status of □P in the case where P is contingent?

Since, by hypothesis, P is contingent, there are some possible worlds in which P is true and others (all the others) in which it is false. Let us, then, divide the set of all possible worlds into two mutually exclusive and jointly exhaustive subsets, W_t and W_f, those possible worlds in which P is true and those possible worlds in which P is false.

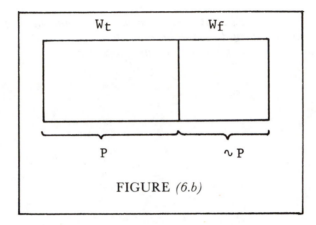

FIGURE *(6.b)*

Arbitrarily pick any possible world in W_t. Let us call that world "W_{t1}".

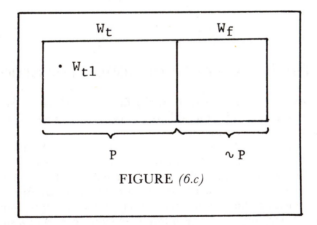

FIGURE *(6.c)*

What is the truth-value of □P in W_{t1}? Clearly □P is false in W_{t1}, for □P asserts that P is true in W_{t1} and in every other possible world as well. But P is false in every world in W_f. And if □P is false in W_{t1}, it is false throughout W_t, for whatever holds for any arbitrarily chosen member of a set (or more exactly, whatever holds of a member of a set irrespective of which member it is), holds for every other member of that set.

This leaves the possible worlds in W_f to be examined. What is the truth-value of □P in W_f? Arbitrarily pick any member of W_f. Call it "W_{f1}".

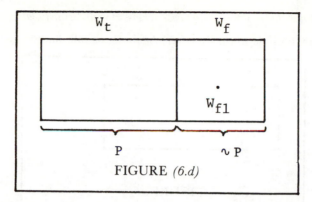

FIGURE *(6.d)*

Clearly □P is false in W_{f1}, for □P asserts that P is true in W_{f1} and in every other possible world as well. But P is false in W_{f1}. Therefore, since W_{f1} is but an arbitrarily chosen member of W_f, it follows that □P is false in every member of W_f. Thus we have shown that □P is false in every member of W_t and have now just shown that □P is false, as well, in every member of W_f. But these are all the possible worlds there are. Hence in the case where P is contingent, □P is false in every possible world, i.e., $\nabla P \rightarrow \square \sim \square P$. As a consequence, if P is contingent, then □P is noncontingent, i.e.,

$$\nabla P \rightarrow \triangle \square P. \qquad \text{[i.e., if P is contingent, then the (modal) proposition that P is necessarily true is itself noncontingent.]}$$

Case 2:   What is the modal status of □P in the case where P is necessarily true?

Arbitrarily pick any possible world whatever. Let us call that world "W_1".

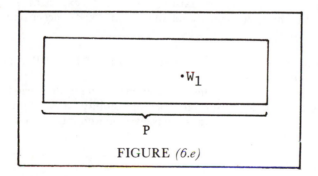

FIGURE *(6.e)*

What is the truth-value of □P in W_1? Clearly □P has the truth-value, truth, in W_1. For, in W_1, the proposition □P asserts that P is true in W_1 and in every other possible world as well, and clearly this is the case. Hence □P is true in W_1. But whatever is true of any arbitrarily selected possible world, is true of every possible world. Hence in the case where P is necessarily true, □P is also necessarily true, i.e., $\square P \rightarrow \square \square P$. As a consequence, if P is necessarily true, then □P is (again) noncontingent, i.e.,

$$\square P \rightarrow \triangle \square P.$$

Case 3:   *What is the modal status of □P in the case where P is necessarily false?*

Again arbitrarily pick any possible world whatever. Again let us call that world "W_1".

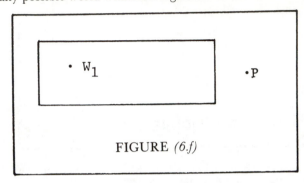

FIGURE *(6.f)*

What is the truth-value of □P in W_1? Clearly □P has the truth-value, falsity, in W_1. For in W_1, the proposition □P asserts that P is true in W_1 and in every other possible world as well. But P is false in W_1. Hence □P is false in W_1. But whatever is false in any arbitrarily selected possible world, is false in every possible world. Hence in the`case where P is necessarily false, □P is also necessarily false, i.e., $□ \sim P \longrightarrow □ \sim □P$. As a consequence, if P is necessarily false, then □P is (once again) noncontingent, i.e.,

$$□ \sim P \longrightarrow \triangle □P.$$

Conclusion: Every modal proposition expressible by a sentence of the form "□P" is noncontingent. If "P" expresses a necessary truth, then "□P" likewise expresses a necessary truth; if "P" expresses either a contingency or a necessary falsity, then "□P" expresses a necessary falsity. In short, a sentence of the form "□P" never expresses a contingency.

This last result holds as well for sentences of the form "◊P", "▽P", and "△P"; i.e., no such sentence ever expresses a contingency.

We can sum up this section by saying that propositions ascribing the various members of the family of properties, necessary truth, necessary falsehood, possibility, impossibility, noncontingency, and contingency, to other propositions, are always themselves noncontingent. (Later, in section 6, we shall put the point by saying that these properties are *essential* properties of those propositions which instance them.)

EXERCISES

1.   *Under what conditions of modal status for P will "◊P" express a necessary truth? Under what conditions, a necessary falsity?*

2.   *Under what conditions of modal status for P will "▽P" express a necessary truth? Under what conditions, a necessary falsity?*

3. *Under what conditions of modal status for P will "$\triangle P$" express a necessary truth? Under what conditions, a necessary falsity?*

4. *Under what conditions of modal status for P will "$\sim \square P$" express a necessary truth? Under what conditions, a necessary falsity?*

5. *Under what conditions of modal status for P will "$\square \sim P$" express a necessary truth? Under what conditions, a necessary falsity?*

5.   THE OPERATOR "IT IS CONTINGENTLY TRUE THAT"

In chapter 1 we introduced the concept of modal status and allowed various predicates to count as attributions of modal status, viz., "is possible", "is impossible", "is necessarily true", "is necessarily false", "is noncontingent", and "is contingent". However, we did not allow the predicates "is contingently true" and "is contingently false" to be so counted (p.13, fn. 10). We now have the conceptual techniques in hand to show how these two concepts differ from all the others just referred to. What, exactly, is it about the concepts of contingent truth and contingent falsity (as opposed to contingency itself) which sets them apart from the concepts of possibility, necessary truth, necessary falsity, and the like?

It is an easy matter to define operators representing the concepts of contingent truth and contingent falsity respectively in terms of the modal monadic operators already introduced. These definitions are, simply,

$$\text{"}\triangledown P\text{"} \quad =_{df} \quad \text{"}\nabla P \cdot P\text{"} \qquad \text{[i.e., P is contingently true if and only if P is contingent and true]}$$

$$\text{"}\triangledown P\text{"} \quad =_{df} \quad \text{"}\nabla P \cdot \sim P\text{"} \qquad \text{[i.e., P is contingently false if and only if P is contingent and false]}$$

From a syntactical point of view there is nothing in these definitions to suggest that there is anything odd or peculiar about the concepts of contingent truth and contingent falsity. But when we come to examine the possible-worlds explication of these concepts the peculiarity emerges.

Let us ask, "What is the modal status of a proposition expressed by a sentence of the form "$\triangledown P$" or "$\triangledown P$"? (We will here examine only the first of these two cases. The conclusions we reach in the one will apply equally to the other.) Concentrating our attention on "$\triangledown P$", there are three cases to consider:

1. The modal status of $\triangledown P$ in the case where P is contingent;

2. The modal status of $\triangledown P$ in the case where P is necessarily true; and

3. The modal status of $\triangledown P$ in the case where P is necessarily false.

Case 1:   What is the modal status of $\triangledown P$ in the case where P is contingent?

As before, we begin by dividing the set of all possible worlds into two mutually exclusive and jointly exhaustive subsets, W_t and W_f, those possible worlds in which P is true and those possible worlds in which P is false. Arbitrarily pick any world in W_t. Let us call that world "W_{t1}", (see figure *(6.c)*). What is the truth-value of ▽ P in W_{t1}? ▽ P will be true in W_{t1}, for ▽ P in W_{t1} asserts that P is true in W_{t1} and is false in some other possible world. Since both these conjuncts are true in W_{t1}, ▽ P is true in W_{t1}. But if ▽ P is true in W_{t1}, it is true throughout W_t. This leaves the possible worlds in W_f to be examined. What is the truth-value of ▽ P in W_f? Choose any arbitrary member of W_f. Call it "W_{f1}" (see figure *(6.d)*). What is the truth-value of ▽ P in W_{f1}? ▽ P will be false in W_{f1}, for ▽ P in W_{f1} asserts that P is true in W_{f1} and is false in some other possible world. (We do not know whether this second conjunct is true or false, that is, whether there is any other possible world besides W_{f1} in which P is false — perhaps there is just *one* possible world, W_{f1}, in which P is false. But, luckily, we do not have to pursue this question or worry about it. For we can confidently assert that irrespective of the truth or falsity of the second conjunct just mentioned, the first is determinately false.) The first conjunct asserts that P is true in W_{f1}, and this we know to be false since W_{f1} is a member of the set W_f, and P is false in every possible world in W_f. Therefore we may conclude that ▽ P is false in W_{f1} and in every other member (if there are any) of W_f. At this point we have shown that ▽ P is true throughout W_t and is false throughout W_f. It follows immediately, then, that in the case where P is contingent, ▽ P is also contingent; or in symbols,

$$\triangledown P \longrightarrow \triangledown \; \triangledown P.$$

Case 2: *What is the modal status of ▽ P in the case where P is necessarily true?*

See figure *(6.e)*. Arbitrarily pick any possible world whatever. Let us call that world "W". What is the truth-value of ▽ P in W? Clearly ▽ P has the truth-value, falsity, in W. For, in W, the proposition ▽ P asserts that P is true in W and is false in some other world. But P is true in every possible world whatever and is false in none. Therefore any proposition which asserts that P is false in some possible world is false. Therefore ▽ P is false in W. But if ▽ P is false in W, it is false in every other possible world as well. Hence in the case where P is necessarily true, ▽ P is necessarily false, and is, ipso facto, noncontingent. In symbols, we have

$$\square P \longrightarrow \triangle \triangledown P.$$

Case 3: *What is the modal status of ▽ P in the case where P is necessarily false?*

See figure *(6.f)*. Arbitrarily pick any possible world, W. ▽ P is false in W. For, in W, ▽ P asserts that P is true in W and is false in some other possible world. But P is false in every possible world including W. Therefore ▽ P is false in W. But if ▽ P is false in W, it is false in every possible world. Therefore in the case where P is necessarily false, ▽ P is necessarily false, and is, ipso facto, noncontingent. In symbols, we have

$$\square \sim P \longrightarrow \triangle \triangledown P.$$

> *Conclusion:* Unlike ascriptions of necessary truth, necessary falsehood, possibility, impossibility, contingency, and noncontingency, which always yield propositions which are *noncontingent*, ascriptions of contingent truth (and contingent falsity) in some instances (viz., those in which the proposition being referred to is itself contingent) will yield propositions which are *contingent*. (See Case 1, this section.)

This difference between ascriptions of contingent truth and contingent falsity, on the one hand, and ascriptions of necessary truth, necessary falsity, possibility, impossibility, contingency, and noncontingency, on the other, is of the utmost importance for the science of logic.

To the extent that logic is an a priori science, and to the extent that an a priori science is incapable of gaining for us the truth-values of contingent propositions,[2] to that extent the truth-values of propositions attributing contingent truth (or contingent falsity) to contingent propositions will be unattainable within the science of logic.

When, earlier in this book, we gave various examples of contingently true propositions, e.g., *(3.10)*, the proposition that Krakatoa Island was annihilated by a volcanic eruption in 1883, we were not (nor did we claim to be) operating strictly within the methodology of the science of logic. For the property attributed to the proposition, viz., the property of being contingently true, is an *accidental* one (see the next section), and the determination that something has an accidental property lies outside the capabilities of the ratiocinative methodology of logic.

Such is not the case, however, when we attribute necessary truth, necessary falsity, possibility, noncontingency, or contingency to a proposition. Ascriptions of these properties, as we showed in the previous section, are always noncontingent. Thus when we attribute any of these latter properties to a proposition we can hope to determine, through the application of the a priori methodology of logic, whether they truly hold or not.

We took some pains to argue in chapter 1 that there are not two kinds of truth, contingent truth and noncontingent truth. There is but one kind of truth. And one should not be tempted to try to make the point of the present section by saying that logic is concerned with noncontingent truth and falsity but not with contingent truth and falsity. Rather we should prefer to put the point this way: Logic is concerned with contingency and noncontingency, and in the latter case, but not in the former, also with truth and falsity. Within Logic one can aspire to divide the class of propositions into three mutually exclusive and jointly exhaustive categories: the necessarily true; the necessarily false; and the contingent. Any attempt to divide further the latter category into true and false propositions, and then to determine which proposition resides in which subclass takes one outside the ratiocinative limits of Logic.

6.   ESSENTIAL PROPERTIES OF RELATIONS

When we first introduced the distinction between *items* and *attributes* (chapter 1, p. 7) we said that an item was anything to which reference could be made, while an attribute is anything that can be ascribed to an item. Now it is clear that attributes can be referred to and that when we do refer to them we are regarding them as items to which still further attributes may be ascribed. For instance, we refer to the relation (two-place attribute) of implication when we say of it that it holds between propositions; we then treat the relation of implication as an item of which something can be said. And when we say of implication that it is a relation between propositions we are ascribing a property (one-place attribute) to it.

Some of the properties of relations are of little general significance. It is of little general significance, for instance, that the relation of *being older than* has the property of holding between the Tower of London and the Eiffel Tower. This, we want to say, is a purely 'accidental' feature of that relation insofar as it is not necessary that the relation have this property.[3]

Other properties of relations, however, *are* of general significance. For instance, it matters a great deal to our understanding the relation of *being older than* that this relation has the property of being

2. Although we have argued in chapter 3, section 6, that there probably are no contingent propositions knowable a priori, we are here leaving the question open in order to accommodate the views of such philosophers as Kant and Kripke.

3. **F** is said to be an accidental property of an item *a* if and only if in some possible world in which *a* exists (or has instances), *a* has the property **F**, and in some (other) possible world in which *a* exists, *a* does not have the property **F**.

asymmetrical, i.e., the property such that if *any* item (the Tower of London, the Sphinx, or anything else) stands in the relation of *being older than* to any other item (the Eiffel Tower, the Premier of British Columbia, or whatnot), then that other item does *not* stand in the same relation to it. Anyone who failed to understand that the relation of *being older than* has this property simply would not understand that relation. It is an 'essential' property of that relation insofar as it is a property which that relation cannot fail to have.[4]

It will help us a great deal in our understanding of relations quite generally, and in our understanding of modal relations in particular, if we get clear about some of the essential, noncontingent, properties that relations have. We shall consider just three sets of such properties of relations.

First, any relation whatever must be either *symmetrical* or *asymmetrical* or *nonsymmetrical*.

A relation, R, has the property of *symmetry* if and only if when *any* item *a* bears that relation to *any* item *b*, it follows that item *b* bears that relation to item *a*. The relation of *being true in the same possible world as* is an example of a symmetrical relation. For given any *a* and *b*, it is necessarily true that if *a* is true in the same possible world as *b* then *b* is true in the same possible world as *a*.

A relation, R, has the property of *asymmetry* if and only if when any item *a* bears that relation to any item *b*, it follows that *b* does *not* bear that relation to *a*. The relation of *being older than* is an example of an asymmetrical relation. For given any *a* and *b*, it is necessarily true that if *a* is older than *b*, then it is false that *b* is older than *a*.

A relation, R, has the property of *nonsymmetry* if and only if it is neither symmetrical nor asymmetrical. The relation of *being in love with* is nonsymmetrical. From a proposition which asserts that some item *a* is in love with some item *b*, it neither follows (although it may be true) that *b* is in love with *a*, nor does it follow that *b* is not in love with *a*.

Secondly, any relation whatever must be either *transitive* or *intransitive* or *nontransitive*.

A relation, R, has the property of *transitivity* if and only if when any item *a* bears that relation to any item *b* and *b* bears that relation to any item *c*, it follows that *a* bears that relation to *c*. The relation of *having the same weight as* is an example of a transitive relation. For given any *a*, *b*, and *c*, it is necessarily true that if *a* has the same weight as *b* and *b* has the same weight as *c*, then *a* has the same weight as *c*.

A relation, R, has the property of *intransitivity*, if and only if when any item *a* bears that relation to any item *b* and *b* bears that relation to any item *c*, it follows that *a* does *not* bear that relation to *c*. The relation of *being twice as heavy as* is an example of an intransitive relation. For given any *a*, *b*, and *c*, it is necessarily true that if *a* is twice as heavy as *b* and *b* is twice as heavy as *c*, then *a* is not twice as heavy as *c*.

A relation, R, has the property of *nontransitivity* if and only if it is neither transitive nor intransitive. The relation of *being a lover of* is an example of a nontransitive relation. From the propositions which assert that some item *a* is a lover of some item *b* and that *b* is a lover of some item *c*, it neither *follows* (although it may be true) that *a* is a lover of *c*, nor does it *follow* that *a* is not a lover of *c*.

---

4. **F** is said to be an essential property of an item *a* if and only if in every possible world in which *a* exists (or has instances), *a* has the property **F**.

Finally, any relation whatever must be either *reflexive* or *irreflexive* or *nonreflexive*.

A relation R, has the property of *reflexivity* if and only if when any item *a* bears that relation to any other item whatever, it follows that *a* bears that relation to itself. The relation of *being a graduate of the same university as* is reflexive. For given any item *a*, it is necessarily true that if *a* is a graduate of the same university as some other item, then *a* is a graduate of the same university as *a*.

A relation, R, has the property of *irreflexivity* if and only if it is impossible that anything should bear that relation to itself. The relation of *being better qualified than* is irreflexive. For given any item *a*, it is necessarily true that *a* is not better qualified than *a*.

A relation, R, has the property of *nonreflexivity* if and only if it is neither reflexive nor irreflexive. The relation of *being proud of* is a nonreflexive relation. From the proposition that *a* is proud of something or someone it does not *follow* (although it may be true) that *a* has self-pride and it does not *follow* that *a* lacks self-pride.[5]

In the light of this classificatory scheme for talking about the essential properties of relations, let us now consider the essential properties of each of the four modal relations we first singled out for attention. In each case we can determine what these properties are by attending once more to the way these relations have been defined.

We can easily prove that *consistency* is symmetrical, nontransitive, and reflexive, if we recall that a proposition, P, is consistent with a proposition, Q, just when there exists at least one possible world in which both are true, i.e., a possible world in which P is true and Q is true. But any possible world in which P is true and Q is true is also a possible world in which Q is true and P is true. Hence if P is consistent with Q, Q must also be consistent with P. That is to say, consistency is symmetrical. Suppose, now, not only that P is consistent with Q but further that Q is consistent with a proposition R. Then not only are there some possible worlds in which both P and Q are true, but also there are some possible worlds in which both Q and R are true. But must the set of possible worlds in which P and Q are true intersect with the set of possible worlds in which Q and R are true? Clearly we have no warrant for concluding either that they do intersect or that they do not. Hence from the suppositions that P is consistent with Q and that Q is consistent with R it does not *follow* that P is consistent with R. Nor does it *follow* that P is not consistent with R. Consistency, then, is a nontransitive relation. Suppose, finally, that P is consistent with at least one other proposition. Then there will exist at least one possible world in which P is true. But any possible world in which P is true will be a possible world in which both P and P itself will be true. Hence, if P is consistent with any other proposition, P is consistent with itself. Consistency, then, is a reflexive relation.[6]

Inconsistency is symmetrical, nontransitive and nonreflexive. If a proposition, P, is inconsistent with a proposition, Q, then not only is there no possible world in which both P and Q are true but also there is no possible world in which both Q and P are true. Hence if P is inconsistent with Q, Q is also

5. A relation, R, is sometimes said to be *totally reflexive* if and only if it is a relation which *every* item must bear to itself. An example is the relation *being identical with*. Likewise a relation, R, may be said to be *totally irreflexive* if and only if it is a relation which *nothing* can bear to itself. An example is the relation of *being non-identical with*. Plainly a relation which is not either totally reflexive or totally irreflexive will be *totally nonreflexive*. Most of the relations which come readily to mind have this latter property.

6. Note, however, that consistency is *not* a *totally* reflexive relation. As we have seen, if a proposition is necessarily false it is not consistent with itself but is self-inconsistent. Moreover, consistency, as we have defined it, is a relation which holds only between items which have a truth-value. Hence, unlike the relation of identity, it is *not* a relation which everything has to itself.

inconsistent with P. That is to say, inconsistency, like consistency, is a symmetrical relation. And, like the relation of consistency, the relation of inconsistency is nontransitive. Suppose not only that P is inconsistent with Q but also that Q is inconsistent with R. Then not only are there no possible worlds in which both P and Q are true but also there are no possible worlds in which both Q and R are true. Does this mean that there are no possible worlds in which both P and R are true? Does it mean that there *are* some possible worlds in which both P and R are true? Neither follows. Hence inconsistency is nontransitive. Where the relation of inconsistency differs from the relation of consistency is in respect of the property of reflexivity. Consistency, we saw, is reflexive. Inconsistency is not. Suppose a proposition, P, is inconsistent with some other proposition, Q. Then it does not follow (although it may be true) that P is inconsistent with itself (i.e., is self-inconsistent) nor does it follow (although it may be true) that P is not inconsistent with itself (i.e., is self-consistent). Inconsistency, then, is neither reflexive nor irreflexive, but nonreflexive.

Implication is nonsymmetrical, transitive, and reflexive. If a proposition, P, implies a proposition, Q, then there are no possible worlds in which P is true and Q is false. Does this mean that there are no possible worlds in which Q is true and P is false? Does it mean that there *are* some possible worlds in which Q is true and P is false? Neither follows. Hence implication is nonsymmetrical. Suppose, now, that P implies Q and that Q implies R. Then in any possible world in which P is true, Q is true; and likewise, in any possible world in which Q is true, R is true. But this means that in any possible world in which P is true, R is also true. Hence implication is transitive. (See Exercise on p. 218.) Further, implication is reflexive. If P implies Q then not only are there no possible worlds in which P is true and Q is false, but also there are no possible worlds in which P is true and P is false (any world in which P is true and P is false is an impossible world). That is, any proposition, P, implies itself. Hence implication is reflexive.

Finally, the relation of *equivalence* is symmetrical, transitive, and reflexive. If a proposition, P, is equivalent to a proposition, Q, then since P and Q are true in precisely the same possible worlds, Q is equivalent to P. Suppose, now, that P is equivalent to Q and Q is equivalent to R. Then not only are P and Q true in precisely the same possible worlds but also Q and R are true in precisely the same possible worlds. Hence P and R are true in precisely the same possible worlds. Equivalence, then, like implication, is transitive. Furthermore, it is reflexive. If P is true in precisely the same possible worlds as Q then P is also true in precisely the same possible worlds as itself. That is, any proposition, P, is equivalent to itself. Hence equivalence is reflexive.

EXERCISES

Part A

1. *Draw a worlds-diagram for three propositions, P, Q, and R, such that P is consistent with Q, Q is consistent with R, and P is inconsistent with R.*

Example:

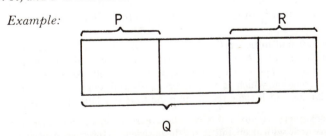

This example is just one among several possible answers.
Find another correct answer to this question.

2. *Draw a worlds-diagram for three propositions, P, Q, and R, such that P is consistent with Q, Q is consistent with R, and P is consistent with R.*

3. *Draw a worlds-diagram for three propositions, P, Q, and R, such that P is inconsistent with Q, Q is inconsistent with R, and P is inconsistent with R.*

4. *Draw a worlds-diagram for three propositions, P, Q, and R, such that P is inconsistent with Q, Q is inconsistent with R, and P is consistent with R.*

5. *See figure (1.i) (p. 51). (a) Which worlds-diagrams represent cases in which P stands to Q in a symmetrical relation? (b) Which are cases of an asymmetrical relation? (c) Which are cases of a nonsymmetrical relation? (d) Which are cases of a reflexive relation? (e) Which are cases of an irreflexive relation? (f) Which are cases of a nonreflexive relation?*

6. *For each of the relations below, tell whether it is (a) symmetrical, asymmetrical, or non-symmetrical; (b) transitive, intransitive, or nontransitive; (c) reflexive, irreflexive, or nonreflexive.*

       i.   *extols the virtues of*

      ii.   *is not the same age as*

     iii.   *is the same age as*

      iv.   *is heavier than*

       v.   *is twice as heavy as*

7. *Suppose that Adams employs Brown, that Brown employs Carter, and that Adams also employs Carter. May we say, then, that in this instance the relation of* employs *is a transitive one? Explain your answer.*

Part B

(The following three questions are more difficult than those in Part A.)

8. *It is possible to define a vast number of different dyadic modal relations in terms of the fifteen worlds-diagrams of figure (1.i). Suppose we were to single out one among this vast number, let us say, the modal relation which we will arbitrarily name "R#": the relation, R#, holds between two propositions, P and Q, if and only if P and Q are related to one another as depicted in worlds-diagram 1, worlds-diagram 2, worlds-diagram 3, or worlds-diagram 4. What are the essential properties of the relation R#?*

9. *What are the essential properties of the relation R!, where "R!" is defined as that relation which holds between any two propositions, P and Q, when P and Q are related as depicted in worlds-diagram 9 or worlds-diagram 10?*

10. *What are the essential properties of the relation R+, where "R+" is defined as that relation which holds between any two propositions, P and Q, when P and Q are related as depicted in worlds-diagram 5 or worlds-diagram 6?*

Part C

On the definitions given here of "transitivity" and "intransitivity", it turns out that some relations are both transitive and intransitive, i.e., the classificatory scheme, transitive/intransitive/nontransitive, while exhaustive of the class of all dyadic relations, is not exclusive.

For example, the relation depicted in worlds-diagram 2 (see figure (1.i)) is both transitive and intransitive. This is so because it is logically impossible that there should be three propositions such that the first stands in just this relation to the second and the second in this same relation to the third. But since this is so, the antecedent conditions of the definitions of both "transitivity" and "intransitivity" are unsatisfiable for any propositions whatever, and thus — in the case of this relation — the two definitions are themselves (vacuously) satisfied. (I.e., any conditional proposition with a necessarily false antecedent is itself necessarily true.)

11. Find all the worlds-diagrams in figure (1.i) which depict relations which are both transitive and intransitive.

12. Consider the relation R$, where "R$" is defined as that relation which obtains between any two integers, x and y, when x is twice y, and y is even. Is R$ transitive, intransitive, or nontransitive?

13. Let R% be that relation which holds between any two integers, x and y, when x is twice y, and y is odd. Is R% transitive, intransitive, or nontransitive?

14. Is the classificatory scheme, reflexive/irreflexive, exclusive?

15. Is the classificatory scheme, symmetric/asymmetric, exclusive?

Part D (discussion questions)

In trying to ascertain the essential properties of relations we must take care not to be conceptually myopic. We must be sure to consider possible worlds other that the actual one, worlds in which natural laws and commonplace events are radically different from those in the actual world. In the actual world, so far as we can tell, travel into the past is physically impossible. But to answer the question whether the relation, for example, being the father of, is intransitive or not, it is insufficient to consider only the actual world. If in some possible worlds, time travel into the past occurs — as described by Heinlein — then in some of these worlds we will have instances in which a person goes back in time and fathers himself or his father. If we are to admit the existence of such possible worlds, then it follows that the relation of being the father of is not, as we might first think, intransitive, but is, we see after more thought about the matter, nontransitive.

If we assume that Heinlein-type worlds in which travel into the past occurs are possible (See chapter 1, section 1), what, then, would we want to say are the essential properties of the following relations?

    i.   is the mother of
    ii.   is an ancestor of
    iii.   was born before

If a person should father himself and then wait around while the child he has fathered grows up, what then becomes of the often heard claim that one person cannot be in two places at the same time?

7.   TWO CASE STUDIES IN MODAL RELATIONS: A Light-hearted Interlude

Case study 1:   The pragmatics of telling the truth

There is a well known saying which goes, "It is easier to tell the truth than to lie." But in what sense of "easier" is it easier to tell the truth than to lie? Some persons find it psychologically or morally very difficult to lie, and when they try to do so are very unconvincing. Other persons can lie blithely and yet appear sincere. From the *psychological* viewpoint, it is simply false that all persons find it difficult to lie. But there is another sense in which lying can be said to be "difficult", and in this sense lying is difficult for *everyone,* saint and sinner alike.

Lying is *logically* difficult. To tell the truth a person need only report the facts; the facts are always consistent. Of course a person may falter in his recollection of them or in his reporting of them, but if he tries to report them honestly he stands a greater chance of relating a consistent story than if he tries to lie. If a person succeeds in relating the facts as they occurred, then consistency is assured; in a metaphorical sense we can say that the facts themselves look after the matter of consistency. But when a person sets out to lie, then his task is very much more difficult. For not only must he bear in mind what actually happened, he must also bear in mind what he has said falsely about those matters, and must try to preserve consistency in everything he says. But to look after the matter of consistency he will need a fair amount of logical prowess, especially if his story is long. The difficulty does not increase linearly with increasing numbers of propositions: it grows, as the mathematician would say, exponentially.

Suppose we wish to check an arbitrary set of propositions for inconsistency. How might we go about it? We would probably begin with the easiest case: checking each individual proposition in the set to see whether it is self-inconsistent or not. Failing to find any self-inconsistent propositions, we would then proceed to the next easiest case, that of searching for inconsistency among all possible pairs of propositions in the set. If we fail to find inconsistency among the pairs of propositions in the set, we would then proceed to all possible triples; and should we happen not to detect inconsistency among the triples, we would pass on to the foursomes, etc. In general, if there are n propositions in a set, then there are m distinct non-empty subsets constructible on that set, where m is given by the formula:

$$m = 2^n - 1$$

Thus in the case where there is one proposition in a set ($n = 1$), the number of distinct non-empty subsets is 1; for a set of two propositions, 3; for a set of three propositions, 7; for a set of four propositions, 15; for a set of five propositions, 31; for a set of six propositions, 63, etc. For a set of only ten propositions, which is a fairly short story — far, far less than one would be called upon to relate in, for example, a typical courtroom encounter — there are no less than 1023 distinct non-empty subsets. And for a still small set of twenty propositions, the number of distinct non-empty subsets jumps to a staggering 1,048,575.

It must be pointed out however, that the person who is telling the story has a somewhat easier task in looking after consistency than does the person hearing the story who is looking for inconsistency. After all, a person telling a story in which he deliberately lies, presumably knows which of his own propositions are true and which false. In order for the teller of the story to ensure that his story is consistent, he need only check for consistency among those subsets which include at least one false proposition. All those other subsets which consist entirely of true propositions he knows to be consistent and he can safely disregard them.

What is the measure of this difference between the difficulty of the tasks of the speaker and of the listener? The speaker is in a slightly more favorable position, but by how much? Let's try an example. Suppose a person were to assert twenty propositions. We already know that there are 1,048,575 non-empty subsets constructible on this set. Also suppose that just *one* of the twenty propositions asserted is false, and of course, that that one is known to be false by the speaker. How many subsets will the speaker have to check? Our naive intuitions tell us that this false proposition will occur in only one-twentieth of all the subsets. But our naive intuitions are wildly wrong in this regard. For the case where there is only one false proposition in a set, the number of subsets which contain that false proposition is always *at least half* the total number of subsets. This quite unexpected result can be made plausible by examining a short example. Suppose we have four propositions, A, B, C, and D, one of which, namely C, is false. In how many subsets does C occur? We list all the non-empty subsets. By the formula above we know that there are exactly 15 distinct subsets:

1.	A	5.	AB	11.	ABC	15.	ABCD
2.	B	6.	AC	12.	ABD		
3.	C	7.	AD	13.	ACD		
4.	D	8.	BC	14.	BCD		
		9.	BD				
		10.	CD				

Proposition C, the single false proposition, occurs in no fewer than eight of these subsets, viz., nos. 3, 6, 8, 10, 11, 13, 14, and 15.

The generalized formula is given as follows, where "q" is the number of subsets which contain one or more false propositions, "f" is the number of false propositions in the set, and "n", as above, is the number of propositions in the set:

$$q = 2^n - 2^{(n-f)}$$

Thus in the case where a liar asserts twenty propositions only one of which is false, he is presented with the task of checking 524,288 subsets for consistency. And if two of the twenty propositions are false the number of subsets containing at least one false proposition, and hence possible sources of inconsistency which would reveal that his story was not entirely true, would jump to 786,432, a number not remarkably smaller than the number of subsets (1,048,575) which his listener would theoretically have to check.

Small wonder, then, that we say that it is difficult to lie. And this fact explains, in part, the wisdom of judicial procedures in which witnesses can be cross-examined. While it is possible for a witness to prepare beforehand a false but consistent story, it is difficult to add to that story or to elaborate it in a short time without falling into inconsistency. Truth-tellers do not have this worry: they merely have to relate the facts and their stories will be consistent. Thus to a certain extent, logical principles, not only moral ones, underpin our judicial system. Indeed, if lying were logically as simple as telling the truth, our legal practice of cross-examination probably would not work at all.

EXERCISES

1. *Consider a set of propositions consisting only of true contingent propositions. Is the set consisting of all and only the negations of those propositions also consistent? Give reasons, and, if possible, illustrations for your answer.*

2. *What difference, if any, is there between lying and not telling the truth?*

Note: The following questions are for mathematically sophisticated students only.

3.   Derive the formula for m.

4.   Derive the formula for q.

5.   If a set of propositions is known to contain s *necessarily true propositions, how shall we modify the formulae for* m *and* q*?*

*   *   *   *   *

Case study 2:   An invalid inference and an unwitting impossible description

In a recent book of so-called "mental exercises" the following puzzle is posed:

> It took 20 days for all of the leaves to fall from a tree. If the number of leaves that fell each day was twice that of the previous day, on which day was the tree half bare?[7]

Most persons, including the author of the book in which this puzzle appears, say that the answer is "on the nineteenth day". The author replies this way:

> If the number of leaves that fell doubled each day, the tree must have been half bare on the 19th day.[8]

This answer, in spite of its initial plausibility, has been reached by a faulty inference. The fact that each number in a series is the double of its immediate predecessor, does *not* imply that it is double the sum of all its immediate predecessors. For a tree to be half bare implies that the number of leaves remaining on it is equal to the sum of the numbers of the leaves which fell on each of the preceding days. For any series of numbers in which each number after the first is double its predecessor, the sum of all of them up to but not including the last is always *less* than the last.[9] The tree cannot be half bare on the nineteenth day: more leaves remain than the sum of all the numbers of leaves which have fallen on each day up to that point. The tree will become half bare only sometime during the last day, the twentieth. (Moreover, the tree will be *exactly* half bare at some time only if there was an even number of leaves on the tree to begin with.)

It would be easy to leave the puzzle at this point, thinking that with this repair all now is in order. All is not in order, however. The puzzle harbors a still more subtle and crippling flaw provided we take the description given of the tree *absolutely literally*. Ask yourself this question: if all the leaves fell from the tree within a twenty-day period, and if on each day the number of leaves which fell was twice

---

7. Alfred G. Latcha, *How Do You Figure It?: Modern Mental Exercises in Logic and Reasoning*, Cranbury, N.J., A.S. Barnes and Co., Inc., 1970, p. 19.

8. *Ibid.*, p. 53.

9. The series at issue is of this sort: n, 2n, 4n, 8n, 16n, . . . One can terminate this series at any point one likes, and one will find that the last term of the terminated series will always be greater than the *sum* of all the previous terms. Thus if one sums through all members of the series up to, but not including, the last term, one will *not* reach one-half of the total sum.

that of the previous day, how many, then, fell on the *first* day? The answer we are forced to give is: "zero". For if all the leaves fell within a twenty-day period, it follows logically that none fell during any time before that period. But if none fell any time before that twenty-day period began, then it also follows logically that none could have fallen on the day before that twenty-day period began. Let's call that day, "Day Zero"; let's call the first day of the twenty-day period, "Day One"; the second, "Day Two"; etc. Since no leaves whatever fell on Day Zero, none fell on Day One; for Day One, like every other day in the twenty-day period, is a day in which twice as many leaves fell as on the previous day. But zero leaves fell on Day Zero, and since twice zero is zero, no leaves fell on Day One. But if no leaves fell on Day One, then no leaves fell on Day Two, for we are told (that is, the description of the tree implies) that on Day Two twice as many leaves fell as on Day One, but again, twice zero is zero. Continuing this line of reasoning (that is, tracing out this line of implications), we can easily show that no leaves fell on Day Three, none on Day Four, and so on, right through and including Day Twenty. In sum, at no time during the twenty-day period did any leaves fall from the tree.

Something (to say the least) is seriously amiss. By two impeccable lines of reasoning we have shown in the first place that the tree was half bare sometime during the twentieth day and in the second place that at no time during that twenty-day period was it half bare. What precisely is wrong?

There is no flaw whatever in any of the implications we have just asserted. The description of the tree *does* imply that the tree will be (at least) half bare sometime during the twentieth day and *does* also imply that the tree will never be half bare anytime during that period. Yet, these conclusions, taken together, are impossible. It is logically impossible both that a tree should be half bare during the course of a certain day and that it should not be half bare at any time during the course of that day.

The trouble with this case lies in the original description of the tree: the description is itself logically impossible, or as we might say, logically self-inconsistent. *Just because* this description implies an impossibility, we know that it itself is impossible. It is logically impossible that there should be a tree which is both half bare and not half bare at a certain time. Yet this is the kind of tree which has been described in the statement of the puzzle. Obviously the author of the puzzle book didn't see this implication; he didn't see that the description implied two logically inconsistent propositions.

Many inconsistent descriptions are of this sort. To the untrained eye, and oftentimes to the trained one as well, the inconsistency does not stand out. And indeed it may take a very long time for the inconsistency to be revealed—if it ever is. Cases are known where inconsistency has escaped detection for many, many years. Classical probability theory invented by Pierre Simon LaPlace was inconsistent. But this inconsistency went unnoticed for seventy-five years until pointed out by Bertrand in 1889.[10] Even now, many teachers of probability theory do not know that this theory is inconsistent and still persist in teaching it in much the form that LaPlace himself stated it.

Every inconsistent set of propositions shares with the case being examined here the feature of implying a contradiction. Indeed, that a set of propositions implies a contradiction is both a necessary and sufficient condition for that set's being inconsistent.

It is easy to underestimate the grievousness of an inconsistent description. We can imagine a person following the two lines of reasoning we have gone through which lead to two different, incompatible answers to the puzzle, and then asking naively, "Well, which one is the *correct* answer?"

What are we to make of such a question? How are we to answer it?

Our reply is to reject a presupposition of the question, viz., that there *is* a correct answer to this question. Not all apparent questions have 'correct' answers. 'The' answer to the puzzle posed is no more the first (repaired) one given (viz., "on the twentieth day") than it is the latter (viz., "the tree is

---

10. A detailed treatment of the so-called "Bertrand Paradox" occurs in Wesley Salmon, *The Foundations of Scientific Inference*, University of Pittsburgh Press, 1967, pp. 65–68.

never half bare"). Both answers follow logically from the description of the tree; but neither is true, simply because there can be no such tree answering to the description given.[11]

Finally, before we turn our attention away from these case studies, let us glean one further point from our discussion. We have said that the original description as quoted is self-inconsistent: it is logically impossible that there should be a tree which is both half bare and not half bare at a certain time. But note carefully: the original description of the tree did not say *precisely* this. Indeed, most persons, unless they are prompted, would not see that this latter description also fits the tree as originally described. The latter, the obviously impossible description, is *implied* by what was written, but was not stated explicitly. Yet, for all that, any person who subscribes to the original description is committed to the explicitly contradictory one. We are, in a quite straightforward sense, committed to *everything* that is logically implied by what we say. This is not to say that we *know* everything that is implied by what we say, or even that we are dimly aware of these things. The point is, rather, that if we are shown that something does logically follow from what we say or believe, then we are logically committed to it also. If an explicit contradiction logically *follows* from something we've asserted, then we can be accused of having asserted a contradiction just as though we had asserted that contradiction explicitly in the first instance.

EXERCISES

1. *Finding that a set of propositions implies a contradiction suffices to show that that set is inconsistent. But failure to show that a set of propositions implies a contradiction does* not *suffice to show that that set is consistent. Why?*

2. *Repair the description of the tree in the quotation from the puzzle book so that it is consistent and so that the correct answer to the question will be, "Sometime during the twentieth day."*

3. *(This question is somewhat more difficult than question 2.) Repair the description of the tree in the quotation from the puzzle book so that it is consistent and the correct answer will be, as the author suggested, "At the end of the nineteenth day."*

4. *The following paragraph is inconsistent. Proceeding in a stepwise fashion (as we have done in the preceding discussion), validly infer from it two obviously inconsistent propositions.*

> *John is Mary's father. John has only two children, one of whom is unmarried and has never been married. Mary has no brothers. Mary is married to Simon who is an only child. Mary's son has an uncle who has borrowed money from John.*

11. Upon analysis, it turns out that these two answers are contraries of one another, and although they are inconsistent with one another, it is not the case that one is true and the other false; they are both false. The pertinent logical principle involved is the following: any proposition which ascribes a property to an impossible item is necessarily false. Clearly we can see this principle illustrated in the present case. Since there is no possible world in which a tree such as the one described exists, it follows that there is no possible world in which such a tree exists and has the property **F**, *and* it follows that there is no possible world in which such a tree exists and has the property **G**.

5.   Is the following description consistent or inconsistent?

> *It took twenty days for all of the leaves to fall from a tree.*
> *The number of leaves which fell each day was 100 more*
> *than fell the previous day.*

8.   USING WORLDS-DIAGRAMS TO ASCERTAIN THE VALIDITY OF MODALIZED FORMULAE

The results of section 4 — in which we proved that every propositional-variable modalized by any one of the operators, "□", "◊", "▽", or "△" can be instantiated to express only a noncontingent proposition — provide the opportunity to state some additional rules for the interpretation of worlds-diagrams so as to allow these diagrams to be used in intuitively appealing ways to demonstrate whether a modalized formula, either fully modalized or partially modalized, is valid, contravalid, or indeterminate.

These additional rules for the width ("W") of brackets are:

Rule WA:

Whenever a bracket for a proposition, P, spans *all* (hence the "A" in "WA") of the rectangle representing the set of all possible worlds, i.e., whenever P is necessarily true, we may add additional brackets for □P, ◊P, and △P each also spanning the entire rectangle. If we wish to add ▽P to the diagram, it will have to be relegated to the external point representing the impossible worlds.

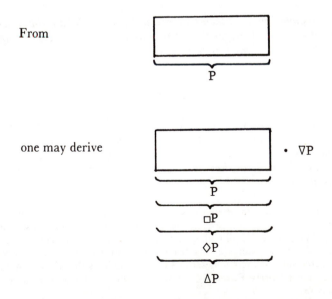

Rule WS:

Whenever a bracket for P spans only part (i.e., *some* but not all) of the rectangle, i.e., whenever P is contingent, we may add additional brackets for ◊P and ▽P each also spanning the entire rectangle. □P and △P will each have to be relegated to the external point.

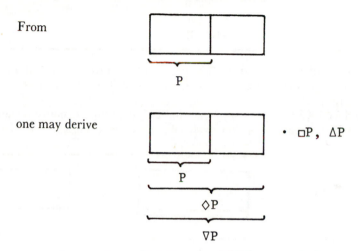

From

one may derive   • □P, △P

Rule WN:

Whenever P spans *none* of the rectangle representing all possible worlds, i.e., whenever P is necessarily false, we may add a bracket for △P spanning the entire rectangle. □P, ◊P, and ▽P will each have to be relegated to the external point.

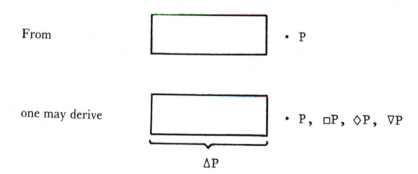

From   • P

one may derive   • P, □P, ◊P, ▽P

Let us see, now, how the addition of these rules facilitates our use of worlds-diagrams in the ascertaining of the validity of modalized formulae.

Applications

Case 1:   Determine the validity of "□P ⊃ ◊P".

Since there is but one sentence-variable type instanced in the formula "□P ⊃ ◊P", we need examine only three worlds-diagrams. They are:

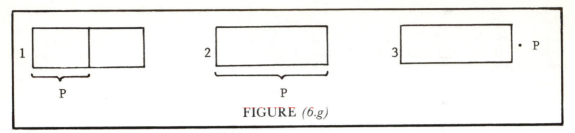

FIGURE (6.g)

Rule WA allows us to place a bracket for □P spanning the entire rectangle in diagram 2. Rule WS allows us to place □P on an external point in diagram 1, and Rule WN allows us to place □P on an external point in diagram 3.

By Rules WA and WS we may place a bracket for ◇P spanning the entire rectangle in diagrams 1 and 2, and by Rule WN we place ◇P on the external point in diagram 3.

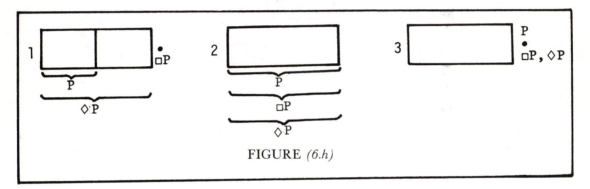

FIGURE (6.h)

Now we are in a position to place □P ⊃ ◇P on our worlds-diagrams. To do this all we need do is remember the rule (from chapter 5) for the placement of material conditionals: represent a material conditional by a bracket spanning all possible worlds except those in which the antecedent of the conditional is true and the consequent false. Immediately we may write

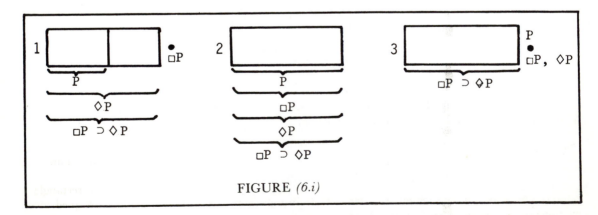

FIGURE (6.i)

By inspection we can see that □P ⊃ ◇P spans all possible worlds in every possible case. Therefore "□P ⊃ ◇P" is *valid:* every possible substitution-instance of this formula expresses a necessary truth.

Case 2:   Determine the validity of "◊P ⊃ □P".

In the previous example we have already placed □P and ◊P on the relevant three worlds-diagrams (see figure *(6.h)*). It remains only to add ◊P ⊃ □P.

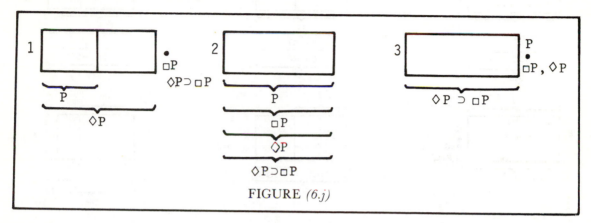

FIGURE *(6.j)*

By inspection we can see that "◊P ⊃ □P" is *not* a valid formula: some of its substitution-instances will express necessary falsehoods (see diagram 1 in figure *(6.j)*) while others will express necessary truths (see diagrams 2 and 3). It is, then, an indeterminate form. (However, as one would expect in the case of a fully modalized formula, none of its substitution-instances can express a contingency.)

Case 3:   Determine whether "(□(P ⊃ Q) · ◊P) ⊃ ◊Q" is valid.

Since there are two sentence-variable types instanced in this formula, we shall have to begin by constructing the fifteen worlds-diagrams required for the examination of the modal relations obtaining between two arbitrarily selected propositions. On each of these we shall have to add a bracket depicting the possible worlds in which P ⊃ Q is true. This we have already done in the previous chapter in figure *(5.i)* (p. 265). In seven of these cases, viz., 1, 3, 4, 6, 8, 9, and 11, the bracket for P ⊃ Q spans the entire rectangle and hence, by Rule WA above, we may add a bracket for □(P ⊃ Q) which also spans the entire rectangle. In all other cases, viz., 2, 5, 7, 10, 12, 13, 14, and 15, by either Rule WS or Rule WN we place □(P ⊃ Q) on the external point.

Next we add a bracket for ◊P. Rules WA and WS allow us to add brackets for ◊P spanning the entire rectangle in diagrams 1, 2, 5, 6, 7, 9, 10, 11, 13, 14, and 15. Only in diagrams 3, 4, and 8 (in accordance with Rule WN) will we place ◊P on the external point.

The placement of these first five formulae on the set of fifteen worlds-diagrams is shown in figure *(6.k)* on p. 354.

Next we are in a position to add □(P ⊃ Q) · ◊P to our diagrams. We recall from chapter 5 that the rule for placing a conjunctive proposition on a worlds-diagram is to have its bracket span just those worlds *common* to the brackets representing its conjuncts. Thus the bracket for □(P ⊃ Q) · ◊P will span the entire rectangle in cases 1, 6, 9, and 11, and will be relegated to the external point in all other cases, viz., 2, 3, 4, 5, 7, 8, 10, 12, 13, 14, and 15.

Now we add the bracket for ◊Q. By WA and WS, this bracket will span the entire rectangle in cases 1, 3, 5, 6, 8, 9, 10, 11, 12, 13, 14, and 15. In accordance with WN, it will be assigned to the external point in cases 2, 4, and 7.

Finally we are in a position to add a bracket for (□(P ⊃ Q) · ◊P) ⊃◊Q to each of our diagrams by invoking the rule for placing material conditionals on a worlds-diagram. The completed figure appears on p. 355.

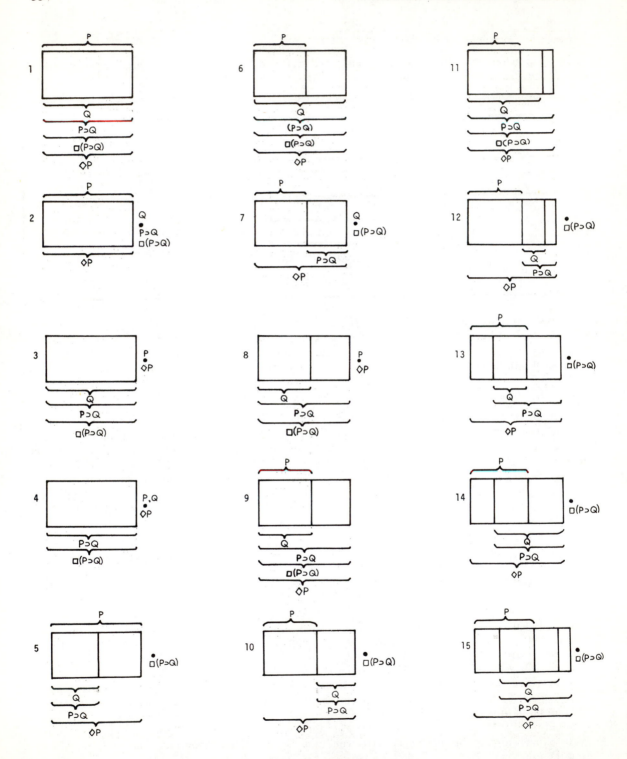

FIGURE *(6.k)*

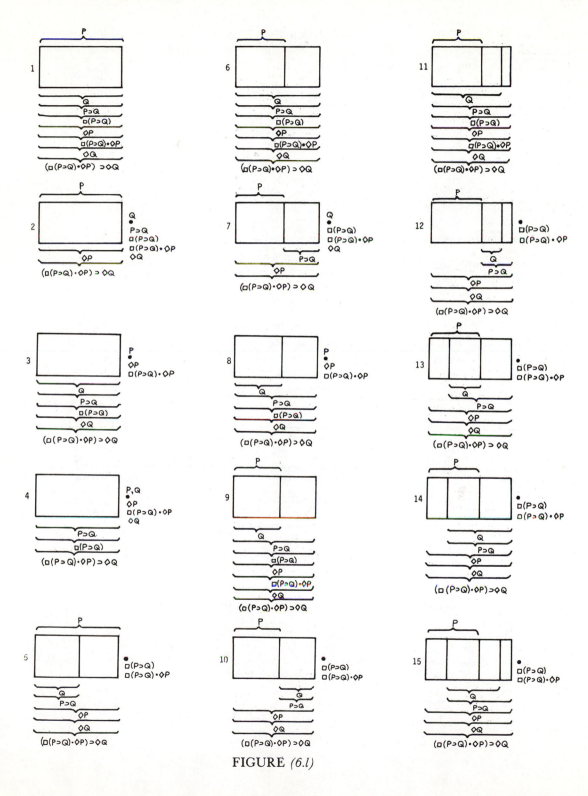

FIGURE *(6.l)*

On examining each of the 15 worlds-diagrams we find that in every case the bracket for $(\square(P \supset Q) \cdot \Diamond P) \supset \Diamond Q$ spans the entire rectangle. This shows that $(\square(P \supset Q) \cdot \Diamond P) \supset \Diamond Q$ is valid, i.e., every possible instantiation of it is necessarily true.

The validity of the axioms of S5.

We have spoken in chapter 4 of the modal system S5. Let us now use the methods just established to test the validity of its axioms. One axiomatization of S5 (that provided by Gödel) consists of any set of axioms of Truth-functional Propositional Logic[12] subjoined to the following three:

(A1) $\square P \supset P$

(A2) $\square(P \supset Q) \supset (\square P \supset \square Q)$

(A3) $\sim\square P \supset \square \sim \square P$

It is a trivial matter (using truth-tables, for example) to demonstrate the validity (tautologousness) of any axiom-set for Truth-functional Propositional Logic. It remains only to determine the validity of (A1)–(A3).

Axiom 1: $\square P \supset P$

Since there is only one sentence-variable type instanced in this formula, we need examine only three worlds-diagrams. It is a simple matter, invoking only the rules WA, WS, and WN, and the rule for placing material conditionals on worlds-diagrams to add brackets first for $\square P$ and then for $\square P \supset P$.

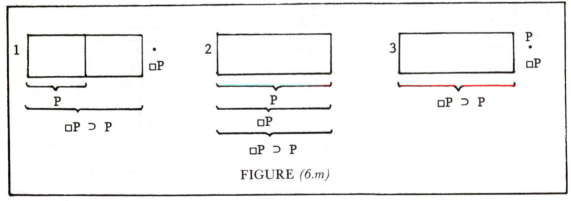

FIGURE *(6.m)*

By inspection one can see that every possible instantiation of $\square P \supset P$ is necessarily true. Hence $\square P \supset P$ is valid.

12. For example, the following axioms, due to Whitehead and Russell, are sufficient (along with their rules of inference) to generate every valid wff of Truth-functional Propositional Logic.

(PC1) $(P \lor P) \supset P$

(PC2) $Q \supset (P \lor Q)$

(PC3) $(P \lor Q) \supset (Q \lor P)$

(PC4) $(Q \supset R) \supset ([P \lor Q] \supset [P \lor R])$

Axiom 2: $\square (P \supset Q) \supset (\square P \supset \square Q)$

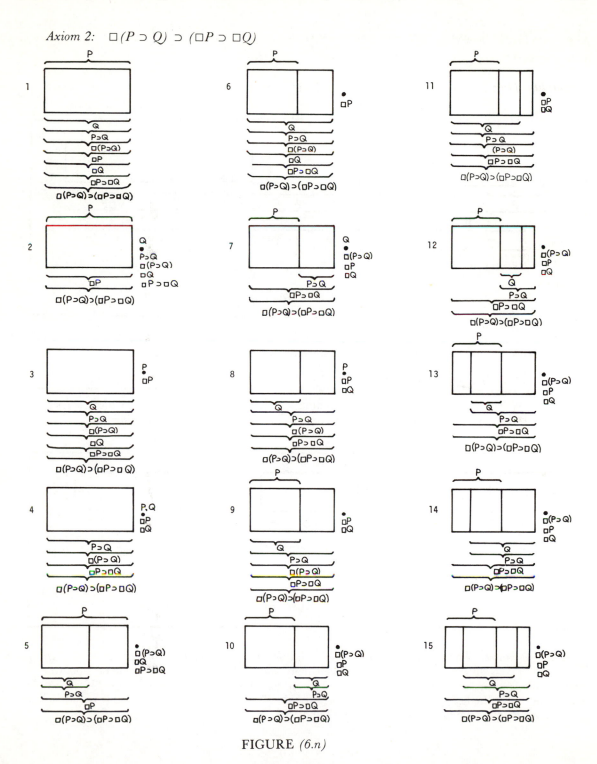

FIGURE *(6.n)*

Figure *(6.n)* reveals, as expected, that Axiom 2 is valid.

Axiom 3: $\sim \Box P \supset \Box \sim \Box P$

As with Axiom 1, only three worlds-diagrams need be considered.

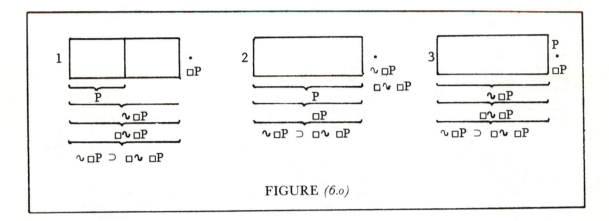

FIGURE *(6.o)*

Just as was the case in testing Axioms 1 and 2, we find that Axiom 3 is also valid.

The nonvalidity of the axiom set for S6

The modal system S6 can be obtained by subjoining a certain subset of the theses of S5 to the single axiom, $\Diamond\Diamond$P. Let us examine the validity of this axiom. Immediately we may write down:

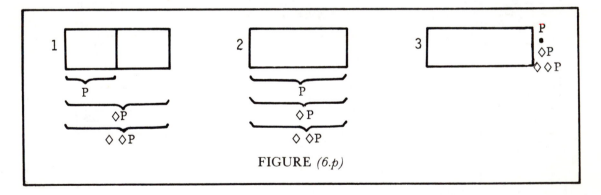

FIGURE *(6.p)*

Here we can see that the axiom $\Diamond\Diamond$P is *not* valid on that interpretation of "$\Box$" and "$\Diamond$" which interprets "$\Box$" as "it is true in all possible worlds that" and "$\Diamond$" as "it is true in some possible worlds that". This is not to deny that on some *alternative* interpretation (e.g., reading "$\Diamond$" as "it is possibly known by God whether", or "it is possibly believed that"), this formula may be valid. (And similar conclusions hold for the distinctive axioms of S7 and S8.)

EXERCISES

Use worlds-diagrams to determine of each of the formulae 1 through 5 whether it is valid, contravalid, or indeterminate.

If a formula contains a dyadic modal operator, first find a formally equivalent formula (using the methods of section 2) containing no modal operators other than "◊" and/or "□".

1. $P \supset \Box P$

2. $\Box (P \supset Q) \supset (P \supset \Box Q)$ *[the so-called 'modal fallacy']*

3. $(\Diamond P \cdot \Diamond Q) \supset (P \circ Q)$

4. $\Diamond (P \cdot Q) \supset (\Diamond P \cdot \Diamond Q)$

5. $(P \supset Q) \supset (P \rightarrow Q)$

6.   *Consider the S6 axiom, $\Diamond \Diamond P$. A substitution-instance of this axiom is $\Diamond \Diamond (P \cdot \sim P)$, which is the negation of $\sim \Diamond \Diamond (P \cdot \sim P)$. Use worlds-diagrams to show that this latter wff is S5-valid.*

   (Note that if $\Diamond \Diamond P$ were, contrary to fact, S5-valid, then it would be possible to derive in S5 both $\Diamond \Diamond (P \cdot \sim P)$ and its negation $\sim \Diamond \Diamond (P \cdot \sim P)$, and thus S5, contrary to fact, would be inconsistent.)

9.   A SHORTCUT FORMAL METHOD FOR DETERMINING THE VALIDITY OF MODALIZED FORMULAE: Modal reductios[13]

The method of utilizing worlds-diagrams, as outlined in the previous section, is *effective*: by the mechanical application of its rules, one can determine the validity of *any* well-formed modalized formula. In this regard it is the analog of truth-table techniques in Truth-functional Propositional Logic. And like truth-table techniques, it suffers from the fault of being excessively burdensome. Indeed it is a more aggravated case. In truth-functional logic, in cases where there is only one sentence-type instanced in a formula, we require a 2-row truth-table; two sentence-types, a 4-row table; 3 sentence-types, an 8-row table; and 4 sentence-types, a 16-row table. But when we come to examine modalized formulae, the complexity explodes. For if we wish to ascertain the validity of a modalized formula instancing one sentence-type, we require 3 worlds-diagrams; 2 sentence-types, 15 worlds-diagrams; 3 sentence-types, 255 worlds-diagrams; and 4 sentence-types, 65,535. Small wonder, then, that logicians have sought other methods to ascertain the validity of modalized formulae.

One of these methods may be regarded as the modal version of the Reductio Ad Absurdum method we have already examined. Like the earlier Reductio method, it works well for some cases, allowing us

---

13. The general method described in this section is the product of many years' work by many persons, some heralded and some not. Among its pioneers must be numbered Beth, Hintikka, and Kripke. Our own method owes much to some unpublished notes of M.K. Rennie. Stylistic variants, closely resembling ours, are to be found in M.K. Rennie, "On Postulates for Temporal Order", in *The Monist* (July 1969) pp. 457–468, and in G.E. Hughes and M.J. Cresswell, *Introduction to Modal Logic*, London, Methuen & Co. Ltd., 1968.

to ascertain the validity of some formulae very easily and rapidly; but for some other cases it works poorly and cumbersomely, at best. Nonetheless, it is so much easier to use in certain instances than is the effective method of worlds-diagrams, that it is useful to pursue it, in spite of its shortcomings.

The strategy of Reductio methods has already been described. One makes an initial assignment to a formula and then looks to see what its consequences are: whether in any possible world that assignment leads to assigning both truth and falsity to one proposition. If it does, then the initial assignment was an impossible one.

To construct the method we need to call upon all those earlier rules we used for making assignments to the components of truth-functional sentences on the basis of assignments having been made to the compound sentences themselves, e.g., if "T" is assigned to "P · Q", then "T" should be assigned to "P" and "T" should be assigned to "Q"; if "F" is assigned to "P ⊃ Q", then "T" should be assigned to "P" and "F" to "Q"; etc.

Since all dyadic modal operators can be 'defined away' in terms of the monadic modal operators, "◊" and "□" (see section 2, this chapter), it will suffice to stipulate rules for handling formulae modalized by just these two operators.

We require rules which tell us how to make assignments to the components of modalized formulae on the basis of assignments having been made to the modalized formulae themselves. For example, suppose the formula "□P" has been assigned "T"; what, then, shall we assign to "P"? There are in all, four cases. Let us examine the appropriate rule in each case. We shall call the rules, "RA-rules", where the "RA" stands for "Reduction to Absurdity".

Rule RA1

If □P is true in W_n, then P is true in W_n and in all other possible worlds as well. Thus we assign "T" to "P" in W_n, and record the fact that this latter assignment is to persist throughout all other possible worlds we examine as well, both those previously examined and those yet to be. To show this, we write immediately below this assignment, the symbol,

$$\text{"T}\updownarrow\text{"}$$

The double-stroke arrow indicates that this assignment is to persist throughout *all* possible worlds. Thus RA1 may be stated this way:

RA1:   *If in W_n we have, "□P", then we may write, "□P".*
            T   TT⟰

Rule RA2

If □P is false in W_n, then P is false in some possible world (it need not be W_n, however.) Given just the information that □P is false in W_n, the truth-value of P is indeterminate in W_n. (This is not to say, however, that some other, additional information might not determine P's truth-value in W_n.) In sum, Rule RA2 may be stated this way:

RA2:   *If in W_n we have, "□P", then we may write, "□P".*
            F   F
                                                                     ⬇F

The 'weak' arrow under "P" indicates that the assignment "F" is to be made in at least one possible world to be examined subsequently. Note that no assignment has been made in W_n itself to "P" and we do not assign "F" to P in a world previously examined. Nothing sanctions that, since we know *only* that P is false in *some* world.

Rule RA3

If ◇P is true in W_n, then P is true in some possible world (it need not be W_n itself.)

RA3:   *If in W_n we have, "◇P", then we may write, "◇P"*
                            T   T
                                                             $\overline{|T}$

Rule RA4

If ◇P is false in W_n, then P is false in W_n and in all other possible worlds as well.

RA4:   *If in W_n we have, "◇P", then we may write, "◇P".*
                        F $F\underline{F}\mathord{\updownarrow}$

Example 1:   *Is the formula "□ (P ⊃ ◇P)" valid?*

We begin by assigning "F" to this formula in possible world W_1.

$$\square\ (P\ \supset\ \Diamond P)$$

$$W_1 \left\{ \begin{array}{ccc} F & & \\ & \overline{|F} & \\ & & \\ \end{array} \right.$$

                  (1)   (2)

The assignment at step (2) was made in accordance with RA2. Step (2) is as far as we can go in W_1: no further assignments are determined in W_1. But one assignment *is* determined for some *other* possible world; for we have written down " $\overline{|F}$ " at step (2). So let us now examine such a world. We will call it "W_2".

$$\square\ (P\ \supset\ \Diamond\ \ \ P)$$

$$W_1 \left\{ \begin{array}{cccc} F & & & F \\ & \overline{|F} & & \\ \end{array} \right.$$

$$W_2 \left\{ \begin{array}{cccc} ① & F & F & Ⓕ\mathord{\updownarrow} \\ & & & \\ & & & \\ \end{array} \right.$$

            (2)   (1) (2)   (3)

The assignments at step (2) were made in accordance with the truth-functional rule for material conditionals. The assignments at step (3) [in W_1 and in W_2] were made in accord with Rule RA4. At this point we discover an inconsistent assignment in W_2: "P" has been assigned both "T" (at step (2)) and "F" (at step (3)). Thus the initial assignment of "F" to "□(P ⊃ ◇P)" is an impossible one, and we may validly conclude that this formula is *valid*.

Example 2:   Is the formula "$[(P \to Q) \cdot \Box P] \to \Box Q$" valid?

The first step must here consist of replacing the two occurrences of dyadic modal operators with monadic modal operators. This is easily done and we may rewrite the formula this way:

$$\text{"}\Box\,([\,\Box\,(P \supset Q) \cdot \Box P\,] \supset \Box Q)\text{"}$$

Just as in Example 1, not a great deal is revealed about this formula in W_1:

$$W_1 \left\{ \begin{array}{l} \quad \Box \;\; (\;[\;\Box\;(P \supset Q)\; \cdot\; \Box P\;]\; \supset\; \Box\; Q) \\[6pt] \quad\; F \\[12pt] \qquad\qquad\qquad\qquad\qquad\qquad\qquad \text{𝕋F} \\[6pt] \quad (1) \qquad\qquad\qquad\qquad (2) \end{array} \right.$$

We turn, then, to W_2.

$$\begin{array}{l} W_1 \left\{ \begin{array}{l} \Box \;\;(\;[\;\Box\;\;(P\;\; \supset\;\; Q)\;\; \cdot\;\; \Box\; P\;]\;\; \supset\;\; \Box\;\; Q) \\[4pt] F \qquad\qquad\quad T \qquad\qquad\quad T \\[4pt] \qquad\qquad\qquad\qquad\qquad\qquad\quad \text{𝕋F} \end{array} \right. \\[30pt] \rule{9cm}{0.4pt} \\[4pt] W_2 \left\{ \begin{array}{l} \quad T\;\; T\;\; T\!\!\uparrow\! T \quad T\;\; T\;\; T\!\!\uparrow\quad F\;\; F \\[4pt] \qquad\qquad\;\;\downarrow \qquad\qquad\qquad\;\downarrow \\[4pt] \qquad\qquad\qquad\qquad\qquad\qquad\qquad\qquad \text{𝕋F} \\[6pt] \quad (3)\;\;\; (5)\;\;\; (4)\dagger\; (6)\quad (2)\;\; (3)\;\; (4)\dagger\;\; (1)\;\; (2)\;\; (3)\text{*} \end{array} \right. \end{array}$$

       *   in accord with Rule RA2   †   in accord with Rule RA1

No inconsistent assignment occurs in W_2, nor was one necessitated in W_1 by the upward pointing arrows at step (4); but there are conditions in W_2 laid down for some subsequent world. In particular, we have not yet examined the consequences of having written " 𝕋F " under the last occurrence of "Q" in the formula. Let us now turn to a possible world in which Q is false:

$$\begin{array}{l} W_1 \left\{ \begin{array}{l} \quad \Box \;\;(\;[\;\Box\;(P\;\; (\;P\;\; \supset\;\; Q)\;\; \cdot\;\; \Box\;\; P\;]\;\; \supset\;\; \Box\;\; Q\;) \\[4pt] \;F \qquad\qquad\quad T \qquad\qquad\;\;\; T \\[4pt] \qquad\qquad\qquad\qquad\qquad\qquad\quad \text{𝕋F} \end{array} \right. \\[30pt] \rule{9cm}{0.4pt} \\[4pt] W_2 \left\{ \begin{array}{l} \quad T\;\; T\;\; T\!\!\uparrow\! T \quad T\;\; T\;\; T\!\!\uparrow\quad F\;\; F \\[4pt] \qquad\qquad\;\;\downarrow \qquad\qquad\qquad\;\downarrow \\[4pt] \qquad\qquad\qquad\qquad\qquad\qquad\qquad\qquad \text{𝕋F} \end{array} \right. \\[30pt] \rule{9cm}{0.4pt} \\[4pt] W_3 \left\{ \begin{array}{l} \qquad\quad T\;\; T\;\; ⓉT \qquad\qquad T \qquad\qquad\qquad Ⓕ \\[6pt] \qquad\quad (3)\;(2)\;\; (4)\text{*}\qquad\qquad (2) \qquad\qquad\qquad (1) \end{array} \right. \end{array}$$

      *   "T" has been assigned to "$(P \supset Q)$" and to "P", hence "T" must be assigned
         to "Q". But "Q" has already been assigned "F" in step (1).

In W_3 an inconsistent assignment is necessitated for "Q". Hence we may validly infer that the initial assignment of "F" to the formula represents an impossible assignment, and thus may infer that the formula is *valid*.

Example 3: Is the formula "$\Diamond P \to P$" valid?

Again we begin by replacing the dyadic operator with a monadic one: "$\Box(\Diamond P \supset P)$". The assignments in W_1 are straightforward.

$$\Box \quad (\Diamond P \quad \supset \quad P)$$

$$W_1 \left\{ \quad F \right.$$

$$\overline{T}F$$

We turn, next, to W_2.

$$\Box \quad (\quad \Diamond \quad P \quad \supset \quad P \quad)$$

$$W_1 \left\{ \quad F \right.$$

$$\overline{T}F$$

$$W_2 \left\{ \qquad T \quad F^* \quad F \quad F \right.$$

$$\overline{T}T\dagger$$

$$(2) \quad (3) \quad (1) \quad (2)$$

    *   required by our having assigned "F" to "P" in step (2)
    †   required by our having assigned "T" to "$\Diamond P$" in step (2) [Rule RA3.]

At this point all assignments have been made in W_2 and no inconsistent assignments have been made. But a condition has been laid down in W_2 for some other possible world: the " $\overline{T}T$ " which occurs under the first occurrence of "P" requires that we examine a possible world in which "P" is assigned "T". We call that world "W_3".

$$\Box \quad (\quad \Diamond \quad P \quad \supset \quad P \quad)$$

$$W_1 \left\{ \quad F \right.$$

$$\overline{T}F$$

$$W_2 \left\{ \qquad T \quad F \quad F \quad F \right.$$

$$\overline{T}T$$

$$W_3 \left\{ \qquad T \quad T \quad T \quad T \right.$$

$$(3) \quad (1) \quad (4) \quad (2)$$

In W_3 no inconsistent assignment has been necessitated. Moreover, in W_3, all earlier downward pointing arrows have been satisfied or 'discharged'. Our test is at its end and no inconsistent assignment has emerged. We may validly infer, then, that the initial assignment of "F" to the formula does not represent an impossible assignment. The formula, thus, is *not* valid. However, it remains an open question whether it is contravalid or indeterminate. To choose between these two alternatives we would have to examine the consequences of assigning "T" to the formula. If that assignment leads to a subsequent inconsistent assignment, then the formula is contravalid; if it does not lead to a subsequent inconsistent assignment, the formula is indeterminate.

Example 4:   Is the formula "$(\Box P \vee \Box Q) \supset \Box (P \vee Q)$" valid?

$$(\Box P \ \vee \ \Box Q) \ \supset \ \Box (P \ \vee \ Q)$$

$$W_1 \left\{ \begin{array}{ccccc} & T & & F\ F & \\ & & & & \underline{T}F \\ & (2) & & (1)\ (2) & (3) \end{array} \right.$$

In W_1 we have three choice points: having assigned "T" to "$\Box P \vee \Box Q$" we can assign "T" to "$\Box P$" and "T" to "$\Box Q$"; "T" to "$\Box P$" and "F" to "$\Box Q$"; or "F" to "$\Box P$" and "T" to "$\Box Q$". Only if *each* of these assignments leads to an inconsistent assignment in some world or other can we validly infer that the formula is valid. At this point, other methods, e.g., worlds-diagrams, seem more attractive as a means to test this particular formula.[14]

EXERCISES

Part A

Using the method of Modal Reductio, determine which of the following formulae are valid.

1. $\Box (P \vee \sim P)$

2. $\Box (P \vee Q)$

3. $\Diamond (P \cdot \sim P)$

4. $(P \supset Q) \supset (P \rightarrow Q)$

5. $(P \supset Q) \rightarrow (P \supset Q)$

6. $(P \supset Q) \rightarrow (P \rightarrow Q)$

7. $(P \rightarrow Q) \supset (P \supset Q)$

8. $(P \rightarrow Q) \supset (P \rightarrow Q)$

9. $(P \rightarrow Q) \rightarrow (P \supset Q)$

10. $(P \rightarrow Q) \rightarrow (P \rightarrow Q)$

11. $\sim P \rightarrow \sim \Diamond P$

12. $\Box P \rightarrow P$

13. $[(P \rightarrow Q) \cdot \sim \Diamond Q] \rightarrow \sim \Diamond P$

14. $[(P \rightarrow Q) \cdot \sim \Diamond P] \rightarrow \sim \Diamond Q$

15. $\sim \Diamond P \rightarrow (P \rightarrow Q)$

16. $\Box P \rightarrow (Q \rightarrow P)$

14. Natural deduction techniques for S5 (as well as for the systems T and S4) are to be found in Hughes and Cresswell, *An Introduction to Modal Logic*, pp. 331 – 334.

17. $\square \lozenge P \rightarrow \lozenge P$

18. $\lozenge \square P \rightarrow \square P$

19. $\square P \rightarrow \square \square P$

20. $\sim \lozenge P \rightarrow (P \phi Q)$

21. $(\lozenge P \cdot \lozenge Q) \rightarrow \lozenge (P \cdot Q)$

22. $(\square P \cdot \square Q) \rightarrow \square (P \cdot Q)$

23. $\square (P \vee Q) \rightarrow (\square P \vee \square Q)$

24. $(P \rightarrow Q) \rightarrow (P \circ Q)$

25. $\triangle \lozenge P$

Part B

26. *Determine whether the formula in* Example 3 *is contravalid or indeterminate.*

27. *Construct a Modal Reductio which proves that the Augmentation Principle (viz.* $(P \rightarrow Q) \rightarrow [(P \cdot R) \rightarrow Q]$ *) cited in chapter 4, section 5, is valid.*

28. *Construct a Modal Reductio which proves that the Collapse Principle (viz.,* $(P \rightarrow Q) \rightarrow [(P \cdot Q) \leftrightarrow P]$ *) cited in chapter 4, section 5, is valid. Note that there is a two-pronged branch-point in this reductio. It will be necessary to examine both branches.*

10. THE NUMBER OF FORMALLY NON-EQUIVALENT SENTENCE-FORMS CONSTRUCTIBLE ON N SENTENCE-VARIABLES[15]

Two sentence-forms will be said to be formally equivalent if and only if, for any uniform substitution of constants for the variables therein, there result two sentences which express logically equivalent propositions. Sentence-forms which are not formally equivalent are said to be formally non-equivalent.[16] For example, according to these definitions, the two sentence-forms, "P $\vee \sim$ P" and "P $\supset$ P", are formally equivalent, while the two sentence forms, "P" and "P $\vee \sim$ P", are formally non-equivalent.

The formation rules of propositional logics allow us to concatenate symbols into strings of indefinite length. We may have a wff containing as few as one symbol (e.g., "P" standing alone) or as many as a trillion or more. Clearly some of these strings will be formally equivalent to others and will be formally non-equivalent to all the remaining ones. The question arises whether the number of distinct formal equivalence-sets of sentence-forms is finite or infinite. As we shall now see, the answer to this question depends on the number of sentence-variables one has in one's symbolic language.

Let us begin with the simplest case, that in which we construct sentence-forms, α, in which there appear sentence-variable tokens of one and only one sentence-variable type. These would include such wffs as

15. Instructors may find that the material in this section is best reserved for their mathematically more proficient students.

16. Note that equivalence tout court (or logical equivalence or 'strict' equivalence) is a property of propositions. *Formal* equivalence is a property of sentence-forms.

"P"

"P ⊃ (P ∨ ∼ P)"

"▽P · P"

"□P ⊃ P"

Into how many distinct formal equivalence-classes may this (in principle) infinite list be subdivided? Interestingly, the answer is: a mere 16. Let us see how we arrive at this figure.

When we wish to put a formula, α, on a set of worlds-diagrams, that formula must be placed on each rectangle so that it spans none of its segments, some but not all of them, or all of them. This fact immediately sets an upper limit to the number of formally non-equivalent formulae which may be depicted on a set of worlds-diagrams: this maximum number is simply the number of ways one can distribute brackets over the total number of segments in the set of worlds-diagrams.

In the case of one sentence-variable type (as we saw in chapter 1) there are three worlds-diagrams comprising a total of four segments. The number of ways that brackets may be distributed over four segments is 2^4, i.e., 16. Each of these ways is shown below and some members from the equivalence-class defined by that particular distribution of brackets are written alongside.

1   α = P ∨ ∼P; □(P ⊃ P); □P ⊃ P; etc.

2   α = ∼□P; ▽P ∨ □∼P; etc.

3   α = □P ∨ ∼P; ∼(▽P · P); etc.

4   α = ∼P; (▽P · ∼P) ∨ (□ ∼P); etc.

5   α = P ∨ □ ∼P; ∼ (▽P · ∼P); etc.

6   α = (▽P · P) ∨ □∼P; etc.

7   α = ∆P; (∆P · P) ∨ (∆P · ∼P); etc.

8   α = □ ∼P; ∼P · ∼▽P; etc.

9   α = ◇P; P ∨ (▽P · ∼P); etc.

10   α = ▽P; ◇P · ◇∼P; etc.

11   α = □P ∨ (▽P · ∼P); etc.

12   α = ▽P · ∼ P; ∼(◇P ⊃P); etc.

13   α = P; □P ∨ P; etc.

14   α = ▽P · P; etc.

15   α = □P; ∆P · P; etc.

16   α = P · ∼P; ∼□(P ⊃ P); (P · ∼ P) · ◇P; etc.

FIGURE (6.q)

The rules which have been given in the course of the preceding and present chapters for depicting formulae on worlds-diagrams allow us to generate a set of brackets for any arbitrarily chosen wff in truth-functional and modal propositional logic. But we have not given any rules for passing the other way. How can one generate an appropriate formula, as has obviously been done in figure *(6.q)*, to match any arbitrarily drawn set of brackets on a set of worlds-diagrams? Here we are faced with a problem, for the number of distinct ways of distributing brackets is finite (in this particular case, sixteen), while the number of distinct formally non-equivalent formulae corresponding to each of these sets of brackets is infinite. While various rules can be given for the generation of at least *some* formula for each set of brackets, no set of rules can generate all the formulae, nor is any simple set of rules known to us which in each case generates the *shortest* formula appropriate for a given set of brackets. In the case of figure *(6.q)* the formulae appearing in the right-hand column were not generated by the application of an effective method, but were instead found by insight, understanding, and trial and error — in short, by a 'feel' for the material.[17]

Each of the rows of figure *(6.q)* defines a class of formally equivalent sentence-forms; these classes are mutually exclusive of one another and are jointly exhaustive of the entire class of sentence-forms which contain only one sentence-variable type. Each formula occurring in the right-hand column of figure *(6.q)* is formally equivalent to every other formula occurring in the same row, and is formally non-equivalent to each formula occurring in each of the other rows. Any wff, α, which contains variables of only one type, and which does not occur explicitly on figure *(6.q)*, can be placed in one and only one row of that figure. Consider, for example, the formula "P ⊃ □P". Depicting this formula on a set of worlds-diagrams gives us:

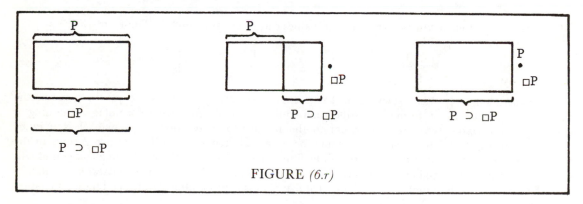

FIGURE *(6.r)*

By inspection, we can see that the brackets for "P ⊃ □P" in figure *(6.r)* are distributed exactly as are the brackets in row 3 of figure *(6.q)*. This tells us immediately that the formula "P ⊃ □P" and the formulae occurring on row 3 of figure *(6.q)*, viz., "□P ∨ ∼P" and "∼(∇P · P)", are formally equivalent. Similarly, any other wff, α, containing propositional variables of only one type, must prove to be a member of exactly one of the sixteen equivalence-classes defined on figure *(6.q)*.

Glancing down the right-hand column of figure *(6.q)*, we notice that four rows, viz., 1, 4, 13, and 16, contain wffs which are unmodalized (i.e., are formulae of truth-functional logic). The question arises: Are these all the rows which contain at least one unmodalized formula? Do any of the other

---

17. A great deal, if not indeed the bulk, of advanced work in both logic and mathematics is precisely of this sort in that it demands insight and creativity and is not attainable by the rote following of recipes. The generation of proofs, the finding of axiom sets, the solving of partial differential equations, etc. etc., lie, like most of logic and mathematics, in the realm of creativity, not in the realm of assembly-line procedures. Textbooks — since they are usually geared to displaying solved problems and effective procedures — tend to obscure this point.

classes, defined by the remaining 12 rows, contain any unmodalized formulae? The answer is: No. That there are exactly four classes of formally non-equivalent truth-functional formulae containing one propositional variable follows immediately from the fact that the truth-table for any unmodalized formula, μ, containing one propositional variable-type, contains exactly two rows.

"μ" is any unmodalized wff containing one propositional variable type, "P".

FIGURE *(6.s)*

There are exactly four distinct ways that truth-values can be assigned to "μ". These are

T	F	T	F
T	T	F	F

These assignments represent rows 1, 4, 13, and 16 respectively in figure *(6.q)*. In general, the number, u, of classes of formally distinct non-equivalent truth-functional formulae containing n propositional variable types will be equal to the number of ways that "T"s and "F"s may be distributed in the last column of a truth-table for n variable-types. Thus if there are 2 rows in the truth-table (i.e., one variable-type), there will be four ways to assign "T" and "F" to a compound wff, α; if 4 rows (i.e., two variable-types), then 16 ways; etc. In short, the number of classes, u, is equal to 2^m, where m equals the number of rows in a truth-table for n propositional-variable types. In chapter 5, m was defined equal to 2^n; thus $u = 2^{2^n}$.

Eight rows (viz., 1, 2, 7, 8, 9, 10, 15, and 16) of figure *(6.q)* contain wffs which are fully modalized. Looking at the configurations of brackets on each of these rows, it is easy to see what property it is on the worlds-diagrams by virtue of which a formula is itself (or is formally equivalent to) a formula which is wholly modalized: the brackets for such a formula will, on each rectangle in a set of worlds-diagrams, span all or none of that rectangle. (This fact follows from the rules WA, WS, and WN. [See section 8.]) That fully modalized formulae map onto worlds-diagrams in this fashion allows us immediately to calculate the maximum number of distinct classes of fully modalized formulae: this number is simply the maximum number of ways brackets may be distributed so that on each rectangle in a set of worlds-diagrams the bracket spans all or none of that rectangle. Letting "k" equal the number of rectangles in a set of worlds-diagrams, the maximum number of ways of distributing brackets in this fashion is, simply, 2^k. Of this number, two configurations are found to be appropriate for two truth-functional formulae as well: the case where the brackets span every rectangle in the set (corresponding to "$P \vee \sim P$"); and the case where the brackets span no rectangle in the set (corresponding to "$P \cdot \sim P$"). Thus the number of distinct classes, f, of formally equivalent wffs which contain at least one wholly modalized formula and no unmodalized formulae is $2^k - 2$.

The total number of distinct classes, t, of formally equivalent formulae — that is, the number of distinct classes without regard being paid to whether those classes contain any unmodalized or any fully modalized, formulae — is equal to the maximum number of ways that brackets may be distributed over the total number of *segments* occurring in a set of worlds-diagrams. In a set of 3 diagrams, there are 4 segments; in a set of 15 worlds-diagrams, there are 32 segments; in a set of 255 worlds-diagrams, there are 1024 segments. Thus the total number of distinct classes, t, of formally equivalent sentence-forms constructible on one sentence-variable type is 2^4 (i.e., 16, as we have already seen); on two sentence-variable types, 2^{32} (i.e., 4,294,967,296); and on three sentence-variable types, 2^{1024}.

We may generalize on these results. If we let n = number of sentence-variable types, we have

Total number of
worlds-diagrams $k = 2^{2^n} - 1$ [See chapter 1, p. 57]

Total number of segments in
a set of k worlds-diagrams[18] $s = 2^{2^n} \times 2^{n-1}$

Total number of ways
which brackets may be
distributed over s segments $t = 2^s$

Total number of distinct
classes of formally equivalent sentence-forms such
that the class contains at
least one unmodalized
formula (truth-functional
formulae) $u = 2^{2^n}$ [See chapter 5, p. 272; $u = 2^m$]

Total number of distinct
classes of formally equivalent sentence-forms such
that no member of the class
is unmodalized and at least
one member is fully
modalized $f = 2^k - 2$

The total number of formally distinct classes of sentence-forms constructible on n sentence-variables is t. Of this number t, a certain number, viz., u, of these classes contain at least one unmodalized formula, and a different number, f, of these classes contain at least one wholly modalized formula. For every value of n, the sum of u and f is smaller than t. This means that for every value of n, there must exist a number of distinct classes, p $(= t - u - f)$, which contain neither an unmodalized formula nor a wholly modalized formula, i.e., which contain *only* partially modalized formulae. As n increases, this number, p, approaches closer and closer to t. What this means is that by far the greater number of classes of formally equivalent wffs are classes whose members are all partially modalized, and hence are classes whose members are formally indeterminate, i.e., neither valid nor contravalid formulae.

We may see some of these results more clearly by actually calculating these various parameters for the first few values of n:

---

18. The derivation for the formula for s is not given here. Mathematically adept students are invited to try to derive it themselves.

n Sentence-variable types	k Worlds-diagrams	s Total segments	u Truth-Functional formulae	f Fully modalized formulae	p Partially modalized formulae	t Formally distinct formulae
1	3	4	4	6	6	16
2	15	32	16	32,766	4,294,934,514	4,294,967,296*
3	255	1,024	256	$2^{255}-2$	$\approx 2^{1024}$	2^{1024}
4	65,535	524,288	65,536	$2^{65,535}-2$	$\approx 2^{524,288}$	$2^{524,288}$
5	etc.					

FIGURE *(6.t)*

By the time we have reached sentence-forms containing as few as four sentence-variable types we can construct (in principle, if not in fact,) $2^{524,288}$ formally non-equivalent sentence-forms. When we pass on to five, six, and seven variables, the numbers become so large as to beggar the imagination.

EXERCISE

How many of the rows of figure (6.q) *represent classes of formally equivalent* valid *formulae?*

11.   LOOKING BEYOND MODAL LOGIC TO INDUCTIVE LOGIC

Modal logic, as presently conceived, concerns itself with those modal attributes which can be explicated in terms of the concepts: (1) *being true (false) in* all *possible worlds;* (2) *being true (false) in* no *possible worlds;* and (3) *being true (false) in* some *possible worlds.*

Inductive logic tries to refine the latter of these three concepts. For intuitively we have the idea that the notion of "some possible worlds" admits of further elaboration: that there is some sense of "size" which allows us to say, of some pairs of contingent propositions — each of which is true in some but not all possible worlds — that one is true in a set of possible worlds which is larger in 'size' than the set of possible worlds in which the other is true. For example, we have a natural disposition to say that the set of possible worlds in which it is true that today is Tuesday is greater in 'size' than the set of possible worlds in which it is true that today is the second Tuesday in November.

---

* Gerald Massey, in his book, *Understanding Symbolic Logic* (New York, Harper & Row, 1970, pp. 188 – 190), derives through matrix methods this same number as the total number of formally non-equivalent formulae containing propositional variables of two types. He, like the present authors, remarks in effect that 16 of these formulae are formally equivalent to truth-functional formulae. But he, unlike the present authors, does not further subdivide the remaining class into those subclasses in which every member is a partially modalized formula, and those in which at least one member is not partially modalized, i.e., in which at least one member is a fully modalized formula.

The cardinality of a class and other concepts of class size

Our first inclination probably would be to identify this notion of 'size' with the number of members (i.e., possible worlds) in each class, with what mathematicians call the "cardinality" of the class. But this simple notion won't do. It comes to grief on the fact that contingent propositions may be true, not in finite classes of possible worlds, but in infinite classes. Consider, for example, the two propositions, (a) that today is Tuesday, and (b) that today is Tuesday or Wednesday. Intuitively we might feel inclined to say that the former is true in a *fewer* number of possible worlds than the latter. But we are barred from saying this. Each of these propositions is true in an infinite number of possible worlds and moreover, even though the former is true in a proper subset of the latter, the two sets have the *same* cardinality.[19]

If the requisite sense of the 'size' of a class cannot, then, for present purposes, be identified with the cardinality of the class, with what property *can* it be identified? This is no easy question, and one which has no obvious answer. Many solutions have suggested themselves to researchers in inductive logic.

In certain ways the problem is reminiscent of a problem in geometry. In geometry, we want to be able to say of two lines, for example, that they differ in 'size' even though (of necessity) each of the two lines contains exactly the same number of points. Happily, geometers have sought and found ways which allow us to do just this; to invoke a notion of the 'length' of a line which does *not* depend on the number of points in that line.[20]

The goal in inductive logic is to define a measure which stands to an infinite set of possible worlds much as the notion of length stands to the set of points which comprise a line: two lines containing the same number of points may yet differ in length (size). Similarly we should like to find a way to say that two sets of possible worlds each containing an infinite number of worlds may yet differ in "size". As just one example of how this measure might be constructed consider the following. The cardinality of the class of all integers is $\aleph_0$ (read "Aleph-nought"). Similarly the cardinality of the class of all *even* integers is $\aleph_0$. In *one* sense of "size"; viz., that in which cardinalities are compared, the class of all integers is *equal* in size to the class of even integers. But we can define a *different* notion of "size" which makes the latter class half the size of the former. Consider the two classes {even integers less than n} and {integers less than n} and let "N{α}" stand for "the cardinality of the class {α}". For any even integer n, the ratio

$$\frac{N\{\text{even integers less than } n\}}{N\{\text{integers less than } n\}}$$

is less than ½. As n increases, the value of this ratio approaches ever closer to ½. The value, ½, is the *limit* of this ratio as n approaches infinity:

$$\lim_{n \to \infty} \frac{N\{\text{even integers less than } n\}}{N\{\text{integers less than } n\}} = ½.$$

We can use this latter formula to define a second notion of 'size' such that — using this latter notion — it is correct to say that the 'size' of the class of even integers is half the 'size' of the class of all integers.

19. Recall that in chapter 3, pp. 146–47, it was shown that an infinite set and a proper subset of that infinite set may each have the same number of members, i.e., the same cardinality.

20. To be more specific: The length "L" of a line which lies in a two-dimensional orthogonal coordinate system and which has end points at (x_1, y_1) and at (x_2, y_2) is given by the formula:

$$L = \left| [(x_1 - x_2)^2 + (y_1 - y_2)^2]^{½} \right|$$

Difficult as it may be to give a rigorous explication of the precise sense of 'the size of a class' which we presuppose when we say, e.g., that the 'size' of the class of possible worlds in which it is true that today is Tuesday is greater than the 'size' of possible worlds in which it is true that today is the second Tuesday in November, the concept of 'size' nonetheless figures as the intuitive foundation of much thinking in inductive logic.

The concept of contingent content

Every proposition satisfies both the Law of the Excluded Middle and the Law of Noncontradiction. The first says that every proposition is either true or false, that there is no 'middle' or third truth-value. The second law says that no proposition is both true and false. Together these two laws say that the properties of truth and falsehood are mutually exclusive and jointly exhaustive of the entire class of propositions.

Corresponding to each of these two laws just cited we can state two analogues for modal status. In the first place we can say that every proposition is either contingent or noncontingent. And in the second, we can say that no proposition is both contingent and noncontingent. The two properties, contingency and noncontingency, are mutually exclusive and jointly exhaustive of the class of propositions.

Between contingency and noncontingency there is no 'middle' or third category. Contingency and noncontingency, like truth and falsehood, do not come in degrees. No proposition is 'half contingent' or 'three-quarters noncontingent' or any other fractional measure, just as no proposition is half or three-quarters true (or false). No contingent proposition is more contingent or less contingent than any other contingent proposition; and no noncontingent proposition is more noncontingent or less noncontingent than any other noncontingent proposition.

None of this means, however, that we cannot talk cogently of one proposition being *closer to being necessarily true* than another. To explicate this latter concept we shall introduce the concept of the *contingent content* of a proposition. And to do this we begin by noticing a curious fact about necessary truths.

In a memorable passage in *Through the Looking Glass*, Alice and the White Knight have the following conversation:

> "You are sad," the Knight said in an anxious tone: "let me sing a song to comfort you."
> "Is it very long?" Alice asked, for she had heard a good deal of poetry that day.
> "It's long," said the Knight, "but it's very *very* beautiful. Everybody that hears me sing it — either it brings *tears* into their eyes, or else — "
> "Or else what?" said Alice, for the Knight had made a sudden pause.
> "Or else it doesn't, you know. . . . "[21]

Although Lewis Carroll doesn't tell us Alice's reaction to this piece of 'information', we can well imagine that Alice would have been somewhat annoyed in being told it. There is a certain sense in which being told that a particular song brings tears to everyone's eyes or it doesn't, is vacuous. Like all necessary truths, in being true of all possible worlds, this proposition of the Knight's tells us nothing specific about his world, about how his song is usually met in his world, which makes that song different from any other song. In its bringing or not bringing tears to the eyes of everyone who hears it, it shares a property in common with every song everywhere, in the past as well as the future and in this, the actual world, in the imaginary world of *Through the Looking Glass,* and in every other possible world as well.

---

21. Lewis Carroll, *Alice's Adventures in Wonderland & Through the Looking Glass,* New York, Signet Classics, 1960, pp. 211 – 212.

Although what the Knight said to Alice is true, it lacks what has come to be called, "contingent content". The contingent information, or the contingent content, of the Knight's declaration is nil or zero.

Philosophers have gone a long way in inductive logic toward constructing measures for the amount of contingent content in a proposition. The basic idea is this: *the smaller the 'size' of the set of possible worlds in which a proposition is true, the greater its amount of contingent content.* A more specific version of this would be: the contingent content of a proposition is *inversely proportional* to the 'size' of the set of possible worlds in which that proposition is true.

Suppose someone were to ask us how many stars there are. If we were to reply,

(6.15)   "There are a million or fewer, or between one million and a billion, or a billion or more",

what we would express would be true. Indeed it would be necessarily true, and we would have succeeded not at all in telling our questioner specifically how many stars there are. Our answer would be true in all possible worlds and we would run no risk of being wrong in giving it. If, however, we were to omit one of the disjuncts, asserting only the remaining two, our answer would no longer be necessarily true. It could be false. For example, if we were to say,

(6.16)   "There are a million or fewer, or between one million and a billion",

then if in fact there were 10 billion stars, we would speak falsely. But whether we in fact end, in this latter case, speaking truly or falsely, our listener would be in receipt of contingent information. He would be entitled to infer that we are asserting (the contingent fact) that there are no more than a billion stars. As we reduce the number of alternatives in our answer, the contingent content (as well as our risk of being wrong) correspondingly increases. The proposition that there are a million or fewer stars, or between one million and a billion, or a billion or more, is true in all possible worlds and contains the least amount of contingent content. The proposition that there are a million or fewer stars or between a million and a billion, is not true in all possible worlds and contains a considerable amount of contingent content. And the proposition that there are a million or fewer stars is true in a set of possible worlds of yet smaller 'size' and contains still more contingent content. The more a proposition *excludes* (rather than includes), the *greater* its amount of contingent content. (Our naive intuitions might have suggested that the relation would be 'the other way round', but it is not.) The more a proposition excludes, the greater is the 'size' of the set of possible worlds in which it is false, and the greater is our risk, in the absence of other information, in holding to it.

From an epistemic point of view the most useful contingent truths are those that are most risky (in the sense just mentioned), for they carry the greatest amount of contingent content. Just notice how we prefer answers with as few disjuncts, with as much contingent content, as possible. When we ask someone, "Where are the scissors?", we would prefer to be told something of the sort, "They are in the cutlery drawer", than to be told something of the sort, "They are in the cutlery drawer, or beside the telephone, or in the desk, or in the sewing basket, or in the woodshed among the gardening tools." And when we ask someone what time it is, we would prefer to be told something of the sort, "It is three minutes past nine" than to be told something of the sort, "It is either three minutes past nine, or six minutes past eleven, or twenty minutes before eight."

Our intuitions in these matters can be captured by appeal to worlds-diagrams. Consider once more figure *(5.f)* (p. 258) which illustrated the relation of disjunction. It can there be seen that the bracket representing the disjunction of two propositions is never smaller than the bracket representing either one of those propositions. What that shows is that a disjunctive proposition (which as we have just seen generally has *less* contingent content than either of its disjuncts) is true in a set of possible worlds which is equal to, or greater in size, than either of the sets of possible worlds in which its disjuncts are true. Choosing one diagram (no. 15) as illustration from among all of those of figure *(5.f)* gives us:

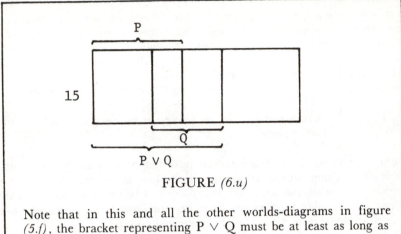

FIGURE *(6.u)*

Note that in this and all the other worlds-diagrams in figure *(5.f)*, the bracket representing P ∨ Q must be at least as long as the bracket representing P and must be at least as long as the bracket representing Q.

As we disjoin more alternatives onto the proposition that there are a million or fewer stars, the content of the proposition systematically decreases. It reaches its lowest point when we say that there are a million or fewer stars, between a million and a billion, or a billion or more. At this point the proposition ceases to have *any* contingent content whatever. This latter proposition is necessarily true, and we can view the process by which we passed from the highly contentful proposition that there are a million or fewer stars, to this latter one in which the contingent content is nil, as passing through an ordered list of propositions each one of which is systematically closer to being a necessary truth. Of course only the last in this list *is* a necessary truth, but the others can be thought to be close or far from that proposition in the list.

The two concepts, closeness to necessary truth and contingent content, can be defined in terms of the size of the set of possible worlds in which a proposition holds.

1. The greater the size of the set of possible worlds in which a proposition is true, the closer it is to being necessarily true.

2. The greater the size of the set of possible worlds in which a proposition is true, the smaller its amount of contingent content.

Closeness to being necessarily true can be seen to vary inversely with the contingent content of a proposition.[22]

22. Let us mention one point which is a source of potential confusion. In recent years there has been a remarkable growth in the science of cybernetics or information theory. In cybernetics, a certain parameter has been defined which bears the name, "information content". But it should be pointed out explicitly that this latter concept is distinct from the concept of contingent content which has here been defined. For one thing, information content is a measure of a property of *sentences*, while contingent content is a measure of a property of *propositions*. This being so allows the information content of a sentence-token expressing a noncontingent truth, on occasion, to be quite high, while the contingent content of the corresponding proposition would, as we shall see, in all cases remain precisely zero.

Monadic modal functors

The contingent content of a proposition is a property of a proposition which comes in various degrees. It cannot, therefore, be symbolized by a single fixed symbol, after the fashion of "□", "◊", "▽", and "△". Instead, in order to symbolize the concept of contingent content and allow for the fact that propositions may have varying degrees of contingent content we use a *functor* rather than a sentential operator.

A functor, like an operator, takes as its argument a wff; but unlike an operator, the result of applying a functor to a wff is not the generation of a sentential wff, but rather the generation of a *numerical* wff, i.e., a wff which stands for a number.

The functor we shall introduce to signify the concept of contingent content will be "$\mathfrak{C}$" (German "C"). Its argument is to be written in parentheses immediately to the right of it, e.g.,

$$\text{``}\mathfrak{C}(P)\text{''},$$
$$\text{``}\mathfrak{C}(P \supset (Q \cdot R))\text{''}.$$

The expression "$\mathfrak{C}(P)$" is to be read as: "The contingent content of P". Both the expressions, "$\mathfrak{C}(P)$" and "$\mathfrak{C}(P \supset (Q \cdot R))$", represent numbers. Such numerical wffs may be used in arithmetical sentential wffs in the standard way that *any* symbol designating a number may be used, for example:

$$\text{``}\mathfrak{C}(P \supset Q) = \mathfrak{C}(\sim P \vee R)\text{''}$$
$$\text{``}\mathfrak{C}(A \supset B) > 0.67\text{''}$$

The first of these is the sentential wff which says that the contingent content of $P \supset Q$ is the same as the contingent content of $\sim P \vee R$. The second says that the contingent content of $A \supset B$ is greater than 0.67.

The amount of contingent content which a proposition has is measured on a scale of 0 to 1, with 0 being the contingent content of the least contentful proposition, and 1, the greatest. On this scale it is obvious that noncontingent truths rate a value of 0. For example,

$$\mathfrak{C} \text{ (It is raining or it is not raining)} = 0, \text{ and}$$

$$\mathfrak{C} \text{ (All aunts are females)} = 0$$

Contingent propositions will assume a value between 0 and 1.

$$0 < \mathfrak{C} \text{ (It is raining)} < 1$$

But what value do we assign to noncontingent *falsities?* In accordance with the above so-called 'basic idea' (p. 373), the amount of contingent content in necessarily false propositions would seem to be 1. Does this make sense? Or should the amount of contingent content of all noncontingent propositions (both those that are true as well as those that are false) be the same, i.e., zero?

While philosophers assert that necessarily true propositions are contingently empty, they assert in contrast that necessarily false propositions are full.

Consider these two propositions:

(6.17)   It is raining or it is not raining. [necessarily true]

(6.18)   It is raining and it is not raining. [necessarily false]

From *(6.17)* nothing logically follows about the distinctive state of the weather in this or any other possible world — it does not follow that it is raining nor does it follow that it is not raining. *(6.17)* is a useless piece of information if we want to know how today's weather conditions differ from those of any other day or any other place or any other possible world for that matter. *(6.18)*, on the other hand, does contain the information we desire. For from *(6.18)* it follows that it is raining. Unfortunately, where *(6.17)* had a dearth of contingent content, *(6.18)* is afflicted with a surfeit of it. For not only does *(6.18)* imply that it is raining; it also implies that it is not. Be that as it may, *(6.18)* certainly does have contingent content. How much exactly is dictated by a fairly standard condition that is imposed on the numerical values for measures of contingent content. This condition is specifically:

$$(6.19) \quad \mathfrak{C}(P) = 1 - \mathfrak{C}(\sim P)$$

or alternatively,

$$(6.20) \quad \mathfrak{C}(P) + \mathfrak{C}(\sim P) = 1$$

Roughly, what this condition says is that whatever contingent content one proposition lacks, any of its contradictories has. Since we have already assigned the value of zero to necessarily true propositions, we must assign the value of one to their contradictories, which are, of course, all those propositions which are necessarily false. In symbols we have:

$$(6.21) \quad \Box P \rightarrow [\mathfrak{C}(P) = 0]$$

$$(6.22) \quad \Box \sim P \rightarrow [\mathfrak{C}(P) = 1]$$

$$(6.23) \quad \triangledown P \rightarrow [0 < \mathfrak{C}(P) < 1]$$

If we allow the 'sizes' of sets of possible worlds to range from zero (for the case of necessarily false propositions) to one (for the case of necessarily true propositions), then it seems perfectly natural to identify the contingent content of a proposition with the 'size' of the set of possible worlds in which that proposition is *false*.

It is sometimes useful to have available a second functor which measures the size of the set of possible worlds in which a proposition is *true*. Its definition, in terms of the functor "$\mathfrak{C}$", is trivial. We shall call this second functor "$\mathfrak{M}$":

$$\text{``}\mathfrak{M}(P)\text{''} =_{df} \text{``}1 - \mathfrak{C}(P)\text{''}, \text{ or alternatively,}$$

$$\text{``}\mathfrak{M}(P)\text{''} =_{df} \text{``}\mathfrak{C}(\sim P)\text{''}$$

We may read "$\mathfrak{M}(P)$" as "P's closeness to necessary truth", or alternatively, "the size of the set of possible worlds in which P is true".

The problem of finding an appropriate sense for the concept of "size" being invoked in this context comes down to devising a suitable formula for assigning numerical-values to the $\mathfrak{M}$-functor. Intuitively we can represent the $\mathfrak{M}$-value of a proposition (the size of the class of possible worlds in which that proposition is true) by a segment on a worlds-diagram whose *width* is proportional to that $\mathfrak{M}$-value.

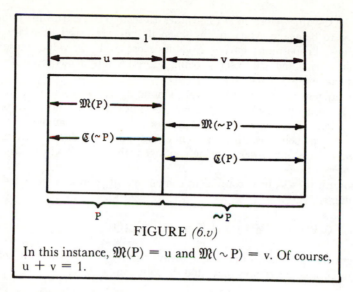

FIGURE *(6.v)*

In this instance, $\mathfrak{M}(P) = u$ and $\mathfrak{M}(\sim P) = v$. Of course, $u + v = 1$.

Much of what we have been saying about contingent content, closeness to necessary truth, $\mathfrak{C}$-values and $\mathfrak{M}$-values, may be organized on one illustrative figure.

Proposition is necessarily false	There are ten stars and it is not the case that there are ten stars	Maximum Contingent Content $\mathfrak{C}(P) = 1$ $\mathfrak{M}(P) = 0$	
Propositions are contingent	There are ten stars		
	There are ten stars or there are nine stars	Increasing closeness to necessary truth	Decreasing contingent content
	There are ten stars or there are nine stars or there are eight stars		
Proposition is necessarily true	There are no stars or there is one star or there are two stars or .... or .... (etc.)	Minimum Contingent Content $\mathfrak{C}(P) = 0$ $\mathfrak{M}(P) = 1$	

FIGURE *(6.w)*

Note that the measure of the contingent content of a *contingent* proposition is *independent* of that proposition's truth-value. A false proposition may have a greater contingent content than a true one.

Propositions having $\mathfrak{C}$-values close to 0 ($\mathfrak{M}$-values close to 1) are true in 'large' sets of possible worlds and are closer to being necessary truths (even if they are false) than are other propositions having higher $\mathfrak{C}$-values. Propositions having $\mathfrak{C}$-values close to 1 ($\mathfrak{M}$-values close to 0) are true in 'small' sets of possible worlds and are closer to being necessary falsehoods (even if they are true) than are other propositions having lower $\mathfrak{C}$-values.

Note that while contingent propositions may vary among themselves as to their respective 'distances' from being necessarily true (or false), i.e., in their $\mathfrak{M}$-values, there is no corresponding feature for noncontingent propositions. Necessarily true propositions do *not* vary among themselves as to their respective 'distances' from being contingent. They are all 'equi-distant' from contingency. No necessarily true proposition is any closer to being contingent than is any other. (And mutatis mutandis for necessarily false propositions.)

A few rather important theses about contingent content might profitably be noted. The first of these we have already explained, viz.,

$$(6.24) \quad \mathfrak{C}(P \lor Q) \leq \mathfrak{C}(P) \text{ and } \mathfrak{C}(P \lor Q) \leq \mathfrak{C}(Q)$$

That is, the contingent content of a disjunction is always equal to or less than the contingent content of either of its disjuncts. To this theorem we may add the following ones:

$$(6.25) \quad \mathfrak{C}(P \cdot Q) \geq \mathfrak{C}(P) \text{ and } \mathfrak{C}(P \cdot Q) \geq \mathfrak{C}(Q)$$

[A conjunction tells us the same as or more than either of its conjuncts]

$$(6.26) \quad \mathfrak{M}(P \cdot Q) \leq \mathfrak{M}(P) \text{ and } \mathfrak{M}(P \cdot Q) \leq \mathfrak{M}(Q)$$

and

$$(6.27) \quad (P \rightarrow Q) \rightarrow [\mathfrak{C}(P) \geq \mathfrak{C}(Q)]$$

[If P implies Q, then Q has the same or less contingent content than P]

Each of these theses may easily be proved by inspecting the fifteen worlds-diagrams (figure *(1.i)*) in chapter 1.

The last of these theses is particularly important: it tells us that in cases where one proposition implies another, the former has the same or more contingent content than the latter, i.e., that the relation of implication can at most preserve contingent content, but that there can never be more contingent content in the consequent than in the antecedent.

These latter facts present a seeming puzzle. Why should we be interested in examining the consequences of propositions once we realize that these consequences can, at best, have the same contingent content, but will, in a great many cases, have less contingent content than the propositions which imply them? Why should we be interested in passing from propositions with high contingent content to propositions with lesser contingent content?

The answer lies wholly in the character of human knowledge. Although a person may know a proposition P, which implies another proposition Q, it does not follow that that person knows Q. Remember (from chapter 3) that four conditions must be satisfied in order for a person to know a proposition. In the case where P implies Q, one's having knowledge that P satisfies one and only one of the four conditions necessary for knowing that Q: one's knowing that P guarantees the *truth* of Q, for as we have earlier seen (1) one cannot know a false proposition, and (2) the relation of implication preserves truth. But one's knowing that P does not guarantee any of the other three conditions, viz., that one believe Q, that one have good evidence that Q, and that this justified belief be indefeasible. If, however, one does know both that P and that P implies Q, then one is in a position to have an indefeasibly justified true belief that Q, i.e., is in a position to know that Q. When a person learns that Q, on the basis of having inferred Q from the known proposition P, even though Q may have less contingent content than P, he adds a further item of knowledge to his store of knowledge.

What are the prospects for a fully developed inductive logic?

Inductive *propositional* logic is a going concern and has been for many years. Vast numbers of important theses in this logic are easily provable. Although rigorous proofs can be given for all of its theses, many of them, virtually by inspection, can be 'read off' worlds-diagrams. It is, for example, a trivial matter to establish any of the following theses simply by examining the set of fifteen worlds-diagrams for two propositions.

$$(6.28) \quad \mathfrak{M}(P \vee \sim P) = 1$$

$$(6.29) \quad \mathfrak{M}(P \cdot \sim P) = 0$$

$$(6.30) \quad (P \Phi Q) \rightarrow [\mathfrak{M}(P \vee Q) = \mathfrak{M}(P) + \mathfrak{M}(Q)]$$

$$(6.31) \quad (P \Phi Q) \rightarrow [\mathfrak{M}(P \cdot Q) = 0]$$

$$(6.32) \quad (P \rightarrow Q) \rightarrow [\mathfrak{M}(P \cdot Q) = \mathfrak{M}(P)]$$

$$(6.33) \quad (P \rightarrow Q) \rightarrow [\mathfrak{M}(P \vee Q) = \mathfrak{M}(Q)]$$

$$(6.34) \quad (P \leftrightarrow Q) \rightarrow [\mathfrak{M}(P) = \mathfrak{M}(Q)]$$

$$(6.35) \quad [\nabla P \cdot (P \rightarrow Q) \cdot \sim (Q \rightarrow P)] \rightarrow [\mathfrak{C}(P) > \mathfrak{C}(Q)]$$

$$(6.36) \quad (P \circ Q) \rightarrow [\mathfrak{M}(P \vee Q) = \mathfrak{M}(P) + \mathfrak{M}(Q) - \mathfrak{M}(P \cdot Q)]$$

So far as it goes, inductive propositional logic is a very attractive logic. But the trouble is that it does not go very far. To be more specific, it never assigns $\mathfrak{M}$- or $\mathfrak{C}$-values to propositions expressed by *simple* sentences, but only to propositions — and then only to some, not all — which are expressed by *compound* sentences.[23] In the above examples we can see that inductive propositional logic sometimes assigns $\mathfrak{M}$-values to propositions expressed by compound sentences solely on the basis of the *forms* of those sentences (see, for example, theses *(6.28)* and *(6.29)*). In other cases, such assignments can be made only upon the specification of the $\mathfrak{M}$- or $\mathfrak{C}$-values of the propositions expressed by their simple sentential components *together with* a specification of certain information about the modal attributes of the latter propositions (see, for example, theses *(6.30)* – *(6.35)*). And in still other cases, inductive propositional logic is unable to do even the latter as can be seen in thesis *(6.36)* which expresses the $\mathfrak{M}$-value of $P \vee Q$ in terms of the $\mathfrak{M}$-value of a proposition (viz., $P \cdot Q$) which is itself expressed by a *compound* sentence and whose own $\mathfrak{M}$-value is *not* calculable within this logic from the $\mathfrak{M}$-values of P and of Q.

It would seem, then, that the next development one would want to see in an inductive logic would be a means of assigning $\mathfrak{M}$- and $\mathfrak{C}$-values to propositions expressed by *simple* sentences, and to those compound sentences the calculation of whose $\mathfrak{M}$- and $\mathfrak{C}$-values apparently lies beyond the capabilities of a propositional logic.

How can these assignments be made?

On the interpretation which has here been suggested for $\mathfrak{M}$- and $\mathfrak{C}$-values, it would appear that the only way to make such assignments would be a priori. Empirical techniques confined to the actual

---

23. Note that in its inability to assign $\mathfrak{M}$- and $\mathfrak{C}$-values to propositions expressed by simple sentences, inductive propositional logic is analogous to truth-functional propositional logic which give us no logical grounds for assigning truth-values to propositions expressed by simple sentences.

world are not going to be able to tell us, for example, the size of the set of all the *other* possible worlds in which some particular contingent proposition is true. But how, exactly, is this a priori program to be carried out?

In the early 1950s Rudolf Carnap made a valiant attempt at constructing a logic to do just this.[24] His, of course, was a logic of *analyzed* propositions; for without analyzing propositions, there can be no basis for assigning one proposition one value, and another proposition some other value. To make these assignments, Carnap constructed what he called "state-descriptions". Although he did not use the possible-worlds idiom, we may regard a state-description as a description of a unique possible world (or as a set of possible worlds which share in common all of a stipulated set of attributes).

The trouble with Carnap's pioneering work, however, was that he was never able to extend his analysis to the entire set of possible worlds. He found it necessary, in each case, to examine only those possible worlds which were describable by very impoverished languages. Within small, highly artificially restricted sets of possible worlds, he was able to assign $\mathfrak{M}$- and $\mathfrak{C}$-values to individual propositions relative to those restricted sets of possible worlds. He was not able to extend his analysis to the unrestricted, full set of all possible worlds.

To date, no completely satisfactory solution has been found to the general problem. The construction of a fully-developed inductive logic remains a challenging, tantalizing goal.

In their search for an inductive logic of analyzed propositions, logicians are guided by a number of paradigm cases, i.e., examples about whose appropriate $\mathfrak{M}$- and $\mathfrak{C}$-values many logicians have shared and strong convictions. For example, we would want our logic to assign much higher $\mathfrak{C}$-values to so-called 'positive' propositions, than to 'negative'. Virtually all of us intuitively feel that the set of possible worlds in which it is false that there are 31 persons in room 2b, is greater in size than the set of possible worlds in which it is true: there are vast numbers of ways for it *not* to be the case that there are 31 persons in room 2b (e.g., there are none; there are 2; there are 17; there are 78; there are 455,921; etc., etc.); but there is only one way for there to *be* 31 persons in that room.

There are, of course, countless numbers of other propositions about whose $\mathfrak{M}$- and $\mathfrak{C}$-values our intuitions fail us. Consider, for example, the two propositions, A, that oranges contain citric acid, and B, that the Greek poet Homer wrote two epics. Is the set of possible-worlds in which A is true, larger, equal to, or smaller in size than the set in which B is true? This question has no *obvious* answer. But this is not a cause for despairing of the possibility of an inductive logic. If an inductive logic can be satisfactorily achieved which yields the 'right' $\mathfrak{M}$- and $\mathfrak{C}$-values for the paradigm cases, then we can simply let it dictate the $\mathfrak{M}$- and $\mathfrak{C}$-values for those propositions about which we have no firm intuitions. Indeed this is one of the motivating factors in searching for any logic, whether it be an inductive logic or any other kind: the constructing of a new powerful logic holds out the promise of providing new knowledge, knowledge beyond knowledge of the paradigm cases which are used to test its mettle.

EXERCISES

1. a. *Which, if either, has more contingent content: the proposition that today is Sunday or the proposition that today is not Sunday?*

    b. *Which, if either, has more contingent content: the proposition that Mary Maguire is over twenty-one years of age, or the proposition that Mary Maguire is forty-two years of age?*

24. Rudolf Carnap, *The Logical Foundations of Probability,* 2nd ed., Chicago, The University of Chicago Press, 1962.

2.   *Find a* contingent *proposition which has* more *contingent content than the proposition that today is Sunday.*

3.   *Suppose that A implies B, that* $\mathfrak{M}(A) = 0.3$ *and* $\mathfrak{M}(B) = 0.5$. *What is the value of* $\mathfrak{M}(A \supset B)$? *the value of* $\mathfrak{M}(A \cdot B)$? *the value of* $\mathfrak{M}(A \vee B)$? *and the value of* $\mathfrak{M}(A \equiv B)$? *[Hint: Study figure (6.u) and reread pp. 313–315.]*

4.   *Suppose that A ⬦ B, that* $\mathfrak{M}(A) = 0.12$ *and* $\mathfrak{M}(B) = 0.43$. *What is the value of* $\mathfrak{M}(A \supset B)$?

5.   *Philosophers often talk about the 'absolute probability' of a proposition, and by this they mean the probability of a proposition in and of itself without regard to any other contingent information whatever. Which do you think is the more appropriate concept with which to identify this notion of absolute probability: the contingent content of the proposition or its complement, closeness to necessary truth? Explain your answer. In seeking answers to questions do we want answers with high or low absolute probability? Again, explain your answer.*

6.   *A question to ponder: We have said that necessary truths have no* contingent *content. Does this mean that. they all lack* informative *value? Can some* different *sense of "content" be devised such that necessary truths will have some sort of informational (epistemic) value?*

*   *   *   *   *

The concept of probabilification

Whether a proposition P implies a proposition Q, is an 'all-or-nothing-affair'; that is, either P implies Q or it is not the case that P implies Q. Implication — like consistency, like truth, like falsity, etc. — does not come in degrees. No proposition *partially* implies another; no implicative proposition is partially true or, for that matter, partially false.

Nonetheless it would be a boon to logical analysis if we could define a somewhat weaker notion than implication, a notion which shares various features in common with that concept, but which *does* 'come in degrees'. Intuitively we can distinguish among various cases of non-implication: some of them *do* seem to 'come closer' to being cases of implication than others. For example, neither of the following cases is a case of implication:

(6.37)   If repeated, diligent searches have failed to find a Himalayan Snowman, then Himalayan Snowmen do not exist;

(6.38)   If Admiral Frank's July 1923 expedition did not find a Himalayan Snowman, then Himalayan Snowmen do not exist.

Many of us would intuitively feel that *(6.37)* is somehow 'closer' to being an instance of implication than is *(6.38)*.

In the case where the relation of implication obtains between two propositions, the truth of the former *guarantees* the truth of the latter. But might there not be a somewhat weaker logical relation such that if *it* were to obtain between two propositions the truth of the former would — if not guarantee — at least *support* the latter?

Philosophers have christened this latter relation "probabilification" (alternatively, "confirmation"). It is allegedly illustrated in the example *(6.37)* above: the proposition that repeated, diligent searches have failed to find a Himalayan Snowmen, is thought to 'probabilify' (to support, warrant, or confirm)— even though it does not imply — the proposition that Himalayan Snowmen do not exist.[25]

A dyadic modal functor for the concept of probabilification

Let us introduce a functor, "$\mathfrak{P}$" (German "P"), to symbolize the concept of probabilification. The functor, "$\mathfrak{P}$", is dyadic: it takes two arguments, written in parentheses and separated by a comma.

$$\text{"}\mathfrak{P}(P,Q)\text{"} =_{df} \text{"the degree to which P probabilifies Q"}$$

To construct a wff using such an expression, one may use it in any way in which one would use any other symbol in arithmetic which expresses a numerical value, for example,

(6.39)   "$\mathfrak{P}(A \lor B, A \supset B) = \mathfrak{P}(A, A \equiv C) - 0.45$"

The probabilification-functor is to assume numerical values between 0 and 1 (inclusive). If P provides utterly no support for Q, as would be the case, for example, if P and Q were both contingent and inconsistent with one another, then the corresponding $\mathfrak{P}$-value would be zero. If, on the other hand, P implies Q, then the $\mathfrak{P}$-functor is to have the maximum value possible, viz., one. All other cases will be assigned numerical values between these two limits.

In terms of worlds-diagrams, how is the $\mathfrak{P}$-functor to be interpreted?

Let us begin with an example. We will choose two logically independent propostions: A, the proposition that there are fewer than 30 persons in room 2A, and B, the proposition that there are at least 25 but fewer than 40 persons in room 2A. The relevant worlds-diagram is the fifteenth.

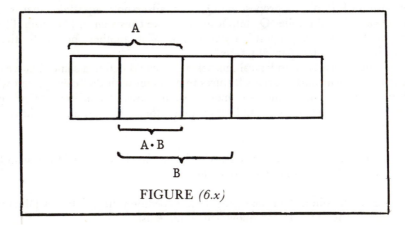

FIGURE *(6.x)*

Arbitrarily pick a world, W, in the set of possible worlds in which A is true. What are the 'chances' that this will be a world in which B is also true? The 'chances' will depend on what proportion of the segment representing A overlaps the segment representing B. More specifically, the 'chances' of W's lying in the segment representing A · B is simply the 'width' of that segment compared to the total width of the segment representing A itself. But the 'widths' of segments are nothing other than the associated $\mathfrak{M}$-values. Hence in this case we may immediately write down the following formula:

25. Rudolf Carnap argued at length that there are *at least* two *different* concepts standardly designated by the term "probability": what he called "confirmation" and "relative frequency" respectively. It is the first alone of the two different concepts which we are examining. For more on Carnap's views see esp. pp. 19 – 36, *op. cit.*

$$(6.40) \quad \mathfrak{P}(P, Q) = \frac{\mathfrak{M}(P \cdot Q)}{\mathfrak{M}(P)}$$

This formula is not fully general, however. It cannot be applied to all cases. Recall that division by zero is a disallowed operation in arithmetic. Thus we must not allow $\mathfrak{M}(P)$ in the above formula to assume the value zero. While *(6.40)* can be used in cases in which P is possible, it cannot be used in cases where P is impossible, for when P is impossible, $\mathfrak{M}(P)=0$. Thus we need a formula different from *(6.40)* to cover the cases where P is necessarily false. What that formula should be is obvious. In cases where P is necessarily false, P *implies* Q, and we have already said that in cases of implication, the $\mathfrak{P}$-functor is to bear the numerical value, one. Thus we replace formula *(6.40)* with the following two formulae:

$$(6.41) \quad \Diamond P \rightarrow [\mathfrak{P}(P, Q) = \frac{\mathfrak{M}(P \cdot Q)}{\mathfrak{M}(P)}],$$

and

$$(6.42) \quad \sim \Diamond P \rightarrow [\mathfrak{P}(P, Q) = 1]$$

It is interesting to calculate the value of $\mathfrak{P}(P,Q)$ in the case where P is necessarily true. The formula we use is *(6.41)*. In cases where P is necessarily true, $\mathfrak{M}(P \cdot Q)=\mathfrak{M}(Q)$, and $\mathfrak{M}(P)=1$. Substituting these values in formula *(6.41)* we find:

$$(6.43) \quad \Box P \rightarrow [\mathfrak{P}(P, Q) = \mathfrak{M}(Q)]$$

The $\mathfrak{M}$-value of a proposition may be considered its 'absolute' or 'degenerate' probability, i.e., the degree to which it is probabilified by a proposition having *no* contingent content. Or putting this another way, the absolute probability of a proposition is its probability in the absence of any contingent information about that proposition.[26]

Given the above explications of probabilification, we can see that there are no further problems in incorporating such a notion into inductive logic than those already mentioned in regard to the calculation of $\mathfrak{M}$- and $\mathfrak{C}$-values. For the problem of actually assigning numerical values to the $\mathfrak{P}$-functor comes down to the problem of assigning $\mathfrak{M}$-values. If we are able to solve that problem, we will automatically be able to assign probabilification-measures.

EXERCISE

Let "C"= "There are at least 25, but fewer than 100, persons in room 2A". Add C to figure (6.x). Does A probabilify C less than, equal to, or more than the degree to which it probabilifies B?

26. What we are here calling the "absolute" probability, is sometimes called the "a priori" probability. We eschew this particular use of the latter term. Although the absolute probability of a proposition can be known *only* a priori, it seems to us misleading to favor this particular probability-measure with that name. For on our account, *all* measures of degree of probabilification, whether absolute or relative (i.e., whether on the basis of propositions having no, or some, contingent content) are — if knowable at all — knowable a priori.

Index